HUMAN AGING

Staff of Research and Education Association

Research and Education Association
505 Eighth Avenue
New York, N. Y. 10018

HUMAN AGING

Printed in the United States of America

Library of Congress Catalog Number 82-80748

International Standard Book Number 0-87891-536-2

PREFACE

The aging process described in this reference book is a challenging field in which to be knowledgeable, as it affects almost everyone. An understanding of the important factors associated with the aging process enables us to deal better with the over 20 million persons aged 65 and older in the United States.

This reference book describes the physiological, psychological, and social changes which attend the normal aging process. A separate section is provided on the patterns of use of psychoactive drugs by the elderly. Included are the effects of psychoactive drugs on physiology and behavior in relation to age.

The information in this reference volume was originated by leading investigators in the field, who carried out observations on healthy persons over a period of years. The investigations were sponsored by the U. S. Public Health Service, and the results from the many researchers which have been incorporated in this reference book, are gratefully acknowledged.

CONTENTS

PART I

PART II

PART III

BIOMEDICAL and BEHAVIORAL CHARACTERISTICS – PART I

CHAPTER 1

Introduction to
The Study of Human Aging

by James E. Birren, Robert N. Butler,

Samuel W. Greenhouse, Louis Sokoloff,

and Marian R. Yarrow

BACKGROUND

Aging is a process of change involving all aspects of the organism. Its consequences range from altered structures and functions of the component tissues of the body to an altered relationship of the organism to its physical and social environment. The purpose of the present research was to examine a broad spectrum of processes in advanced age, in individuals in whom disease is absent or minimal. This volume reports an intensive study of healthy men over the age of 65 years. Data on physical, physiological, psychological, psychodynamic, and social processes were obtained. Selection of variables was determined by specific questions within each of the disciplines collaborating in the study and by interdisciplinary interests. There were the dual research purposes of testing specific hypotheses and obtaining empirical data of a wide range for descriptive purposes.

Many prevailing ideas and facts about aging and the aged come from studies of the sick and institutionalized. Because of the nature of the studies and of the populations studied, the dominant theme has been one of *decline*. Thus cerebral metabolism and circulation have generally been regarded as declining with advancing age; senility, regression, and rigidity are often regarded as unavoidable concomitants of growing older. The contributions of factors of disease, en- vironmental changes, and preexisting personality need also to be disentangled from changes more properly regarded as aging.

Many basic questions about human aging remain unanswered in research; indeed the lack of reliable information about aging in many instances results in poorly defined questions. From a review of the past research it is safe to draw two general conclusions: (1) hypotheses about aging are more or less general in nature, and (2) mechanisms are essentially unknown (see Birren, 1959). Behind the changes associated with advancing age undoubtedly lies a complex of factors, heredity, cultural patterns, exposure to disease, etc.; determination of the precise contribution of these factors will require considerable research. Different strategies and methods of study are necessary for this difficult task and for isolating the effects of aging from other factors having little or no relation to the age of the individual.

Definition of Aging

The intent of the present study was to focus on the essentially normal process of aging; however aging is such a diffuse topic that it is often difficult to communicate to others what aspects are to be discussed. Depending upon one's interests and purposes, different definitions of aging may be used with implications for various antecedents of a biological, environmental, social, or random nature. Here aging is looked upon as a characteristic pattern of late-life change ultimately distinguishable from disease and adventitious consequences of existence. The term "aging" is meant to denote determinate patterns of late-life changes, changes eventually shown by all persons though varying in rate and degree. In this usage, aging lies close to concepts of growth and development in which most members of a species are regarded as showing a representative pattern of change. Use of the term "aging" to denote determinate or predictable changes of advancing age does not imply that these changes are necessarily larger or more important than random events. In contrast to the invariant transformations of aging most diseases are not experienced by all members of the population. On the other hand, a process of aging could be manifested by all members of a population and yet be relatively small in its influence compared with adventitious events; thus health and/or certain social changes may assume pervasive significance in later life and become the major determinants of an older individual's behavior. The problem then is to determine which possible variables have to be considered to explain the complex manifestations of aging. There is certainly no evidence at present to justify defining aging as a result of a single pacemaker which controls change in a broad range of anatomical, physiological, and psychological characteristics.

Much reported research in aging is concerned with limited aspects of the organism. Little attention has been given to matters of the congruence and dependencies of the simultaneous changes in individuals as they grow older. Systems of integration and control in aging, whether at the biochemical, psychological, or social level, have yet to be elucidated by research. The nervous system is undoubtedly an important factor in human aging, since through its integrative functions the organism compensates for changes and regulates itself so it can survive as a totality. Some literature indicates that there are genetic factors controlling the development of pathological changes of the nervous system in later life and to a limited extent, genetic control appears in changes in the more "normal" range. At yet another level, temperament and experience in the development of the individual personality may give rise to a form of control which might enhance, modify, or suppress age changes induced by endogenous or exogenous factors. The present study gives detailed attention to a variety of specific aspects of the organism, and examines them also in terms of the interdependencies with one another.

Nature of This Report

This study began in 1955 with a focus on the interrelations between cerebral physiological changes of advancing age and psychological capacities and psychiatric symptoms. As the study evolved it expanded in a number of ways. Social psychological aspects of old age were included. Also, within each discipline problems and questions developed in areas particularly of interest to the discipline. These extended interests in turn affected the interdisciplinary data available for examination. The resulting study combined the efforts of 22 investigators and their collaborators.

The individual investigator was free to choose the particular variables in his discipline which were of special interest to him. Examples of the questions raised in various disciplines follow:

Psychiatry:

What kinds of psychopathology are present in older persons relatively free from physical disease and living in the community?

What is the character of senility and is it an inevitable consequence of the "aging process"?

What kinds of changes do the noninstitutionalized and basically healthy older people observe in themselves, and how do they react to them?

What personality factors contribute to adaptation and maladaptation of the community-dwelling older individual to the crises of late life?

Social psychology:

What are the characteristics of social behavior in the healthy aged?

How do environmental factors, of cultural background and of immediate circumstances, contribute to adaptation (maladaptation) of the aged?

How do characteristics of daily living and social behavior relate to measured physical and psychological capacities, and where discrepancies occur how can they be accounted for?

Physiology:

Are the changes in cerebral blood flow and cerebral metabolic rate previously described in the literature the result of aging of the nervous system or the result of disease?

When these changes occur, does the circulation fail first because of vascular disease and the metabolism secondarily because of circulatory insufficiency, or is there a primary decline in metabolic rate with a secondary adjustment of the circulation to the reduced metabolic demand?

Are the changes in blood flow and metabolism, when they occur, correlated with other aspects of cerebral functioning and clinical symptoms?

Psychology:

Which psychological capacities show most and which least difference with advancing age?

To what extent is the slowing in speed of psychomotor skills the result of a general process of change in the nervous system?

To what extent are age changes in psychological capacities related to concomitant changes in health, cerebral physiology, social behavior, and psychopathology?

During the 5 years of this project, a continuous research seminar operated. During the last 2 years a committee continued this function; it served an editorial function and reviewed the substantive findings of the various contributors. This involved lengthy discussions about different ways of conceptualizing aging and interpretations of the data; these discussions were always lively, sometimes heated. It was primarily through these meetings that the representatives of the various disciplines had an impact on the thinking of others with the result that concepts were discarded or modified and issues were seen more clearly.

The detailed research issues of the study are presented in the following chapters. The subjects are described in their social and medical characteristics in chapters 2 and 3, and the general research design is described in chapter 4. It should be pointed out that the subjects of this study were not only favored in health with respect to their living peers, they have been subjected to a severe survivorship bias; less than 50 percent of peers of these men were alive at the time of the study. It is difficult to specify the effects of survivorship bias in terms of measured characteristics of these men, although we have, in chapter 2 and 3, described many of the characteristics of these men insofar as they are a "sample" of individuals.

Chapter 3 describes the conditions under which these men lived for 2 weeks in the Clinical Center of the National Institutes of Health during which time the studies of them were made. The schedule of the daily activities of the men while under study is given on page 20. While the schedule may seem full, it was arranged with continuous awareness of the subjects' advanced age and their possible reactions to a totally new and strange environment. The investigators were perhaps overly self-conscious in their estimates of the subjects' capacity for sustained interest and activity. In point of fact, the subjects were not only able to participate fully but generally enjoyed the research program.

Chapters 5 through 14 present the research of separate disciplines. In chapter 15 the view of the data is interdisciplinary.

There are many possible comparisons of the data and the reader may wish to make other analyses of the data than those discussed in chapter 15. Many of the raw data on the subjects are presented in the appendices, following certain chapters. Chapter 16 attempts to integrate the information from the entire study and offer some generalizations, from a broad perspective, about how man grows old.

REFERENCES

BIRREN, J. E. (*ed.*). Handbook of Aging and the Individual: Psychological and Biological Aspects. Chicago: University of Chicago Press, 1959, pp. 939.

CHAPTER 2

Description of Subjects: Social Characteristics

by E. Grant Youmans

The ideal population with which the research was concerned was that of the physically healthy, socially independent aged. This ideal, however, does not lead directly to definitions of the characteristics or methods by which such subjects can be selected and obtained for study. How healthy, how independent, how old shall the subjects be? Shall variables such as sex, intellectual level, and others be considered? How should cultural variables enter into selection? Can one research design truly meet needs as many and diverse as those reflected in the multidisciplinary problems represented here? Blood pressure level, for example, is a necessary sampling criterion in the design of physiology; social origins and statuses are significant in the evaluation of social aspects of aging. With this range of requirements, is it possible to find subjects who meet all criteria, and who are interested in research participation? Decisions on sample thus represent resolutions of theoretical problems, as well as practical problems.

This research relied on volunteer subjects who responded to publicity released through two interested agencies, the Home for the Jewish Aged in Philadelphia and the Association for Retired Civil Employees in Washington, D.C. Volunteers through these sources, each of which represents rather unique social characteristics, comprise the population on which medical and social sampling criteria could be imposed.

Males were chosen as the subjects in the present study because of the predominant use of male subjects in the research literature on aging, with the existence, therefore, of control groups for purposes of comparison. Limiting the study to males also simplified research administration. The choice of an age minimum of 65 years rests mainly with tradition. A sample size of approximately 50 was set by the practical limitations of time required for the detailed study of each case, and by the desire to have a sufficiently large number to permit correlational analyses within and across disciplinary lines.

Subjects were evaluated medically at two points, by a referring physician when volunteering for the study, and by a series of examinations at the Clinical Center at the time of entering the study. The medical screening is described in chapter 3.

One major social criterion—independent living in the community—was used in sample selection. As has been pointed out, the sick and institutionalized aged have been the major sources of subjects in reported research and the basis of many of our conceptions of old age. The present sample attempts to exclude those sources of debilitating effects. A range of variation was permitted in the man's social independence, from independent householder status, to somewhat dependent status in the households of friends, and, in three cases,

TABLE 1.—*Age of subjects*			
Age	Group I[1]	Group II[1]	Total
65–69...........	11	7	18
70–74...........	12	8	20
75 and over......	4	5	9
Total.....	27	20	47
Mean age.......	70.8	72.4	71.5

[1] Group I and II refer to medically differentiated groups. Group I meets all the medical criteria set by the research. Group II represents a subclinical or asymptomatic disease group. The groups are described in detail in ch. 3.

to recent entrance into the Home for the Jewish Aged. Other social variables, such as education, social class, cultural backgrounds, were allowed to vary—a decision reached mainly of necessity. These constitute, then, uncontrolled sources of variation, contributing in unknown ways to the findings. Where possible, analyses have been done of subgroups in the sample.

The final sample consists of 47 men, 65 years or older, with a median age of 71 and a range from 65 to 91 years. (See table 1.) The following social characteristics are represented.

Cultural Backgrounds

All subjects lived in urban environments at the time of the study, and, in most cases, for long periods previously. Twenty of the men were born in foreign countries, having migrated in childhood or early youth. In religious background, 20 of the subjects were Jewish, 23 were Protestant, and 4 were Catholic. The foreign born included a much larger proportion of the Jewish than of the non-Jewish men (75 percent and 25 percent, respectively). (See tables 2 and 3.)

There was an extremely wide range of educational background in the sample, from men with college degrees to men with

TABLE 2.—*Cultural backgrounds*

Background	Group I (N=27)	Group II (N=20)	Total (N=47)
Origin:			
Foreign born......	11	9	20
Native born........	16	11	27
Religion:			
Jewish.............	9	11	20
Protestant.........	16	7	23
Catholic...........	2	2	4
Education:			
Grade school or less.	11	9	20
Some high school or high school graduate..............	7	4	11
Some college or college graduate.....	9	7	16
Occupation:			
Professional........	5	6	11
Business, managerial.	6	4	10
Clerical...........	10	0	10
Skilled and semi-skilled..........	6	10	16

almost no formal education. Educational level of an aged group is difficult to assess in terms of our present educational structure. Particularly this is true of men who received their educational training in Europe 50 to 70 years ago. It is also true that 10 years of formal education in the United States half a century ago and today are not equivalent. Therefore, the educational description (and comparisons with present norms and young control groups) must be viewed cautiously.

TABLE 3.—*Nativity, educational level, and religion*

Nativity and religion	High school education or less	Some education beyond high school
Foreign born:		
Jewish..............	13	2
Protestant and Catholic..	2	3
Native born:		
Jewish..............	3	2
Protestant and Catholic..	13	9
Total..............	31	16

The subjects described their formal schooling in diverse terms, including religious schools, night schools, tutoring, home study, correspondence courses, and apprenticeships in skilled trades, as well as public grammar schools, high school, and college. The foreign-born subjects obtained their education often in religious schools, the native born mainly in public schools. Slightly over one-third of the men in the sample had some college education or were college graduates. The estimated median years of formal education of the 47 men was 9.5 years. This is somewhat higher than the median indicated by the 1950 census for the same age group in the general urban population of the United States (8.3 years).[1]

The sample includes men from many classifications of occupation, overrepresenting the higher status white-collar occupations and underrepresenting the lower status manual occupations. Twenty-three percent of the men had been professional persons during their work careers; 21 percent had been business entrepreneurs or managers; 21 percent had been clerical workers. Thirty-five percent had been skilled or semiskilled workers.

Economic and Work Status

At the time of the study, 32 of the 47 men were fully retired. They had been retired for an average of 7 years, several for as long as 30 years. Ten of the men were in semiretired status. Five were currently employed in their major occupation (table 4).

The men were asked to estimate the average annual income they had received between 40 and 60 years of age. The median for these estimates was $4,300, and the

[1] U.S. Bureau of the Census, *U.S. Census of Population 1950.* Vol. II, *Characteristics of the Population,* Part I, U.S. Summary (U.S. Government Printing Office, 1953), pp. 1–240.

TABLE 4.—*Economic and work status*

Status	Group I (N=27)	Group II (N=20)	Total (N=47)
Income level:			
Under $2,000......	5	9	14
$2,000 to $4,000....	10	4	14
Over $4,000........	9	7	16
Don't know........	3	0	3
Retirement status:			
Not retired........	1	4	5
Semiretired.......	8	2	10
Retired...........	18	14	32

range was $1,200 to $10,000. The men also reported income during the last 5 years before retirement, the median being $4,600 and the range $900 to $13,000. At the time of the study (when 42 of the men were in full or semiretirement status), the median annual income of the subjects was $3,100, and the range was $500 to $14,000. (The subject's report on his income is probably quite unreliable. This is suggested in internal evidence in the data, in discrepencies in the subject's reports at different times in the interviews, and differences in report of subject and informant. Memory errors, intentional upgrading or downgrading, and changing economic periods of inflation and deflation contribute to the unreliability.)

The later years of life brought fairly severe reductions in income for slightly less than half the men; the others suffered no financial loss. Thirty-six of the men reported that they relied entirely on their own incomes (including pensions and social security), and 11 men said they received some financial assistance from their families or from welfare agencies.

Marital Status and Living Arrangements

The majority of the men were living in intact families at the time of admission to the study; 31 in their own households with their wives, 6 in the households of relatives. Seven were living alone in apartments or roominghouses. Three were living in the home. Thirty-two of the men were married or remarried; 14 were widowed, divorced, or separated; and 1 had never married (table 5).

SUMMARY

The men in this sample appeared to be in somewhat more fortunate social circumstances than the general aged population. They had not only the good health for which they had been chosen; but they had better-than-average educational backgrounds as a group, they had earned better than average incomes, and three-quarters of them had retired with fair economic comfort in private households. Within the sample, however, were subgroups from the extremes of educational achievements and from widely divergent cultural backgrounds. The sample is neither representative of the aged population as a whole, nor is it a purposive sample in social and cultural characteristics.

TABLE 5.—*Marital status and living arrangements*

Status	Group I (N=27)	Group II (N=20)	Total (N=47)
Marital status:			
Married or remarried.........	21	11	32
Widowed..........	4	6	10
Divorced or separated...........	1	3	4
Never married......	1	0	1
Household:			
In own home, with wife.............	20	11	31
In home of relative or friend.........	4	2	6
Living alone, not in own home........	3	4	7
Home for Jewish Aged............	0	3	3
Type of residence:			
Private home.......	23	9	32
Apartment.........	3	6	9
Roominghouse......	1	2	3
Institution.........	0	3	3

CHAPTER 3

Medical Selection, Evaluation, and Classification of Subjects

by Mark H. Lane and Thomas S. Vates, Jr.

INTRODUCTION

Since the major emphasis of this multidisciplinary project was the investigation of the effects of normal aging, it was of paramount importance to evaluate the health status of each subject. This chapter will describe the process of selection, the medical criteria for selection, the methods and procedures used in the medical evaluation, the results of the medical examinations, and the classification of the subjects on the basis of the medical evaluation.

A major objective of the medical examination and selection procedure was the recognition and exclusion of disease. In spite of a rigorously selected initial group, it became apparent upon more careful examination after admission that it was almost impossible to obtain a completely disease-free sample in this age range. We therefore found it expedient to classify the acceptable subjects into two main groups: the first, an optimally healthy group, as free of diagnosable disease as could conceivably be obtained in this age group; and another group which exhibited some objective evidence of underlying, although minimal and asymptomatic, disease. A third group was completely disqualified on the basis of the medical findings.

Sources of Subjects

The social background of the subjects is described in chapter 2. They were recruited for these investigations chiefly through the agency of the following organizations: (1) The Home for the Jewish Aged of Philadelphia, Pa., whose physicians screened volunteer subjects from the Philadelphia area; (2) the National Association of Retired Civil Service Employees, Washington, D.C., chapter. Subjects applying from the District of Columbia area were screened directly by the investigators at the National Institutes of Health.

A total of 54 subjects were admitted for study to the National Institutes of Health, 41 through the auspices of the Home for the Jewish Aged, 12 from the Retired Civil Service Employees, and 1 from Florida, who, after reading a newspaper article about the project, volunteered for the study, passed a preliminary screening examination by his local physician, and was found acceptable after arrival at the National Institutes of Health.

PROCESS OF SELECTION

The design of the project required the selection of a group of elderly subjects who could be considered optimally healthy aged men. Acceptable criteria for health were therefore established for each of the research areas by the respective investigators at NIH. These set the standards at all levels of the screening and selection process. To initiate recruitment of volunteers, the purposes and requirements of the project were publicized. The requirements were listed as follows: (1) Men, 65 years or older; (2) absence of known or symptomatic disease; (3) community residence. Of those who responded to this publicity, many were immediately rejected because of evidence of gross defects obtained by simple inquiry. The remainder were accepted for careful medical examination on an outpatient basis. This procedure resulted in the elimination of a number of subjects who were found to be suffering from disqualifying disease.

The subjects who passed the first two stages of screening were then admitted to NIH for research investigations as well as further, more intensive, examination and evaluation of their health status. At the conclusion of their 2-week stay their medical status was again reviewed on the basis of the same criteria, which were now even more rigorously applied. The methods and problems concerning the final disposition of these subjects into clinical groups are discussed below in the section on "Medical Criteria for Aged Subjects."

The judgment of medical "normality" is notoriously difficult, and particularly so in aged persons because of the relatively fewer reliable qualitative and quantitative criteria. In large part the difficulty arises because of inability to distinguish between changes resulting from normal aging and those resulting from pathological processes. The concept of "normality," particularly as related to the elderly, therefore always requires qualification to be meaningful.

Our subjects were not representative of the medical and physical characteristics of the population for their age. This group was optimally healthy for their age. Although not completely successful, the goal was to select subjects who were free of diagnosable conditions without relaxation of standards because of their age. It was soon

clear, however, that the acquisition of a group of subjects of respectable size in this age range with complete absence of disease was an impractical matter. Therefore, in addition to the subjects with no symptoms or objective evidence of disease, there were accepted a few with doubtful evidence of truly trivial disease (i.e., partial deafness, cataracts, varicose veins, or benign prostatic hypertrophy) (group I). Following study and examination at NIH, some subjects were found to have definite evidence of disease with more serious implications, but since in these cases the disease was minimal and asymptomatic, they were included in the study but as a separate group (group II). In a few instances serious or advanced disease was discovered by the medical examinations; these subjects were rejected outright from the study (group III). Details of the findings and diagnoses are discussed below.

All information for medical classification of the subjects was gathered in routine clinical procedures and maintained in files unavailable to the other investigators. Data from the other disciplines in this study were not known or utilized for purposes of classification with two exceptions: special psychiatric evaluation to rule out functional psychoses and mean arterial blood pressure measurements obtained during the cerebral blood flow procedure. Only after all the medical information was available on all subjects were the results reviewed completely and the original criteria applied as rigidly as possible to the satisfaction of all the investigating groups.

It is apparent that some subjects were difficult to classify. It was the intent of the study to keep the optimally healthy group (group I) as uncontaminated with disease as possible.

Therefore, when borderline decisions were required, the tendency was to classify the subjects in the next lower level of health status. Some of these decisions were undoubtedly arbitrary but necessary for operational purposes.

GROUP I. OPTIMALLY HEALTHY SUBJECTS

The medical criteria considered acceptable for designation of optimal health (group I) are described below. Twenty-seven subjects fulfilled these criteria.

1. *Cardiovascular.*—Absent historical, physical, or electrocardiographic evidence of myocardial infarction, angina pectoris, clinical arrhythmias, rheumatic, or any other heart disease. Absent clinical or radiological evidence of enlargement of any of the chambers of the heart. All X-ray and fluoroscopic interpretations of the heart size and contour to be within normal limits. No pathological cardiac murmurs to be heard. Systolic blood pressure below 170 and diastolic blood pressure below 95 mm Hg; and no previous history of hypertension or treatment for hypertension. Negative history of peripheral vascular insufficiency. No retinal arteriosclerotic changes beyond grade I. The abnormalities which were accepted in group I are listed in table 1a.

2. *Pulmonary.*—No history of dyspnea at rest or with mild exertion, nocturnal dyspnea, orthopnea, asthma, chronic productive cough, hemoptysis, cyanosis, or pulmonary surgery. Absent radiological evidence of significant pulmonary abnormalities. Evidence of minimal emphysematous changes and healed minimal old fibrocalcific disease was acceptable.

3. *Central nervous system.*—Absent history or evidence of any vascular "accidents." No pathological changes in sensation, motor function, muscle size, coordination, muscle tone, reflexes, speech, or mentation. No history of severe or recurrent headache, mi-

TABLE 1a.—*Associated findings of note in group 1 subjects*

Subject number	
1	Absent anal sphincter from surgery 10 years prior to investigation.
7	Healed chronic retinitis.
12	Osteoarthritis of spine.
	Ptosis of kidney.
13	Gastrectomy for peptic ulcer 5 years prior.
	Right bundle-branch block (incomplete).
15	Decreased hearing acuity.
	Sinusitis.
	Mild, diffuse EEG abnormality.
16	Right bundle-branch block.
	Osteoarthritis of spine.
19	Mild, diffuse EEG abnormality.
20	Right bundle-branch block.
26	Decreased hearing acuity, mild.
36	Macular degeneration in right eye.
47	Bilary calculus.
49	Decreased hearing acuity.
50	Decreased hearing acuity.
	Osteoarthritis of spine.
51	Decreased hearing acuity.
	Mild pulmonary emphysema.
	Osteoarthritis of spine.
53	Decreased hearing acuity.
54	Chronic, noncongestive glaucoma.
	Right bundle-branch block (incomplete).
55	Right bundle-branch block.
56	Diverticulosis of esophagus.
	Mild pulmonary emphysema.
59	Osteoarthritis.
	Diverticulosis of colon.

graine attacks, unexplained or recent syncope, seizures or involuntary movements. No ophthalmalogical evidence of ocular palsies, increased intracranial pressure, field defects, optic atrophy or abnormal reflexes. Slight "benign" tremor of the hands, symmetrically diminished virbration sensibility in the feet, symmetrically diminished ankle jerks or abdominal cutaneous reflexes were acceptable.

4. *Endocrine.*—No history or evidence of diabetes mellitus, nor evidence of pituitary, thyroid, parathyroid, or adrenal disease. No history or evidence of marked weight change, obesity, or malnutrition.

5. *Genitourinary.*—No history or evidence of chronic renal disease. Specifically, normal urine concentrating ability with no

evidence of proteinuria, glucosuria, pyuria, or hematuria. Some degree of prostatic hypertrophy was anticipated; significantly symptomatic or clinically serious prostatic disease was not present in any subject at the time of the investigation. Prior prostatic surgery without complications was not disqualifying.

6. *Gastrointestinal.*—No history of active or recent ulcer, hematemesis, severe dyspepsia, or dysphagia. No history or evidence of recent or recurrent jaundice, hepatomegaly or splenomegaly, melena, or marked change in bowel habits.

7. *Skeletal.*—No absence of limbs. No evidence of active inflammatory disease of bone or joint. Some degree of osteoarthritis was anticipated, but in no case was it found to be severe or limiting.

8. *Other general considerations.*—Absent history and evidence of anemia or treatment for anemia, polycythemia, or other blood dyscrasias. Negative blood serology with no history or evidence of syphilis.

Some of the subjects in group I revealed what were considered to be minor or minimal degrees of pathological change. These are listed in table 1a.

Group II. Subjects With Mild Asymptomatic Disease

Although having no major disqualifying medical findings, 20 subjects had defects that disqualified them from the "optimally healthy" aged group according to the previous criteria. (See table 1b.) These were consigned to group II. Two subjects who were inadvertently admitted for study were found not to fulfill the original requirement of community residence. Five demonstrated mean arterial blood pressures during the cerebral blood flow measurement procedure which were three standard deviations away from the mean of normal young

control values. (See chap. 6.) The abnormalities in this group were mild, did not inhibit the physical or social functioning of the subjects, and were generally asymptomatic. These subjects were believed to approximate more closely the usual medical concept of a "normal" aged group.

Group III. Rejected Subjects

Despite the multiple screening procedures, it was found after more extensive medical evaluation at NIH that seven subjects could not be classified in either group I or group II because of excluding pathological findings. These disqualifying findings are listed in table 2. Data presented in this monograph were derived only from the studies carried out on subjects in groups I and II.

PROCEDURES AND METHODS FOR MEDICAL EVALUATION

Volunteer subjects who passed the initial screening procedures were admitted to the Clinical Center of the National Institutes of Health for a 2-week period. They were assigned to an open unit with a capacity of 16 beds. The remainder of the individuals in this unit were mostly young normal control subjects for other NIH investigations and a few patients with mild psychoneurosis. The aged subjects shared attractively decorated semiprivate rooms with ample closet space and private baths. There was also a living room area with television, record player, magazines, and books available on the unit. Meals on the unit were served "family style" at tables in a large common dining area. A late evening snack was available, if desired. Although there was a minimum amount of free time for social activities between 8 a.m. and 5 p.m. on weekdays, opportunities to

TABLE 1b.—Group II abnormalities

Principal findings excluding subjects from group I	Associated significant abnormal findings
Subject number	
8 Mild chronic alcoholism.	Liver palpable 3 cm below costal margin.
10 Auricular flutter.	Diaphragmatic hernia of stomach.
Pericardial calcification.	Slight, diffuse dysrhythmia on EEG.
Enlarged heart.	Mild pulmonary emphysema.
11 Bronchiectasis.	Right bundle-branch block.
Enlarged heart.	Cataract of left eye.
	Aphakia of right eye.
18 Labile hypertension.	Osteoarthritis of spine.
23 Enlarged heart (left ventricle).	Solitary thyroid adenoma.
Abnormal EKG.	Mild pulmonary emphysema.
Labile hypertension.	Decreased hearing.
24 Old myocardial (diaphragmatic) infarction, 11 years prior.	
25 Rare angina pectoris (normal EKG).	Intermittent claudication of left leg.
	Mild pulmonary emphysema.
27 Abnormal EEG, with mild diffuse abnormalities.	Chronic sinusitis.
Hypertensive on CBF study.	
28 Institutionalized in home for aged.	Cataracts.
Elevated mean arterial blood pressure during CBF study.	Decreased hearing acuity.
29 Diabetes mellitus, mild (controlled by diet alone).	Mild pulmonary emphysema.
	Bell's palsy.
	Decreased hearing ability.
31 Increased mean arterial blood pressure during CBF study.	Right bundle-branch block (incomplete).
32 Institutionalized in home for aged.	Decreased hearing ability.
Elevated mean arterial blood pressure during CBF study.	
33 Elevated mean arterial blood pressure during CBF study.	Osteoarthritis.
	Esophageal hiatus hernia.
35 Elevated mean arterial blood pressure during CBF study.	Mild pulmonary emphysema.
	Aphakia.
	Osteoarthritis.
38 Mildly enlarged heart.	Mild rheumatoid arthritis.
Rheumatoid arthritis.	Right bundle-branch block.
	Decreased hearing ability.
39 Diabetes mellitus, mild (controlled by diet alone).	Abnormal EKG.
Old myocardial infarction, 5 years prior.	
41 Peptic ulcer history.	Osteoarthritis.
42 Gout.	
52 Left bundle-branch block.	"Duodenitis".
57 Marked calcification of cerebral blood vessels.	Mild pulmonary emphysema.
Intermittent claudication.	Decreased hearing ability.

TABLE 2.—*Group III disqualifying findings*

Subject
number

4 Probable multiple myeloma.
   Paralysis agitans, mild.
   Right bundle-branch block.
17 Paralysis agitans.
   Arteriosclerotic heart disease. Abnormal *t*
      waves on EKG. Enlarged heart size.
   Bronchiectasis.
21 Schizophrenic reaction, paranoid type.
   Arteriosclerotic heart disease.
   Auricular fibrillation and intraventricular con-
      duction defect on EKG. Enlarged heart
      size.
22 Polycythemia vera.
   Splenomegaly.
34 Hypertensive cardiovascular disease, associ-
      ated with angina pectoris. EKG changes of
      premature ventricular contractions, and of
      left ventricular ischemia.
   Arteriosclerosis obliterans of foot.
37 Schizophrenic reaction, undifferentiated type.
   EKG showed left ventricular conduction de-
      fect and left axis deviation.
   Kyphoscoliosis, congenital.
   Pulmonary emphysema, mild.
43 Adjustment reaction of late life with tran-
      sient psychotic state.
   Pulmonary nodular fibrosis of unknown eti-
      ology.
   Cardiac enlargement.
   Obesity.

enjoy the many recreational facilities of the NIH Clinical Center, and, indeed, the entire Washington, D.C., area, were provided and facilitated on evenings and weekends. Volunteer subjects did not incur any expenses during their visit to the National Institutes of Health.

I. MEDICAL HISTORY AND PHYSICAL EXAMINATION

Detailed histories and physical examinations, including a thorough systemic review, were carried out on each subject. Particular attention was paid to any signs or symptoms which might relate to the cardiovascular or central nervous system. Expert opinions available at the NIH were obtained whenever indicated.

II. NEUROLOGICAL EXAMINATION

A detailed examination of the motor, sensory, reflex, speech, and coordination status, as well as funduscopic examination, was performed by the medical physician in charge. An ophthalmological examination, which included a funduscopic examination, slit lamp, and visual field measurements, was performed by an opthalmologist from the Ophthalmology Branch of the National Institute of Neurological Diseases and Blindness. An audiogram was obtained, the procedures and results of which are described in chapter 9. The neurological evaluation included electroencephalograms. The details of the EEG examination are discussed in chapter 7. Tracings and clinical interpretations were performed by the Clinical EEG Branch of the National Institute of Neurological Diseases and Blindness.

III. BLOOD STUDIES

A. *Hemogram:* Hematocrit (Wintrobe, 1933), hemoglobin (Drabkin, 1949), white blood count, white cell differential, and erythrocyte sedimentation rate were performed by the Hematology Section of the Clinical Pathology Laboratory, National Institutes of Health.

B. *Blood Chemistry:* The following determinations were performed: (1) fasting blood sugar by a modified Nelson-Somogyi method (Reinhold, 1953a); (2) blood urea nitrogen by direct Nesslerization after urease incubation (Vanselow, 1940; (3) total cholesterol (Abell et al., 1952); (4) creatinine (Bonsnes and Taussky, 1945); (5) total protein by a modified Kingsley biuret method (Reinhold, 1953b); (6) serum albumin by precipitation (Rutstein, 1954); (7) protein bound iodine (Barker, 1951); (8) serum protein electrophoresis, by filter paper technique.

IV. Urinalysis

Specific gravity, pH, glucose (qualitative enzymatic method), protein sulfosalicylic acid method), and a microscopic examination were performed.

All chemical analyses, except the serum protein electrophoresis, were performed in the Clinical Chemistry Section, Clinical Pathology Laboratory, National Institutes of Health. The serum protein electrophoresis was performed by the Metabolism Service, National Cancer Institute.

V. X-Rays

Study of the chest included PA and lateral views and fluoroscopy with barium swallow. Particular attention was paid to abnormalities of heart size and to changes of the thoracic aorta, such as calcification, tortuosity, and widening. Skull films included PA, lateral and stereoscopic views with special attention to calcifications, particularly of blood vessels.

VI. Electrocardiograms

Three routine 12-lead recordings were taken during the period of admission: on the day of admission, immediately after the cerebral blood flow study, and a final tracing just before discharge. These tracings were interpreted by spatial vector analysis (Grant, 1957) in the EKG Laboratory of the National Heart Institute. No subject had any significant change among the three tracings taken during the 2-week period.

VII. Ventilatory Function Tests

These included: (1) Total vital capacity; (2) timed vital capacity; (3) maximum breathing capacity (Baldwin et al., 1948); measured vital capacity and maximum breathing capacity values were compared to their predicted values according to the formulas of Baldwin et al. (1948). They are expressed as the percent of deviation from the calculated predicted value. These tests were administered by the Pulmonary Function Service of the National Heart Institute.

VIII. Vital Signs

Daily 8 a.m. and 8 p.m. reclining auscultatory blood pressure, pulse rate, respiration rate, and oral temperature were recorded by the ward nursing personnel.

IX. Physical Measurements

Daily weight before breakfast was recorded by the ward nursing personnel. The subject's height without shoes was measured on admission.

SCHEDULING OF PROCEDURES

A 2-week period of investigation was agreed upon as being desirable by the investigating groups. An hour-by-hour schedule was prepared by the medical physician to coordinate the activities of all investigating groups. Two subjects were studied simultaneously during the 2-week period. Schedules for the two subjects are noted in figure 1 as "A" and "B." An attempt was made, as far as possible, to keep the sequence of examinations similar in the two schedules, although obviously this could not always be attained. If only one subject was being studied in a particular 2-week period, the "B" schedule was followed. The ward physician was always directly responsible for the subject's welfare during the period of investigation and could cancel or modify investigating procedures if in his opinion this was indicated for the well-being of the subject. It was rarely necessary to do so. A physician was available at all times of day and night to see any subject if the need arose.

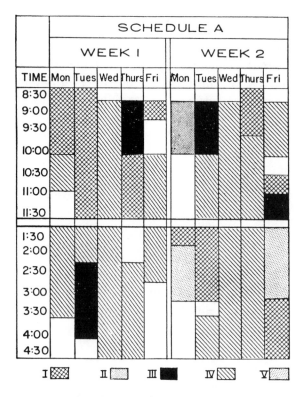
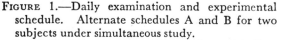

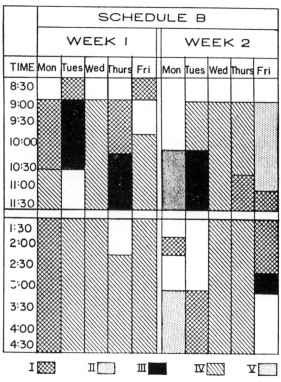

FIGURE 1.—Daily examination and experimental schedule. Alternate schedules A and B for two subjects under simultaneous study.

I. Medical Evaluation. All procedures described in this chapter, including electroencephalography, described in chapter 7.

II. Physiological studies. Cerebral blood flow and metabolism studies, described in chapter 6.

III. Psychiatric Evaluaton. Studies described in chapter 11.

IV. Psychological evaluations as described in chapters 8, 9, 10, 12, and 13.

V. Social Psychology Evaluation. Described in chapters 2 and 14.

RESULTS

I. MEDICAL HISTORY

As required by the criteria for the group, no subject in group I had a medical history suggesting disease of the cardiovascular, respiratory, renal, or nervous systems, or of any metabolic disorder of any significance. No subjects in group II had any history suggestive of present illness. One, however, had had vague chest discomfort which might conceivably have been angina pectoris. Two had historical evidence suggesting a previous myocardial infarction at least 5 years prior to this investigation. None of the subjects had a history of previous illness suggestive of hypertension, renal disease, cardiac failure, cerebral vascular accident, or chronic pulmonary disease. Slightly less than 25 percent of group I denied the use of tobacco during their lifetime, as compared to 10 percent of group II; 15 percent of group I were deemed heavy smokers, as compared to 40 percent of group II. The small numbers involved, however, do not permit any reliable statistical comparisons between them.

Twenty-five percent of group I and 10 percent of group II had never indulged in the use of alcohol during their lifetimes. Fifteen percent of group I and 25 percent of group II admitted to drinking some form of alcoholic beverage daily. Only one subject in group II admitted to being a "problem drinker." The remainder indulged in occasional or "social" drinking only. No significant difference in the history of use of laxatives was noted, with approximately half of both group denying their use at all. Twenty-five percent of each group used them regularly or frequently, the remainder only occasionally. Only 10 percent of subjects in either group took sleeping medication frequently.

II. PHYSICAL EXAMINATION

No subjects in group I were noted to have any abnormalities of the lungs or of heart size. No significant cardiac murmurs were heard. Venous varicosities of the legs were noted in 13 subjects in group I and 6 in group II, but these were not symptomatic in any case. Most subjects had sublingual venous varicosities. Only rare spider nevi or skin angiomas were noted in either group.

A palpable liver edge on deep inspiration was noted in 11 subjects of group I and 2 of group II. In none of these was the liver tender. None of the palpable liver edges was considered to reflect hepatomegaly; there were no abnormalities in liver function tests. Prostatic hypertrophy, never greater than moderate, was noted in 63 percent of the subjects in group I and 35 percent of group II. No significant anal or rectal abnormalities were noted in any of the subjects. There were no symptomatic hemorrhoids.

Half of the subjects in group II (10 out 20) were placed there because of demonstrable arteriosclerosis. The clinical differentiation of those with and without arteriosclerosis in the aged is extremely difficult and inexact. However, because of the implications to the processes of aging, it was deemed important to attempt such a separation. The clinical findings used in arriving at this classification included: (1) historical, physical, or electrocardiographic evidence suggestive of arteriosclerotic heart disease, i.e., left bundle-branch block (one subject), and old myocardial infarction (two subjects); (2) chest X-ray revealing calcification of the thoracic aorta, often accompanied by widening and/or dilatation; (3) historical or physical evidence of partial obliteration of peripheral circulation (arteriosclerosis obliterans); (4) retinal arteriosclerosis which when found unassociated with criteria 1–3, was not considered meaningful in the classification.

For operational purposes it was assumed that the probability of the presence of significant arteriosclerosis was greater in individuals demonstrating some or all of the criteria listed above, than in individuals with none of these findings.

III. NEUROLOGICAL EXAMINATION

There were no findings of serious clinical significance uncovered by the neurological examination. Diminished or absent vibratory sensation was found in seven subjects in group I and two in group II. One subject in group II was found to have an old Bell's palsy.

IV. BLOOD STUDIES

The means, standard errors, and ranges of the various blood measurements in both groups I and II are presented in table 3. All mean values were within the normal range, and there were no statistically significant differences between the mean of any of the variables measured in groups I and II.

V. URINE

Except for mild albuminuria (1+) in one subject in group II, there were no significant abnormalities or differences be-

TABLE 3.—Medical data

Variable	Group I				Group II				Units
	Number	Mean	S.E.	Range	Number	Mean	S.E.	Range	
Hematocrit	27	44	0.6	38 –50	20	44	0.7	38 –51	Percent.
Hemoglobin	27	14.8	.2	12.6 –16.7	20	14.9	.2	13.2 –16.7	gm./100 ml.
White blood count	27	6,552	278	4,300 –10,900	20	6,660	315	4,000 –10,400	cells/mm.³
E.S.R.	27	22	3	2 –46	20	19	2	4 –48	mm. in 1st hour.
Blood urea nitrogen	27	17.9	.6	13 –24	20	17.3	.7	11 –23	mgm./100 ml.
Creatinine	27	1.1	.03	0.6 –1.4	20	1.1	.03	0.8 –1.4	mgm./100 ml.
Fasting blood sugar	26	77.5	1.7	64 –101	17	77.2	2.2	66 –167	mgm./100 ml.
Protein-bound iodine	26	5.4	.2	2.9 –7.4	20	5.2	.2	4.1 –7.3	µgm./100 ml.
Total cholesterol	27	226	6	171 –313	20	243	10	176 –387	mgm./100 ml.
Total protein	27	6.67	.08	5.8 –7.6	20	6.72	.10	6.0 –7.5	gm./100 ml.
Albumin	27	3.52	.05	3.1 –3.9	20	3.46	.06	2.9 –3.8	gm./100 ml.
Globulin	27	3.14	.07	2.4 –3.9	20	3.20	.13	1.6 –4.1	gm./100 ml.
Electrophoresis:									
Total protein	24	6.97	.12	5.20–8.00	19	6.87	.11	6.07–7.52	gm./100 ml.
Albumin	24	3.30	.06	2.60–3.88	19	3.24	.06	2.71–3.70	gm./100 ml.
Alpha 1 globulin	24	.39	.02	0.25–0.50	19	.37	.01	0.29–0.46	gm./100 ml.
Alpha 2 globulin	24	.89	.03	0.60–1.20	19	.88	.03	0.70–1.19	gm./100 ml.
Beta 1+2	24	1.14	.03	0.88–1.50	19	1.13	.03	1.00–1.37	gm./100 ml.
Gamma	24	1.35	.07	0.78–2.10	19	1.25	.07	0.88–2.00	gm./100 ml.

tween groups I and II in any of the variables measured.

VI. X-rays

Chest films revealed no evidence of significant pulmonary disease. There was nonvascular calcification in seven subjects in group I and six subjects in group II. A few subjects in both groups I and II showed minimal flattening of the diaphragms and increased translucency suggestive of mild emphysematous change.

There were no patterns of heart shadow suggestive of serious cardiac pathology. Borderline cardiomegaly, based on the ratio of heart diameter and transverse chest diameter, was observed in 12 percent of the subjects in group I and 55 percent in group II. The incidence in the two groups is statistically significantly different ($p \leqq 0.01$). Aortic calcification was noted in 15 subjects in group I and 9 in group II.

Skull X-rays revealed vascular calcification in 30 percent of group I and 70 percent of group II subjects which is a statistically significant difference ($p \leqq 0.05$).

VII. Electrocardiograms

Thirty-five of the 47 subjects in groups I and II had no significant ECG abnormalities. Of the remaining 12 subjects, 5 were in group I; in all, the abnormality was right bundle-branch block (2 incomplete, 3 complete). The abnormalities in the seven subjects in group II were as follows: three right bundle-branch blocks, one incomplete; two tracings suggestive of old posterior wall myocardial infarction; one instance of left bundle-branch block; and one case of auricular flutter.

VIII. Ventilatory Studies

As seen in table 4, mean measured vital capacity and deviation from predicted values were not significantly different in the two groups. On the other hand, measured maximum breathing capacity values and deviation from predicted values were significantly higher in group I than in group II. Timed vital capacity mean values were not significantly different between the two groups; the values were about 76 ± 8 percent in 1 second and 90 ± 6 percent in 3 seconds for the combined groups.

IX. Vital Signs

Daily blood pressures in the two groups differed statistically significantly only in regard to systolic blood pressure (table 5). Distribution of the blood pressure readings according to age are presented in table 6.

X. Physical Measurements

The average height of both groups was 65 inches. The average weight of group

TABLE 4.—*Ventilatory function*

	Vital capacity		Maximum breathing capacity	
	Measured liters±S.D.	Percent deviation from predicted value	Measured liters/min. ±S.D.	Percent deviation from predicted value
Group I (*N*=27)....................	3.5±0.7	+6	99±26	+13
Group II (*N*=18)....................	3.2±0.7	−2	**76±22	**−9

** Significantly different from group I, at the 0.01 level.

TABLE 5.—*Mean blood pressure*

	Mean Systolic B.P.±S.E. mm Hg	Mean iastoli B.P.±S.E mm Hg
Group I (*N*=26)............................	127±2	75±1
Group II (*N*=20)............................	** 140±4	78±1

** Significantly different from group I, at the 0.01 level.

I (69.7±2.0 kg.) was statistically significantly greater than that of group II (64.6± 1.7 kg.). In comparison with the height-weight chart for Americans 65 to 94 years of age, compiled by Master et al. (1960), the subjects in both groups I and II did not deviate significantly from the average population.

SUMMARY

The purpose of this chapter has been to describe the medical characteristics of the subjects used in this multidisciplinary study of human aging and the means employed to recruit, screen, evaluate, and classify them. The study was designed chiefly to evaluate the relative contributions of normal aging processes and disease to many of the changes observed in aged human individuals. This necessitated the extensive medical evaluation procedures described in this chapter. By the application of such detailed methods, it was possible to select from a very large but indeterminate population of volunteers over 65 years of age a group of 27 men who by almost any standard could be considered remarkably healthy for their age (group I). In addition, there was a group of 20 men who, although they exhibited signs but no symptoms of disease, more closely approximated what is generally considered to be normal for their age (group II). This chapter summarizes the results of the diagnostic and medical evaluation procedures applied to these two groups.

ACKNOWLEDGMENTS

We are indebted for our subjects from the Philadelphia area to Mr. Arthur Waldman, executive director of the Jewish Home for Aged, and to Drs. Nathan Blumberg and Stanley Tauber for their preliminary medical evaluation. We are indebted for the recruiting of subjects in the Washington,

TABLE 6.—*Mean blood pressure by age groups*

Age group	Group I			Group II			Total		
	Number	Systolic B.P.	Diastolic B.P.	Number	Systolic B.P.	Diastolic B.P.	Number	Systolic B.P.	Diastolic B.P.
65–69.......	10	130	77	7	129	75	17	130	76
70–74.......	12	124	74	9	146	79	21	134	77
75–79.......	13	122	67	3	153	83	6	138	75
80–84.......	1	146	91	0	......	......	1	146	91
85–89.......	0	......	......	0	......	......	0	......	......
90–94.......	0	......	......	1	125	75	1	125	75

D.C., area to Mr. Frank Wilson, president, and his staff of the National Association of Retired Civil Service Employees.

For aid in the clinical evaluation of the subjects for this study, we wish to acknowledge the help and cooperation of many people: The Clinical Center of the National Institutes of Health: To Dr. George Z. Williams and the staff of the Department of Clinical Pathology for numerous blood and urine examinations; Dr. Theodore Hilbish and staff of the Diagnostic X-ray Department for radiological procedures and interpretations. To the National Heart Institute: Dr. Robert Hyatt and staff for the pulmonary ventilation studies; Dr. Robert Grant and staff for recording and interpreting the many electrocardiograms. To the National Institute of Neurological Diseases and Blindness: To Drs. George Goodman and Ralph Gunkel of the Ophthalmology Branch for ophthalmoscopic and visual field determinations; and to Dr. Cosimo Ajmone-Marsan and staff of the Clinical Electroencephalography Branch for the routine and special EEG's. To the National Cancer Institute: Dr. John Fahey of the Metabolism Laboratory for the serum protein electrophoresis.

And not least of all, we wish to express our thanks to Mrs. Mary Bradeson and her staff of nurses and attendants of Nursing Unit 4—West of the National Institute of Mental Health for making the subjects comfortable during their stay at the National Institutes of Health.

REFERENCES

ABELL, L. L. A simplified method for the estimation of total cholesterol in serum and demonstration of its specificity. *J. Biol. Chem.,* 357–365, *195,* 1952.

BALDWIN, E. DeF., COURNAND, A., and RICHARDS, P. W., Jr. *Pulmonary Insufficiency* I. Physiological classification, clinical methods of analysis, standard values in normal subjects. *Medicine,* 243, *27,* 1948.

BARKER, S. E., HUMPHREY, M. J., and SOLEY, M. H. The clinical determination of protein-bound iodine. *J. Clin. Invest.,* 55–61, *30,* 1951.

BONSNES, R., and TAUSSKY, H. On the colorimetric determination of creatinine by the Jaffe Reaction. *J. Biol. Chem.,* 581–590, *158,* 1945.

DRABKIN, D. Nucleic acids and antibody production by plasma cells. *Am. J. Med. Sci.,* 710, *217,* 1949.

GRANT, R. P. *Clinical Electrocardiography: The Spatial Vector Approach.* The Blakiston Division, McGraw-Hill Book Co., Inc., New York, 1957.

KINGSLEY, G. R., and SCHAFFERT, R. R. *Standard Methods in Clinical Chemistry.* Academic Press, New York, 1957, pp. 55.

MASTER, A. M., LASSER, R. P., and BECKMAN, G. Tables of average weight and height of Americans aged 65 to 94 years. *J.A.M.A.,* 658–662, *172,* 1960.

———— and JAFFE, I. Blood pressure in white people over 65 years of age. *Ann. Int. Med.,* 284–297, *48,* 1958.

REINHOLD, J. G. *Standard Methods in Clinical Chemistry.* Academic Press, New York, 1953a, pp. 65.

———— *Standard Methods in Clinical Chemistry.* Academic Press, New York, 1953b, pp. 88.

RUTSTEIN, D. D., INGENITO, E. F., and REYNOLDS, W. E. The determination of albumin in human blood plasma and serum. A method based on the interaction of albumin with anionic dye-2-(4-Hydrozy-Benzeneazo) Benzoic Acid. *J. Clin. Invest.,* 211, *33,* 1954.

VANSELOW, A. P. Preparation of Nessler's Reagent. *Ind. Eng. Chem. Anal. Ed.,* 516–517, *12,* 1940.

WINTROBE, M. M. Microscopic examination of the blood. *Am. J. Med. Sci.,* 58–70, *185,* 1933.

CHAPTER 4

Statistical Methodology

by Samuel W. Greenhouse and Donald F. Morrison

Introduction

The use of statistical methods is essential to a multidisciplinary study of the kind described in this monograph. If the statisticians are an integral part of the research team, they are also in a position to contribute to the project beyond mere experimental design and analysis of data. It is the purpose of this chapter to present the varied roles and functions served by the statistician in such efforts. In addition, certain technical comments will be made concerning the methods used in summarizing and analyzing the research data, and also relating to the limitations and generality of the conclusions drawn from the project.

This chapter will present discussions in five areas: (1) design of the study, (2) handling and storage of data, (3) analysis of data, (4) problems in statistical and research methodology, and (5) general comments on multidisciplinary research. In some of these areas, it will be our intent to point out problems that appear to be peculiar to multidisciplinary research. For certain of these problems, we offer no solution other than to make their statement explicit.

Design of the Study

Since the purpose of the investigation was to study aged individuals who were normal in the sense of being free from physical or mental illness, the customary sources of subjects for aging studies, namely, homes for the aged and other institutions, were excluded. It was therefore important to obtain subjects who were able to maintain themselves in the general community.

There were several reasons for not considering formal sampling designs during the planning stage of this study, the principal ones being: (1) the requirement that all subjects be optimally healthy, that is, free from known, symptomatic physical or mental illness, and residing in the community; (2) the relatively small number of subjects (a maximum of 60) that could be brought to the Clinical Center for a 2-week examination over the proposed 2-year study period; and (3) an awareness among the participating investigators of the primarily exploratory nature of the study. Although in a definitive research inquiry, statistical considerations would have demanded a procedure of probability sampling, the expected recovery of usable subjects meeting all the criteria

¹ We are indebted to Mrs. Annie Randall for maintaining the files and performing innumerable statistical calculations throughout most of the study, and to Mrs. Norma Johnston for setting up the central files and performing necessary computations during the early part of the study.

would be low. So large a population would have to be examined that it would entail too great a cost for an exploratory study.

Because of the nonrandom selection of the sample, it is clear that great caution must be exercised in interpreting the results. This admonition applies whether a value of some trait obtained in this study is to be taken as holding for all normally healthy aged or whether a comparison presented between our aged group and a group of young individuals is to be interpreted as what would have been found in the respective populations of old and young. On the other hand, it seems reasonable to believe that biases resulting from a nonrandom sample do not affect all types of variables measured in the same way. Whereas certain social, demographic, and psychological data may be considerably affected, other psychological and physiological measurements may be slightly biased, if at all, with respect to a population of optimally healthy aged.

Estimates of population parameters, e.g., means and variances of population traits, may be, and probably are, biased, but relationships among traits need not be. For example, a sample estimate of the correlation between two biochemical measurements or between biochemical and psychomotor measurements may very well be an unbiased estimate of the relationship between the same two variables in the population of normal aged. This lack of bias may exist despite the fact that both variables under consideration are biased in their averages.

In view of the failure to achieve a completely biased sample for health, it is possible that correlations between certain variables may be spurious because of the existence of unrecognized, asymptomatic disease in some subjects. The presence of debilitants may cause deviant observations on a number of scales or measurements,

with the result that those features might be significantly correlated.

To maintain homogeneity, two groups were distinguished, one the optimally healthy individuals and the other the subclinical and asymptomatic group. It should be made clear that this classification of subjects was made on the basis of the descriptive medical and psychiatric examinations. With one exception, none of the research variables reported in this monograph was used to make this classification. The exception involved five cases who were found to have excessively high blood pressure readings during the course of the research procedure which measured cerebral blood flow.

Further, it was necessary in screening and classifying the subjects to make arbitrary decisions with respect to the values of those variables known to change with age that were to be considered as pathological. For example, it was decided to consider any blood pressure reading above three standard deviations from the mean of normal young as hypertensive.

During the 2 years in which each subject was observed and studied in the Clinical Center for a period of 2 weeks, several investigators, primarily in psychology and physiology, were making control observations on groups of young males. These control observations served to maintain some control over the techniques used and also to provide comparative values in a young group.

Maintenance of a Central Data File

Since a major objective of the study was to determine relationships between variables studied by different disciplines, it was felt that investigators should not have access to, or discuss, each other's data when they were being collected and in coding the data after collections. Conceivably, exchange of diagnosis and observations might induce biases in future measurements and evaluations. For example, after the first 10 subjects were studied, it could well happen that the physiologist measuring cerebral metabolism might mention to the psychiatrist that 2 subjects had rather low oxygen consumption values. Not unreasonably, the psychiatrist would ask for the names of the two, and upon their identification would also search his memory for psychiatric features in which these two were also peculiar. Unfortunately, he might find some scale or characteristic on which the two subjects appeared to stand out from the other individuals. The effect of such interactions during the data collection and coding phase could easily result in spurious and biased correlations between variables. The confidentiality of each investigator's observations on subjects currently on the ward was maintained throughout the study.

One clerk of the Statistics Section was assigned the task of keeping a central data file. This clerk received protocols and data from the investigators after each pair of patients had been seen on the ward, and transferred the measurement and categorical observations to worksheets for each discipline. Without this central clerical service it is certain that the exchange of data and coordination of efforts for the interdisciplinary analyses would have been slow and cumbersome.

Analysis of the Data

Over 600 characteristics were measured and observed on each of the 47 subjects used in the study. The decision was made to reduce the number of continuous (physiological measurements, psychological test scores and scale values, ratings on psychiatric scales) variables obtained on each medically acceptable subject to a smaller complex of operationally and statistically independent measures. Each investigator grouped his continuous variables into blocks on some rational basis so that a matrix of product moment correlation coefficients might be computed for each block. Representative variables or weighted combinations of them were selected from each block according to the correlation patterns. The IBM 650 computer library program available in the fall of 1957 dictated that the largest block contain no more than 49 variables. Sixteen blocks representing experimental psychology, clinical psychology, psychiatry, and cerebral circulation and metabolism were submitted for computation of their intrablock correlations. Block size ranged from 5 to 49 variables. Missing data proved to be a troublesome problem: small gaps, as in the case of three Minnesota Multiphasic Personality Inventory scores on a single patient, were closed by inserting the variables' averages. For larger sets of missing values (e.g., those psychological testing procedures introduced after the first few patients had been seen), the nonexistent scores and measures were recorded as "0" and the required correlations were computed on desk calculators from the subsidiary machine output of sums of observations and sums of squares and cross products. The correlation computed in this manner between two given measures was based only upon those patients with observations on both variables, although the means and variances reported for descriptive purposes utilized all patients. The experience of the Statistics Section with these computations led to the preparations of a useful IBM 650 program for intercorrelating large sets of such incomplete data on virtually any number of subjects (Cramer, 1959).

Hotelling principal components (Hotelling, 1933) were extracted directly from the correlation matrices of the psychiatric, cerebral metabolic, and clinical psychology blocks. The Hotelling procedure is a mathematically well-defined type of factor analysis that attempts to account for most of the total variation in a complex of variables by a few uncorrelated weighted averages of the original variables. Unfortunately, this parsimonious ideal seldom follows from matrices with small to moderate correlations; furthermore, it is often difficult to give conceptual or operational meaning to the ensuing components. Components analyses were not carried out upon the experimental psychology and audiometric correlations; instead, a smaller complex of 32 variables (23 cognitive and psychomotor, 9 audiometric) was constructed, and its principal components were extracted. Those analyses formed the basis for chapter 15. The general interdisciplinary complex finally compiled from the correlational study consists of the 40-odd variables treated in chapter 15.

The course of the statistical analyses within the complexes followed a pattern characterized by evolution and feedback. Significant correlations suggested other variables, often outside the complex, whose common variance with the original measures might account for their dependence. It was then necessary to compute the partial correlations between the original variables to determine their degree of relationship if the third variable had in fact remained constant. Dichotomous and categorical variables (diagnosis, medical group) were also referred to for that purpose, although their simultaneous use usually left some cells vacant or with but one or two subjects, so that a complete assessment of all factors was not possible. Some additional principal component analyses and multiple regressions were also computed in an attempt to determine the structure of the data.

Concurrent with the search for small complexes of significant variables, the Statistics Section collaborated in several specific interdisciplinary analyses. An attempt was made to find physiological and psychological correlates with the psychiatric features of depression, denial, and senile quality. Extensive analyses were made of suspected EEG-cerebral physiological relationships. Differences between normal and hypertensive patients were investigated on a host of nonphysiological measures.

Problems in Research and Statistical Methodology

In the majority of the analyses standard statistical techniques were adequate. The product moment correlation coefficient was used extensively. Since this measure generally overstates significance when used in place of the chi-square statistic (with Yates' correction) for categorical or 0–1 observations, the risk of missing significant relationships in the screening process was minimal. Relationships found to be significant in this manner were verified by other techniques.

The many possible cross-classifications of subjects in the study suggested two- and three-way analyses of variance on a number of continuous variables, such as reaction time, Wechsler subtest scores, and similar psychological modalities. However, the unequal numbers of subjects in the different cells of the double and triple dichotomies usually made the classical multiway analysis of variance inexact, so that tests for significant main effects were usually made by t statistics, after it had been ascertained that the ways of classification were "additive" in their effect upon the continuous response variable, and did not produce interactions. Three-way classifications within a given medical group often left empty cells, so that certain comparisons could not be made.

The orthogonality of the Hotelling principal components permits evaluation of factor scores for each subject much more easily than with centroid factors. One merely computes standard (T) scores for each subject on all variables included in the complex, and multiplies the standard score for a particular subject and variable by that variable's coefficient in the given component vector.

Because of the exploratory nature of many of the analyses, two-sided probability levels were generally used in determining the significance of most test statistics. However, the psychological or physiological nature of some variables implied that a change could reasonably be expected in only one direction, so that in some cases one-sided significance with a smaller value of the test statistic was proper. Little attention was devoted to the determination of the probability of the "Type II error," or the failure of detecting a significant result when one actually existed.

A problem arises in the analysis of categorical data, as commonly found in the clinical and behavioral sciences, in relating such data to each other and to continuous variables. A difficulty in applying statistical techniques here is that they do not take account of the inherently different scaling of the various traits being measured. This is a problem to which we certainly do not present any clear-cut solution. Futhermore, it would seem that no solution to this problem can be effected through the mere device of more elaborate statistical techniques of analysis. The problem is in part basic to the content being studied by these disciplines and can only be resolved with additional information leading to more refined scaling in measurement. In the simpler situation where a scaled variable is used for comparing different groups, it is the function of the statistician to point out the appropriate technique to be used which may require the investigator to bring into focus

the kind of scaling such as ordinate, nominal etc., being assumed by his measurement.

Problems in multidisciplinary research

From the statistical point of view, the matter of multiple testing or multiple comparisons constitutes the most troublesome problem of this investigation. Research in the behavioral sciences is generally of the type where there are a great many observations on each of a relatively small number of individuals. It is inevitable that the investigator becomes involved in a great many tests of significance or confidence intervals.

Before pursuing this problem further, however, it is important to emphasize that this study was initiated by definite questions and hypotheses both inter- and intra-disciplinary in nature. It is characteristic of much research in the behavioral sciences that although specific questions and hypotheses may exist and constitute the reason for the study, observations are not restricted to those questions. Many more data are collected than would seem necessary merely to answer the questions posed. The reason for this is probably twofold. First, much of the cost, both in economic and in scientific effort, in human behavioral research, is in obtaining the human subject. The second reason is probably a consequence of the nature of the variables and measurements in these sciences. The behavioral scientist defines a human trait or factor but is uncertain of the sharpness of available rulers in measuring that characteristic and may therefore add other measurements which purport to assess the same trait or perhaps related traits. As a result, many statistical tests of significance are performed, on differences between means, on correlation coefficients, on chi-square statistics, etc.

Investigators in these fields are generally aware of the hazards inherent in multiple testing based on a large number of statistics derived from the same set of data. If 100 such independent tests were made in the same experiment, each at the 100 α percent level of significance, it is clear that 100 α percent of these can be expected to be significant on the basis of chance deviation from the null hypotheses tested. However, independent tests can be handled in more or less approximate fashion. The case where the various statistical tests are correlated is much more complicated. The very least that can be said then is that the investigator loses control of the risk of rejecting null hypotheses, that is, he no longer can state the level of significance of his conclusions. Similarly if, rather than tests of significance, many confidence intervals are computed on the same data, then the degree of confidence associated with the interval conclusions can no longer be given (Scheffé, 1959).

There is no clear-cut solution to this problem other than blind insistence that such studies without a defined group of *a priori* questions not be undertaken at all. Short of any such extreme solution is the alternative of performing studies which are exploratory in that they arrive at many conclusions whose inferential potential may be questionable but which are more than pilot studies in that some inferences are permissible and valid. It is in this sense that we consider this investigation to be an exploratory study. For those variables in "the fishing expedition" significant or nonsignificant relations can only be suggestive. A whole chain of these observed interrelationships may lead to a tentative theory.

In reading the various chapters, it may be observed that statements are made which may appear to be unqualified generalizations and that P values are given as the stamp of authority. The former are to be interpreted in the light of the comments made here concerning the exploratory nature of this research and the latter as an aid and guide to the reader of the strength of the evidence against the null hypothesis.

REFERENCES

CRAMER, E. 1959. Personal Communication.

HOTELLING, H. 1933. Analysis of a Complex of Statistical Variables into Principal Components, *J. Educ. Psych.*, 24, pp. 417–441, 498–520.

SCHEFFÉ, H. 1959. Analysis of Variance, John Wiley & Sons, N.Y., p. 30.

CHAPTER 5

Medical Investigation of The Processes of Aging

by Leslie S. Libow

What is aging? Are the changes in mentation, physical state, and physiology, commonly observed in aged individuals, a reflection of inevitable natural changes evolving with time, or are they the manifestations of disease states, and thus potentially alterable? Disease was defined operationally in this study as those pathological processes occurring occasionally in the young and not universally in the aged. Aging by contrast is defined as a progression of adult changes characteristic of the species and which should occur in all individuals if they live long enough.

The aims of this study were first, to distinguish more clearly the medically significant changes due to time per se from the pathological states which so often obscure our view of the process of aging; second, to present data to help establish age relevant "normal" values for many measurements of medical significance. This chapter is the author's medically oriented analysis of the total data obtained by the several collaborating disciplines in this study.

As described in chapters 2 and 3, these healthy aged (65 to 92 years) male volunteers were screened in their home communities and then admitted to the National Institutes of Health for 2 weeks of study. After all of the medical data was available, it was clear that the group was not homogeneous for health and they were divided into two

subgroups. Group I, composed of 27 men, represents the optimally healthy aged, with largely insignificant and asymptomatic abnormalities, such as X-ray evidence of osteoarthritis, senile cataracts and minimal conduction defects in the electrocardiogram. Group II contains 20 men who showed definite evidence of disease with more serious implications, though completely asymptomatic. These changes included diastolic blood pressures of 90 to 94 mm of mercury, elevated mean arterial blood pressures (MABP) during cerebral blood flow studies, certain completely asymptomatic electrocardiographic abnormalities (see section on E.C.G.) as well as such abnormalities as a mild case of gout. Also included in this definition of disease was arteriosclerosis, which was not viewed as an inevitable part of the aging process. Ten of the 20 individuals in group II demonstrated what was judged as significant, clinically demonstrable, generally asymptomatic, involvement of the vascular system with arteriosclerosis and were placed into a subgroup of group II, termed "arteriosclerotic." The criteria employed in this classification (see ch. 3) included some or all of the following: historical, physical, or electrocardiographic evidence suggestive of arteriosclerotic heart disease; chest X-ray evidence of calcification of the thoracic aorta with or without tortuosity and/or widening; historical and/or physical evidence of interference with peripheral circulation ("arteriosclerosis obliterans"); ophthalmoscopic evidence of retinal arteriosclerosis. This latter finding alone was not considered sufficient evidence for classification into the "arteriosclerotic" subgroup.

The chapters concerning selection of subjects and medical screening and examination (ch. 2 and 3) indicate the care given to achieve the separation of "normal aging" from the effects of disease. It is obvious that this aim could only be partially fulfilled because of limitations in detecting known diseases as well as the existence of as yet undescribed disease states. Unquestionably, too, the clinical recognition of arteriosclerosis is imprecise. There probably were some subjects judged to be free of this disease who had a greater degree of arteriosclerosis than those classified in the "arteriosclerotic" group. However, to understand the process of aging, it is essential to attempt a delineation of the effects of arteriosclerosis. Thus, for operational purposes it was assumed that the probability of the presence of significant arteriosclerosis was greater in individuals demonstrating some or all of the criteria listed, than in individuals with none of these findings. It appears quite certain that our subjects were healthier than average individuals of this age group and that the optimally healthy aged (group I) were as a group healthier than the asymptomatic disease group (group II).

This division of the subjects into two groups, based on our earlier definition of disease, permitted two major approaches to be employed in this study: a comparison of the healthy aged with the young to determine variables altered by the aging process; and a comparison between the optimally healthy group and the asymptomatic subclinical disease group in order to determine the extent to which disease influenced observed differences.

The research design of this interdisciplinary study, especially in its approach to the organic aspects of aging, has focused on the central nervous system. The medical aspect of the study was largely that of total medical evaluation for the purpose of classification in regard to overall health status in general and central nervous system status specifically. The medical investigation was exhaustive and utilized many of the facilities available at the NIH.[1]

HEMATOLOGICAL AND BLOOD CHEMISTRY PROFILE OF THE HEALTHY AGED

There is a striking similarity between the hematological and blood chemical values of these healthy aged men and those values considered normal by the clinical chemistry laboratory of the NIH for a younger adult group (table 1). Furthermore the hemoglobin, hematocrit, and white blood count, did not correlate significantly with age for the age range covered by our group (65–92 years).

The erythrocyte sedimentation rate is elevated compared to the young. Several reports of a similar finding have previously been reviewed (Reinbourne, 1952). Since group I (22±4.2 mm./1st Hr.) and II (19±4.2 mm./1st Hr.)[2] do not differ from each other in regard to this measurement, the increased sedimentation rate suggests an age related change, perhaps reflecting the distribution of serum proteins described below.

---

[1] The medical histories, physical examinations, and laboratory values used by the author in his analyses were obtained through the efforts of Dr. Mark Lane and Dr. Thomas Vates. They have described their methods in ch. 3.

[2] Values given in this chapter are means and standard error of the means, unless otherwise noted.

TABLE 1.—*Hematology and chemistry profile of the healthy aged*

		Healthy aged (group I and II: $N=47$)				Healthy adults [1]
		Mean	S.D.	Range [2]	r	Range
Hematology:						
Hematocrit	Percent	44	3	38–50	N.S.	45–50.
Hemoglobin	gm/100ml	15	1	13–17	N.S.	14–18.
White blood cell count	(Cells) mm³	}6,600	1,400	3,800–9,400	N.S.	4,500–11,000.
Differential white cell count						
Neutrophiles	Percent	57.08	8	41–73	N.S.	59.
Lymphocytes	Percent	35.09	8	19–51	N.S.	34.
Basophiles	Percent	.44	.3	0–1.4	N.S.	0.5.
Monocytes	Percent	3.75	2.4	0–8.5	N.S.	3.8.
Eosinophiles	Percent	3.64	2.3	0–7.2	N.S.	2.7.
Erythrocyte sed. rate	mm/1st Hr.	20.63	13.1	0–46	N.S.	0–15.
Chemistry:						
Glucose, fasting	mg/100ml	77	9	59–95	N.S.	65–110.
Blood urea nitrogen	mg/100ml	17	3.0	11–23	N.S.	8–22.
Total cholesterol	mg/100ml	233	40.0	153–313	N.S.	150–250.
Creatinine	mg/100ml	1.1	.20	0.7–1.5	N.S.	0.6–1.1.
Total protein	gm/100ml	6.7	.40	5.9–7.5	** −0.38	6.7–8.2.
Serum albumin	gm/100ml	3.5	.26	3.0–4.0	** −0.48	50 percent total protein.
Protein bound iodine	μg/100ml	5.3	1.0	3.3–7.3	* −0.33	3.4–8.0.

[1] These are the normal adult values of the NIH Clinical Pathology Laboratory which performed the determinations on the aged as listed in this table. The exact age ranges for these comparative values of younger adults are not available.
[2] Range = mean ± 2 S.D.
* Statistically significant at the 0.05 level.
** Statistically significant at the 0.01 level.

S.D. = Standard deviation.
N.S. = Not statistically significant.
r = Coefficient of correlation with age.

The fasting blood glucose, blood urea nitrogen, and creatinine values, also show ranges similar to younger adult values as well as an absence of statistically significant correlations with age.

The serum cholesterol has previously been shown by Keys to have a distinct trend with age in healthy men (Keys, 1952a). He showed that between the ages of 20 and 55 the level of serum cholesterol rises continually from a mean of 170 to a mean of 250 mg percent. In the late 50's this trend is reversed and the decline continues to age 75, the limit of the study. Though the abrupt decline in the mid-50's can be shown to be unrelated to the selective morbidity and mortality effect of coronary artery disease, this selective factor has a greater influence on age groups beyond the mid-50's (Keys, 1952a). With increasing years, those with coronary disease and the associated higher cholesterol values would be eliminated from the studies of "normal" serum cholesterol levels and consequently contribute to the negative trend with age of observed cholesterol values in the general population.

The cholesterol data for our entire aged group (table 1), while showing a mean and standard deviation similar to that of the men 65 to 75 years in the Keys study, fails to show a significant trend with age. The lack of a negative correlation of cholesterol over our age range may reflect the unique state of health of these men. That is, when a "steady state of health" is maintained, the elevated cholesterol values may not affect the total system in an adverse manner.

Serum Proteins

A change basic to the process of aging is suggested in the highly significant decrease ($p \leq 0.001$) of serum albumin in our healthy aged (3.27 ± 0.04 gm percent) as compared to young adults (3.81 ± 0.09 gm percent), as measured by filter paper electrophoresis (table 2). That this change reflects a process evolving with time rather

TABLE 2.—*Serum protein electrophoreses* [1]

Serum protein		Healthy aged group I and II combined (N=43; 65–92 years)			Healthy young males (N=22; 18–36 years)			Significance of group difference
		Mean	S.E.	Range [2]	Mean	S.E.	Range [2]	
Total protein	gm/100 ml	6.93	0.07	5.84–8.92	7.19	0.10	6.21–8.17	N.S.
Albumin	gm/100 ml	3.27	.04	2.69–3.85	3.81	.09	2.99–4.63	(***)
Alpha 1 globulin	gm/100 ml	.38	.01	.24–.52	.37	.10	.23–.54	N.S.
Alpha 2 globulin	gm/100 ml	.88	.02	.58–1.18	.76	.04	.38–1.13	(**)
Beta globulin	gm/100 ml	1.13	.02	.87–1.39	.99	.05	.67–1.7	(***)
Gamma globulin	gm/100 ml	1.30	.05	.66–1.94	1.25	.06	.73–1.7	N.S.

[1] All determinations (filter paper electrophoresis) presented here were performed by Dr. John L. Fahey, National Cancer Institute.
[2] Range=mean ±2 S.D.
** Statistically significant at the 0.01 level.
*** Statistically significant at the 0.001 level.

S.E.=Standard error.
N.S.=Not statistically significant.

than disease states is suggested, since there is no statistically significant difference between the mean serum albumin concentration in our group of excellent health (group I: 3.30 ± 0.06 gm percent) compared with our group of average health (group II: 3.24 ± 0.06 gm percent). Further evidence that this change does not reflect subclinical chronic disease is the lack of a statistically significant difference in the gamma globulin fraction of our aged (1.30 ± 0.05 gm percent) as compared to the healthy young (1.25 ± 0.06 gm percent). Gamma globulin has been reported as frequently elevated in a broad spectrum of chronic disease states including infections, neoplasms, collagen diseases and cirrhosis of the liver (Gutman, 1948; Gross, Gitlin, and Janeway, 1959).

A decreased serum albumin concentration in the aged, electrophoretically measured, has previously been reported, (Karrel, Wilder, and Beber, 1956).

As is well known, proteins are in a state of continuous flux and the serum protein concentration is a reflection of this process as well as of the circulatory dynamics. Thus, the conditions that could decrease serum albumin concentration include deficient intake or absorption, catabolic predominance via increased protein breakdown or diminished protein production, albumin loss into body fluids, and finally a dilutional effect secondary to a relatively increased plasma volume.

The significantly lower serum albumin in these healthy, active, community-resident and well-nourished elderly men suggests a change in overall body protein metabolism or a specific change in the ability of the liver to synthesize serum albumin. Alternative possibilities have not been supported by previous studies reported by others in the literature. There are no differences between aged individuals and younger persons in terms of: dietary protein requirements (Horwitt, 1953; Keys, 1952b); extent of protein digestion and absorption (Chinn, Lavik, and Cameron, 1956); or blood volume (Sklaroff, 1956; Smith, 1958). Furthermore, in our subjects there is no clinical or laboratory evidence for chronic wasting disease, liver disease, hypermetabolic states, or protein loss via urine, edema fluid, or gastrointestinal tract.

Isotope tracer techniques on healthy aged individuals would shed much light on the dynamic state of protein turnover and aid in the understanding of this change. The use of I^{131} labeled polyvinyl-pyrolidine (PVP) (Gordon, 1959) or chromium 51 labeled albumin (Waldmann, 1961) to investigate any possible subtle protein loss into the gastrointestinal "compartment" might also be revealing.

The serum total protein (6.93 ± 0.07 gm percent) is not significantly different from the normal younger adult value (7.19 ± 0.10 gm percent). The alpha 1 globulin values are almost identical in both groups (aged: 0.38 ± 0.01 gm percent; young: 0.37 ± 0.10 gm percent). The alpha 2 globulin (0.88 ± 0.02 gm percent) is significantly ($p \leq 0.01$) elevated as compared to the young (0.76 ± 0.04 gm percent). The beta globulin is very significantly ($p \leq 0.001$) increased (1.13 ± 0.02 gm percent) as compared to the younger adults (0.99 ± 0.05 gm percent). Some part of this increase is probably related to the reported elevation of beta lipo-proteins with age (Lindgren and Nichols, 1960). The increase of the alpha 2 and beta globulins explains the maintenance of total protein levels in the presence of the diminished serum albumin.

The alpha globulin group, as determined by paper electrophoresis, is known to include glycoproteins, mucoproteins, ceruloplasmin, alpha-lipoproteins, and at least one macroglobulin. The beta globulin group includes beta-lipoproteins, the iron-binding protein (transferrin), a protein of plasma cell origin (Petermann, 1960), and probably several unknown quantitatively smaller specific components. Although the beta-lipoproteins comprise about one-third of the beta globulin fraction it cannot be concluded with any certainty that a quantitative change in the total fraction is related to any one component. Our data do not provide any evidence on the mechanisms of the increases in alpha 2 and beta globulin fractions. With methods such as starch-gel electrophoresis (Poulik and Smithies, 1958) and immunoelectrophoresis (Bieler, Ecke, and Spies, 1949) the specific components of the altered globulin fractions can be more clearly delineated.

Protein Bound Iodine

The data reveal a significant negative correlation ($r = -0.33$; $p \leq 0.5$) of the protein bound iodine and age (table 1). Previous studies based largely on institutionalized subjects have disagreed regarding the existence of this relationship (Kountz, Chieffi, and Kirk, 1949; Gaffney, Gregerman, Yiengst, and Shock, 1960).

Thyroid hormone circulates in the plasma loosely bound to precipitable protein, and its level is reflected by the PBI test (Robbins and Rall, 1960). That the significant negative trend of the PBI with age is a reflection of a decrease in circulating thyroid hormone and not in the transporting serum proteins is suggested by the lack of significant correlation between levels of PBI and levels of electrophoretically determined serum albumin, alpha 1 globulin, alpha 2 globulin, beta globulin, and gamma globulin. However, undetectably minute changes in the level of the transporting proteins or alterations in the binding ability of the transporting proteins have not been ruled out.

Blood Pressure

There was no significant correlation between clinically recorded systolic or diastolic blood pressure and age (table 3a). However, the mean arterial blood pressure (MABP), measured directly in the femoral artery with a mercury manometer, shows a significant, positive correlation with age ($r = +0.30$; $p \leq 0.5$), for the combined groups.

Systolic and diastolic blood pressures have been reported to increase between ages 16 and 60 (Master, Garfield, and Walters, 1952). The study was continued on a large number of older healthy males between the ages of 65 and 106 (Master, Lasser, and Jaffe, 1957). Blood pressures were recorded by family physicians from men whom they considered free of cardiovascular disease. These results are shown in table 3a. In the older group, these investigators found no significant correlation of the systolic blood pressure with age. Their data show a significant decrease of the diastolic blood pressure with age.

The mean of the clinical blood pressure measurements for the entire older group in Master's study was 145/82 while the mean blood pressure for the NIH group I was 127/75, and that for group II, 140/78 (table 3b). Thus, the mean systolic blood pressure in our group II closely resembles that of the older Master's group. In contrast, the mean systolic blood pressure in group I resembles the level of Master's 20–40-year-old group (table 3a). The mean diastolic blood pressure for both groups I and II are similar to those of Master's younger group.

There is an impressive trend toward an increasing mean systolic and diastolic blood pressure in group II (over the age range of

Master data [1]

Age	Systolic	Diastolic	Age	Systolic	Diastolic
5 [3]	92	62	65–69	143	83
10 [3]	103	69	70–74	145	82
15	119	74	75–79	146	81
20	123	76	80–84	145	82
30	126	79	85–89	145	79
40	129	81	90–94	145	78
50	135	83	95–106	146	78
60	142	85			

NIH data [2]

Group I (N=27)				Group II (N=20)			
Age	Systolic	Diastolic	Number	Age	Systolic	Diastolic	Number
65–69	130	77	10	65–69	129	75	7
70–74	124	74	13	70–74	146	79	10
75–79	121	67	3	75–79	155	86	2
80–84	146	91	1	80–84			
85–89				85–89			
				90–92	125	75	1

NIH: Group I and group II combined (N=47)

Age	Mean systolic	Mean diastolic	Number
65–70	130	76	17
70–74	134	76	23
75–79	135	74	5
80–84	146	91	1

[1] Master, A. M., et al., 1952, 1957.
[2] NIH data: Blood pressure recorded twice daily for 2 weeks on each subject.
[3] The data for these age groups (5 and 10 years) were drawn from Handbook of Circulation, National Academy of Sciences—National Research Council, p. 105, 1959.

65 to 80 years (table 3a). An opposite trend exists over this age range for group I (table 3a). This may reflect the influence of the greater degree of arteriosclerosis in group II. That this trend toward an increasing blood pressure serves to preserve the functional integrity of the brain in the presence of arteriosclerosis is suggested by the electroencephalographic (E.E.G.) findings. In group I, with its cerebral blood flow not differing from the young controls (ch. 6), no correlations exist between blood pressure and E.E.G. variables. However, in group II, with its cerebral blood flow diminished as compared to the young, there is a significant negative correlation between percent slow wave activity and blood pressure (ch. 7), suggesting that in the presence of vascular disease (group II) elevation of the blood pressure tends to preserve the electrical ac-

TABLE 3b.—*Mean blood pressure of healthy aged*

Blood pressure	NIH [1]				Master [2]	
	Group I		Group II		Mean	S.E.
	Mean	S.E.	Mean	S.E.		
Systolic........................	* 127	2	140	4	145	0. 41
Diastolic.......................	* 75	1	* 78	1	82	. 18

[1] NIH: Blood pressure recorded twice daily for 2 weeks on each subject.
[2] Master, A. M., et al., 1957. Age range: 65–106 years.
* Significantly different at the 0.05 level from values obtained by Master.

S.E.=Standard error.

tivity of the brain. With the increased peripheral vascular resistance often associated with arteriosclerosis, the arterial blood pressure is increased if the cardiac output is maintained at the same level. This would, however, require an increased cardiac work. A lack of a rise in blood pressure in the presence of arteriosclerosis, indicates the failure to increase the cardiac work adequately to maintain the cardiac output. This ability to increase cardiac work may be an important survival characteristic for the total organism and for the central nervous system in particular.

Blood pressure elevations accompanying depressive states have long been noted. Usually such reports refer to psychotic depressions (Miller, 1939; Igersheimer and Stevenson, 1951). Those individuals manifesting chronic depressive trends in otherwise well-integrated personalities are rarely hospitalized. Thus, little physiological data is available on such a group.

This study afforded an opportunity to evaluate clinical blood pressures, mean arterial blood pressures, and pulse rates on a group demonstrating subtle manifestations of depression.

The entire group of 47 men were interviewed by 2 independently-rating psychiatrists. Thirteen of these subjects showed evidence of depression. The criteria for such categorization has been described in chapter 11.

The group with diagnosed depression had a mean arterial blood pressure (MABP = 108.36 mm Hg) that borders on being significantly greater ($0.1 \geq p \geq 0.05$) than the remaining men who exhibited no depression (mean = 97.30 mm Hg).

The systolic blood pressure in the depressed group was elevated (mean = 140) as compared to the remainder of the subjects (mean = 129). The elevation also approaches significance ($0.1 \geq p \geq 0.05$).

The diastolic blood pressure and pulse rate of the depressive group did not differ significantly from the other subjects.

It is of interest that even subtle depression in otherwise healthy and well-integrated individuals is accompanied by a suggestion of increased blood pressure.

Vascular System

In this study the diagnosis of retinal arteriosclerosis, by funduscopic examination, does not correlate with cerebral blood flow (CBF) or cerebral vascular resistance (CVR) nor with any clinical findings such as blood pressure, X-ray evidence of calcification of the aorta or calcification of the internal carotid artery siphon as seen on skull X-ray.

The appearance of the retinal arterioles by funduscopic examination has long been considered a reflection of the state of the cerebral vasculature. This derives in part from the close anatomical relationship of the retinal and cerebral vessels. Duke-Elder in his text (1940) states "the best way to obtain information about the cerebral vessels is by means of ophthalmoscopic examination." Other textbooks of ophthalmology state similar views (May, 1937; Walsh, 1957). However, a detailed post mortem study by Alpers, Forster, and Herbut (1948), failed to reveal a correlation between retinal arteriosclerosis and arteriosclerosis of most of the major branches of the cerebral vasculature.

In the NIH study, the fundi of all 47 subjects were evaluated ophthalmoscopically by an internist and ophthalmologist. Thirty-eight of these 47 very healthy men were judged to have minimal arteriosclerotic changes, characterized chiefly by narrowing of the arterioles and increased light reflex, often with tortuosity of the vessels. By ophthalmoscopic examination, arteriosclerotic changes of the retina are, of course, difficult to differentiate from early arteriolar changes accompanying hypertension.

There was no statistically significant difference between the mean cerebral blood flow or the mean cerebral vascular resistance of the group with retinal arteriosclerosis as compared to the small remainder of the group without this ophthalmoscopic finding (CBF=55.5 and 57.0, respectively; CVR= 1.75 and 1.72, respectively).

The high incidence of minimal retinal arteriosclerotic changes in these healthy subjects, together with the lack of correlation with quantitative cerebral circulatory changes and any clinical findings, indicates that this funduscopic finding is of little significance in an accurate evaluation of the state of overall health and/or of physiological function of elderly individuals.

Cerebral Vascular Calcification

There is a significantly decreased ($p \leq$ 0.05) cerebral blood flow in the group with skull X-ray evidence of internal carotid artery siphon [3] calcification as compared to the remainder of the subjects who did not demonstrate this finding. Further delineation reveals this difference to be largely related to the presence within this group, showing calcification, of subjects from group II; group II having a significantly lower cerebral blood flow than group I (ch. 6). However, when dividing the subjects into subcategories of groups I and II, with and without internal carotid artery siphon calcification (table 4), the suggestion of diminished cerebral blood flow and diminished internal jugular venous oxygen tension (reflection of the oxygen tension of the brain) associated with the calcification, persists, even within group I.

Pulmonary Function

The central nervous system is extremely sensitive to changes in oxygen and carbon dioxide, and such changes may constitute important factors resulting in changes of brain function, which in turn influence manifestations of human aging.

To understand the effect of changing pulmonary function on the aging process, as well as to establish adequate norms for these latter years, results of tests of vital capacity, timed vital capacity, maximum breathing capacity, arterial pH, arterial CO_2 and arterial oxygen saturation have been analyzed.

---

[3] The "carotid siphon" is an angiographic term denoting the internal carotid artery in its intracranial course through the carotid canal and the cavernous sinus up to the point immediately prior to joining the Circle of Willis.

TABLE 4.—*Comparison of cerebral circulatory and metabolic functions [1] in groups with and without calcification of the internal carotid artery siphon [2]*

	Calcification of internal carotid artery siphon	CBF (ml/100g/min)	CVR (mm Hg) (ml/100g/min)	VPO$_2$ (mm Hg)
Group I.............	O:			
	Mean..................	59. 27	1. 53	36. 28
	S.D...................	11. 13	. 33	2. 9
	+:			
	Mean..................	[3] 55. 07	1. 66	[3] 34. 7
	S·D...................	9. 70	. 37	2. 6
Group II...........	O:			
	Mean..................	56. 60	2. 14	37. 0
	S.D...................	10. 59	. 34	3. 6
	+:			
	Mean..................	[3] 50. 13	1. 96	[3] 33. 58
	S.D...................	10. 08	. 51	4. 79

[1] The individual values for these measurements are presented in ch. 6.

[2] As seen on skull X-rays.

[3] Note lower levels of CBF and VPO$_2$ for subgroups with calcification. When considered together, the group with calcification has a significantly lower cerebral blood flow than the group without this calcification (CBF: mean=52.6, 57.9, respectively; significant at the 0.05 level).

O=Group without calcification of the carotid artery "siphon."
+=Group with calcification of the carotid artery "siphon."
S.D.=Standard deviation.
CBF=Cerebral blood flow.
CVR=Cerebral vascular resistance.
VPO$_2$=Jugular venous oxygen tension.

There was no clinical evidence of pulmonary disease. One man gave a history of bronchial asthma, and another complained of shortness of breath, which remained unexplained.

Recordings were made on a Collins 9-liter recording spirometer which had a ventilograph attachment. All respiratory tests were performed with the subjects in a sitting position. All gas volumes were measured at room temperature and corrected to body temperature and pressure saturated with water vapor. The methods for the determination of arterial oxygen saturation and arterial CO$_2$ tension are described in chapter 6.

Tables 5, 6, and 7 give the pulmonary function results.

Maximal Breathing Capacity (M.B.C.)

The maximal breathing capacity in both group I (98.5 ± 3.97 liters/min) and group II (76.2 ± 3.36 liters/min) reflects adequate respiratory ability. The values resemble somewhat younger age groups in previous studies (Baldwin, Cournand, and Richards, 1948; Norris, Shock, Landowne, and Falzone, 1956), and agree closely with the values predicted for this age group as extrapolated from a regression formula by the recent combined Veterans Administration study (Kory, Callahan, Boren, and Syner, 1961). The lower values reported in previous studies probably reflect, in part, the hospitalized populations used in establishing those representative values.

The M.B.C. for the combined group, and for group I and group II separately, does not correlate significantly with height for this age range. This result differs from previously reported correlations of the M.B.C. with height for a wider age range extending from young adults to older subjects (Baldwin, Cournand, and Richards, 1948; Kory, Callahan, Boren, and Syner, 1961).

TABLE 5.—*Pulmonary function in healthy aged men*

Pulmonary function	Group I (N=27; age 65–84)		Group II (N=18; age 65–92)		Group total (N=45; age 65–92)	
	Mean	S.D.	Mean	S.D.	Mean	S.D.
Total vital capacity (ml)	3,505	226	3,192	707	3,380	721
Maximum breathing capacity (liters/minute)	*98.5	26	*76.2	22	89.6	27
Height (cm)	146.5	7.0	145.8	5.7	146.3	6.4
Weight (kg)	69.7	10.4	64.6	7.5	67.5	9.6
Timed vital capacity (percent of total vital capacity) 1st second (N=43)	....	....	....	....	75.4	6.8
1st, 2d, plus 3d second	....	....	....	....	90.3	5.7

* Group II significantly different from group I, at the 0.05 level.

S.D.=Standard deviation.

The mean M.B.C. in group II is significantly lower ($p \leqq 0.01$) than the mean M.B.C. in group I. The M.B.C. for the entire group, as well as group II alone, decreases significantly with age ($r = -0.43$; $p \leqq 0.01$). However for group I alone, although there is a trend toward decreasing M.B.C. with age, it is not significant. The M.B.C. has previously been reported to decrease with age over these later years (Norris, Shock, Landowne, and Falzone, 1956). There was no obvious difference, clinically, between these two groups in regard to their pulmonary systems. It is of interest, though not surprising, that the difference in ventilatory ability is in a direction consistent with the minimal difference in the overall state of health. This difference between groups I and II suggests the influence of disease states, subtle nonpulmonary and/or occult pulmonary, beyond the effects of time, per se, in producing this so-called "age-change" in pulmonary function.

Vital Capacity

The average vital capacity of the entire group reflects adequate levels (3380 cc ± 109.9 cc). The vital capacity does not differ significantly between group I and group II. The correlation of vital capacity with age in the entire group is −0.50. This is a significant decrease with age, thus confirming at these later ages the decline in vital capacity with age, reported in other studies (Baldwin, Cournand, and Richards, 1948; Kory, Callahan, Boren, and Syner, 1961).

The vital capacity also showed a significant decrease with age in group II alone ($r = -0.69$). The vital capacity for group I ($r = -0.31$) reveals a declining, though nonsignificant, trend with age. These findings may be explained on the same basis as those offered for the maximum breathing capacity.

The vital capacity for the entire group correlates significantly and positively with height ($r = 0.56$) and with M.B.C. ($r = 0.71$).

Vital capacity has not usually been considered a very meaningful reflection of ventilatory ability. When the element of time is added (timed vital capacity: T.V.C.) the test assumes greater usefulness as a reflection of airway obstruction. It is recorded as percent of the total vital capacity expired in a given period of time. This study reveals a 1 second T.V.C. of 75 percent, with a range (±2 S.D.) of 60–90 percent and a 3 second T.V.C. of 90 percent with a range of 79–100 percent. The values reported by Gaensler (1951) for young healthy adults are 83 percent in 1 second, with a range of 72–98 percent and 97 percent in 3 seconds with a range of 92–100 percent.

It is difficult to evaluate these differences because there is no comparative data for the same age group within the same laboratory.

In these subjects, arterial CO_2 tension and pH of group I, group II, and the combined group I and II, do not differ significantly from the values obtained for younger healthy control subjects. The data is presented in table 6.

The arterial oxygen saturation in both group I (96.9±0.55 percent) and group II (97.6±0.4 percent) is significantly lower (p≤.05) than the value for the healthy young controls (98.9±0.3 percent). Conclusions from previous studies on the effects of aging on arterial oxygen saturation have been controversial (Greifenstein, King, Latch, and Comroe, 1952; Tenny and Miller, 1956).

The reduced, though adequate, maximal breathing capacity and timed vital capacity in these aged subjects certainly do not explain the significantly diminished arterial oxygen saturation. This decrease in arterial oxygen saturation indicates that a signif-icant drop in oxygen tension has occurred, while the arterial CO_2 tension has been maintained at levels similar to the young. Among the possible causes of such a change are an abnormal ventilation—perfusion ratio, diminished diffusion capacity or venous—arterial shunting. A decrease in the maximal diffusing capacity of the lung correlated with increasing age has been reported (Cohn, Carrol, Armstrong, Shepard, and Riley, 1953). This decrease in arterial oxygen saturation, occuring in both groups I and II suggests a spontaneous change evolving with time rather than the influence of disease.

Physiological Effects of Chronic Smoking

Chronic cigarette smoking has been associated with an increased cardiovascular death rate (Doll and Hill, 1956; Hammond and Horn, 1958). The data from this study affords an opportunity to evaluate possible relationships between chronic smoking and physiological measurements ranging from clinically recorded blood pressures to cerebral circulatory and metabolic values.

This group of 47 men was divided into three categories of smoking history: 11 nonsmokers, 28 chronic cigarette smokers, and 8 chronic cigar or pipe smokers. The 28

TABLE 6.—*Arterial blood studies* [1]

Measurements	NIMH normal young subjects [2] (N=15)		NIMH normal elderly subjects [3]			
			Group I (N=26)		Group II (N=17)	
	Mean	S.D.	Mean	S.D.	Mean	S.D.
Arterial hemoglobin (concentration grams %)...	13. 87	0. 36	14. 01	0. 20	14. 27	0. 22
Arterial O_2 saturation (percent)...............	98. 9	.3	*96. 9	.5	*97. 6	.4
Arterial CO_2 tension (mm Hg)...............	42. 4	1. 6	42. 7	.08	41. 4	1. 2
Arterial pH...............................	7. 39	.02	7. 14	.01	71. 40	.01

[1] The individual values for these measurements are presented in ch. 6.
[2] Mean age of young subjects=20 years.
[3] Mean age of elderly subjects=Group I, 71.0 years; group II, 72.8 years.
* Significantly different from normal, young subjects, at the 0.05 level.

TABLE 7.—*Pulmonary function correlations*

Pulmonary function	Group I r	Group II r	Total r
Vital capacity vs. height	0.09	* 0.56	* 0.56
Vital capacity vs. weight	.24	** .60	** .40
Vital capacity vs. age	—.31	** —.69	** —.50
Maximum breathing capacity (M.B.C.) vs. height	.07	.31	.15
MBC vs. weight	.06	* .39	.32
MBC vs. age	—.31	** —.59	** —.43
Height vs. age	.09	* —.55	—.20
Weight vs. age	*** .60	.40	*** .54
Vital capacity vs. MBC	*** .75	** .61	*** .71
Height vs. weight	*** .60	.40	*** .54

* Significant at the 0.05 level.
** Significant at the 0.01 level.
*** Significant at the 0.001 level.

r = Coefficient of correlation.

cigarette smokers have the following smoking histories: 19 of these men continued smoking up to the time of this study, over a period of 35 to 60 years, with a mean duration of 47.2 years.[4] The remaining 9 had stopped smoking 1 to 6 years prior to this study. The cigar and pipe smokers had a smoking history also extending over 35 to 60 years, with a mean of 47.6 years.

---

[4] 15 of these subjects smoked more than 20 cigarettes per day; the other 4 smoked 10–20 cigarettes per day.

As seen in table 8, there are no significant differences between nonsmokers and chronic cigarette smokers in regard to systolic blood pressure, diastolic blood pressure, mean arterial blood pressure, pulse rate, cerebral blood flow, cerebral oxygen utilization ($CMRO_2$), and total serum cholesterol levels. This lack of significant difference for these physiological variables might appear to minimize their importance as indicators of the pathological processes responsible for the increased mortality rates among

TABLE 8.—*Effect of chronic smoking on physiological variables*[1]

	Nonsmokers (N=11)	Chronic cigarette smokers		Chronic cigar and/or pipe smokers (N=8)
		(N=19 [2])	(N=9 [3])	
Systolic blood pressure (mm Hg)	133.62	134.32	124.78	134.25
Diastolic blood pressure (mm Hg)	79.40	74.16	74.67	76.62
Mean arterial blood pressure (mm Hg)	98.58	97.50	98.38	110.00
Pulse rate (beats/min)	74.08	73.16	72.11	72.50
Total cholesterol (mgm/100ml)	217.31	232.84	252.22	230.62
Cerebral blood flow (ml/100g/min)	56.29	56.01	54.66	53.12
Arterial oxygen saturation (percent)	97.07	96.28	97.78	98.40
Cerebral oxygen utilization ($CMRO_2$) (ml/100g/min)	3.36	3.32	3.36	3.40
Maximal breathing capacity (liters/min)	97.77	82.47	101.78	79.12
Vital capacity (ml)	3,427.08	3,293.76	3,602.07	3,402.00

[1] The 4 groups shown above do not differ significantly for any of the variables presented.
[2] 19 chronic smokers; mean duration 47.2 years.
[3] 9 chronic smokers who had stopped smoking 1 to 6 years prior to this study.

the smokers who have survived to this age range. However, one is reluctant to draw inferences from these data in regard to the influences of smoking, primarily because of the many possible selective and survival biases that may have been operating.

When comparing nonsmokers with the entire group of 28 chronic cigarette smokers, these data fail to reveal any differences in M.B.C., vital capacity, and arterial oxygen saturation. Moreover, no correlations were found between these variables and the duration of smoking. Other studies have reported definite decreases in pulmonary function with chronic smoking (Blackburn, Brozek, and Taylor, 1959; Wilson, Meador, Jay, and Higgens, 1960).

Senile Emphysema

The findings suggest that the term "senile emphysema" with its implication of functional decline, is inappropriate. Many of our subjects demonstrated rounding of the thoracic cage as well as increased resonance on percussion of the chest wall, and a suggestion of an increased A–P diameter. However, none of these individuals presented symptoms of pulmonary disease, such as dyspnea, chronic cough, or X-ray evidence of significant lung pathology.

The maintenance of ventilatory ability as reflected in adequate vital capacity, maximal breathing capacity and timed vital capacity, as well as the lack of significant differences from the young in arterial CO_2 and pH indicates the functional insignificance of these "physical abnormalities" so commonly observed in aged individuals.

Pierce and Ebert (1958) have demonstrated that even the more pronounced abnormality of chest contour, the so-called "barrel deformity of the chest," is not accompanied by any significantly greater functional impairment of pulmonary function when compared to a random sample of aged. Those individuals with true obstructive emphysema have more severe and far different pulmonary function abnormalities. Convincing evidence for the existence of a senile nonobstructive emphysema is lacking.

ELECTROCARDIOGRAPHIC FINDINGS IN HEALTHY AGED MEN

Method and Subjects

Standard 12 lead electrocardiographic tracings from unipolar and bipolar limb leads and 6 anterior chest leads were taken with direct writing instruments. Each subject had an ECG on 2 separate days. The records were analyzed for QRS interval, QRS axis in the frontal plane, QRS transition, T-wave axis in the frontal plane and T-wave transition, QRS–T angle, amplitude of S wave in VI and amplitude of the R wave in V5. The interpretations represent a consensus of two physicians, employing the vector method of Grant (1957).

Findings

The data are presented in table 9. The results of a previous study (Simonson and Keys, 1952), also obtained by use of unipolar, bipolar, and chest leads, on groups of men 18 to 25 and 45 to 55 years, are presented in the same table for general illustrative purposes. Because they were done in different laboratories, no statistical comparisons were made.

Thirty-five of the 47 subjects were considered to have no ECG abnormalities and were used to compile the age relevant normative data. Of the remaining 12 subjects, 10 had completely negative cardiac histories but demonstrated the following ECG abnormalities: right bundle-branch block (5 complete, 3 incomplete); left bundle-branch block (1); auricular flutter (1).

The two other subjects had histories suggestive of myocardial infarction 5 to 10

TABLE 9.—*Electrocardiographic data of healthy elderly men*

	QRS interval (seconds)		QRS axis (degrees)		QRS transition	T axis (degrees)		T transition
	Mean	S.D.	Mean	S.D.		Mean	S.D.	
Young men [1] 18–25 (N=157).	0.08	0.01	66.8	21.3	V2/V3.....	42.8	21.1	V1
Middle aged men [1] 45–55 (N=233).	.08	.01	37.8	34.8	V2/V3.....	32.9	23.3	V1
NIH elderly men [2] 65–94 (N=35).	.07	.01	17.0	35.2	V2/V3.....	33.3	21.9	V1

[1] Simonson, E., and Keys, A., 1952—Healthy Adults.
[2] NIH—Healthy Elderly Men; see text for description of subjects.

S.D.=Standard deviation.

years prior to this study and had electrocardiograms consistent with such a diagnosis.

The mean QRS duration is 0.07 seconds, which is similar to the 0.08 seconds in the younger groups of the comparative series.

The mean QRS axis in the frontal plane is 17°. This suggests a continuation of the leftward shift of the QRS axis noted in the comparative studies, which reveal a mean QRS axis of 66° for age range 18 through 25 and a mean QRS axis of 37° for the age range 45 through 55. This leftward axis trend with increasing age, as well as the range of values noted in our older age groups is also consistent with the data obtained by the United States Air Force Aerospace School (Lamb, 1959), in a study of a large population of healthy men between the ages of 18 to 63.

The QRS axis is commonly viewed as being influenced by the total body weight. In our group there is no statistical correlation between QRS axis and total body weight. However, there was a negligible incidence of obesity in our subjects. Similarly, the total serum cholesterol level is not significantly correlated with the QRS axis.

The QRS transition is at V2–V3 for 31 of these men and at V3–V4 for 4 of the subjects and this agrees with the findings for all age groups in the Air Force study (Lamb, 1959). Though there is a leftward shift with age of the QRS axis in the frontal plane, there is no accompanying shift of the vector in the transverse plane.

The mean T axis is 33° and is not shifted as compared with the data of Simonson and Keys (1952), for age 45 to 55. This is relevant to the disagreement in the literature concerning the leftward shift of the T axis with age. One group (Packard, Graettinger, and Graybiel, 1954) did not observe a significant shift in the T axis in their followup study of naval aviators, while other studies (Lamb, 1959; Simonson and Keys, 1952) indicate a leftward shift with age.

The T transition in largely at V–1. This is consistent with previous studies (Simonson and Keys, 1952; Lamb, 1959).

The finding in all the subjects but one of a QRS–T angle of 70° or less is in agreement with the Air Force study (Lamb, 1959).

Right Bundle-Branch Block

Among those of our subjects who were not included in the statistical analyses of the normal electrocardiogram of the aged were five with complete right bundle-branch block (RBBB). The criteria employed for the diagnosis of complete right bundle-branch block were as follows: QRS duration of 0.12 seconds or more in the standard leads, a broad S wave in lead 1 and an R-prime in V1 and/or V2. This incidence of RBBB is unusually high.

The prognostic significance of RBBB has not been clearly established. There is a lack of information available regarding the pathological significance of this electrocardiographic finding, and the literature does not reveal any clear-cut autopsy study directed at this problem. In an attempt to clarify this issue, the Armed Forces Institute of Pathology has undertaken a study of the relationship between the electrical abnormality of RBBB and the pathological correlates in autopsy specimens (Manion, 1961). Early medical attitudes toward RBBB derive from a paper by Graybiel and Sprague in 1933 who studied 395 cardiac patients and concluded "bundle-branch block almost invariably indicates serious organic disease of the heart, usually coronary disease." That study by virtue of their patient population was biased in the direction of poor prognosis. Soon afterward, a report on 64 patients with RBBB (Wood, Jeffers, and Wolferth, 1935) concluded that the prognosis depended on the presence or absence of other definite heart disease and not on the isolated finding of RBBB. In 1947, a review of 100 cases of RBBB (Langley, Reed, and Utz) concluded that RBBB had a far different and less serious prognostic significance than left bundle-branch block. They stressed the growing number of reports of 10-year followups on RBBB. In 1950 a report on 281 patients with RBBB concluded that the significance of RBBB depended entirely on accompanying demonstrable heart disease (Shreenivas, Messer, Johnson, and White). A report of an increased incidence of RBBB in asymptomatic Air Force men after the age of 40 appeared in 1959 (Johnson, Averill, and Lamb).

The incidence reported was 2.9 per thousand after 40 as compared to 1.5 per thousand before 40. This increased incidence of RBBB with age does not necessarily point to occult coronary artery disease as the etiological agent. Changes in connective tissue and ground substance with increasing age have been reported (Kaplan and Meyer, 1959; Kolin and Rollerson, 1960). Furthermore, the opportunity for viral and other infectious diseases to affect the conduction system increases with length of life. In our aged population, none of the men with RBBB had historical or clinical evidence of any definite heart disease or obvious major infectious processes. In addition, the mean serum cholesterol was not significantly different for the group with RBBB as compared to the remainder of the subjects.

Why the right bundle should be selectively affected by an as yet uncertain etiological process is not clear. On the basis of present evidence it does not appear that RBBB represents an electrical manifestation of coronary artery disease or a sign of other significant heart disease.

DISCUSSION

What we have learned about aging in this study depends upon the success we have had in separating the effects of normal aging processes from disease.

The results reported in the other chapters have tended to validate the medical evaluation and classification procedures. Though the research data from all other disciplines were not used in classifying the subjects, the results of the studies in cerebral circulation and metabolism, electroencephalography, psychology, social psychology, and psychiatry, confirm the superior state of the optimally healthy group (group I), and the lesser performance of the asymptomatic disease group (group II).

The presence of these two groups has permitted a partial separation of the influence of time and of disease on the aging process.

There were a considerable number of variables showing no difference between our group of healthy aged and younger adults. Therefore, when differences in such variables may be observed they are presumably the result of disease. Such reported differences in the literature, for example the cerebral blood flow and the blood pressure by auscultation, may be implicitly the consequences of undetected disease in the aged subjects studied.

On the other hand there were several variables which were significantly different between our aged and the young. These differences, when present to the same degree in both groups I and II, are viewed as more likely to be a reflection of the passage of time, although the effects of undetected diseases must always be suspected. Some of the variables differed from the young to the same magnitude in groups I and II (serum albumin), and others did not (maximum breathing capacity). The interpretation of those characteristics which differed from the young, but also between groups I and II, raises additional questions.

The cerebral blood flow, which differs from the young controls only in group II (ch. 6), certainly makes salient the influence of disease rather than time in producing this central nervous system change.

It should be emphasized that from a medical point of view these were strikingly healthy, vigorous, alert, and independently functioning individuals. Our evidence strongly suggests that with the aproach of an era in which arteriosclerosis and other diseases occurring frequently with increasing age may be reversible and/or preventable, the present picture of human aging, with its behavioral manifestations of central nervous system change, may be markedly altered.

SUMMARY

1. A variety of medical data were obtained on 47 men over the age of 65 (mean 71.5 years, S.D.=4.8). The subjects were divided into two groups; group I, 27 men of excellent health, and group II, 20 men of more nearly average health. Differences between groups I and II are viewed largely as disease related changes, while the absence of group differences in the presence of significant alterations in comparison with young controls are viewed as time related changes.

2. Comparisons between values for the healthy aged with those for healthy younger adults indicate no differences in hemoglobin, hematocrit, white blood count, fasting blood glucose, blood urea nitrogen, and creatinine values. Furthermore, none of these measurements revealed any correlation with age. The erythrocyte sedimentation rate is elevated in the aged and this may be related to the serum protein changes described below.

3. Serum cholesterol did not correlate with age. The fact that the negative trend with age, as previously reported for individuals 55 and over, was lacking in our group may reflect the unique state of health of these subjects.

4. Serum albumin was decreased to the same degree in both groups I and II when compared with young controls. Gamma globulin levels, however, were not significantly different. Low serum albumin levels, without altered gamma globulin levels, in the absence of any pathological conditions which could explain the hypoalbuminemia suggests a metabolic change basic to the aging process rather than a change secondary to disease.

5. Serum total protein and the alpha 1 globulin were not significantly different, whereas serum alpha 2 globulin and beta

globulin were significantly elevated in the aged as compared to the young control group.

6. Protein bound iodine (PBI) correlated negatively with age. No correlations were observed between PBI and serum albumin, alpha 1 globulin, alpha 2 globulin, beta globulin and gamma globulin levels, suggesting that the decrease in PBI reflects a diminution of circulating thyroid hormone rather than a decrease in transporting protein. However, subtle quantitative or qualitative changes in protein binding cannot be ruled out.

7. Mean systolic blood pressure in group I was similar to the mean systolic blood pressure in the 20–40 year group studied by Master (1957), while the mean systolic blood pressure of group II closely resembles the mean systolic blood pressure in the older age group studied by Master (1957). The mean diastolic blood pressures in both groups I and II were more like those of the younger groups in Master's series (1957).

8. Thirty-eight of the 47 subjects evidenced minimal retinal arteriosclerosis. Retinal arteriosclerosis did not correlate with cerebral blood flow or cerebral vascular resistance, nor with such clinical findings as blood pressure, X-ray evidence of calcification of the aorta, or X-ray evidence of calcification of the internal carotid artery siphon. The high incidence of retinal arteriosclerosis in this healthy group, together with the lack of correlation with cerebral circulatory and X-ray changes suggests that the funduscopic finding of retinal arteriosclerosis is of little significance in an evaluation of the state of overall health or of physiological function of the elderly.

9. Calcification of the internal carotid artery siphon, as viewed on skull X-ray, correlates significantly with a decreased cerebral blood flow. A diminution in cerebral venous oxygen tension was observed in the subgroups evidencing internal carotid artery siphon calcification.

10. Maximum breathing capacity in both groups I and II reflects adequate ventilatory ability though the levels are diminished compared with younger adults.

11. Maximum breathing capacity in group II was significantly lower than in group I. This suggests the influence of subtle disease states, including nonpulmonary or undetected pulmonary pathology, rather than simply a change evolving with time.

12. Vital capacity for the combined group decreased significantly with age although the mean values obtained reflect adequate function. Vital capacity in group II decreased significantly with age, whereas that for group I did not. These findings may be explained on the same basis as that offered for the maximum breathing capacity.

13. Arterial CO_2 tension and pH for both groups I and II did not differ when compared with young controls. On the other hand, arterial oxygen saturation in both groups I and II was significantly lower than the value for young controls. This decrease of the same magnitude in both groups I and II suggests a change evolving with time rather than a consequence of disease.

14. The entire group was subdivided on the basis of their smoking habits: 11 nonsmokers; 19 cigarette smokers (mean duration of smoking, 47.3 years); 9 cigarette smokers who had stopped smoking 1 to 6 years prior to this study; and 8 subjects who smoked pipes and cigars. There were no consistent relationships among these groups with respect to vascular, respiratory, and cerebral metabolic variables, and smok-

ing. It is difficult to draw inferences from these data about the influences of smoking both in the few instances where significant differences were found and more particularly in the larger number of cases where no differences were found between smokers and nonsmokers, primarily because of the many possible selective and survival biases that may have been operating.

15. Electrocardiographic values for these healthy aged subjects differed in some respects from values for the young and not in others. The mean QRS axis in the frontal plane was 17°, suggesting a continuation of the leftward trend with age reported in comparative series of younger subjects. The QRS axis did not correlate with weight or with total serum cholesterol levels. The QRS transition for the majority of subjects was at V2–V3 and for a small group at V3–V4. Thus, although there was a leftward shift in the QRS axis in the frontal plane, there was no accompanying shift of the vector in the transverse plane. The mean T axis was 33° and was not shifted in comparison with the data for younger groups. The T transition was largely at V1.

16. Evidence is presented suggesting that right bundle-branch block may not represent an electrical manifestation of coronary artery disease or a sign of other significant heart disease.

ACKNOWLEDGMENTS

The author wishes to express his appreciation to Mrs. Ann Randall for her extremely competent and untiring efforts in the statistical analyses.

To Dr. Joseph C. Greenfield of the National Heart Institute for his aid in the interpretations of the electrocardiograms.

To Mrs. Dorothy Oest, Mrs. Virginia Marbley, and Mrs. Joyce Horwath, for their invaluable technical assistance.

REFERENCES

ALPERS, B. J., FORSTER, F. M., and HERBUT, B. A. 1948. Retinal, cerebral and systemic arteriosclerosis. *Arch. Neurol. and Psychiat.*, 60, 440–456.

BALDWIN, E. DeF., COURNAND, A., and RICHARDS, D. W. 1948. Pulmonary insufficiency. *Medicine,* 27, 243–278.

BIELER, M. M., ECKER, E. E., and SPIES, T. D. 1949. Serum proteins in hypoproteinemia due to nutritional deficiency. *J. Lab. Clin. Med.*, 32, 130–138.

BLACKBURN, H., BROZAK, J., and TAYLOR, H. L. 1959. Lung volume in smokers and nonsmokers. *Ann. Int. Med.*, 51, 68–77.

CHINN, A. B., LAVIK, P. S., and CAMERON, D. B. 1956. Measurement of protein digestion and absorption in aged persons by a test meal of I^{131}-labelled protein. *J. Geront.*, 11, 151–153.

COHN, J. E., CARROLL, D. G., ARMSTRONG, B. W., SHEPARD, R. H., and RILEY, R. L. 1953. Maximal diffusing capacity of the lung in normal male subjects of different ages. *J. Appl. Physiol.*, 6, 588–597.

DOLL, R., and HILL, A. B. 1956. Lung cancer and other causes of death in relation to smoking. Second report on mortality of British doctors. *Brit. Med. J.*, 2, 1071–1081.

DUKE-EDLER, W. S. 1940. *Textbook of Ophthalmology.* London, Henry Kimpton.

GAENSLER, E. A. 1951. Analysis of the ventilatory defect by timed vital capacity. *Am. Rev. Tuberc.*, 4, 256–278.

GAFFNEY, G. W., GREGERMAN, R. I., YIENGST, M. J., and SHOCK, N. W. 1960. Serum protein-bound iodine concentration in blood of euthyroid men aged 18–94 years. *J. Geront.*, 15, 234–241.

GORDON, R. 1959. Clinical staff conferences. *Ann. Int. Med.*, 51, 553–576.

GRANT, R. P. 1957. *Clinical Electrocardiography; the Spatial Vector Approach.*

GRAYBIEL, A., and SPRAGUE, H. B. 1933. Bundle branch block—an analysis of 395 cases. *Am. J. Med. Sci.*, 185, 395–401.

GREIFENSTEIN, F. E., KING, R. M., LATCH, S. S., and COMROE, J. H., JR. 1952. Pulmonary function studies in healthy men and women 50 years and older. *J. Appl. Physiol.*, 4, 641–648.

GROSS, A. M., GITLIN, D., and JANEWAY, C. A. 1959. The gamma globulins and their clinical significance. III. Hypergammaglobulinemia. *N. Engl. J. Med.*, 260, 121–125.

GUTMAN, A. B., 1948. The plasma proteins in disease. *Advances in Protein Chem.*, 4, 156–250

HAMMOND, E. C., and HORN, D. 1958. Smoking and death rates. Report on 44 months of followup of 187,783 men. II. Death rates by cause. *J.A.M.A.*, 156, 1294–1308.

HORWITT, M. K., 1953. Dietary requirements of the aged. *J. Am. Diet. Assoc., 29*, 443–448.

IGERSHEIMER, W. W., and STEVENSON, J. A. F. 1951. Effect of electroshock on the blood pressure in psychotic patients. *Arch. Neurol. & Psychiat., 65*, 740–751.

JOHNSON, R. L., AVERILL, K. H., and LAMB, L. E. 1954. Electrocardiographic findings in 63,375 asymptomatic individuals. Part VI: Right bundle-branch block. The First International Symposium on Cardiology in Aviation conducted at the School of Aviation Medicine, pages 271–288.

KAPLAN, D., and MEYER, K. 1959 Aging of human cartilage. *Nature, 183*, 1267–68.

KARREL, J. L., WILDER, V. M., and BEBER, M. 1956. Electrophoretic serum protein patterns in the aged. *J. Am. Geriat. Soc., 4*, 667–68.

KEYS, A. 1952. Nutrition of the later years of life. *Pub. Health Rep., 67*, 484–489.

————. 1952. The age trend of serum concentrations of cholesterol and of S_f 10–20 ("G") substances in adults. *J. Geront., 7*, 201–206.

KOLIN, R. R., and ROLLERSON, E. 1960. Aging of human collagen in relation to susceptibility to the action of collagenase. *J. Geront., 15*, 10–18

KORY, R. C., CALLAHAN, R., BOREN, H. G., and SYNER, J. C. 1961. The Veterans' Administration—Army cooperative study of pulmonary function. *Am. J. Med., 30*, 243–258.

KOUNTZ, W. B., CHIEFFI, MARGARET, and KIRK, J. E. 1949. Serum protein-bond iodine and age. *J. Geront., 4*, 132–135.

LAMB, L. E. 1959. The first International Symposium in Cardiology in Aviation conducted at the School of Aviation Medicine, pp. 377–379.

LANGLEY, R. W., REED, J. C., and UTZ, D. C. 1947. Bundle-branch block—a review of 100 cases. *Am. Ht. J., 33*, 730.

LINDGREN, F. U., and NICHOLS, A. V. 1960. Structure and function of human serum lipoproteins—*The Plasma Proteins*. Vol. II. Ch. II. Academic Press, New York and London.

MANION, W. C. 1961. Personal communication, Armed Forces Institute of Pathology.

MASTER, A. M., GARFIELD, C. I., and WALTERS, M. B. 1952. Normal blood pressure and hypertension. Lea & Febiger, Philadelphia.

———— LASSER, R. P., and JAFFE, H. E. 1957. Blood pressure in apparently healthy aged 65 to 106 years. *Proc. Soc. Exp. Biol. Med., 94*, 463–467.

MAY, C. H. 1937. *Manual of Diseases of the Eye for Students and General Practitioners.* Ed. 15. William Wood & Co., Philadelphia.

MILLER, M. L. 1939. Present conception of essential hypertension. *Psychosom. Med.* I, 101–117.

NORRIS, A. H., SHOCK, N. W., LANDOWNE, W., and FALZONE, J. A. 1956. Pulmonary function studies: Age differences in lung volumes and bellows functions. *J. Geront., 11*, 379–387.

PACKARD, J. M., GRAETTINGER, J. S., and GRAYBIEL, A. 1954. Analysis of the electrocardiogram obtained from 1,000 young healthy aviators. Ten year followup. *Circ., 10*, 384–400.

PETERMAN, M. L. 1960. Alterations in plasma proteins in disease. In, *The Plasma Proteins.* Vol. II. Putuam, F. W. Academic Press, New York and London.

PIERCE, J. A., and EBERT, R. V. 1958. The barrel deformity of the chest, the senile lung and obstructive pulmonary emphysema. *Am. J. Med., 25*, 13–22.

POULIK, M. D., and SMITHIES, O. 1958. Comparison and combination of the starchgel and filter paper electrophoretic methods applied to human sera: two dimensional electrophoresis. *Biochem. J., 68*, 636–643.

REINBOURNE, E. T. 1952. Some blood changes in old age—a clinical and statistical study. *Human Biol., 24*, 57.

ROBBINS, J., and RALL, J. E. 1960. Proteins associated with the thyroid hormones. *Phyisologic Rev., 40*, 415–489.

SHREENIVAS, MESSER, A. L., JOHNSON, R. P., and WHITE, P. D. 1950. Prognosis in bundle-branch block; factors influencing the survival period in right bundle-branch block. *Am. Ht. J., 40*, 891–902.

SIMONSON, E., and KEYS, A. 1952. Effect of age and body weight on the electrocardiogram of healthy men. *Circ., 6*, 749–761.

SKLAROFF, D. M. 1956. Isotopic determination of blood volume in the normal aged. *Am. J. Roentgen., 75*, 1082–1083.

SMITH, R. H. 1953. Normal blood volumes in men and women over 60 years of age as determined by a modified Cr^{51} method. *Anesthesiology, 19*, 752–756.

TENNEY, S. M., and MILLER, R. M. 1956. Dead-space ventilation in old age. *J. Appl. Physiol., 9*, 321–327.

WALDMANN, T. A. 1961. Gastrointestinal loss demonstrated by Cr^{51}-labelled albumin. *Lancet, 2*, 121–122.

WALSH, F. B. 1957. *Clinical Neuro-ophthalmology.* Williams and Wilkins, Baltimore, pp. 883.

WILSON, R. H., MEADOR, R. S., JAY, B. E., and HIGGENS, E. 1960. The pulmonary pathologic physiology of persons who smoke cigarettes. *N. Engl. J. Med., 262*, 955–960.

WOOD, F. C., JEFFERS, W. A., and WOLFERTH, C. C. 1935. Followup study of 64 patients with a right bundle-branch conduction defect. *Am. Ht. J., 10*, 1056–1066.

Effects of Aging on Cerebral Circulation and Metabolism in Man

by Darab K. Dastur, Mark H. Lane,

Douglas B. Hansen, Seymour S. Kety,

Robert N. Butler, Seymour Perlin, and

Louis Sokoloff

The commonly expressed idea that "man is as old as his arteries" reflects the widely accepted view that the state of the circulatory system plays a major role in the pathogenesis of human aging. Since many of the more prominent clinical features of old age are attributable to changes in the central nervous system, considerable attention has been directed in the last few years to the circulation and gross metabolism of the aged human brain. Most studies have indicated a decline in cerebral blood flow and metabolic rate, and a rise in cerebrovascular resistance with advancing age (Fazekas, Alman, and Bessman, 1952; Fazekas, Kleh, and Finnerty, 1955; Fazekas, Kleh, and Witkin, 1953; Scheinberg, Blackburn, Rich, and Saslaw, 1953; Schieve and Wilson, 1953); several have failed to confirm such age-dependent changes (Gordan, 1956; Shenkin, Novak, Goluboff, Soffe, and Bortin, 1953); and Shenkin and his coworkers have concluded that there are no significant alterations in cerebral circulation and metabolism in old age except in the presence of both hypertension and arteriosclerosis. In a recent critical and comprehensive review of the subject, Kety (1956) has interpreted the available evidence as indicating rapid decreases in overall cerebral blood flow and oxygen consumption during childhood and adolescence, and more gradual but nonetheless progressive declines in these functions in the remaining lifespan.

Several pertinent questions appeared, however, to remain unanswered. In his review Kety (1956) attempted, as far as possible, to exclude from consideration all studies performed on patients with a diagnosis of hypertension, arterioclerosis, or senile psychosis. The remaining series were composed almost entirely of hospitalized patients; they included, therefore, a variety of diseases even if they were of a type deemed unlikely to alter cerebral circulation and metabolism. As he himself pointed out, studies on such patients represented "only an approximation of the normal aging process." Furthermore, vascular disease such as arteriosclerosis, which is known to impair the cerebral circulation (Fazekas, Kleh, and Finnerty, 1955; Shenkin, Novak, Goluboff, Soffe, and Bortin, 1953; Schieve and Wilson, 1953), is so frequently and often so subtly intertwined with the aging process that it is doubtful if it can be successfully excluded without the exercise of the most stringent criteria for its detection and rejection. There is little evidence to indicate that adequately rigorous measures to exclude less than clinically obvious arteriosclerosis were employed in any of the previously cited studies. The possibility remained, therefore, that their results reflected more the effects of vascular or other types of diseases commonly associated with aging rather than the effects of chronological or physiological age per se.

The objectives of the present study were several. First, it was hoped to ascertain clearly and conclusively whether reductions in cerebral blood flow and metabolic rate were inevitable accompaniments of the aging process and occurred in the absence of any detectable cardiovascular or other diseases so often present in the aged. In the event that such changes did indeed occur, evidence was sought which might indicate whether the primary defect was cerebral circulatory insufficiency with secondary neuronal damage and reduced cerebral metabolic rate or, contrariwise, primary neuronal or metabolic impairment followed by secondary diminution in blood flow in response to the reduced metabolic demand. Finally, in view of the rare opportunity afforded by the broad multidisciplinary nature of this project, possible correlates of cerebral circulatory and metabolic functions in the aged were sought in their clinical state, electroencephalographic patterns, cognitive, perceptual, and behavioral functions, psychiatric signs and symptoms, and sociological status and performance. The results of the latter investigations are reported elsewhere in this volume.

METHODS

Subject Material

In order to isolate the effects of aging per se from those of other common age-associated variables on the cerebral circulatory and metabolic functions studied, a highly selected group of normal male subjects over 65 years of age were chosen for these investigations. A detailed description of the group and the exact criteria for acceptance or rejection are presented in chapters 2 and 3. Two stages of selection were carried out, a careful preliminary screening in the field and then a thorough, rigorous series of examinations and evaluations after admission to the National Institutes of Health. Fifty-four subjects met the criteria of the preliminary selection and were admitted for study. Of these, only 27 fulfilled the exacting requirements of the second-stage evaluations for consideration as noninstitutionalized, normal elderly men as free of any apparent disease as possible, and functioning normally in their communities (group I). Twenty subjects were found to be suffering from minimal subclinical or asymptomatic diseases of various types, mainly vascular, and, therefore, did not meet the standards of group I. However, since their medical status was at least equal to and probably better than that of average men of similar age, they were included in the study as a separate group (group II). Seven of the admitted subjects were found to be suffering from serious or advanced diseases which, it was felt, might themselves influence the results of the experimental studies; they were, therefore, excluded from either of the preceding groups (group III).

Cerebral circulatory and metabolic studies were successfully accomplished in 26 of the 27 subjects in group I, 17 of the 20 subjects in group II, and 4 of the 7 subjects in group III. Except for mean arterial blood pressure, none of the data obtained in these studies played any part in the evaluation and classification of the subjects into their respective groups. The normal range of mean arterial blood pressure was defined as the mean value ± three standard deviations (84±23) obtained during similar cerebral circulatory and metabolic studies performed simultaneously on a group of 15 normal young subjects for the purpose of obtaining comparative data. On the basis of this definition, 5 elderly subjects (Subjects Nos. 8, 18, 28, 33, and 35), who fulfilled all the clinical requirements for inclusion in group I, were found to be hypertensive at the time of the cerebral blood flow determinations and were, therefore, relegated to group II. In addition to the previously described groups of elderly men and normal young subjects, a series of 10 patients suffering from chronic brain syndrome with psychosis were admitted from St. Elizabeths Hospital (Washington, D.C.) and Spring Grove Hospital (Catonsville, Md.), and studied in a similar fashion in order to investigate further the relationship between this clinical condition and cerebral circulatory and metabolic functions.

Procedures

Cerebral blood flow (CBF) was determined by the nitrous oxide method as described by Kety and Schmidt (1948), except that the measurement period was extended to 15 minutes to allow more time for equilibration between brain tissue and cerebral venous blood. Mean arterial blood pressure (MABP) was measured directly in the femoral artery by means of an air-damped mercury manometer adjusted to the level of the carotid artery; mean internal jugular venous blood pressure (MJVP) was measured directly in the internal jugular vein by means of a Statham strain gauge (Model No. P23B) and Brush Universal Analyser (Model No. BL–320) and oscillograph (Model No. BL–202).

Blood oxygen and carbon dioxide contents were determined by the manometric method of Van Slyke and Neill (1924), but blood oxygen saturation was measured directly by the Triton X–100 spectrophotometric technique (Deibler, Holmes, Campbell, and Gans, 1959). Blood pH

was measured anaerobically at ambient temperature with a MacInnes-Belcher glass electrode and Cambridge potentiometer (Model R), and was then corrected to its value at 37° C by means of the factors of Rosenthal (1948). The Nelson-Somogyi method (Nelson, 1944) was employed for the determination of blood glucose concentration, and arterial hemoglobin concentration was determined by conversion to cyanmethemoglobin and photometric measurement (Evelyn and Malloy, 1938).

The following functions were computed from the directly measured variables described above. Cerebral oxygen consumption (CMR_{O2}) and glucose utilization (CMR_G) were calculated as the products of the CBF and the arteriovenous oxygen ($[A–V]_{O2}$) and glucose ($[A–V]_G$) differences, respectively. The O_2/glucose ratio ($O_{2/G}$) was determined from the molar values of $(A–V)O_2$ and $(A–V)_G$, and the cerebral respiratory quotient (R.Q.) was obtained by division of $(A–V)_{O2}$ into the cerebral arteriovenous carbon dioxide difference. Cerebral vascular resistance, the ratio of cerebral blood pressure gradient to blood flow, was calculated as the ratio of the MABP–MJVP difference to the CBF. Blood carbon dioxide tension (pCO_2) was determined by means of the nomogram of Van Slyke and Sendroy (1928), and the nomogram based on the data of Dill (National Research Council, 1944) was employed for the determination of the internal jugular venous oxygen tension (pO_2).

Results

In tables 1a and 1b are presented the individual data obtained in the normal elderly men (group I); these include not only the values of the cerebral circulatory and metabolic functions but also of a variety of blood constituents known to influence these

Table 1a.—*Cerebral circulation, metabolism, and related functions in normal elderly men*

Subject No.	Age	MABP (mm Hg)	MIJVP (mm Hg)	CBF (ml/100 g/min)	CVR (mm Hg/ml/100g/min)	$(A-V)O_2$ (Vol. %)	CMR_{O_2} (ml/100g/min)	$(A-V)_G$ (mg %)	CMR_G (mg/100g/min)	Cerebral R.Q.	O_2/G (mMole/mMole)	Int. Jug. Ven. pCO_2 (mm Hg)	Int. Jug. Ven. pO_2 (mm Hg)
							26 NORMAL ELDERLY MEN						
1	69	97	6	43	2.1	6.61	2.9	7.4	3.2	1.03	7.2	53	33
2	79	89	7	75	1.2	5.29	4.0	6.8	5.1	.95	6.2	43	34
3	66	94	3	72	1.3	5.41	3.9	7.3	5.3	.96	5.9	51	33
5	69	89	5	56	1.4	7.00	3.1	8.5	4.8	.78	6.6	50	33
6	72	89	9	58	1.6	5.56	3.2	6.8	3.8	.97	6.6	47	33
7	67	101	8	50	2.0	5.56	3.1	9.8	5.7	.95	4.6	52	35
9	67	104	4	51	1.5	6.25	3.2	6.5	3.2	.99	4.7	52	38
12	70	81	3	70	1.5	6.26	3.4	6.3	3.2	1.00	8.0	48	37
14	69	88	6	63	1.1	4.81	3.1	8.1	3.6	.85	4.8		39
15	75	98	5	75	1.5	4.91	3.9	5.7	4.7	1.04	6.9	56	
16	71	95	9	48	2.0	5.25	3.1	6.2	4.4	1.02	6.8	53	40
19	70	101	4	46	1.7	6.50	3.3	9.2	3.9	1.01	5.7	53	37
20	73	94	17	51	2.0	7.25	3.4	8.4	4.3	.94	6.9	50	34
26	76	104	4	66	1.3	6.30	3.3	8.0	5.3	.79	6.0	49	34
30	73	86	4	61		5.09		6.8	4.1	.81	5.2	49	43
36	69	103		73		5.52				.86	6.5	57	37
47	65	79	6	73	1.0	5.78	4.2	5.8	4.3	.94		45	37
49	72	96	7	52	1.2	4.26	3.1	8.7	4.6	.85	5.9	53	35
50	72	99	6	66	1.8	5.87	3.1	11.0	7.2	.87	5.5	57	36
51	71	96	12	42	1.3	6.14	3.0	15.5	6.5	.90	4.5	58	38
53	81	91	4	50	2.1	7.19	3.4	10.0	5.0	.89	3.7	49	34
54	72	93	5	56	1.8	6.76	2.8	6.1	3.4	.97	5.0	41	32
55	65	86	5	52	1.5	4.98	3.3			.83	6.5	52	40
56	69	93	10	57	1.6	6.36	2.6	10.3	4.3	.82		55	36
58	71	90	5	42	1.5	4.58				.84		54	37
59	74	96	6		2.2	7.49	3.1			.81	5.9		33
Mean	*71.0	*93.2	6.4	57.9	*1.58	5.88	3.33	8.2	*4.6	.91	6.0	51.2	35.9
S.E.	±.8	±1.3	±.6	±2.1	±.07	±.17	±.08	±.5	±.2	±.02	±.2	±.8	±.6
							15 NORMAL YOUNG SUBJECTS						
Mean	20.8	84.2	7.1	62.1	1.29	5.70	3.51	9.3	6.0	0.92	5.5	51.9	37.5
S.E.	±.4	±1.9	±.5	±2.9	±.06	±.30	±.21	±.8	±.7	±.02	±.5	±1.5	±1.5

* Significantly different from normal young subjects at the 0.05 level.

TABLE 1b.—*Blood constituents in normal elderly men*

Subject No.	Art. Hemoglobin Concentration (grams %)	Blood O₂ Content (Vol. %)		Blood CO₂ Content (Vol. %)		Blood Glucose Concentration (mg. %)		Blood pH		Blood CO₂ Tension (mm. Hg.)		Blood O₂ Saturation (in percentage)	
		Arterial	Int. Jug.	Arterial	Int. Jug.	Arterial	Int. Jug.	Arterial	Int. Jug.	Arterial	Int. Jug.	Arterial	Int. Jug.
						26 NORMAL ELDERLY MEN							
1	16.04	19.92	13.31	48.40	55.20	91.8	84.4	7.42	7.35	41	53	97.0	60.1
2	13.78	17.38	12.09	47.91	52.94	94.9	88.7	7.43	7.41	38	43	95.8	64.5
3	13.49	16.78	11.37	49.64	54.86	86.8	79.5	7.41	7.33	41	51	90.8	59.3
5	15.09	18.93	11.93	47.52	53.01	106.0	97.5	7.39	7.35	42	50	92.5	58.6
6	13.28	16.76	11.20	50.13	55.47	87.8	81.0	7.38	7.34	44	52	93.8	59.6
7	14.56	18.65	13.09	49.22	54.49	89.9	80.1	7.41	7.39	41	47	98.3	66.6
9	14.35	18.56	12.31	44.87	51.04	96.5	90.0	7.38	7.31	40	52	97.2	65.7
12	14.68	19.10	12.84	45.32	51.58	96.9	90.6	7.41	7.31	38	52	97.9	64.1
14	14.27	18.17	13.36	51.79	55.89	99.7	91.6	7.43	7.40	42	48	97.5	72.2
15	14.68	17.94	13.03	50.11	55.23	83.5	77.8					96.1	68.4
16	13.12	17.36	12.11	53.08	58.44	83.3	77.1	7.36	7.34	49	56	98.1	69.7
19	14.27	18.66	12.16	45.38	51.93	87.4	78.2	7.36	7.30	42	53	98.6	63.8
20	13.98	18.64	11.39	46.33	53.15	84.8	76.4	7.39	7.32	41	53	97.1	59.4
26	13.20	17.28	10.98	50.03	55.01	92.9	84.5	7.40	7.36	42	50	96.7	61.8
30	12.46	16.35	11.26	52.20	56.34	74.0	66.0	7.41	7.37	45	49	99.0	74.6
36	14.89	18.67	13.15	48.91	53.68	85.3	78.5	7.37	7.36	47	57	98.9	66.3
47	11.94	15.85	10.07	52.58	58.00			7.36	7.31	39	45	98.6	63.6
49	14.35	17.53	13.27	50.99	54.63	77.3	71.5	7.46	7.41		53	91.8	66.0
50	14.07	17.93	12.06	51.78	56.89	85.9	77.2		7.33	49	57	97.6	64.2
51	13.28	17.36	11.12	51.10	56.62	75.6	64.6	7.35	7.30	52	58	99.0	66.1
53	14.27	18.21	11.02	50.21	56.60	97.4	81.9	7.32	7.31	39	49	97.5	58.9
54	13.98	18.23	11.47	48.88	55.41	82.9	72.9	7.43	7.37	37	41	98.8	60.0
55	16.04	20.70	15.72	45.38	49.53	82.7	76.6	7.44	7.42	43	52	98.5	74.0
56	14.68	18.63	12.27	48.26	53.46			7.38	7.33	48	55	96.6	63.2
58	11.94	15.12	10.54	53.26	57.12			7.35	7.31	43	54	95.8	63.8
59	13.49	17.72	10.23	49.43	55.48	81.0	70.7	7.38	7.32			99.4	57.8
Mean	14.01	17.94	12.05	49.34	54.69	88.0	*79.9	7.39	7.35	42.7	51.1	*96.9	64.3
S.E.	±.20	±.24	±.24	±.48	±.43	±1.7	±1.7	±.01	±.01	±.8	±.9	±.5	±.9
						15 NORMAL YOUNG SUBJECTS							
Mean	13.87	18.24	12.52	48.12	53.38	83.2	73.8	7.39	7.33	42.4	51.9	98.9	63.1
S.E.	±.36	±.42	±.46	±.56	±.57	±3.3	±1.1	±.02	±.01	±1.6	±1.5	±.3	±2.3

* Significantly different from normal young subjects at the 0.05 level.

functions. The mean values and standard errors obtained in similar measurements in the group of normal young subjects are included for comparison. It is immediately apparent that, despite an age difference of five decades, there is a striking paucity of statistically significant differences between the two groups. Significant increases in both mean arterial blood pressure (MABP) and cerebral vascular resistance (CVR) were observed in the aged group, suggesting that vascular changes are so closely associated with aging that they cannot be avoided even by the stringent selection process employed in these studies. Similarly, the slight but significant decrease in arterial O_2 saturation probably indicates some pulmonary changes with age. Cerebral blood flow (CBF) and oxygen consumption (CMR$_{O2}$) in both groups were well within the ranges generally observed in normal young people (Sokoloff, 1960), and although they were slightly lower in the elderly than in the young, the differences were far from being statistically significant. On the other hand, cerebral glucose utilization (CMR$_G$) in the aged was significantly reduced (p, approximately 0.05), and in association with the discrepancy between the changes in CMR$_{O2}$ and CMR$_G$, the oxygen:glucose ratio (O_2/G) was correspondingly though not significantly increased; the possible implications of these findings will be discussed below. No other distinguishing features were observed.

The results of the same studies in the elderly men with asymptomatic or subclinical disease (group II) are summarized in tables 2a and 2b. Since the criteria for selection and classification relegated to this group all those subjects who were rejected from group I only because of an elevated blood pressure at the time of the cerebral flow studies, it is, of course, not surprising that the MABP of group II was markedly higher than observed in either the young or normal elderly groups. In line with the generally observed relationship between arterial blood pressure and cerebral vascular resistance (Lassen, 1959), CVR was also elevated, but the rise in CVR in this group was disproportionately greater than that of the MABP, resulting in a statistically significant 16-percent fall in CBF below the level of the normal young subjects and a 10-percent decline, just short of statistical significance, below that of group I. CMR$_{O2}$, however, was negligibly lower than that of group I and not significantly different from that of the normal young group. As might be expected from a fall in blood flow without a proportionate decrease in oxygen consumption, there were tendencies though not quite statistically significant, for the $(A-V)_{O2}$ to widen and the internal jugular venous pO_2, which probably reflects the O_2 tension of the brain tissues, to fall. Cerebral glucose utilization (CMR$_G$) was similar to that of group I and significantly lower than that of the normal young subjects. In all other respects, group I was similar to the normal elderly and normal young subjects.

Evidence of vascular disease was by far the most common cause of assignment of subjects to the group II category. In order to assess better the influence of such disease on the cerebral circulation and metabolism of the aged, subjects in group II so diagnosed were classified into several smaller but homogeneous subgroups based on the nature of their vascular disease. These subgroups included: (1) normal hypertensives, who manifested elevated mean arterial blood pressure (above 107 mm Hg) (see "Methods"), but no noteworthy evidence of arteriosclerosis; (2) normotensive arteriosclerotics, who showed clear evidence of arteriosclerosis but no hypertension; and (3) hypertensive arteriosclerotics who, of

TABLE 2a.—*Cerebral circulation, metabolism, and related functions in elderly men with miscellaneous asymptomatic disease*

Subject No.	Age	MABP (mm Hg)	MIJVP (mm Hg)	CBF (ml/100 g/min)	CVR (mm Hg/ml/100g/min)	$(A-V)_{O_2}$ (Vol. %)	CMR_{O_2} (ml/100g/min)	$(A-V)_g$ (mg %)	CMR_g (mg/100g/min)	Cerebral R.Q.	O_2/g (mMole/mMole)	Int. Jug. Ven. pCO_2 (mm Hg)	Int. Jug. Ven. pO_2 (mm Hg)
8	71	112	11	40	2.5	9.58	3.8	11.4	4.6	.93	6.8	48	24
10	92	114	4	46	2.4	5.69	2.6	8.0	3.6	.83	5.7	51	39
11	73	106	14	44	2.1	5.98	2.6	11.7	5.1	.99	4.1	56	33
18	66	111	10	50	2.0	6.98	3.5	10.4	5.2	1.06	4.0	52	33
25	74	112	7	65	1.6	5.46	3.6	6.3	4.1	1.05	7.0	50	36
28	73	170	11	69	2.3	4.87	3.4	7.8	5.4	.93	5.0	56	42
29	77	116	5	49	2.3	6.33	3.1			1.02		52	37
31	72	117	5	62	1.8	4.92	3.1	7.1	4.4	.98	5.6	52	36
32	76	127	9	43	2.8	5.62	2.4	7.0	3.0	.94	6.4	51	37
33	72	132	7	51	2.4	6.57	3.4	9.5	4.8	.85	5.6	50	37
35	74	116		67		6.09	4.1	12.2	8.2	.81	4.0	49	34
38	74	104		44		5.66	2.5	9.6	4.2	1.00	4.7	44	35
39	68	90	7	62	1.3	6.42	4.0	6.6	4.1	.91	7.8	46	33
41	65	80	8	61	1.2	5.62	3.4	4.5	2.7	.88	10.0	51	37
42	68	96	7	49	1.8	5.65	2.8	10.6	5.2	.95	4.3	52	37
52	69	91	5	34	2.5	10.68	3.6	19.7	6.7	.96	4.4	40	24
57	74	90	8	49	1.7	5.89	2.9			.86		57	35
Mean	*72.8	*¹110.8	7.9	*52.1	*¹2.05	6.35	3.22	9.5	*4.8	.94	5.7	50.4	34.7
S.E.	±1.5	±5.0	±.7	±2.5	±.12	±.37	±.13	±.9	±.4	±.02	±.4	±1.0	±1.1

¹ Significantly different from normal elderly men (group I) at the 0.05 level.
* Significantly different from normal young subjects at the 0.05 level.

TABLE 2b.—*Blood constituents in elderly men with miscellaneous asymptomatic disease*

Subject No.	Art. Hemoglobin Concentration (grams %)	Blood O$_2$ Content (Vol. %)		Blood CO$_2$ Content (Vol. %)		Blood Glucose Concentration (mg. %)		Blood pH		Blood CO$_2$ Tension (mm. Hg.)		Blood O$_2$ Saturation (in percentage)	
		Arterial	Int. Jug.	Arterial	Int. Jug.	Arterial	Int. Jug.	Arterial	Int. Jug.	Arterial	Int. Jug.	Arterial	Int. Jug.
8	13.86	18.14	8.56	45.49	54.38	90.4	79.0	7.47	7.38	34	48	98.8	44.4
10	13.49	17.78	12.09	47.11	51.81	84.2	76.2	7.34	7.31	45	51	96.9	67.2
11	13.98	18.19	12.21	51.71	57.62	94.8	83.1	7.41	7.33	42	56	96.2	58.9
18	14.56	19.10	12.12	46.72	54.09	90.7	80.3	7.35	7.33	44	52	98.6	60.5
25	13.37	17.74	12.28	49.28	55.02	81.0	74.7	7.39	7.36	43	50	97.9	65.9
28	14.27	18.64	13.77	53.91	58.44	76.6	68.8	7.37	7.34	49	56	98.5	73.2
29	15.71	19.91	11.58	47.13	53.58			7.38	7.34	43	52	97.6	66.6
31	13.12	16.59	11.67	51.80	56.63	83.2	76.1	7.40	7.36	44	52	98.2	66.0
32	13.57	17.87	12.25	49.79	55.05	77.6	70.6	7.39	7.35	44	51	99.7	66.1
33	15.71	20.75	14.18	44.59	50.16	82.9	73.4	7.38	7.32	41	50	99.5	64.8
35	13.12	17.10	11.01	50.88	55.81	90.4	78.2	7.41	7.38	41	49	96.8	62.9
38	15.30	18.90	13.24	48.31	53.97	82.6	73.0	7.42	7.36	40	44	95.0	64.0
39	14.89	18.64	12.22	46.44	52.39	151.0	144.4	7.44	7.39	37	46	94.7	63.1
41	14.15	18.05	12.43	49.97	54.87	100.0	95.5	7.44	7.35	40	51	96.7	65.7
42	13.98	18.22	12.57	50.06	55.44	85.5	74.9	7.41	7.35	41	52	98.2	65.9
52	15.63	20.76	10.08	41.29	51.53	84.4	64.7	7.52	7.45	28	40	100.0	45.5
57	13.86	17.08	11.19	50.24	55.32			7.35	7.30	47	57	95.2	59.8
Mean	14.27	18.44	12.09	48.51	54.48	90.4	80.9	7.40	7.35	41.4	50.4	*97.6	62.4
S.E.	±.22	±.29	±.33	±.75	±.52	±4.6	±4.9	±.01	±.01	±1.2	±1.0	±.4	±1.8

* Significantly different from normal young subjects at the 0.05 level.

course, manifested both conditions. These subgroups included 14 of the 17 subjects studied in group II; in addition, one subject (No. 17), who had been rejected altogether because of moderately severe arteriosclerosis, was added for the purposes of this analysis to the normotensive arteriosclerotic subgroup. The results obtained in these individuals are presented in tables 3a and 3b, as well as the means and standard errors of the normal young subjects, normal elderly subjects, and the patients suffering from chronic brain syndrome, which are included for comparison. Despite the limited size of the subgroups, it is clear that it was the arteriosclerotic subjects who were chiefly responsible for the finding of a significant reduction in the CBF of group II. Except for the expected higher values for MABP and CVR and a significant increase in the arteriovenous glucose difference, the results in the normal hypertensive subjects were essentially the same as in the normal young and normal elderly groups. On the other hand, the arteriosclerotic subjects, both hypertensive and normotensive, revealed significant, indeed considerable, reductions in CBF which could account for almost all of the decrease observed in group II as a whole (table 2a). One of the normotensive arteriosclerotic subjects (No. 32) obviously hyperventilated at the time of the study, and it was probably his contribution which was mainly responsible for the significant reductions in the mean values for arterial pCO_2 and cerebral venous pO_2 observed in this subgroup; although in this one subject the hyperventilation undoubtedly contributed to cerebral vasoconstriction and reduced cerebral blood flow, it does not account for the low mean cerebral blood flow of the subgroup as a whole, which remains significantly reduced even when he is excluded from the data. Although there were no statistically significant changes in cerebral oxygen consumption and glucose utilization in the subgroups with vascular disease, CMR_{O2} tended to be substantially lower in the arteriosclerotic subjects and might, perhaps, have been found to be significantly so had the series been larger. In general, all the vascular disease subgroups tended to have increased arteriovenous oxygen and glucose differences, and the internal jugular venous pO_2 tended to fall progressively in going from the normal young group through the normal elderly and hypertensive groups, and finally, to the arteriosclerotic subjects.

In the patients with chronic brain syndrome and psychosis, there was unequivocal evidence of disturbances in both cerebral circulation and metabolism. Cerebral circulatory functions were essentially the same as in the arteriosclerotic subgroups of group II, but there were in addition marked reductions in cerebral oxygen consumption and glucose utilization. Internal jugular venous pO_2 was statistically significantly below that of the normal young and normal elderly subjects, but the arteriovenous oxygen and glucose differences were similar to those of the normal subjects and considerably less than those of the subjects with vascular disease. The combination of a low CBF, low CMR_{O2}, and normal $(A-V)_{O2}$ fails to distinguish between the possibilities of a reduced cerebral oxygen supply or a reduced cerebral oxygen demand in the pathogenesis of these changes; however, the additional finding of a low cerebral venous pO_2 suggests an anoxia of the cerebral tissues and a deficiency in supply relative to demand which in these patients was undoubtedly aggravated by a significant reduction in their arterial O_2 saturation, presumably secondary to pulmonary dysfunction.

TABLE 3a.—Comparison of cerebral circulatory and metabolic functions in various categories of elderly men and normal young subjects

Subject No.	Age	MABP (mm Hg)	MJVP (mm Hg)	CBF (ml/100 g/min)	CVR (mm Hg/ml/100g/min)	(A-V)O₂ (Vol. %)	CMRO₂ (ml/100g/min)	(A-V)_G (mg %)	CMR_G (mg/100g/min)	Cerebral R.Q.	O₂/G (mMole/mMole)	Int. Jug. Ven. pCO₂ (mm Hg)	Int. Jug. Ven. pO₂ (mm Hg)
NORMAL YOUNG (15 SUBJECTS)													
Mean	20.8	84.2	7.1	62.1	1.29	5.70	3.51	9.3	6.0	0.92	5.5	51.9	37.5
S.E.	±.4	±1.9	±.5	±2.9	±.06	±.30	±.21	±.8	±.7	±.02	±.5	±1.5	±1.5
NORMAL ELDERLY MEN (26 SUBJECTS)													
Mean	*71.0	*93.2	7.1	*57.9	*1.58	5.88	3.33	8.2	*4.6	.91	6.0	51.2	35.9
S.E.	±.8	±1.9	±.5	±2.1	±.07	±.17	±.08	±.5	±.2	±.02	±.2	±.8	±.6
NORMAL HYPERTENSIVES (5 SUBJECTS)													
8	71	112	11	40	2.5	9.58	3.8	11.4	4.6	.93	6.8	48	24
18	66	111	10	50	2.0	6.98	3.5	10.4	5.2	1.06	4.0	52	33
28	73	170	11	69	2.3	4.87	3.4	7.8	5.4	.93	5.0	56	42
33	72	132	7	51	2.4	6.57	3.4	9.5	4.8	.85	5.6	50	37
35	74	116		67		6.09	4.1	12.2	8.2	.81	4.0	49	34
Mean	*71.2	*¹128.2	*¹9.8	*¹55.4	*¹2.30	6.82	3.64	¹10.3	5.6	.92	5.1	51.0	34.0
S.E.	±1.4	±11.1	±.9	±5.5	±.11	±.77	±.14	±.8	±.7	±.04	±.5	±1.4	±2.9
NORMOTENSIVE ARTERIOSCLEROTICS (6 SUBJECTS)													
11	73	106	14	44	2.1	5.98	2.6	11.7	5.1	.99	4.1	56	33
17	75	83	7	58	1.3	6.66	3.9	9.9	5.7	.97	5.4	43	35
38	74	104		44		5.66	2.5	9.6	4.2	1.00	4.7	44	35
39	68	90	7	62	1.3	6.42	4.0	6.6	4.1	.91	7.8	46	33
52	69	91	5	34	2.5	10.68	3.6	19.7	6.7	.96	4.4	40	24
57	74	90	8	49	1.7	5.89	2.9			.86		57	35
Mean	*72.2	*94.0	8.2	*¹48.5	*1.78	6.88	3.25	¹11.5	5.2	.95	5.3	47.7	*¹32.5
S.E.	±1.2	±3.7	±1.5	±4.2	±.23	±.77	±.27	±2.2	±.5	±.02	±.7	±2.9	±1.7

HYPERTENSIVE ARTERIOSCLEROTICS (4 SUBJECTS)

25	74	112	11	40	2.5	9.58	3.8	11.4	4.6	.93	6.8	48	24
29	77	116	5	49	2.3	6.33	3.1	...	...	1.02	...	52	37
31	72	117	5	62	1.8	4.92	3.1	7.1	4.4	.98	5.6	52	36
32	76	127	9	43	2.8	5.62	2.4	7.0	3.0	.94	6.4	51	37
Mean	*74.8	*¹118.0	7.5	*48.5	*2.35	6.61	3.10	8.5	4.0	.97	6.3	50.8	33.5
S.E.	±1.1	±3.2	±1.5	±4.9	±.21	±1.03	±.29	±1.5	±.5	±.02	±.4	±.9	±3.2

CHRONIC BRAIN SYNDROME WITH PSYCHOSIS (10 PATIENTS)

Mean	*71.8	*¹101.7	6.2	*¹48.5	*¹2.11	5.69	*¹2.72	7.06	*13.6	.94	5.7	50.5	*¹33.1
S.E.	±1.8	±6.2	±.3	±3.8	±.25	±.23	±.18	±.87	±.6	±.02	±.8	±1.0	±1.1

[1] Significantly different from normal elderly men (group I) at the 0.05 level.
* Significantly different from normal young subjects at the 0.05 level.

TABLE 3b.—*Comparison of blood constituents in various categories of elderly men*

Subject No.	Art. Hemoglobin Concentration (grams %)	Blood O$_2$ Content (Vol. %)		Blood CO$_2$ Content (Vol. %)		Blood Glucose Concentration (mg. %)		Blood pH		Blood CO$_2$ Tension (mm. Hg.)		Blood O$_2$ Saturation (%)	
		Arterial	Int. Jug.	Arterial	Int. Jug.	Arterial	Int. Jug.	Arterial	Int. Jug.	Arterial	Int. Jug.	Arterial	Int. Jug.
NORMAL YOUNG (15 SUBJECTS)													
Mean.........	13.87	18.24	12.52	48.12	53.38	83.2	73.8	7.39	7.33	42.4	51.9	98.9	63.1
S.E..........	±.36	±.42	±.46	±.56	±.57	±3.3	±1.1	±.02	±.01	±1.6	±1.5	±.3	±2.3
NORMAL ELDERLY MEN (26 SUBJECTS)													
Mean.........	14.01	17.94	12.05	49.34	54.69	88.0	*79.9	7.39	7.35	42.7	51.1	*96.9	64.3
S.E..........	±.20	±.24	±.24	±.48	±.43	±1.7	±1.7	±.01	±.01	±.8	±.9	±.5	±.9
NORMAL HYPERTENSIVES (5 SUBJECTS)													
8............	13.86	18.14	8.56	45.49	54.38	90.4	79.0	7.47	7.38	34	48	98.8	44.4
18...........	14.56	19.10	12.12	46.72	54.09	90.7	80.3	7.35	7.33	44	52	98.6	60.5
28...........	14.27	18.64	13.77	53.91	58.44	76.6	68.8	7.37	7.34	49	56	98.5	73.2
33...........	15.71	20.75	14.18	44.59	50.16	82.9	73.4	7.38	7.32	41	50	99.5	64.8
35...........	13.12	17.10	11.01	50.88	55.81	90.4	78.2	7.41	7.38	41	49	96.8	62.9
Mean.........	14.30	18.75	11.93	48.32	54.58	86.2	75.9	7.40	7.35	41.8	51.0	98.4	61.2
S.E..........	±.43	±.60	±1.02	±1.76	±1.35	±2.8	±2.1	±.02	±.01	±2.4	±1.4	±.4	±4.7
NORMOTENSIVE ARTERIOSCLEROTICS (6 SUBJECTS)													
11...........	13.98	18.19	12.21	51.71	57.62	94.8	83.1	7.41	7.33	42	56	96.2	58.9
17...........	15.71	20.14	13.48	42.37	48.80	85.2	75.3	7.40	7.33	37	43	94.4	63.0
38...........	15.30	18.90	13.24	48.31	53.97	82.6	73.0	7.42	7.36	40	44	95.0	64.0
39...........	14.89	18.64	12.22	46.44	52.39	151.0	144.4	7.44	7.39	37	46	94.7	63.1
52...........	15.63	20.76	10.08	41.29	51.53	84.4	64.7	7.52	7.45	28	40	100.0	45.5
57...........	13.86	17.08	11.19	50.24	55.32	....	....	7.35	7.30	47	57	95.2	59.8
Mean.........	¹14.90	18.95	12.07	¹46.73	53.27	99.6	88.1	7.42	7.36	¹38.5	49.3	*95.9	¹59.1
S.E..........	±.33	±.54	±.52	±1.72	±1.26	±13.0	±14.4	±.02	±.02	±2.6	±2.5	±.9	±2.8

HYPERTENSIVE ARTERIOSCLEROTICS (4 SUBJECTS)

25	13.37	17.74	12.28	49.28	55.02	81.0	74.7	7.39	7.36	43	50	97.9	65.9
29	15.71	19.91	13.58	47.13	53.58	......	......	7.38	7.34	43	52	97.6	66.6
31	13.12	16.59	11.67	51.80	56.63	83.2	76.1	7.40	7.36	44	52	98.2	66.0
32	13.57	17.87	12.25	49.79	55.05	77.6	70.6	7.39	7.35	44	51	99.7	66.1
Mean	13.94	18.03	12.45	49.50	55.07	80.6	73.8	7.39	7.35	43.5	51.3	98.4	66.2
S.E.	±.60	±.69	±.40	±.96	±.62	±1.6	±1.7	±.00	±.01	±.3	±.5	±.5	±.2

CHRONIC BRAIN SYNDROME (10 PATIENTS)

Mean	13.81	17.54	11.86	48.02	53.38	*92.1	*85.1	7.38	7.34	42.3	50.5	*194.7	[1]59.4
S.E.	±.41	±.32	±.35	±.87	±.89	±2.1	±1.9	±.01	±.01	±.7	±1.0	±.9	±1.9

[1] Significantly different from normal elderly men (group I) at the 0.05 level.
* Significantly different from normal young subjects at the 0.05 level.

DISCUSSION

To a great extent, the results almost speak for themselves. Despite a 50-year difference in age, cerebral blood flow and oxygen consumption in normal elderly men (group I) were essentially the same as in normal young subjects. The slight declines that were observed in the aged, 7 percent in CBF and 5 percent in CMR_{O2}, may lead some to speculate concerning their possible meaningfulness. It must be emphasized, however, that these were statistically insignificant changes in series of rather appreciable size. Furthermore, even if these changes could be construed to reflect something more than random variation, it would, in view of our findings in the arteriosclerotic subjects, most likely be the impossibility of completely ruling out the variable of arteriosclerosis from a presumably healthy aged population.

On the other hand, these results do not refute the previous evidence (Kety, 1956) that these functions usually decrease in the aged. The subjects comprising our group of normal elderly men were highly selected according to rigorous criteria and could hardly be considered representative of the aged population at large; they were, as regards relative freedom from vascular and other diseases, far superior. Group II, the subjects with asymptomatic or subclinical disease, were probably more representative of their age group, and, indeed, in this group CBF was significantly reduced, and CMR_{O2} tended to be lower though still not statistically significantly. The possibility may be entertained that our normal old men in group I may, because they were so select, have suffered declines in CBF and CMR_{O2} from initially higher than average values which could have been detected only by longitudinal studies. However, the basis of their selection was general freedom from disease, and since there is no evidence to in-

dicate that high values for CBF and CMR_{O2} tend to promote general good health, it would indeed be fortuitous if such were the case. It is, therefore, difficult on the basis of our results to avoid the conclusions that blood flow and oxygen consumption of the cerebral tissues during adulthood is not a function of chronological age, and that the decreases in these functions so often observed in the elderly are not directly attributable to the process of aging per se but rather to some frequent accompaniment of old age.

The possible nature of this deteriorative concomitant of old age is suggested by the results obtained in the group of elderly men with asymptomatic or subclinical disease (group II). This group differed from the normal elderly only in that they exhibited evidence of mild subclinical disease, generally vascular, when subjected to an exacting clinical examination; yet in contrast to the normal elderly men, their CBF was significantly reduced below that of the young subjects. On further examination of the subgroups with vascular disease (table 3a), it is clear that this reduction was not associated with hypertension, but could be accounted for entirely by the findings in the subjects with arteriosclerosis. In the subjects with hypertension alone, CBF and CMR_{O2} were like those of the normal young and elderly subjects. On the other hand, in the arteriosclerotic patients, both normotensive and hypertensive, CBF was significantly reduced by about 16–20 percent, and CMR_{O2} also tended to be lower though not statistically significantly so in this small series. Furthermore, in all of the subjects with vascular disease there was a tendency for the arteriovenous oxygen difference to increase and the internal jugular venous pO_2 to fall. The latter change was particularly pronounced and statistically significant in the normotensive arteriosclerotic subjects; inasmuch as this function reflects the oxygen tension of the cerebral tissues, the observed changes suggest cerebral ischemia and anoxia in the arteriosclerotic group. It would appear then from these results that it is arteriosclerosis which is responsible for the decline in cerebral blood flow in the aged; secondarily there is an anoxia of the cerebral tissues and ultimately a fall in oxygen consumption which, although not statistically significant in these studies, has frequently been observed by others (Fazekas, Alman, and Bessman, 1952; Fazekas, Kleh, and Finnerty, 1955; Fazekas, Kleh, and Witkin, 1953; Heyman, Patterson, Duke, and Battey, 1953; Kety, 1956; Lassen, Feinberg, and Lane, 1960), Schieve and Wilson, 1953. We are, therefore, essentially in agreement with Shenkin and his coworkers (Shenkin, Novak, Goluboff, Soffe, and Bortin, 1953) who concluded that cerebral blood flow and metabolism are impaired in the aged only in the presence of both hypertension and arteriosclerosis; our results also implicate vascular disease but suggest that it is arteriosclerosis alone which is responsible. They are, however, at variance with the recent findings in a small group of normal aged men by Lassen and his coworkers (Lassen, Feinberg, and Lane, 1960) of a slight but significant reduction in CMR_{O_2} without any comparable impairment of CBF.

Cerebral blood flow in the patients with chronic brain syndrome and psychosis was reduced, but no more so than in the arteriosclerotic subjects. However, in the former group cerebral O_2 consumption was markedly depressed below the levels found in any of the other groups, resulting in the restoration of a more or less normal proportion of oxygen utilization to supply. Similar results have been reported by Freyhan and his associates (Freyhan, Woodford, and Kety, 1951). Such a situation could have resulted from a primary decrease in metabolic rate, except that in this series the cerebral venous pO_2 was also significantly reduced, suggesting a primary circulatory deficit, tissue anoxia, and secondary reduction in metabolic rate. It is conceivable that the changes observed in our chronic brain syndrome patients merely reflect the ultimate consequences of those occurring in arteriosclerosis, that after a prolonged period of cerebral ischemia and hypoxia the cerebral tissues lose their ability to utilize or extract from the blood the quantities of oxygen necessary to maintain normal metabolic processes and mental function. There may, perhaps, even be an acceleration in the loss of neuronal elements reported to occur in the cortex in association with aging (Brody, 1955).

The significance of the differences in cerebral glucose utilization observed in several of the groups of elderly men is difficult to evaluate. Usually glucose and oxygen are consumed by the brain in almost stoichiometric amounts (Kety, 1957; Sokoloff, 1960). In these studies, however, CMR_G was significantly reduced in both the normal elderly men and in the subjects with asymptomatic or subclinical disease, while the CMR_{O_2} in both groups was only negligibly altered. In the subgroups with vascular disease, there did appear to be a correlation between the two metabolic rates; the hypertensive arteriosclerotics showed the greatest reductions in both, although only the change in CMR_G was statistically significant. In the chronic brain syndrome series also, both CMR_{O_2} and CMR_G were significantly and almost proportionately reduced. It may be that CMR_G is a more sensitive indicator of cerebral metabolic rate than CMR_{O_2}, but this would indeed be surprising, for blood glucose determinations in our laboratory, and probably in most others, are far less accurate or reliable than blood oxygen measurements. On the other hand, it is not inconceivable that there are with aging subtle changes in cerebral metabolism which result in a lowering of glucose utilization before a reduction in CMR_{O2} becomes apparent. Normally there is slightly more glucose utilized by the brain than can be accounted for by the oxygen consumption, assuming complete oxidation of glucose (Kety, 1957; Sokoloff, 1960). The fate of this excess glucose is at present uncertain. Himwich and Himwich (1946) have accounted for it by the cerebral pyruvate and lactate production, but others have failed to confirm this (Kety, 1957). It is likely that some of this glucose and its derivatives are incorporated into the complex chemical constituents constantly being re-synthesized by the brain (Geiger, 1958). In any case, there may be, in the aged, alterations in these aspects of cerebral carbohydrate metabolism which would not be reflected in cerebral oxygen consumption, but until there is confirmation of our findings and additional experimental evidence, further speculation would be unjustified.

As in most studies of this type, our data were obtained by means of the nitrous oxide method, and, therefore, apply only to a representative fraction of the brain as a whole rather than to the total brain. They are completely independent of changes in brain weight, but are more relevant to the events occurring within the tissues of the brain. The question of the total quantity of brain tissue or the amount of functioning tissue in the aged brain is an entirely different problem.

The absence of any significant changes in cerebral blood flow and oxygen consumption in the normal elderly men (group I) should not be construed as evidence that there are no age changes in the central nervous system in the absence of disease. The fact that such changes do occur is demonstrated by the findings of alterations in their cognitive and perceptual functions (chs. 8 and 9) and electroencephalographic activity (ch. 7). It suggests rather that these functions may be more sensitive indicators of the aging phenomenon in the brain or that they involve processes too subtle to be reflected in the gross blood flow and metabolic rate of the brain as a whole. On the other hand, when vascular disease is present and leads to reductions in cerebral blood flow and oxygen tension, as it did in the arteriosclerotic patients, then it becomes the pacemaker of the aging process in the brain and results in more rapid deterioration of these other functions (chs. 7, 8, and 9).

SUMMARY

1. Studies of cerebral circulation and metabolism revealed no significant differences in cerebral blood flow and oxygen consumption between a group of normal young subjects (mean age, 20.8 years) and a group of highly selected normal elderly men (mean age, 70.0 years) who were functioning effectively in their communities and were as free of evidence of disease, including vascular disease, as was possible to obtain in their age group.

2. In a similar group of elderly men differing from the previous one only in that they exhibited clear evidence of mild asymptomatic or subclinical disease, chiefly vascular, there was a statistically significant decline in cerebral bloow flow of 10–16 percent. Cerebral oxygen consumption also tended to be lower but not statistically significantly.

3. All of the reductions in cerebral blood flow and oxygen consumption in the group of elderly men with asymptomatic disease could be accounted for by the results obtained in the arteriosclerotic subjects. Hypertensives without arteriorsclerosis were normal with regard to these functions.

4. The cerebral arteriovenous oxygen difference tended to be increased and the cerebral venous oxygen tension tended to fall in all the categories of vascular disease, particularly the arteriorsclerotic groups. These changes, though not quite statistically significant probably because of the small size of the individual categories, were pronounced and were, therefore, interpreted as evidence of relative cerebral circulatory insufficiency and hypoxia.

5. Although cerebral oxygen consumption was not decreased, there was a considerable and statistically significant fall in cerebral glucose utilization in the normal elderly subjects. The possible implications of this discrepancy between the two metabolic rates are discussed.

6. In patients with chronic brain syndrome and psychosis, cerebral blood flow was markedly reduced, but no more so than in the arteriosclerotic subjects. However, in contrast to the arteriosclerotics, cerebral oxygen and glucose utilization was proportionately depressed so that the arteriovenous differences were within normal limits. Cerebral venous pO_2 remained low, however, indicating relative cerebral anoxia.

7. It is suggested that decreases in cerebral blood flow and oxygen consumption are not the consequences of chronological aging per se, but rather of arteriosclerosis which causes first a relative cerebral circulatory insufficiency and anoxia and then ultimately a secondary reduction in cerebral metabolic rate.

ACKNOWLEDGMENTS

The authors wish to express their appreciation to Mrs. Mary S. Holmes, Mrs. Gladys E. Deibler, and Miss Phyllis L. Campbell for their outstanding technical assistance in the experimental procedures; to Dr. Samuel Greenhouse and Mr. Donald F. Morrison, for the statistical analyses; and to Miss Carol L. Talley for the preparation of the tables.

REFERENCES

BRODY, H. 1955. Organization of the cerebral cortex. III. A study of aging in the human cerebral cortex. *J. Comp. Neurol., 102,* 511.

DEIBLER, G. E., HOLMES, M. S., CAMPBELL, P. L., and GANS, J. 1959. Use of Triton X–100 as a hemolytic agent in the spectrophotometric measurement of blood O_2 saturation. *J. Appl. Physiol., 14,* 133.

EVELYN, K. A., and MALLOY, H. T. 1938. Microdetermination of oxyhemoglobin, methemoglobin, and sulfhemoglobin in a single sample of blood. *J. Biol. Chem., 126,* 655.

FAZEKAS, J. F., ALMAN, R. W., and BESSMAN, A. N. 1952. Cerebral physiology of the aged. *Am. J. Med. Sciences, 223,* 245.

FAZEKAS, J. F., KLEH, J., and FINNERTY, F. A. 1955. Influence of age and vascular disease on cerebral hemodynamics and metabolism. *Am. J. Med., 18,* 477.

———, ———, and WITKIN, L. 1953. Cerebral hemodynamics and metabolism in subjects over 90 years of age. *J. Am. Geriat. Soc., 1,* 836.

FREYHAN, F. A., WOODFORD, R. B., and KETY, S. S. 1951. Cerebral blood flow and metabolism in psychoses of senility. *J. Nerv. & Ment. Dis., 113,* 449.

GEIGER, A. 1958. Correlation of brain metabolism and function by the use of a brain perfusion method in situ. *Physiol. Rev., 38,* 1.

GORDAN, G. S. 1956. Influence of steroids on cerebral metabolism in man. *Recent Progress in Hormone Research, 12,* 153.

HEYMAN, A., PATTERSON, J. L., DUKE, T. W., and BATTEY, L. L. 1953. The cerebral circulation and metabolism in arteriosclerotic and hypertensive cerebrovascular disease. *N. England J. Med., 249,* 223.

HIMWICH, W. A., and HIMWICH, H. E. 1946. Pyruvic acid exchange of the brain. *J. Neurophysiol., 9,* 133.

KETY, S. S. 1956. Human cerebral blood flow and oxygen consumption as related to aging. Neurologic and Psychiatric Aspects of the Disorders of Aging. *Res. Publ. Assoc. Res. Nerv. & Ment. Diseases, 35,* 31. Baltimore: Williams & Wilkins Co.

———. 1957. The general metabolism of the brain in vivo. In the *Metabolism of the Nervous System,* edited by D. Richter. London: Pergamon Press.

———, and SCHMIDT, C. F. 1948. The nitrous oxide method for the quantitative determination of cerebral blood flow: theory, procedure, and normal values. *J. Clin. Invest., 27,* 476.

LASSEN, N. A. 1959. Cerebral blood flow and O₂ consumption in man. *Physiol. Rev., 39*, 183.

——, FEINBERG, I., and LANE, M. H. 1960. Bilateral studies of cerebral oxygen uptake in young and aged normal subjects and in patients with organic dementia. *J. Clin. Invest., 39*, 491.

NATIONAL RESEARCH COUNCIL. 1944. Oxygen dissociation curves of normal human blood (Chart B–1 a and b). *Handbook of Respiratory Data in Aviation*, Washington, D.C.

NELSON, N. 1944. A photometric adaptation of the Somogyi method for the determination of glucose. *J. Biol. Chem., 153*, 375.

ROSENTHAL, T. B. 1948. The effects of temperature on pH of blood and plasma in vitro. *J. Biol. Chem., 173*, 25.

SCHEINBERG, P., BLACKBURN, I., RICH, M., and SASLAW, M. 1953. Effects of aging on cerebral circulation and metabolism. *Arch. Neurol. and Psychiat., 70*, 77.

SCHIEVE, J. F., and WILSON, W. P. 1953. The influence of age, anesthesia, and cerebral arteriosclerosis on cerebral vascular reactivity to carbon dioxide. *Am. J. Med., 15*, 171.

SHENKIN, H. A., NOVAK, P., GOLUBOFF, B., SOFFE, A. M., and BORTIN, L. 1953. The effects of aging, arteriosclerosis, and hypertension upon the cerebral circulation. *J. Clin. Invest., 32*, 459.

SOKOLOFF, L. 1960. The metabolism of the central nervous system in vivo. In the *Handbook of Physiology*, Vol. III, American Physiological Society.

VAN SLYKE, D. D., and NEILL, J. M. 1924. The determination of gases in blood by vacuum extraction and manometric measurement. *J. Biol. Chem., 61*, 523.

——, and SENDROY, J., Jr. 1928. Studies of gas and electrolyte equilibria in blood. XV. Line charts for graphic calculations by the Henderson-Hasselbalch equation, and for calculating plasma carbon dioxide content from whole blood content. *J. Biol. Chem., 79*, 781.

CHAPTER 7

The Electroencephalogram of Healthy Aged Males

by Walter D. Obrist

Although the literature contains many references on the electroencephalogram (EEG) of aged psychiatric patients, there are relatively few investigations of brain wave patterns in "normal" senescence. Most of the reports are based on average people with the usual chronic diseases of old age. In contrast, the present project was designed to observe optimally healthy old people and to compare them with elderly subjects who are less healthy. Information could thus be gained on the degree to which factors of health contribute to EEG changes in later life. This phase of the study is reported in the current chapter.

The interdisciplinary aspect of the investigation made it possible to pose several additional questions. Of particular interest was the correlation of senescent EEG changes with alterations in cerebral metabolism. It also seemed desirable to determine the relation of EEG findings to early signs of mental deterioration. Results from the interdisciplinary studies are presented in chapter 15. The literature and hypotheses relevant to these issues are reviewed in the following sections.

EEG CHANGES ASSOCIATED WITH AGING

It is apparent from previous research that electrocortical activity does not undergo dramatic changes in senescence. Except for psychiatric patients, who are likely to have severe abnormalities, the average old person's EEG differs only in minor respects from that of youth.

Obrist (1954) studied a group of retired men in a fraternal home and noted that frequency of the alpha rhythm was significantly slower than in young adults. Alpha waves of 7 to 9 cps were more prevalent in elderly subjects, while rhythms of 10 to 12 cps were less common. Similar results have been obtained by Mundy-Castle et al. (1954) on mentally normal volunteers, and by Friedlander (1958) on general hospital patients with normal EEG's. Other characteristics of the alpha rhythm may also show age differences. Mengoli (1952) noted a diminution of amplitude and a tendency for discontinuity in healthy seniles. When normal old and young subjects were compared by Mundy-Castle et al. (1954), slight but significant reductions in both amplitude and percent-time alpha were obtained for the elderly group.

Using a low anterior temporal lead, Silverman, Busse, and Barnes (1955) discovered abnormal foci over the temporal lobe in one out of three aged community volunteers. The foci consisted of slow waves and amplitude asymmetries, sometimes accompanied by spikes, occurring predominantly on the left side (Busse et al., 1956). These observations were subsequently confirmed by Obrist and Busse (unpublished data),[1] who reported temporal delta or theta activity in 30 percent of elderly community subjects and in 3 percent of young controls.

Focal slow waves outside the temporal area are less common during normal senescence. Obrist and Busse found only 4 percent nontemporal foci in community volunteers,[1] whereas Obrist (1954) obtained an incidence of 10 percent for a slightly older, institutionalized group. In both studies, the frontal area was most frequently involved.

Diffuse, nonfocal slowing has been reported as an abnormality in 15 to 20 percent of aged control subjects (Gibbs and Gibbs, 1950; Silverman, Busse, and Barnes, 1955; Maggs and Turton, 1956). These figures probably include cases with a slow alpha rhythm of 7 to 8.5 cps. When the upper limit of abnormality is reduced to 7 cps or less, the reported incidence of diffuse slowing is smaller. Thus, Mundy-Castle et al. (1954) found theta rhythms in only 8 percent of elderly volunteers, a value comparable to that of young adults. Similarly, Obrist (1954) observed diffuse delta waves in only 2 percent of mentally normal old people. The latter emphasized that the higher incidence of slow activity in advanced age groups is mainly due to the presence of abnormally slow alpha rhythms. Although there are many slow alpha variants between 6 and 8 cps, diffuse activity below this frequency seldom occurs in nonhospitalized elderly subjects.

A number of authors have commented on the prevalence of fast, beta activity during normal senescence (Mundy-Castle, 1951; Mengoli, 1952; Obrist, 1954; Maggs and Turton, 1956). This is consistent with the observation of Gibbs and Gibbs (1950) that the proportion of predominantly fast tracings increases during middle life, reaching 25 percent between age 60 and 70 in normal controls. That it may decrease again in advanced old age is suggested by Silverman, Busse, and Barnes (1955) on the basis of their group over 80 years.

From the literature just cited, certain tentative generalizations can be made concerning the EEG in average, nonhospitalized elderly people: (1) The alpha rhythm is slower in old than in young adults, with a tendency toward decreased amplitude and percent-time. (2) Slow wave foci are prevalent over the temporal lobe, other areas being involved only occasionally. (3) Diffuse slow activity of 6 cps or less seldom occurs in normal senescence, although waves of 7 and 8 cps are common. (4) Fast activity is prominent up to age 80, after which the incidence declines.

The major problem posed in the current study is whether the above age differences are simply a function of poor health, or whether they occur independently of physical disease. If the former is true, little or no EEG difference would be expected between normal young adults and a select group of healthy old people. Differences would be expected, however, between elderly subjects who varied in physical health. To test these predictions, the records obtained here were evaluated in terms of young adult norms, and healthy old subjects were compared with those having diagnosable disease. For reasons advanced in the next section, special attention was given to a subgroup with clinical evidence of arteriosclerosis.

Relation of EEG to Cerebral Circulation and Metabolism

One of the purposes for including electroencephalography in this project was to in-

---

[1] Obrist, W. D., and Busse, E. W. 1960. Temporal lobe EEG abnormalities in normal senescence. *EEG Clin. Neurophysiol., 12,* 244.

vestigate its relation to cerebral circulatory and metabolic variables. It is well known that anoxia and hypoglycemia are associated with a definite slowing of brain potentials (Davis, Davis, and Thompson, 1938; Gibbs, Williams, and Gibbs, 1940; Brazier, 1948). Disturbances in cerebral circulation also produce abnormal slow waves in the EEG, presumably because they interfere with delivery of oxygen and glucose. Diffuse delta and theta activity is prominent in patients with congestive heart failure (Ewalt and Ruskin, 1944; Stuhl, Cloche, and Kartun, 1952), and focal slowing is prevalent in cerebral thrombosis (Strauss and Greenstein, 1948; Roseman, Schmidt, and Foltz, 1952). These EEG changes may be reversed when adequate circulation is reestablished. In studies on cerebral vascular insufficiency, Corday, Rothenberg, and Putnam (1953) produced slow wave abnormalities in animals by combined arterial ligation and hypotension. Similar EEG changes have been brought about in humans with cerebral vascular disease by cartoid artery compression and tilting (Skillicorn and Aird, 1954; Meyer, Leiderman, and Denny-Brown, 1956).

The above studies all point to a direct effect of impaired cerebral circulation on the EEG, specifically the production of slow waves. Since a shift in frequency to the slow side is a common feature of the senescent EEG, the question arises whether this could result from undetected circulatory deficiencies, known to be prevalent among old people. It is clear that reversible abnormalities in the EEG can be precipitated by acute cardiovascular crises, such as heart failure, cerebral thrombosis, or a sudden drop in blood pressure. It is not at all clear whether the more permanent EEG changes associated with aging could result from chronic circulatory impairment, particularly cerebral arteriosclerosis.

Direct EEG correlations with postmortem evidence of arteriosclerotic brain disease have been reported by Sheridan et al. (1955) on five aged psychiatric patients. Diffuse slow wave abnormalities were present in four cases, three of whom also had focal slowing. In a clinical study, Obrist and Bissell (1955) compared elderly cases of cardiac and cerebral vascular disease with healthy age-matched controls. A significant reduction of alpha frequency and increased delta activity was found in the group with cardiovascular disease, even in the absence of acute circulatory disturbances. Although low correlations were obtained between ophthalmic vascular pathology and EEG (Mars, Morpurgo, and Serra, 1955), electrocardiographic irregularities (Morpurgo, Serra, and Mars, 1955), and X-ray evidence of cardiomegaly (Obrist and Bissell, 1955) were frequently associated with abnormal brain waves. It is probable that many patients with coronary heart disease have cerebral arteriosclerosis (Young et al., 1956; Giongo and Minoni, 1959), which may partially explain the concordance of cardiac and EEG findings.

More recently, Obrist, Busse, and Henry (1961) found an inverse relationship between blood pressure and diffuse slow wave abnormalities among aged psychiatric patients. The correlation did not apply to mentally normal subjects who had minimal EEG changes. On the assumption that psychiatric patients have increased cerebral vascular resistance, mild elevations in blood pressure might help preserve EEG normality by maintaining adequate cerebral circulation. In normal subjects, vascular resistance is presumably lower, so that blood pressure may not be as critical in the maintenance of either cerebral circulation or normal brain potentials.

The question arises whether the lesser electroencephalographic slowing of healthy old people can be explained on the basis of minor circulatory deficiencies. In the current study an attempt was made to explore the possibility that age-related shifts in EEG frequency might be associated with a reduction of cerebral blood flow and oxygen consumption in normal senescence.

There are few previous studies relevant to this question. Heine (1953) found a correlation between EEG abnormality and decreased CBF and $CMRO_2$ in patients with cardiovascular disease. Lassen, Munck, and Tottey (1957) recorded EEG's in six cases with organic dementia and decreased $CMRO_2$. All had abnormal EEG's, five of them revealing slow wave disturbances. On the other hand, in normal physiological conditions of sleep and mental activity, the EEG and cerebral metabolism vary independently (Mangold et al., 1956; Sokoloff et al., 1956). Whereas the latter undergoes little change with alterations of mental state, the EEG may show profound shifts in frequency. It should be noted that predictions made here concerning the relationship between EEG and cerebral metabolism apply only to the basal, waking state.

Relation of EEG to Psychological Function

Research on psychiatric patients has consistently revealed relationships between senile deterioration and EEG abnormality. The most common finding is an association of diffuse slow waves with evidence of chronic brain syndrome; specifically, disorientation, memory disturbance, and intellectual deficit (Barnes, Busse, and Friedman, 1956; Obrist and Henry, 1958a). Furthermore, the severity of diffuse slowing is positively correlated with the degree of psychological impairment (McAdam and Robinson, 1956; Weiner and Schuster, 1956). Organic mental signs are also associated with a slow alpha rhythm of less than eight cycles (Luce and Rothschild, 1953)

and a decrease in percent-time alpha (Mundy-Castle et al., 1954; Obrist and Henry, 1958b). Memory test performance varies directly with the dominant frequency of a record (Hoagland, 1954). The fact that outcome of illness is reasonably predicted from EEG (McAdam and Robinson, 1957; Pampiglione and Post, 1958), emphasizes the significance of the correlations on psychiatric patients.

In contrast to these findings, EEG-psychological studies on mentally normal old people are notably negative. Obrist [2] related performance on standard intelligence and memory tests to alpha frequency and presence of slow waves in the EEG. Low correlations were found, which disappeared when age was partialed out. Busse et al. (1956) and Thaler (1956) were unable to differentiate normal EEG's from focal temporal abnormalities on the basis of intelligence test scores or tests of abstract-concrete behavior. Thaler did obtain a slight difference in Wechsler-Bellevue performance between individuals with diffuse abnormalities and normal tracings. However, these findings could not be confirmed by Busse and coworkers, using the Wechsler Adult Intelligence Scale.

The EEG and mental ability are poorly correlated when each is within normal limits (Ostow, 1950). The presence of organic brain disease, however, may increase the degree of relationship by virtue of its adverse effect on both functions. If brain pathology is permitted to vary, as when senile patients are mixed with community subjects, a significant relationship is obtained between EEG and intelligence test performance (Silverman et al., 1953).

---

[2] Obrist, W. D., Busse, E. W., Eisdorfer, C., and Kleemeier, R. W. 1962. Relation of the electroencephalogram to intellectual function in senescence. *J. Geront., 17,* 197–206.

Recently, McAdam and Robinson (1958) noted a tendency for minor EEG abnormalities to be associated with psychiatric ratings of mild intellectual impairment in socially adjusted old people. This suggests the desirability of a continuing search for EEG correlates of *early* senile mental changes. The present investigation offers a unique opportunity to explore the correlation of EEG with a wide variety of intellectual, behavioral, and personality variables in healthy senescence.

METHODS

Subjects

The EEG results described here are based on 47 white males over age 65. These individuals enjoyed better than average health for their age, being selected from a larger group that had been screened for the absence of physical disease. All lived in the community, except three who resided in a home for the aged. The subjects were divided into two categories on the basis of health: Group I, consisting of 27 cases with little or no evidence of physical disease, mean age 70.8 years; group II, comprising 20 individuals with asymptomatic, subclinical evidence of pathology, mean age 72.3 years. In accordance with the question previously raised, a special subgroup of 12 subjects with evidence of arteriosclerosis was selected from group II for special study. Eleven had a diagnosis of arteriosclerotic heart disease, four revealed evidence of intracranial vascular calcification and two showed signs of peripheral arteriosclerosis, some subjects having more than one finding. The diagnoses were based on a medical history, physical examination, electrocardiogram, X-rays of the chest and skull, and special examinations when indicated. A complete description of the subjects and their physical findings may be found in chapters 2 and 3.

Testing Procedure

EEG's were recorded on an eight-channel Grass Electroencephalograph, using both bipolar and monopolar techniques. Nineteen scalp and two ear electrodes were applied according to the international system of placement (Jasper, 1958). Approximately 30 minutes of routine waking record was obtained, followed by 5 minutes of overbreathing. Intermittent photic stimulation was administered in many cases, and sleep tracings were secured on a few. For those sections of the record subjected to quantitative analysis, particular care was taken to insure constant recording conditions. Subjects were encouraged to relax but remain awake, and extraneous stimuli were carefully controlled. Testing was carried out after a light breakfast of fruit juice and toast, comparable to the procedure used in the blood flow studies. None of the subjects had taken medication during the week preceding their EEG.

EEG Clinical Evaluation

The routine tracings were interpreted by a qualified electroencephalographer,[3] who had no knowledge of the subjects other than age, race, and sex. A rating of normal or abnormal was assigned, with a description given of the type and location of any abnormality. Judgments were based on generally accepted adult criteria (Gibbs and Gibbs, 1950; Hill and Parr, 1950), except that mild slowing of the alpha rhythm and minor amounts of fast activity were not regarded as abnormal. Since these characteristics are prevalent in senescence, the judgments tended to be relative to age. EEG's were also rated independently by the author, who was in 91 percent agreement

[3] The author is indebted to Dr. Cosimo Ajmone-Marsan for his interpretation of the recordings and for the generous use of EEG facilities at the National Institutes of Health.

with the original evaluations (43 out of 47). The few discrepancies were resolved by consultation between the two interpreters.

EEG Frequency Analysis

Because research of this type requires more precise discrimination of subjects, the clinical EEG ratings were supplemented by quantitative measurement. This was facilitated by recording brain potentials on frequency-modulated magnetic tape (Cox, Obrist, and Henry, 1955). The tapes were later played back at three times the original amplification and twice the standard paper speed. The magnified waves thus obtained were subjected to a manual frequency analysis.

The method of frequency analysis was originally devised by Brazier and Finesinger (1944), and subsequently used in studies on aged psychiatric patients (Daneman, Chornesky, and Haycox, 1955; Obrist and Henry, 1958b). Samples of parieto-occipital tracing, totaling 40 to 60 seconds, were selected when the subject was relaxed, fully awake, and had his eyes closed. The frequency of every wave from 1 to 30 cps was measured by a transparent rule. Complex waves were broken down into component parts in an attempt to register fast superimposed activity. The number of waves at each frequency was counted and multiplied by the duration of that frequency, which gave the amount of time occupied by such waves. Finally, percent-time scores were obtained by determining the proportion of time each frequency was present during the interval sampled.

Since the percent-time method disregards amplitude, a further technique was employed. The amplitude of every wave in the sample was measured to the nearest millimeter (2.5 microvolts). These measurements were summated for each frequency over the time interval analyzed and then converted to voltage per second by multiplying by the appropriate constant.

An individual's EEG could be characterized by plotting either percent-time or summated voltage measurements against frequency, thus forming a frequency spectrum. By averaging measurements from individuals, mean frequency spectra could be determined for each diagnostic group, as shown in figures 1 and 2. Comparison of groups was facilitated by dividing the spectra into three frequency bands. Indices of slow activity (1 through 7 cps), alpha activity (8 through 12 cps), and fast activity (13 through 30 cps) were computed for each individual by summating measurements within these bands. This permitted differentiation of alpha waves from slower and faster frequencies, a technique that has both clinical and statistical meaning (Gibbs and Gibbs, 1950; Hill and Parr, 1950). An index of total activity was also obtained, which is the sum of measurements over the entire spectrum from 1 to 30 cps. Eight indices were therefore available for statistical analysis, four involving percent-time scores and four based on summated voltage.

According to Kaufman and Hoagland (1946), one of the most sensitive indicators of the physiologic state of the brain is "dominant" or "peak" frequency; i.e., the modal point of an individual's frequency spectrum. In the present study, peak frequency was defined as the mode of percent-time measurements, calculated to the nearest tenth of a cycle by interpolation. In five subjects with flat multimodal spectra (low voltage fast tracings), a peak frequency score could not be determined.

Split-half reliability coefficients based on measurements from the same tracing varied from 0.80 for percent-time delta to 0.95 for percent-time alpha. These are quite high, considering the homogeneous nature of the

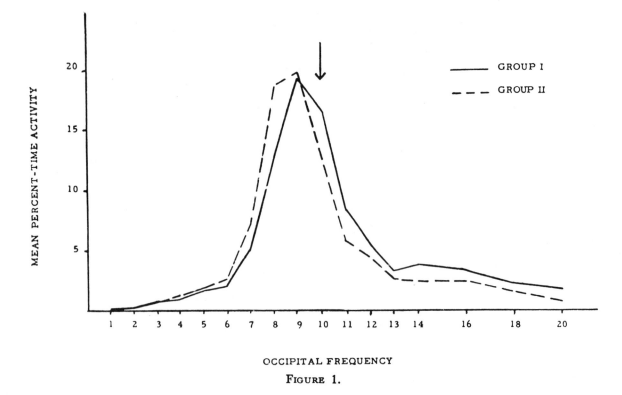

OCCIPITAL FREQUENCY

FIGURE 1.

sample. Day-to-day reliabilities were not obtainable, but there is reason to believe they are not much lower (Brazier and Finesinger, 1944; Kaufman and Hoagland, 1946). Intercorrelations between indices of slow, alpha, and fast activity were generally low (-0.28 to $+0.22$), indicating independence of the three frequency bands. On the other hand, percent-time indices were highly correlated with voltage scores derived from the same frequency band ($+0.71$ to $+0.96$). The latter is not surprising, since

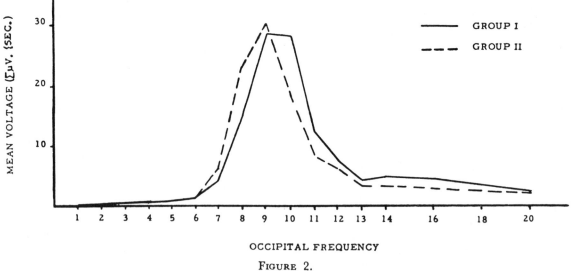

OCCIPITAL FREQUENCY

FIGURE 2.

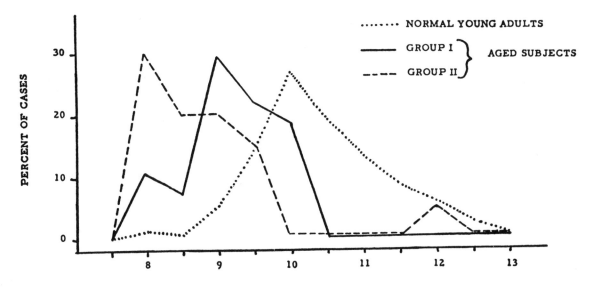

PEAK OCCIPITAL FREQUENCY

FIGURE 3.

both types of measurement are a function of wave number. A methodological paper on the interrelationship of these various types of measurement will be published separately.

RESULTS

The clinical EEG findings are summarized in table 1 for each of the diagnostic groups and for the total sample. Normal tracings are classified according to whether alpha activity or low voltage fast waves predominate, and abnormal records are characterized by the type of abnormality. The overall incidence of normal EEG's is 81 percent, which compares favorably with figures obtained on healthy young adults (Cohn, 1949; Gibbs and Gibbs, 1950). Of special interest, is the infrequent occurrence of slow wave abnormalities. Only 9 percent of the subjects (four cases) revealed focal slow waves, including one mixed record with both focal and diffuse disturbances. In all instances the slowing was localized to the anterior and middle portions of the temporal lobe. Diffuse slow waves also appeared in 9 percent of the sample (one

mixed and three diffuse cases). Groups I and II did not differ significantly with respect to overall incidence or type of abnormality.

It should be pointed out that the low proportion of abnormal ratings reflects the use of age-relative criteria. Although tracings with a slow alpha rhythm or excess fast activity were considered normal here, some of them would have been classified abnormal by strict young adult standards. Alpha rhythms of less than 8.5 cps were recorded in 19 percent of the subjects, while fast activity was prominent in 11 percent. Groups I and II did not differ with respect to fast activity, but a slow alpha rhythm occurred three times more frequently in group II than in group I (30 percent versus 11 percent). These clinical observations are in agreement with results of the frequency analysis.

Frequency spectra based on percent-time and summated voltage measurements are presented in figures 1 and 2, respectively. Each graph gives the mean curves for the two diagnostic groups. Regardless of sub-

TABLE 1.—*Incidence and type of normal and abnormal EEG's by subject group* [1]

EEG measurement	Group I		Group II		Total	
	Percent	(N)	Percent	(N)	Percent	(N)
Normal:						
Alpha....................	67	(18)	70	(14)	68	(32)
Low voltage fast...........	15	(4)	10	(2)	13	(6)
Total................	82	(22)	80	(16)	81	(38)
Abnormal:						
Asymmetrical.............	7	(2)	0	(0)	4	(2)
Focal slow................	4	(1)	10	(2)	7	(3)
Mixed focal and diffuse slow...........	0	(0)	5	(1)	2	(1)
Diffuse slow..............	7	(2)	5	(1)	6	(3)
Total................	18	(5)	20	(4)	19	(9)

[1] None of the differences between groups is statistically significant.

ject group or type of measurement, all of the mean spectra have a peak frequency of 9 cps. The arrow in figure 1 indicates a frequency of 10 cps, which is the average peak for young control subjects (Gibbs, 1942; Johnson and Ulett, 1959). In comparison with young adults, the mean curves for the old people have shifted to the slow side by approximately one cycle. The entire spectrum appears to be involved, particularly the major side frequencies. There is more 7- and 8-cycle activity among the elderly subjects, but fewer waves in the 10- and 11-cycle range.

Although small systematic differences may be seen, the spectra for groups I and II are quite similar. Table 2 presents an analysis of group differences by frequency band. Mean percent-time and summated voltage measurements of slow, alpha, fast, and total activity are shown for each diagnostic group. None of the differences are statistically significant. When comparisons are made at each individual frequency along the spectrum, a significant t is found at only one point; namely, 8 cps. The t-tests for intergroup differences in 8-cycle activity are presented in table 3. This table

also gives values for the arteriosclerotic subgroup of 12 cases within group II. Both of the groups with subclinical disease have more 8-cycle activity than group I, with the arteriosclerotics showing the largest difference. It is interesting that voltage scores yield less significant results than percent-time measurements, primarily because of their greater variability. The relatively poor differentiation of clinical groups by voltage has been noted elsewhere (Obrist and Henry, 1958b).

The EEG measure that best differentiates groups I and II is peak occipital frequency. In most cases this corresponds to the frequency of the alpha rhythm. Figure 3 shows the percent of cases that peak at each frequency in the two diagnostic groups and in a sample of normal young adults studied by Brazier and Finesinger (1944). A significant chi-square is obtained when the young people are compared with the combined older groups. Table 4 presents an analysis of differences within the present sample. Significant chi-squares result when either group II or the arteriosclerotic subgroup is compared with group I. Whereas most of the individuals in group I

TABLE 2.—*Average percent-time and voltage measurements for 2 groups of subjects* [1]

EEG measurement	Group I (*N*=27)		Group II (*N*=20)	
	Mean	S.D.	Mean	S.D.
Percent-time:				
Slow (1–7 cps)...........................	11.0	7.9	13.8	5.4
Alpha (8–12 cps)...........................	62.6	20.2	60.9	17.6
Fast (13–30 cps)...........................	15.2	10.3	10.4	7.0
Total activity (1–30 cps) [2]...................	88.8	17.9	85.1	19.2
Voltage ($\Sigma\mu$V/sec):				
Slow (1–7 cps)...........................	7.0	5.7	9.4	6.5
Alpha (8–12 cps)...........................	92.3	55.3	86.8	64.5
Fast (13–30 cps)...........................	21.4	16.8	14.3	12.8
Total activity (1–30 cps)...................	120.7	54.1	110.5	74.1

[1] None of the differences between groups are statistically significant.
[2] Total percent-time is less than 100 because portions of many EEG's had no measurable waves.

have peak occipital frequencies of 9 cps or more, group II subjects tend to have peak frequencies of 8.5 cps or less. Again, it is the arteriosclerotics that reveal the more significant trend.

Since a difference was found between arteriosclerotic and healthy subjects, it seemed desirable to relate EEG findings to objective laboratory evidence of cardiovascular disease. Electrocardiograms and X-ray determinations of heart size were used for this purpose. Whereas EEG and EKG abnormalities gave only chance asso-ciations, heart size appeared to be correlated with peak EEG frequency. Seven out of nine cases with cardiomegaly had peak frequencies of 8.5 cps or less, while only 8 out of 33 subjects with normal heart size had values this low.

DISCUSSION

The results indicate that even among healthy old people, the electroencephalo-gram undergoes certain changes with age. In contrast to the more severe abnormalities of elderly patients with psychiatric, neuro-

TABLE 3.—*Amount of 8-cycle activity in relation to physical health*

EEG measurement	Group I (healthy)		Group II (subclinical disease)		*t*—test of difference	
			Total	Arterio-sclerotic	I vs. II	I vs. arterio-sclerotic
Percent-time............	Mean........	12.8	18.6	21.4	* 2.1	*** 3.9
	S.D...........	8.9	9.1	7.0	....	....
Voltage ($\Sigma\mu$V/sec).......	Mean........	15.3	23.2	26.0	N.S.	N.S.
	S.D...........	14.6	17.0	16.6	....	....

* Significant at the 0.05 level (d.f=45).
*** Significant at the 0.001 level (d.f=37).

N.S.=Not significant.

I-88

TABLE 4.—*Relation of peak occipital frequency to physical health* [1]

Peak occipital frequency (cps)	Number of cases [2]		
	Group I (healthy)	Group II (subclinical disease)	
		Total	Arterio-sclerotic
8.0 and 8.5	5	10	8
9.0 and 9.5	14	7	4
10.0 or more	5	1	0
Total	24	18	12

[1] Groups I and II differ significantly at the 0.05 level with respect to proportion of cases below 9 cps ($x^2=4.0$; d.f.$=1$). Group I and the arteriosclerotic subgroup are significantly different at the 0.02 level ($x^2=5.4$; d.f.$=1$).

[2] 5 subjects with low voltage fast EEG's are omitted.

logic, and cardiovascular disease, the deviations from youthful norms observed here are quite minor. Since most of the EEG changes in healthy subjects are within the young adult range of normality, it is not possible to characterize a given record as senescent.

Using age-relative criteria, only 19 percent of the present tracings were classified abnormal, a value comparable to that of young people. When stricter criteria were employed, however, the percentage increased twofold. For example, raising the cutoff point of alpha frequency from 8.0 to 8.5 increased the incidence of abnormal EEG's to 34 percent. A further rise to 40 percent was obtained when persistent fast activity of more than 20 microvolts was regarded as deviant. Reports by Lascalea (1957) and by Jaffe and Reisman (unpublished data)[4] of a low incidence of abnormality in elderly people may reflect the use of less strict criteria, similar to those employed in table 1. From the clinical point of view, there is probably no justifi-

[4] Jaffe, R., and Reisman, E. 1960. EEG and Mental Status: A correlative study in 100 aged subjects. *EEG Clin. Neurophysiol.*, *12*, 245.

cation for stricter criteria, since slight deviations in alpha frequency and fast activity are not known to be of diagnostic or prognostic significance.

Failure to obtain age trends on the basis of loose clinical standards may lead to the conclusion that age and EEG are unrelated. On the contrary, if careful *quantitative* measurements are performed, such as a frequency analysis, statistically significant differences can be observed. Although these minor changes are of little interest clinically, they may have considerable import for the study of aging in the nervous system.

The major finding, based on quantitative measurement, is that the average frequency spectrum of the old person is approximately one cycle slower than the comparable young adult curve. This is especially obvious in the case of peak occipital frequency, the dominant alpha rate in most subjects. It is well known that the alpha frequency of healthy young people ranges from 8.5 to 12.0 cps, with a mean of approximately 10.2 cps (Lindsley, 1938; Henry, 1944). Yet only six cases in the entire sample had a dominant rhythm of 10 cps or more. Two-thirds of the elderly subjects had peak frequencies of 8 or 9 cps, clearly a full cycle slower than the average for young adults. These results are consistent with previous reports of alpha slowing in senescence (Obrist, 1954; Mundy-Castle et al., 1954; Friedlander, 1958). Age differences are not confined to peak frequency, but involve the major adjacent frequencies as well. There is an increase of 7- and 8-cycle activity, with a corresponding decrease of 11- and 12-cycle waves. Thus, it might be inferred that the entire frequency spectrum shifts to the slow side in old age.

Within the present sample, variations in health status are associated with minor EEG differences. Less healthy subjects (group II) have frequency spectra that show a slight but systematic shift to the slow side in comparison with healthy individuals (group I). The difference between groups is most marked at 8 cps, the only point on the spectrum yielding a statistically significant result. Because the spectra are quite similar, intergroup differences by frequency band (slow, alpha, fast) are not statistically reliable. On the other hand, when groups are compared with respect to peak occipital frequency, a significant difference is obtained. Subjects with subclinical disease have generally lower peak frequencies than healthy people. This measure discriminates groups well because it reflects the increase in 8-cycle activity associated with poorer health.

Although the results do not permit the conclusion that circulatory disease is an important factor influencing EEG, it is probably significant that most of the cases in group II had evidence of arteriosclerotic pathology. The fact that the arteriosclerotic subgroup revealed even greater EEG changes than the total group II is consistent with such a speculation. Furthermore, the inverse correlation of heart size with peak frequency lends support to a cardiovascular hypothesis. These findings are in agree-ment with previous observations on the EEG in cardiovascular disease (Obrist and Bissell, 1955; Morpurgo, Serra, and Mars, 1955), with the exception that no relationship was found between brain waves and the electrocardiogram. In view of the limited range of pathology in the present sample, it is surprising that positive results were obtained.

It is interesting to note that the EEG's of people with subclinical disease differ from their healthy controls in the same direction as the general age trend. It is as if the age changes apparent in the healthier individuals had been accentuated by the occurrence of subclinical disease. Because electrocortical activity is related to health status, the question arises whether differences between healthy young and old people are in fact due to aging, *per se*. Is it possible that undetected subclinical pathology exists even among the healthiest old people in group I, and that this might be responsible for the subtle EEG changes observed? An alternative explanation is that some endogenous age factor produces a shift in EEG frequency, which coincidentally is of the same kind and direction as that associated with pathology. Although the latter interpretaion seems less plausible, the issue is by no means settled.

One of the unexpected results of this investigation is the low incidence of temporal lobe abnormalities (9 percent), previously reported in one-third of elderly community subjects. Although not identical, the particular electrode placement and recording technique are similar to that described earlier, making it unlikely that this is the cause of the discrepancy. A possible explanation is that temporal foci indicate underlying cortical pathology, which presumably is rare in healthy subjects. In the original study, Silverman, Busse, and Barnes (1955) observed that low income patients from a hospital clinic had 50 percent more foci than upper class subjects who were actively working. Since subsequent investigation failed to confirm the socioeconomic difference,[5] it was concluded that factors of health probably account for the earlier findings. The lack of difference obtained here between groups I and II does not argue against such an interpretation because of the very mild pathology involved.

One of the serious limitations of the current study is the restriction of frequency analysis to the parieto-occipital lead. This was necessitated by the impracticability of performing tedious hand measurements on more than one channel of recording. Since waves from only a small part of the cortex were measured, a word of caution is in order concerning the applicability of the analysis to other brain areas. Although previous work would suggest comparable results from different head regions (Obrist and Henry, 1958b), it remains for future research to determine the scope of the present findings.

SUMMARY

Electroencephalograms were recorded on 47 male subjects over age 65, selected on the basis of sound health. Twenty-seven cases had no evidence of physical pathology (group I), while 20 cases had asymptomatic, subclinical disease (group II). In addition to a standard EEG interpretation, the parieto-occipital tracing was subjected to a manual frequency analysis.

The incidence of clinically normal EEG's was 81 percent, which is comparable to figures reported for young people. In contrast to earlier aging studies, only 9 percent of the cases had temporal lobe foci. Groups I and II did not differ with respect to incidence or type of abnormality.

Frequency analysis gave a mean spectrum with a peak frequency of 9 cps, a full

cycle slower than previously found in young adults. The entire spectrum, especially the major frequencies, appeared to have shifted to the slow side.

Group II (subclinical disease) showed significantly more eight-cycle activity than group I (healthy subjects), although other points along the spectrum did not differ appreciably. This was associated with slower individual peak frequencies in group II, which was the major EEG difference between diagnostic categories. A subgroup of 12 cases with arteriosclerosis revealed similar, slightly more significant trends.

It was concluded that the EEG undergoes changes with age, even in the absence of any detectable physical disease. Because the group with subclinical pathology had slower tracings, it was suggested that health status, particularly cardiovascular disease, is an important factor influencing brain potentials.

The present chapter has been concerned with a description of the EEG and its relation to age and health. Intercorrelations of EEG with cerebral metabolic and psychological variables will be given in chapter 15.

REFERENCES

BARNES, R. H., BUSSE, E. W., and FRIEDMAN, E. L. 1956. The psychological functioning of aged individuals with normal and abnormal electroencephalograms. II. A study of hospitalized individuals. *J. Nerv. Ment. Dis.*, 124, 585–593.

BRAZIER, M. A. B. 1948. Physiological mechanisms underlying the electrical activity of the brain. *J. Neurol. Neurosurgery Psychiat.*, 11, 118–133.

——— and FINESINGER, J. E. 1944. Characteristics of the normal electroencephalogram. I. A study of the occipital cortical potentials in 500 normal adults. *J. Clin. Invest.*, 23, 303–311.

BUSSE, E. W., BARNES, R. H., FRIEDMAN, E. L., and KELTY, E. J. 1956. Psychological functioning of aged individuals with normal and abnormal electroencephalograms. I. A study of nonhospitalized community volunteers. *J. Nerv. Ment. Dis.*, 124, 135–141.

---

[5] Obrist and Busse, op. cit.

Cohn, R. 1949. *Clinical Electroencephalography.* New York: McGraw-Hill, 639 pp.

Corday, E., Rothenberg, S. F., and Putnam, J. J. 1953. Cerebral vascular insufficiency. *Arch. Neurol. Psychiat., 69,* 551–570.

Cox, R. R., Obrist, W. D., and Henry, C. E. 1955. Application of magnetic tape recording to automatic frequency analysis. *EEG Clin. Neurophysiol., 7,* 472.

Daneman, E. A., Chornesky, G., and Haycox, J. A. 1955. Psychosomatic investigations of cerebral arteriosclerosis with psychosis. *Dis. Nerv. Sys., 16,* 165–173.

Davis, P. A., Davis, H., and Thompson, J. W. 1938. Progressive changes in the human electroencephalogram under low oxygen tension. *Amer. J. Physiol., 123,* 51–52.

Ewalt, J. R., and Ruskin, A. 1944. The EEG in patients with heart disease. *Texas Reports on Biol. Med., 2,* 161–174.

Friedlander, W. J. 1958. Electroencephalographic alpha rate in adults as a function of age. *Geriatrics, 13,* 29–31.

Gibbs, F. A. 1942. Cortical frequency spectra of healthy adults. *J. Nerv. Ment. Dis., 95,* 417–426.

—— and Gibbs, E. L. 1950. *Atlas of electroencephalography. Volume I. Methodology and controls.* Addison-Wesley Press, Cambridge, Mass., 2d ed., 324 pp.

——, Williams, D., and Gibbs, E. L. 1940. Modifications of the cortical frequency spectrum by changes in CO_2, blood sugar and O_2. *J. Neurophysiol., 3,* 49–58.

Giongo, F., and Minoni, G. 1959. Contributo clinico allo studio della sindrome cerebro-cardiaca. *L'Ospedale Maggiore, Milano, 47,* 393–401.

Heine, G. 1953. Comparison of EEG, cerebral blood flow and cerebral O_2—consumption in 113 cases with heart, circulatory and vascular diseases. *EEG Clin. Neurophysiol. (Supp. 3),* 28.

Henry, C. E. 1944. Electroencephalograms of normal children. *Monogr. Soc. Res. Child Develop., 9,* 71 pp.

Hill, D., and Parr, G. (Ed.). 1950. *Electroencephalography.* London, Macdonald & Co., 438 pp.

Hoagland, H. 1954. Studies of brain metabolism and electrical activity in relation to adrenocortical physiology. In G. Pincus (Ed.), *Recent Progress in Hormone Research.* New York, Academic Press, Inc., *10,* 29–63.

Jasper, H. H. 1958. The ten-twenty electrode system of the international federation. *EEG Clin. Neurophysiol., 10,* 371–375.

Johnson, L. C., and Ulett, G. A. 1959. Quantitative study of pattern and stability of resting electroencephalographic activity in a young adult group. *EEG Clin. Neurophysiol., 11,* 233–249.

Kaufman, I. C., and Hoagland, H. 1946. Dominant brain wave frequencies as measures of physicochemical processes in cerebral cortex. *Arch. Neurol. Psychiat., 56,* 207–215.

Lascalea, M. C. 1957. Elettroencefalogramma nella vecchiaia. In *Fourth Cong. Internat. Assoc. Gerontol., Vol. IV:* International Symposium on Medical-Social Aspects of Senile Nervous Diseases, 17–53.

Lassen, N. A., Munck, O., and Tottey, E. R. 1957. Mental function and cerebral oxygen consumption in organic dementia. *A.M.A. Arch. Neurol. Psychiat., 77,* 126–133.

Lindsley, D. B. 1938. Electrical potentials of the brain in children and adults. *J. Genet. Psychol., 19,* 285–306.

Luce, R. A., and Rothschild, D. 1953. The correlation of electroencephalographic and clinical observations in psychiatric patients over 65. *J. Geront., 8,* 167–172.

Maggs, R., and Turton, E. C. 1956. Some EEG findings in old age and their relationship to affective disorder. *J. Ment. Sci., 102,* 812–818.

Mangold R., Sokoloff, L., Therman, P. O., Conner, E. H., Kleinerman, J. I., and Kety, S. S. 1955. The effects of sleep and lack of sleep on the cerebral circulation and metabolism of normal young men. *J. Clin. Invest., 34,* 1092–1100.

Mars, G., Morpurgo, M., and Serra, C. 1955. Sul valore diagnostico dell'esame oftalmoangioscopico ed elettroencefalografico in soggetti di eta' avanzata. *Progr. med., Napoli, 11,* 193–197.

McAdam, W., and Robinson, R. A. 1956. Senile intellectual deterioration and the electroencephalogram: A quantitative correlation. *J. Ment. Sci., 102,* 819–825.

——, ——. 1957. Prognosis in senile deterioration. *J. Ment. Sci., 103,* 821–823.

——, ——. 1958. Psychiatric and electroencephalographic studies in socially adjusted old people. *J. Ment. Sci., 104,* 840–843.

Mengoli, G. 1952. L'elettroencefalogramma nei vecchi. *Riv. Neurol., 22,* 166–193.

Meyer, J. S., Leiderman, H., and Denny-Brown, D. 1956. Electroencephalographic study of insufficiency of the basilar and carotid arteries in man. *Neurology, 6,* 455–477.

Morpurgo, M., Serra, C., and Mars, G. 1955. Sull'analisi comparativa dei dati electroencefalografici ed elettrocardiografici in pazienti di eta' senile. *Min. Med., 46,* 361–372.

Mundy-Castle, A. C. 1951. Theta and beta rhythm in the electroencephalograms of normal adults. *EEG Clin. Neurophysiol., 3,* 477–486.

MUNDY-CASTLE, A. C., HURST, L. A., BEER-STECHER, D. M., and PRINSLOO, T. 1954. The electroencephalogram in the senile phychoses. *EEG Clin. Neurophysiol., 6*, 245–252.

OBRIST, W. D. 1954. The electroencephalogram of normal aged adults. *EEG Clin. Neurophysiol., 6*, 235–244.

——, and BISSELL, L. F. 1955. The electroencephalogram of aged patients with cardiac and cerebral vascular disease. *J. Geront., 10*, 315–330.

——, BUSSE, E. W. and HENRY, C. E. 1961. Relation of electroencephalogram to blood pressure in elderly persons. *Neurology, 11*, 151–158.

——, and HENRY, C. E. 1958a. Electroencephalographic findings in aged psychiatric patients. *J. Nerv. Ment. Dis., 126*, 254–267.

——, ——. 1958b. Electroencephalographic frequency analysis of aged psychiatric patients. *EEG Clin. Neurophysiol., 10*, 621–632.

OSTOW, M. 1950. Psychic function and the electroencephalogram. *Arch. Neurol. Psychiat., 64*, 385–400.

PAMPIGLIONE, G., and POST, F. 1958. The value of electroencephalographic examinations in psychiatric disorders of old age. *Geriatrics, 13*, 725–732.

ROSEMAN, E., SCHMIDT, R. P., and FOLTZ, E. L. 1952. Serial electroencephalography in vascular lesions of the brain. *Neurology, 2*, 311–331.

SHERIDAN, F. P., YEAGER, C. L., OLIVER, W. A., and SIMON, A. 1955. Electroencephalography as a diagnostic and prognostic aid in studying the senescent individual. A preliminary report. *J. Geront., 10*, 53–59.

SILVERMAN, A. J., BUSSE, E. W., and BARNES, R. H. 1955. Studies in the processes of aging: Electroencephalographic findings in 400 elderly subjects. *EEG Clin. Neurophysiol., 7*, 67–74.

——, ——, ——, FROST, L. L., and THALER, M. B. 1953. Studies on the processes of aging. 4. Physiologic influences on psychic functioning in elderly people. *Geriatrics, 8*, 370–376.

SKILLICORN, S. A., and AIRD, R. B. 1954. Electroencephalographic changes resulting from carotid artery compression. *Arch. Neurol. Psychiat., 71*, 367–376.

SOKOLOFF, L., MANGOLD, R., WECHSLER, R. L., KENNEDY, C., and KETY, S. S. 1955. The effect of mental arithmetic on cerebral circulation and metabolism. *J. Clin. Invest., 34*, 1101–1108.

STRAUSS, H., and GREENSTEIN, L. 1948. The electroencephalogram in cerebrovascular disease. *Arch. Neurol. Psychiat., 59*, 395–403.

STUHL, M. L., CLOCHE, Mlle., and KARTUN, M. P. 1952. Interet de l'electroencephalographie dans l'etude des insuffisances cardiaques avec cyanose. *Arch. Mal. Coeur, 45*, 921–926.

THALER, M. 1956. Relationships among Wechsler, Weigl, Rorschach, EEG findings, and abstract-concrete behavior in a group of normal aged subjects. *J. Geront., 11*, 404–409.

WEINER, H., and SCHUSTER, D. B. 1956. The electroencephalogram in dementia. —Some preliminary observations and correlations. *EEG Clin. Neurophysiol., 8*, 479–488.

YOUNG, W., GOFMAN, J. W., MALAMUD, N., SIMON, A., and WATERS, E. S. G. 1956. The interrelationship between cerebral and coronary atherosclerosis. *Geriatrics, 11*, 413–418.

CHAPTER 8

Mental Abilities and Psychomotor Responses in Healthy Aged Men

by Jack Botwinick and James E. Birren

INTRODUCTION

Cognition is perhaps the most thoroughly investigated of the psychological aspects of aging, and already there has been sufficient information to warrant reviews of the literature (e.g., Inglis, 1958; Jones, 1959). This is not to say that present information is definitive; but theoretical issues have been defined, concepts have been developed, and hypotheses have been tested experimentally.

Early studies of cognitive processes in the elderly were almost solely descriptive investigations. More recently, however, descriptive data have been analyzed with respect to mechanism or antecedent conditions, and questions are beginning to be asked regarding behavioral consequences. For example, when intelligence tests are given to elderly adults, it is found usually that general information and vocabulary abilities rise or are maintained, while decline is seen in functions that require speed. And even in verbal skills it has been shown that differential changes occur with age (Ricks, 1957; Riegel, 1959). There is, therefore, the task of explaining why some psychological functions increase and others remain the same or decline with age. When age changes in speed of response are investigated, it is found that central nervous processes may be involved (e.g., Birren, 1955; Birren and Botwinick, 1955a).

Organization of Cognitive and Psychomotor Processes

Two related questions may be raised about the organization of cognitive and psychomotor processes in the elderly. One question involves the degree of intercorrelation of abilities, and the second question involves the changes in pattern that may occur with age. If various measures of cognitive and psychomotor function in the elderly can be described by means of relatively few parameters or factors, then we may conceptualize the abilities as an ordered or structured phenomenon rather than ". . . a patternless mosaic of an infinite number of elements without functional groupings" (Thurstone, 1947, p. 57). The question then becomes one of parsimony—the smallest number of factors which explain the data and the relative proportion that is explained by the various major factors. The second question concerns how this organization changes with age. It has been suggested in three studies that the various factors contribute different amounts of variance in different age groups (Cohen, 1957; McHugh and Owens, 1954; Balinsky, 1941). However the results lead to the conclusion that, in general, test intercorrelations tend to increase in the later adult years. Birren (1952) reported high intercorrelations of Wechsler-Bellevue subtests in subjects aged 60–74 years; median correlation (r) was 0.53. In 31 senile patients the median correlation rose to 0.63.

In factor analysis, or in other similar techniques, there is the possibility that an age-relevant factor might be neglected if the analyses are done within limited age groups. For example, when elderly subjects are compared to younger ones in a wide variety of performances that involve speed, almost always the older group is slower than the younger one. If the measures on a wide age range sample were correlated and factor-analyzed, a large speed factor or several speed factors might be extracted. However, if the scores of only one age group, say, an older one, were factor-analyzed, a speed factor might not be extracted; or if it were, the extracted speed factor might be small.

The factor of set may also be pertinent to the organization of cognitive processes. A relevant hypothesis was discussed in a recent study (Botwinick, Brinley, and Robbin, 1958b). Indices of alteration (AI's) referring to an ability to alternate or shift from one arithmetic operation to another were derived from performance scores of a series of simple arithmetic problems. Elderly subjects alternated more slowly than did younger subjects. The AI's were correlated with the arithmetic performance scores themselves and relation between them was found within a younger group but not within an older one. It was hypothesized from this that in youth, alternation is related to other abilities. With advancing age, however, ability to alternate or change set may become an important limiting factor in itself, which is independent to a degree from other factors.

Purpose

The purpose of this chapter is to describe a sample of healthy elderly men by the use of standard and newly devised measures of cognitive and psychomotor functioning. Explanations of the individual differences in the various measures have been sought within the context of psychological findings (the data of this chapter) and within the context of physiological, psychiatric and social findings (the data of the other chapters). The latter information is presented in chapter 15.

METHOD

Subjects

The present sample of elderly subjects is described in chapters 2 and 3 while the previously studied elderly and young subjects that were compared with the present subjects are described in the indicated references. In general, the present elderly subjects met more rigorous health requirements than previous samples and appeared to be more alert, active, and adequate, than previous subjects of similar age.

Data Reduction

Subjects were examined with procedures that yielded approximately 170 numerical values or scores from which a reduced number of 23 scores was derived. In the final analyses only experimentally independent scores were used. For example, the WAIS (Wechsler Adult Intelligence Scale, 1955) was used as one of the procedures and yielded 11 scores; the additional 3 scores of verbal, performance, and total IQ's, were not used.

Data reduction becomes a sizable problem with as many as 170 variables. The first step in the reduction was to exclude data that would give rise to spurious correlations, as for example, part-whole relationships. The second step was to exclude data of those procedures that were not completed, for various reasons, on a sufficient number of subjects.

The third step of reducing the data to interpretable dimensions included intercorrelation of variables within each of four blocks or groupings. The largest block of intercorrelations was a 50 x 50 matrix. Two other blocks were 24 x 24, and one block was 28 x 28. Blocks were not independent since many variables appeared in more than one block.

The final step in choosing the most pertinent variables involved an inspection of the correlations within the four blocks. A choice of variables was made from among those that were independent and also from among those that were logically similar and correlated with each other to a large extent (e.g., the vocabulary scores of the WAIS and of the Mill Hill vocabulary test, or reaction time measurements under various experimental conditions). The one variable representing the group of interrelated variables was chosen on the basis of its reliability, generality, or psychological significance. It was most often an observed score, but derived measures were not excluded (e.g., ratios of two conditions of one procedure wherein the elements of the ratios were not included as separate variables).

The Chosen Procedures

The 23 procedures which represent the reduced set are listed below. Henceforth each one will be referred to as a test.

1. Information (WAIS)
2. Comprehension (WAIS)
3. Arithmetic (WAIS)
4. Similarities (WAIS)
5. Digit Span (WAIS)
6. Vocabulary (WAIS)
7. Digit Symbol (WAIS)
8. Picture Completion (WAIS)
9. Block Design (WAIS)
10. Picture Arrangement (WAIS)
11. Object Assembly (WAIS)
12. Raven Progressive Matrices
13. Wisconsin Card Sorting
14. Speed of Card Sorting
15. Learning
16. Addition Rate
17. Arithmetic Alternation Rate
18. Speed of Copying Digits
19. Word Fluency
20. Perception of Line Difference
21. Reaction Time
22. Mirror Tracing
23. Stroop Test

Description of Tests and Related References

Tests 1–11. The first 11 tests are those of the *Wechsler Adult Intelligence Scale (WAIS)*. This scale (Wechsler, 1955) is a revised version of the Wechsler-Bellevue Scale (Wechsler, 1944) with which a dozen or more studies on aging have been concerned. A general summary of several of these studies (e.g., Norman and Daley, 1959; Botwinick, 1953; Botwinick and Birren, 1951a, b; Fox and Birren, 1950) is that stored information (for example, Vocabulary) tends to show relatively little or no deficit with advanced age while psychomotor skills (for example, Digit Symbol) and perceptual-integrative abilities (for example, Picture Arrangement or Block Design) hold up less well. Those tests that are sensitive to normal aging are not necessarily best for reflecting the senescent psychoses.

The scores of the WAIS tests that were used in this study are the scaled scores not corrected for age. The age scaled scores would alter spuriously the basic relationships among the measures.

Test 12. The *Progressive Matrices Test* is a nonverbal, nonmotor test of "immediate capacities for observation and clear thinking." It assesses "a person's capacity for intellectual activity" (Raven, 1954). The mental abilities as measured by this test have been found to decline with advanced age (Foulds and Raven, 1948). The test consists of 60 problems divided equally into 5 sets graded progressively in difficulty.

Test 13. The *Wisconsin Card Sorting Test* (*WCST*) assesses aspects of thinking and reasoning by measuring some combination of the ability to abstract or to form concepts and the ability to shift set. The WCST includes 64 response cards, each in some combination of one of four geometric forms (circles, triangles, crosses, and stars), one of four colors (red, blue, green, and yellow), and one of four numbers of geometric forms (one, two, three, and four). There are four stimulus cards placed in front of the subject. Going from left to right, the stimulus cards are one red triangle, two green stars, three yellow crosses, and four blue circles. The subject places the response card in front of one of the four stimulus cards and is told whether he is correct or wrong. The correctness of the sort is related to whether the concept to be formed is color, form, or number. After 10 correct sorts, the concept is changed or shifted by the experimenter without notice. The test is completed when the subject forms each concept twice, i.e., makes five shifts, or uses 64 cards in a single concept. Early versions of this test were reported by Berg (1948) and Grant and Berg (1948).

The procedure was changed in the present study by utilizing two sets of response cards (128 cards) and going through all of them regardless of the number of shifts, number of perseverative errors, and number of concepts formed. In the present study, one score was used and this was the number of concepts attained with the 128 cards. Morrow's study (1946) indicates that the

type of function measured by WCST declines with age.

Test 14. *Speed of Card Sorting* is an experimental procedure described in a recent study by Botwinick, Robbin, and Brinley (1960). Card sorting tasks were varied in three dimensions of difficulty but in the present investigation, performance on one level of one dimension of difficulty was used. The procedure measures an aspect of perceptual matching. Subjects sorted 71 playing cards as quickly as possible into one of nine slots by matching the numbers of the sorting card to the number of the stimulus card. When no match was possible, the sorting card was placed in a 10th slot. The 71 cards comprised two complete decks minus the 24 face cards, the 5 stimulus cards (5H, 9C, 3C, 8S and 6S,) and 4 additional cards (4D, 10S, 2D, and 7C). The sorts were done four times and the score for each subject was the median sorting time in seconds of the four trials.

Test 15. *The Learning Test* comprises a a list of five meaningful words each presented for 1 second at the rate of one word every 2 seconds in a Hull-type memory drum. The list was presented once for viewing and 12 additional times for the subject to anticipate the word next on the list. The score was the number of words anticipated correctly during the 12 trials. The maximum score possible was 60 words. Lists longer than five words have been used successfully with college students as subjects but pilot experimentation suggested five as sufficiently long for older subjects—especially with lists of nonsense words that were used for a different purpose. Learning even a few nonsense words of a list containing 12 words appeared too difficult a task for many elderly subjects.

Test 16. This test, *Addition Rate,* was used originally in a study which indicated that normal individuals of two different age groups, and individuals of one age group but of two different groups of mental status, could be differentiated by the parameters of the functional relation between problem length and speed of simple addition (Birren and Botwinick, 1951a). The problem length uesd in the present study was seven single digits. Problems were presented on a single page. Subjects added continuously for approximately 2 minutes going from problem to problem stopping only to write with pencil the sum of each under the column of seven digits. The score was in terms of operations per second or the number of digits added per second multiplied by 6/7 (see rationale and subject description in study by Birren and Botwinick, 1951a).

Test 17. Arithmetic Altenation Rate is a test involving continuous altenation from subtraction to addition to subtraction and so on. This procedure was used in a study discussed earlier (Botwinick, Brinley, and Robbin, 1958b). Problems were seven digits in length with the first digit being double and the remaining six being single. All problems were on one page. Arithmetic altenation proceeded continuously for approximately 2 minutes except for stops to record the computation. Scores were in terms of altenation operations per second, or the number of digits added and subtracted per second multiplied by 6/7.

Test 18. Performance on the speed of *Copying Digits* test was studied in relation to age by Birren and Botwinick (1951b). Subjects between 16 and 89 years copied single digits with pencil as quickly as they could. The digits were arranged on standard size typing paper in 12 rows and 8 columns for a total of 96. Scores were digits copied per second. It was found that the correlation (r) between age and scores was 0.81. For subjects 20 years and older the correlation was 0.78, and 0.65 after level

of education was partialled out. Identical procedures were used in this study.

Test 19. The *Word Fluency Test* in relation to age was reported by Birren (1955). In that study, subjects in eight age groups ranging from 16 to 89 years wrote as many words in a column as they could in a 2 minute period. The test instructions specified the first letter of the words to be written. In general it was found that older subjects were less fluent in this verbal ability, and the age difference in fluency was most apparent when the number of available words in the category was greatest. One of the tests was to write as many words that begin with the letter "S" as quickly as possible. This test was used in the current investigation.

Test 20. Perception of *Line Difference Test* in relation to age was reported by Birren and Botwinick (1955b) and by Botwinick, Brinley, and Robbin (1958a). Two vertical lines systematically varied in length were presented tachistoscopically for 2 seconds. One line was the standard 88 mm. long, and the other line, the variable, was shorter. There were six variable lines shorter than the standard by 1, 2, 3, 5, 10, and 20 percent. The subject had to report as quickly as possible which line, the right or the left, was the shorter. Speed of making the judgment response was measured to the nearest 0.01 second. Each subject responded eight times to each of the 6 percent line length differences. The median of the eight responses was computed and the score for each subject was the mean of the six medians.

Test 21. Reaction Time has been investigated in relation to age in various ways, and consistent is the finding of increased slowness with advancing age (e.g., Birren and Botwinick, 1955a, and Botwinick, Brinley, and Robbin, 1959b). In the present investigation, finger reaction times were recorded to a 1000 cycle, 85 db tone stimulus separated from a visual warning light by preparatory intervals of 1.0, 1.5, 2.0, 2.5, 3.0, 4.0, 5.0, and 6.0 seconds. These eight intervals were each presented three times in fixed quasi-random order. The score for each subject was the mean of the 24 reaction times.

Test 22. Ruch (1934) was perhaps the first to present experimental evidence which indicated that a deficit of the elderly may exist in reorganizing or reversing an old habit. His subjects performed on a pursuit-rotor task and then did this by mirror vision or *Mirror Tracing.* It was found that older subjects found the mirror task relatively more difficult than the direct vision task.

In the present study, a 12-sided (6-pointed) star was traced as quickly as possible by direct vision and by mirror vision. The differences between mirror and direct vision scores were sufficiently large as to make them largely a function of the mirror vision scores. The mirror vision task was so difficult for many, that frequently, even with errors it could not be completed. Accordingly, the scoring involved estimated time for the completion of mirror tracing the 12-sided star. At first each subject was allowed a maximum of 360 seconds on one side of the star, or 1,080 seconds for the total mirror-tracing task. Later subjects were allowed 360 seconds for the total task because it was found that more time did not contribute to improved scores, but only made for discomfort. The measured time was multiplied by 12 and divided by the number of sides actually completed. To make for zero or near zero performance scores, the reciprocal of the estimated time scores was used for each subject. The reciprocal scores were multiplied by 100 for convenience in computation.

Test 23. The *Stroop Ratio* is a test of interference or blocking. The original version of this test was reported in 1935 by Stroop. This test involves three aspects: (1) reading printed names of colors, e.g., "red," (2) naming colors of printed colored circles, e.g., red, and (3) naming the color of ink of printed words which spell the name of different colors. For example, the latter task might have the word "red" printed in green ink. Subjects were required to disregard the word "red" and name the color "green." Each of the three tasks was presented in 10 rows and 10 columns for a total of 100 times each. The score for each subject was the time taken to name the color in the third task, divided by the time taken to name the color in the second task. The higher the ratio, the greater the interference effect or blocking.

RESULTS

Performances on the 23 tests are compared between subjects in group I and group II, and between these samples and others that have been described in previous studies concerned with the same measurements. The means, standard deviations, and numbers of the present and previous comparable studies are presented in table 1. In addition, some unpublished data of young subjects are also presented.

It is significant that of the 23 tests given to the subjects of this study, scores were poorer for group II than for group I in all but 2 tests. Group II made a better score on the Digit Span test of the WAIS and made an equal score on Mirror Tracing. On all the remaining tests, group I performed more adequately than group II. The statistical significance level of this group difference is far less than 0.01 as determined by chi square on the basis of a 50–50 hypotheses ($x^2 = 14.08$, $df = 1$). However, when difference tests were performed between groups for each of the 23 tests, reliable differences were found in only 6 tests: Line Difference, Stroop, Comprehension, Similarities, Block Design, and Picture Arrangement. The significance levels are less than 0.01 for the Block Design test and less than 0.05 for the other 5 tests. Total and Performance WAIS score were different for both groups ($p<0.05$), but the Verbal WAIS group difference just missed significance ($t=1.92$, $df=45$).

The performance of the present sample compares favorably to previous samples of similar age. With the WAIS, for example, table 1 shows groups I and II made total scaled scores of 102.59 and 86.25 respectively while a previous sample made a score of only 77.36 (Doppelt and Wallace, 1955). Even with these superior performances, however, the classic aging pattern of cognitive function was once again seen. Verbal abilities were high while psychomotor abilities were lower; the Verbal score was approximately twice that of the Performance score in both groups I and II. The Digit Symbol test was again found to be especially sensitive to normal aging and in addition, performance on the Picture Arrangement test in the present sample was particularly poor relative to the other scores. This classic aging pattern appears to be independent of sex, race, I.Q., socioeconomic status and mental health (Eisdorfer, Busse, and Cohen, 1959). Variations in WAIS performances were small with standard deviations of scaled scores ranging from 1.93 on the Digit Symbol subtest for group I to 4.05 on the Vocabulary subtest for group II.

Although the present sample was found in general to be superior to previous samples of similar age, the effects of aging were apparent when comparisons were made with younger samples. It may be seen in table 1 that performance scores on the Raven indicate deficit with age. Concept formation (WCST) scores were not available for young control subjects but the previous literature (e.g., Berg, 1948) suggests three concepts with 128 cards to be a very poor score. Speed of perceptual matching by card sorting clearly dimished with age, and learning, as already indicated in the description of the test, was difficult with 12 nonsense words so that it was necessary to make the task simpler.

Table 1 shows that the present sample was quicker than the young in simple addition and about the same in rate of alternation from an addition to a subtraction operation. As indicated in the introduction of this section, however, when an index of alternation was computed which equated age groups for their rates of addition and subtraction, the older sample, a sample comprised of many subjects of the present study, was found to be slower in alternating than was the younger group of subjects (Botwinick, Brinley, Robbin, 1958b).

In speed of copying digits and in speed of word fluency, the present sample was found to be better than the previous sample of similar age but poorer than the young samples. In perceiving or judging the differences in line lengths, the present population is clearly slower than the young control sample. Analyses of the total line difference data from which the current scores were derived indicate that the older group is relatively slower with the more difficult discriminations or judgments. It was suggested that older persons may require a relatively high level of confidence before responding (Botwinick, Brinley, Robbin, 1958a). Nevertheless, when the situation requires a response where choice or judgment is not involved, the elderly are still slower. In simple auditory reaction time, previous and present samples responded in

TABLE 1.—*Test scores of the present sample compared with scores of other samples*

| Test | Present sample [1] | | | | | | Elderly samples [2] | | | Young samples [3] | | |
| | Group I | | | Group II | | | | | | | | |
	Mean	S.D.	Number	Mean	S.D.	Number	Mean	S.D.	Number	Mean	S.D.	Number
Raven	25.59	9.32	27	24.00	9.19	20	Median=24			48	8.2	44
WCST	3.81	3.37	26	2.25	2.29	20						
Card Sorting	116.50	25.54	24	122.05	34.29	20				88.03	11.22	34
Learning	43.35	16.25	20	34.53	19.82	17						
Addition Rate	.94	.30	24	.83	.38	20	0.60 (approx.)			.78 (approx.)	(approx.)	58
Alternation Rate	.36	.13	24	.29	.12	20				.70	.14	58
Copy Digits	1.11	.25	27	.96	.32	20	.82	.32	66	.32	.26	57
Word Fluency	17.22	8.28	27	16.33	9.21	18	9.7	4.6	43	24.9	7.0	41
Line Difference	*1.09	.20	27	*1.26	.26	19				1.42	.37	31
Reaction Time	.22	.03	23	.24	.06	19	.23	.05	32	.18	.03	26
Mirror Tracing	.32	.39	27	.32	.49	18				.18	.02	32
Stroop	*1.57	.70	25	*2.21	1.09	14				.78	.45	17
WAIS:												
Comprehension	*12.70	3.92	27	*10.15	3.33	20	8.14	2.27	51	10	3	500
Information	12.30	3.78	27	10.95	3.24	20	8.61	3.11	51	10	3	500
Vocabulary	11.96	3.41	27	10.25	4.05	20	8.37	2.80	51	10	3	500
Arithmetic	11.74	3.60	27	9.80	3.25	20	8.69	3.66	51	10	3	500
Similarities	*9.74	3.82	27	*7.20	3.73	20	7.47	2.90	51	10	3	500
Digit Span	8.81	2.67	27	9.05	2.80	20	7.57	2.97	51	10	3	500
Block Design	*8.00	2.64	27	*5.55	2.82	20	6.02	2.62	44	10	3	500
Picture Completion	7.74	2.36	27	6.75	2.66	20	6.87	2.65	47	10	3	500
Object Assembly	7.07	2.60	27	6.05	2.66	20	6.25	2.95	40	10		500
Picture Arrangement	*6.30	2.27	27	*4.95	2.42	20	6.37	2.51	41	10	3	500
Digit Symbol	6.22	1.93	27	5.55	2.84	20	3.00	2.50	44	10	3	500
Verbal	67.26	17.58	27	57.40	17.26	20	48.85			60		500
Performance	*35.33	9.07	27	*28.85	10.90	20	28.51			50		500
Total	*102.59	24.22	27	*86.25	25.76	20	77.36			110		500

[1] Mean ages of group I and group II subjects were approximately 71 and 73 years, respectively.

[2] Scores of the Raven Progressive Matrices from Raven (1938). Age of subjects was approximately 65 years. Subjects of the Addition Rate and Copy Digit studies (Birren and Botwinick, 1951a, b) and of the Word Fluency study (Birren, 1955) were between 60 and 69 years. Data of reaction time of subjects aged 70 years were obtained by Birren and Botwinick (1955a) with a method slightly different from that used with the present sample. WAIS scores of male subjects aged 70–74 years from Doppelt and Wallace (1955).

[3] Scores of Raven Progressive Matrices from Foulds and Raven (1948); Card Sorting from Botwinick, Robbin, and Brinley (1960); Addition and Alternation Rate from Birren and Botwinick (1951a), and Botwinick, Brinley, and Robbin (1958b); Copy Digits from an unpublished study and from Birren and Botwinick (1951b); Word Fluency from Birren (1955); Line Difference from Botwinick, Brinley, and Robbin (1958a); Reaction Time from Birren and Botwinick (1955a), and Botwinick, Brinley, and Robbin (1958c, 1959a); Mirror Tracing from an unpublished study. Age range of subjects of these studies varied between 18 and 37 years. WAIS scores of subjects aged 20–34 years (Wechsler, 1955).

* Groups I and II significantly different at 0.05 level.

0.23 seconds as compared to 0.18 seconds for the young controls.

Mirror Tracing and Stroop scores were not available for younger samples. Both tests measure aspects of blocking or ability to inhibit behavioral tendencies. There is much evidence that such abilities diminish with age (Botwinick, Robbin, and Brinley, 1959).

DISCUSSION

It must be kept in mind that in the present study an attempt was made to select a group of healthy noninstitutionalized elderly men. The results, therefore, are not representative of the level of functioning of all men over the age of 65. In general, this population of men compares more favorably with the test results of young subjects than do the aged men of previous studies who were less rigorously selected for health. But changes with age were found and these are regarded as being especially significant. Two points may thus be made: (1) healthy men over 65 do better on psychological tests than men unselected for health, and (2) age differences in patterns of abilities were found even in a population devoid of apparent disease.

From the present study it is impossible to state whether the behaviors which seem intimately associated with aging are simple or multiple phenomena. Loss of speed, for example, may result from a change in component capacities rather than in a general overall loss. In advanced age does one hear less well because one cannot put words together sufficiently rapidly, or does one hear less well because one cannot receive the input? In the former case a general mediating process is suggested, and in the latter case a deficit in a specific sensory modality is implied.

In the course of research new problems become apparent and these are not neces-

sarily anticipated from the questions that are originally asked. In the present study a question arose that concerned the extent to which memory ability influenced the test performances. Were instructions remembered equally well by the poor and superior performers? Did a test that presumed to measure, for example, ability to alternate, really measure—in part or in full—ability to recall the previous and next operation? Are the learning scores distinguishable from scores of memory performances? Is concept formation largely a matter of being able to keep in mind many facets of information over a period of time? Many other questions are possible, but unfortunately the present data do not provide answers, since only one memory test—digit span (an inadequate sample of memory function)—was given. Had one or more additional memory tests been included in the battery, correlations and partial correlations would possibly have answered some of the questions. It is noted that Inglis (1959) found elderly patients suffering from memory disorders to perform more poorly with tasks of new learning than control patients of similar age.

Another question that arose had already been alluded to in the problem of general mediating processes versus specific sensory modalities, as accounting for the major portion of behavioral age changes. Was poor vision responsible for poor performance on the Raven, or speed of perceptual judgment on the Line Difference test? Was the Digit Symbol test more a test of visual acuity than of some other ability? Answers to these questions would be possible had measurements of visual acuity been made.

These two problems, memory and sensory acuity, are important ones for both theoretical and practical concerns. In view of this, it would seem that future studies of performance changes with age would do well to include measures of various types of memory and acuity. It would then be important to determine not only the extent of contribution of these variables to the remaining measurements of cognitive and psychomotor function but to determine whether the extent of contribution itself changed with age.

Regardless of the contribution of memory and acuity to the present data the two points discussed earlier still hold. Elderly men selected for health tend to function more adequately than do unselected elderly men with respect to cognitive and psychomotor processes. Even with the selected sample, however, age differences in these processes are seen when comparisons are made with younger persons.

REFERENCES

BALINSKY, B. 1941. An analysis of the mental factors in various age groups from nine to sixty. *Genet. Psychol. Monogr., 23,* 191–234.

BERG, ESTA A. 1948. A simple objective technique for measuring flexibility in thinking. *J. Gen. Psychol., 39,* 15–22.

BIRREN, J. E. 1952. A factorial analysis of the Wechsler-Bellevue scale given to an elderly population. *J. Consult. Psychol., 16,* 399–405.

————. 1955. Age changes in speed of simple responses and perception and their significance for complex behavior. *In Old Age in the Modern World.* Edinburg and London: E & S Livingstone, Ltd. pp. 235–247.

———— and BOTWINICK, J. 1951a. Rate of addition as a function of difficulty and age. *Psychometrika, 16,* 219–232.

————. 1951b. The relation of writing speed to age and to the senile psychoses. *J. Consult. Psychol., 15,* 243–249.

———— ————. 1955a. Age differences in finger, jaw, and foot reaction time to auditory stimuli. *J. Geront., 10,* 429–432.

———— ————. 1955b. Speed of response as a function of perceptual difficulty and age. *J. Geront. 10,* 433–436.

BOTWINICK, J. 1953. Wechsler-Bellevue split-half subtest reliabilities: differences in age and mental status. *J. Consult. Psychol., 17,* 225–228.

————. 1959. Drives, expectancies, and emotions. In, J. E. Birren (Ed.) *Handbook of aging and the individual: psychological and biological aspects.* University of Chicago Press.

BOTWINICK, J. and BIRREN, J. E. 1951a. The measurement of intellectual decline in the senile psychoses. *J. Consult. Psychol., 15,* 145–150.

———— ————. 1951b. Differential decline in the Wechsler-Bellevue subtests in the senile psychoses. *J. Geront., 6,* 365–368.

————, BRINLEY, J. F., and ROBBIN, J. S. 1958a. The interaction effects of perceptual difficulty and stimulus exposure time on age differences in speed and accuracy of response. *Gerontologia, 2,* 1–10.

———— ————. 1958b. Task alternation time in relation to problem difficulty and age. *J. Geront., 13,* 414–417.

———— ————. 1958c. The effect of motivation by electrical shocks on reaction-time in relation to age. *Amer. J. Psychol., 71,* 408–411.

———— ————. 1959a. Further results concerning the effect of motivation by electrical shocks on reactiontime in relation to age. *Amer. J. Psychol., 72,* 140.

———— ————. 1959b. Maintaining set in relation to motivation and age. *Amer. J. Psychol., 72,* 585–588.

————, ROBBIN, J. S., and BRINLEY, J. F. 1959. Reorganization of perceptions with age. *J. Geront., 14,* 85–88.

———— ————. 1960. Age differences in card sorting performance in relation to task difgence Scale for older persons. *J. Abnorm. Soc. 59,* 10–18.

COHEN, J. 1957. The factorial structure of the WAIS between early adulthood and old age. *J. Consult. Psychol., 21,* 283–290.

DOPPELT, J. E., and WALLACE, W. L. 1955. Standardization of the Wechsler Adult Intelligence Scale for older persons. *J. Abnorm. Soc. Psychol., 51,* 312–330.

EISDORFER, C., BUSSE, E. W., and COHEN, L. D. 1959. The WAIS performance of an aged sample: the relationship between verbal and performance IQs. *J. Geront., 14,* 197–201.

FOULDS, G. A., and RAVEN, J. C. 1948. Normal changes in the mental abilities of adults as age advances. *J. Ment. Sci., 94,* 133–142.

FOX, CHARLOTTE, and BIRREN, J. E. 1950. The differential decline of subtest scores of the Wechsler-Bellevue Intelligence Scale in 60–69 year old individuals. *J. Genet. Psychol., 77,* 313–317.

GRANT, D. A., and BERG, ESTA A. 1958. A behavioral analysis of shifting to new responses in a Weigl-type card-sorting problem. *J. Exp. Psychol., 38,* 404–411.

INGLIS, J. 1958. Psychological investigations of cognitive deficit in elderly psychiatric patients. *Psych. Bull., 55,* 197–214.

INGLIS, J. 1959. Learning, retention, and conceptual usage in elderly patients with memory disorder. *J. Abnorm. Soc. Psychol., 59,* 210–215.

JONES, H. E. 1959. Intelligence and problem-solving. In, J. E. Birren (Ed.) *Handbook of aging and the individual: psychological and biological aspects.* University of Chicago Press.

McHUGH, R. B., and OWENS, W. A. 1954. Age changes in mental organization—a longitudinal study. *J. Geront., 9,* 296–302.

MORROW, MARY A. 1946. Performance on the Hunt test with differential vocabulary scoring compared with performance on a card sorting test. M.A. Thesis, University of Wisconsin.

NORMAN, R. D., and DALEY, M. F. 1959. Senescent changes in intellectual ability among superior older women. *J. Geront., 14,* 457–464.

RAVEN, J. C. 1954. *Guide to Using Progressive Matrices (1938).* Beverly Hills, Calif.: Western Psychological Services.

RICKS, J., JR. 1957. Age and vocabularly test performance: a qualitative analysis of the responses of adults. Ph. D. dissertation, Columbia University.

RIEGEL, K. F. 1959. A study of verbal achievements of older persons. *J. Geront., 14,* 453–456.

RUCH, F. L. 1934. The differentiative effects of age upon human learning. *J. Gen. Psychol., 11,* 261–286.

STROOP, J. R. 1935. Studies of interference in serial verbal reactions. *J. Exp. Psychol., 18,* 643–662.

THURSTONE, L. L. 1947. *Multiple-factor Analysis.* Chicago: University of Chicago Press.

WECHSLER, D. 1944. *The Measurement of Adult Intelligence.* (3d ed.) Baltimore: Williams and Wilkins.

———. 1955. *Manual for the Wechsler Adult Intelligence Scale.* New York: Psychological Corporation.

CHAPTER 9

Auditory Perception in Relation to Age

by Alfred D. Weiss

One major problem in the study of the psychophysiology of aging is to distinguish changes which are due to central as opposed to peripheral processes; viz, functional changes attributable to the sense organs and their associated nervous pathways. Since purely psychological experimental methods require the participation of processes from the sensory receptor to some effector mechanism, the localization by such means probably can be little more than indicative. However, the complexity of the nervous system makes it difficult to relate anatomical and physiological to psychological findings. A more precise psychological differentiation will ease the considerable task required of physiology and anatomy. Extensive reviews of sensory (Weiss, 1959) and perceptual (Braun, 1959) changes with age have been reported.

A working definition of sensory and perceptual processes has been proposed by Weiss (1959). This definition is based on the concept of "symbolic transformation." The sense organs act as transducers of physical energy, transforming them into coded patterns of nerve impulses in the associated nerve tract. These patterns of impulses will eventually reach the appropriate primary sensory area of the brain, although they may become modified en route (Hernandez-Peon et al., 1955; Galambos et al., 1955). This may be due to centrifugal impulses from different levels and to feedback mechanisms.

Impulses also may reach various subcortical areas of the brain. Various psychological concomitants of these neurophysiological processes are possible: (1) The propagation of the signal is blocked and shortly no trace of the occurrence of the original event remains; there is no overt or covert response by the organism. (2) There may be an overt or covert response without any subjective awareness by the organism. (3) There may be a simple subjective awareness that a stimulus has occured; here it might be said that the stimulus has been "sensed" but not "perceived." (4) Symbolic transformation of the stimulus may occur, so that the organism is consciously aware of the more complex information conveyed by the stimulus and categorizes it in symbolic terms. (5) Qualitatively or quantitatively inadequate stimuli may produce miscategorization and hence an incorrect perception. This may also occur when the subject has a set biased in favor of some categories.

Case 1 is self-explanatory. The homeostatic mechanisms, such as those involved in breathing, may be cited as an example of the second case. Another example of case 2 may be the normal auditory feedback control of speech intensity. An example of case 3 is where a word is spoken suddenly to an inattentive subject—he is aware only that he has been spoken to. The experiment reported by Cherry (1953) where subjects attended only to the message in one ear, disregarding the message in the other ear, can be cited as another example. An example of case 4 is normal speech, where the subject is aware primarily of symbolic content. It is likely that the greater the load on the perceptual mechanism, the greater the rejection of irrelevant aspects of the stimulus prior to the symbolic transformation. Overloading may produce rejection or loss of relevant aspects of the stimulus as well. As an example of case 5, a subject may misunderstand a speaker with a strong, unfamiliar accent, or he may interpret a statement in terms of what he expects or wishes to hear.

Aging has been shown to be a useful variable in differentiating "central" and "peripheral" processes in hearing. Pestalozza and Shore (1955) found that discrimination for speech may be poor in the aged, even in the presence of only a mild hearing loss by tone threshold audiometry. On the basis of these and similar findings by other methods, the authors suggested that this "phonemic-regression syndrome" of the aged may have a central basis. Fleischer (1956) reached similar conclusions.

The present series of experiments on age changes in auditory processes was designed to differentiate "sensory" and "perceptual" processes, and to see how such measures might relate to physiological, psychiatric, sociological, and other psychological measures.

SUBJECTS

The population of old subjects has been described elsewhere in this monograph. In this chapter, group I refers to the sample of healthy elderly subjects. Group II refers to those elderly subjects who had asymptomatic and/or subclinical diseases. Group II–H refers to a subsample of group II. This subsample consisted of subjects who qualified for group I, except for the finding of an elevated mean arterial blood pressure during the cerebral blood flow procedure described elsewhere in this monograph. Elderly subjects who were not included in the above groups of normal subjects because of the presence of clinical disease states are separately indicated as group III. Group Y refers to the young control group, which consisted of 15 healthy young males between 18 and 30 years of age, median age of 20. These young men were volunteers for medical research at the Clinical Center, National Institutes of Health.

THE CLINICAL EVALUATION OF HEARING

The rise in the auditory threshold with age has been extensively studied (e.g., Montgomery, 1932; Steinberg et al., 1940; Beasley, 1940). This rise becomes more marked toward the higher frequencies. The work of Rosée (1953) on 360 subjects, all carefully selected for absence of known pathology, showed a parallel rise in bone- and air-conduction thresholds, indicating that the loss was not of the conductive type. All of his subjects had positive Rinné's, indicating the normal greater sensitivity of air conduction over bone conduction. Studies by Fleischer (1956), Pestalooza and Shore (1955), and de Bruïne-Altes (1946) showed that older subjects usually show no recruitment, indicating that the primary pathology lay in the ganglion cells rather than in the organ of Corti.

A clinical evaluation of hearing, testing primarily the "sensory" functions, was performed on all subjects, in order to differentiate "sensory" from "perceptual" auditory changes in aging. The latter were tested by the experimental procedures to be described later.

Methods

A medical history pertinent to the auditory and vestibular systems was obtained. An otoscopic examination was performed, with removal of cerumen when necessary. This was followed by Rinné and Weber tests with a 128 cps tuning fork, and a Romberg test. Then air-conduction audiograms were obtained, using an Audivox 7–B audiometer with a Western Electric 705–A earphone in a sound-treated room.

Results

For purposes of analysis, the subjects were divided into five groups: four groups of old subjects designated as the normal (group I), the hypertensive normal (group II–H), the asymptomatic and/or subclinical disease group (group II, less group II–H), the rejected "apparent disease" (group III), and the normal young (group Y). The criteria for grouping the older subjects were discussed earlier in this monograph (chs. 2, 3).

The air conduction audiograms were categorized as the hearing loss in the better ear at each frequency, and the difference between ears at each frequency. The means for each group at each frequency are shown in figures 1 and 2.

The hearing loss in the better ear at each frequency is well within the normal standards given by Rosée (1953) for all groups except group II, which included several subjects with severe hearing loss.

The analysis of variance (table 1) showed that the groups and frequencies differed highly significantly, and the groups x frequency interaction was also highly significant, all at minimum degrees of freedom. (Manipulation of degrees of freedom in a mixed model variance analysis is discussed by Geisser and Greenhouse, 1958.) A Scheffé (1953) test ($p = 0.05$) on group

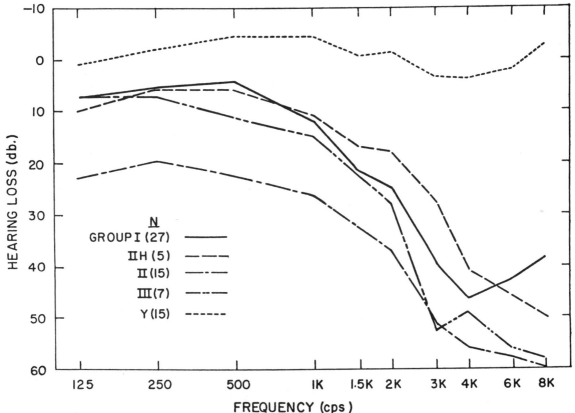

FIGURE 1.—Hearing loss in decibels in the better ear at each frequency. The four old groups and one young group are described in the text.

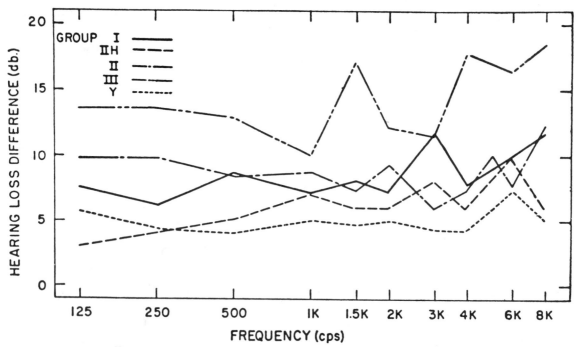

FIGURE 2.—The difference in hearing loss between pairs of ears.

means showed that group Y differed from all other groups and group II differed from groups I and II–H. The only significant interactions were between group Y and all other groups.

A similar variance analysis of the difference between pairs of ears showed that the groups differed ($p<0.01$ max. d.f., $p.<0.05$ min. d.f.) A Scheffé test ($p=0.05$) showed that group Y differed from group III.

The results of the audiograms showed, (*a*) the expected difference in hearing loss between young and old subjects; (*b*) that the degree of hearing loss in latently hypertensive subjects (group II–H) did not differ from that in healthy old subjects (group I), but did differ significantly from that found in subjects with other asymptomatic and subclinical disease states (group II); and (*c*) that difference in hearing loss be-

TABLE 1.—*Audiometric hearing loss (better ear)—analysis of variance*

Source	Sums of squares	Degrees of freedom	F
Frequencies (F)	115, 039. 456	9	*** 137. 891
Groups (G)	123, 904. 807	4	*** [1] 17. 763
Ind. w.g. (I w.g.)	111, 603. 092	64	....
F×G	28, 364. 203	36	*** [2] 8. 499
F×I w.g.	53, 393. 841	576	....
Total	432, 305. 399	689	....

[1] Scheffé multiple comparison test on group means shows that group Y differs significantly ($p<0.05$) from all other groups and group II differs significantly from groups I and II–H.

[2] Scheffé test on frequency X group interactions (shapes of the curves) shows that the shape of the Y group is significantly different ($p\times0.05$) from the curve shapes of all other groups.

*** Significant at the 0.001 level.

TABLE 2.—*Audiometric difference between pairs of ears—analysis of variance*

Source	Sum of squares	Degrees of freedom	F
Frequencies (F)..	745. 834	9	N.S.
Groups (G)..	4, 515. 775	4	[1][2] 2. 53
Ind. w.g. (I w.g.)...	28, 536. 907	64	....
F×G...	1, 396. 350	36	N.S.
F×I w.g...	32, 255. 316	576	....
Total...	67, 450. 182	689	....

[1] Significant at the 0.05 level with minimum degrees of freedom; at the 0.01 level with usual degrees of freedom. (See text, p. 5.)

[2] Scheffé test on group means shows that group Y differs from group III only ($p < 0.05$).

N.S.=Not significant.

tween pairs of ears did not change with age per se, but changed significantly in subjects with clinical disease states (group III).

All young subjects had positive Rinné tests in both ears. Among older subjects, every ear showing an air-conduction loss greater than 25 db had a negative Rinné. There was no consistent pattern of lateralization on the Weber test in terms of the results of the Rinné test and air-conduction audiograms at 125 cps.

CLICK PERCEPTION

One function of the auditory analyzer is to make temporal discriminations. In the simplest case, this would be expressed in terms of the minimum temporal interval required for the discrimination of two discrete stimuli. Such a measurement was reported as early as 1875 by Exner, who found a minimum interval of 2 milliseconds. Electrophysiological measurements at the round window and auditory cortex of cats in response to clicks have shown similar values when the clicks were of moderate intensity (Rosenzweig and Rosenblith, 1953). At a delta (interclick) interval of 2 milliseconds, the nerve response to the second click at the round window was 60 percent the amplitude of the response to the first click. At a delta interval of about 5 milliseconds, the auditory

cortex response to the second click had an amplitude about 20 percent as large as the response to the first click.

The rise of intensity thresholds with age has been discussed earlier. The following experiment was designed to test the age changes in the threshold of auditory temporal discrimination and their relation to intensity threshold changes.

Methods

The apparatus consisted of a click stimulator which could deliver square wave pulses. The duration and amplitude of the click, delta interval, and the number of clicks could be controlled independently. Acoustic calibration of 0.25 millisecond click in a 9–A coupler showed a frequency response from 150 to 10,000 cycles per second, with the peak response ranging from 1 to 6 kilocycles.[1]

Using 0.25 millisecond clicks, the subject's threshold to 2,000 clicks per second was measured by the method of limits. (All determinations were made diotically. In diotic presentations, the stimuli to both ears are identical; in dichotic presentations, the stimuli are different for each ear.) The threshold for one click per second was deter-

[1] Kindly performed by M. D. Burkhard at the National Bureau of Standards (Burkhard and Corliss, 1954).

mined similarly. All subsequent stimuli to a subject were delivered at 30 db above that subject's threshold for one click per second.

Using a modified method of limits, the subject's two-click discrimination threshold was determined. The subject was instructed to distinguish between two clicks and one click, regardless of whether or not the two clicks sounded clearly separated. During the stimulus series of decreasing and increasing delta (interclick) intervals, the subject was intermittently presented with a single click to assure good stimulus control and to reinforce the subject's criterion of difference between one and two clicks. The smallest delta interval at which the subject responded correctly to two clicks was taken as the reading, and the mean of five decreasing and five increasing series readings was obtained. Each stimulus presentation proceeded as follows: After making the necessary settings, the experimenter closed the switch, initiating a brief (about 0.3 second) warning tone of the same intensity as the clicks to follow. Three seconds later, the click stimuli would be delivered. After recording the subject's response the experimenter would make the settings for the next presentation.

Results

The results of the intensity threshold determinations are shown in table 3A. The values shown are decibels of attenuation; higher values indicate lower thresholds. Groups I and II do not differ significantly for either 2,000 clicks per second or 1 click per second; group Y differs highly from group I with these measures.

The results of the two-click discrimination are shown in table 3b. The values shown are the mean minima (in milliseconds) at which two clicks were differentiated from one click. Because of the skewed distributions, the table shows the median and the first and third quartiles for each group; the old subjects are shown both as independent groups I and II, and as the combined group O. The medians of groups Y and I are virtually identical; how-

TABLE 3a.—*Thresholds*

[Intensity thresholds (db attenuation)]

Threshold	Groups					
	Young group ($N=15$)		Group I ($N=27$)		Group II ($N=16$)	
	Mean	S.D.	Mean	S.D.	Mean	S.D.
2,000 clicks per second...........	93.7	5.31	75.5	14.86	71.8	18.33
1 click per second................	80.5	4.69	67.9	7.20	64.0	13.07

Results of t-tests

	Y vs. I	I vs. II
2,000 clicks per second..	*** 6.67	N.S.
1 click per second...	*** 5.62	N.S.

*** Significant at the 0.001 level.

TABLE 3b.—*Thresholds*

[2-click discrimination] [1]

Groups	Number	Median	Q_1	Q_3
Y..	15	1.80	0.86	2.77
I...	27	1.72	1.35	5.56
II..	16	3.20	2.20	10.65
(I+II)...	43	2.69	1.44	9.58

[1] Values in milliseconds:

Mann-Whitney U tests (single tailed)

Comparisons: *P*

Y vs O... (**)

Y vs. I... N.S.

Y vs. II.. (***)

I vs. II.. N.S.

    ** Significant at the 0.01 level.
    *** Significant at the 0.001 level.

ever, the Q_3's do differ. The Mann-Whitney U test (as given by Siegel, 1956) shows the single tailed p value for rejection of the null hypothesis to be 0.06. Groups I and II differ at a p of 0.07, groups Y and II at a p of 0.0003, and groups Y and O at a p of 0.01. It is noteworthy that the Q_1 of group II lies outside the Q_3 of group Y and the Md. of group I. The highest mean value for a young subject was 4.19 milliseconds. These results indicate that healthy older men do not differ from healthy young men in the two-click discrim-

ination, and that the less healthy old tend to have larger discrimination times. It should be added that, with a little practice, two-click discrimination becomes a relatively stable measure.

That this increase in two-click discrimination threshold in the old is not related to pure tone audiometric or click intensity thresholds is shown in table 4. This correlation matrix shows clearly that, while all intensity threshold measures are highly correlated, none of them correlate with the two-click discrimination threshold.

TABLE 4.—*Correlation matrix of threshold measures in older subjects (groups I and II)*
(*N*-43)

	Mean	S.D.
1. Audiogram, HL in db at 2,000 cps, left ear.......................	29.65	18.47
2. Audiogram, HL in db at 2,000 cps, right ear......................	28.26	17.25
3. 2,000 clicks/sec, threshold in db att............................	74.24	16.19
4. 1 click/sec, threshold in db att................................	66.45	9.98
5. 2-click discrimination threshold in m sec.......................	6.80	9.06

	1.	2.	3.	4.	5.
2.	** 0.81				
3.		** —0.82	** —.91		
4.			** —0.80	** —.80	
				** .86	—0.06
					—.04
					—.06
					.11

    ** Significant at the 0.01 level.

After the determination of the two-click discrimination threshold, each subject was presented with trains of clicks, varying in number from 1 to 10, and presented at various rates of speed. The delta intervals used were 160, 130, 100, 80, 63, and 25 milliseconds, designated A through F, respectively. (At 25 milliseconds, only two through five clicks were presented.) The stimulus number and the rates were simultaneously quasi-randomly varied, and five determinations of each number at each rate were obtained. The presentation of each stimulus train of clicks was preceded by a warning signal 3 seconds earlier. Response latencies were measured to the nearest 0.1 second by means of a voice key.

The subject was instructed to report as accurately as possible how many clicks he heard. He was not informed of how many clicks there might be, nor that the latency of his response would be measured.

The means of responses for each stimulus number across rates A through E are shown for the two age groups in figure 3. It is evident that the under estimation for both groups increased with increasing stimulus number, more so for the old than for the young. (At the fastest rate, F, there was considerable overestimation by the young and underestimation by the old.) Rates A through E did not differ significantly from each other, as shown by analysis of variance. However, the click $\times$ rate interaction was

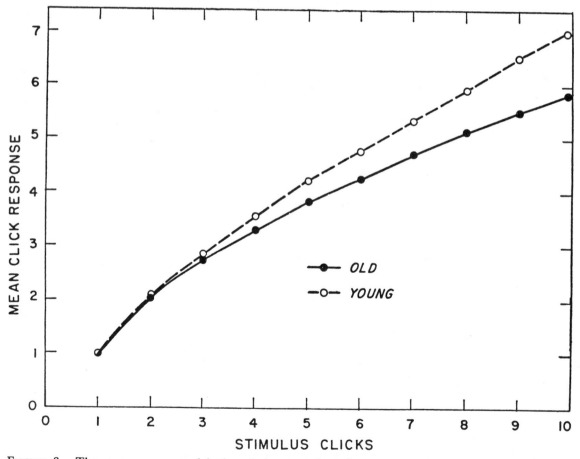

FIGURE 3.—The mean responses (absolute judgments of number) as a function of the number of clicks presented for groups of young and old subjects.

significant. This interaction is shown in figure 4.

The curves have been smoothed by means of three point-moving averages. It appears that the fastest rate, E, shows relatively greater overestimation at low stimulus numbers, and relatively greater underestimation at high stimulus numbers than the slower rates. (The rate designations used are: A, 160 millisecond delta interval; B, 130 milliseconds; C, 100 milliseconds; D, 80 milliseconds; and E, 63 milliseconds.)

The analysis of variance of the click response numbers is shown in table 5. The method of evaluation of significance in a mixed model by manipulating degrees of freedom is discussed by Geisser and Greenhouse (1958). The import of the method is that the minimum degrees of freedom give the conservative limits of p, while the maximum degrees of freedom show the usual bounds of p under the usual analysis of variance assumption of uncorrelated errors (or equally correlated errors).

Clicks, age, clicks $\times$ rate, and clicks $\times$ age were found to be significant at minimum degrees of freedom. The clicks $\times$ rate $\times$ age interaction was highly significant at maximum degrees of freedom, and had a p of less than 0.10 at minimum degrees of freedom. This second order interaction therefore is likely to be significant.

The means of response latencies across rates are shown for the two groups in figure 5. There was no significant statistical difference between the age groups. However,

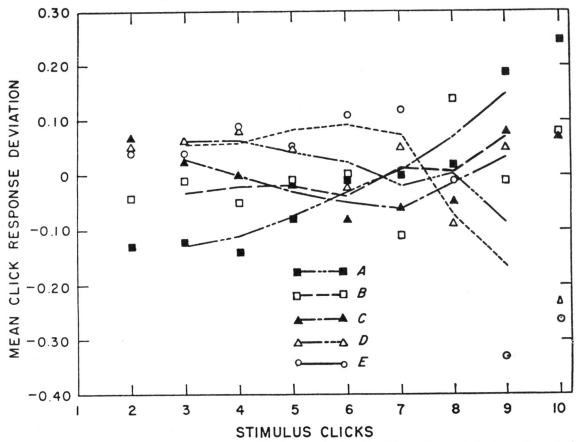

FIGURE 4.—The click $\times$ rate interaction for all subjects combined. The point symbols show the actual values; the curves have been smoothed by three-point moving averages. The rate of presentation of clicks increases from A to E; the delta intervals are specified in the text.

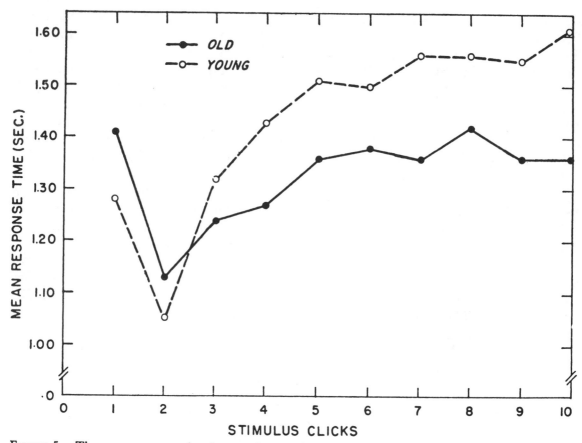

FIGURE 5.—The mean response time in seconds as a function of the number of clicks presented for old and young age groups.

it is of interest to note that the older subjects had shorter mean response latencies for all click stimulus numbers except one and two. The fact that the latency to one click was greater than the latency for two clicks may well be due to the subjects' having to assure themselves that no second click would follow; while for two clicks, the subject needed to wait only for an interval after the second click equal to that between the first and second click. To see if the decreased response time of the old relative to the young might be due to the smaller responses, a product-moment correlation was run. A correlation of 0.305, with a p value of 0.05, was obtained. There is a rise in response time for both groups up to about five clicks, with a subsequent plateau.

The effect of presentation rate on response time for all subjects combined is shown in figure 6. (The delta intervals for rates A through E are the same as previously described. The delta interval for rate F is 25 milliseconds.) It is apparent that response time increases as presentation rate increases from A through F.

The variance analysis of the response time is shown in table 6. Both clicks and rate are significant at the conservative level. The click×rate interaction is significant (0.01 level) only at the maximum degrees of freedom, the p value being close to 0.25 at the minimum degrees of freedom. Therefore, the possible significance of this interaction must be viewed with the greatest caution.

The results for the young subjects on num-

TABLE 5.—*Analysis of variance of click response number*

Source	Degrees of freedom	Sums of squares	Formula	F	d.f.[1] Max.	d.f.[1] Min.
Clicks (C)..............	8	4,329.75	$\dfrac{C}{C \times \text{Ind. w.g.}}$	569.71	....	(***)
Rate (R)...............	4	10.72	$\dfrac{R}{R \times \text{Ind. w.g.}}$	2.39	(*)	....
Age (A)................	1	146.23	$\dfrac{A}{\text{Ind. w.g.}}$	5.19	....	(*)
Individuals w.g..........	53	1,493.12	....	....	...	...
C×R...................	32	26.88	$\dfrac{C \times R}{C \times R \times \text{Ind. w.g.}}$	19.76	....	(*)
C×A...................	8	70.14	$\dfrac{C \times A}{C \times \text{Ind. w.g.}}$	9.23	....	(**)
C×Ind. w.g............	424	403.05	....	....	...	...
R×A...................	4	3.50	$\dfrac{R \times A}{R \times \text{Ind. w.g.}}$	<1	....	...
R×Ind. w.g............	212	237.18	....	....	...	...
C×R×A..............	32	5.31	$\dfrac{C \times R \times A}{C \times R \times \text{Ind. w.g.}}$	3.89	(***)	....
C×R×Ind. w.g.........	1,696	72.13	....	....	...	...
Total..............	2,474	6,798.01	....	....	...	...

[1] See text, p. 9, for explanation of varying degrees of freedom.
* Significant at the 0.05 level.
** Significant at the 0.01 level.
*** Significant at the 0.001 level.

ber judgment are generally in agreement with those found by Taubman (1944), Cheatham and White (1952), and Garner (1951). The main difference lies in the somewhat higher response levels found by other experimenters. This may have been due to either more practice by their subjects, or to their having run one presentation rate at a time, which may have led to time-rate judgments rather than to number judgments per se. Garner (1951) found a statistically significant difference in results between these two methods.

For purposes of comparison of click response results with the results of other procedures, the mean responses for each stimulus were summed for each subject. The same was done for response latency. These sums represent the area under the curves and are reasonably representative of each subject's performance. Comparison ("*t*"-test) of groups I and II for these two measures proved nonsignificant.

The two-click discrimination measure was originally conceived of as representing the limit of delta interval, below which click

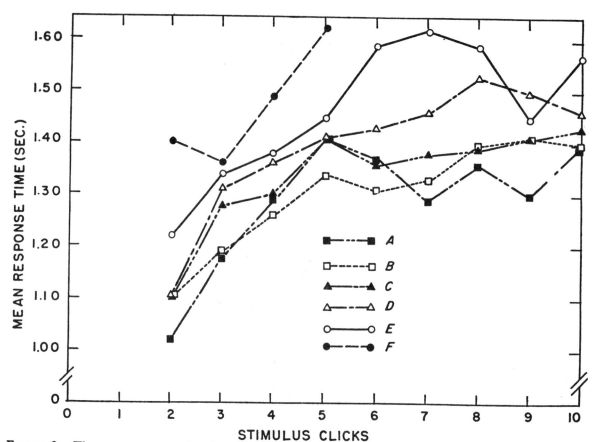

FIGURE 6.—The mean response time for all subjects as a function of the stimulus number for each stimulus presentation rate.

perception would not be possible. A correlation run between the two-click discrimination threshold and the sum of click perception proved to be not significant. A partial correlation, leaving out hearing loss, did not affect this lack of significance. Evidently, the age changes measured by pure tone audiometry, two-click discrimination, and click perception are not significantly related to each other.

DIOTIC AND DICHOTIC DIGIT SPANS

The decline in conventional (diotic) digit span with age has been noted (ch. 8 in this monograph; Doppelt and Wallace, 1955; Wechsler, 1955). There is some question as to the homogeneity of decline in the digits forward—digits backward type of presentation; Bromley (1958) has found that only digits backward shows decline with age. Only the digits forward span will be considered here.

Digit span may be considered to be a test of immediate memory. Broadbent, in a series of papers (1954, 1955,[2] 1956, 1957a, 1957b) has presented another method by which he has sought to separate what might be called a sensory memory from a perceptual memory, and has presented a theoretical model to account for his findings. [Broadbent (1958) has provided an excellent summary of the literature in this area].

---

[2] Broadbent, D E. Comments on successive responses to simultaneous stimuli in unpublished letter to Medical Research Council, 1955. (Other dates refer to published materials listed in chapter bibliography.)

TABLE 6.—*Analysis of variance of click response time*

Source	Degrees of freedom	Sums of squares	Formula	F	d.f.[1] Max.	d.f.[1] Min.
Clicks (C)...............	8	27. 5004	$\dfrac{C}{C \times \text{Ind. w.g.}}$	10. 32	(***)	(**)
Rate (R)................	4	10. 2878	$\dfrac{R}{R \times \text{Ind. w.g.}}$	21. 53	....	(***)
Age (A)................	1	9. 2794	$\dfrac{A}{\text{Ind. w.g.}}$	<1	....	....
Individuals w.g...........	53	555. 7180	....	....	....	....
C×R..................	32	4. 2780	$\dfrac{C \times R}{C \times R \times \text{Ind. w.g.}}$	1. 75	(**)	....
C×A..................	8	3. 8141	$\dfrac{C \times A}{C \times \text{Inc. w.g.}}$	1. 43	....	....
C×Ind. w.g...........	424	141. 1746	....	....	....	....
R×A..................	4	. 2746	$\dfrac{R \times A}{R \times \text{Ind. w.g.}}$	<1	....	....
R×Ind. w.g...........	212	25. 3199	....	....	....	....
C×R×A..............	32	2. 3614	$\dfrac{C \times R \times A}{C \times R \times \text{Ind. w.g.}}$	<1	....	....
C×R×Ind. w. g.........	1,696	129. 5567	....	....	....	....
Total..............	2,474	909. 5649	....	....	....	....

[1] See text, p. 10.
** Significant at the 0.01 level.
*** Significant at the 0.001 level.

The basis of Broadbent's method was the simultaneous presentation of different numbers to the two ears (dichotic presentation). The method used in this experiment was quite similar. In one instance, the subject would be required to repeat the numbers serially, one ear at a time, which is here called the "S" response. In the other instance, the subject would be required to repeat the digit pairs in the order in which they were heard, which is here called the "P" response. To illustrate, the number 1 2 3 might be presented to the right ear, and the number 4 5 6 would be simultaneously presented to the left ear, so that the digits 1 and 4 arrived simultaneously, as would the digits 2 and 5, and 3 and 6. For the "S" response, the subject would repeat, "1 2 3 4 5 6," or "4 5 6 1 2 3." For the "P" response, the subject would repeat, "1 4 2 5 3 6," or any other pattern that repeated the digit pairs in proper order. The rate of presentation of digit pairs was varied, with digit pairs being presented every ½, 1, 1½, or 2 seconds.

Broadbent found that accuracy of repetition was virtually nil for the P response at the faster presentation rates, but quite good at the slower rates. The S response accuracy seemed little affected by rate. He hypothesized that the difficulty in the P response at the fast rates was due to the time required to switch the perceptual mechanism from one input channel to the other. He hypothesized that inaccuracies in the S response mode were due to the time decay in a kind of sensory storage mechanism—the longer the information had to be stored in the secondly responding channel, the greater the likelihood of its loss.

Methods

In this experiment, all stimulus material was recorded on a dual-channel tape recorder. In the diotic digit span, numbers were presented in blocks, beginning with a three-digit number, then a four-digit number, etc., up to an eight-digit number. After hearing each number, the subject repeated the number with all the digits in proper sequence. All the digits in any number were different. Each block of numbers was presented at one of four rates, with digits occurring every ½, 1, 1½, or 2 seconds. A group consisted of four blocks of numbers, representing all four rates. Four such groups were given, with the rates being in counterbalanced order.

In the dichotic presentation, each block consisted of two- and three-digit pairs (four and six digits, respectively). Groups were arranged in the same fashion as in the diotic presentation. In two groups, the subject was required to give the S response, and in the other two groups, the P response. The response orders were balanced among the subjects.

The experimental presentation was always a group of diotic numbers, a group of dichotic numbers, and then another group of diotic and a group of dichotic numbers. After a 10-minute rest period, the group order was dichotic, diotic, dichotic, and diotic. Before the first dichotic presentation in both halves of the experimental session, a single-digit pair would be presented for the purpose of balancing the subjective intensities in the two ears.

Of the older subjects tested, only one was incapable of distinguishing the single-digit pair; his data are not included. None of the 15 young subjects experienced this difficulty.

In the diotic span, subjects were scored on (1) the largest correct span in a block, and (2) the total number of errors made in a block. The mean score at each presentation rate for each subject was used.

Results

The results are shown in table 7; the analyses of variance are shown in table 8. For the scores on the digit span, only the groups differed significantly: a Scheffé on group means showed that the young differed from both old groups, but the two old groups did not differ from each other. The age difference is that the old have a significantly smaller span than the young, differing by about one digit.

The analysis of variance of the error scores showed that the groups differed significantly: a Scheffé showed that groups Y and I differed significantly. The rates difference and the rate $\times$ group interaction are questionably significant, having p values less than 0.025 for maximum degrees of freedom, and less than 0.10 for minimum degrees of freedom. A Scheffé on rates showed that the error difference between rates 2.0 and 1.5 had a p value of about 0.05. The lack of clear trend in the rate $\times$ group interaction and its questionable significance makes further analysis of this point dubious.

Correlations between spans and errors were uniformly highly negative, ranging around -0.9. Tests for homogeneity did not show any significant differences in correlations among the age groups. A Fried-

TABLE 7.—*Diotic digit spans, mean spans, and errors*

			Presentation rate				
	Group	Number	0.5	1.0	1.5	2.0	Across rates
Span...........	I.............	27	6.02	5.80	5.99	5.94	[1] 5.94
	II...........	15	6.13	5.84	5.80	6.13	[1] 5.98
	Y...........	15	6.82	6.98	7.23	6.90	[1] 6.98

[1] Scheffé shows that groups I and Y differ at 0.01 level; II and Y differ at 0.05 level.

Errors.............	I................		5.69	6.56	5.90	6.96	* 6.28
	II................		6.05	6.12	6.05	5.87	6.02
	Y................		5.32	5.68	5.08	5.79	* 5.45

* Scheffé test shows that groups I and Y differ at the 0.05 level.

TABLE 8.—*Analysis of variance of diotic digit spans*

SPANS Source	Degrees of freedom	Sums of squares	F	P [1]	
				Max. d.f.	Min. d.f.
Rates (R).....................	3	0.82	0.97	....	....
Groups (G).....................	2	47.29	7.10	....	(**)
Individuals w.g..............	54	179.70	....	....	....
R×G.......................	6	2.94	1.75	....	....
R×Ind. w.g................	162	45.36	....	....	....
Total.....................	227	276.11	....	....	....

ERRORS Source	Degrees of freedom	Sums of squares	F	P	
				Max. d.f.	Min. d.f.
R...........................	3	17.82	3.77	(*)	....
G...........................	2	332.57	4.99	....	(**)
Ind. w.g...................	54	1,800.20	....	....	....
R×G.......................	6	25.16	2.66	(*)	....
R×Ind. w.g................	162	255.48	....	....	....
Total.....................	227	2,431.23	....	....	....

[1] See text, p. 14.
* Significant at the 0.05 level.
** Significant at the 0.01 level.

man two-way analysis of variance (as given by Siegel, 1956) of the correlations on groups and presentation rates failed to show significant differences in the correlations with rate of presentation. This analysis had been made to test the null hypothesis against the alternative hypothesis that older subjects would make more errors relative to their digit spans; viz, the old groups would show lower magnitudes of correlation between spans and errors than the young. The null hypothesis was not rejected. It had been hypothesized further that the faster presentation rates would produce higher magnitudes of correlations than the slower rates (except possibly at the 2.0-second rate where rehearsal during presentation was possible). Here also the null hypothesis could not be rejected. A correlation matrix of spans at different presentation rates for the old subjects showed correlations ranging between 0.61 and 0.80, all significant at the 0.01 level.

The dichotic presentation responses were scored on the bases of (1) the average highest correct span, called the Score, and (2) the average number of correct fragments, called the Partial Score, both obtained at all presentation rates and at both response modes. The Scores had a possible range of 1 through 3, and the Partial Scores had a possible range of zero through 10. The medians for each group at each presentation rate and response mode are shown in table 9. The medians for the combined old groups (I+II) are also shown.

Because all distributions seemed strongly skewed, generally positively skewed for the old groups and negatively skewed for the young, nonparametric methods of analysis were applied to the data. The methods used are given by Siegel (1956).

The results are in general agreement with those reported by Broadbent (1955). A summary of the overall analyses is shown in table 10.

To see if the groups differed significantly from each other in the procedure as a whole, sign tests were applied to the median values shown in table 9. Single tailed

TABLE 9.—*Dichotic digit spans* [1]

Procedure	Group [2]	Presentation rate			
		0.5	1.0	1.5	2.0
S Scores	I	1.0	1.5	1.5	1.0
	II	1.0	1.0	1.0	1.0
	I+II	1.0	1.25	1.25	1.0
	Y	2.0	3.0	2.5	2.0
P Scores	I	1.0	1.5	1.5	1.5
	II	1.0	1.0	1.0	1.5
	I+II	1.0	1.5	1.5	1.5
	Y	2.0	2.5	2.5	2.5
S Partial Scores	I	2.5	3.0	3.5	2.5
	II	3.0	2.0	2.0	2.0
	I+II	2.5	2.5	3.25	2.5
	Y	6.0	9.0	7.5	4.5
P Partial Scores	I	3.0	5.0	5.0	5.0
	II	1.0	3.0	4.0	4.0
	I+II	2.0	4.0	4.0	5.0
	Y	5.0	7.0	8.0	9.0

[1] Median values.
[2] Group size: I (N=27), II (N=15), Y (N=15).

TABLE 10.—*Dichotic digit spans*

Sign tests between groups for all measures [1] (single tailed probabilities)

Groups	II	Y	I+II
I.............	(**)	(***)	....
II...........	....	(***)	....
Y.............		....	(**)

Median test among groups for each measure [1] (averaged across rates) (χ^2, 2 degrees of freedom)

	S procedure	P procedure
Scores..............	* 8. 90	*** 13. 94
Partial scores........	* 7. 04	** 10. 27

[1] Group size: I(N=27), II(N=15), Y(N=15).
* Significant at the 0.05 level.
** Significant at the 0.01 level.
*** Significant at the 0.001 level.

probabilities, shown in table 10, tested the null hypothesis against the alternate hypothesis that the old groups, both separately and combined, would have lower values than the young, and that group II would have lower values than group I. The null hypothesis was rejected in all cases. A me-dian test for each procedure and measure to test for group differences showed that the groups differed significantly in all of these conditions.

Friedman Two-Way Analyses of Variance were used to test the null hypothesis that speed of presentation would not significantly affect responses under either procedure or measure. The results are shown in table 11. For all subjects combined, the null hypothesis could be rejected for both measures of the P procedure, but could not be rejected for either measure of the S procedure. Similar analyses for each group separately are also shown in table 11. In the S procedure, only the Partial Scores of group Y were significant. In the P procedure, all except the Scores of group II were significant. In short, presentation rate did not affect either Scores or Partial Scores in the S procedure, but significantly affected both measures in the P procedure. This seemed to hold both for the groups separately and for the pooled subjects. However, adding the χ^2 (and the degrees of freedom) indicated significance for the Partial Scores of the S procedure.

TABLE 11.—*Dichotic digit span*

Friedman 2-way analyses of variance on the effects of presentation rates (χ^2_R, 3 degrees of freedom)

Source	Number	S procedure		P procedure	
		Score	Partial Score	Score	Partial Score
All subjects.....................	57	4. 15	3. 45	*** 21. 49	*** 43. 25
Group Y.......................	15	6. 86	* 8. 42	** 12. 56	*** 16. 82
Group I.......................	27	3. 44	6. 03	* 9. 14	*** 17. 13
Group II......................	15	1. 46	3. 62	3. 70	** 14. 66
Sum of groups [1].............	....	11. 76	* 18. 07	** 25. 40	*** 48. 61

[1] With 9 degrees of freedom.
* Significant at the 0.05 level.
** Significant at the 0.01 level.
*** Significant at the 0.001 level.

Since the groups differed significantly in both procedures, and since the presentation rates differed significantly in the P procedure, some further breakdown of the data was required. Unfortunately, the author knows of no nonparametric techniques which would be analogous to a parametric mixed model analysis of variance with subsequent evaluation of significant differences and interactions by means of the Scheffé (or a similar test). Therefore, Kolmogorov-Smirnov tests were performed, at each presentation rate for each procedure. Sixty-four tests were required, which would give rise to the possibility of spurious significances. To guard against beta errors (falsely rejecting the null hypothesis), the discussion of significant differences in table 12 will be restricted to those differences that are in a sense fragments of significant differences found in the overall tests.

As was discussed earlier, the sign test showed that the groups differed significantly from each other in dichotic digit spans. The K–S tests show that group Y differs significantly from group O (groups I and II combined) in 15 out of 16 conditions, from group I in 12 out of 16, and from group II in all 16 conditions. Group I differs significantly from group II in only 2 out of 16 conditions. Therefore, the difference between the young group and both old groups is far greater than that between the two old groups. However, group Y tends to differ more from group II than from group I. The only condition in which no significant group differences appear is the Partial Scores, S procedure, 2.0-second rate. In the S procedure Partial Scores, this is the rate at which the young group shows its worst performance, as shown in table 9. Since the summed χ^2 over groups (with summed degrees of freedom, viz, 9) for the S procedure Partial Scores was significant, while the χ^2 for all subjects pooled in this condition was not significant, it is possible that there was a significant interaction between groups and presentation rates.

TABLE 12.—*Dichotic digit span*

Comparison of groups in each procedure and measure at each presentation rate
[Kolmogorov-Smirnov Test]

Procedure	Presentation rate	D Y vs. O	D Y vs. I	K_D Y vs. II	D I vs. II
S procedure scores............	2.0	** 0.462	0.385	** 9	0.216
	1.5	** .543	** .547	** 10	.364
	1.0	** .677	** .644	** 11	.156
	.5	** .543	** .547	* 8	.169
S procedure partial scores........	2.0	.356	.332	6	.178
	1.5	** .538	** .540	** 9	.393
	1.0	** .724	** .681	** 12	.186
	.5	** .566	** .621	* 7	.214
P procedure scores............	2.0	** .623	** .599	** 10	.112
	1.5	** .490	.392	** 10	.341
	1.0	** .552	* .488	** 10	.341
	.5	** .462	* .421	* 8	.134
P procedure partial scores........	2.0	** .605	** .533	** 11	.326
	1.5	** .557	* .422	** 12	.393
	1.0	** .599	* .488	** 12	* .430
	.5	** .385	.303	** 10	* .460

* Significant at the 0.05 level.
** Significant at the 0.01 level.

Only group Y showed a significant rate effect in this condition, which would support this inference. (Unfortunately, the author knows of no direct way of testing for interactions in this type of analysis.) In the P procedure, all groups showed a parallel tendency for Scores and Partial Scores to decrease as the presentation rate increased. The failure of group II to show significance in the P Scores probably was due to the extreme clustering of values at the minimum Score.

The reason that both Scores and Partial Scores were obtained in the dichotic digit span was to test the null hypothesis against the alternative that older subjects would tend to have lower Scores relative to their Partial Scores than the young. This could mean that older subjects were less able to organize properly the fragments of information they had obtained. Therefore, the correlation between Scores and Partial Scores should be lower for the old than for the young. Because of the nonnormal distribution of the data, Spearman rank correlations were computed (table 13). All the correlations were significant.

The next problem was to determine whether these significant correlations differed significantly from each other. The rationale for using Cochran's Q test for this is described below.

Kendall (1955, p. 63) stated that the nonnull distribution of r_s is not known, and that the limit of the variance of the nonnull r_s is $\frac{3}{n}(1-p^2)$. Any test of difference between two nonnull r_s that uses this variance is extremely conservative. Therefore, a more powerful method was devised by the author. The usual formula for the Spearman rank correlation coefficient is:

$$r=1-\frac{6\Sigma d^2}{N^3-N}$$

where Σd^2 is the sum of the squares of differences in the two ranks, and N is the number of subjects. This shows that for a fixed N, the magnitude of the r_s depends purely on the sum of the d^2, if no correction for ties is made. The greater disparity in the rank ordering of the two variables, the greater the absolute rank differences and the square of the differences. Any two r_s obtained from samples of equal N's (or from the same sample) will be related by the distributions of their d^2. Therefore a distribution-free test of the distribution of the two samples of d^2 can be used to determine the probability that the two samples have come from the same population. For two samples, the McNemar test for the significance of changes (McNemar, 1955) can be applied to the distribution of d^2 around their combined median. (The sign test is better when N is small.) When there are more than two samples, Cochran's Q test (Cochran, 1950) can be used. For simplicity of computation, the absolute magnitudes of d ($/d/$) can be used. The advantage of these tests lies in their applicability to multiple determinations (two or more sets of $/d/$) obtained from one sample of subjects. As Cochran (1950) has pointed out, these tests do not depend on the total number of N, but only on those rows (subjects) which do not have uniform signs in the k conditions. In order to maximize the latter group, it is desirable to fix the boundary of division as close to the actual median as possible; i.e., to have the number of 1's and 0's as nearly equal as possible. If the Q test proves significant, it is interpreted to mean that the distribution of $/d/$ above the median, (or below the median) differs significantly among the k conditions. One may then infer that the degrees of association (the r_s) are different under the different conditions. When $k>2$, and the Q test has been found significant, it is possible to partition the Q in the manner described by Cochran (1950), and/or apply the McNemar or Sign test to any two of the k conditions, in order to ascertain which conditions differ significantly in the distributions of their $/d/$, and therefore presumably in the magnitude of their r_s.

The results of the Q tests are shown in table 13. In the S procedure, only group I showed significance. Since Q tends to distribute as chi-square with appropriate degrees of freedom, and since the three groups are independent, the Q's and degrees of freedom were summed across groups. This Q was significant. A Q obtained by combining all subjects was not significant. This probably indicates that there is an interaction between groups and presentation rates. Only group I showed significant differences among rates. Group I showed a steady decrease in the r_s as presentation rate increased. Although neither group Y nor

TABLE 13.—*Dichotic digit span*

Spearman rank correlation of Scores and Partial Scores

S procedure

Source	Presentation speed r_s				Friedman $\chi^2 R$	Cochran Q	Fisher group χ^2	p of σ_{sD} Max. vs. min. r_s	Sign test (2 tailed) of significantly different speeds
	2.0	1.5	1.0	0.5					
Group Y................	** 0.89	** 0.94	* 0.95	** 0.96	2.66	6.32	1.53	≤ .39	....
Group I................	** .87	** .77	** .74	** .66	4.72	** 15.54	3.25	≤ .24	{2.0 vs. 0.5.** / 1.5 vs. 0.5.*
Group II...............	** .66	** .78	** .67	** .83	1.10	.63	1.25	≤ .35	....
Y+I+II................ (9 d.f.)					8.48	** 22.49			
All subjects........... (3 d.f.)					1.03	6.55			

P procedure

Source	Presentation speed r_s				Friedman $\chi^2 R$	Cochran Q	Fisher group χ^2	p of σ_{sD} Max. vs. min. r_s	Sign test (2 tailed) of significantly different speeds
	2.0	1.5	1.0	0.5					
Group Y................	** 0.99	** 0.93	** 0.79	** 0.83	** 11.66	** 16.84	** 14.71	≤ 0.25	{2.0 vs. 1.0.* / 2.0 vs. 0.5.** / 1.5 vs. 0.5.*
Group I................	** .75	** .84	** .91	** .75	5.41	7.22	5.46	≤ .26	....
Group II...............	** .90	** .84	** .82	** .69	5.46	* 10.00	2.31	≤ .29	1.0 vs. 0.5.*
Y+I+II................ (9 d.f.)					** 22.53	** 34.06			
All subjects........... (3 d.f.)					*** 17.49	** 24.63			

* Significant at the 0.05 level.
** Significant at the 0.01 level.
*** Significant at the 0.001 level.

group II showed significant differences for presentation rates, the r_s tended to increase with increasing presentation rate.

The Friedman Two-Way Analysis of Variance technique can be used instead of the Cochran Q. The advantage of the Friedman over Cochran Q is that it utilizes the ordinal nature of the $/d/$ and does not require the dichotomization of the $/d/$ around the common median. In addition, the Friedman is dependent on the size of the N. The Friedman $\chi^2 R$ values are shown in table 13. Using the additive nature of χ^2, the combined group $\chi^2 R$ was also computed, as well as the $\chi^2 R$ for all subjects combined. It is immediately apparent that the $\chi^2 R$ is more conservative than the Q. In order to have a standard of comparison, it was assumed that r_s was equivalent to a Pearson r, and a Fisher χ^2 test for homogeneity was obtained for each group in each procedure (Snedecor, 1946, pp. 151–155). These values are shown also in table 13. It is apparent that these values correspond rather closely to those obtained by the Friedman $\chi^2 R$. Several points should be kept in mind. The χ^2 test for homogeneity of r assumes that the different r's are independent. The values of r_s tend to be lower than the values of r when both are applied to the same data. Both of these factors tend to make the Fisher χ^2 test conservative. Therefore, the Friedman $\chi^2 R$ is probably a reasonable and conservative test of the homogeneity of several r_s. The Q test probably represents the less conservative confidence bounds.

Testing the rates against each other for group I using the Sign test on the Q test tabulation showed that the 0.5 rate differed significantly from the 1.5 and the 2.0 rates. Testing the difference between the 0.5 and 2.0 rates by a standard error of difference techniques, using the formula,

$$c_eD = \frac{r_{s1}-r_{s2}}{\sqrt{\frac{3}{n_1}(1-r_{s_1}{}^2)+\frac{3}{n_2}(1-r_{s2}{}^2)}}$$

a $p \leq 0.24$ was obtained. This is an ultraconservative estimate, compared to the $p < 0.01$ obtained by the Sign test. If one were to assume that the r_s are equal to Pearson r, the two r fall close to each other's 0.01 confidence limits, which is roughly the same as found by the author's technique. The advantage of the latter technique is that no assumption need be made about the distributions. The Sign test was then repeated on all rates within every group and procedure where the Q test had been significant. Those speeds which showed significant differences by this technique are shown in table 13. Repeating the Sign tests using the tabulation obtained for the Friedman test on the speeds for group Y, P procedure (the only case where the $\chi^2 R$ was significant) showed somewhat higher p values (two-tailed) than were found by the aforementioned method on the Q distribution. Only speed 2.0 vs. 0.5 was significant, with a $p < 0.01$. For this comparison, the seD had $p \leq 0.25$.

Comparing groups for all speeds in both procedures, the young group had higher r_s than either old group in seven out of eight comparisons. As was mentioned earlier, the proposed alternative to the null hypothesis was that group Y would have higher r_s than group I which would have higher r_s than group II. The single-tailed p value of comparison between young and either old group is 0.035. Therefore, the first null hypothesis is rejected in favor of the alternative. Group I has r_s larger than group II five out of eight times, which has a single tailed p of 0.855. Therefore, the second null hypothesis cannot be rejected.

Summarizing the dichotic digit span results, it appears that old subjects perform significantly worse than the young, and group II slightly worse than group I. In agreement with the findings of Broadbent (1955), the speed of presentation has little effect in the S-type response but a large effect on the P-type response. In the S response, speed seems to affect the young groups more than the old, perhaps because of the generally worse performance of the old. The effect of speed seems to be about the same for all groups in the P procedure. There is a higher degree of association (r_s) between dichotic span Scores and fragments that compose it (Partial scores) for the young than for the old. Speed of presentation affects the r_s only in the P procedure, and the effect is specifically demonstrable only for group Y.

It was desired to relate diotic digit span to dichotic digit span by testing the null hypothesis against the alternative that old subjects would do disproportionately worse than young subjects in the two channel (dichotic) situation as compared to the single channel (diotic) situation. Ratios of average dichotic span/average diotic span were obtained for all subjects. The alternative to the null hypothesis was that group Y would have higher ratios than group I, and that group I would have higher ratios than group II. Using the Mann-Whitney U test, the null hypothesis was rejected with $p < 0.001$ and $p < 0.04$, respectively. Evidently, the two-channel situation is disproportionately more difficult for the old, especially the less healthy old, than for the young, compared to the single channel situation.

DELAYED SPEECH FEEDBACK

Since the initial report of the effects of delayed speech feedback on speech by Lee (1950), there have been various reports of studies on the nature of this phenomenon. Black (1951) showed that the effect was dependent on the length of the delay, being maximal at 0.18 second. Butler and Galloway (1957) found that higher feedback intensities were required to show the length of delay effect. Spilka (1954) sought to relate the phenomenon to various personality characteristics; of particular note was the lack of correlation with measures of rigidity. Kline, Guze, and Haggerty (1954) found that hypnotic deafness reduced but did not abolish the effect. Beaumont and Foss (1957) found a low but significant correlation between delayed speech feedback effects and star tracing; and a significant difference in effect between showing and not showing Einstellung on Luchin's test. Weiss [3] found that the effect was significantly increased under the influence of secobarbital, but unaffected by the influence of chlorpromazine. The present experiment was designed to explore the effects of age on delayed speech feedback.

Methods

The basic instrument used was a dual-channel tape recorder, adapted to provide a continuously variable time delay from recording to playback. The delays used were 0.1, 0.2, and 0.3 second. A normal feedback time was obtained by tapping the recording amplifier. During most of the experiment, amplifier gains were so adjusted as to give an amplification of unity on both normal and delayed feedback conditions. During those parts of the experiment designated "high," the gain was so adjusted as to give an output of 85 db for an input of 60 db on both normal and delayed feedback. With this gain, as input rose, output rose rapidly to a plateau of about 110 to 115 db. Input to the ears was diotic. By means of a toggle switch, the experimenter could quickly switch the output from nor-

[3] Weiss, A. D. The effects of chlorpromazine and secobarbital on delayed speech feedback. (Unpublished, in preparation.)

mal feedback to the preset delayed feedback.

The subject was seated in front of a microphone, wearing earphones. He also wore a throat microphone, the output of which was fed to a penrecorder. The pen record was used only for timing purposes. The subject was given a standard paragraph, which consisted of many common polysyllabic words and was neutral in content. He was instructed to read the paragraph out loud as he would normally read out loud. He was told that he would hear his own voice through the earphones, sometimes as he would normally hear himself and sometimes like an echo, but simply to disregard what he heard and to continue to read the passage as normally as possible.

There were two orders of experimental conditions, each given to alternate subjects.

Order I: normal, 0.1 second delay, 5 minutes rest; normal, 0.2 second delay, 5 minutes rest; normal, 0.3 second delay, 5 minutes rest; normal, normal (high intensity), 0.2 second delay (high intensity).

Order II: same as order I, except that the order of delays was 0.3 second, 0.2 second, 0.1 second, and 0.2 (high intensity).

Because many of the older subjects were foreign born and did not read as fluently as the younger subjects, a speech disruption ratio was devised. This ratio was computed by dividing the reading time at a given delay condition by half the sum of the reading times obtained with the two immediately adjacent normal conditions. The high intensity delay was divided by the high intensity normal.

The second measure used in this experiment was the voice intensity. This was measured by means of a sound level meter, set to curve C with a heavily damped response. Measurements were made by playing back the tape with the earphone approximated to the microphone of the sound level meter. The average of the three peak responses during each reading

was used for the intensity measure. All intensity measures during unity gain are comparable, as are those during high gain; however, high gain and unity gain measures are not comparable.

Results

The mean time derived speech disruption ratios are shown in table 14.

TABLE 14.—*Mean speech disruption time ratios*

[Delay (seconds)]

Group	Number	Unit gain feedback			0.2 high gain feedback
		0.1	0.2	0.3	
I.........	20	1.22	1.32	1.27	1.53
II.........	14	1.15	1.20	1.24	1.52
Y.........	14	1.18	1.23	1.28	1.44
Total.....	......	1.19	1.26	1.27	1.50

The analysis of variance performed on these data (table 15) showed that only the delay conditions were significantly different. A Scheffé on the delay conditions showed that the high gain feedback at 0.2 second differed ($p < 0.05$) from each of the unitary gain delay conditions, which did not differ among themselves. This lack of difference due to different delays at normal speech feedback intensity and the increased effectiveness of high intensity speech feedback is in accord with the findings of Butler and Galloway (1957).

The results of the vocal intensity measurements are shown in table 16. Since the vocal intensity measurements under unitary gain and high gain feedback conditions were not directly comparable, two analyses of variance were performed. In the first (table 17), only the unitary gain feedback delays were compared. Only the delay conditions were found to differ significantly at minimum degrees of freedom.

The delay $\times$ group interaction was highly significant ($p<0.001$) at maximum degrees of freedom but not quite significant ($0.05<p<0.10$) at minimum degrees of freedom. A Scheffé on the delay conditions showed that all the delayed feedback conditions differed significantly from all the normal feedback conditions ($p<0.05$), but that neither the delays nor the normal conditions differed significantly among themselves. The nature of the questionably significant group $\times$ delay interaction was not readily apparent on inspection of the means. There was a tendency in both groups to show increasing vocal intensities as the delay period increased. However, none of the simple contrasts between any two pairs of means reached the 0.05 level of significance in a Scheffé test, using maximum degrees of freedom.

As was mentioned earlier, the vocal intensity measures under unitary gain conditions were not directly comparable to those under high gain conditions. However, it was thought desirable to make such a comparison in order to test the null hypothesis against the alternative that there would be an interaction between groups and feedback intensities, the older subjects showing a greater difference between unitary and high gain than the young. The mean intensity measurements are shown in table 17. The difference scores, $D_{.02}=$ normal$_2$ and $D_{.02\,high}=$ normal$_{high}$ were computed for each subject and subjected to an analysis of variance (table 18).

It was found that the gain conditions differed significantly, as did the groups. However, there was no significant conditions $\times$ groups interaction. Perusal of the group means showed the young group was less affected by the feedback delay than either old group; the two old groups differed very little between themselves. All groups were more affected by the high gain condition than by the unitary gain condition.

In summary, there appeared to be no age differences in delayed speech feedback effects, except for vocal intensity at 0.2 second feedback delay when both unitary and high gain feedback were employed. At normal feedback intensities, variation in feedback delay (within the range of 0.1 to 0.3 second) showed no significant effect. Increased feedback intensity significantly affected the measured responses.

INTERCORRELATIONS OF MEASURES

The nine variables, Nos. 24 through 32, listed on tables 1 and 2 of chapter 10, were chosen as being representative of major fac-

TABLE 15.—*Analysis of variance of time ratios*

Source	Degrees of freedom	Sums of squares	F
Delays (D)	3	2. 7586	*** 49. 44
Groups (G)	2	. 1239	<1
Order (O)	1	. 2008	1. 36
G×O	2	. 2039	<1
Individuals within groups and orders	42	6. 1915	....
D×O	3	. 0363	<1
D×G	6	. 1176	1. 05
D× Ind. w.g.o.	126	2. 3432	....
D×G×O	6	. 1056	<1
Total	191	12. 0814	....

*** Significant at the 0.001 level with minimum degrees of freedom.

TABLE 16.—*Mean delayed speech feedback vocal intensities (db)*

Group	Number	Unitary feedback gain							High gain [1]	
		Normal$_1$	$D_{.1}$	Normal$_2$	$D_{.2}$	Normal$_3$	$D_{.3}$	Normal$_4$	Normal$_{high}$	$D_{.2\ high}$
I............	20	58.8	67.0	59.1	67.6	59.2	67.7	59.3	84.0	95.4
II...........	14	62.4	71.6	63.1	72.3	61.9	72.7	62.7	87.2	97.5
Y...........	14	61.8	67.1	62.0	66.6	61.4	66.6	62.6	81.7	90.9
Total........	48	60.8	68.2	61.0	68.6	60.5	68.7	61.6	84.7	94.7

[1] The db values in the high gain conditions are not directly comparable to those in the unitary gain conditions.

I-135

TABLE 17.—*Analysis of variance of vocal intensity in the unitary gain conditions*

Source	Degrees of freedom	Sums of squares	F	p [1]	
				Max. d.f.	Min. d.f.
Delays (D)	6	4,919	86.63	....	(***)
Groups (G)	2	922	2.70	....	....
Orders (O)	1	2	<1	....	....
Individuals within groups and orders	42	7,177	....	....	....
G×O	2	274	<1	....	....
D×O	6	16	<1	....	....
D×G	12	326	2.87	(***)	....
D×G×O	12	62	<1	....	....
D×Ind. w.g.o	252	2,385	....	....	....
Total	335	16,083	....	....	....

[1] See text, p. 24.
*** Significant at the 0.001 level.

tors seemingly involved in the experiments. Discussion here will be limited to these variables.

Variable 24, audiometric hearing loss in the better ear at 2,000 cps, is considered important in that hearing at this frequency is important in normal communication. It does not correlate significantly with any of the other variables.

Variable 25, two-click discrimination, which measures simple auditory temporal discrimination, also shows no significant correlations with the other variables.

Variable 26, sum of click responses, correlates significantly with variable 29, the "S" response. Variable 29 also correlates significantly with variable 27, the sum of click response time. These variables may conceivably represent a sensory storage system, the capacity of which tends to decline with age.

Variable 28, the diotic digit span at 1 second, correlates significantly with variable 30, the "P" response. These variables may conceivably represent a perceptual storage system, the capacity of which declines with

TABLE 18.—*Analysis of variance of the effect of feedback gain on vocal intensity*

Source	Degrees of freedom	Sums of squares	F
Delays (D)	1	190	*6.44
Groups (G)	2	172	*4.20
Orders (O)	1	1	<1
G×O	2	41	<1
Individuals within groups and orders	42	1,239	....
D×G	2	43	1.57
D×O	1	1	<1
D×G×O	2	32	1.17
D×Ind. w.g.o	42	574	....
Total	95	2,293	....

*Significant at the 0.05 level.

age independently of the sensory storage system. The significant correlation holding between variable 28 and variable 31, the speech disruption time ratio at 0.2-second delay, is difficult to explain; particularly since variable 31 does not change with age, while variable 28 shows an age related decline. In order to explore further the nature of this significant relationship, the 1.0-second diotic digit span condition was correlated with the 0.2-second delay high feedback gain (table 19). For control, the unitary gain and high gain feedback conditions were correlated also. The same correlations were obtained for the young group. The digit span correlation with $D_{.2}$ was positive and significant for both age groups, and the two correlations did not differ significantly from each other. The correlations between digit span and $D_{.2\ high}$ were lower for both groups; the correlation for the old was not significant, while that for the young was negative and significant. These two correlations did differ significantly. The correlations between $D_{.2}$ and $D_{.2\ high}$ were positive and significant for both groups, but were not significantly different from each other. Evidently, digit span and sensitivity to speech feedback interference are not uniformly related, since low spans tend to go with low sensitivity in moderate

feedback interference but with high sensitivity in strong interference.

The significant correlation between variable 31 and variable 32, the speech disruption intensity ratio, 0.2-second delay, shows that there is some commonality of these two response measures; it is rather surprising that the correlation is only 0.33. The small number of significant correlations found among these eight variables, plus their seeming representativeness of other variables not carried forward into the matrix, should allow for a goodly representation of the factors involved in the experiments on auditory perception to be carried forward into the interdisciplinary correlations.

SUMMARY AND CONCLUSIONS

A series of experiments on age changes in auditory processes was conducted in order to differentiate better between "sensory" and "perceptual" processes, and to see how such measures might relate to physiological, psychiatric, sociological, and other psychological measures. The subjects for these experiments were 47 male volunteers over 65 years of age and 15 healthy young male volunteers. The older group was subdivided into group I of 27 clinically healthy men, and group II of 20 men with asymptomatic or subclinical diseases, five of whom

TABLE 19.—*Some relationships between the diotic digit span and the delayed speech feedback time ratio*

Variables	Correlations		χ^2 for homogeneity
	Old (I+II)	Young	
1 second digit span vs. $D_{.2}$ [1]	** 0.42	** 0.68	. . . .
1 second digit span vs. $D_{.2\ high}$	.27	* −.53	** 6.67
$D_{.2}$ vs. $D_{.2\ high}$	** .42	** .74	2.11

[1] $D_{.2}$ is the time ratio at 0.2 second delay for the delayed speech feedback procedure, using unitary feedback gain. $D_{.2\ high}$ refers to the same procedure at the high feedback gain, 0.2 second delay.
* Significant at the 0.05 level.
** Significant at the 0.01 level.

had only latent hypertension. An additional group of seven men with evidence of clinical diseases of various diagnoses was studied for special purposes.

1. In the clinical study, consisting of otological examination and air conduction audiometry, all groups save one showed findings consistent with those normally described for their ages; the asymptomatic disease group included several subjects with severe hearing loss. The degree of hearing loss in latently hypertensive subjects did not differ from that in healthy old subjects. There was no greater difference in hearing between pairs of healthy old ears than between pairs of healthy young ears; however, the clinically diseased old did show an increased difference between the two ears.

2. In the click perception study, measurements of intensity thresholds and the temporal discrimination threshold, and judgments of numerousness were obtained. Age changes in intensity thresholds corresponded closely to those found audiometrically. The temporal discrimination threshold of the healthy old did not differ from that of the healthy young; the less healthy old showed a rise in this threshold. This rise was not shown to be related to changes in intensity threshold. In the judgment of numerousness, in which the subjects were required to count the number of clicks presented, all subjects showed increasing perceptual loss as the number of stimuli and their rate of presentation were increased, the old subjects to a greater degree than the young. This age difference correlated neither with intensity threshold nor with temporal discrimination threshold. In terms of the definitions stated in the introduction, intensity and temporal discrimination thresholds are measures of sensory functions, while number judgment is a measure of perception. Therefore, age changes in sensation and perception are not necessarily correlated. The speed of the subjects' responses decreased as stimulus number and presentation rate increased, but no age differences were found here.

3. In the diotic digit span experiment, old subjects were found to have a digits forward span of about six digits, and the young subjects of about seven digits. In the dichotic digit span experiment, where subjects were presented with a different number to each ear simultaneously, the old subjects performed considerably worse than the young. The healthy old performed better than the other old subjects. Further analysis showed that the old subjects had difficulty not only in retaining the digits but also in maintaining them in proper order. The nonparametric method developed by the author to make this comparison is discussed in detail in the text.

The two types of responses required in the dichotic digit span were thought to measure a type of sensory storage system and a type of perceptual storage system. Both of these systems seem to decline with age, but independently of each other. The measure of the sensory storage system correlated significantly with the judgment of numerousness; the measure of the perceptual storage system correlated significantly with the diotic digit span.

Comparing the ratios of dichotic spans/ diotic span for the different groups showed that the old had a disproportionate decrease in the dichotic spans, more marked for the less healthy old. Evidently, the old subjects had disproportionate difficulty in simultaneously monitoring two channels.

4. In the delayed speech feedback experiment, very little difference was found among the groups. Evidently, the speech feedback mechanisms show little if any change with age, at least in comparison with the large interindividual variability found in all age groups.

REFERENCES

BEASLEY, W. C. 1940. The general problem of deafness in the population. *Laryngoscope.* 50, 856–905.

BEAUMONT, J. T., and FOSS, B. M. 1957. Individual differences in reacting to delayed auditory feedback. *Brit. J. Psychol., 48,* 85–89.

BLACK, J. W. 1951. The effect of delayed sidetone upon vocal rate and intensity. *J. Speech & Hearing Disorders, 16,* 56–60.

BRAUN, H. 1959. Perceptual processes. Chapter XVI in *Handbook of Aging and the Individual: Psychological and Biological Aspects.* J. E. Birren (ed.), Chicago: The University of Chicago Press.

BROADBENT, D. E. 1954. The role of auditory localization in attention and memory span. *J. Exp. Psychol., 47,* 191–196.

————. 1956. Successive responses to simultaneous stimuli. *Quart. J. Exp. Psychol., 8,* 145–152.

————. 1957a. A mechanical model for human attention and immediate memory. *Psychol. Rev., 64,* 205–215.

————. 1957b. Immediate memory and simultaneous stimuli. *Quart. J. Exp. Psychol., 9,* 1–11.

————. 1958. *Perception and communication.* New York: Pergamon.

BROMLEY, D. B. 1958. Some effects of age on short term learning and remembering. *J. Gerontol., 13,* 398–406.

DE BRUÏNE-ALTES, J. C. 1946. The symptom of regression in different kinds of deafness. Thesis, Groningen: Wolters.

BURKHARD, M. D., and CORLISS, E. L. R. 1954. The response of earphones in ears and couplers. *J. Acoust. Soc. Am., 26,* 679–685.

BUTLER, R. A., and GALLOWAY, F. T. 1957. Factoral analysis of the delayed speech feedback phenomenon. *J. Acoust. Soc. Am., 29,* 632–635.

CHEATHAM, P. G., and WHITE, C. T. 1954. Temporal numerosity: III. Auditory perception of number. *J. Exp. Psychol., 47,* 425–428.

CHERRY, E. C. 1953. Some experiments on the recognition of speech, with one and with two ears. *J. Acoust. Soc. Am., 25,* 975–979.

COCHRAN, W. G. 1950. The comparison of percentage in matched samples. *Biometrika, 37,* 256–266.

DOPPELT, J. E., and WALLACE, W. L. 1955. The performance of older people on the Wechsler Adult Intelligence Scale, *Am. Psychol., 10,* 338–339.

EXNER, S. 1875. Experimentelle Untersuchung der einfachsten psychischen Prozesse. *Pflüg. Arch. Ges. Physiol., 11,* 403–432.

FLEISCHER, K. 1956. Histologische und audiometrische Studie über der Alternsbedingten Struktur- und Funktionswandel des Innenohres. *Arch. Ohren-usw. Heilk, u.Z. Hals-usw. Heilk., 170,* 142–167.

FRIEDMAN, M. 1937. The use of ranks to avoid the assumption of normality implicit in the analysis of variance. *J. Am. Statist. Assoc., 32,* 675–701.

GALAMBOS, R., SHEATZ, G., and VERNIER, V. G. 1955. Electrophysiologic correlates of a conditioned response in cats. *Science, 123,* 376–377.

GARNER, W. R. 1951. The accuracy of counting repeated short tones. *J. Exp. Psychol., 41,* 310–316.

GEISSER, S., and GREENHOUSE, S. W. 1958. An extension of Box's results on the use of the F distribution in multivariate analysis. *Ann. Math. Statist., 29,* 885–891.

HERNANDEZ-PEON, R., SCHERRER, H., and JOUVET, M. 1955. Modification of electric activity in cochlear nucleus during "attention" in unanesthetized cats. *Science, 123,* 331–332.

KENDALL, M. G. 1955. *Rank correlation methods.* 2d ed. New York: Hafner.

KLINE, M. U., GUZE, H., and HAGGERTY, A. D. 1954. An experimental study of the nature of hypnotic deafness effects of delayed speech feedback. *J. Clin. Exp. Hypnosis, 2,* 145–156.

LEE, B. S. 1950. Some effects of side tone delay. *J. Acoust. Soc. Am., 22,* 639–640.

McNEMAR, Q. 1955. *Psychological Statistics.* 2d ed. New York: Wiley.

MONTGOMERY, H. C. 1932. Do our ears grow old? *Bell Lab. Rec., 10,* 311–313.

PESTALOZZA, G., and SHORE, I. 1955. Clinical evaluation of presbycusis on the basis of different tests of auditory function. *Laryngoscope, 65,* 1136–1163.

ROSÉE, B. Graf de la. 1953. Untersuchungen über das normale Hörvermögen in den verschiedenen Lebensaltern, unter besonderer Berücksichtigung der Prüfung mit dem Audiometer. *Zeitschrift f. Laryngol. Rhinol. u. Otol., 32,* 414–420.

ROSENZWEIG, M. R., and ROSENBLITH, W. A. 1953. Responses to auditory stimuli at the cochlea and at the auditory cortex. *Psychol. Monog., 67,* No. 13.

SCHEFFÉ, H. 1953. A method for judging all contrasts in the analysis of variance. *Biometrika, 40,* 87–104.

SIEGEL, S. 1956. *Nonparametric statistics for the behavioral sciences.* New York: McGraw-Hill.

SNEDECOR, G. W. 1946. *Statistical methods.* 4th ed. Ames, Iowa: The Iowa State College Press.

SPILKA, B. 1954. Relationships between certain aspects of personality and some vocal effects of delayed speech feedback, *J. Speech & Hearing Disorders, 19,* 491–503.

STEINBERG, J. C., MONTGOMERY, H. C., and GARDNER, M. B. 1940. Results of the World's Fair Hearing Tests. *Bell Telephone System Technical Publications, Monograph B 1256.*

TAUBMAN, R. E. 1950. Studies in judged number; I. The judgment of auditory number. *J. Gen. Psychol., 43,* 167–194.

WECHSLER, D. 1955. *Manual for the Wechsler Adult Intelligence Scale.* New York: The Psychological Corporation.

WEISS, A. D. 1959. Sensory functions. Chapter XV in *Handbook of Aging and the Individual: Psychological and Biological Aspects.* J. E. Birren (ed.). Chicago: The University of Chicago Press.

CHAPTER 10

Interrelations of Mental and Perceptual Tests Given to Healthy Elderly Men

by James E. Birren, Jack Botwinick,
Alfred D. Weiss, and Donald F. Morrison

INTRODUCTION

The purpose of this analysis and discussion is to develop a parsimonious description of what the present data on mental and perceptual measurements reveal about aging. With repeated reports in the literature of significant changes with age in sensory, perceptual, and intellectual functions, interest has developed in typifying the changes in terms of general processes.

The first task was to account for the intercorrelations of the previously described test variables (ch. 8, 9) on the basis of some smaller number of factors or components. In turn the components were to be interpreted in terms of the presumed psychological processes involved. On the one hand, the present attempt is to determine the minimum number of factors necessary to account for the common variance in a wide range of psychological measurements in older men; and on the other, to reduce a wide range of test scores to a few summarizing independent component scores which could be correlated with physiological, personality, and social psychological variables measured on the same subjects.

MEASUREMENTS

The 32 variables subjected to analysis are described in chapters 8 and 9 and are identified here only by name or phrase. As described previously, all measurements were made individually on each subject and were distributed over a 2-week period during which time the subjects were living within the National Institute of Health Clinical Center. All subjects took the tests in a prescribed order with some variations in time per session depending upon working speed and allowance for possible "fatigue." In the group of 32 variables are many commonly used psychometric devices such as the Raven Progressive Matrices and the WAIS. The majority are less commonly used tests and experimental procedures; these reflect the intent to define the nature of the psychological processes measured by the standard tests as well as contribute to the more abstract problem of describing the organization of cognitive processes in elderly men (table 1).

Methods of Analysis

The 32 measurements obtained on the 47 male subjects were all intercorrelated by computing product-moment correlation coefficients. Missing or incomplete measurements results in some correlations being based on less than 47 subjects: the smallest number of subjects for a single correlation was 33. The correlation matrix is presented in table 2.

The correlation matrix was analyzed using Hotelling's Principal Component Method. About 58 percent of the variance is accounted for by the first five components, and about 30 percent by the first component alone. In table 3 the results of the Principal Component Analysis are given showing the coefficients of each test on the five components.

Computation of Component Scores

On the basis of the Principal Component Analysis, component scores were computed for each subject by multiplying the individual's standard scores on the tests by the coefficients of the tests on the components. In order to derive component scores which would be experimentally independent, an individual test was used in deriving only one component score. Variables having coefficients of 0.23 or higher were used in deriving the component scores. In using a criterion level of 0.23 as a cut-off, three variables were dropped from the 32 variables in computing the component scores (variables, 5, 22, and 30, of table 3). The use of 0.23 as a criterion level also minimized the number of variables which might qualify for use in more than one component score. Only five variables (6, 8, 12, 16, and 17, of table 3) were above 0.23 in more than one component. For these five, the variables were only used in computing the component score of the highest coefficient. In table 4 the tests used in deriving the five component scores and the associated coefficients are given. The principal component scores for each subject are presented in table 5.

Results

The means of groups I and II on the five components are presented in table 6. As might be expected from the method of derivation, the component scores are essentially independent measures. In table 7 it may be seen that the highest correlation of the five component scores is only 0.15. In view of this independence it is worth noting that all of the differences in the five component scores were in favor of group I; however, only the difference in component score I

TABLE 2.—*Correlation matrix [1] product moment correlations between all variables of table 1*

	1	2	3	4	5	6	7	8	9	10	11	12	13	14	15	16	17	18	19	20	21	22	23	24	25	26	27	28	29	30	31	32
1	1	76	68	79	35	82	52	49	55	62	38	40	47	-24	46	19	27	04	47	01	-36	02	-16	-35	20	37	42	45	34	31	19	00
2		1	72	71	39	78	37	38	40	49	28	31	43	-17	45	33	41	17	48	11	-36	-10	-20	-46	42	14	39	48	25	17	19	-04
3			1	61	32	63	55	38	48	55	24	28	41	-47	59	57	73	33	46	04	-37	-17	-04	-23	14	03	17	35	07	39	29	07
4				1	39	87	45	44	48	64	40	33	38	-25	58	25	33	18	41	-11	-45	02	-05	-44	12	25	44	47	23	31	17	-08
5					1	41	35	33	39	56	34	49	33	-34	51	43	22	29	33	-11	-20	-13	-01	-32	-08	24	13	61	05	32	21	23
6						1	49	33	42	70	40	35	34	-13	50	29	37	18	54	10	-38	04	-19	-43	14	30	42	56	38	23	20	-13
7							1	40	65	72	53	17	20	-51	40	45	43	-09	45	-10	-53	00	30	-37	03	16	06	25	12	27	23	-04
8								1	46	52	40	53	15	-30	29	19	16	13	08	01	-25	02	-02	-01	13	38	14	35	08	17	10	02
9									1	56	49	56	43	-50	46	37	37	-12	28	-25	-39	10	-07	-28	08	17	07	33	17	48	26	05
10										1	66	51	58	-43	46	41	35	21	40	-18	-37	10	03	-35	-02	22	15	42	-01	41	33	00
11											1	49	15	-25	37	-01	-02	09	07	-07	-35	11	17	-15	04	14	17	26	07	10	04	10
12												1	20	-29	41	23	11	11	19	-22	-13	05	-09	-08	05	21	12	28	17	19	02	10
13													1	-33	24	30	28	-08	30	-19	-08	-21	-08	-30	-22	-05	24	44	03	40	31	18
14														1	-32	-48	-40	-13	-19	32	23	10	-16	16	14	-02	10	-12	09	-31	-08	-09
15															1	40	51	26	44	-18	-33	-06	-08	-34	08	35	23	51	-04	41	27	-02
16																1	78	34	45	04	-21	-04	-15	-18	-10	-30	-08	33	01	37	26	14
17																	1	27	45	07	-29	-10	-07	-27	13	00	-07	31	02	49	21	01
18																		1	-02	17	-07	-01	-13	12	02	00	00	08	12	08	06	02
19																			1	01	-28	07	-09	55	01	20	20	45	15	15	28	-01
20																				1	32	-03	-06	17	-01	-04	13	-11	11	-27	-14	-01
21																					1	-11	-28	60	-11	-06	05	-16	-04	-18	-09	-04
22																						1	08	-15	-03	13	-06	-11	-34	-10	-04	-26
23																							1	-17	-14	-07	-17	-12	-10	07	-07	05
24																								1	05	-01	-19	-27	01	-10	-10	-01
25																									1	07	-15	08	38	14	-17	02
26																										1	29	24	42	29	-22	-04
27																											1	12	-09	-12	-15	-09
28																												1		35	42	14
29																													1	08	-11	-28
30																														1	21	00
31																															1	33
32																																1

[1] Decimal points omitted.

I-145

Tests	Component I	Component II	Component III	Component IV	Component V
1. Information..........................	0.26	0.22	0.00	−0.03	0.04
2. Comprehension.....................	.24	.16	−.18	−.08	.04
3. Arithmetic..........................	.25	−.08	−.20	.00	−.18
4. Similarities.........................	.26	.17	.00	−.12	.00
5. Digit-Span..........................	.20	−.07	.03	.21	.16
6. Vocabulary.........................	.26	.24	−.10	−.09	−.14
7. Digit-Symbol.......................	.23	−.11	.16	−.17	−.11
8. Picture Completion.................	.18	.07	.24	.26	−.16
9. Block Design.......................	.24	−.08	.21	.08	−.01
10. Picture Arrangement...............	.26	−.02	.12	.03	−.02
11. Object Assembly...................	.16	.04	.39	.10	−.02
12. Raven.............................	.17	.03	.24	.30	−.05
13. Wisconsin.........................	.18	−.08	−.08	.04	.40
14. Card Sorting A5 [1]...............	−.16	.27	−.11	−.06	.11
15. Learning DM......................	.23	−.02	−.04	.06	−.06
16. Addition 6........................	.18	−.30	−.29	.07	−.16
17. Alternation 6......................	.19	−.22	−.30	.04	−.27
18. Digits/Sec........................	.06	−.04	−.22	.22	−.30
19. Words Beginning "S"..............	.19	.01	−.19	−.24	.10
20. Line Difference (2.0 Sec. Exp.) [1].	−.04	.18	−.30	.08	−.18
21. Reaction Time [1].................	−.16	.11	−.19	.40	.13
22. Mirror............................	−.01	.09	.15	−.19	−.17
23. Stroop-Ratio [1]..................	−.02	−.21	.27	−.28	−.04
24. Hearing Loss Audio [1]............	−.16	.00	00	.47	−.14
25. 2-Click Discrimination [1].........	.02	.08	.02	.03	−.31
26. Σ of Clicks	.09	.30	.18	.14	−.05
27. Σ of Click Response Time	.09	.38	−.07	−.01	.20
28. 1-Sec. Digit Span.................	.20	−.02	−.07	.12	.29
29. Dichotic Span 1 pr/1.5 Sec.......	.07	.36	−.09	.05	−.01
30. Dichotic Span 1 pr/2.0 Sec.......	.16	−.16	.01	.13	−.05
31. Read T. D–2.....................	.11	−.22	−.12	.03	.32
32. Int. D–2.........................	.02	−.22	.01	.20	.31
Latent Roots.........................	9.68	2.87	2.37	1.90	1.70
Proportion of Variance due to Component percent....	30.25	8.98	7.42	5.95	5.34
Cumulative Proportion of Variance percent....	30.25	39.23	46.65	52.60	57.94

[1] High test score reflects poor performance.

was significant. This leads to the question that will be considered later of whether the difference between groups I and II on component one should be regarded as a superiority of group I or as a deficit related to the health status of group II.

The difference between groups I and II was further explored by regarding each test as a separate item in computing mean standard scores for each subject. In this computation all tests were weighted equally and the individual's standard scores for all tests were averaged. Of the tests listed in table 1, the first 23 tests and the last 9 tests (24–32) were thus combined to yield two mean standard scores for each subject. The last nine tests were those involving aspects of auditory perception.

Table 8 presents the mean standard scores for subject groups I and II. Again the direction of the difference was in favor of group I (better scores) but the differences in means were not statistically significant. A further analysis was made of the mean standard scores by considering subjects with cardiovascular disease as a separate cate-

TABLE 4.—*Tests and coefficients entering into the computation of component scores*

[In computing an individual's component scores, his standard scores on the particular test were multiplied by the appropriate coefficients, and the products summed]

Components

I Stored information achievement		II Enumeration speed		III Flexibility in set		IV Speed of association and reasoning		V Concept formation or stimulus orientation	
Information	0.26	Card Sorting	0.27	Object Assembly	0.39	Picture Completion	0.26	Wisconsin Card	0.40
Comprehension	.24	Addition (6)	−.30	Alternation (6)	−.30	Raven Matrices	.30	Digits/second	−.30
Arithmetic	.25	Clicks	.30	Line Difference	−.30	Verbal Fluency	−.24	2 Click Discrimination	−.31
Similarities	.26	Clicks Response Time	.38			Reaction Time	.40	1 Sec. Digit Span	.29
Vocabulary	.26	Dichotic Span 1 pr/1.5 sec	.36			Stroop-Ratio	−.28	Delayed Speech:	
Digit Symbol	.23					Hearing Loss	.47	Read T. D–2	.32
Block Design	.24							Int. D–2	.31
Picture Arrangement	.26								
Learning	.23								

TABLE 5.—*Standardized principal component scores for each subject*

Subject number	Group	I	II	III	IV	V
1	I	−0.66	−0.44	0.40	0.11	0.14
2	I	−.41	−.29	.18	.49	.70
3	I	−.70	.05	.32	−.61	.15
5	I	1.08	2.32	.64	−.25	1.37
6	I	−.67	.09	−.65	−.27	−.34
7	I	.66	−.28	.46	1.24	.12
8	II	−.84	−1.00	1.34	.29	.15
9	I	−.44	−1.18	−.59	1.62	−.56
10	II	−2.09	−.43	−.20	.12	−.80
11	II	−2.39	1.41	−.24	−1.46	−.10
12	I	−.14	−.17	1.42	.31	1.34
13	I	.10	.78	.53	.70	.07
14	I	−.05	−.38	−.98	−.64	−.65
15	I	.32	−.55	.88	−.38	−.08
16	I	.30	−.71	.30	−1.50	−.07
18	II	.33	.92	−1.34	−.80	.39
19	I	.54	−1.29	−2.59	−1.36	.64
20	I	.37	2.25	.49	.37	−.06
23	II	−.36	−1.77	1.05	1.06	.44
24	II	.92	−.60	−1.42	−1.24	−.42
25	II	−.66	−.06	.49	−.67	.12
26	I	−.96	−.24	1.05	.61	.22
27	II	1.32	.84	−.77	−.78	.62
28	II	−.50	−.14	−.86	1.95	.13
29	II	−.13	−.31	−.89	1.80	−.28
30	I	−2.16	.01	−.65	.93	−.70
31	II	.05	.18	−1.98	−.57	.10
32	II	−.95	.12	−.23	.99	−.11
33	II	.46	1.70	−.76	.65	−1.42
35	II	−.18	−1.99	−.47	−.68	−.66
36	I	−.36	−.26	−.01	−1.93	−.06
38	II	−2.04	.73	−1.42	.12	−1.14
39	II	−.14	−.93	.41	.59	.60
41	II	−1.01	−.28	1.53	−.64	−1.15
42	II	.27	−.10	1.52	−.23	−1.26
47	I	1.93	−.24	1.24	−.55	2.51
49	I	1.30	.04	−.62	.78	.08
50	I	.66	−.72	−.90	−.74	−1.11
51	I	.56	−1.23	−1.14	−.26	1.99
52	II	.69	−.82	.29	−2.78	1.61
53	I	.56	−.45	.89	.88	−1.37
54	I	1.50	.12	−.26	.46	1.81
55	I	2.00	−.09	.79	.88	2.10
56	I	.67	2.22	1.15	−.36	−.89
57	II	−.37	1.31	.74	1.32	.47
58	I	.64	2.01	1.16	.90	−1.42
59	I	1.09	−.08	.63	−.23	−1.10

gory. The point of interest was whether subjects in group II with cardiovascular disease had a different "overall" performance on the various tests than the nonvascular disease subjects. When the subsample of group II with vascular disease was compared with group I the results were significant (table 8). This is seen graphically in figure 1. Figure 1 shows the two mean standard scores for each subject.

In figure 2 the mean WAIS subtest scores of groups I and II have been plotted in relation to the mean of the young standardization group. The subtests with verbal content tend to be high, both relatively and absolutely, in comparison with the subtests

TABLE 6.—*Mean component scores of subjects in groups I and II*

Subjects	Component				
	I	II	III	IV	V
Group I:					
Mean	0.52	0.04	0.10	0.04	0.15
S.D.	1.68	.93	.59	.73	.88
Group II:					
Mean	−.69	−.06	−.10	−.04	−.11
S.D.	1.79	.92	.67	.99	.66
Mean dif.	1.21	.10	.20	.08	.26
t	*2.37	N.S.	N.S.	N.S.	N.S.

*Significant at the 0.05 level.

N.S.=Not significant.

TABLE 7.—*Intercorrelation of component scores of table 5*

Component	I	II	III	IV	V
I		0.01	0.01	−0.01	0.04
II			.13	.09	−.13
III				.15	.15
IV					−.10
V					

TABLE 8.—*Comparison of mean standard scores of tests 1–23 (A) and 24–32 (B) for subjects in groups I and II*

		A Tests 1–23	B Tests 24–32
Group I	Mean	0.16	0.13
	S.D.	0.50	0.39
	Number	27	27
Group II	Mean	−0.22	−0.08
	S.D.	0.59	0.43
	Number	20	16
t I–II		* 2.26	1.55
Group II (vascular disease)	Mean	−0.30	−0.04
	S.D.	0.59	0.31
	Number	14	10
t I–II vascular disease		* 2.36	1.14

* Significant at the 0.05 level.

S.D.=Standard deviation.

I-149

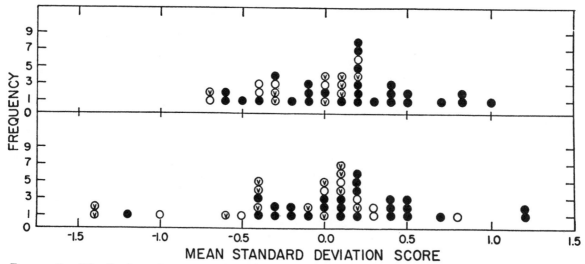

FIGURE 1.—Distribution of mean standard scores for each subject as distributed about the mean expected score of 0. Upper distribution contains the scores on the auditory perception measures (tests 24–32): lower distribution contains the scores on the mental tests (1–23). A plus score lies above the mean (better) and minus score below the mean (poorer) of the distribution. Solid points are subjects in group I: circles are subjects in group II; those containing a *V* represent subjects with some form of vascular disease.

which involve the manipulation of non-verbal symbols or materials. In the "verbal" subtests, the group II mean was almost identical to that of the young standardization group; the mean for group I was somewhat higher. Thus, in general, the older subjects tend to do as well or better than young subjects on verbal tests. Two exceptions occurred as can be seen in figure 2. The similarities subtest of group II and the digit span subtest of both groups were below the mean of the young group. The similarities test appears to be more a matter of manipulation of stored verbal material than it is a measure of the amount of stored information per se. The digit span test seems to be primarily a measure of short-term auditory memory rather than a verbal test: also, it showed little variance in common with the other tests (table 3).

Interpretation

Both groups I and II were lower in the WAIS "performance" subtests than were the young standardization subjects, and the

groups were also significantly different from each other. The difference between group I and young subjects was almost twice as large as that between groups I and II: a mean difference of 2.94 vs. 1.29 respectively. Thus in this sample a greater difference was associated with chronological age than with the difference in health status of the two groups of subjects.

Such inferences were also suggested by the principal component analysis. Table 6 shows that groups I and II differed significantly only in component I. The verbal tests are heavily weighted in this component as can be seen in table 4. The first component is large in the amount of total variance associated with it (30 percent). Tests high in this component, e.g., general information, verbal similarities, vocabulary, and picture completion, which measure achievement which appears to be related to general experience in our culture. In tests of this component, the test or situation always seems simple and unambiguous; the subject either knows or doesn't know or recognize what is called for. If he does not have the answer in his repertoire of experience it is hard for the subject to use context for clues.

Either stored information or general intellectual achievement seem to be an acceptable descriptive phrase for what is being measured in the first component. In young adults this component would be closely related to present level of intellectual functioning, although in older adults there may exist some recession from a previously higher level of functioning. Thus a high first component score would not necessarily be the best index to present level of functioning of perceptual, acquisitive, and manipulative functions, although it would remain a useful measure of achievement or stored information.

Groups I and II did not differ significantly on components II to V. This should not be interpreted as necessarily indicating unchanged functioning with age but merely that the two samples did not differ. Both groups differ from young subjects on many tests, e.g., on speed measures (table 1, ch. 8). When one examines the content of components II through V, there is an impression that the level of performance of the psychological tasks is a matter of the nature of the critical aspects of the task and the individual differences in the subject task approach or work methods. For example, the tasks vary in the extent to which concern with immediate perceptual characteristics of the stimuli is important or conducive to good performance. Some tests such as the

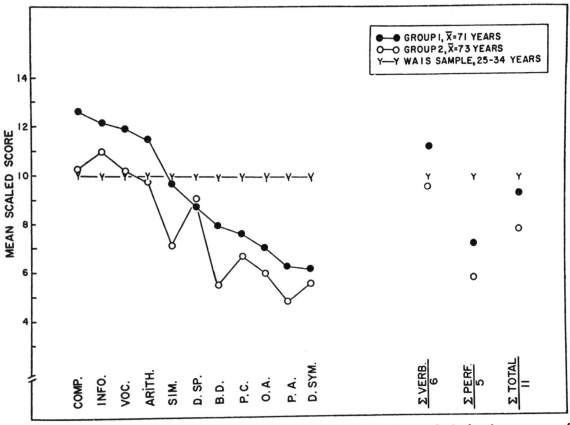

FIGURE 2.—Comparison of subtest scores of the Wechsler Adult Intelligence Scale for three groups of subjects: young adult standardization group and groups I and II of the present study. The expected mean value for young adults (25–34 years) is 10 on each subtest.

Picture Arrangement, require abstraction or integration of perceptual material, the latter being constantly available for review. In still other tasks, such as the Wisconsin Card Sorting test, the process of selection and rejection of mental sets seems to play a role. In this connection the deferral of responses and the resistance to an urge to rapid response is sometimes advantageously made when review of stimuli and manipulations of associations will yield a more general solution.

The interpretations of the psychological content of the components, or what is being measured, is necessarily approached with caution as the common variance becomes increasingly small. In table 3 it is seen that components II to V, respectively, have 8.98, 7.42, 5.95, and 5.34 percent, of the variance associated with them. While a small common variance is not necessarily associated with low reliability, tentativeness is called for before considerable confidence is placed on the generality of the findings.

Component II appears to be a measure of the speed of assimilation of numbers or enumeration and the rapidity of the associated response. In card sorting one must quickly recognize the number of the card and promptly place it into the correct bin. In speed of addition one must also recognize the numbers quickly and perform the familiar operation of arithmetic addition. The component appears to be more of a measure of the speed of association of the relevant response to familiar stimuli than it is a matter of speed of perception of familiar stimuli.

Component III seems to be measuring some aspect of ability to maintain a decision set vs. set flexibility. The Object Assembly of the WAIS and the Line Difference test require a constant set: in the first case some hypothesis must be maintained in order to proceed; in the second case, the

subject must continue to be set to judge which line is smaller, right or left, despite changes in relative size. In contrast to these two, the alternation score is related to the ability to shift sets rapidly, in this instance between addition and subtraction operations.

In component IV, the tests having to do with reasoning or perceiving relations between components (Raven Matrices, WAIS Picture Completion) have opposite signs from those measuring speed (simple auditory reaction time). Given a rapid disposition to respond, performance on a reasoning task might suffer. Hearing loss shows a relation in component IV possibly because the reaction time signal was auditory. Thus some subjects are slow because the stimulus may not be intense despite the attempt to adjust for level of auditory acuity. However, there is an aspect of response speed which is apparently independent of auditory acuity since the verbal fluency scores and Stroop-ratio are also related. What seems to be implicated is the balance between disposition to rapid responses and reasoning, the latter being adversely affected if the subject responds quickly rather than after a period of review and reflection.

Component V appears to involve some feature of concept formation since the highest coefficient is associated with the Wisconsin Card Sorting test. Task vigilance or attention is important. The speed of copying digits is low or negative possibly because a conventional set is advantageous here; the subject recognizes and does the usual in a rapid manner. In the other tests the stimuli are not so familiar hence the subject must attend closely. In this connection it seems plausible that concept formation requires close scrutiny of a class of stimuli and deferral or inhibition of response. It is uncertain whether the component as a whole is measuring concept formation or the ability to maintain a perceptual or stimulus orientation. The latter is favored here since some of the tests represented apparently have little to do with concept formation: although a stimulus orientation is a necessary prerequisite to concept formation.

DISCUSSION

The most general question which can be asked of studies such as the present one is: How do mental abilities change with advancing age? Related is the question of what are the antecedents of the age changes. Although only partial answers are obtained from any single study, the results point to significant differences in psychological performance associated with advancing chonological age, physiological well being, and mental diseases of the senium. The present results show: (1) physiological well being in older men, as might be associated with presence or absence of nonincapacitating conditions of hypertension and arteriosclerosis, is related to differences in performance of tests of mental abilities, and (2) healthy aged men show significant differences in their performance of psychological tests in comparison with young adults.

In the present data the age differences appeared more impressive than the health differences. This point, however, can easily lead to misconceptions if not properly qualified in terms of the sample. That is, health differences in the present study were rather small compared to the range which would likely be found in a large random sample of the population. Disease of advanced state must necessarily lead to a restriction of function, but in older persons apparently many illnesses of a nonapparent or nonincapacitating character are not associated with large psychological differences.

The healthy aged showed both increments and decrements in comparison with previous data from young adults. This is in agreement with previous reports that with advancing age, increases are seen in some verbal abilities and decreases in "perceptual" or nonverbal aspects of mental performance. Literate healthy adults tend to accrue verbal information with advancing age, and perhaps increase storage of nonverbal information as well. The subjects of this study had verbal intelligence scores above the mean of young adults, suggesting that as they advanced in age they had an expanding amount of organized stored information. In the sense that older persons have more information "inside" they know more than young adults. The manipulation and use of this information is an additional issue.

If we characterize the healthy group as having an expanding storage of verbal information with advancing age, it is necessary to account for the lower verbal scores of the group II subjects. Specifically group II subjects showed a verbal performance in several tests lower than group I but about equal to that of the standardization population of young adults. Psychologically the issue is whether the lower scores of group II represents: (1) a failure to gain, (2) a loss, or (3) a sampling or selection difference. The latter seems unlikely since the educational attainment in the two groups is about the same, as was the distribution of occupations (see ch. 2). It seems reasonable to expect that the duration of an illness is related to its effect on the pattern of mental abilities. Gain of verbal information might be expected to take place during all the adult years before the onset of late life illnesses which might restrict the uptake and storage of information. The mean age of the present sample was about 72 years and while the presence of illness might restrict the acquisition of information in the later years, it would be expected, for example, that by the sixth decade a mean vocabulary would be attained that would be higher than young adults. This interpretation gives rise to the hypothesis that late life illnesses of the kind and severity found in group II subjects result in a loss of previously stored information. To some extent gains and losses of information, as in words in the vocabulary, are always going on although the extent of normal turnover in words is an unknown process. What is being said here is that only moderately severe late life illness may be associated with a greater loss than gain in vocabulary.

Not all of verbal ability is described in terms of the age changes in vocabulary. Riegel (see reference in ch. 8) has shown that older persons do best in a synonym test, but less well in tests where the process of selection enters or when a specific relationship has to be recognized as in an analogies test. We should thus distinguish between that which is organized and stored from the manipulation and elicitation of the information in some present context.

It is suggested that the age difference in psychological test performance increases with increased necessity for searching the stimulus field, searching for present meanings and manipulation of materials in novel ways. In the Raven Matrices test and in some of the WAIS subtests, what is required is manipulation or integration of information. In such tests both present groups of subjects were below young adult means. In these tests the age difference was clearly larger than the group or presumed health difference.

While it is premature to try to specify in detail the nature of the "aging principle" involved in differential changes in performance, one generalization seems possible. That is, the magnitude of age differences in psychological test performance varies with the extent to which previously organized and stored information can be used

in response to present stimulus situations. Two known facts are relevant to differential psychological change with age. Sensory and perceptual limitations with advancing age of the kind measured in these studies often result in a lessened opportunity for the older subject to gather what is "being called for." The older person might be characterized as being perceptually more distant from his environment. The older subject is also slower and may thus be less able to scan and evaluate the environment in an optimum period of time. There is the possibility that the well established psychomotor slowing of advancing age is a consequence of reduced physiological activation. This agrees with what limited literature exists on age differences in activity and drive levels. Assuming a less energized or activated organism with age, in any unit of time there will be less interaction between the individual and his environment. This reduces the opportunity for all psychological processes to take place, e.g., perception, acquisition, manipulation of symbols, and storage.

The concept of a less activated older organism may be further refined to allow for distinctions in behavior which result from less interest, i.e., lower motivation, from those which result from a decline in set or expectancy. The latter have been discussed by Botwinick (see reference in ch. 8) but it is still too early to determine if the phenomena of set and expectancy in the aged are a part of or separate from psychomotor slowing and lower drive level.

As adults grow older there is selective overlearning of some skills, e.g., social behavior, and a decline in use and opportunity for reinforcement of other psychomotor and mental skills. In addition to changes in the kind and frequency of transactions which engage the adult in daily living, the organism itself appears to change in a way which is to a large extent independent of use. Visual changes for example, probably neither favor nor disfavor the avid reader, but of this we have little evidence.

In the interest of simplicity and ease it is tempting to invoke a change in only one or at most a few antecedent variables which might account for the striking age differences in psychological performance. It does not seem possible at this stage to go much further in interpretations of the results. Further specification of the changes of normal aging await more insight into the measurements, improved and larger samples of subjects, and perhaps experimental studies in which the implicated variables are manipulated.

SUMMARY

1. The analysis attempted to develop a parsimonious description of the results obtained from a broad range of mental and perceptual tests described in previous chapters. Results were examined both with respect to differences between subjects groups I (healthy) and (II (some health impairment) which would presumably reflect the influence of health status, and between the present elderly subjects and previously studied young subjects.

2. Three methods of comparing data were used: (a) standard scores were computed for each subject for all tests; these were averaged to yield a mean standard score reflecting each subject's general level of performance, weighting all tests equally, (b) all 32 tests were intercorrelated and five principal components were derived; for each of the five components, individual scores were computed which were essentially independent measures, and (c) data on the verbal and performance portions of the Wechsler Adult Intelligence Scale were compared.

3. Group II subjects tended to have lower psychological performance than subjects of group I. Health differences in the range studied thus presumably make a difference in psychological functioning. These psychological differences were most apparent in verbal abilities or general achievement level. Groups I and II were different in performance on principal component I which was interpreted to be storage of previously organized information, primarily, but not exclusively, verbal. The problem of interpretation of the results involved the issue of whether the lower scores of group II were a result of: (a) a failure to gain information over the adult years, (b) a loss of information, or (c) a sampling artifact. The tentative interpretation was advanced that the lower values of group II reflected a late life loss of information. The illnesses observed in group II would presumably not be prevalent during the early and middle adult years when they would be expected to show an increase in score above that for young adults.

4. On perceptual and manipulative types of tests the older subjects were in general lower in performance than young subjects. Comparable control subjects however were not available for all comparisons. For available data the age difference was greater than the group I–II difference. Older subjects tend to have sensory limitations and are also slow in responses. In many situations where the task requires operation on or manipulation of symbolic materials, it is not clear whether the slower output and errors result from the necessity to take additional time to perceive the pertinent information, or whether the older organism is less "activated" or "energized." In the present results both groups I and II were slower than young subjects but did not differ significantly from each other. This leads to the unanswered question why age is more im-

portant in speed measures, and health in vrebal measures.

5. The present results call for further analyses of the data in relation to the physiological and personality aspects of the individuals. Within the limitations of the present data it is not clear, for example, to what extent older subjects are slow because: (a) they require more time to perceive externally presented information; the deficiency being perceptual and the time change an adaptive consequence, (b) they do not "need" to be slow but are so because of a commonly adopted set or habit pattern, and (c) they are slow because of a lower level of activation. Further specification of the factors which lie behind the psychological changes with advancing age requires correlations with measures of physiological and social functioning.

CHAPTER 11

Psychiatric Aspects of Adaptation to The Aging Experience

by Seymour Perlin and Robert N. Butler

Although the psychiatrist is familiar with community-resident aged in situations of crisis, his contact is ordinarily brief and directed towards referral to an old age home or State mental hospital. The emotionally-disturbed, community-resident aged rarely receive psychiatric treatment (Bowman, 1959). Consequently, psychotherapy, an important source of data and theory in other age groups, has not substantially contributed to the understanding of the non-hospitalized aged. Moreover, the latter have not been the subject of research investigations until recently (Busse et al., 1954a, 1954b).

The following questions broadly define the interests of the participating psychiatrists in this multidisciplinary investigation of aging and the aged:

What kinds of psychopathology are present in older persons who are relatively free from physical disease and living in the community? What is the character of senility, and is it an inevitable consequence of the "aging process"? What kinds of changes do the noninstitutionalized and basically healthy older people observe in themselves, and how do they react to them? What personality factors contribute to the adaptation and maladaptation of the older individual, living in the community, to the crises of late life?

Psychiatric contributions to the characterization of the aged, the experience of aging, and the adaptive processes involved, have been primarily derived from examination of the institutionalized aged and the treatment of the mentally-ill (Abraham, 1927; Butler, 1960; Galpern, Turner, and Goldfarb, 1952; Ginsberg, 1955; Goldfarb and Turner, 1953; Grotjahn, 1955; Hollender, 1952; Kaufman, 1940; Kay, Roth, and Hopkins, 1955; Linden, 1953; Perlin, 1958; Rechtschaffen, Atkinson, and Freeman, 1953; Roth, 1955; Roth and Kay, 1956; Stern, Smith, and Frank, 1953). These developments, in turn, have been partly stimulated by studies suggesting reevaluation of the presumed relationship of clinical symptomatology to neuropathology in the organic brain disorders of the aged and also suggesting that the influence of psychological and social variables must be investigated (Rothschild, 1937, 1942). Despite these contributions, however, the psychiatrist remains limited in his empirical and theoretical knowledge as well as in his methods of assessment when confronted with the much larger number of elderly persons who are neither institutionalized nor so severely mentally ill.

Psychiatric study of the aged has been largely dependent upon concepts and techniques either derived from theories emphasizing organic origin or selected because of their successful application in other age periods. The older person has been most commonly investigated "neuropsychiatrically" where the perspective has been principally limited to the assessment of organic changes, the knowledge of which is insufficient. When the older person has been evaluated psychologically, there has been a distinct tendency to extrapolate techniques and concepts originally applied successfully in the earlier periods of the life cycle. Although psychological understanding of the child and young adult contributes to the understanding of the elderly, the elderly themselves require investigation in their own right as well as in the context of the experience of aging.

Despite these limitations in knowledge due to the nature of samples studied, basic concepts, and methods of assessment employed, an impressive body of information regarding the more severe functional and organic disorders of the aged has accumulated. A high incidence of depression and the occurrence of the neuroses and psychoses of youth have been recognized in the aged (Clow and Allen, 1951). Interest has been shown in the natural history of functional disorders whose origins predate the later life period. Alterations (amelioration or exacerbation) of such disorders have been described (Cameron, 1956; Clow and Allen, 1951; Fenichel, 1945; Weinberg, 1955). Nonetheless, such data are incomplete, and theoretical formulations accounting for such disorders and changes within them are limited. In addition, the possible relations of psychopathology and personality to successful and unsuccessful adaptation in aged persons residing in the community have not been comprehensively examined.

Considering our present state of knowledge, it was our wish to examine in detail the mental status and personality functioning of the community-resident, medically healthy, nonpsychotic aged individual and to explore *with* him his aging experience and his adaptation to it. Although we proceeded within a broad psychodynamic framework and preselected numerous variables that we, or others, assumed to be age-relevant for special consideration, we attempted to obtain as full a picture of the aging experience as possible. We emphasized the exploratory nature of our interviewing.

It was our belief that the selection of a sample of this kind would permit emphasis upon the relationship of psychiatric variables to chronological age per se, as well as aid in clarifying potentially obscuring medical and social variables. At the same time, it was our view that a multidisciplinary approach would extend our total understanding of the aged.

In addition to acquiring descriptive data, our fundamental purpose was directed towards the construction of a working psychodynamic model of patterns of adaptation-maladaptation within the aging experience.

In keeping with the multidisciplinary character of the overall project, a second objective was to look for intercorrelations among the several disciplines in order to define further the interrelations and relative weighting of various factors contributing to a multifactorial model of the aged individual. We were interested in finding what biological, medical and social variables affected the psychological status and adaptation of the aged, and vice versa. (See ch. 15.)

A third goal was to find ways of describing and defining this "normal" population to aid in the selection of potential control groups for comparative research into various mental disorders of the aged, such as Chronic Brain Syndrome. (See ch. 15.)

Finally, it was necessary to adapt, develop and test methods and concepts in order to facilitate the carrying out of the above objectives. It was also anticipated that this experience might have application in the psychiatric diagnostic evaluation of the aged.

These several objectives reflected two basic intentions—a theoretical inquiry into the psychological nature of the aged and of aging; and the acquisition of empirical and theoretical knowledge which could be applied to the considerable practical problems inherent in the evaluation, care and treatment of the large numbers of the mentally disturbed aged.

The nature of both the interviewing and the analyses undertaken was focused on the assessment of mental status (functional psychopathology and organic change), the individual's subjective experience of changes within the aging period, and psychodynamic evaluation of adaptation and maladaptation.

METHODS

In chapters 2 and 3, the social and medical criteria for selection of the sample are provided. The sample comprised 47 white males 65 years and older (mean age 71) in good medical health and free of psychoses. Further medical characterization resulted in the division of the basic sample into two groups: group I—subjects with no apparent medical disease; group II—subjects with subclinical and/or asymptomatic disease.

Three interviews (2 to 3 hours in length) were conducted with each subject under standard conditions.[1] Sessions occurred at fixed times in the schedule of procedures for each subject during his 2-week stay at the

---

[1] Our modification of the traditional psychiatric interview and setting and its rationale has been described elsewhere: Perlin, S., and Butler, R. N. The use of the interview in psychiatric evaluation of the aged. Presented at the 5th Annual Meeting, Gerontological Society, Baltimore, Md., Oct. 27, 1955. Mimeographed.

Institute. The interviews were observed through a one-way vision mirror by an observer-psychiatrist, and were recorded and audited in an adjoining room.

The first interview, while for the most part free and nondirective, included questions designed to obtain a personal history and a record of psychiatric symptomatology. This interview was in essence the usual method of psychiatric evaluation. The second interview was structured and designed to explore concepts believed to be highly relevant to the aged; e.g., adaptation to age-relevant changes, attitudes toward the future and toward death (Krapf, 1953; Schilder, 1940). In addition, a mental status examination adapted from several testing procedures (Lewis, 1943; Terman and Merrill, 1937; Wechsler, 1955) was administered. The third interview allowed for the development of material obtained in the previous sessions. (The interview outline and the adapted mental status examination are found in app. A.)

Systematic rotation of the roles of interviewer and observer was introduced in order to minimize systematic bias. The psychiatrist who was not interviewing became the observer-auditor. Simultaneous observations underlie the independent and consensual judgments (scaled where possible) of symptoms and behavior. Judgments or ratings were made on the following: psychiatric diagnosis, symptoms and characteristics considered "age-relevant" in the literature, psychiatric symptoms and interview behavior. (See app. A.) Denial of aging changes and status was also evaluated (Butler and Perlin, 1957). An impression concerning the presence or absence of senile qualities was recorded and individual psychodynamic formulations were written. Recordings of verbal content provided protocols for further analyses. Manifest self-reported changes were thus studied and independent psychiatric judgments were obtained. (See app. A, Independent Protocol Analysis.)

RESULTS

General Description And Evaluation of Sample

The 47 aged men had led interesting and varied lives and our interviews were rarely dull. As a group they were vigorous, candid, and intelligent; many of them were psychologically-minded and most of them were well-motivated to participate in this study. They were generally cooperative and showed curiosity about and understanding of individual procedures as well as project goals. In marked contradiction to the usual stereotype of "rigidity" of the aged, these individuals generally demonstrated mental flexibility and alertness in interviews. They continued to be constructive in their living; they were resourceful and usually optimistic.

Those individuals who showed evidence of recent and even profound decline still gave evidence of active engagement in personal and circumscribed social pursuits. Those who showed neurotic symptoms, including depression, were not seeking treatment, and except for rare instances, treatment was not indicated. With the exception of those showing prodromal indications of senility, the mental and emotional responsiveness of these people was not diminished.

An important corollary to the candor of these individuals was their revelation of their character structure as well as their innermost experiences. The life histories which they gave appeared to be unusually direct, coherent, and lucid. They were generally willing to explore in depth material which clearly made them anxious; e.g., they were willing to explore the meaning of death, a topic the authors had felt guarded about. Although members of the group varied in

psychological insight and in their acceptance or denial of aging changes, it was usually feasible to "get behind" the individual's defenses and develop a reasonably comprehensive picture of his aging experience. Although minimal memory disturbances were present, patience and careful questioning as well as active self-correction suggested that memory was an insignificant barrier to realizing the aims of the study. Indeed the impression was that failure in memory was seldom primary but that interest and attention, preludes to memory, were often directed either to inner experiences or to special features of the environment.

The foregoing evaluation of this sample should be held in mind during the course of reading the detailed analyses of data to follow. As part of the "microscopic" examination of functional psychopathology, changes in intellectual and other functions occurring with advancing age, and aspects of maladaptation, could give the impression of considerable pathology in the sample. The fact that this is a medically-healthy group of aged men who are functioning well in the community and do not require psychiatric treatment should be emphasized.

Functional Psychopathology

How prone to the development of psychopathology in late life is the older individual who is relatively free from physical disease and living in the community?

What kinds and how much functional psychopathology are present in such a sample?

What differences and similarities may be observed between the psychopathology of the young and the old?

What changes in the natural history of psychopathology may be observed? Is there an amelioration or worsening in certain disorders with advancing age?

Does health influence psychopathology, or vice-versa?

Thirteen (28 percent) of the 47 volunteers had psychoneuroses. Twenty-nine (62 percent) presented diagnosable functional psychopathology including personality disorders. Thirteen subjects warranted multiple diagnoses. Psychoneurosis constituted the most common diagnostic class, followed closely by personality disorders. The single most common diagnosis was depressive reaction which was found in nine subjects. The depressions found were mild and reactive in nature; the affected individuals had usually experienced major crises such as recent death of wife or a disturbing retirement (Butler and Perlin, 1957). These individuals with neuroses, including depression, may differ (not only in the severity of their condition) from individuals with similar disorders who are seeking treatment or are institutionalized.

Basic differences were not observed in the psychological structure of the neuroses of these older persons compared to younger subjects. For example, the same mechanisms, as currently understood, occurred in depression. Nonetheless, lifelong psychopathology was observed to have been modified with advancing years in some cases. Both exacerbation (e.g., paranoid isolation) and amelioration (e.g., mellowing of obsessional-compulsive neurosis) occurred. A third development was the occurrence of entirely new disturbances, not classified in the current nomenclature, in which lifelong psychopathology and/or personality characteristics were predisposing (e.g., identity crises) (American Psychiatric Association, 1952).

Diagnosable psychopathology had its origin in the aging period (after 65) in 11 subjects (23 percent). Age-relevant psychopathology included the nine depressive reactions, one Chronic Brain Syndrome without psychosis and one Adjustment Reaction of Late Life.

Table 1 summarizes the primary psychiatric diagnostic findings of the 47 aged men, divided into groups I and II according to medical criteria. (In table 1 of app. B, diagnosis by individuals in group I and group II is provided.) No significant differences were found among the psychiatric diagnostic subgroups with respect to age.

The presence of psychopathological symptoms in the sample is summarized in table 2. These symptoms were distributed among 38 of the volunteers; 9 subjects had no symptoms. Three subjects reported past suicidal attempts at some time in their lives;

TABLE 1.—*Primary diagnoses in 47 aged subjects*

Diagnostic category	Groups I (N=27)	Groups II (N=20)	Total (N=47)
No psychiatric diagnosis	12	6	18
Psychoneurosis	5	8	13
Depressive reaction	4	5	9
Obsessive-compulsive reaction	1	3	4
Adjustment reaction of late life	0	1	1
Chronic brain syndrome with senile brain damage without psychosis	0	1	1
Personality disorders	8	4	12
Psychophysiological reaction	1	0	1
Special symptom reaction	1	0	1

TABLE 2.—*Incidence of functional psychopathological symptoms in 47 aged subjects*

Symptom	Groups		Total (N=47)
	I (N=27)	II (N=20)	
No symptoms	6	3	9
Depressive trend	8	5	13
Nightmares	8	3	11
Obsessions	3	8	11
Hypochondriacal ideas	7	3	10
Suspiciousness	6	4	10
Psychosomatic symptoms	4	3	7
Anxiety	3	3	6
Compulsions	4	1	5
Schizoid symptomatology	3	1	4
Sexual maladaptation	1	3	4
Conversion symptoms	0	2	2
Tendency toward elation	1	1	2
Grandiose ideas	2	0	2
Conduct aberrations [1]	2	0	2
Persecutory trend	0	1	1
Illusions	0	1	1
Phobias	1	0	1
Past suicidal attempts	2	1	3
History of auditory and visual hallucinations	1	0	1

[1] Not of recent origin.

seven others had either considered suicide or had made a gesture. Depression was the most common symptom as well as the most common diagnosis. Other common symptoms were: nightmares, obsessions, hypochondriacal ideas, suspiciousness, psychosomatic symptoms, and anxiety. These were likely to occur in isolated fashion as well as in groupings; e.g., with depression.

Five members of the sample had received psychiatric treatment whereas 35 reported no prior psychiatric contact. No information is available for seven subjects. Reasons for treatment included depression in three cases, personality disorder in one, and alcoholism in another.

No statistically significant differences were found in the relative incidence of either diagnosable psychopathology or symptomatology between the medical groupings (group I and II), but individual study indicated that illness aggravated or contributed to the depressions of several of the subjects. The relation of psychopathology to morale and adaptation are considered later. (See pp. 177–83.)

Senile Manifestations

What characteristics contributed to the clinical impression of early senile manifestations?

What criteria may be offered for the recognition of early senile manifestations, and for their separation from senescence and depression?

Is senility an inevitable consequence of chronological age per se?

Might senility, or certain forms of it, represent prodromal manifestations of Chronic Brain Syndrome?

Eleven subjects (23 percent of the sample) were evaluated as showing "Senile Qualities" on the basis of clinical impression of recent and profound decline in the mental status and in the function of the patient, rather than by the use of specific signs and symptoms. Each psychiatrist recorded his impression separately at the end of each individual case study; there was complete agreement on 11 subjects; disagreement on 3. The designation "border-line senile quality" was applied to three individuals where agreement was lacking.

Correlating significantly ($r=0.718$) with the overall interview impression of Senile Quality by the psychiatrists were the independent ratings of senile qualities by the nonpsychiatric members of the research team (internist, psychologist, nursing staff, etc.) who observed the subjects in experimental situations which varied in duration, objective, and stress. Such agreement could reflect stereotypes regarding age which are significantly shared by all members of the research team. Physical appearance could also be contributory to the agreement obtained.

A very important problem for psychiatry is to determine the critical variables and factors which can be objectively used to distinguish between normal aging changes and "senile" deteriorative changes. This section will attempt to isolate such factors. Since all the evidence relating to this methodological study is internal to our study, the factors being isolated were possibly the very ones involved in clinical impression of "Senile Quality." Therefore the findings and suggestions in this section are tentative. Further validation is required. We are reporting interview and mental status results of subjects whom we have judged as Senile Quality and non-Senile Quality.

In the interview situation the Senile Quality subjects seemed to be less involved with their environment, human and non-human, than the non-Senile Quality subjects. Their attention and set were impaired. There was an overall lack of comprehension of "purpose," limitation of ideas and an impairment of abstraction ability. These subjects often made assumptions which were not based on inquiry into, and manipulation of, the experimental situation; there was failure to recall the interviewer, the room, etc. Communication often consisted of highly personal associations, serving to create further distance between the subject and interviewer. Such associations led to drift and irrelevancy. There was decreased "responsivity" in the interpersonal situation; i.e., decreased direct, immediate, affective interaction. (This, as will be noted, does not mean lack of "emotional lability.") The tempo of thought processes tended to be reduced. Direct communications were appropriate, but stereotyped and relatively uncomplicated. Under stress, crying and confusion might result; such "disintegration" occurred more frequently in Senile than non-Senile Quality subjects, especially in association with depression. Emotional lability as a criterion seemed useful only in extreme cases. Severely impaired judgment, disorientation and confabulation were found only in the Senile Quality subgroup of this sample.

In order to delineate further the criteria for Senile Quality, clinically evaluated impairments of cognitive function in the Senile and non-Senile Quality subgroups were analyzed. A 34 item check list of symptoms and characteristics considered "age-relevant" in the literature was used in the interview. The occurrence of signs among the Senile Quality and non-Senile Quality subjects differed significantly. These signs probably contributed to the global impression but may not have totally accounted for it. In the hope of making more definitive possible criteria for diagnosing Senile Quality from non-Senile Quality by others, table 3 reports these data. The impairments, when present, tended to be more severe as well as more frequent in the Senile Quality than in the non-Senile Quality subgroup. (Fig. 1.)

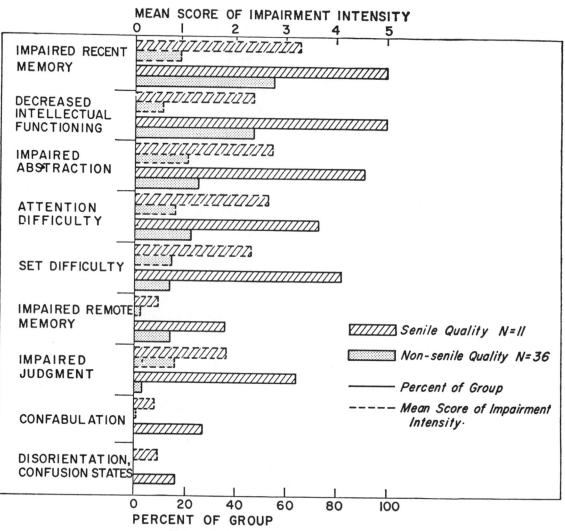

FIGURE 1. Impairments in senile quality.

The clinical categories of Senile Quality and non-Senile Quality were checked against the individual mental status scores on the psychiatric examination. Table 4 presents mean scores showing significant differences between the judged Senile and non-Senile Quality subjects for logical memory, opposites, proverbs, absurdities, and the following verbal Wechsler Adult Intelligence Scale Items: information, similarities, digit span, vocabulary, and the verbal score. There were discrepancies between certain mental status scores and clinical impressions. For example, memory scores were not significantly different, although the subjects in interview had given impressive evidence of their increasing loss of memory, which apparently was not "tested." They had difficulty in remembering a variety of items simultaneously, in keeping an appointment, and in dressing appropriately for the occasion. Differences between clinical appraisal and mental status scores on certain functions may reflect differences in the technique of evaluation as well as in the definition of the function undergoing evaluation.

TABLE 3.—*Clinically-evaluated impairments of cognitive functions: sample of 47 aged subjects, Senile Quality subgroup and its complement*

Impairment	Senile Quality (N=11)	Non-Senile Quality (N=36)	Total sample (N=47)
Impaired recent memory	11	20	31
Decreased intellectual functioning	11	17	28
Impaired abstraction	10	19	19
Attention difficulty	8	8	16
Set difficulty	9	5	14
Impaired remote memory	4	5	9
Impaired judgment	7	[1] 1	8
Confabulation	3	0	3
Disorientation, confusion states	2	0	2

[1] "Borderline Senile Quality" subject.

Significant differences were obtained between the Senile and non-Senile Quality groups on a variety of psychological tests secured independently of the psychiatrists. (See related chs. 12 and 15 for psychological test data.)

In summary, cognitive dysfunction, alterations in behavior, and disturbances in affective expression, appear to have been the areas of importance in the clinical evaluation of Senile Quality. (See p. 182, Case No. 11 for case illustration.) Early characteristics are believed to include mild impairments in comprehension, in recent memory and in maintaining of attention and set, and reduced responsiveness, as well as greater liability to "disintegration" during stress. Characteristics which appear to

TABLE 4.—*Mean score differences between the Senile Quality and non-Senile Quality subgroups on the psychiatric mental status examination*

Subtest	Senile [1] Quality (N=9)	Non-Senile [2] Quality (N=35)	Significance of group differences
Total orientation	8.2	8.9	N.S.
Retention	3.4	3.8	N.S.
Recent memory	7.7	8.1	N.S.
Remote memory	8.2	8.2	N.S.
Logical memory	8.3	10.3	* 0.05
Opposites	7.4	10.9	** .01
Proverbs	2.3	3.8	* .05
Absurdities	6.3	8.1	** .005
Selected WAIS items:			
Information	8.7	13.1	** .01
Comprehension	12.3	14.1	N.S.
Arithmetic	10.5	12.1	N.S.
Similarities	8.3	12.5	N.S.
Digit span	7.8	11.4	*** .001
Vocabulary	10.1	12.9	*** .001
Verbal score	109.8	121.9	N.S.

[1] Data unavailable for 2 subjects.
[2] Data unavailable for 1 subject.
* Significant at the 0.05 level.
** Significant at the 0.01 level.
*** Significant at the 0.001 level.

develop later are emotional lability, impaired orientation and impaired judgment. (In this study, these characteristics were only found in two extreme Senile Quality subjects.) Potential signs and symptoms suggesting progression of the aforementioned characteristics would include perseveration, lack of comprehension, irrelevance, withdrawal, isolation, apathy ("pseudo-depression"), inappropriate affect, emotional incontinence and confusion (see table 5).

Depression may present a very similar clinical picture to the one described for Senile Quality, and differentiation may not always be possible. Depression did coexist in five Senile Quality subjects. We examined the following groupings: Senile Quality subjects with depressive symptoms alone ($n=6$), Senile Quality subjects without other diagnoses ($n=5$); non-Senile Quality, depressive symptoms alone ($n=7$); and non-Senile Quality subjects without other diagnoses ($n=13$) (table 6, table 7, ch. 15 and app. C). Presenting sympto-

matology of the Senile Quality subgroup is more likely to emphasize an adaptation (or maladaptation) to intellectual decline and memory loss. Depressive elements of a reactive nature may occur in association with "insight" (Butler and Perlin, 1957). While both groups may appear apathetic, the Senile Quality subjects are more likely to be "uninvolved" regardless of content while the depressed subject may become involved and responsive in relation to content, such as death of spouse.

Preoccupation in the depressed may appear similar to the set difficulties in the Senile Quality subjects. In contrast to the Senile Quality subgroup, the depressed are apt to exaggerate signs of aging and also to relate such signs to the dynamic meaning of their depression; e.g., as punishment for treatment of deceased spouse, and the like. When "disintegration," crying, etc., did occur, it was more apt to be "inappropriate" relative to the stress exerted, for the Senile Quality subject; in the depressed subject, responses to the interview were linked

TABLE 5.—*Characteristics of the Senile Quality Subgroup*

Early characteristics	*Potential signs and symptoms* [1]
I. *Cognitive*	
1. "Intellectual" decline:	
Reduced tempo of stream of thought.	
Impoverishment of ideas.	Perseveration.
Concreteness: impaired abstraction.	Increasing impaired comprehension.
2. Decline of recent memory:	Increasing memory loss (recent and remote).
Registration, recall; organization. [2]	Confabulation.
3. Difficulty maintaining attention and set.	Perseveration, irrelevance.
II. *Behavioral and affective*	
4. Reduced attentiveness.	
5. Reduced Responsiveness:	Progressive withdrawal and self-isolation.
Decreased interpersonal interaction.	Apathy:
Less direct, immediate affective expression.	Pseudo-depression vs. depression.
6. Liability to "disintegration" during stress.	"Inappropriate" affect.
III. *Later characteristics*	
1. Emotional lability.	Emotional incontinence.
2. Impaired orientation.	Confusion.
3. Impaired judgment.	

[1] A 1-to-1 relationship between presenting characteristic and potential symptom is not implied. Other symptoms may include irritability, apathy, suspiciousness, slovenliness, etc.

[2] Impaired organization refers to the inability to remember (and utilize) items in a time-related sequence.

to variables which were relevant to the depression. Table 6 contrasts the interview behavior of the Senile Quality subgroup with the depressed sample.

There was no significant difference in the mean chronological age of the Senile and non-Senile Quality subgroups. We may hypothesize that the Senile Quality subgroup exhibits malfunctions which are associated with the aging period but are not a consequence of aging per se; i.e., at least within the age range studied. Nor was there a simple relationship between Senile Quality and medical status as defined by groups I and II; however, among the Senile Quality group, there were individuals with arteriosclerosis (ch. 15).

The clinical description of these subjects is reminiscent of certain aspects of the Chronic Brain Syndrome. On the premise that Senile Quality might represent early Chronic Brain Syndrome, each individual characterized as Senile Quality was reevaluated at the end of the project in terms of the five major features of the Chronic Brain Syndrome, as defined in the diagnostic manual of the American Psychiatric Association (1952). Disturbance of memory, judgment, orientation, comprehension, and affect, were therefore reevaluated. A Chronic Brain Syndrome score (1–6) was devised in which a score of one was given in the presence of Senile Quality and an additional point for each of the Chronic Brain Syndrome features present. The distribution of the 11 Senile Quality subjects according to this measure was as follows: 4 subjects had 2 of the features; 6 showed 3 of them; and 1 revealed 4 of the 5 classic signs.

Appendix B, table 2, indicates the presence of the clinically evaluated impairments of cognitive function according to a rating for intensity (severity) for the entire sample. Mild intellectual changes were also

found in the non-Senile Quality group. (See tables 3 and 4 in this chapter, and tables 2 and 3 in app. B.) Although these findings may reflect the nature of clinical appraisal, they agree with the psychological test findings, obtained independently, which revealed some cognitive changes with advancing age in this sample. The amount of decline found was much less than has usually been reported in the aged. (See ch. 8.)

Manifest Reactions to Change

What kinds of changes do noninstitutionalized and basically healthy older people observe in themselves and how do they react to them?

Do older people observe constructive qualities in any of their changes—or do they consider them to be deficiencies?

What kinds of changes are seen as inevitable and unalterable and what kinds as reversible? Are there specific modes of reaction favored for specific kinds of change?

Do the nature and number of changes relate to psychopathology, personality structure, medical and social variables?

Specific questioning elicited reports pertaining to changes (see app. A for focussed interview), but spontaneous reports concerning changes occurred throughout the interviews. All manifest content statements by the subject referring to changes and reactions were extracted from the interview material. A change was defined as the subject's statement that he had perceived a change with advancing age either within himself or in his social-psychological environment. A reaction to change was defined as the behavioral or emotional or attitudinal response to the reported change. In order to systematize basic abstracting and categorizing of the abstracted units, operational definitions and rules were developed which are reported in full elsewhere (Werner, Perlin, Butler, and Pollin, 1961).

Changes were characterized as being Physical, Cognitive, Personality-Affective and Social-Psychological.

TABLE 6.—*Interview behavior of the Senile Quality and depressed subgroups*

Interview behavior scale	No psych. diagnosis no Senile Quality Mean (N=13)	Senile Quality only Mean (N=5)	Depression only Mean (N=7)	Depression with Senile Quality Mean (N=6)	Senile Quality only effect F	Depression effect F	Interaction between Senile Quality and depressive features F
Responsivity.	12.00	8.40	10.71	8.67	* 5.83	<1	<1
Depression.	8.23	10.00	12.57	22.71	* 4.50	*** 45.64	1.1
Somatic reactivity.	1.15	5.20	1.14	5.43	* 4.43	<1	<1
Disintegration.	4.46	3.40	5.29	12.29	3.04	** 8.13	* 5.71
Integration.	25.23	22.60	21.00	15.86	2.00	* 5.71	<1
Fear-anxiety.	8.54	8.40	12.43	18.00	2.69	*** 16.54	3.35
Anger-out.	8.31	9.40	17.71	17.67	<1	*** 18.16	<1
Anger-in.	7.69	4.20	15.71	18.00	<1	*** 22.18	1.67

* Significant at the 0.05 level.
** Significant at the 0.01 level.
*** Significant at the 0.001 level.

Physical changes referred to general health, appearance, strength, speed of movement, body organs and function, including sexual changes. Cognitive changes included alterations in orientation, memory, attention, set, and learning. Personality-Affective changes referred to affectivity, mood states, emotional well-being, characterological and personality traits. Social-Psychological changes included loss of spouse and friends, retirement, and changes in social and familial roles (e.g., growing up of children).

The abstracted changes were further categorized as decreases or declines, increases, or unratable. (Less than 1 percent of all reported changes were found to be unratable.)

Reactions to decreases were categorized on the basis of five selected reaction-modes:

1. *Compensation* referred to a reaction which repairs, modifies, avoids, or substitutes for a decrease. (Examples: To the change of decreased hearing—"I got myself a hearing aid;" to a decline in memory—"I use a memory pad;" to the loss of wife—"I got remarried" or "I go out and meet people;" to retirement—"I attend to my hobbies" or "I do part-time work, civic work, church work, etc.").

2. *Acceptances* referred to a reaction in which the change was seen as "unavoidable," "inevitable," and "beyond changing." (Often such statements were introduced or accompanied by such phrases as "of course" and "naturally." Example: To a decrease in sexual activity—"Of course you will slow down with age," or "I take this as a course of nature;" to the loss of contemporaries—"Well, death is the end of life.")

3. A rating of *Limitation* was made where a subject reported interference with some of his explicitly stated needs or his necessary daily functions. (Example: When a subject reported the decrease—"diminished hearing" and added the statement, "I no longer can attend concerts," this was taken to indicate that "attending concerts" was a wish, the fulfillment of which was interfered with by his perceived change. Another example: a subject in reaction to the observed change "slowed-down gait," reported subsequently, "I am afraid of crossing a street and being run over by traffic.")

4. The rating *Complaint* was made when a subject reported that a decrease provoked an emotional response such as "discomfort," "pain," "annoyance," or "embarrassment." A Complaint was distinguished from a Limitation by virtue of emphasis on emotional effects rather than on direct interference with a performance or need fulfillment. (Examples: In reaction to a change in "name-memory" a subject uttered, "You tell me a name and I am embarrassed.")

5. A rating *Qualification* was given when a subject minimized the importance of the loss by indicating that the degree of the decrease was so small that the change was insignificant in its effects. (Example: A lawyer reports that "he is almost as good as he was years ago in interpreting legal passages." The statement, "just a little bit less," was often made in a qualifying reaction to a decrease.)

A subject seldom reported more than one reaction to a change. If more than one reaction was reported, a preferential order of rating was established so that only one reaction was coded. Compensation was given preference above the other reactions. A decrease was rated according to the following order, giving primary emphasis to the more healthy and adaptive reaction: Compensation, Acceptance, Limitation, Complaint, Qualification. Example: After a subject reported the change of "deteriorated memory" and the reaction that he "used a memory pad," he then added that he "naturally expected to be more forgetful at this age." In this case the decrease was seen as being "compensated." The Acceptance reaction is regarded as being overridden by the act of Compensation and was not rated.

For each subject, the percentage agreement on content codings was computed on codings of decreases, increases, and unratables. The percentage agreement on 20 randomized individual subjects selected independently of the judges ranged from 89 to 100 percent (mean 97 percent). On types of change (where five choices, including that of unratable, were possible for each of the raters), the range in the percentage of exact agreement over the 20 subjects was from 75 to 96 percent (mean 88 percent). Finally, in the case of Compensation and Acceptance, agreement in all cases was 100 percent.

Every subject reported some changes. The mean number of changes of any type reported by an individual was 15 (range 8–32). Changes in the physical area were the most common (mean=6). Personality-affective, social-psychological and cognitive changes followed in that order. Table 7 lists the number of subjects in the sample as a whole and in groups I and II specifically reporting these kinds of changes. Due to technically unsuitable recordings, two subjects could not be included in this analysis; the data reported thus pertains to 45 subjects.

Positive and constructive changes were reported as developing in the geriatric period. Changes were not uniformly viewed as deficiencies or losses, as it is frequently implied or described in the literature pertaining to old age. This finding probably reflects the character of this sample which contrasts with the more commonly studied sick and institutionalized old. Although physical and cognitive changes were overwhelmingly reported as decreases, personality-affective and social-psychological changes were frequently reported as increases. For example, 14 subjects (32 percent) reported 100 percent of their personality-affective changes as increases. Table 8 details the means (and standard deviations) of decreases and increases in the total sample and in groups I and II.

Changes were not uniformly viewed by the aged subjects as inevitable and unalterable. There was a relationship between the area of change and the mode of reaction reported. Acceptance was the most common mode of reaction to physical decreases, compensation to social-psychological decreases, and both to cognitive and personality-affective decreases. Limitations were noted primarily in the physical area. Table 9 shows the number of subjects utilizing a particular mode of reaction to decreases (expressed as percent of decreases to which reactions have been reported by each subject in a given area. (App. B, table 4, gives these data in terms of groups I and II.)

Not everyone reported reactions to their decreases. Altogether, there were 314 reactions to the 521 decreases reported by the total sample. Subjects tended to report reactions to their physical decreases; on the other hand, one-half the subjects reported no reactions to their personality-affective decreases. The largest number of subjects reported reactions (especially compensation) to all their social-psychological decreases, suggesting their view that the latter were modifiable. Twenty-seven subjects reacted to 100 percent of their social-psychological decreases.

A person's awareness of changes with advancing age would not appear to depend upon physical health within the narrow range studied here. No statistically significant relationships were found between medical health (groups I and II) and the number or character of changes or reactions to them, although group II tended somewhat to report more changes, more decreases, and less increases, with one exception (namely, a tendency toward reporting more personality-affective increases in group II). The Senile Quality group did report a significantly greater number of decreases among the changes reported than the non-Senile (0.01 level of confidence). (A summary of the total changes, increases and decreases reported by the 45 subjects is provided in app. B, table 5.)

Adaptive and Maladaptive Patterns

This section is concerned with questions relative to the adaptive and maladaptive responses to the changes associated with advancing years.

TABLE 7.—*Number of subjects reporting physical, cognitive, personality-affective and social-psychological changes in the total sample and groups I and II*

Category	Physical			Cognitive			Personality-affective			Social-psychological		
	Groups		Total	Groups		Total	Groups		Total	Groups		Total
	I	II		I	II		I	II		I	II	
Number of subjects reporting changes.......	26	19	45	21	18	39	26	18	44	26	17	43
Number of subjects reporting no changes.....	0	0	0	5	1	6	0	1	1	0	2	2
Total...............	26	19	45	26	19	45	26	19	45	26	19	45

TABLE 8.—*Mean numbers of physical, cognitive, personality-affective and sound-psychological decreases and increases in the total sample and groups I and II*

Subjects	Physical Decreases		Physical Increases		Cognitive Decreases		Cognitive Increases	
	Mean	Standard deviation	Mean	Standard deviation	Mean	Standard deviation	Mean	Standard deviation
Group I (N=26)	5.38	2.33	0.12	0.32	1.35	1.17	0.07	0.26
Group II (N=19)	6.57	2.26	.05	.22	1.68	.80	.05	.22
Total group (N=45)	5.39	2.36	.09	.28	1.49	1.04	.07	.25

Subjects	Personality-affective Decreases		Personality-affective Increases		Social-psychological Decreases		Social-psychological Increases	
	Mean	Standard deviation	Mean	Standard deviation	Mean	Standard deviation	Mean	Standard deviation
Group I (N=26)	1.62	1.80	2.96	1.90	2.27	1.37	0.92	1.21
Group II (N=19)	2.26	2.19	3.37	3.61	2.37	1.59	.47	.88
Total group (N=45)	1.89	2.06	3.13	2.79	2.31	1.47	.73	1.11

TABLE 9.—*Number of subjects reporting mode of reaction to reported decreases* [1]

Number of subjects reporting decrease	Physical (N=44)					Cognitive (N=38)				
Percentage of decreases	A	B	C	D	E	A	B	C	D	E
0	24	9	38	39	22	26	23	36	38	29
1–100	20	35	6	5	22	12	15	2	0	9

Number of subjects reporting decrease	Personality-affective (N=30)					Social-psychological (N=41)				
Percentage of decreases	A	B	C	D	E	A	B	C	D	E
0	24	24	28	30	27	7	29	32	39	40
1–100	6	6	2	0	3	34	12	9	2	1

[1] Expressed in percent of decreases to which reactions have been reported by each subject.

A=Compensation; B=Acceptance; C=Complaint; D=Limitation; E=Qualification.

What factors contribute to the adaptation and maladaptation of the community-dwelling older individual to the crises of the aging period?

How important are psychosocial losses and disruptions compared to psychological predisposition, structure and defense? What kinds of psychological defense measures are observed?

How predictive of adjustment is diagnosis in this age group? How does morale relate to adjustment and upon what does morale depend?

To help study adaptive and maladaptive patterns, three psychiatrists, who had no knowledge of the subjects, each reviewed approximately one-third of the transcribed interviews and recorded their judgments using a questionnaire (see app. A, Independent Protocol Analysis). This questionnaire represented factors hypothesized by the authors to be of particular salience to the adaptation of the aged and to be of particular importance in assessment. The completed questionnaires of the independent consultants were reviewed by the authors and contributed to their final consensual judgments.

It was found that past life experiences, personality predisposition, and defensive structure, as well as the nature, incidence, and number of stresses, contributed to present adaptation. Persons who had experienced manifestly similar stresses varied widely in their reactions. Illustrative was depression in an obsessive-compulsive (Subject no. 7) compared to increased hypomania in a cyclothymic personality (Subject no. 8) in response to retirement.

Certain adaptive patterns were especially prevalent in this sample. The use of activity (to the extreme of counterphobic activity), denial of aging changes and status, and the adaptive use of lifelong psychopathology were prominent adaptive or defensive measures. These appeared or were intensified following stresses; in our judgment these adaptive techniques were of paramount importance in maintaining adjustment and averting depression; in ex-

istent depressions these mechanisms were reparative.

The counterphobic attitude (Fenichel, 1943) was recognized in the repetitive pattern of engagement in physical activities obviously excessive and even potentially dangerous to life and limb in old age. Individuals with this attitude displayed their youth and vigor daily, apparently to continually reassure themselves against their fears of aging and dying. Subjects No. 14 and 16 illustrate these men who would "not grow old." The former had belonged to a gymnastic group devoted to body culture and preservation since childhood. During his stay at the Institute he participated in vigorous competitive sports with young normal control volunteers. The other subject had not undertaken such a strenuous round of activities until after a stressful retirement and widowhood; the subject himself stated that his activities "keep me going and free of depression."

The phenomenon of denial of aging changes and status (Butler and Perlin, 1957) was observed in the minimization and/or direct refusal to "see" such changes within oneself which were obvious to others. This pattern occurred both in persons who had manifested denial (in the psychodynamic sense of denial as a mechanism of defense) in the past and in persons in whom no such history could be obtained.

The changing adaptive-maladaptive value or function of personality and psychopathology with advancing age and in a changing environment was an intriguing phenomenon. Diagnosis alone was not an adequate measure of adaptation. Obsessive-compulsive mechanisms were helpful in an enforced retirement vacuum. Schizoid detachment appeared to protect individuals from the inevitable losses of this period in life. Passive-dependent personality features often led to successful adaptation in a protected family situation, or in a home for the aged (Perlin, 1958).

These several adaptive measures frequently occurred in the same individual. For example, in eight individuals both counterphobia and denial coexisted. Similarly, the adaptive use of past psychopathology was often associated with denial and/or counterphobia. In table 10, the prevalence of these various techniques is shown; no relationship to groups I and II were found. (The data are given for individual subjects in app. B, tables 6 a and b.)

None of these mechanisms was observed in 16 of the 47 subjects. These individuals were characterized by their effective use of insight. Their perception of their changed circumstances of old age was accurate; their realistic and well-planned modification of their activities and goals was impressive. These subjects either had no psychiatric disorder or a mild personality disorder. Although the effective use of insight would appear to be the highest mode of adaptation, the constructive contributions of denial and counterphobia to adaptation were clear.

Past psychopathology was not always adaptive; exacerbation also occurred. Increasing isolation in a paranoid personality is illustrative; as his sphere of life activities and relationships contracted, his suspiciousness and paranoid ideas increased (Case No. 33). As described earlier (p. 163), new psychopathology (including nondiagnostic) developed in the geriatric period. Both exacerbation of old disorders and the emergence of new maladaptive patterns were found in the same individual. Psychological isolation and identity crises occurred in association with both new and exacerbated psychopathology, of both nondiagnostic and diagnostic proportions.

Identity crises (Erikson, 1959a) of significant proportions were present in 13 subjects. Most of these had diagnosable psychopathology which was either lifelong or new to the aging experience.

One subject (Case No. 24) had been orphaned at an early age, and following a period at an asylum, had been shifted from one foster home to another before final adoption. The subject apparently made a pretense of carrying out the usual roles of marriage, family, etc., within which he existed in isolation; only in his job, with the utilization of the "company" as a symbolic parent and overidentification with authority figures, was his sense of identity maintained. With retirement, there was a crisis in this aspect of his ego integration; he devoted considerable time and money to searching out records of who his "real mother" was in a rather feeble attempt to re-establish his sense of identity. This problem was further accentuated by the departure of his children to establish their own family units.

TABLE 10.—*Adaptive patterns in 47 aged subjects*

Adaptive pattern	Groups		Total (N=47)	Percent
	I (N=27)	II (N=20)		
Passivity-activity:				
1. Average passivity	14	8	22	47
2. Passive dependent	5	4	9	19
3. Counterphobic	8	8	16	34
Denial of aging status:				
Denial	11	6	17	36
No denial	16	14	30	64
Lifelong psychopathology useful	11	6	17	36

TABLE 11.—*Maladaptive patterns in 47 aged subjects*

Maladaptation	Groups		Totals (N=47)	Percent
	I (N=27)	II (N=20)		
New functional psychopathology	4	4	8	17
Exacerbation psychopathological reaction	6	7	13	28
Psychological isolation—severe	4	5	9	19
Age crisis in identity	6	7	13	28
Prediction of functional breakdown:				
1. Not expected	13	9	22	47
2. Any likelihood	12	7	19	40
3. Likely	2	4	6	13

"Functional Breakdown" was judged to be "likely" in six subjects, most of whom were depressed and had become psychologically isolated. In table 11, the prevalence of these maladaptive patterns[2] is given; there was frequent coexistence of these features in the same subject. There is a suggestive trend towards a greater prevalence of these features in group II (no statistical significance).

Two indices of present adjustment were developed. An index of adaptation, based on psychiatric ratings, pertains to current overall adjustment to the intrinsic and environmental aspects of the aging experience, irrespective of the adaptive techniques (which could be, as observed, psychopathological). (See app. A, VI, items 3 a, b, c.)

An Index of Morale was developed to reflect the self-evaluation of the subjects. It was intended to obtain some measure of what is seen as positive in the aging experience by the aged themselves. The Index refers to the percentage of personality-affective changes reported as increases. The High Morale subgroup is composed of subjects who reported over 50 percent of their personality-affective changes as increases.[3]

Twenty-six individuals fulfilled the definition of High Morale and 19 of Low Morale. (It will be recalled that two protocols were unavailable for content analysis.) Seventeen subjects were rated "excellent-very good" and 17 "fair-poor" in adaptation. No relationships were found between the medical groupings and morale, adaptation, or diagnosis.

The absence of a significant difference in morale between the Diagnosis and No Diagnosis subgroups indicated that diagnosis per se was not a crucial factor for low morale as defined here, nor was adaptation significantly associated with diagnosis. But adaptation and morale were significantly associated ($p < 0.005$).

Table 12 shows the occurrence of adaptive and maladaptive features in the Diagnosis and No Diagnosis groups. Denial of

[2] These patterns refer to the Independent Analysis Protocol Questionnaire (App. A, VI). Thus, the phrase, "New functional psychopathology" refers to a "reaction to aging," may or may not be a formal diagnosis, and should be distinguished from the "age-relevant" psychopathology discussed earlier, although overlap is present. The questionnaire was concerned with psychodynamics rather than nosology.

[3] Another measure of "morale", the inverse of the proportion of decreases to total changes reported, was compared to this Index. Agreement in the placement of individuals between these two procedures was 83 percent.

TABLE 12.—*Adaptive and maladaptive features found in No Diagnosis and Diagnosis subgroups*

Adaptive characteristic	No Diagnosis ($N=18$)	Diagnosis ($N=29$)	Significance of group difference
Adaptive patterns			
Passivity-activity:			
1. Average passivity	12	10	} N.S.
2. Passive-dependent	1	8	
3. Counterphobic	5	11	
Denial of aging status	2	15	} (*)
No denial of aging status	16	14	
Lifelong psychopathology useful	2	15	(**)
Maladaptive patterns			
New functional psychopathology	0	8	(*)
Exacerbation psychopathological reaction	3	11	(*)
Psychological isolation—severe	1	8	N.S.
Age crisis in identity	1	12	(*)
Prediction of functional breakdown:			
1. Not expected	13	9	} (*)
2. Any likelihood	5	14	
3. Likely	0	6	

* Significant at 0.05 level.
** Significant at 0.01 level.

aging status was significantly related to diagnosis. Although passive-dependent and counterphobic activity tended to occur in subjects with a diagnosis, the relationship of diagnosis to the passivity-activity continuum was not statistically significant. Severe psychological isolation and age crises in identity were almost always associated with diagnosis. Prediction of functional breakdown was significantly related to diagnosis.

There was a trend toward denial and counterphobic activity in the High Morale subgroup as compared to the Low Morale subgroup. There was no significant difference in the usefulness of psychopathology in the two subgroups; however, new psychopathology and severe psychological isolation were associated with low morale. Finally, the prediction of a functional breakdown was significantly related to morale. (See table 13.)

High Adaptation was significantly associated with high morale and with no diagnosis. Counterphobic activity tended to be associated with high adaptation, while denial did not. Lifelong psychopathology was present and useful in both groups, but more likely to be new and to be in exacerbation in the Low Adaptation subgroup. In this latter group, severe psychological isolation and the prediction of functional breakdown were significantly related. (See table 14.)

Although morale and adaptation varied together, there was no significant relationship between morale and diagnosis; diagnosis and adaptation were not consistently related. It was observed that diagnostic (and nondiagnostic) psychopathology may be overridden by an individual's morale and/or adaptation; moreover, such psychopathology may contribute to an individual's morale and/or adaptation. In order to help clarify the interrelationships between morale, adaptation, diagnosis and adaptive-maladaptive patterns groups were formed out of the

TABLE 13.—*Comparison of High Morale and Low Morale subgroups with respect to selected adaptive and maladaptive features*

Adaptive characteristics	High morale[1] (N=26)	Low morale (N=19)	Significance of group differences
Adaptive patterns			
Passivity-activity:			
1. Average passivity	12	10	
2. Passive-dependent	3	5	N.S.
3. Counterphobic	11	4	
Denial of aging status	12	5	N.S.
No denial of aging status	14	14	
Lifelong psychopathology useful	11	6	N.S.
Maladaptive patterns			
New functional psychopathology	1	7	(**)
Exacerbation psychopathological reaction	3	11	(**)
Psychological isolation—severe	1	8	(**)
Age crisis in identity	6	7	N.S.
Prediction of functional breakdown:			
1. Not expected	17	4	
2. Any likelihood	8	10	(**)
3. Likely	1	5	

[1] 2 protocols were unavailable for content analyses.
** Significant at 0.01 level.

TABLE 14.—*Comparison of high adaptation and low adaptation subgroups with respect to selected adaptive and maladaptive features*

Adaptive characteristics	High adaptation (N=17)	Low adaptation (N=17)	Significance of group differences
Adaptive patterns			
Passivity-activity:			
1. Average passivity	8	7	
2. Passive-dependent	0	7	(**)
3. Counterphobic	9	3	
Denial of aging status	7	8	N.S.
No denial of aging status	10	9	
Lifelong psychopathology useful	8	6	N.S.
Maladaptive patterns			
New functional psychopathology	1	5	N.S.
Exacerbation psychopathological reaction	1	8	(*)
Psychological isolation—severe	0	7	(**)
Age crisis in identity	2	6	N.S.
Prediction of functional breakdown:			
1. Not expected	13	2	
2. Any likelihood	4	9	(***)
3. Likely	0	6	

* Significant at 0.05 level.
** Significant at 0.01 level.
*** Significant at 0.001 level.

various combinations of Morale, Adaptation, and Diagnosis. Individual case descriptions follow.

The following description is of a subject without diagnostic psychopathology in the High Adaptation-High Morale subgroup, which was composed of 15 subjects, 8 without a diagnosis.

Subject No. 35 reported 60 percent of his personality-affective changes as increases, had no psychiatric diagnosis and was regarded as showing excellent adaptation to aging and the aging period.

Mr. C., a 74-year-old retired manufacturer, was spontaneous, garrulous, and relevant. His affect was variable and appropriate. There was no psychomotor retardation. During the interview he was integrated and frankly boastful of his accomplishments. There was no evidence of marked intellectual decline. Some general forgetfulness was reported on history; no impairments of memory were noted on the adapted mental status exam. He was not overly concrete, but performed irregularly on tests involving proverbs and similarities.

He was born in a small town in Eastern Europe, the first of a large number of children. He began work at age 9 and ran away from home at age 13. He did not regard his parents as "ideal" and indicated greater closeness to his mother. With reference to his father, a weaver, he indicated greater understanding over the years. He emigrated to the United States at age 24, the year of his marriage. He described his marriage as exemplary; his wife is living and well. Following a prostatectomy at 56, there was decreased sexual desire and in the past 10–15 years, no sexual intercourse. He has children and grandchildren with whom he has a satisfactory relationship and moderate interaction. The rebellion of his own children he regards as having helped him to view anew his own childhood and adolescence.

He planned for the aging period and makes plans for the future, about which he is optimistic. He is concerned about death, and prays he will die in his sleep. He denies belief in an afterlife and denies increased religious interest. He has made out his will and has selected a burial site.

There was reasonable recognition of his aging status and no denial. He "accepted" his physical changes. He was rated as having average passivity. The evaluation of the usefulness of lifelong psychopathology was regarded as "not relevant," and there was no new psychopathological reaction. There was no psychological isolation and no age identity crisis. He was not regarded as likely to have a functional breakdown.

The case description of a subject with a diagnosis in the High Adaptation-High Morale subgroup follows and illustrates the adaptive value of psychopathology.

Subject No. 54 was a 72-year-old professor of political science, diagnosed as a Schizoid Personality with obsessive and compulsive features.

In the interview, the subject was withdrawn and distant. His verbal productivity was increased with much circumstantiality and occasional irrelevance. There were lapses of attention with breaking of set. No language deviations were present. Reaction time seemed increased. Affect was appropriate but impressively shallow. He was guarded in the interview; he was assertive and controlling. Although he was of superior intelligence, he gave some evidence of decline. There were no impairments of orientation, memory, and judgment. He emphasized detachment-avoidance and a suspiciousness of close relationships.

Mr. L. was the first of six children. His father was a farmer; his mother died when he was age 10. For a time he lived with an uncle and then was sent to a home for indigent children. He states he was not close to either parent; and he recalls no reaction to his mother's death. He states he has always been a "detached onlooker." He emphasizes that his adult life, including graduation from college, resulted from "not letting things happen— I don't knock on wood and hope." Following graduation, he had a successful career. He married at age 27 and has one son. He appears to have had a relationship with his wife in which he assumed the role of a distant protector. He states: "She's never had a normal share of my time and activity." There has been little sexual interest for many years. In general, he sees life as a "scientific experiment," and people as "harsh and effecting their own tragedies." He is well-defended against the realization of limitations in his own life.

The subject retired 3 years ago and takes part-time assignments. He sees being aged as an "accumulated experience." He is planning activity for the future, which he views "scientifically." He gives evidence that in contrast to his earlier life, in which he was forced into interpersonal relationship with resulting suspiciousness, emotional crises, etc., his schizoid makeup together with retirement "freedom" permits the setting up of a psychologically comfortable distance between himself and the rest of the world. His very lack of interpersonal relationships seems to protect him from the reactions to loss found in other subjects.

He did not deny his aging status. His lifelong psychopathology was regarded as useful in the aging period. There was no new psychopathological reaction to aging. There was some counterphobic activity. Psychological isolation existed, and in the aging period was attributed to self and not to his environment; this was not severe. A problem of identity was present which, however, was not regarded as likely to lead to a functional breakdown. He utilized acceptance to over 50 percent of his changes in the physical area and compensation for over 50 percent of his changes in the social-psychological area.

Reference may be made to cardinal features of other subjects in the High Adaptation-High Morale group. Case No. 8 exhibits a hypomanic denial of his aging "role"; his morale is high and he adapts well. Case No. 14 is engaged in counterphobic activities to maintain and, when necessary, to compensate, for changes of age and the aging period. Case No. 42 has an obsessive-compulsive neurosis which interfered with work efficiency during earlier years; in his retirement there seems to be a "mellowing" of his neurosis, which contributes to filling in the vacuum brought about by enforced retirement. His obsessive-compulsive approach to life keeps him occupied with house, garden, workshop. His satisfaction with his routine, and its meaning, are expressed in his statement: "My house—is now in order."

In an "intermediate" subgroup of seven subjects there was no consensus between self-evaluation (as indicated by the Index of Morale) and psychiatric evaluation of adaptation. The high morale of five High Morale-Low Adaptation subjects (all with diagnoses) appeared in itself to be part of the defense against impending crisis and change. In one subject (Case No. 9), the ability to coerce the environment via the threat of disowning his children was still present; at such time that this manipulative ability is no longer present or relevant, a severe depression seems likely. Another subject (Case No. 3), fearful of retribution for past misdeeds, achieved a state of tentative security by obsessive-compulsive expiatory rituals. In another subject (Case No. 30), marked denial and counterphobic activity may have accounted for the high Index of Morale in the face of a depression,

which related to the death of wife and retirement; here, too, the wherewithal to manipulate the environment made for a precarious sense of security. In general these subjects were marked by increasing passivity in the "hands of fate" (in spite of the utilization of denial and counterphobic activity as reparative mechanisms), increasing psychological isolation, a sense of unfulfillment, and a growing awareness of an age crisis in identity with overall anxiety and concern regarding the future.

There were two subjects showing Low Morale but evaluated as showing excellent adaptation. One subject (Case No. 2), whose passive-dependent personality characteristic interfered with function during the "work-years" and in marriage, was secure in the knowledge of a forthcoming admission to a home for the aged despite his poor morale.

For purposes of comparison, the following cases will be selected from the Low Morale-Low Adaptation subgroup, comprising 11 individuals. Subjects, with and without diagnosis, will be described; 8 of the 11 had a psychiatric diagnosis.

Case No. 57 was a 74-year-old, retired, widowed engineer without a diagnosis. He appeared somewhat apathetic in interview. He seemed not to be involved in much of the questioning (decreased responsiveness) but was for the most part relevant and appropriate. His attention occasionally "wandered." Affect was variable and appropriate, but of limited range. He gave a history of some decrease in intellectual function as well as in recent memory. There were some slight difficulties in abstraction. He was considered to be borderline Senile Quality.

The subject's mother and five of his siblings were killed in a flash flood when the subject was aged 7. Thereafter he lived (alternately) with each set of grandparents. He denies overt reactions at the time of this family tragedy and indicates "distance" to such events. He married for the first time at age 30 and separated 5 years later; his second wife committed suicide after 8 years of marriage. To the latter event, he withdrew markedly in what he called a "shell-shock" state. He has been a widower for the past 30 years. There were no children.

Although interacting with others, there was apparently decreased pleasure. In each instance, there had been a history of a critical episode (long past), which seemed to relate to a subsequent state of apathy, sadness, and withdrawal.

He prospered in his career and whatever friendships he had were mostly among professional colleagues. Here, too, there was a sense of distance in his relationships. He showed concern for loss of friends and his own eventual death. He reports decreased sexual potency with maintained desire. He indicated numerous affairs over the years; in such relationships he was apt to let the woman "take the lead." He expressed regret in not remarrying. He had anticipated retirement, which was mandatory at age 70, but finds boredom in his "freedom."

There is no denial of aging status. There is no new reaction to aging and no exacerbation of past psychopathology. Passive dependent features are present but not marked. He is seen as psychologically isolated; age crisis in identity is not regarded to be present. He is not seen as likely to have a functional breakdown. (He was the first subject known to have died since the project's completion; his coronary death occurred about 1 year after study.)

In common with the above subject, two others also showed a picture of low morale and inability to compensate for losses while at the same time being unable to accept the status quo. There seemed to exist a "deadlock," resulting in isolation and the clinical picture of intense apathy and sadness without overt depression. These diagnosis-free Low Morale-Low Adaptation subjects (as well as the two Low Morale-High Adaptation subjects) seem to have lost their belief in the "integrity" of their own life cycle, and its meaning and place in relationship to familial and societal life cycles. Clinically, Erikson (1959a) has described the situation in which there is a "lack or loss of accrued ego integration . . . signified by despair and an often unconscious fear of death: the one and only life cycle is not accepted as the ultimate of life. Despair expresses the feeling that the time is short, too short for the attempt to start another life and to try out alternate roads of integrity. Such a despair is often hidden behind a show of disgust, a misanthropy, or a chronic contemptuous displeasure with particular institutions and particular people—a disgust and displeasure which . . . only signify the individual's contempt of himself." This description appears relevant to a number of the 11 Low Morale-Low Adaptation subjects found in this study, but not to all.

In contrast to the previous case, the following two subjects in the Low Morale-Low Adaptation subgroup suffered from overt depressions.

Case No. 11 was a 74-year-old tailor who suffered from a depression since the death of his wife 1½ years prior to admission.

In the interview, he was anxious, distrusting, irritable, and hostile. He had difficulty in maintaining attention and set. He revealed tangentiality, perseveration, and frequent flight of ideas. There was some psychomotor retardation. Affect was reduced in variability, but appropriate and of sufficient depth.

He was regarded as a member of the Senile Quality subgroup. There was a history of a progressive decrease in intellectual functioning. He tended to be concrete. Memory was impaired, especially for recent events. There was also impairment in all spheres of orientation as well as in judgment. Emotional lability was also present.

He presented clearly the agitation and anger of his depression which dated from the death of his wife. He revealed no feeling of guilt toward her, nor did he speak of her as a love object from whom he was now separated. Rather, he expressed open resentment that she should have existed at all; and following a description of his wife's supportive role, he expressed resentment that she should have left him to fend for himself. He expressed his anger at himself for having failed to coerce her, and his "rejecting" children.

The personal history is relevant insofar as he had apparently outcompeted his three siblings for his mother's attention and support. In his marriage he seemed to have outcompeted his children for sole attention from his wife; with her absence he finds himself defeated and depressed.

Another picture of depression is provided by Case No. 23, a 74-year-old former plumbing inspector who was also in the Low Adaptation-Low Morale group.

In the interview, he frequently lapsed into silence. There was little spontaneity. There was difficulty in maintaining attention and set. Perseveration occurred. He showed impairments in memory, abstraction, and judgment. Psychomotor retardation was marked. He was evaluated as showing Senile Quality, and his depression was the most severe of those observed.

Relevant to the current depression was the death of his 93-year-old mother, with whom he lived after the death of his wife 25 years ago. His anxiety was further increased by the increase in physical signs of aging and recent minor illnesses. He saw himself as defeated by the world on which he had depended. He pointed up his anger at being uncared for as well as the anger at himself for needing and demanding care at this time. (There are no children.)

He has no plans for the future; he sees death as the only event to be faced. He is cognizant of his dissolution, which extends to slovenliness, etc.; such recognition increases his feelings of despair. There is no denial of his present status. Lifelong psychopathology has not been useful. His marked passive dependency (which might become "useful" in a Home for the Aged) overshadows any attempts to compensate for losses. There is severe psychological isolation. Functional breakdown is regarded as a "most likely" possibility.

In a previous report (Butler and Perlin, 1957) the depressed subgroup was considered in detail; of especial interest was the continued community residence, lack of treatment, and the maintenance of adequate social functioning. The reactively depressed subjects were noted to have sustained major losses, particularly death of wife and enforced retirement. The depressed tended to be widowed, separated, divorced, or single. The data indicated that denial of aging losses was an early reparative mechanism which might precede or *modify* depression in the aged. Counterphobic activity was a particularly effective therapeutic measure. When denial, use of activity and other mechanisms of defense failed, awareness of personal, social, and aging losses aggravated the depressive process. In the diagnosed, Low-Morale-Low-Adaptation subjects, crises had already occurred and the reparative processes (such as denial and counterphobic activity) have been unsuccessful though they may have modified the end results.

Senile Quality and Adaptation

Five of the Senile Quality subjects also suffered from depression. The wide range of reactions to presumed senile changes, based on individual history, has been described before (Butler and Perlin, 1957; Hollender, 1959). Where awareness or insight takes precedence over denial, depression may develop or be aggravated by the development of senile changes. In the two extreme Senile Quality subjects (Chronic Brain Syndrome), depression was not present, suggesting that with advancement of the process an incapacity to perceive may be operating rather than the utilization of denial. Senile changes may interfere with an individual's self- and outer-perception and may affect as well others' perception of him. Simple, direct relationships were not found to exist between Senile Quality and the adaptation score, morale, and adaptive patterns; the Senile Quality subject was not found to be more liable to psychological isolation and identity crises; nor were predictions of functional breakdown more likely.

DISCUSSION

Selection of a medically-healthy, community-resident, nonpsychotic aged sample was the fundamental methodological feature of this multidisciplinary project. It provided the psychiatrists the opportunity to compare the findings in this population with the prevailing views about the aged which principally derive from studies of the sick and institutionalized. Our initial assumptions concerning methods of conceptualization and investigation seem to us to have been sufficiently useful to warrant reemphasis.

We assumed that psychiatric evaluation should lay stress upon the current life situation as well as upon the past, for adaptation does not occur in a vacuum. We emphasized the multifactorial viewpoint; we believed that many factors determine the normal and abnormal behavior of the aged. We viewed psychiatric evaluation as one part of an overall (extensive and intensive) evaluation of the aged person which would also include medical, neurophysiological, psychological tests and sociological assessment. We considered it necessary to know both what the aged individual brings into the aging experience and the nature of this experience. Our methods of assessment and analyses focused upon the following major variables: (1) current psychopathology, whether functional or "organic" (designated here as senile quality), whether new or old, and whether diagnostic or symptomatic; (2) age-relevant changes, whether intrinsic or environmental; (3) subjective response, including personal reports of modes of adaptation and morale; (4) overall adjustment; and (5) the adaptive and maladaptive functions and consequences of psychopathology and personality structure in the context of the aging experience.

Although quantitative evaluation of etiological factors would require further investigation, we believed qualitative delineation to be an essential prelude. Nonetheless, attempts to quantify certain of the major variables were made. Utilizing a standardized mental status examination and symptom and behavioral rating scales, tentative criteria for senility were offered. A drawback to this methodological study was the circumstance that the evidence examined in this attempt to delineate characteristics of senility may have been implicit in the clinical impression. A second methodological development was the application of content analysis towards finding a reliable and valid technique for obtaining the older person's conscious recognition of changes occurring with advancing years. It is suggested that both the method of eval-uating senility and the technique for obtaining self-reported changes with age might be usefully employed in the study and comparison of other aged samples selected along various lines such as diagnosis, institutionalization, and the like.

Although representativeness cannot be claimed for this volunteer sample, the substantive results, such as diagnostic findings, may be compared to other studies. The prevalence of psychopathology in this aged sample is similar to that reported in younger volunteer samples (Lasagna and von Felsinger, 1954; Perlin, Pollin, and Butler, 1958), but higher than that reported from various community surveys (Pasamanick, Roberts, Lemkau, and Krueger, 1959). (However, the methods employed in community surveys and their results have been quite variable.) In fact, the mental health of this group as a whole was impressive. Existent psychopathology was not associated with serious impairment. As a group they more than adequately functioned in the community and showed effective insight and/or other adaptive patterns. Mental alertness, flexibility, and candor were characteristic.

Further evaluation of the fixed, prevailing ideas and stereotypes about the aged is made obvious by our findings. It was notable, for example, that many of the aged considered their "aging" changes to be increases, not deficits. It was also impressive how many individuals with signs of depression and/or senility continued to function adequately in the community. Theoretical and practical consequences can be expected to follow from the study of the functioning aged which, in fact, comprise the majority of the aged and do not constitute a "problem." Since the greater number of aged do reside in the community, are not psychotic and are in functional medical health, this sample is probably less exceptional and more representative than previously studied samples of the aged.

It is recognized that the kinds of discoveries in the psychodynamics and psychopathology of the aged are inevitably linked to the selection of subjects investigated (Perlin, Pollin, and Butler, 1958) and that the meaning of volunteering is of significance (Pollin and Perlin, 1958; Butler and Perlin, 1958). The frequency of counterphobia and denial of aging changes may partly have been a reflection of one motivation for volunteering, "tested" assurance of physical and mental well-being.

In our view, the impressive incidence of depression reflected the increased incidence of environmental stresses and crises so prevalent in the old age period. There was no evidence linking depression to organic variables or the "aging process." Why certain individuals were disposed to develop depression in response to certain stresses while others did not, emphasizes the importance of personality structure. To consider a social variable (e.g., death of spouse) to have equivalent effects is unjustified.

The variation in the nature and function of psychopathology as well as of mature, "healthy" modes of adaptation was a striking finding. It suggested the need to reconsider current nosology and diagnostic evaluation. In certain individuals there was amelioration; in others, exacerbation of old psychopathology. In still other individuals, psychopathology was seen to be useful, for example, as a defense against depression. The fact that psychopathology could be adaptive in one period and not in another implied that current psychiatric nosology is not invariably predictive. The psychological understanding of the individual (that is, psychodynamic formulation) is important to assessment, in addition to standard classification (diagnosis) and phenomenological description. Moreover, qualification must be taken to such textbook views as "the more immature and maladjusted . . . have been the adaptations of earlier life, the smaller is the stress required in old age to produce disorganized or disturbed behavior," (Noyes and Kolb, 1958).

The occurrence of age-crises in identity in this sample was of theoretical as well as practical interest. Erikson (1959b) has defined the personal sense of identity and ego identity as follows: "The conscious feeling of having a personal identity is based on two simultaneous observations: the immediate perception of one's selfsameness and continuity in time; and the simultaneous perception of the fact that others recognize one's sameness and continuity. . . . Ego identity, then, in its subjective aspect, is the awareness of the fact that there is a selfsameness and a continuity to the ego's synthesizing methods and that these methods are effective in safeguarding the sameness and continuity of one's meaning for others."

In our subjects experiencing an age-crisis in identity there was an apparent substitution of one or more features of identity for the whole of identity. Thus, the utilization of a role, the obsessive-compulsive community "helper," which permits expiation of guilt or of an overidentification, as with the "powerful" therapist, may function as a substitute for a more complex and probably more stable sense of identity. Because of the equating of a part for the whole, any change in this segment of the individual's existence may precipitate a crisis and potential loss of "going concern" status. For example, a marked shift in role or in body structure (and in the relationship of physical self-representation to identity) or in the relationship to a parental figure may each threaten crisis.

In our opinion, the retention of a psychodynamically *functional* sense of identity is particularly important to the adaptation of the aged. It seems clinically crucial in the maintenance of a transition phase or barrier between, for example, the depression of a community-resident old person and that depression which might necessitate his hospitalization. Just as schizoid withdrawal may not be a mature mode of reaction to postretirement freedom, so too this functional sense of identity may deviate from a theoretical normality or maturity and still be a sound mechanism for survival.

For all our subjects there had been a crisis in identity in the very "sensing" of themselves as old. However, to paraphrase Erikson's statement regarding adolescence (Erikson, 1959b), finding oneself old has been a normative crisis, not an affliction, for most if not all of our subjects. Nevertheless, for 13 of our sample, an "age-crisis in identity" seemed to threaten such affliction. Needless to say, not all our subjects, even prior to the aged years, had attained fully a sense of identity. Further, such failure may not have been recognized until the retirement period. With aging, too, there seems to be further corroboration of the concept that "identity," once achieved, cannot be taken for granted.

At that point at which the individual faces the possibility of identity diffusion (that is, the shattering of a sense of identity), a "stereotype" of an aged individual may be chosen as a personal identity. This "stereotype identity" is a partial counterpart of what Erikson designates as the "negative identity; e.g., an identity perversely based on all those identifications and roles which at critical stages of development had been presented to the individual as most undesirable or dangerous, and yet also as most real" (Erikson, 1959b). Thus, "stereotype identity" seems to have been the substitute for identity diffusion; self-perception and "other-perception" thus remain unified in the service of identity.

The finding that a substantial number of this sample considered many of their changes associated with advancing age as positive and other changes as modifiable was contrary to prevailing views. We believe these features are significant to the characterization of the physical and emotional health of our sample. We postulate an Acceptance-Compensation continuum of reaction based on the degree of "reparability" of change in aging and the aging period. The organic and psychological capacities (in addition to motivation) to perceive and pay attention to what is reparable, as well as the ability to plan and act accordingly, would appear important. Self-perceived, manifest Acceptance may have such psychodynamic counterparts as insight, detachment, or even denial; and Compensation includes activity which may be regarded as counterphobic. We suspect that Acceptance and Compensation (and their psychodynamic counterparts) are importantly related to the maintenance of personal identity.

The effects of social, medical, neurophysiological, and other factors are considered elsewhere in the volume (ch. 15). In this generally healthy functioning sample, global measures of health (groups I and II) had little apparent effect upon adaptation. Similarly chronological age per se did not appear to be the potent explanatory variable in the psychopathology of the aged that it has so often been considered to be. Within the limits of this study, senility did not appear to be an inevitable consequence of aging but a morbid process. The usefulness of distinguishing senility from senescence is suggested.

The importance of direct evaluation of the aged subject, not evaluation in the shade of fixed ideas such as "irreversibility," "second childhood," "organicity," "rigidity," must be emphasized. Evaluation, of course, must always precede treatment and should occur early in the course of disturbance. Early recognition of and distinction between senescence, senility, and depression, for example, has been neglected in the aged. Since it is our view that neither depression nor senility would appear to be inevitable consequences of the "aging process," but rather morbid conditions, their treatability should not be dismissed. The similarity of functional disorders of old age to those of the younger adult, as well as the mental flexibility observed, suggests that the aged are more accessible to psychotherapeutic intervention than has been usually recognized. The community-resident aged are rarely seen by psychiatrists (Bowman, 1959) and when they are finally seen, are often considered untreatable and are relegated to custodial care (Hollingshead and Redlich, 1958).

In a pilot study of this kind, generalization is limited. Followup of this sample (such as of the Senile Quality subjects), as well as extension into other populations, would be desirable. For example, there are likely to be differences in adaptation to the aging experience between the female and male aged.

The varieties of adaptation and psychopathology described may be taken as approximate models (e.g., tentative criteria of senility) of functioning aged subjects against which comparisons may be made with other community as well as institutionalized samples; e.g.: hospitalized depressions to these ambulatory depressions; hospitalized Chronic Brain Syndrome cases to these Senile Quality and senescent subgroups. The identification of certain adaptive techniques can be compared in other samples. Further exploration of variables

of special significance to the psychology of the aged is indicated.

The final psychological development of man is largely ignored by contemporary personality theory. The study of those who have attained the final period of life, in terms of survival and the character of the survivors, should enlarge our everyday concepts of stress and defense. The meanings of death, of time, of self-perceived changes, of losses, and of grief, of loneliness, and of isolation, are among the "themes" with which the aged are particularly experienced, but which remain to be systematically investigated.

SUMMARY OF RESULTS

1. In this group of 47 nonpsychotic and predominantly, medically healthy, community-resident volunteers, 28 percent had psychoneuroses and 62 percent presented diagnosable functional psychopathology, including personality disorders.

   a. Mild reactive depression constituted the most common single diagnostic class (19 percent of the sample).

   b. Diagnosable psychopathology, including depression, had its origin in the aging period in 23 percent.

   c. Modification of psychopathology including exacerbation and amelioration had occurred with advancing age.

   d. Existent psychopathology was not associated with serious impairments. None of these subjects sought treatment nor was treatment indicated.

2. Among the individuals who were evaluated as exhibiting "Senile Qualities," a commonality of characteristics was observed involving intellectual functions and feelings; namely, decreased comprehension, memory, attention and set, as well as reduced emotional responsiveness. It is postulated that these individuals represent early senility.

a. Criteria are offered for the early separation of depression from senescence and senility; their use for the selection of control groups in the study of severe psychopathological states, and in the search for interdisciplinary relationships is also suggested.

b. Senile Quality may reflect diverse etiology and subcategories may vary in their subsequent course. Among the alternatives it was hypothesized that Senile Quality represents an early Chronic Brain Syndrome which would progress to the completed picture seen in the hospitalized case. Clinical evidence suggesting this relationship was provided.

c. It was further hypothesized that neurophysiological and medical correlation would further illuminate Senile Quality. There was no relationship between the presence and degree of Senile Quality and global measures of medical health (groups I and II). (See ch. 15).

d. Chronological age did not differ between the senile and senescent groups.

3. The importance of chronological age per se as an overriding factor in the psychiatric disorders of the aging appears questionable; the significance of other factors, including personality, psychosocial disruptions and losses, diseases and the like, is emphasized.

4. Efforts were directed toward further defining the aging experience of an individual, in terms of intrinsic and environmental changes, and reactions to them.

a. All subjects described changes. The mean number of changes reported by a subject was 15, the greatest number of these being physical changes (mean = 6). Personality-affective, social-psychological and cognitive changes followed.

b. Changes were not uniformly viewed as deficit in character by the aged subject, as they are so frequently described in the literature pertaining to old age. Changes were often reported as increases. Increases were especially described in the personality-affective sphere, where 14 subjects, or 32 percent, reported all of these changes as increases. Social-psychological changes were also frequently reported as increases, whereas physical and cognitive changes were almost wholly reported as deficits.

c. Changes were not uniformly viewed as inevitable and unalterable by the aged subject. There was a relationship between the kind of change and the mode of reaction reported. Acceptance was the most frequently reported reaction to physical decreases; compensation was to social-psychological decreases; and both were to cognitive and personality-affective decreases. This mode of Acceptance-Compensation may reflect the selection of and be characteristic of this sample; i.e., healthy and noninstitutionalized.

5. Medical health (within the narrow range in this sample) was not significantly related to diagnostic psychopathology, Senile Quality, changes, morale, and adaptation.

6. The personal meaning or psychological significance of psychosocial losses and disruptions appeared to be as important as the nature, incidence or number of such stresses per se in the adaptation of the aged.

7. Effective use of insight involving accurate perceptions of the changed circumstances of old age and appropriate behavioral modifications was a common occurrence. Other adaptive patterns included the use of activity (to extreme counterphobic activity), denial of aging changes and status, and the adaptive use of lifelong psychopathology (e.g., schizoid and obsessive mechanisms). Prior to the aging period, such psychopathology had often been maladaptive.

8. Maintenance of a functional sense of identity seemed to be crucial to successful

adaptation. For most subjects, finding oneself old was a normative crisis, not an affliction. In 13 subjects experiencing an age-crisis as an affliction, one or more features of identity often substituted for the whole of identity. An apparent alternative to the shattering of functional identity was the acceptance of the stereotyped identity of an aged person.

9. In addition to age-crises in identity, severe psychological isolation and depression were especially maladaptive clinical patterns.

10. In contrast to other age groups where diagnosis is reasonably predictive of adaptation, in the aged the discrepancy between diagnosis and adaptation seems to be much greater, suggesting a need for revision in assessment and diagnosis in the aged. Evidence was presented suggesting the importance of evaluating the relationship of morale to the nature and effectiveness of adaptive techniques in the contemporary aging experience.

ACKNOWLEDGMENTS

The authors wish especially to express their appreciation to Mrs. Martha Werner and Mr. Walter Ladusky for their contributions of ideas and research assistance in the course of this work. To Dr. Edward S. Fleming, Mrs. June T. Caldwell, Mr. Kenneth Haun, Mr. Bert Brenner, Mr. Sidney Haddad, and Mrs. Lillian Sulliman, we are also indebted for research assistance.

To Dr. Donald F. Morrison and Dr. Samuel Greenhouse we are especially indebted for contributions towards the design of the study as well as for aid in the statistical analyses.

Dr. William Pollin contributed to the conceptualization and conduct of the content analysis of self-reported changes.

Drs. Reneal C. Cobb, A. Russell Lee, and Frederick Snyder provided independent psychiatric evaluations of the interview transcriptions.

Miss Margaret A. O'Brien and Miss Barbara DuBois transcribed the interviews and Mrs. Eunice B. Powers and Mrs. Elizabeth K. Porter provided invaluable technical assistance.

We were continually stimulated by the thoughtful comments and suggestions of Dr. Leon Yochelson, Medical Care Consultant to the Clinical Center, National Institutes of Health, and Professor and Chairman of the Department of Psychiatry, George Washington University School of Medicine.

The Fellows at the Center for Advanced Study in the Behavioral Sciences, Stanford, Calif., provided stimulating discussions of the material. The secretarial and research staff members of the Center were also most generous in their assistance during the Fellowship in 1959 of one of the authors (S.P.).

REFERENCES

ABRAHAM, K. 1927. The applicability of psychoanalytic treatment to patients at an advanced age. (First published in German, 1927; now available in English in the following book published in 1949.) *Selected Papers of Psychoanalyses.* London: Hogarth Press. pp. 312–317.

AMERICAN PSYCHIATRIC ASSN. 1952. Mental Disorders, *Diagnostic and Statistical Manual.* Washington, D.C.

BOWMAN, K. M. 1959. Geriatrics. Review of Psychiatric Progress, 1958. *Amer. J. Psychiat.* *115*: 621–23.

BUSSE, E. W., BARNES, R. N., and SILVERMAN, A. J. 1954a. Studies in the processes of aging: I. Behavior patterns in the aged and their relationship to adjustment. *Dis. Nerv. System,* 15: 22–26.

———— ———— ————, SHY, G. M., THALER, MARGARET, and FROST, L. L. 1954b. Studies of the process of aging: Factors that influence the psyche of elderly persons. *Amer. J. Psychiat.,* *110*: 897–903.

BUTLER, R. N. 1960. Intensive psychotherapy for the hospitalized aged. *Geriatrics.* 15: 644–653.

BUTLER, R. N. and PERLIN, S. 1957. Depressive reactions in the aged: the function of denial, awareness and insight. Presented at 113th Annual Meeting, American Psychiatric Assn., Chicago, Ill. Mimeographed.

————. 1958. Psychiatric consultation in a research setting, *Med. Annals D.C.* 27: 503–06.

CAMERON, N. 1956. Neuroses of later maturity. In O. J. Kaplan (ed.), *Mental Disorders in Later Life.* (2d ed.) Stanford, Calif.: Stanford Univ. Press, pp. 201–243.

CLOW, H. E. 1940. A study of 100 patients suffering from psychosis with cerebral arteriosclerosis. *Amer. J. Psychiat.,* 97: 16–26.

———— and ALLEN, E. B. 1951. Manifestations of psychoneuroses occurring in later life. *Geriatrics,* 6: 31–39.

ERIKSON, ERIK H. 1959a. Growth and Crises of the Healthy Personality. *Psychological Issues,* Vol. 1, No. 1. New York: International Universities Press, Inc.

————. 1959b. The Problem of Ego Identity. *Psychological Issues,* Vol. 1, No. 1. New York: International Universities Press, Inc.

————. 1959c. Ego Development and Historical Change. *Psychological Issues,* Vol. 1, No. 1. New York: International Universities Press, Inc.

FENICHEL, O. 1944. Remarks on the common phobias. *Psychoanal. Quart.* 13: 313–326.

————. 1945. *The Psychoanalytic Theory of Neurosis.* New York: W. W. Norton.

GALPERN, MARIE, TURNER, HELEN, and GOLDFARB, A. 1952. The psychiatric evaluation of applicants for a home for the aged. *Soc. Casework, 33:* 152–160.

GINSBERG, R. 1955. Psychiatric and psychological techniques in the treatment and management of elderly psychotics. International Association of Gerontology, Third Congress. *Old Age in the Modern World.* London: E. and S. Livingstone, p. 115.

GOLDFARB, A. I. 1955. Psycotherapy with aged persons: Patterns of adjustment in a home for the aged. *Ment. Hyg., 36:* 608–621.

———— and TURNER, HELEN. 1953. Psychotherapy of aged persons. II. Utilization and effectiveness of "brief" therapy. *Amer. J. of Psychiat., 109:* 916–921.

GROTJAHN, M. 1955. Analytic psychotherapy with the elderly. I. The sociological background of aging in America. *The Psychonal. Rev., 42:* 419–427.

HOLLENDER, M. H. 1952. Individualizing the aged. *Soc. Casework, 33:* 337–342.

————. 1959. Early psychologic reactions associated with organic brain disease in the aged. *N.Y. State J. Med., 59:* 802–809.

HOLLINGSHEAD, A. B., and REDLICH, F. C. 1958. *Social Class and Mental Illness.* New York: John Wiley & Sons, Inc.

KAUFMAN, M. R. 1940. Old age and aging; the psychoanalytic point of view. *Amer. J. Orthopsychiat., 10:* 73–84.

KAY, D. W., ROTH, M., and HOPKINS, B. 1955. Affective disorders arising in the senium. I. Their association with organic cerebral degeneration. *J. Ment. Sci., 101,* 423: 302–316.

KRAPF, E. E. 1953. On aging. *Proc. Roy. Soc. Med.* 46: 957–964.

LASAGNA, L., and VON FELSINGER, J. M. 1954. The volunteer subject in research. *Science, 20:* 359–361.

LEWIS, N. D. C. 1943. Outlines for Psychiatric Examinations (3d ed.) Albany, N.Y.: N.Y. State Dept. of Mental Hygiene.

LINDEN, M. E. 1953. Group psychotherapy with institutionalized senile women; study in gerontologic human relations. *Int. J. Group Psychother., 3:* 150–170.

NOYES, A. P., and KOLB, L. C. 1958. *Modern Clinical Psychiatry.* (5th ed.). Philadelphia and London: W. B. Saunders.

PASAMANICK, B., ROBERTS, D. W., LEMKAU, P. W., and KRUEGER, D. E. 1959. A survey of mental disease in an urban population; prevalence by race and income, in *Epidemiology of Mental Disorder,* Ed. B. Pasamanick, Washington, D.C., Publ. No. 60, Amer. Assn. Advancement Sci., pp. 183–196.

PERLIN, S. 1958. Psychiatric screening in a home for the aged: I. A followup study. *Geriatrics, 13:* 747–751.

————, POLLIN, W., and BUTLER, R. N. 1958. The experimental subject. I. The psychiatric evaluation and selection of a volunteer population. *A.M.A. Arch. of Neur. & Psychiat., 80:* 65–70.

POLLIN, W., and PERLIN, S. 1958. Psychiatric evaluation of "normal control" volunteers. *Amer. J. Psychiat., 115:* 129–133.

RECHTSCHAFFEN, A., ATKINSON, S., and FREEMAN, J. G. 1953. An intensive treatment program for state hospital geriatric patients. *Geriatrics, 9:* 28–34.

ROTH, M. 1955. The natural history of mental disorder in old age. *J. Ment. Sci., 101,* 423: 281–301.

———— and KAY, D. W. 1956. Affective disorders arising in the senium II. Physical disability as an etiological factor. *J. Ment. Sci., 102,* 426: 141–150.

ROTHSCHILD, D. 1937. Pathological changes in senile psychosis and their psychiatric significance. *Amer. J. Psychiat., 93:* 757–788.

ROTHSCHILD, D. 1942. Neuropathologic changes in arteriosclerotic psychosis and their psychological significance. *Arch. Neurol. & Psychiat., 48:* 417–436.

SCHILDER, P. 1940. Psychiatric aspects of old age and aging. *Amer. J. Orthopsych., 10:* 62–69.

STERN, K., SMITH, J., and FRANK, M. 1953. Mechanism of transference and counter-transference in psychotherapeutic and social work with the aged. *J. Geront., 8:* 328–332.

TERMAN, L. M., and MERRILL, M. A. 1937. *Measuring Intelligence.* Boston: Houghton-Mifflin Co.

WECHSLER, D. 1955. *The Measurement of Adult Intelligence.* (3d ed.). Baltimore: Williams & Wilkins.

WEINBERG, J. 1955. Personal and social adjustment. In *Psychological Aspects of Aging.* Proceedings of a Conference on Planning Research, Division of Maturity and Old Age. Bethesda, Md., April 1955, edited by Anderson, J. E., American Psychological Association (publisher). pp. 17–21.

WERNER, MARTHA, PERLIN, S., BUTLER, R. M., and POLLIN, W. 1961. Self-perceived changes in community-resident aged: "Aging Image" and adaptation. *Archives of General Psychiatry, 4:* 501–508.

APPENDIX A

PSYCHIATRIC INTERVIEW

INTERVIEW I

I. *Explanation:* An initial, standardized explanation is made to each subject at the time of introduction on the ward.

II. *History of Psychiatric Contact*

III. The first interview, while for the most part free and nondirective, does include questions designed to obtain (1) a personal history, and (2) a record of psychiatric symptomatology. (See Psychiatric Symptom Check List). Check lists are used for reference to increase comparability of data.

1. *Personal History Checklist*
   A. *Early family life:*
   B. *Kind of Child: Disposition*
   C. *Parents or substitutes:*
   D. *Siblings:*
   E. *Sex, marriage, children:*
   F. *Work:*

2. *Psychiatric Symptom Checklist:*

3. At the end of the first interview, the interviewer will ask the subject: "How long have we been talking together?" to assess subjective appreciation of time duration.

INTERVIEW II

"Structured" Interview

I. Formal Mental Status Evaluation (including one-half of the verbal Wechsler Adult Intelligence Scale).

II. Psychiatric Evaluation of Concepts of Potential Age Relevance.
   A. Futurity
   B. Death
   C. Self-Concept:
      1. Self-Perceived Changes.
      2. Ideal Parents.

NAME: _____ DATE: _____ SUBJECT NO.: _____

INTERVIEWER: _____ OBSERVER: _____ SCORER: _____

I. MENTAL STATUS EVALUATION

I. *RETENTION:*
   "I am going to tell you an address which I want you to remember. I will ask for it at a later time. This is the address: (Alternate)
   Apartment C   Room 7
   Arbor Estates   Carrier Hotel
   "Repeat that for me now." Continue with II. (Time interval: 5 minutes)
   Then, "Do you remember the address I gave you a few minutes ago?"
   Raw Score: (−1, 0, 1, 2, 3, or 4)   _____

II. *REMOTE MEMORY:*
   (Write out subject's response. Score 1 point for each correct answer.)   *Score*
   1. Where were you born?
   _____ _____
   2. Where did you go to school?
   _____ _____

3. Highest grade completed?
   _____ _____
4. How old were you when you finished school?
   _____ _____
5. How old were you when you began work?
   _____ _____
6. Name of first employer?
   _____ _____
7. Address of first employer?
   _____ _____
8. Mother's maiden name?
   _____ _____
9. Who was President of United States when you began your first job? (In this country when foreign born.)
   _____ _____

Remote Memory Score: Sum of correct answers

III. *ORIENTATION:*

(Rate 1, 2, or 3 for A, B, and C)

A. *TIME:* _____ _____

What is the date today? (If not complete)
What year (month, day) is it? What season is it?
1. No awareness of correct time (e.g., does not know month, season, or year.)
2. Disturbed orientation, but some degree of awareness (e.g., knows season or year, etc.)
3. Knows exact time (month, approximate day, year, and season.)

B. *PLACE:* _____ _____

What is the name of this place?
Where is it?
1. No awareness of location.
2. Disturbed orientation, but can give an approximation that is reasonably accurate.
3. Knows exact location.

C. *PERSON:* _____ _____

What is my job? (other members of the staff?)
1. No knowledge of who or what the examiner or staff is.
2. Some knowledge of above.
3. Knows exactly who and what they are.

Orientation Score: Sum of A, B, C. _____

IV. *RECENT MEMORY:*

(Check when you are certain he is correct, otherwise write in subject's response. Leave blank if incorrect. 1 point for each correct response.)
1. Where do you live?_____ _____
2. How long have you lived there?__ _____
3. How long have you been here?____ _____
4. Where were you a week ago?_____ _____
5. How many meals have you had today?

_____ _____
6. What did you have for breakfast? _____
7. What is my name?_____ _____
8. When did you see me for the first time?

_____ _____
9. Have you been in this room before?

_____ _____

Recent Memory Score: Sum of correct answers

_____ _____

V. *READING* (Logical Memory):

"I am going to read you a story. Listen carefully." Then, "Now tell me what I read. Begin at the beginning and tell me everything that you can remember" . . . "and what else?"

(21 possible memories. Check every memory. Leave spaces beside wrongly remembered or omitted facts blank. When in doubt write out response. 1 point for each memory.)

From: Terman, L. M., and Merrill, M. A., Measuring Intelligence, Houghton-Mifflin Co., 1937, pp. 255–256.

Logical Memory Score: Sum of memories

_____ _____

VI. *ABSURDITIES:*

"I am going to read to you some foolish statements and I want you to tell me what is foolish about them." (Check when you are certain he is correct. Leave blank when you are certain he is incorrect. When interpretation is necessary, write down subject's response.)

(Directions: Read each statement and ask, "What is foolish about that?")

From: Terman, L. M., and Merrill, M. A., ibid., pp. 235–239; 244–248.

A. Absurdities I: (4 questions)
(Ask if subject misses 3 or more of Section B items.)

Score_____ _____

(Score 4 if not given) No. correct: _____

B. Absurdities II: (5 questions) (ASK THESE FIRST) No. correct: _____ _____

VII. *OPPOSITES:*

"I am going to say some words and I want you to tell me the word that has the opposite meaning."

(15 word list. Check when correct opposite is given. Otherwise write his error or "Don't know." When subject gives logical opposite, but grammatical error, write out. Delayed response is acceptable.)

From: Lewis, N. D. C., Outlines for Psychiatric Examinations, Albany, N.Y., New York State Department of Mental Hygiene, 3d edition, 1943, p. 85; ultimately derived from Kent, Grace H., Emergency Battery of One-Minute Tests, J. of Psych., vol. 13, 1942, pp. 141–164.

Sum _____ _____

(Up to the item where subject "broke set.")

VIII. *PROVERBS:*

(Write in subject's response. Score 0, 1, 2.)

From: Three items: 7, 13, and 14 of Comprehension, in Wechsler, D., WAIS Manual, Psychological Corp., 1955, p. 36.

Proverbs Score_____ _____

IX. *INFORMATION:*

(15 items. Discontinue after 3 failures. 1 point for each correct answer)

From: Items 1, 3, etc., from Information, in Wechsler, D., ibid., p. 33–35.

Total Raw Score_____ _____

X. *COMPREHENSION* (judgment):

(7 items. Item 1 is scored 2 or 0 points. The remaining items are each scored 2, 1, or 0. Credit 2 points for subjects for whom the first item was not administered. If in doubt, write down subject's response for later interpretation.)

Score:
1. Why do we wash clothes?_____ _____

From: Items 3, 5, 6, 8, 10, 12 of Comprehension, in Wechsler, D., ibid., p. 36.

Total Raw Score_____ _____

XI. *CALCULATIONS:*

(6 problems. Record time for each response from the end of the first presentation. Full credit for correct numerical quantity, even if units unstated or wrong.)

From: Items 3, 5, 7, 9, 11, and 13, from Arithmetic, Wechsler, D., ibid., p. 37–38.

Number correct: _____ _____

Number of Bonus Credits: _____ _____

Total Raw Score: _____ _____

XII. *SIMILARITIES:*

(Abstraction Ability) (7 pairs. Write subject's response. Score 2 points each.)

From: Items 1, 3, 5 etc., from Similarities, in Wechsler, D., ibid., p. 39.

Total Raw Score: _____ _____

XIII. *DIGIT SPAN:*

From Wechsler, D., ibid., p. 40–41. No changes introduced.

XIV. *VOCABULARY:*

(20 words. Check if correct. Blank if incorrect. Write "Don't know" when subject so indicates. 2 points for each correct definition.)

From: Items 1, 3, etc., from Vocabulary, in Wechsler, D., ibid., p. 42–43.

Total Raw Score: _____ _____

Special List:

    21. Eyelash _____

    22. Puddle _____

    23. Muzzle _____

XV. "How do you feel you did in answering these questions?"

Answer: _____

I. CONCEPT EVALUATION

A. FUTURITY

I.

1. Do you think of yourself as young, middle-aged, old, or very old?
   a. Why? Anything else?
   b. Why don't you think of yourself as old? (If question applies.)
2. Years ago, did you prepare yourself for being older either emotionally or financially?
   a. Why or why not?
   b. Do you wish you had? If so, why?
3. Did your parents or friends make plans for their future, especially old age?
4. Are you making plans for the future now? Why or why not?
5. a. Do you plan for things as they come along? Or do you simply do the best you can under the circumstances?
   b. Do you feel planning is within your control? Or does it depend on other people, Social Security, etc.?

6. Did you plan for retirement—in recent years?
   a. What did you plan to do during retirement?
   b. Was your retirement voluntary, forced, other?
   c. What were your anticipations about the retirement period?
   d. What did you think retirement would be like?
   e. Is retirement similar to the way you visualized it?

II.

1. When you were young, what were the attitudes of your parents and family about older people?
2. When you were a child, what were your attitudes and feelings re older people?
   a. When you were in your twenties?
3. How were older people treated when you were young?
   a. How has this changed?
4. What are the advantages of being_____years old for you?
5. What are the disadvantages of being_____years old for you?
6. Do some of the problems you are having now remind you of another period in your life? Or are they specific for this period?
   a. Are the adjustments you are making to an older age similar to another period? (Do you handle or meet problems in a different way now?)

III.

1. What are your plans for the future?
2. What are your feelings about your future?
3. Can you picture or see yourself 10 years from now?
4. Do you think much about (your) future?
   a. What do you think about when you do?
5. What do you think will happen to you as you grow older?
   a. What are your hopes as to what will happen as you grow older?
   b. What are your fears as to what will happen as you grow older?
6. How do you spend your time now?
   a. What are your interests? Hobbies?
   b. Are you doing what you like to do?
7. What gives you pleasure?

IV.

1. Are you especially conscious about time? And its passing? Faster? Slower?
   Illustration: Subject No. 26

[Abridgment]

I. "How do you feel you did in answering these questions?" S. "Well, ahhh, there were some words that I missed."

I. "What percentage?" S. "I would say about 75%".

I. "You're modest." S. Laughs.

I. "As I mentioned before, these questions are routine. Now I'd like to return to questions concerning how you feel, your ideas, opinions, personal approach to life. Do you think of yourself as young, middle-aged, old, or very old?" S. "I'm an old man—76—I'm not sickly, although I'm not a hero. According to my age I'm doing pretty well."

I. "Do you feel old, middle-aged, . . .?" S. "About middle-aged."

I. "Years ago, did you prepare yourself for being older either emotionally or financially?" S. "No."

I. "Why was that?" S. "I didn't have any, enough sense to do it, and circumstances . ."

I. "Emotionally?" S. "Yes, I was thinking, ahh, why often, and I tried to keep my health as much as humanly possible, and not to bring the old age too soon."

I. "How did you do that?" S. "By living a normal life . . . no abuse . . . no over-indulgence . . . I haven't been in a hurry to die, cause when we are dead they're not going to miss us."

I. "Did your parents or friends make plans . . ?" S. "Not in my time . . ."

I. "Are you?" S. "No. . . . I can't . . . how many more years I'm going to live anyway . . . If something comes along I try to make the best of it."

I. "Rather than long-range planning?" S. "Yes . . . anyway, things don't always turn out as you planned it." (Later describes some financial planning near time of retirement.) S. "I knew after I was retired, I'd have financial difficulties." (Later)

I. "What are your worst fears about the future?" S. "That I should be in good health until I die, so I wouldn't have to depend on anybody else to light my cigarettes or put on my shoes." (Goes on to state that he does not want to burden others; suggests euthanasia instead.) (It is of some interest that many subjects such as this man brought up death while discussing the future. A person's ideas and feelings about various topics spontaneously emerge in a variety of contexts; this is informative about the person and also provides material for cross-reference and comparison.)

B. DEATH

I.

1. Do you think much about death?
   a. When?
   b. At night?
2. Do you fear death?
3. Would you welcome death?
4. Do you think others would welcome your death?

5. How would your death affect others?
6. How do you feel about their reacting this way?
7. How does the death of others affect you? Explore grief and its handling. How is it manifested? Do you feel angry?
   (a) self?
   (b) others? Feel unworthy? Feel guilty?

II.

1. How do you envision death?
   a. As an end?
   b. As immortality?
2. Do you believe in Heaven and Hell?
3. Have you become more or less interested in religion since you have become older or is your interest the same?
   a. Is this similar to your religious training in childhood?
   b. How frequently do you go to church now and formerly?
   c. (If applies) Do you believe you go to church more frequently to meet people?

III.

1. What preparations or provisions have you made for your death?
   a. Funeral arrangements.
   b. Particular plot.
   c. Will.

II. CONCEPT EVALUATION

C. SELF-CONCEPT

1. Self-Perceived Changes

1. How would you describe a typical older person?
   a. Does anyone in your family or among your friends fit this description?
   b. Is there a critical chronological age beyond which all persons are old regardless of age?
2. Would you describe yourself? (If patient gives a physical description, ask) How would you describe yourself emotionally? (Vice versa, as indicated.)
3. How would your friends describe you?
   a. Your enemies?
   b. Your spouse?
   c. Do others think of you as old?
4. Explain to me as best you can in what way there have been changes since you have become older? (Date and specify changes.) (Check list below.)
   a. *Physically?* Tremor. Gait. Slowed down. Strength.
   b. *Emotionally?* More sentimental? Less? Shifts of mood? Irritable? Argumenta-

tive? Feel good generally or tired? Restless? Less apt to be moved by unpleasant or "tragic" events? Do noise, people, outside events and excitement in general bother you more, less or same since older? Do you avoid such activity or seek it out? Can you picture yourself in the future? (Cross-check with A. Futurity.)

c. *Mentally?* Episodes of confusion? Progressive slowing? Memory? Recent or Remote? Think a great deal about the past? (Compare with present and future.) Find it hard to adapt to a new experience? Difficult to maintain attention?

d. *Sexually?* Frequency? Changed desire, ability? Masturbation? Unusual sexual experiences? (This is a recheck.)

e. *Eating?*

f. *Sleeping?*

5. Do you see any connection between your physical, emotional, mental, sexual changes?
   a. Which came first?
   b. Did anyone cause any of the others?
   c. Are you conscious of these changes? Acutely or rarely think of them?

6. Do you pay more attention to what you say now that you are older? Talk more or less? Trust people more or less? Why?

7. Do you pay more attention to your appearance now? Why?

8. Do you feel that you or parts of your body look unusual to other people since you are older?
   a. Do you think your organs are all right?
   b. Do you pay more attention to your health?
   c. Do you pay more attention to sickness?

9. How do you explain these changes you have described?

10. How have you handled these changes? What have you done about them? (For instance, if "memory" is "bad") How do you make up for this disability? (Clarify with subject: Write things down, make up story, etc.)
    a. Do you act in accordance with these changes? Take them into account?
    b. Have you had to change your way of doing things?
    c. Do you substitute?

11. How do these changes make you feel?
    a. Have they restricted you from doing things?
    b. What problems do they create?

12. Looking back, do you feel you've been the same person all along? Or completely different?

13. Do you feel you've been the sort of person you wanted to be?

14. In your teens or early twenties, did you have an ideal you hoped to live up to?
    a. Who influenced you the most? At what age? Why?

b. (If no ideal) Can you account for the fact that you did not?

c. (If yes) In what way did you live up to or fail to live up to your ideal?

d. Have the demands upon yourself—standards, aspirations—been excessive —plaguing you?

15. What do you feel you ought to have been?

16. What do you feel you ought to have done that you didn't?

17. a. What would you have liked to do that you didn't do?
    b. Did you do everything you wanted to do in your life?
    c. Are there certain things you want to do yet?
    d. Are there things you wish you had not done?
    e. Do you like yourself?
    f. What ought you do in the future?

Illustration: Subject No. 19

[Abridgment]

I. "Is there some age at which you would say you would have to be considered old?" S. "Yes, I would think when I hit 80 I would think that I begin to get in the old age class."

I. "Regardless?" S. "But I hope that I will never be an invalid nor a burden to my family. I may be physically slowed down or something like that but I'll never be a tyrant and I'll never expect too much from my family. I don't want them to make me the whole center. Don't interfere in their daily lives and all that I ask is that I be just taken care of in the ordinary way. Many times away back that I can remember whenever I had anything the matter with me I never wanted anybody to be fussing with me."

I. "You've described yourself, how would your friends describe you? S. "Let's see. I should think that they would say that physically, would you say? In general or what way?"

I. "Either or both?" S. "Physically, my neighbors said that they hoped that they will be in as good physical condition when they reach my age. As far as anything else, I think they think I am a little above the average for an old man of my age. I'm sure that they do. They see me out with my boy."

I. "What about emotionally, how would they describe you?" S. "I don't think that they ever figure me in that respect as an old man. I have never showed, as far as I know, any signs of being an old man. I look at things always from a young man's point of view."

I. "In what way do you consider yourself older?" S. "Just my age and experience."

I. "Age and experience?" S. "Age and experience. When I think of my experiences then I realize that I am old. Outside of that I don't think about it at all."

Change	Reaction

Change   *Reaction*

I. "Are there any other ways in which you have aged? Physically?" S. "Yes, physically. Of course I can't run as much as I used to. I can't walk as much as I used to. The other night this buddy and I walked about 5 miles. Last Wednesday night we took a 5-mile walk down Wisconsin Avenue and down through the town and up around this way. About a 5-mile jaunt. It didn't seem to hurt either of us." "That's all I wanted to say is that physically I have noticed just a few changes inasmuch as *I can't run as much as I used to.* I would be puffing more. *I don't have any trouble going up and down stairways or anything like that.*"

Decrease—Physical

Qualification
Increase in Memory
(Cognitive)

I. "What about memory?" S. "Memory I think is better. *I think my memory is better because I have more occasion to use it now.*" I. "What about emotionally?" S. "Emotionally I think maybe I am a little bit more softer inasmuch as I know so much more. I can realize a thing. Just as an illustration, if I saw someone hurt in an accident, crippled, I can sort of visualize the life that is in front of them. Before when I was younger I didn't. When I was young I took it as a matter of fact. That fellow got hurt or he is going to be blind and that was about all *but now from an older point of view I can see, visualize what that fellow is going to be up against.*"

Increase: More sympathetic
to other people's problems.
(Personality-Affective)

2. *Ideal Parents*

1. What would the ideal mother be like?
2. What would the ideal father be like?
3. *a.* Did your mother and father live up to these ideals?
   b. Did you live up to these ideals?

INTERVIEW III

A. "Structured Conclusion."
   1. What were the most important topics to you that we discussed together?
      a. What was the most upsetting topic?
      b. What was the most pleasant topic?
   2. What is the most important thing (or things) that happened to you in your life?
      a. Best?
      b. Worst?
      c. Comment on choice?
   3. Review II Major "Age Relevant" Check List.
B. "Ages of Aspiration."
   1. *a.* How old do you expect to live to be?
      b. Why did you choose that age?
   2. *a.* How old would you like to live to be?
      b. Why did you choose that age?
   3. *a.* What age would you like to be?
      b. Why did you choose that age?
   4. *a.* What age do you feel is the prime of life?
      b. Why?
      c. How long should a person live?
   5. What do you feel about the aging process? i.e., growing old.
C. 1. What questions would you like to suggest that we ask older people in this study?
   2. What should the public know about older people?
   3. What can young people do to make older people happy?
   4. What is the secret of your success? Motto?
   5. What advice do you have for younger people? In terms of preparing for being old?
   6. What advice do you have for people of your own age?
   7. What questions should I have asked you in order to understand you better?
D. "Free" Period: to pursue areas developed in previous interviews, check out psychodynamic hypotheses, etc.

NAME: _____ DATE: _____ SUBJECT NO.: _____

I. DIAGNOSTIC CATEGORY

A.P.A. Nomenclature [1]

A.P.A. No.

Qualifying phrase: (Rate 1–7)

	Psychotic	Neurotic	Behavioral	Acute	Subacute	Chronic	Mild	Mod.	Sev.	Dur.
1. No Psychiatric Diagnosis:										
2. CBS c̄ Arteriosclerosis: [2]										
3. CBS c̄ Senile Brain Disease:										
4. CBS c̄ Ascl. and Senility: (mixed)										
5. CBS, Unknown Cause:										
6. Other Organic:										
7. Neurosis:										
8. Functional Psychosis:										
9. Other Diagnoses of APA classification:										
10. Does he have or show "senile qualities?"										
Borderline?										

[1] Diagnostic and Statistical Manual Mental Disorders, 1952.
[2] CBS—Chronic Brain Syndrome.

Rater: _____

NAME: _____ DATE: _____ SUBJECT NO.: ____

II. "AGE RELEVANT" CHECKLIST [1]

1. Progressive decrease of intellectual functions (0–6) _____ _____
*2. Late onset (state age) _____ _____
3. "Childish" emotionality (0–6) __ _____
4. Blunting (0–4) _____ _____
   Unresponsiveness of emotions (5, 6) _____ _____
5. Lack of insight (0–6) _____ _____
6. Sense of well-being (0–1) _____ _____
   Euphoria (2, 3, 4) _____ _____
   Excessive laughing (5, 6) _____ _____
7. Relevant (0, 1) _____ _____
   Irrelevant (2, 3, 4) _____ _____
   Incoherence (5, 6) _____ _____
8. Self-centered (demanding for self) (0–6) _____ _____
9. Difficulty in assimilating new experiences (0–6) _____ _____

*10. Fluctuating, remitting course ___ _____
   (yes, no) _____ _____
11. Emotional lability (0, 1) _____ _____
   Shifts of mood (2, 3, 4) _____ _____
   Marked shifts of mood (5, 6) __ _____
12. Occasionally emotionally incontinent (0, 1) _____ _____
   Emotional incontinence (2, 3, 4) _____ _____
   Stimulus-bound (5, 6) _____ _____
13. Complaints of some weakness (0, 1) _____ _____
   Fatigue (2, 3, 4) _____ _____
   Exhaustion (5, 6) _____ _____
*14. Nocturnal wandering (yes, no) __ _____
*15. Patchy performance (yes, no) __ _____
16. Clouding of consciousness (0–6) _ _____
*17. Confusion states (yes, no) _____ _____

18. In this subject, how relevant to aging were the above positive ratings (0, 2, 4, 6) _____ _____

19. Delayed relevant response (0–6) _ _____
20. Perseveration of ideas (0–6) ____ _____
21. Impaired recent memory (0–6) __ _____
22. Impaired remote memory (0–6) __ _____
23. Occasional substitution for memory loss of fantasy (interwoven with reality) or of reality that is not true for the occasion (0, 1) _____ _____
   Frequent replacement (2, 3, 4) __ _____
   Marked confabulation (5, 6) ____ _____
24. Occasionally brings up past (0, 1) _____ _____
   Frequently brings up past (2, 3, 4) _____ _____
   Absorbed in past (5, 6) _____ _____
25. Normal verbal productivity (0) __ _____
   Increased (1) _____ _____
   Overproductive (2, 3, 4) _____ _____
   Garrulous (5, 6) _____ _____

26. Restlessness (0, 1) _____ _____
   Incessant activity (2, 3, 4) _____ _____
   Agitation (5, 6) _____ _____
27. Occasionally irritable (0, 1) _____ _____
   Frequently irritable (2, 3, 4) ____ _____
   Constantly irritable (5, 6) _____ _____
28. Ability to generalize versus concrete (0–6) _____ _____
29. Impaired judgment (0–6) _____ _____
30. Difficulty in maintaining attention (0–6) _____ _____
31. Difficulty in maintaining set (0–6) _____ _____
32. Flight of ideas (0–6) _____ _____
*33. Decreased potency (yes, no) ____ _____
*34. Decreased sexual desire (yes, no) _____ _____

Score range: 0–162

*7 items were not scaled.

[1] The first 17 items were placed in separate columns on the basis of the possible differentiation between "senile" (left column) and "arteriosclerotic" (right column) psychoses.

NAME: _____ DATE: _____ SUBJECT NO.: _____

EXAMINER: _____ OBSERVER: _____ SCORER: _____

III. MENTAL STATUS SCORE

			Final score	Scale range
I.	RETENTION: Raw score sum 0–4 plus 2......................	I.	_____	0–6
II.	REMOTE MEMORY: Sun of correct answers......................	II.	_____	0–9
III.	A. Orientation to TIME: Rating..........................	IIIA.	_____	0–3
III.	B. Orientation to PLACE: Rating........................	IIIB.	_____	0–3
III.	C. Orientation to PERSON: Rating.......................	IIIC.	_____	0–3
III.	TOTAL ORIENTATION SCORE: Sum of A, B, and C..............	III.	_____	0–9
IV.	RECENT MEMORY: Sum of correct answers....................	IV.	_____	0–9
V.	READING: Number of correctly remembered facts.............. (Logical Memory)	V.	_____	0–21
VI.	ABSURDITIES: Score for A 4 plus score for B 5..............	VI.	_____	0–9
VII.	OPPOSITES: Number correct............................	VII.	_____	0–15
VIII.	PROVERBS: Total Score..............................	VIII.	_____	0–6
IX.	INFORMATION: Total raw score 15. Convert to scaled score.......	IX.	_____	0–19
X.	COMPREHENSION: Total raw score 14. Convert to scaled score....	X.	_____	0–19
XI.	CALCULATIONS: Number correct 6 plus bonus points (up to 2) plus 1–9 raw score. Convert to scaled score....................	XI.	_____	0–17
XII.	SIMILARITIES: Total raw score 14. Convert to scaled score.......	XII.	_____	0–19
XIII.	A. Dig. Forward: Highest number repeated correctly...........	XIIIA.	_____	0–9
XIII.	B. Dig. Backward: Highest number repeated correctly..........	XIIIB.	_____	0–8
XIII.	DIGIT SPAN: Sum of A, and B, 17 correct to scaled score..........	XIII.	_____	0–19
XIV.	VOCABULARY: Total raw score 40. Convert to scaled score.......	XIV.	_____	0–19
1.	Verbal IQ = Sum of Scores below double line = 112. Convert..........	1.	_____	0–157
2.	Total Score = Sum of all scores................................	2.	_____	0–196

NAME: _____ DATE: _____ SUBJECT NO.: _____

IV. PSYCHIATRIC SYMPTOMS CHECKLIST

	Int. I	Columns	Consensus
1. Conversion Symptoms		(1)	
2. Hypochondriacal Ideas		(2)	
3. Somatic Delusions		(3)	
4. Suspiciousness		(4)	
5. Persecutory Trend		(5)	
6. Idea of Unreality		(6)	
7. Depersonalization		(7)	
8. Nihilistic Ideas		(8)	
9. Depressive Trend		(9)	
10. Suicidal Attempts		(10)	
11. Elation		(11)	
12. Grandiose Ideas		(12)	
13. Hallucinatory Experiences:		(13)	
(a) Auditory		(a)	
(b) Visual		(b)	
(c) Tactile		(c)	
(d) Gustatory		(d)	
(e) Olfactory		(e)	
14. Illusions		(14)	
15. Misinterpretations (including ego hallucinations)		(15)	
16. Obsessions (including death)		(16)	
17. Compulsions		(17)	
18. Phobias		(18)	
19. Anxiety; fear (including death)		(19)	
20. Nightmares: Dreams		(20)	
21. Sexual Maladaption: Homosexuality or other		(21)	
22. Psychosomatic Symptoms		(22)	
23. Exacerbation of Somatic Pathology		(23)	

Rater: _____

Scale: None........ 0
Mild........ 1, 2
Moderate.... 3, 4
Marked..... 5, 6
Unratable... U

NAME: _____ SUBJECT NO.: _____

V. INTERVIEW BEHAVIOR AS RATED BY INTERVIEWER AND OBSERVER

	Interview I— Date: _____	Interview II— Date: _____	Interview III— Date: _____
*1. Fear (Anxiety)................................	(1)	(1)	(1)
*2. Anger—out....................................	(2)	(2)	(2)
*3. Anger—in.....................................	(3)	(3)	(3)
*4. Depression....................................	(4)	(4)	(4)
5. Pleasure......................................	(5)	(5)	(5)
*6. Responsiveness................................	(6)	(6)	(6)
7. Assertiveness.................................	(7)	(7)	(7)
8. Compliance...................................	(8)	(8)	(8)
a) Passive.................................	(a)	(a)	(a)
b) Active..................................	(b)	(b)	(b)
9. Cs. Suppression...............................	(9)	(9)	(9)
10. Uncs. Repression..............................	(10)	(10)	(10)
11. Use of Fantasy................................	(11)	(11)	(11)
*12. Integrating...................................	(12)	(12)	(12)
*13. Disintegrating................................	(13)	(13)	(13)
*14. Somatic Reactivity............................	(14)	(14)	(14)

CHECK:

Observer: _____   _____   _____

Interviewer: _____   _____   _____

*Items used in statistical analyses; sums of ratings of 3 interviews by both raters used.

VI. INDEPENDENT PROTOCOL ANALYSIS

NAME: _____ DATE: _____ SUBJECT NO.: _____

Psychiatric Rater: _____

1. Diagnosis (APA Nomenclature): _____
2. Summary Dynamic (Diagnostic and Descriptive) Formulation:

	P	F	G	E
*3. *a.* Present Adjustment as "general" concept	0	1	2	3
b. Adaptation to Biological Aging	0	1	2	3
c. Adaptation to Changes Associated with Aging (incl. retire.)	0	1	2	3
d. Lifelong Adjustment	0	1	2	3

4. Is there any evidence for concept of mellowing of neurosis: Yes_____ No_____
   Explain:
5. Of what needs and desires (psychological and tangible) does subject feel most deprived or frustrated?
   List:
6. *In reaction to aging:* (Psychopathology is used here in its broadest sense, to include psychopathology which would not warrant diagnosis).
     a. Has lifelong psychopathology been useful or adaptive?   Not rel.____ Yes____ No____
       1. Most prominent adaptive p-p_____
       2. Describe psychopathology and indicate in what way it has been useful.
     b. Is there a new psychopathological reaction to aging?   Yes____ No____
       1. Most prominent new psychopathological reaction to aging_____
       2. Describe and justify_____
     c. Is there an exacerbation of past psychopathology in reaction to aging?
       Not rel.____ Yes____ No____
       1. Most prominent psychopathological exacerbation_____
       2. In what age period was this psychopathology prominent?
         Childhood_____ Adol._____ Maturity_____
       3. In what way had it been suppressed or in what way had there been remission?_____
7. What mechanisms of defense or reparative mechanisms are presently characteristic of this individual?
   Describe: _____
   _____
     a. Are these lifelong or age-relevant?_____
     b. Which is most characteristic of life history?_____
     c. Which is most characteristic of aging period?_____
     d. Are these useful or adaptive in the aging period?_____
*8. Does psychological isolation exist?   0 1 2 3
     a. Does this seem to stem from himself?_____
     b. Or the circumstances of his life?_____

*Items used in analyses.

I-202

*9. Does a counterphobic attitude[1] to age exist (Hinsie and Shatsky)? 0 1 2 3
    a. Normal amount of passivity, ego-integrated and accepted:
       Acceptance of passivity:_____
    b. Open excessive passivity; open wish to be taken care of:
    _____

    c. Passivity utterly rejected and not accepted; counterphobic stress of activity:_____
*10. Is there a problem in "Identity" or of "Self?"   Yes_____ No_____
    Explain:
    a. Note type of previous identity pattern (e.g., work)_____
    b. Note history of difficulties and explain (e.g., parental, etc.)_____

11. What are the strengths of this individual in dealing with aging period?
    a. Most prominent_____
    b. Describe in general (refer to ego strengths; i.e., includes personality assets as well as environmental
       assets)_____

                                    P F G E
12. *a.* Prediction of organic breakdown   0 1 2 3
    b. What is future diagnosis of CBS   ASCL   Yes_____ No_____
                                  SBD   Yes_____ No_____
                                  Uncertain of type   _____
                                  Unratable   _____
    c. Prediction of functional breakdown   0 1 2 3
       (Why or why not) (Liability)
    d. What is stress situation likely to be?
13. Estimate of rater's confidence in his ratings (i.e., reliability)
14. Special Comments.

    *Items used in analyses.
    [1] Evaluator was referred to Hinsie, L. E., and Shatzky, J., Psychiatric Dictionary, 2d ed., New York,
Oxford University Press, 1953.

APPENDIX B

TABLE 1.—*Psychiatric disorders in 47 aged subjects*

Group I (N=27) Subject		Diagnostic category	
Number	Age	Primary psychiatric diagnosis	Other psychiatric diagnoses
1	69	None...................................	
2	79	Psychophysiological musculoskeletal reaction...	
3	65	Obsessive-compulsive reaction................	
5	70	Schizoid personality.........................	
6	72	None....................................	
7	67	Depressive reaction.........................	Obsessive-compulsive reaction.
9	67	.....do....................................	
12	70	None....................................	
13	66	Personality trait disturbance.................	
14	68	Cyclothymic personality, hypomanic type......	
15	75	Compulsive personality......................	
16	71	Special symptom reaction (kleptomania).......	
19	70	None....................................	
20	73	.....do....................................	
26	76	.....do....................................	
30	73	Depressive reaction.........................	Compulsive personality.
36	69	.....do....................................	Personality trait disturbance.
47	65	Schizoid personality.........................	
49	72	Compulsive personality......................	
50	72	None....................................	
51	71	.....do....................................	
53	81	.....do....................................	
54	72	Schizoid personality.........................	
55	65	None....................................	
56	69	Passive-aggressive personality...............	Special symptom reaction (premature ejaculation).
58	71	None....................................	
59	74	.....do....................................	
Group II (N=20)			
8	71	Cyclothymic personality, hypomanic type......	
10	92	Chronic brain syndrome, associated with senile brain disease without psychosis.	
11	73	Depressive reaction.........................	
18	66	None....................................	
23	74	Depressive reaction.........................	
24	67	Obsessive-compulsive reaction...............	Personality trait disturbance (schizoid trait).
25	74	Personality trait disturbance.................	Special symptom reaction (impotence).
27	66	Obsessive-compulsive reaction...............	Passive-aggressive (dependent) personality: special symptom reaction (premature ejaculation).
28	73	Depressive reaction.........................	
29	77	None....................................	

TABLE 1.—*Psychiatric disorders in 47 aged subjects*—Continued

Group II (N=20) Subject		Diagnostic category	
Number	Age	Primary psychiatric diagnosis	Other psychiatric diagnoses
31	72	Personality trait disturbance..................	
32	77	Depressive reaction.........................	Paranoid personality.
33	72	....do...................................	Do.
35	74	None....................................	
38	76	....do...................................	
39	73	....do...................................	
41	65	Compulsive personality.....................	Psychophysiologic gastrointestinal reaction.
42	68	Obsessive-compulsive reaction...............	Schizoid personality.
52	69	Adjustment reaction of late life.............	
57	74	None....................................	
Group III (N=7)			
4	68	Depressive reaction........................	
17	75	None....................................	
21	74	Schizophrenic reaction, paranoid type........	
22	69	Schizoid personality.......................	
34	79	Chronic brain syndrome, associated with senile brain disease without psychosis.	Passive-aggressive (dependent) personality.
37	67	Schizophrenic reaction......................	
43	76	Adjustment reaction of late life with transient psychotic episodes.	

TABLE 2.—*Presence of clinically-evaluated impairments of cognitive function according to individual subject in 51 aged subjects*

Subject number	Impair. recent memory	Impair. intell. function	Impair. Abstract.	Attn. diffi- culty	Set diffi- culty	Impair. remote mem- ory	Impair. judg.	Con- fabula- tion	Confus. states Disorient.	Marked lability	Total changes	Pres. of senile quality
GROUP I												
1		X	X			X					3	
2	X	X	X								3	X
3											0	
5		X									1	
6	X	X	X	X	X			X			6	X
7	X	X	X								3	X
9	X			X							2	
12											0	
13		X	X	X							3	
14											0	
15	X	X		X							3	
16	X	X			X						3	
19											0	
20		X	X	X	X						4	Border. X
26	X										1	
30	X	X	X	X	X	X	X	X			8	X
36	X										1	
47			X								1	
49		X									1	
50											0	
51			X								1	
53	X	X		X	X	X					5	X
54		X		X	X	X					4	Border. X
55											0	
56	X										1	
58	X										1	
59											0	

I-206

Scalogram table (Group II, Group III, Total sample). The rightmost column is marked "Border. X".

	35	32	22	18	15	11	9	4	2	2	14	No.
GROUP II												
8	X	X	X	X	X	X						0
10	X	X	X	X	X	X	X		X		X	8
11	X	X	X	X	X							9
18	X	X	X	X	X	X	X					1
23	X	X	X	X								6
24	X	X										1
25	X	X	X	X	X							5
27	X											1
28	X	X	X	X	X	X	X					5
29	X	X	X	X	X							4
31	X	X	X									3
32	X	X	X	X	X	X	X					6
33	X	X										2
35	X											1
38	X	X	X	X	X	X	X					6
39	X	X										1
41	X		X	X	X							3
42	X		X	X								3
52	X	X	X	X	X	X	X					6
57	X	X	X	X	X	X	X					6
GROUP III												
4	X	X	X	X	X							4
17	X	X	X									4
22	X	X	X	X	X	X	X	X	X		X	1
34	X	X	X	X	X	X	X			X		8
Total sample	35	32	22	18	15	11	9	4	2	2	14	

TABLE 3.—*Distribution of 51 aged subjects according to the intensity of clinically evaluated impairments of cognitive function*

Rated intensity of impairment	Impair. recent memory		Impair. intell. function		Impair. Abstract.		Attention difficulty		Set difficulty		Impair. remote memory		Impair. judg.		Confabulation		Disorientation	
	Number	Per cent of total	Number	Per cent of total	Number	Per cent of total	Number	Per cent of total	Number	Per cent of total	Number	Per cent of total	Number	Per cent of total	Number	Per cent of total	Number	Per cent of total
0	16	31	19	37	30	58	33	64	36	70	40	78	42	82	47	92	49	96
1	15	29	20	39	4	8	4	8	3	6	9	18	3	6	3	6		
2	9	18	5	10	5	10	4	8	1	2	2	4	0	0				
3	4	8	4	8	5	10	3	6	3	6			0	0	1	2		
4	4	8	2	4	4	8	3	6	3	6			3	6			2	4
5	2	4	1	2	2	4	1	2	2	4			2	4				
6	1	2			1	2	3	6	3	6			1	2				
Total	51	100	51	100	51	100	51	100	51	100	51	100	51	100	51	100	51	100

TABLE 4.—*Numbers of subjects in groups I and II reporting mode of reaction [1] to reported decreases*

[Percent of decreases [2]]

Number of subjects reporting decreases	Physical (N=25)					Cognitive (N=20)					Personality-affective (N=17)					Social-psychological (N=25)				
	A	B	C	D	E	A	B	C	D	E	A	B	C	D	E	A	B	C	D	E
0.........	14	3	23	22	9	12	10	20	20	15	12	13	17	17	14	2	19	24	21	24
1-100.....	11	22	2	3	16	8	10	0	0	5	5	4	0	0	3	23	6	1	4	1

GROUP II

Number of subjects reporting decreases	(N=19)					(N=18)					(N=13)					(N=16)				
0.........	10	6	16	16	13	14	13	18	16	14	12	11	13	11	13	5	10	15	11	16
1-100.....	9	13	3	3	6	4	5	0	2	4	1	2	0	2	0	11	6	1	5	0

[1] Expressed in percent of decreases to which reactions have been reported by each subject.

[2] A=Compensation; B=Acceptance; C=Limitation; D=Complaint; E=Qualification.

TABLE 5.—*Summary of number of total changes, increases, and decreases reported by 45 aged subjects*

	Changes [1]					Increases [1]				
	I	II	III	IV	Total	I	II	III	IV	Total
Total.............	269	70	226	137	702	4	3	141	33	181
Mean.............	5.98	1.56	5.02	3.04	15.6	.09	.07	3.13	.73	4.02
Standard deviation...	2.31	1.03	3.85	1.81	5.31	.28	.25	2.79	1.11	3.17

	Decreases [1]					Unratable changes
	I	II	III	IV	Total	
Total..................................	265	67	85	104	521	7
Mean..................................	5.89	1.49	1.89	2.31	11.58	....
Standard deviation........................	2.36	1.04	2.06	1.47	4.37	....

[1] I=Physical; II=Cognitive; III=Personality-Affective; IV=Social Psychological.

TABLE 6a.—*Adaptive and maladaptive features present in 27 group I aged subjects*

Subject number	Index morale	Composite adaptation score (1, 2, 3)	Denial	Passivity-activity (1, 2, 3)	Psychopathology			Psychological isolation	Identity crisis	Predicted functional breakdown
					Useful	New	Exac.			
1	0	2		2						
2	25	2		2		X	X		X	
3	100	3	X	2	X					
5	43	2	X	1	X	X		X		
6	75	1	X	3		X		X		
7	0	3		1	X		X			X
9	66	3	X	2		X	X	X		X
12	80	2		1	X		X	X		
13	14	3	X	2	X		X		X	
14	100	1	X	3	X				X	
15	63	1	X	1	X					
16	100	1	X	3	X				X	
19	75	1	X	1						
20	25	2		1						
26	80	2		1						
30	100	3	X	3					X	
36	45	3	X	1						
47	75	3		1					X	
49	100	1		3	X					
50	50	1		1						
51	100	1		3	X					
53	75	1		1	X					
54	100	1		3			X			
55	100	1		1						
56	Unav.	3		1						
58	50	1		3						
59	100	3		1						
Total	17>50%		11	[2] 8 c.p.	11	4	6	4	6	2

[1] 1 = Excellent-very good; 2 = Good; 3 = Fair-poor. [2] 1 = Average passivity; 2 = Passive-dependency; 3 = Counterphobia (c.p.).

TABLE 6b.—*Adaptive and maladaptive features present in 20 group II aged subjects*

Subject number	Index morale	Composite adaptation score (1, 2, 3)	Denial	Passivity-activity (1, 2, 3)	Psychopathology			Psychological isolation	Identity crisis	Predicted functional breakdown
					Useful	New	Exac.			
8	100	1	X	1	X					
10	80	2	X	3		X	X	X		X
11	25	3	X	2			X			
18	45	2		3			X		X	
23	0	3		2		X		X		X
24	50	3	X	3	X		X		X	
25	78	2		1					X	
27	100	2		3					X	
28	66	3		2						
29	40	3		1						
31	50	2		1					X	
32	14	3		2	X	X	X	X	X	X
35	60	1		1						
38	50	2		1						
39	100	1		1						
41	Unav.	1		3	X	X	X			
42	100	1	X	3	X					
52	100	2	X	3						
57	10	3		3	X			X		
33	20	3		1			X	X	X	X
Total	9 > 50%	············	6	8 c.p.	6	4	7	5	7	4

[1] No psychological changes.

I-212

APPENDIX C

1. *Comparison of mental status assessment made in psychiatric interview with psychological test results.*

There was substantial agreement, correlations ranging from 0.69 to 0.89 between WAIS-derived psychiatric mental status scores and corresponding full WAIS scores obtained by psychologists.

2. *Brief testing of intellectual functions.*

An attempt was made to adapt and quantify the mental status examination which is a traditional (and unquantified) part of psychiatric evaluations assessing cognitive functioning. The adapted mental status examination was not wholly satisfactory. Sections III Remote Memory and IV Recent Memory (app. A) were especially unsatisfactory; there is no way to directly check the former and the latter was "too easy" for this population, although items eight and nine seemed especially useful for discrimination.

The introduction of abbreviated versions of the verbal WAIS subtests appeared to be more satisfactory. These were included within the mental status and were administered by the psychiatrist (see app. A); the previous day, the full WAIS had been administered by the psychologist. The product-moment correlations computed between the results of the separate administrations were all significant at the 0.001 level. These data are given in table 1. Although the possible use of the abbreviated WAIS as a screening device is suggested, it is concluded from this study that only Information and Vocabulary would be sufficiently reliable for individual interpretation.

3. *Cognitive Test Differences between Senile Quality and Depression*

Within the sample of mild cases of depression and potentially early cases of senile disorder, there were associations between depression and mean reaction-time contrasted with the relative absence of depressive effect upon cognitive and perceptual tests, in turn affected by senility. The possibility that depression of greater severity may affect cognitive and perceptual tests is not, of course, ruled out and, in fact, is likely. Similarly, with advancing senility speed of response is probably affected. But in the early stages this relative differential may be useful diagnostically. Subjects with the diagnosis of Depressive Reaction did not differ significantly from the No Psychiatric—non-Senile Quality group on the Mill Hill Alpha and Beta, verbal fluency, speed of copying words or Raven Matrices, nor were there any relationships between depression and the WAIS (table 7, ch. 15).

On the other hand, there were associations between senile changes (Senile Quality Subgroup) and scores on the Mill Hill Alpha and Beta, verbal fluency, speed at copying words and the Raven Matrices as well as the verbal performance WAIS and most of its subtests (table 7, ch. 15). Subjects with senile manifestations did *not* have increased reaction-time.

TABLE 1.—*Correlations between WAIS-derived psychiatric mental status scores and corresponding full WAIS scores obtained independently by psychologists* [1]

Verbal subtests	Product moment correlations
Information	0.89
Comprehension	.69
Arithmetic	.72
Similarities	.76
Digit span	.62
Vocabulary	.85
Mental status scaled verbal I.Q. vs. total verbal WAIS	.85

[1] Each correlation is based upon 48 observations. All are significantly different from zero at better than the 0.001 probability level.

CHAPTER 12

Personality Measurements In the Aged

by Margaret Thaler Singer

One of the dilemmas in psychological assessment of the aged, as in other groups, is that tests sample aspects of behavior, but not the "overall effect"; the "global essence" of the personality of any one individual or group may be lost. It was the aim in this study to process test behaviors obtained from a group of healthy aged men in ways that might more nearly parallel this overall impact or impression of an individual as he appears to a clinically trained observer. The position taken here was to view aging as a process and to focus upon aspects of adjustment and integration from an inner point of view. The verbal tests were analyzed as communication tasks, with both formal and content features (Frenkel-Brunswick, 1948; Frenkel-Brunswick, 1950; Rapaport and Schafer, 1946; Rapaport, 1942). Here the formal features of performance on the tests, and not the content as such, will be emphasized. Formal features of perceptual and thought processes appeared to be the more important, enduring and discriminating aspect of performance. In contrast, affective tone varies in tests and interviews over brief time periods. It was assumed that the formal aspects of the communication process, the programing of behavior, in handling projective tests would relate to physiological functioning and to overall functioning level, and that the dynamic interpersonal content in the tests would relate to the affective aspects of interpersonal interactions.

FORMAL ASPECTS OF COMMUNICATION

Projective tests are essentially a series of communication tasks. The subject is asked to interpret some sample situations. On the basis of what and how he communicates in responding, four aspects of his performance were rated: (1) his comprehension of and set toward the instructions, (2) his formal style of perceiving as well as the content of his apperceptions, (3) his reasoning, and (4) his communication as it reflects the foregoing components of the interaction process with the materials, instructions, and the examiner. These tasks, items, and material, are regarded as sample situations and interpretive inferences are made predicting a subject's adequacy in handling similar *actual* situations. The rating procedures later described were designed specifically to assess how well a man "programs" or plans his thinking and behavior in relation to the test interaction. The ratings as they are presented here were derived from our own past experience with groups of aged (Silverman, Barnes, Frost, and Thaler, 1953; Thaler, 1952; Thaler, 1956; Thaler and Frost, 1953; Thaler, Reiser, and Weiner, 1957) and from work with the present group.

It was our impression from this previous work that well-functioning aged persons can handle test interactions with the examiner much as do adequately functioning younger persons. It is possible that the great numbers of relatively unhealthy, possibly brain damaged, individuals in large samples of aged persons are responsible for some of the cultural stereotypes in our society about what to expect of the aged (garrulousness or impoverished output, pointless ruminating in the past, poor memory, etc.).

The performances of aged persons who differed from younger normal persons appeared to have an ineffective programing of behavior. The input or reception of instructions, the subsequent memory search and response selection procedures, and the proper stopping or termination of performance, seemed to have inefficiencies or breakdowns at one or all stages. The response behavior of these more poorly performing aged persons suggested that breakdowns in the planning of performance, as it could be inferred from assessment of verbalized thought productions, differentiated these individuals from persons demonstrating normal adult performances during testing. For example, at an input level instructions may not be clearly and properly received (only parts get in, an incorrect level of meaning is assigned them, either a more literal or personal meaning than is the intent of the instructions and test interaction is taken). Performance often begins well, but the intent, purpose, and goal of the performance blurs. The instructions seem to have become lost. The focus of the memory search broadens or unduly constricts in two major ways: "drifting" or perseveration occurs. Drifting is noted when the point of the memory search is lost, and the subject drifts from topic to topic. Perseveration is either blatant in that an idea stays in mind too long and is repeated and the memory search seems

t. bog down openly, or a more subtle and often unrecognized thing happens; a high redundancy is present in the ideas given. The final characteristic of the inefficient planning of behavoir is poor termination. The impaired aged subjects seem not to have programed the proper time and point for stopping, either ending their performance too soon, or going on until fortuitously stopped by an outside person or distracting event, seeming to forget to plan an end to a purposive performance. These impressions of how to conceptualize the test behavior of aged subjects whose planning and thought programing seemed deviant from younger normals, led us to formulate the ratings discussed subsequently.

METHODS

General Problems of Testing Aged Subjects

From our experience with aged persons, ranging from superior normals to deteriorated senile individuals, three features of the testing procedures appear to be especially important: certain roles must be taken by the tester; on the whole, projective-type tests are difficult for aged persons to comprehend and enter into in the expected manner; and the sequence of test presentation has to be carefully planned. It is desirable for the examiner to structure quickly by actions and words what he and the subject are going to be doing. Optimally, testing should begin with a concrete test where the aged person "does" something. This should be an obvious "test" type task which is nonthreatening, not too difficult, not too "childish" in its simplicity. For example, we generally begin with tasks in which the aged subject can readily see why there might be age-relevant features (speed of making X's, figure 8's, tapping, etc.), rather than tasks connoting childishness (Weigl blocks, cubes, sticks, drawing, etc.). These tests get the person "doing something" and also set roles for the examiner and the subject. Two other problems are waylaid by this beginning. The aged person often treats interviews and testing situations as conversational and social times. He may not perceive that there has been a break in ongoing activity in which he was engaged in the ward, clinic, reception room, or the home.

The young adult tester may experience countertransference feelings and preconsciously cast himself in a role which permits the obvious parent-position of the aged subject to rule and control the procedure. Loss of control of the situation may result in tangentiality, prolonged testing, boredom, the loosening of defenses, etc.

Introducing projective tests is easy with young adults and adolescents familiar with the concepts from books, school, job, television, etc. To the aged, what is expected in the way of performance, the idea of a "personal answer" rather than right-wrong-type answers, etc., can be very puzzling, particularly if the aged person is concrete and literal. The tester can become very perceptive, in diagnostic impressions of senile qualities, "brain damage" type behavior, perceptual-associative impoverishment, depression, and the like, by evaluating the difficulties the aged subject encounters in getting the "set" for projective and other test or interview items. The amount of effort needed by the tester to get the stage set and the testing proceeding may be related to the extent of impairment revealed in subsequent behavior. The drifting content of the garrulous in a controlled situation and the seeming self-centered unawareness of time schedules in many aged persons has considerable clinical usefulness.

The Tests Used

Eleven tests were used; six were of the "projective" type, two were more purely verbal manipulation (proverbs and homonyms), and three were more "performance" than verbal tests (Draw a Person, Weigl Sorting Test, and Level of Aspiration Test). While some are more cognitive in nature than the others, all are used at various times to assess aspects of personality functioning.

The tests were given in an order thought to minimize perseveration of set on certain tests and to maximize set where it was helpful to do so, and to structure the roles of tester and examinee quickly and easily. It begins with easy items to reduce threat and ends with easy items when boredom and fatigue may be occurring in a testing session. Ten tests were given in a session lasting 1 hour and a half for most subjects. The Rorschach was given in a separate session.[1] The tests were given in the order in which they are described in the following discussion.

The *Level of Aspiration Test* (see app. B), a simple paper-and-pencil procedure, was an easy, quick way to set the stage for the testing session. It required the subject to fill squares with X's, as many as possible in a limited time. About 3 minutes are needed for the entire procedure. Two quantitative scores are obtained: the total number of X's made during four trials and an aspiration index (the ratio of the S's guesses about his forthcoming performance in relation to his actual performance).

The *Draw a Person Test* easily followed the preceding paper-and-pencil test. The subject was asked to "draw a picture of a person, the best one you can, make it a whole person." Occasionally a subject demurred momentarily saying it had been years since he had drawn anything, but mild reassur-

_____
[1] We wish to thank Dr. Conan Kornetsky, who administered the Rorschach test, for his generous sharing of the material so that multiple use could be made of it. We also greatly appreciate the assistance of Ogretta Humphries and Ronald D. Wynne.

ance was sufficient. If he asked whether it should be a man or woman, he was told, "either one." Upon completion of the drawing he was asked to "now draw a woman (or man)."

Two scoring procedures were used. Goodenough's (1926) scoring criteria for itemizing body and clothing features were used by two raters independently. Difference between final total scores was averaged. Secondly, two raters classified the drawings into nine groups, with the lower numbers assigned to drawings from individuals "supposedly free of effects of 'brain damage'" and higher numbers to drawings which showed greater indications of the effects of "brain damage, senility, and intellectual deterioration" (Albee and Hamlin, 1950; Jones and Rich, 1957; Lakin, 1956; Machover, 1948; and Schilder, 1935).

The *Weigl Color-Form Sorting Test* was included to assess the skill at shifting mental set toward a task, and to contrast language and performance. A five-point rating was used (app. C).

The *Emotional Projection Test* was the first of the "projective tests" used. It was put in this position because it is easy to comprehend, the responses required are simple, and it led into the somewhat more complex subsequent tests. A series of 30 pictures, 15 of a man and 15 of a woman, each showing various facial expressions are shown one at a time. The subject is asked to tell "what is the emotion, what is the feeling the person in the picture has" (Glad, 1956; Glad and Shearn, 1956).

While this test offers the clinician considerable material for individual case analysis, only three features were given primary attention in the formal assessment. These were the variety or lack of it in the subject's associations, the amount of interaction with other persons read into the pictures, and the amount of bewilderment, puzzlement, and severe indecision read into the pictures. The first feature was regarded as an index of the subject's skill at meeting the demands put forth in the instructions and his inferred skill at perceiving and labeling subtle changes in facial (i.e., emotional) expression (Bruner and Tagiuri, 1954; Thaler, Reiser, and Weiner, 1957). The interaction feature was considered an index of social responsiveness, and was deemed the most important content feature; the subject's "self" was reflected as he tried to empathize with the person in the picture. This depends primarily on long-term style of personality and does not vary as mood tone changes.

Raters were given the criteria which appear in appendix D and were asked to class a man's total test performance into one of six groups (one good, six very poor). A second scoring was made of the content of the responses assessing the interpersonal affective qualities present, following the system developed by Leary (1957). Sixteen interpersonal behavior qualities are rated, and two scores, Love and Dominance, emerge. The more positive the orientation toward others, the larger the Love score. The more dominating the orientation toward others, the larger the Dominance score. A third score used was the actual number of the Emotional Projection Test responses which were scorable at an interpersonal level (it is possible on this test to give purely intra-self-responses).

The *Thematic Apperception Test* followed next. Sixteen cards were selected from the early Murray series, which was to our knowledge the first Harvard Psychological Clinic small-format, photographed edition (Murray, 1943; Rapaport, Gill, and Schafer, 1946). These pictures are reproduced in Rapaport, *Diagnostic Psychological Testing,* volume II, pp. 400–401.

The following cards were used. The Murray card designations appear in parentheses.

1. (M11) A young man and an old woman.
2. (F20) A very ancient man holding his head.
3. (MF2) An old woman in the doorway of a room.
4. (F13) Two young girls and a boy in old-fashioned garb.
5. (MF5) A man and woman embracing.
6. (MF1) A boy with a violin.
7. (M14) A hypnotist.
8. (F15) A girl with her hand over her face, head downcast.
9. (M20) A well-dressed older man in a derby hat, and a young roughly dressed man.
10. (MF4) A silhouetted figure at an open window.
11. (M15) An older and younger man.
12. (MF3) An old man in a cemetery.
13. (F17) Two women by stairs.
14. (M18) A man face down on a bed.
15. (F16) An old man at a window frame.
16. (F11) An old woman in the background, a young woman in the foreground.

This edition, rather than later ones, was used for several reasons. The photographic edition makes the depicted person seem more real and this assists the very concrete aged person in talking about the people, rather than saying merely, "It's a drawing." However, this very feature can also be viewed as a test of the better preserved person's ability to maintain his distance and keep an interpretive attitude toward the cards, rather than slipping into a concrete attempt to "recognize" the situation. Further, the early TAT edition depicted the older persons as clearly aged, and included pictures, no longer in the series, of very aged persons.

Usually the content of the TAT stories is given primary attention. Here, however, five main formal features were rated: interpretation versus card description; perseveration versus nonperseveration; appearance of misperceptions; variety among themes; and clarity and continuity of roles and identities. The instructions to the

raters appear in appendix E. The Leary scoring system, which was used in the prior section on the Emotional Projection Test, was used here also. The Love, Dominance, and number of interpersonal tales were quantified.

A *Family* Scene, a specially designed TAT-type card,[2] depicts a close view of a scene in which an old man and young woman are standing, and an old woman and young man are seated in the foreground.

Neugarten (1955) and Neugarten and Gutmann (1956) report findings on this card from 140 adults, 40 to 70 years of age, from the Kansas City Studies of Adult Life, nonclinical population. They found that "role descriptions vary significantly with age of respondent, although not with sex or social status."

The old man is seen in terms of uncritical affiliation, identification with the needs of others, and denial of interpersonal intrusiveness. Younger respondents (40–54) see him as one who exercises some measure of intrafamilial authority, but older respondents (50–70) see him as object of aggressive domination by his wife, whose only mode is to "think" and who has no effective familial role.

The old woman is seen in terms of the need for intimacy, and for unlimited control over the interpersonal environment. Younger respondents see her as one who has a submissive familial role; but older respondents see her as wielding unilateral control over the family and as increasingly aggressive in implementing her needs.

The role descriptions are partly artifacts of the projective process, but the age shift is undoubtedly based upon changes in real behavior. The implication is that deep-seated psychosexual development occurs in late adulthood, development which follows a different pattern in men than in women.

Responses were rated, following, in general, the procedure used with the TAT (app. F). The "interpersonal role" of each of the four depicted persons was also scored, using the Leary (1957) procedure.

Problem Situations, from the Sargent (1953) Insight Test, were presented which

[2] We wish to thank Dr. Bernice Neugarten for supplying us with this card used in the Kansas City Studies of Adult Life.

explore attitudes toward mothers and fathers, and toward group exclusion.

The three items used were:

1. A young man is working or studying away from home. He gets a letter from his mother, after the death of his father, asking him to move back home.
   a. What did he do and why?
   b. How did he feel?
2. A young man's father has always looked forward to having his son take over his business and has educated him for it. The son becomes interested in another vocation.
   a. What did he do and why?
   b. How did he feel?
3. A man gets the impression that others are discussing him. On several occasions he thinks conversation has stopped or the subject changed when he entered the room.
   a. What did he do and why?
   b. How did he feel?

The subject had just finished the Family Scene picture and was instructed as follows: "Here is a problem situation. I want your opinion about what should be done. Here is the first one." The subject was given a printed card with this one problem situation on it and the examiner slowly read the item aloud while the subject read it to himself. The examiner then said: "What is your opinion here?" The other two items were subsequently given. The verbatim responses were recorded.

Overall performance was rated on a three-point scale of the general adequacy of responses, as outlined below:

1. All the instructions were comprehended and carried out. No perseveration from story to story is noted. An actual solution or selected alternative paths are presented.
2. Some drift in reasoning toward personal interpretation can occur. The man is not openly confused, but never does much with the three tales.
3. Misperceives the point, reads in personal background meaning, perseverates from tale to tale. Confused.

The *Homonyms Test* was given, consisting of 10 simple, often used words which are homonyms (fire, spring, fly, hide, lie, match, box, loaf, diamond, and drill). The sub-

ject was asked to give as many *different* meanings for these words as he could. In order to secure the proper set toward the task, the examiner illustrated with the word "lead," saying that "there are lead pipes; a person who is easily influenced is said to be easily led; and one can say, the fireman led the children to safety." The test words were then presented one at a time orally, and the subject's responses recorded verbatim until he indicated he had completed the item. This test was chosen to assess skill at shifting set, and to measure roughly the amount of "information" contained in the spontaneous answers by contrasting the number of statements with the number of task-relevant, nonredundant definitions given. Scoring consisted of (1) counting the number of remarks or statements made to each word, and (2) obtaining the ratio of number of nonredundant definitions given to total number of statements. The less adequately functioning subjects would be the garrulous, low information group, or the impoverished group with little output, but moderate information in their responses.

Nine fairly common *proverbs* (app. G) were presented (selected from 1937 Revised Stanford-Binét Tests of Intelligence). The proverb interpretations were rated on an eight-point scale from good abstract interpretations to concrete responses and lack of comprehension.

The *Sentence Completion Test* was a 28-item test (see app. H) constructed by the writer with starting phrases designed to elicit responses to age-relevant areas. These areas are: anger, depression, parents, wife, wishes, body and health, death, children, religion, generalization about youth, generalization of youths' attitude toward the aged, the future, current attitude toward age, what he used to think about being aged, positive suggestions for his age group, age as a "brake" and negative force.

The order of the items was set to minimize perseveration on certain items and to maximize it on others, to enhance the formal as well as content analysis of responses. For example, the first two items are present tense ("I get angry when . . ." "I feel blue . . ."), but items 3 through 6 necessitate a shift to past tense ("My parents . . ." "My father used to . . ."). It was predicted that the less adequately functioning men would not make the proper shift and would hold the set too long, speaking of their parents in the present tense. Three items on wishes were widely spaced in the order of the test. This was planned as a built-in memory test, since subjects might refer to "this is the one I just did." The items referring to the body were grouped together to see to what extent consistency was shown, how much perseveration occurred, and to what extent the man experienced difficulty staying within an area but trying to give differentiated responses.

Earlier work had indicated that while sentence completion items are easy for young adults, they are not necessarily so for the aged. Literalness can make this test puzzling and difficult if the proper set has not been established. The test was introduced by the examiner covering all but item one and saying, "Here is the first part of a sentence. I want you to finish the sentence by telling me the first thing that comes to mind that will finish the sentence." The examiner read the item aloud while the man read it. If an answer was not forthcoming in a few seconds, the examiner said, "What have you thought of for this one, [repeating] 'I get angry when . . .'." Responses were recorded verbatim by the examiner.

The total production of each subject was coded in one of the following five categories: (1) variety in answers and differing lengths of answers; (2) moderate associative impoverishment or some evasion of the procedure; (3) subject unable to stop himself and talks at length; (4) severe associative impoverishment; and (5) subject confused about what the task demands, or language is confused.

The *Rorschach Test* was scored using Beck (1952) location and populars, Klopfer (1942) determinants, and the DeVos (1952) scoring of affective symbolism in the content. Twenty-seven scores were analyzed because their rationale makes them the logical choice in terms of our overall thinking about what features might differentiate adequately and poorly functioning groups (Ames, Learned, Metraux, and Walker, 1954; Bruner, 1948; Caldwell, 1954; Kutash, 1954; Orme, 1955; Pope and Jensen, 1957; Powers and Hamlin, 1955; Thaler, 1952; Watkins and Stauffacher, 1952). It was thought that the well-functioning men's records would be characterized by a better differentiation of percepts, more variety of content, and clarity in communication. Records from men functioning less adequately would have fewer responses, faster reaction times, fewer details, more space responses, less communication of nuances about what determines associations (i.e., mostly form responses, with few shading, movement, and color responses). The responses would fit blot contours only moderately well ($F+$ percent), and even less well when all responses were considered (extended $F+percent$). Little organization among blot areas would be made. Great stereotypy would be seen among associations and would also be noted in the presence of few content categories. Popular content and human content would be less. It was thought that the affective symbolism scores would indicate that the less adequately functioning men's records contained more neutral, anxious, and dependent content, and less pleasant content than the better functioning men's records.

All tests were scored on a blind basis.[8] When all scoring was completed, each man was given a summary score for his overall performance on the 11 tests. The scores on the individual tests and the summary scores for each subject are given in appendix A.

The Sample and Subgroups Studies

The basic sample consisted of 47 men. The various social features and selection procedures are described in chapter 2; in chapter 3 are found definitions of the medical subgroups. In the section to follow, reference will be made to group I and group II, defined by health criteria, and to the psychiatric groupings of Senile Quality and non-Senile Quality (ch. 11).

RESULTS

In table 1 are presented the test scores and ratings obtained for groups I and II. The statistically significant difference between these groups obtained on only one

[8] Our grateful appreciation is extended to four skillful clinical psychologists who gave extensive time and effort to scoring and rating the various tests: Dr. Nathene Loveland and Miss Betty Shanks, Walter Reed Army Institute of Research; Miss Nancy Herriman, National Institute of Mental Health; and Mrs. Helen Hursch, Berkeley, Calif.

test (the Weigl test rating) is regarded as due to chance. Nonetheless, there was a consistent tendency for the very healthy group to have better scores. These subjects more easily comprehended the instructions, took the intended set toward the tasks and created clearly stated, appropriately varied associative and cognitive productions. Their handling of certain of these tasks (Weigl, Homonyms, Problem Situation, Human Drawings, Proverbs) was relatively concise, focused, and rapid. These particular tasks may be characterized as the more cognitive, factual and performance oriented of those utilized here. The term "rapid" should be qualified, however, for these better functioning men tended to reveal a "sufficient" delay before beginning the tasks; they did not impulsively begin before instructions were completed. It is inferred that "delay mechanisms" for holding incoming instructions are necessary to adequate performance and that their operation in this group is similar to that in younger adults.

In tables 2 and 3 are presented the test scores and ratings obtained for the Senile Quality and non-Senile Quality groups. It was hypothesized that those subjects who were diagnosed as Senile Quality would tend to perform more poorly on these psychological tests than would non-Senile Quality subjects. (It was hoped these tests

TABLE 1a.—*Comparisons of groups I and II on various personality tests*

For Graded Variables

Variable	Group I (*N*=27)		Group II (*N*=19)		Significance of group difference, *t*=value
	Mean	Standard deviation	Mean	Standard deviation	
Level of aspiration performance	66.89	13.29	63.00	21.46	0.76
Draw-a-person score	20.19	9.93	18.37	9.95	.61
Homonyms (number)	25.15	8.03	22.16	7.25	1.29
Homonyms (percentage)	72.04	22.80	62.42	19.13	1.50
Sum of ratings	35.93	13.93	44.42	16.61	1.88

TABLE 1b.—*Comparisons of groups I and II on personality tests rating variables*

Variable	Group 1 (N=27)		Group II (N=19)		Significance of group difference, t
	Number	Percent of total	Number	Percent of total	
Level of aspiration:					
Index less than 1.33....................	14	52	13	68	N.S.
Index greater than 1.33................	13	48	6	32	
Weigl:					
Score 1 or 2..........................	16	59	4	21	(*)
Score 3 or above......................	11	41	15	79	
Draw a person:					
Score 1–4............................	13	48	7	37	N.S.
Score 5 or above......................	14	52	12	63	
Rorschach:					
Score 1–3............................	14	54	6	35	N.S.
Score 4 or above......................	12	46	11	65	
Proverbs:					
Score 1–4............................	15	56	7	37	N.S.
Score 5 or above......................	12	44	12	63	
Homonyms:					
Score 1 or 2..........................	13	48	6	32	N.S.
Score 3 or above......................	14	52	13	68	
Sentence completion:					
Score 1..............................	16	59	10	53	N.S.
Score 2 or above......................	11	41	9	47	
Emotional projection test:					
Score 1 or 2..........................	15	56	10	53	N.S.
Score 3 or above......................	12	44	9	47	
Family scene:					
Score 1..............................	15	56	7	37	N.S.
Score 2 or above......................	12	44	12	63	
Problem situation:					
Score 1..............................	18	67	8	42	N.S.
Score 2 or 3..........................	9	33	11	58	
Tat:					
Score 1 or 2..........................	18	67	8	42	N.S.
Score 3 or above......................	9	33	11	58	

N.S.=Not significant.   *Significant at the 0.05 level.

and methods of evaluation used might provide more objective means of delineating and distinguishing "Senile Quality.") Support for the hypothesis is seen in table 2. Of the 16 variable, 9 showed statistically significant differences between the 2 groups. Attention was given to the possible association of Senile Quality and medical status, since of the 11 Senile Quality subjects, 5 were members of group I, and 6 were members of group II. A chi-square test on a fourfold table representing number of subjects in the various groups indicated no association.

Table 3 shows that the sum of ratings [4] on each subject discriminated between the

[4] The rating scales varied in range (see app. A), the majority being five- or seven-point scales. The range was determined by pretesting with a sample of tests from other aged subjects. Certain tests contribute more to the sum of ratings, but inspection of the table suggests no marked shifts in relative success. A man seemed to have his own level of skill on most tests and where he had a score out of line with his average, it was more an idiosyncratic occurrence than that any one set of test scores were discrepant for a large number of men. Each set of tests was scored as a unit (i.e., all TAT's at once, etc.) and the names were coded. Thus the seeming consistency of performance is not due to a halo effect created by performance on one or two tests.

TABLE 2a.—*Comparisons of senile quality and non-senile quality groups on various personality tests*

Graded Variables

Variable	Senile ($N=11$)		Non-Senile ($N=35$)		Significance of group difference, $t=$value
	Mean	Standard deviation	Mean	Standard deviation	
Level of aspiration-performance...............	55.09	20.30	68.49	14.78	* 2.39
Draw a person score.......................	15.55	7.45	20.66	10.31	1.52
Homonyms (number).......................	18.82	8.20	25.51	7.02	* 2.65
Homonyms (percent).......................	54.45	23.05	72.34	19.66	* 2.53
Sum of ratings...........................	53.91	16.91	34.89	12.04	** 4.13

* Significant at the 0.05 level.
** Significant at the 0.001 level.

Senile Quality and non-Senile Quality subgroups of groups I and II. The Senile Quality subgroup of group II had a higher score (indicating a poorer performance) than the Senile Quality subgroup of group I. Also the non-Senile Quality subgroup of group II performed less well than the non-Senile Quality subgroup of group I. This was the case in four of the five test scores selected for analysis. Finally, there was a consistent tendency for the group I, non-Senile Quality subgroup to perform the best of all four groups. This was again the situation in four of the five tests. A two-way analysis of variance however was not found to be statistically significant; therefore this must be viewed only as a trend.

From these analyses of subgroups, it is concluded that broad generalizations about differences between groups I and II and between Senile and non-Senile Quality groups are not warranted. Instead, it is suggested that the interaction between Senile Quality and medical status possibly accounts for differences on test performance. The test behavior of the Senile Quality subgroup in group II approximated the behavior of individuals ordinarily considered "senile." These features are often used to rate indications of "brain damage" (however poorly defined) in younger adults.

Level of Aspiration Test.—Table 4 presents comparisons between the Senile and non-Senile Quality groups on this test. Performance at each stage of the test was significantly lower for the Senile Quality group. It is well to view again table 3 and note the very low score of the Senile Quality segment of group II, and the nearly equal scores of the other three segments of the sample. Visual comparison of the non-Senile Quality men's mean scores in table 4 and the scores of a young control group presented in appendix B indicates that an age difference exists even when the Senile Quality men are removed from the aged group. An interesting feature in table 4 is the somewhat unvarying "guess" score for the Senile Quality group. It seems that these men simply repeated their guessed performance each time, whereas the non-Senile Quality men tended to inspect their performance and realistically raise their goal somewhat on the first three guesses and, then, following the shortened time trial, adjusted their guess realistically.

Draw a Person Test.—The two systems of scoring this test, the average rating and the average Goodenough score, correlated

TABLE 2b.—*Comparisons of senile quality and non-senile quality groups on personality tests rating variables*

Variable	Senile (N=11)		Non-Senile (N=35)		x^2
	Number	Percent of total	Number	Percent of total	
Level of aspiration:					
Index less than 1.33....................	6	55	21	60	N.S.
Index greater than 1.33................	5	45	14	40	
Weigl:					
Score 1 or 2.........................	3	27	17	49	N.S.
Score 3 or above....................	8	73	18	51	
Draw a person:					
Score 1–4...........................	3	27	17	49	N.S.
Score 5 or above....................	8	73	18	51	
Rorschach:					
Score 1–3...........................	1	9	19	59	* 6. 42
Score 4 or above....................	10	91	13	41	
Proverbs:					
Score 1–4...........................	3	27	19	54	N.S
Score 5 or above....................	8	73	16	46	
Homonyms:					
Score 1 or 2.........................	3	27	16	46	N.S.
Score 3 or above....................	8	73	19	54	
Sentence completion:					
Score 1..............................	2	18	24	69	** 6. 72
Score 2 or above....................	9	82	11	31	
Emotional project test:					
Score 1 or 2.........................	1	9	24	69	** 9. 66
Score 3 or above....................	10	91	11	31	
Family scene:					
Score 1..............................	2	18	20	57	N.S.
Score 2 or above....................	9	82	15	43	
Problem situation:					
Score 1..............................	2	18	24	69	** 6. 72
Score 2 or 3........................	9	82	11	31	
TAT:					
Score 1 or 2.........................	2	18	24	69	** 6. 72
Score 3 or above....................	9	82	11	31	

* Significant at the 0.05 level.
** Significant at the 0.01 level.

N.S.=Not significant.

+0.91. Both scoring systems probably assess "differentiation," since a more detailed drawing tended to receive a better rating on the qualitative scale. In the total sample, the mean rating was 4.00 (S.D. 1.87) and the mean Goodenough score was 19.60 (S.D. 9.54). Using the mean of 4 as a cutting point, considering scores of 5 through 7 the poorer drawings, Senile Quality subjects and non-Senile Quality subjects differed significantly (chi-square 5.64, significant at the 0.02 level of confidence). In this manner of scoring the test, 77 percent of the Senile Quality group and 67 percent of the non-Senile Quality subjects were correctly classed.

The DAP scores were correlated with a variety of other psychological tests obtained independently. (See ch. 15.) It is tentatively concluded that the Draw a Person score relates more closely to the Wechsler performance score and the more cognitive tests used in this study, than to the purely verbal tests.

TABLE 3.—*Mean scores for medical and senile factor groupings*

Variable	Non-Senile	Senile	Senile factor, *t*=value	Medical grouping, *t*=value
Level of aspiration-performance:				
Group I...........................	69. 59 (*N*=22)	64. 00 (*N*=5)	} *2. 79	N.S.
Group II..........................	70. 08 (*N*=13)	47. 67 (*N*=6)		
Draw a person score:				
Group I...........................	21. 45	17. 00	} N.S.	N.S.
Group II..........................	20. 23	14. 33		
Homonyms (number):				
Group I...........................	26. 36	20. 20	} *2. 69	N.S.
Group II..........................	24. 23	17. 67		
Homonyms (percent):				
Group I...........................	78. 41	53. 00	} *2. 71	N.S.
Group II..........................	65. 54	55. 67		
Sum of ratings:				
Group I...........................	31. 55	46. 80	} **4. 70	*2. 33
Group II..........................	37. 31	59. 83		

*Significant at the 0.05 level.
**Significant at the 0.001 level.

N.S.=Not significant.

Weigl Color-Form Sorting Test.—This test did not discriminate between the Senile and non-Senile Quality groups. While there was a tendency for the Senile Quality men to score at levels 3 to 5, the poorer performance, the level of confidence is not statistically conclusive. The results may be compared to other studies (Heglin 1956; Hopkins and Post, 1951; Hopkins and Post, 1955; Thaler, 1956; Thaler and Frost, 1953) which have indicated that the aged tend to perform at a concrete level on this test.

Emotional Projection Test.—Content as well as formal thought processes were noted on this test. The content of the responses

TABLE 4.—*Mean level of aspiration test scores*

Tests	Non-Senile Quality	Senile Quality	*t*-value
Guess 1...................................	17. 31	13. 08	*2. 12
Performance 1.............................	16. 78	12. 15	**3. 46
Guess 2...................................	18. 44	13. 54	**3. 23
Performance 2.............................	18. 42	13. 46	***3. 60
Guess 3...................................	19. 28	13. 92	**3. 47
Performance 3.............................	15. 72	11. 69	***3. 60
Guess 4...................................	17. 94	13. 62	**3. 01
Performance 4.............................	18. 81	14. 00	***3. 57
Index of aspiration.......................	1. 26	1. 56	N.S.

*Significant at the 0.05 level.
**Significant at the 0.01 level.
***Significant at the 0.001 level.

N.S.=Not significant.

was scored by the Leary (1957) method of quantifying interpersonal attitudes in verbal material. This method yields two scores, one indicating an attitude conceptualized on a love-hate dimension, and the other revealing a position on a dominance-submission dimension. In addition, responses to the Emotional Projection Test pictures which contained overt references to interpersonal interaction were tallied. Table 5 presents comparisons between the Senile Quality and non-Senile Quality groups and a contrast group of 50 men comprising an army hospital field unit; the mean age of the latter was 25 years.

There was a tendency for the young men and the Senile Quality men to be more positively oriented toward "others" than was the non-Senile Quality group as indicated by their "Love" scores. There were no group differences on the Dominance scores. The interpersonal scores yielded the most marked differences between the Senile Quality and the other two groups. The Senile quality group tended not to read interaction meanings into the feeling states they attributed to the pictures. When they did, they seemed to view others as sources of nurturance. Their responses were more self-centered. From a formal standpoint it may be a more complex task to perceive interpersonal feeling states than to merely describe an intrapersonal state. Thus, what appears to be a "dynamic content feature" may be highly predetermined by a formal aspect of performance.

In summary, the formal scoring of this test tended to depict the Senile Quality group as giving a narrow range of responses, perseverating and repeating answers, while the study of content suggests feelings of puzzlement and uncertainty about themselves and their performance.

The formal scoring of this test correlated 0.69 with the formal TAT scores, indicating a fairly strong consistency of performance on similar tests.

Thematic Apperception Test.—The Leary scoring system was again used to rate the content of the TAT scores. Table 6 indicates that the Senile Quality and non-Senile Quality groups did not differ in the affective interpersonal qualities assigned their stories, but did differ significantly on the number of interpersonal scorings given to the "hero" and to the "other" person in the tale. A "hero" score could be obtained on each of the 16 cards. The means suggest that the non-Senile Quality group failed to develop a main hero or main character on only one card, whereas the Senile Quality group failed to do so on four cards on the average. Since eight of the cards depicted more than one person, the finding of a mean

TABLE 5.—*Comparison of senile quality and non-senile quality aged men and a group of young men on 3 interpersonal scores from the emotional projection test*

Score	Senile Quality ($N=11$)		Non-Senile Quality ($N=36$)		Young men ($N=50$)		F
	Mean	S.D.	Mean	S.D.	Mean	S.D.	
Love..........................	39.64	15.93	30.53	14.61	36.34	16.96	N.S.
Dominance.....................	43.45	21.68	38.75	10.66	41.92	12.96	N.S.
Number of interpersonal scores.......	16.64	9.17	23.22	4.89	23.68	5.27	* 7.11

* Significant at the 0.05 level.

N.S.=Not significant.

TABLE 6.—*Comparison of Senile Quality and non-Senile Quality groups on 3 interpersonal scores from the thematic apperception test*

Scoring	Senile Quality (N=11)		Non-Senile Quality (N=36)		t=value
	Mean	S.D.	Mean	S.D.	
Dominance	49.09	8.07	49.83	6.62	N.S.
Love	42.00	9.09	47.17	11.27	N.S.
Number of hero scores	12.82	3.40	15.89	3.47	* 2.58
Number of "other" scores	2.09	1.87	4.83	2.86	** 2.99

* Significant at the 0.05 level.
** Significant at the 0.01 level.

N.S. = Not Significant.

of 4.83 "other" scores for the non-Senile Quality group indicates that these men neither attended to nor differentiated both persons in the pictures. The mean of the Senile Quality group was even less (2.00). The most parsimonious explanation is that the Senile Quality group tended not to differentiate the elements in the picture as well as the other group.

The formal TAT rating correlated 0.88 with the pooled ratings of the "projective" tests taken as a unit (Rorschach, EPT, Sentence Completion, Family Scene, and Problem Situations), again suggesting that the rating criteria for viewing language and test handling on the various tests was quite similar. This correlation also suggests that performance by a subject was relatively stable from test to test in terms of these criteria.

Family Scene Picture.—Ratings of responses on the Family Scene correlated +0.79 with the TAT formal ratings, and +0.79 with the overall projective rating. This suggests that responses to this one card, when rated formally, might serve as a useful short sampling of thought-verbal processes. On the other hand, offering a series of cards, the TAT, increases the possibility of observing perseveration and provides a variety of responses permitting raters to

better differentiate varying levels of performance, compared to single card test analysis.

The Senile and non-Senile Quality groups were differentiated on the Family Picture ratings at the 0.06 level of confidence. Inspection of the scatter of scores on the TAT and Family Scene revealed that a large majority of the non-Senile Quality men did well. In addition to the overall formal rating, each man's story was scored by the Leary system. Table 7 presents the percentage distribution of the various roles assigned by the total sample to each of the four figures in the scene. The trends noted by Neugarten (1955) and Neugarten and Gutmann (1956) were seen here also. There seemed to be a role reversal for older figures from that found in younger adults; that is, the older man was seen behaving in a passive-compliant way; the older woman was seen as aggressive-domineering. Interesting both from a content and formal standpoint is the relative lack of attention given the young man and young woman figures; they were seen as passive-compliant, conventional, or ignored. It might be inferred that the large number of men who ignored the young persons in the picture merely attests to the formal feature of level of complexity of a tale, in that the men who give a simple tale make note only of the aged figure. It might also be inferred that the aged are less empathic with young persons in this test picture, or finally, it may be an artifact of the card itself.

Problem Situations.—Sixty-nine percent of the non-Senile group had scores of 1 (good), while 82 percent of the Senile Quality group received scores of 3 (poor) on this test. Perusal of the individual records suggested that these problem questions put considerable demand on the subject because of their specificity and the need to formulate their answers fully and quickly. Some of the tasks which used pictures seemed to permit a "warmup" or "wandering" period during which the subject might make "filler" comments, while seeming to come to a decision about the meaning. Here there was a tendency for a number of the Senile Quality men to respond on the basis of only partial comprehension, or to respond too quickly without sufficient integration of their associations, or to begin to drift on about the content of statements seemingly introduced to fill time prior to "really answering."

Examples from a few Senile Quality records of responses to the first problem situation (a young man is working or studying away from home. He gets a letter from his mother, after the death of his father, asking him to move back home. What did he do and why? How did he feel?) illustrate the above comments.

Worst thing he could do. He did wrong to begin with and he feels bad about it. It was wrong to run away from home. His father took it to heart and died on account of him. [Idiosyncratic interpretation, no solution.]

He felt sad. He went back to his mother. Generally you feel sorry for the mother after the death of the father. [Response to only the last phase at the start, then repeats portion of the question as his response.]

[Reads it aloud three times.] It doesn't say the young man has graduated or anything and would be at liberty to come home. He's working and studying . . . [rereads aloud]. The young man, it depends on whether the mother, if she had security in the way of insurance to warrant the young man to leave where he was studying in college, he'd be in a better position to maybe make up his mind to come home to his mother and he would move back home with his mother. [Rereads and notes word "feel."] Very sad because of the vacant chair, the plate that was set down and no father to eat it and go over in his mind his boyhood days and it would take him quite a long while to ever get to feel he did the right thing. We know it was the right thing to do to come home to his widowed mother because she had done so much. [Unsure and puzzled over what task is. Looks for answer within story. Reads further, gives reply based on his own associations. Much drift, inability to come to a stop.]

By way of contrast, replies from two non-Senile Quality records illustrate the clearer comprehension, lack of drift from the main

TABLE 7.—*Interpersonal roles assigned the figures in the Family Scene*

Role	Percent assigning roles to—			
	Older men	Older women	Young men	Young women
Managerial-autocratic	12	41	0	2
Competitive-narcissistic	1	1	3	4
Aggressive-sadistic	0	2	0	0
Rebellious-distrustful	6	9	0	0
Self-effacing-masochistic	45	16	21	20
Docile-dependent	14	7	23	16
Cooperative-overconventional	5	3	5	10
Responsible-hypernormal	3	3	8	4
No interpersonal role given figure	12	16	38	42

task, and the attempted coping with a clear solution.

> The mother is alone you think. It could be a thing where he'd like to come home because she needs him for company and support, but on the other hand he has a job in another city that he is doing well in and would hate to give it up because he can't get anything as good in his home town. Maybe his mother didn't want to move to the city where he is. He'd finally get someone to stay with his mother. He holds his job, is able to send her something each week. [Never handles question of "feel," but comes to grips with the problem and does not drift, etc.] He, surely, in my estimation, is the right kind of a son if he goes back home to mother and comforts her in her hours of distress. While he may have felt going home would temporarily delay his studies, he felt it was his duty in his love for his mother to go home with her until other arrangements could be made, and he'd go back to school and continue his studies.

Analysis of the various contents, such as whether the subject stressed filial obligation, etc., was not differentiating on a group basis, even though it offered a wealth of individual attitude information. The formal qualities, such as the raters were asked to note in the responses, seemed the crucial differentiating features on a group basis.

Homonyms.—As indicated in table 2 the number of definitions given in the Homonyms test differentiated the Senile and non-Senile Quality groups (means 18.82 and 25.51, respectively), and the percentage of "information" contained in the responses (number of nonredundant definitions divided by total number of responses) differentiated the groups. The mean percent information by the Senile Quality group was 54 percent; the non-Senile group's mean was 73 percent. These objective methods of scoring proved to be better ways of handling this material than the impressionistic overall ratings. The latter did not differentiate between groups. Examination of these test responses suggests a relationship between the ability to shift one's

thinking and get new ideas and the ability to control the amount of "gabbiness" or noninformative verbal material given in a test such as this. Illustrations are helpful to contrast group trends. A man who had the largest number of definitions and an information score of 93 percent said for the word "fire": "It's a common word for general air combustion; as a verb, rifle shot, you fire it; a synonym for discharge in handling personnel; in a somewhat different sense, fire the imagination; more or less allegorically, where there's smoke there's fire." Note the lack of filler material sometimes seen when a subject is seemingly waiting for the next idea to fall into awareness. The man first gave the most salient feature, and then seemed to use the examiner's acceptance as a feedback that his performance was satisfactory, as well as his own knowledge that he was "right." A Senile Quality man, whose responses on most tests tended to be rambling, effusive, and diffuse, said: "Fire means calamity; fire is wind and wind is very bad for fire and fire will work through wind." An improverished Senile Quality record contained this: "coal and wood fire; a big fire." A man of moderate educational and intellectual level gave a "to the point" performance similar to that of the man in the first illustration above: "Fire a gun, fire a rifle, fire a slingshot; if you're a foreman in a factory and a man don't [sic] do his job, you can fire him." While four "definitions" were given, only 50 percent information score accrued because of redundancy.

This test is highly cognitively weighted, correlating $+0.72$ with the Wechsler verbal, and $+0.68$ with the performance scale. It might be useful as an estimate of functioning intelligence.

Proverbs Test.—The "objective" scoring of the proverbs tests produced scores ranging from 11 to 109 (low being very good).

Two raters grouped the records into eight categories, considering the presence of increasing degrees of literalness and breakdowns in comprehension and formal reasoning. They were instructed to use a framework of assessing increasing evidence of "brain damage" effects. The average clinical rating was used. Significant discrimination between the Senile and non-Senile groups did not occur.

Because there appeared to be similarities between the Weigl, Proverbs, and Homonyms tests, correlations between these tests were made and appear in table 8. These

TABLE 8.—*Correlation among tests*
(*N*=49)

Test	Weigl	Proverbs	Homonyms
Weigl.........	....	0. 21	—0. 29
Proverbs......	....	....	*** —. 75
Homonyms....	....	....	....

*** Significantly different from 0 at the 0.001 level.

tests do not appear to be measuring the same thing, although the *r*'s are large enough to indicate dependence. The negative correlations are due to the scoring system: the higher the Weigl and Proverb score, the worse the performance; but the higher the Homonym score, the better the performance. Even though the Proverbs and Homonyms correlate highly, this *r* still leaves about 43 percent of the variance unexplained if one tries to predict the Proverbs score from that for Homonyms.

Sentence Completion Test.—This test discriminated between the Senile and non-Senile Quality groups. An item summary of the content was made and appears in appendix I, inspection of which reveals some interesting features. Almost each item had some responses which tended to differentially classify the groups. On the whole,

the "no" responses, the confusion, and concrete replies, and less differentiated responses were given by Senile Quality men. These subjects also tended to refer to their parents in the present tense on item No. 3 as was predicted by the test construction plan. They also said mother was "good to me," and in other places indicated a more dependent, but pessimistic outlook. Thus they miss father (6), think of themselves as dying (14), emphasize loss and lost feeling about wives dying (15), and want their children to treat them better (17). Also their age-relevant associations indicate they envy young people their happiness (20), view being 70 as a negative state (21), are pessimistic about the future (22), want to be young and live their lives over (23), wish they did not have to die (24), and become quite disorderly in handling the topics referring to age (26, 27, 28).

The non-Senile Quality group intended to give the more differentiated, optimistic, altruistic responses, and to intellectualize more about things. They felt their anger was set off when they were opposed, and that blueness was brought on by things limiting activity such as bad weather. They tended cursorily to state that their parents were dead and let it go at that, and when items called for more specific information about parents, identified them by their work, or by types of interaction they had with them. They even gave more differentiated views of their wives than the Senile Quality men. Their wishes were very specific and personal, they denied their body had defects, intellectualized about death, and emphasized a man would be lonely when his wife died. The Senile Quality men had said a man would feel lost and dwelt on the loss, while the non-Senile Quality men's responses created the impression of more independence of self on this and other items.

Their responses about their children were more varied. Two-thirds of them divided their attitudes toward young people between feeling positively toward them, or moralizing about them, rather than envying them as had the Senile Quality men. Being 70 was viewed with more variety and positiveness. The same held true for the future. Their wishes tended to be more altruistic ones. They expressed the desire to live on. They tended to deny there was anything they "had" to do, and had quite specific dislikes. They had not expected to live to be as old as they were in their youthful fantasies. One-third of them gave replies indicating young people regard 60 as "old" and they did not. Nearly half said young people regard the aged as useless. The last two items referring to age in terms of "shoulds" and "should nots" elicited thoughts on conserving health and being moderate in activity.

If anything could be said to have colored all the records, it was the theme of their awareness that younger persons in this society view the aged as they do old objects, as useless, worn out, to be discarded, and that since the aged were just "old things," their feelings, their human life qualities, were no longer vibrant within them. If one were to paraphrase their remarks, it would be to say they felt the current younger society valued newness and sexuality, and since these aged men did not have either quality at a market value level, they were treated as discarded objects.

The Rorschach Test.—As indicated in table 9, 11 of the 27 scores were significantly differentiating between the Senile and non-Senile Quality groups. Eight others showed a trend in the predicted direction. Three concepts can be offered as probable links accounting for the eight differentiating formal scores (the content scores, items 18–27 will be noted later). The first is a qual-ity best termed "skill at communicating nuances about ideas." Items 5 through 8 are essentially redundant ways of assessing how well a man specifies his associations. In particular, it is thought that the human movement component of the EB score, which in itself was also significantly differentiating, was the strongest portion of this item. Thus the other related significant score, the F percent, logically follows as high in the Senile Quality group because it is the remainder of a man's responses which are determined by form with no elaboration.

The stereotypy and content categories can be linked as reflecting the variety or lack of it among a man's associations. The popular percent indicates the amount of conventional, high frequency responses given.

Among the DeVos affective content symbolism scores, the non-Senile Quality group had greater hostile and body content. Trends in the other score indicate that the non-Senile Quality men tended to be more active, aggressive, and positive in their symbolic content, while the Senile Quality men tended to be less able to verbalize nuances (as the earlier scores indicated), were more anxious, particularly in giving content suggesting bound, or perhaps chronic, anxiety, symbolic content, and less pleasant associations.

Here again, as in most of the other tests discussed, better features were seen as an ability to muster a variety of associations which were appropriate, and to communicate clearly about nuances regarding these ideas.

DISCUSSION

The performance of the very healthy segment of the sample, in terms of the conceptual model used, can be characterized as follows: verbal behavior and overall ability to function within the context of the

TABLE 9.—*Rorschach scores*

Score	Non-Senile quality (N=35)		Senile quality (N=13)		t-value	Significant
	Mean	S.D.	Mean	S.D.		
1. Number of responses..........	22.66	11.101	17.57	6.418	1.61	N.S.
2. Time per first responses.......	24.89	....	16.69	....	2.1	(*)
3. d percent...................	5.14	8.012	5.14	7.979	0	N.S.
4. S percent...................	3.51	4.475	6.86	8.457	−1.81	N.S.
5. Sum EB...................	3.69	2.298	1.43	.917	3.55	(**)
6. Sum eb...................	4.37	3.200	2.43	1.989	2.10	(*)
7. $EB+eb$...................	8.06	4.435	4.76	1.998	2.66	(*)
8. $\frac{EB+eb}{R}$ percent.............	38.06	11.359	23.79	18.486	2.13	(*)
9. F percent...................	64.77	17.822	77.57	16.332	−2.32	(*)
10. $F+$ percent.............	70.40	15.578	65.21	15.612	1.05	N.S.
11. Extended $F+$ percent.......	73.29	12.851	65.64	13.670	1.85	N.S.
12. Stereo percent.............	62.54	13.77	73.71	15.04	−2.50	(*)
13. H percent.................	18.43	9.69	16.57	11.59	.57	N.S.
14. $\frac{ad+hd}{R}$ percent.............	16.31	12.44	14.07	13.83	.55	N.S.
15. P percent Beck.............	33.54	14.20	23.29	10.29	2.45	(*)
16. Content categories...........	4.26	2.55	2.50	2.10	2.29	(*)
17. Z........................	20.40	10.69	14.50	9.04	1.82	N.S.
18. N percent.................	39.14	14.93	48.71	17.09	−1.95	N.S.
19. H percent.................	14.97	7.42	8.64	6.18	2.82	(**)
20. A percent.................	17.74	10.30	23.57	11.59	−1.73	N.S.
21. B percent.................	4.86	7.58	.14	.53	2.31	(*)
22. D percent.................	9.83	7.67	9.79	10.41	.02	N.S.
23. P percent.................	12.43	9.04	7.71	6.78	1.76	N.S.
24. M percent.................	2.31	3.075	1.57	3.252	.75	N.S.
25. Sum HAB.................	37.57	14.022	32.36	15.678	1.14	N.S.
26. Ae percent.................	5.86	4.008	6.64	7.078	−.49	N.S.
27. Ab percent.................	11.26	9.930	16.93	9.327	−1.84	N.S.

* Significant at the 0.05 level.
** Significant at the 0.001 level.

N.S.=Not significant.

test situation were not noticeably deviant from performance expected of younger, adequately functioning persons. Their programing or planning ability was adequate. At an input level, instructions appeared to be received clearly and properly. These men were able to wait until the total set of instructions was given; they seemed to receive and weigh properly the various parts of the instructions, to assign a level of meaning that was neither more literal nor more personal than the intent of the instructions. They neither broadened nor constricted the focus of the memory search, neither drifting pointlessly, nor bogging down into repetitiveness or redundance. Finally, they seemed able to plan or program a proper termination. Further, this group seemed to have a wide range of available and appropriate associations, and they seemed able to discuss nuances about ideas.

In contrast, the behavior of the Senile Quality men in group II can serve as a prototype of those features usually considered "senile." The start of their performance was particularly poor. They tended to start too soon, on the basis of partial understanding or seeming to have attended to only part of the instructions. This tendency is worth noting because most performance tasks characterize similar groups as slow. Here, where verbal responses were elicited, a too hasty, impulsive beginning was noted. Further, there was a tendency for these men to respond to directions on an incorrect "level," taking a more literal or personal connotation than was intended. The ability to sense or respond to the proper "intent" of instructions was impaired in this group. Thus input seemed impaired, and the initiation of responding was poorly controlled. There seemed to be a blurring and losing of the point or purpose of the act. It was as if the instructions which had not been too well received became even further deteriorated. These men drifted from one association to another, rather than seeming to direct their memory search with a plan or goal behind the activity. Both drifting and perseveration were often noted in some individuals. In some, whose perseveration was subtle, and labeled here as high redundancy, there was superficial verbal facility, but inspection of their thinking indicated impoverishment. There appeared to be a restricted range of associations to call upon, and a reduced skill at communicating nuances about most ideas. The verbal expressions of the "senile" seemed more stark, primitive, and gross than the nonsenile. The capacity of the "senile" to plan a proper termination to each performance was poor; some stopped after very brief and insufficient responses; others talked endlessly until the tester or an outside event interrupted.

The approach to assessment which has been outlined permits the analysis of verbal behavior on projective-type tests, and it can be easily transposed to clinical behavior ratings. The types of ratings of the formal thought qualities among the various tests suggest a way of studying tests from groups of various ages without content beclouding issues. Even though age-determined associative content was present, the formal characteristics of the very healthy segment of the sample did not seem to differ from that expected of younger well functioning groups. While a large number of projective-type tests were used here, the findings suggest that a shorter series of tests rated in a similar way can be used where a limited amount of testing time is available.

The experiences of testing and studying the responses of this relatively healthy group of aged men, combined with prior work with other groups of aged, gives some indication that, in terms of the conceptual model used, one can roughly consider three groups among the aged. The first of these groups of aged individuals appears to evidence patterns of thought processes similar to what we grossly consider appropriate for younger, adequately functioning adults. A "transition" group appears to be composed of individuals who, in test situations like these, are impulsive and overtalkative in responding, provide a low ratio of "information," and show a tendency to "drift" as they associate. Of course, the range of behavior here is fairly wide. One senses that "something is amiss" about the functioning of these individuals. At one level of interference this behavior may appear "self-centered" in the aged person and be attributed to "personality attitudes, etc." Some of it is even excused as a burst of talking from a somewhat lonely person who has just received positive and inviting attention from a receptive audience. However, the impression remains that impulsive test behavior, combined with marked or obvious drift from topic to topic, combined with moderate to obvious perseveration of ideas within the drift, is not an expected, necessary, and normal component of aging.

The third group, rarely represented in this sample but prominent in institutional samples of aged, is characterized by slow responses, an impoverished range as well as a low output of expressed ideas, and perseveration within thought content.

These groups need further exploration. The problem of assessing and distinguishing depression, "brain damage indications," and psychoses is present in test evaluations of the aged. Some of the formal features rated in the tests reported here, combined with content analysis, might elucidate some distinctions more sharply, and help to define subgroups within the three large clusters of aged described.

SUMMARY

A group of 47 relatively healthy aged men were tested with various psychological tests, mostly of the projective type. Ratings of total test performance focused upon the following response qualities: how well the aged person was able to wait for and comprehend instructions; how many appropriate and varied associations he was able to call up for use in the situation; how well he adhered to the task goal, keeping his thoughts directed without drift from the task goal and without perseveration; how well he ordered the sequence of his thoughts; how appropriately he limited amount of verbalizing; and how appropriately he terminated his responses.

Analysis of the results indicated that when the basic sample of men was sectioned into a group of very healthy and a group with subclinical or asymptomatic disease processes, the less healthy group consistently, although not at a statistically significant level, performed somewhat less adequately on the tests. A further analysis of groupings based upon ratings of Senile and non-Senile Quality behavior indicated the Senile Quality group performed significantly more poorly. In particular it appeared that the group II Senile Quality men contributed heavily to this finding.

REFERENCES

ALBEE, G. W., and HAMLIN, R. M. 1950. Judgment of adjustment from drawings: the applicability of rating scale methods. *J. Clin. Psychol.*, 6, 363–365.

AMES, L. B., LEARNED, J., METRAUX, R., and WALKER, R. 1954. *Rorschach responses in old age.* New York: Hoeber-Harper.

ANDERSON, J. E. 1955. Assessment of aging. *Public Health Reports*, 70, 839–842.

———. 1956. *Psychological aspects of aging.* Washington D.C., American Psychological Association.

BECK, S. J. 1952. *Rorschach's test.* Vols. I, II, and III. New York: Grune & Stratton.

BENJAMIN, J. 1946. A method for distinguishing and evaluating formal thinking disorders in schizophrenia. In J. S. Kasanin, Ed., *Language and thought in schizophreniac.* Berkeley, California: University of California Press.

BENTON, A. L. WINDLE, C. D., and ERDICE, E. 1957. *A review of sentence completion techniques.* ONR Research Report, State University of Iowa, Dept. of Psychology.

BIRREN, J. E. 1955. Age changes in speed of simple perception and their significance for complex behavior. In: *Old age in the modern world.* E. & S. Livingston, Ltd., London, pp. 235–247.

———. 1955. Changes in speed and timing. *Public Health Reports*, 70, 844–846.

BRUNER, J. S. 1948. Perceptual theory and the Rorschach test. *J. Personality*, 17, 157–168.

———. and TAGIURI, R. 1954. The perception of people. In: Lindzey, G., *Handbook of social psychology.* Cambridge: Addison-Wesley Publishing Co.

CALDWELL, B. M. 1954. The use of the Rorschach in personality research with the aged. *J. Gerontol.*, 9, 316–323.

DeVos, G. 1952. A quantitative approach to affective symbolism in Rorschach responses. *J. Proj. Tech.*, 16, 133–145.

FRENKEL-BRUNSWICK, E. 1948. Dynamic and cognitive categorization of qualitative material: application to interviews with the ethnically prejudiced. *J. of Psychol.*, 25, 261–277.

———. 1950. Personality theory and perception. In: R. R. Blake and G. V. Ramsey, *Perception: an approach to personality.* New York: Ronald Press.

GLAD, D. D. 1956. An emotional projection test. *Psychological Test Specialists.* Louisville: Southern University Press.

——— and SHEARN, C. R. 1956. An emotional projection test. *Percep. and Motor Skills* (Sup. 1) 6: 1.

GOLDSTEIN, K., and SCHEERER, M. 1941. Abstract and concrete behavior; an experimental study with special tests. *Psychological Mono.* 239.

GOODENOUGH, F. L. 1926. *Measurement of intelligence by drawing.* Yonkers: World Book Co.

GORHAM, D. R. 1956. A proverbs test for clinical and experimental use. *Psychological Reports,* Monograph Sup. 1.

HEGLIN, H. J. 1956. Problem solving set in different age groups. *J. Gerontol., 11,* 310–317.

HOLZMAN, P. S., and KLEIN, G. S. 1956. Motive and style in reality contact. *Bull. Menn. Clin., 20,* 181–192.

HOPKINS, B., and POST, F. 1951. Abstract and concrete behavior in elderly patients, *J. Gerontol.,* 6, Supp. to No. 3, *104.*

———— ————. 1955. The significance of abstract and concrete behavior in elderly psychiatric patients and control subjects. *J. Ment. Sci., 101,* 841–850.

JACKSON, D. N. 1957. Intellectual ability and mode of perception. *J. Consult. Psychol., 21,* 458–465.

JONES, A. W., and RICH, T. A. 1957. The Goodenough draw-a-man test as a measure of intelligence in adults. *J. Consult. Psychol., 21,* 235–238.

KLEIN, G. S. 1950. The personal world through perception. In: R. R. Blake and G. V. Ramsey, *Perception: an approach to persønality.* New York: Ronald Press.

———— and SCHLESINGER, A. 1949. Where is the perceiver in perceptual theory? *J. Personal., 18,* 32–47.

KLOPFER, B., and KELLY, D. M. 1942. *The Rorschach technique.* New York: World Book Co.

KUTASH, S. B. 1954. Personality patterns of old age and the Rorschach test. *Geriatrics, 9,* 367–370.

LAKIN, M. 1956. Certain formal characteristics of human figure drawings by institutionalized aged and normal children. *J. Consult. Psychol., 20,* 471–474.

LEARY, T. 1957. *Interpersonal diagnosis of personality.* New York: Ronald Press.

LORGE, I., TUCKMAN, J., and DUNN, M. B. 1954. Human figure drawings by younger and older adults. *Am. Psychol., 9,* 420–421.

MACHOVER, K. 1948. *Personality projection in the drawing of the human figure.* Springfield, Ill., Chas. C Thomas.

MURRAY, H. A. 1943. *Thematic apperception test.* Cambridge: Harvard University Press.

NEUGARTEN, B. 1955. Age changes in perceptions of male-female relationships. *Am. Psychol., 9.*

———— and GUTMANN, D. L. 1956. *A study of age changes in adult sex roles.* Paper given at 1956 Gerontological Society annual meeting.

ORME, J. E. 1955. Intellectual and Rorschach test performances of a group of senile dementia patients and a group of elderly depressives. *J. Ment. Sci., 101,* 863–870.

POPE, B., and JENSEN, A. R. 1957. The Rorschach as an index of pathological thinking *J. Proj. Tech., 21,* 54–62.

POWERS, W. T., and HAMLIN, R. M. 1955. Relationship between diagnostic category and deviant verbalizations on the Rorschach. *J. Consult. Psychol., 14,* 120–124.

PRADOS, M., and FRIED, E. A. 1947. Personality structure in the older age groups. *J. Clin. Psychol., 3,* 113–120.

RAPAPORT, D., GILL, M., and SCHAFER, R. 1946. *Diagnostic psychological testing.* Chicago: Yearbook Publishers

————. 1942. Principles underlying projective techniques. *Character and Pers., 10,* 213–219.

SARGENT, H. 1953. *The insight test.* New York: Grune & Stratton.

SCHILDER, P. 1935. *The image and appearance of the human body.* London: Regan, Paul, Franch, Trubner & Co., Ltd.

SILVERMAN, A. J., BUSSE, E., BARNES, R., FROST, L., and THALER, M. 1953. Physiological influence on psychic functioning in elderly people. *Geriatrics, 8,* 370–376.

TERMAN, L. M., and MERRILL, M. A. 1937. *Measuring intelligence.* New York: Houghton Mifflin Co.

THALER, M. 1956. Relationships among Wechsler, Weigl, Rorschach, EEG findings and abstract-concrete behavior in a group of normal aged subjects. *J. Gerontol., 11,* 404–409.

————. 1952. Three theories of personality applied to the Rorschachs of 75 aged subjects. Unpublished dissertation, University of Denver.

———— and FROST, L. L. 1953. Physiological and psychological correlates of aging. *Am. Psychol., 8,* 446.

————, REISER, M., and WEINER, H. 1957. Exploration of the doctor-patient relationship through projective techniques. *Psychosom. Med., 19,* 228–239.

TOMKINS, S. S. 1947. *Thematic apperception test.* New York: Grune & Stratton.

WATKINS, J. G., and STAUFFACHER, J. C. 1952. An index of pathological thinking in the Rorschach. *J. Proj. Tech., 16,* 276–286.

WEIGL, E. 1941. On the psychology of so-called processes of abstraction (translation). *J. Abn. and Soc. Psychol., 36,* 3–33.

WELFORD, A. T. 1951. *Skill and age.* London: Oxford University Press.

WYATT, F. 1942. Formal aspects of the TAT. *Psychol. Bull., 39,* 491.

APPENDIX A

Performance of Each Subject on the Eleven Psychological Tests *

| | Level of Aspiration | | Weigl | Draw a Person (score) | Rating | Rorschach | Proverbs | Homonyms | | Sentence completion | Emotional Projection test | Family scene | Problem situations | TAT | Sum of ratings |
	Index	Performance						Number	Percent						
1	1.00	61^{3}	1	12^{5}	6	3	6	17^{4}	61^{3}	3	3	4	2	3	46
2	1.00	67^{3}	1	14^{5}	7	4	6	17^{4}	52^{4}	1	4	3	2	3	47
3	6.67	81^{1}	4	12^{5}	5	1	5	27^{2}	69^{3}	1	2	1	1	3	33
5	.67	67^{3}	1	26^{2}	1	1	1	36^{1}	90^{1}	1	1	1	1	1	16
6	3.33	49^{5}	1	7^{7}	9	4	6	19^{4}	48^{5}	2	5	3	3	3	57
7	.67	80^{1}	4	24^{3}	4	3	2	26^{2}	41^{5}	3	2	2	1	1	33
8	.33	81^{1}	4	17^{4}	6	1	7	21^{3}	68^{3}	1	2	1	1	1	35
9	1.33	70^{2}	4	22^{3}	5	4	7	15^{5}	39^{6}	1	5	4	2	3	51
10	1.33	24^{7}	5	12^{5}	9	7	8	10^{5}	50^{4}	5	6	5	3	5	74
11	1.33	58^{4}	1	43^{1}	1	2	6	24^{3}	65^{3}	1	2	4	1	2	31
12	−.67	34^{6}	5	7^{7}	9	7	8	9^{5}	47^{5}	5	6	5	3	5	76
13	6.00	83^{1}	1	19^{4}	5	3	4	24^{3}	89^{2}	1	1	1	1	1	28
14	3.33	84^{1}	1	12^{5}	8	2	7	18^{4}	95^{1}	2	2	1	1	2	36
15	2.00	81^{1}	2	26^{2}	4	3	5	21^{3}	54^{4}	1	5	1	1	2	34
16	3.33	83^{1}	2	8^{7}	8	4	6	17^{4}	63^{3}	1	2	2	1	2	43
18	−.67	90^{1}	4	42^{1}	1	3	4	28^{2}	65^{3}	1	1	3	1	3	28
19	3.33	70^{2}	1	19^{4}	3	1	2	24^{3}	52^{4}	1	1	1	1	1	25
20	2.33	82^{1}	4	16^{4}	6	5	3	29^{2}	97^{1}	1	4	1	1	2	35
23	1.67	71^{2}	4	14^{5}	5	4	7	21^{3}	70^{2}	4	5	4	3	4	52
24	.33	92^{1}	1	35^{1}	1	1	3	35^{1}	58^{4}	1	1	1	1	1	18
25	−.33	45^{5}	5	22^{3}	7	5	5	24^{3}	31^{6}	2	3	1	2	2	49
26	1.33	55^{4}	2	15^{5}	7	5	8	19^{4}	49^{5}	1	2	1	1	2	47
27	1.33	77^{2}	4	23^{3}	2	2	2	26^{2}	76^{2}	1	1	1	1	1	24
28	.67	63^{3}	5	12^{5}	8	6	7	23^{3}	92^{1}	1	1	2	1	2	46
29	.67	37^{6}	5	11^{6}	8	6	3	19^{4}	95^{1}	2	2	4	2	5	51
30	2.67	54^{4}	3	14^{5}	9	7	8	12^{3}	24^{7}	3	4	5	3	5	68
31	−.33	64^{3}	1	8^{7}	9	6	6	18^{4}	62^{3}	1	5	2	3	3	53
32	−.33	36^{6}	3	13^{5}	8	6	7	20^{3}	63^{3}	2	6	3	3	4	59
35	−2.33	82^{1}	4	8^{7}	9	7	3	23^{3}	58^{4}	1	2	2	1	3	47
36	−.33	58^{4}	4	11^{6}	7	4	1	27^{2}	68^{3}	1	2	1	1	1	37
38	3.33	38^{6}	4	11^{6}	7	6	8	11^{5}	23^{7}	3	6	1	3	4	66
39	2.33	77^{2}	4	27^{2}	1	1	5	30^{1}	67^{3}	1	1	1	2	1	25
41	1.67	84^{1}	1	26^{2}	4	1	7	25^{2}	38^{6}	4	1	1	1	3	34
42	.00	59^{4}	1	22^{3}	5	....	5	19^{4}	59^{4}	2	1	3	1	3	36
47	1.67	83^{1}	1	45^{1}	1	1	1	38^{1}	100^{1}	1	1	1	1	1	13
49	2.33	77^{2}	3	20^{4}	4	1	1	19^{4}	95^{1}	1	1	1	1	1	25
50	4.00	61^{3}	1	17^{4}	6	4	1	26^{2}	93^{1}	2	2	3	3	3	35
51	2.33	48^{5}	3	27^{2}	2	4	2	23^{3}	100^{1}	1	4	3	1	3	34
52	3.00	83^{1}	4	29^{2}	1	4	2	35^{1}	81^{2}	1	5	3	3	3	32
53	1.00	70^{2}	2	26^{2}	4	5	1	27^{2}	100^{1}	2	4	1	1	2	29
54	−.67	61^{3}	3	18^{4}	3	1	1	41^{1}	93^{1}	3	1	1	1	1	24
55	.33	79^{2}	1	35^{1}	1	1	1	43^{1}	93^{1}	1	1	1	1	1	14
56	1.33	67^{3}	4	29^{2}	2	....	2	28^{2}	90^{1}	2	4	4	3	3	32
57	2.33	60^{3}	3	10^{6}	6	....	3	24^{3}	83^{2}	1	4	4	2	2	39
58	2.33	63^{3}	1	14^{5}	4	2	2	33^{1}	79^{2}	2	1	1	2	2	28
59	1.33	59^{4}	3	26^{2}	3	2	4	31^{1}	91^{1}	1	3	1	1	1	27

* Superscripts, small numbers, are performance ratings.

APPENDIX B

LEVEL OF ASPIRATION TEST

This unpublished test was devised by Dr. Earl Swartzlander. It consists of a page with 4 mimeographed areas of boxes, each box contains 27 half-inch squares arranged in rows. To the left of each of these are two vertical squares. The instructions to a subject are: "Notice that this sheet is made up of boxes or squares and that there are four sections or parts. At the left-hand side of each of these sections there is a large box divided into two parts . . . I want you to put an X in as many of these boxes or squares as you can in the time you are given. I will always say 'ready—begin' and then 'stop.' Don't start writing until I say 'begin' and be sure and stop when I say 'stop.'

"Now before you start I want you to guess how many boxes or squares in this first section you can fill with an X in 10 seconds. Write that number in the top half of the big box at the left." After this has been done ask: "Are you sure you understand what I want you to do?" If necessary the examiner demonstrates on another page the quick making of a few X's in the boxes.

Then say: "Ready—begin." (Start timing with stopwatch when you say "begin.") After exactly 10 seconds, say: "Stop." Now say: "Count how many you did and write that number in the bottom half of the box at the left."

Then say: "Now I want you to try again. Look at the next section, then guess how many you can do in 10 seconds."

After this guess has been recorded say: "Ready—begin." After exactly 10 seconds say: "Stop." Now say: "Count how many you did this time and write that number in the bottom half of the box at the left."

Then say: "Now look at the next section and guess again." (Do not mention the time.)

After this guess has been recorded say: "Ready—begin." After exactly 8 seconds say: "Stop." (No matter what S says about the shortened time, which is rarely ever noted by aged subjects, but quite often by alert young subjects, do not in any way indicate that the time was reduced.)

Now say: "Count how many you did and write that number in the bottom half of the box at the left."

Then say: "Now make your last guess." After this has been recorded in the appropriate place, say: "Ready—begin." After exactly 10 seconds, say: "Stop." Now say: "Count how many you did and write the number in the box at the left."

Scoring index:

$$\frac{(\text{Guess } 2 - \text{Performance } 1) + (G_3 - P_2) + (G_4 - P_3)}{3}$$

Norms for young men:

5.00 and above	Unrealistically high level of aspiration.
3.00—4.99	High level of aspiration.
1.00—2.99	Within normal limits.
—1.49 to —0.99	Low level of aspiration.
—1.50 and below	Unrealistically low level of aspiration.

For individual clinical assessment, the psychologist can make interpretive inferences about questions such as: Was there a rigidity of the Guesses without regard to the Performance? What was the effect of the time reduction? Was the G_1 above or below P_1? Did S count the boxes in section 1 before recording G_1?

During the course of this study the performance on this test of a sample of 120 young men, mean age 25 years, was secured. Table B-1 indicates that with the exception of Guess 1, the young men consistently have significantly higher scores on each subsequent portion of the test. However, it is interesting to note in table B-2 that the Level of Aspiration Index (ratio of aspiration to actual performance) scattering of scores is similar for the two groups, with equal portions of both groups scoring at the various levels as shown.

TABLE B–1.—*Level of Aspiration Test means for aged and young men*

	Young men		Aged men		t	p
	Mean	S.D.	Mean	S.D.		
Guess 1	16.25	5.16	16.18	6.39	0.07	N.S.
Performance 1	18.71	3.63	15.55	4.59	4.74	0.001
Guess 2	19.82	3.45	17.14	5.12	3.94	.001
Performance 2	20.48	3.57	17.10	4.76	5.05	.001
Guess 3	21.12	3.65	17.86	5.28	4.60	.001
Performance 3	17.46	2.70	14.65	3.87	5.38	.001
Guess 4	19.45	3.58	16.80	4.80	3.94	.001
Performance 4	21.06	3.20	17.53	4.64	6.67	.001
	76.63	12.32	67.94	19.05	3.52	.001
	77.70	12.43	64.84	17.38	5.41	.001

N.S. = Not significant.

TABLE B–2.—*Level of Aspiration Index*

Level of Aspiration Index	Percent young men	Percent aged men
Unrealistically high	1	4
High	11	12
Normal	53	46
Low	30	34
Unrealistically low	5	1

APPENDIX C

THE WEIGL COLOR-FORM SORTING TEST

The test (Goldstein and Scheerer, 1941; Weigl, 1941) presents the subject with 12 unarranged, flat plastic figures: 4 each of equilateral triangles, squares, and circles. Each of these forms occurs once in red, green, blue, and yellow. The subject is asked to sort the figures which he thinks belong together. The expected response is a grouping either by color or form. Following the first grouping, the figures are disarranged and the subject is asked to re-sort them in another way (e.g., if the first sorting was by form, the S would then sort on the basis of color).

In earlier work (described in Thaler, 1956) a scoring method was evolved and tested, evaluating both the actual sortings made and the language level used by the subject.

Scores range from 1 to 5.

1. The S made the two sortings (color, as well as form sort) quickly, gave an adequate verbaliza- tion of what he had done, and showed no need to build a pattern with the pieces.

2. The S made the two sortings correctly, ver- balized adequately, but tended to build patterns with the pieces (mild tendency to concreteness in treating the objects, but language skill was adequate).

3. The S correctly sorted the pieces, and may or may not have patterned them, but could not verbalize that color and form were the conceptual sorting principles. Adequate verbal accounting could not be made for the grouping.

4. One sorting with or without patterning was made, but the subject could not voluntarily shift to the other grouping. The examiner then at- tempted to teach the S the shift as a test of learn- ing capacity in this situation, and success ensued.

5. The S could not make a sorting by either color or form, and could not learn the sortings from the examiner. He was unable to learn the features and groupings when shown. Language was either concrete, no verbalization occurred, or it was highly confused.

APPENDIX D

INSTRUCTIONS FOR RATING AN INDIVIDUAL'S PERFORMANCE ON THE EMOTIONAL PROJECTION TEST

The best performances on this procedure are characterized by *variety* among the associations, the presence of *positive* content, and the presence of *interaction* content. The less adequate performances are characterized by associative impoverishment, concrete-literalness, and the usual indications of narrowed, impoverished mental-associative resources, and social interaction potentials.

A suggested sequence of groupings might be: (1) variety, positive content and interaction; (2) some impotence in thinking, running out of vocabulary, saying "I'm just guessing," and a number of doubt-indecision, querulous responses; (3) only moderate variety; (4) uncertain, little variety; (5) continuous tale, monotopic, concrete, no people alluded to; (6) monotopic, severely constricted.

On the whole, verboseness is not a good feature. It is usually a middle-range feature and the content is usually redundant. Feeling there are pictures which are the "same" as ones already seen is again not found in good records.

The following are further qualitative features of adequate performance stated in positive form to assist in rating records where these features apply:

a. The *S* has comprehended the instructions in the sense they were intended, makes efforts to comply with them, and maintains the original set throughout the test. He has the proper set toward "feeling," meaning "emotion." A brief attention span, or a partial understanding, may result in a subject using the word "feeling" to refer to "physical status." So doing suggests the subject's attention and comprehension were partial, concrete, etc., as well as primitive and self-oriented. Prior work with this test suggests the less adequately functioning aged individuals take this orientation to the word "feeling" and create a primitive, literal, self-oriented quality to their performance on this test.

b. The man consistently attempts to interpret the pictures. He does not try to "recognize," but is aware he has an interpretive task to carry out. Further, he does not serialize his responses. Perceptual distortions do not occur.

c. The man feels sure of his own performance. He does not frequently state he is unsure he is doing well, and actually communicates a specific interpretation of the picture. Some aged subjects give a lengthy response, but inspection reveals the man has never come to a definite answer, or even to alternative answers; he has left a series of "possible" answers. Further, the actual state attributed to the depicted persons is not frequently one of bewilderment, being puzzled or severely indecisive in good performances.

d. A good feature, but not a necessary one, is the presence of several good "interaction" responses in which the depicted person is seen having the feeling in relation to a meaningful interaction with another person. Also positive content in which love, fun, good cheer are noted is a good, but again not necesasry, feature.

e. Variety among the responses is, as stated earlier, a crucial feature.

APPENDIX E

INSTRUCTIONS TO RATERS ON THE THEMATIC APPERCEPTION TEST

The following descriptions were given the raters who were asked to class the records into five groups on the basis of their overall impressions of the total responses.

TAT Descriptive Groupings

1. The man actually creates a series of separate interpretative stories. His productions convey to the reader the impression of a unitary experience in which the man integrated the instructions, the card, the examiner, and his story.

He does not perseverate words or themes. Stories are not filled with puzzlement, bewilderment, and not knowing what to do, either regarding the test or as part of the theme about the depicted persons.

The man remains aware of he point of alternative tales and recalls that *he* posed the alternatives.

2. A subtle repetition of themes occurs. Subtle "I don't know what to do" themes emerge in the tales. Alternative tales are given and may not be tied up clearly.

3. Card description occurs, but it is of some length, and the man may even bog down into repetitive chatter over the card.

A moderate language problem is noted. The man has trouble getting the right word; occasionally intrusions may occur of personal experience or personal opinion references.

Personal interest topics cause drift, but there is still a point to the tale.

A mild misperception of a card or cards occurs, but the meaning is close to the usual.

4. Severe associative impoverishment is indicated. Barren card description is given. Role and identity of characters shift. Obvious perseverations of themes and words is present. Misperceptions of card or cards is moderate.

5. The man severely or frequently misperceives the cards. There are pointless card descriptions. Roles and identities shift. He is confused. There is a drift in the point of the tale, or a drift in the language, such as saying a man's head is sore, then drifting to talking about "sorry." Blatant intrusion of tangential thoughts occurs. A marked carry-over from tale to tale occurs.

As a further aid to the raters, the five main features being rated (interpretation versus card description, perseveration versus nonperseverations, misperceptions, themes, and roles and identities) were graded descriptively in the following table and given to the raters along with the earlier five level descriptions.

Graded Features of the TAT Descriptive Groupings

Interpretation vs. Card Description	Perseveration vs. non-perseveration	Misperceptions	Themes	Roles and identities
1. Interprets.........	No perseveration or repetitiveness.	None........	Variety...........	Clear.
2. Interprets.........	Subtle repetition.......	None........	Subtle repetition.....	Clear.
3. Primarily card description.	Mild repetitiveness; may serialize cards into running story.	Mild.........	No particular theme, or mild repetition.	Merely described.
4. Barren card description.	Obvious perseveration of words and themes.	Moderate.....	No particular point to tale.	Some shift.
5. Pointless card description.	Severe perseveration; cards seen as serial story.	Marked......	Pointless or severe repetition.	Gross shifts.

APPENDIX F

INSTRUCTIONS FOR RATING FAMILY SCENE TALE

Rank the stories into five groups (one best, five poorest) on the basis of your overall impression of the extent to which the subject inferred, chose among alternatives, and adequately developed and elaborated a central theme. To what extent did he avoid card description? To what extent does he avoid presenting alternative possible meanings without choosing or having a central theme (i.e., no point to story or merely a collection of possible meanings)? To what extent does he avoid having intrusions of personal "themes," references, and reality conflicts (not to be confused with personal dynamics, but consists of the introduction of "real life" material, rather than keeping the set toward the card)?

APPENDIX G

PROVERBS

1. A burnt child dreads the fire.
2. He who would eat the kernel must crack the nut.
3. A drowning man will catch at a straw.
4. We only know the worth of water when the well is dry.
5. No wind can do him good who steers for no port.
6. Don't judge a book by its cover.
7. Let sleeping dogs lie.
8. A bad workman quarrels with his tools.
9. It's an ill wind that blows nobody good.

APPENDIX H

SENTENCE COMPLETION TEST

1. I get angry when . . .
2. I feel blue . . .
3. My parents . . .
4. My mother . . .
5. My father . . .
6. My father used to . . .
7. My wife . . .
8. I wish . . .
9. My body . . .
10. My eyes . . .
11. The worst thing about my health . . .
12. The best thing about my health . . .
13. When I am sick . . .
14. When I think of people dying . . .
15. When a man's wife dies . . .
16. My children treat me . . .
17. I wish my children . . .
18. When I think of my children . . .
19. To me God is . . .
20. Most young people . . .
21. When a person gets to be 70 . . .
22. To me the future . . .
23. I wish that I could . . .
24. I wish I didn't have to . . .
25. I used to think that when I got to be 70 . . .
26. Most young people think that after a person gets to be 60 years old . . .
27. A person my age should . . .
28. A person my age should not . . .

APPENDIX I

SENTENCE COMPLETION
RESPONSE ANALYSIS

The responses to each item were grouped under the various headings shown beneath the starting phrase. Where the proportion of men in the Senile Quality group tended to differ from that of the non-Senile Quality group on a response, the percentages are given.

Item No. 1—Anger

| | Percent | |
	S	NS
When affronted		
Meals		
Opposed, injustices, etc.	0	42
Idiosyncratic		
Synonyms		
Denies	69	33
No response		
Self-failure		

Item No. 2—Blue

	S	NS
Weather	4	20
Health		
Outside forces		
Lonely		
Deny		
Disappointed, sad		
Nothing to do		
No response		
At times		
Failures	8	14
Money		

Item No. 3—Parents

	S	NS
Dead	0	42
Present tense	46	8
Neutral-negative		
Positive		
Good to me	23	11
No response		

Item No. 4—Mother

	S	NS
Positive		
Dead		19
Attribute, neat		
Hard worker, etc.	23	33
Good to me	46	14
Negative		
No response		

Item No. 5—Father

| | Percent | |
	S	NS
Trade		
Good man		
Provider		
Dead	15	25
Church		
Negative		
Liked me		
Strict		
Intellectual man	15	28

Item No. 6—Father used to—

	S	NS
Advise me		
I miss him, etc.	23	--
His work		25
Worked hard, provider		
Play with me		17
No response		
Chastise me		
Drink	8	28

Item No. 7—My wife

	S	NS
Lovely, capable	46	47
Loves me		
Miscellaneous		
Negative or none	0	22
What she does		
Is dead		

Item No. 8—I wish

	S	NS
Reference to wife		
Be in another city		
Greater pleasure		
Altruistic		
Retain, maintain health		
No response		
Immediate		
Specific personal	0	28

Items No. 9–13—Body health

	S	NS
Sick or rambling reply	45	22
Denial of any defects	55	78

Item No. 14—Think of people dying

	S	NS
Minimize, deny		
Intellectualize	8	36
Feel sorry	38	38
Sorry for family or young deaths	8	17
Thinks of self dying	23	3
No response or confused		
Open acceptance		
Miscellaneous		

I-248

Item No. 15—Wife dies	Percent	
Lonely	0	36
Loss, lost	62	22
Chin up	0	17
Sorry	23	17
Miscellaneous		
No response		

Item No. 16—My children treat me—		
Good, OK, fine	62	69
Qualified or neutral		
Negative		
No children		
No response, confused		

Item No. 17—Wish my children		
Positive	38	61
No response		
Miscellaneous		
No children		
Treat me better	38	6

Item No. 18—Think of my children		
Positive	0	17
Qualified		
Miscellaneous		
None		
No response		

Item No. 19—God		
Quality		
Role		47
Miscellaneous		
Negative		

Item No. 20—Most young people		
No response	23	3
Happy	15	33
Positive	46	14
Miscellaneous		
Negative and Moralizing	15	35

Item No. 21—Gets to be 70		
Negative	62	19
Positive	8	28
Miscellaneous		
No response	0	17
Health		
Regrets		
Live so long		

Item No. 22—The future		
Positive	23	67
Unknown, uncertain	23	28
Pessimistic	38	6
No response		

Item No. 23—Wish I could	Percent	
Altruistic		31
Live longer		
Be young, live over		31
Work		
Do things		
Miscellaneous		
No response		
None		

Item No. 24—Wish I didn't have to		
Nothing	15	33
Money worries		
Old, die		31
No response		31
Personal		44

Item No. 25—Used to think		
No response		
Rich		
Less healthy		
Prepared		
Positive		
Never thought	8	19
Less positive		
Retire		
Miscellaneous		

Item No. 26—Most young people think		
You're old	8	36
Miscellaneous		
Useless	35	44
Perseverate		
No response		
Respect		

Item No. 27—Person my age should		
Positive	31	43
Health }	23	43
Brake }		
No response		
Suicide or die		
Act age		

Item No. 28—Person my age should not—		
Be too active	23	43
Miscellaneous		
Be inactive	0	22
Drink, eat		
Worry		
Act young		
Confused, omit	38	11

Minnesota Multiphasic Personality Inventory: Results Obtained From a Population of Aged Men

by Conan Kornetsky

The present section deals with the responses of the aged sample to the Minnesota Multiphasic Personality Inventory (MMPI). This test is a standardized personality inventory that requires the subject to respond to 550 separate statements as either "true, or mostly true as applied to you, or false, or not usually true." A third alternative is given to the subject: if the statement does not apply at all, it can be placed in a "Cannot say" category. The inventory characterizes personality in terms of a number of clinical syndromes or personality characteristics. These are: hypochondriasis (Hs), depression (D), hysteria (Hy), psychopathic deviate (Pd), masculinity-femininity (Mf), paranoia (Pa), psychoasthenia (Pt), schizophrenia (Sc), hypomania (Ma), and the social (Si). In addition there are four validatory scales: question score (?), lie score (L), validity score (F), and K score (K). The theory construction and use of this test have been adequately described (elsewhere) Welsh and Dahlstrom, 1956).

Although the MMPI is probably the most widely used inventory of personality in the repertoire of the clinical psychologist, there is a paucity of reported studies in a normal aged population. The few isolated studies have generally been confined to the results of scores of aged subjects on single isolated scales (Hathaway and McKinley, 1956) or item analysis of responses to single items on the test (Brozek, 1955).

METHODS

The characteristics of the subjects are described in chapters 2 and 3.

The individual card form of the test was used in this study rather than the booklet and answer sheet form. In the card form, subjects are presented with only a single item at a time, thereby reducing the possibility of errors that are inherent in the booklet form. Complete tests were obtained on 43 of the total sample of geriatric subjects. Subjects were administered the test in their rooms at the Clinical Center. Half of the subjects were given the test on the fourth day of their first week and the other half on the fourth day of their second week of residence at NIH. Care was taken to make sure that subjects understood what was required of them. They were encouraged to make a definitive response to each card so that the number of items in the "Cannot say" category would be small. No time limit was set for completion of the task; however, the subjects were urged not to spend too much time on any single item.

RESULTS

Table 1 shows the mean raw score with K added and the standard deviation (S.D.) for the 43 subjects on all scales with the exception of the "?" scale. Since subjects were urged to make a definitive response, there were not enough subjects who had a score in this latter category to compute means. Figure 1 shows the same data transformed to T scores of the original standardization group (mean of 50 S.D. of 10). Also, one and two S.D.'s of the aged sample are plotted in figure 1.

Only on the D and Mf scale did the means of the aged sample deviate as much as one S.D. or more from the mean of the general population (i.e., the standardization group). The elevated D scale score agrees with the findings of Hathaway and McKinley (1956), who reported that there is an elevated D scale score on males age 56 years and above. They report in this age range a mean raw D scale score of 21.46, with an S.D. of 6.43. Our obtained D scale raw score was 21.88, with a S.D. of 5.43.

McKinley and Hathaway (1956) also reported age changes in the Pt scale. For male age 56 to 65 (13 subjects), they obtained a mean of 12.38 with an S.D. of 8.8. This result, which is without K added, is higher than our obtained Pt scale score of 10.44 with an S.D. of 8.16.

At first glance one is aware of the difference between the present aged sample and the scores obtained in the general population. It appears that the aged individual is deviant of many of the categories; however, this may be an artifact of the sample selection of aged subjects. The mean IQ of our sample was 110 (MMPI subjects), which is above the mean of the general population; and although no direct studies of the relationship between intelligence and score on the MMPI could be found, this relationship can be inferred from the MMPI results obtained in college students. A study of male college students (Goodstein, 1956) found that this group deviated significantly from the general population. Since

TABLE 1.—*Mean MMPI raw scores with K correction for all subjects*

Scale	Group I (N=25) [1]		Group II (N=18)		Total group (N=43)	
	Mean	S.D.	Mean	S.D.	Mean	S.D.
L	5.92	2.75	4.67	1.99	5.44	2.57
F	4.72	4.00	6.94	4.47	5.65	4.34
K	15.44	4.52	12.39	5.68	14.16	5.25
Hs	14.28	4.62	14.78	3.90	14.49	4.35
D	22.36	5.54	22.06	4.72	22.23	5.23
Hy	19.84	4.96	20.00	6.28	19.91	5.53
Pd	20.56	4.41	20.33	4.83	20.47	4.58
Mf	26.12	4.17	24.94	4.83	25.63	4.49
Pa	8.68	2.88	9.39	2.20	8.98	2.65
Pt	24.84	5.17	24.39	5.74	24.65	5.42
Sc	24.60	4.93	25.11	6.54	24.81	5.65
Ma	18.80	3.98	17.89	4.64	18.41	4.28
Si	28.83	8.00	29.40	9.46	29.05	8.57

[1] Group I was superior in health to group II. See chs. 2 and 3 for descriptions of the subjects.

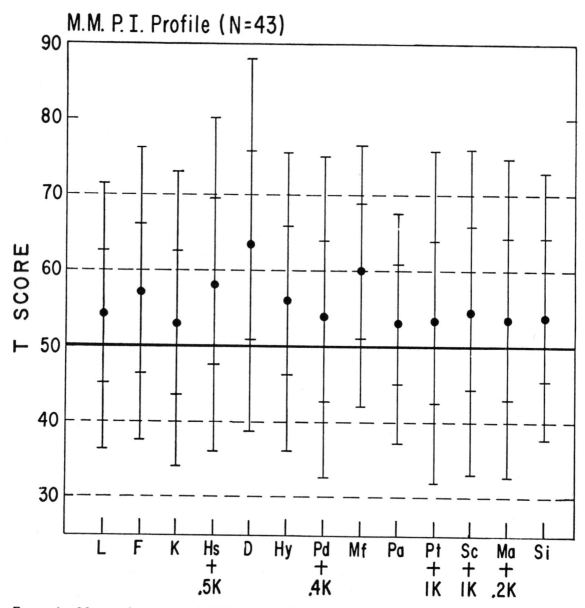

FIGURE 1.—Mean scale scores on the Minnesota Multiphasic Personality Inventory (MMPI). The standardization mean with 50 with an S.D. of 10. Mean scores for the present sample are plotted with plus and minus two standard deviations indicated by the vertical lines.

it is a reasonable assumption that college students generally score higher on tests of intelligence, the elevated MMPI scores in the college population may be attributed to the higher IQ. Our sample, although not a college sample, also had somewhat higher IQ's than the population at large; therefore, a reasonable hypothesis would be that the important independent variable in our sample is IQ and not merely age, with the exception of the elevated D scale score. However, the present sample made higher scores mostly by better performance on the verbal tests; lower scores were seen on non-verbal measures. (See ch. 8.) Further investigation is needed of the relations be-

TABLE 2.—*Comparison of D scale scores in subjects judged by the psychiatrists to be depressed or not depressed*

No depression	Mean D scale score
a. Group I ($N=18$)	21.11
b. Group II ($N=14$)	21.14
Depression	
c. Group I ($N=7$)	25.57
d. Group II ($N=4$)	25.25

$t=2.52$ ($P<0.02$) Combined groups $a+b$ vs. $c+d$.

See chapters 2 and 3 for information about the populations studied.

tween education, intelligence measures, and personality tests in older populations.

It is not clear how to interpret the elevated Mf scale. The Mf is elevated in the college population and the present sample was somewhat more educated than its age group in the general population. About one-third of the present sample had some college training or were college graduates. (See ch. 2.) Thus without other evidence it is not possible to interpret the elevated Mf in terms of a possible age difference in a personality characteristic.

The significant elevation of the D scale score suggests that a number of our subjects may have been pathologically depressed. In order to test this, a *t-test* (Edwards, 1950) was computed on the raw D scale score between subjects who were found to be depressed by the psychiatrists (see ch. 11) and those of whom no diagnosis of depression was made. Table 2 shows the results of this analysis. Although the D scale score difference between "no depression" and "depression" does not reach an acceptable level of significance, the difference is suggestive. (See table 2.)

The results on the MMPI in this aged sample suggest that they do not deviate, with the exception of the D scale, beyond the limits of what might be expected from an above-average-IQ group of subjects. The deviant D scale score indicated more depression among this group than that which could be expected in a group of younger subjects matched for IQ and economic status. The presence of depression in this sample is discussed in more detail in chapter 11.

REFERENCES

BROZEK, J. 1955. Personality changes with age: An item analysis of the Minnesota Multiphasic Personality Inventory. *J. Gerontol., 10,* 194–206.

EDWARDS, A. L. 1950. *Statistical Analysis.* Rinehart & Co., Inc. p. 172.

GOODSTEIN, L. D. 1956. Regional Differences in MMPI Responses Among Male College Students. In Welsh, G. S., and Dahlstrom, W. G. Basic Readings on the MMPI in Psychology and Medicine. University of Minnesota Press. pp. 574–578.

HATHAWAY, S. R., and McKINLEY, J. C. 1956. Scale 2 (Depression) in Welsh, G. S., and Dahlstrom, W. G. *Basic Readings on the MMPI in Psychology and Medicine.* University of Minnesota Press. pp. 73–80.

McKINLEY, J. C., and HATHAWAY, S. R. Scale 7 (Psychasthenia), *ibid.* pp. 81–86.

WELSH, G. S., and DAHLSTROM, W. G. 1956. *Basic Readings on the MMPI in Psychology and Medicine.* University of Minnesota Press.

Social Psychological Characteristics of Old Age

by Marian R. Yarrow, Paul Blank,
Olive W. Quinn, E. Grant Youmans,
and Johanna Stein

Old age, in expectation and reality, brings many changes in the life setting of the individual. Changed physical and psychological capacities, and changed circumstances and opportunities, tend to impose limitations necessitating substitutions and reorganizations in behavior. During earlier adulthood, developmental changes and chronological age, per se, have been of little significance to the individual in his day-to-day functioning and of little influence on how he had been regarded by society. They assume importance, however, in his old age. His concerns about physiological processes and mental functioning tend to be magnified and tend to shape his behavior and attitudes. His environment, in many ways inseparable from the person, is often markedly altered in old age: critical changes in, and losses of, the persons of the immediate environment are likely to occur as the individual enters the sixth, seventh, or eighth decades of life—changes in family members and others through whom his identity has been defined. The predictable structure of day-to-day living, in terms of the routine responsibilities and the motivations relating to family, work, and community, breaks down, and new structure must be built to replace it. In the process of getting old, the individual also grows into new social situations defined by society, through the roles and responsi-

bilities it accords the older person and the restrictions it imposes upon him. Such situations appear in the employment codes for old age, the financial provisions for retirees, the permitted nonwork roles for the elderly, the social valuations of age, and the like.

While not all these changes and stresses are peculiar to old age, in their combination they comprise a relatively unique Gestalt. In this perspective, old age becomes a period requiring active coping with multiple changes in which biological and social components are intimately related. A physical organism, itself experiencing changes, must deal with changes (often major) in its immediate social environment. This paper is directed to some aspects of these changes and requirements. It is concerned (*a*) with the nature of the aged person's social environment, (*b*) with his adaptations to his changed physical and social circumstances, and (*c*) with relationships between certain environmental and behavioral variables.

This is an exploration in a research area which is still at a relatively early stage of development. Descriptive data on the social psychology of old age are incomplete; relatively few antecedent-consequent relationships have been investigated; and concepts and theory in this area are relatively undeveloped. Social psychological studies of old age cannot follow the models of biological studies or those of child development which seek normative age changes. Unlike biological changes with age, which can somewhat more legitimately be investigated as functions of time and maturation, social behavior and attitudinal characteristics of the aged cannot be interpreted meaningfully as functions of time, apart from the environmental settings in which these responses occur. Herein would seem to lie difficult problems for research in the social psychology of old age, for we are, at present, a long way from adequate conceptualizations and analyses of the environment.

Environment can be thought of in terms of the gross settings in which the aged person lives, such as institution or community, retired status or not retired, one social class or ethnic culture or another. Such setting analyses must be further refined, however, before one can see clearly how these settings may be the bases of differences in life adjustments. One step in this direction would be investigation of specific setting dimensions in association with particular behaviors and attitudes of the aged. Thus, class and culture might be investigated more analytically by examining ways in which cultural differences in particular traditions, values, styles of living, and pathologies contribute to given kinds of problems and adjustments in old age. What, for example, are the implications for old age of differences in cultural values regarding achievement and competitive striving, youth and physical prowess, wisdom and reflective pursuits? Where are generational differences most pronounced? How do differing (culturally linked) tendencies in responding to illness and pain (Zborowski, 1952) and meanings of death play a role in old-age adjustments? Environment at another level may be regarded much more in terms of immediate events and situations—the persons present or absent, the threats or obstacles in the immediate circumstances, the material facilities available, the freedom of movement within the environment. In the present research we have been concerned with environments as gross behavior settings and as specific situations.

Although it is too early to find sufficient data from research to develop a systematic body of knowledge concerning environmental effects, there is considerable evidence from varied sources pointing to the fruitfulness of careful analyses of the interaction of old-age adjustments and environmental factors. Granick (1957) discusses some of the adjustments of aged in communities of retirants. There is considerable controversy and concern as to the appropriateness of mental hospitals as environments in which to treat elderly persons with emotional disturbances (Kolb, 1956; Waldman, 1959). Statistical reports from a number of sources (Dunham, 1956; Jones, 1959) on hospitalization and mortality rates for the aged point to the disproportionate number of beds and the higher mortality rates for the single, widowed, and divorced aged. It is likely that these "single" persons generally live in more isolated and lonely circumstances than the married aged—a factor which may contribute to the poorer survival. Thompson and Streib (1958) have shown a relationship between what they term situational resources and adjustment in retirement. They conclude that the retired man who is in poor health and who is economically deprived is more likely to be poorly adjusted than the man hampered by only one or the other of these conditions, and that the man who is economically and physically well off is least likely to be dissatisfied with life and dejected.

A number of community studies have been reported recently in the field of aging; namely: the New York City survey of "Five Hundred Overy Sixty" (Kutner, Fanshel,

Togo, and Langner, 1956), the Kansas City interview studies of middle and old age (Henry, 1959; Cumming, Dean, Newell, and McCaffrey, 1960), the Cornell survey of a wide range of male workers prior to and after retirement (Streib, Thompson, and Suchman, 1958), the interviews with lower economic families in East London (Townsend, 1957). Recurrent in these reports are themes of the importance of family ties and also the complicated nature of family relationships, the frequency of social isolation, loneliness or the fear of loneliness, the shrinkage in social roles, the links between environmental resources and morale. Another common emphasis, that the aged are not a homogeneous group in their adjustments to old age, invites further research which will help to ascertain the biological and social determinants of the variance in adjustments.

Much of what has been mentioned concerning environmental changes correlated with old age has been of changes outside the control of the elderly person himself. In this sense there is a close parallel between his situation and that of the young child. In the child, feeling state is highly dependent upon the characteristics of the immediate situation; development of greater independence from the immediate setting is part of the maturational process. One may ask to what extent the interdependence of person and environment increases in old age, when again environment tends more to be beyond manipulation and control in respects very vital to the individual.

The present research is concerned with four questions which grow out of the general perspectives described above.

(1) Where inroads of physical and psychiatric pathology are minimal (i.e., where ill-health or physical handicaps do not seriously limit the environment and restrict behavior), how is old age lived? What activities, aspirations, and affects make up day-to-day living?

(2) How are cultural differences in life history settings (i.e., educational background, occupational history and national origin) related to adjustments in old age?

(3) How much are behavior and attitudes of the aged person a function of current environmental circumstances? We are concerned particularly with the influence of circumstances over which the person has little or no control: (a) losses, or threats of loss, of significant persons, through death or abandonments; (b) losses in status and functions in family, in work role, in community; (c) changes in physical self which limit the kind of environment and behavior available to the person; and (d) experienced cultural or generational changes which "outdate" the individual.

(4) How are the aged person's measured physical and psychological capacities related to his daily living and social behavior? Does the man's functioning in the community reflect his tested capacities? To the extent that discrepancies occur, how can they be accounted for?

(The findings and discussion relating to question 4 are presented in ch. 15.)

In assessing behavior and attitudes of the aged, we have been concerned with the quality and complexity of daily behavior and of personal relationships, and with the extent of changes from middle adulthood; with the expansiveness or constrictiveness of the individual's perspectives—the nature of goals, the meaning of time, the kinds of interests maintained, the nature of his self-picture; and with the social stimulus-value of the individual to others.

SUBJECTS

In one very important respect the subjects constitute a homogeneous subgroup of the aged population, homogeneous in possessing good physical health. (See ch. 3.) Since old age and failing health are often partners, characteristics of behavior and attitudes attributed to age (exclusion of stimuli, conservation of energy, regression) (Weinberg, 1956) may be the fruits of illness as well. Descriptive data on this healthy group thus provide a partial picture of social and interpersonal sides of old age when the contributions of illness are minimal. We will use less selective samples as reference points in interpreting our data.

Several social subgroups within our sample reflect the sources of our volunteer subjects. (The detailed sample description appears in ch. 2.) There is a foreign-born group of Jewish origin with relatively little formal education; a native-born non-Jewish group with relatively little education; and a native-born non-Jewish group with some college training. (Not all of the men studied fall into these subgroups.) Within the limitations of sample size, some exploration of cultural contributions to old age is made.

PROCEDURES OF DATA COLLECTION AND ANALYSIS

Several sources of data were used. While the subjects lived at the research hospital, two interviews were conducted to obtain social psychological data. Also, ratings were made, by nursing personnel and investigators, of the subject's reactions to ward routines and his sociability and mood on the ward and in the testing procedures. Approximately 1 month later a third interview was conducted in the subject's home. At this time, an interview with an informant was also obtained.

Detailed interview guides rather than a standard set of specific questions structured the interviews. The first interview was conducted during the man's first few days at the Clinical Center. It was designed to obtain the following social history data:

(a) Early family data, including cultural and economic characteristics, place of origin, circumstances surrounding coming to the United States, and characteristics of family constellation and cohesiveness;
(b) Subsequent family history, bringing it up to the present in terms of family members living and present contacts and relationships with them;
(c) Educational history;

(d) Occupational history, including jobs held, occupational motivations and aspirations, and income level at "height" of career, just before and since retirement;
(e) The subject's retirement, including how it took place, his planning for it, his attitudes at the point of retirement, and his subsequent work;
(f) The subject's marital history and current marital status, a description of his children; and
(g) The subject's present living arrangements.

The second interview which took place a week later focused primarily on the subject's current situation. He was asked to talk about an average day. This was the basic context for probes which followed a variety of directions, exploring—

(a) The sequence of daily events;
(b) The way in which time is spent (duties and pleasures);
(c) The persons around, the kinds of relationships (particularly in the family);
(d) The degree of fulfillment and frustration in the day-to-day events; and
(e) The nature of goals which structure living.

This kind of probing was extended to a typical month of time, with additional inquiries into the kinds of contacts and activities in the community. In the context of the typical day and month, he was asked for comparisons and contrasts with earlier adult years. There were two other areas of questioning. One concerned the persons in the subject's adult life with whom he had meaningful relationships, and the presence or absence of such persons in his old age. The other area concerned his feelings about the "good old days" compared with the present.

The home interview dealt again with current living. Its purposes were:

(a) To fill in gaps in the preceding interviews;
(b) To obtain a picture of relationships with his children (what contacts, at whose initiative, what is done for whom, by whom, what do they do together, what is his assessment of his children's "success," what are the sources of trouble, of satisfaction); and
(c) To discuss directly his reactions to retirement and being old. ("How do you feel about not working?" "What problems that you face now are different from problems in your life earlier?"

"How does one feel oneself changing from middle age to old age?"—probing for specific decrements. "What are some of the advantages and disadvantages you have felt in being old?")

The subject's willingness to be interviewed at home was ascertained while he was at the Clinical Center. At that time, too, he was asked to enlist the cooperation of someone who had known him for a long time, who was willing to be interviewed about him. The subjects, with one exception, cooperated in the home interview and in obtaining an intimate informant, most often a son or daughter. The latter interview obtained the informant's assessments of—

(a) The critical turning points and crises in the aged subject's life;

(b) The nature of his shift from employment to retirement, his problems and adjustments regarding retirement;

(c) Significant losses of persons and statuses with old age (such as deaths of family members, conflicts with family, etc.);

(d) His relationships with his wife and children, affection and authority roles, strains and strengths;

(e) The typical day and month now compared with his most active period of life; and

(f) The important physical and mental changes observed in his growing old.

Interviews were tape recorded and transcribed. Data were coded independently by 2 of the investigators on 27 of the cases; 83 percent was set arbitrarily as the necessary level of coder agreement. A few areas of coding (aspects of early family relationships, present egocentric or altruistic attitudes) did not reach this level, and therefore have not been reported. A small number of variables concerning current family interactions were coded through consensual judgments of the members of the research team. Throughout the analysis, information derived from the responses of the subject and his informant has been used. In most cases this double source has resulted in elaborations which clarify coding issues. In a few instances irreconcilable contradictions led to uncodable categories. The concepts and codes used in analysis are described in the report of the findings.

FINDINGS

Our first research question, it will be recalled, deals with the day-to-day functioning of this group of healthy men. How does old age look from the viewpoint of these men? What is their ordinary living like? How does it compare with survey data on more representative but less healthy men 65 years and older? We will look first at the transition from active work years to retirement, then at the concrete aspects of how time is spent, then at the subjective sides of living in old age.

THE PROCESS OF RETIRING

From a social point of view, retirement generally defines the beginning of old age. It is often thought of as a clear-cut status change unlike many other changes with age (Streib, et al., 1958, p. 5). Data from this group of men suggest something quite contrary, however, many of the men "grew into" retirement, much the same as children grow into adolescence. Voluntary and compulsory aspects entered in; fuzzy margins between retired and not retired status persisted; and little planning of how retirement would be spent was reported. At the time of the study, retirement or semiretirement was a condition in the lives of all but five of the men. For all who considered themselves retired, save one, retirement had occurred more than 1 year earlier, for some as long as 30 years (an average of 7 years). Hence, the data are retrospective and from varying vantage points during retirement.

A sharp break from all to none in work was characteristic of only half the group.

For roughly half the group, retirement developed as a gradual, sometimes long-drawn-out process. This is typified by the garment worker who shifted from running his own tailoring shop to working for the man who bought his shop to taking "odd jobs" until "no one would have me." Others made trial excursions into retirement, by briefly quitting a job, hiring back into it, quitting for something less taxing, and so on. A number of men in the semi-retired group were persons who had formally retired from a main job or career at a compulsory retirement age, but who had replaced it with some other full or part-time "retirement" job, and were thus retiring gradually.

Although our data do not have the answers, the question arises as to differences in the immediate concomitants of a break from work which is sharp and one which is gradual and probably unclearly defined over a long period of time. Sharp versus gradual is often associated with another variable, voluntary versus compulsory retirement. We found that a surprisingly large number of men could not be classified in either category. Table 1 which presents the decision variable indicates that "pure" choice or "pure" compulsory retirement classified only 50 percent of this group.

The other men (and their informants) reported strong conflicting impulses and pressures making it difficult to say what was chosen and what was imposed retirement (whether or not an age limit was institutionally enforced).

A prototype of the "pure" compulsory cases is the man who had been stably employed as a railway brakeman for many years, who had moved up through the company, measuring his years of work against his pension eligibility, expectant and ready at 65 to retire promptly on a known and secure income. As far as his estimate of capabilities was concerned, however, he could have continued to work. Another example is the government employee who was retired unwillingly at 70 by government policy, feeling fully able to continue the kind of work he had been doing. After leaving the government job he established himself on his own in the same field in which he had been employed, but considered himself, nonetheless, retired. In these instances the decision point seemed determined purely by the company code, sometimes welcomed and sometimes resented by the men.

A purely voluntary retirement is illustrated by the man who saw a good opportunity for a continued income on retirement and who took advantage of it. Another

TABLE 1.—*Characteristics of the retirement process*

[Percent of retired men with reported characteristic] [1]

Retirement process	Group I (N=26)	Group II (N=16)	Total group (N=42)
How retirement was achieved:			
"Pure" choice	39	0	24
Pressures and choice	42	50	45
Denial of actual retirement	0	13	5
"Pure" compulsory	19	37	26
Transition from employment to retirement:			
Gradual tapering off	46	63	52
Definite point of change	54	37	48

[1] 5 men had not retired; 1 was from group I, 4 from group II.

decided to retire in order to try another occupation that he liked.

Other men, however, retiring at age limits set by the employer or sometimes earlier, showed greater ambivalence, subjectively needing or wanting to retire and at the same time wanting or trying to continue work. There was an overwhelming coincidence of many different feelings and circumstances: the feelings of going "downhill," of wanting leisure and freedom from worries of work, of wanting to "keep in the stream," the arrival at an age when social security benefit payments can begin or when company policy permits or requires retirement, the urgings of wife or children.

In reporting retrospectively on their retirement, the men, on the whole, tended to recall "smoother" transitions, and decisions which fell more neatly into the dichotomy of compulsory or voluntary than the accounts of the informants suggested. Elements of indecision and conflict were documented very fully by their sons and daughters.

Although retirement brings a man face to face with many new problems, such as how to reschedule his time and energies, how to provide for his economic needs, how to relate to persons in his new role (or lacking his old role), etc., few men reported having planned ahead for their old age. Thirteen percent described plans made prior to retirement which included social and interpersonal as well as financial aspects of old age. Another 30 percent of the group referred to financial plans alone. Usually this meant being part of a retirement system, such as social security or an industrial pension. The correlates or consequences of the different avenues to retirement are discussed later. (See p. 263.)

The Daily Living of the Aged Men

Ignoring for the moment the attitudes and feelings of the men in meeting life as aged persons, we will look at the ways in which time is occupied. The men described the kinds of activities which were part of the typical day and month. It was not uncommon for the men (30 percent) to say of their earlier years that work took all their time and energy, that they could recall "nothing special" in the way of leisure-time activities in the average day or month. The leisure activities filling much of their time now, therefore, had been acquired or expanded in old age (table 2). Reading newspapers and listening to the radio or watching TV were reported almost universally as being regular and often sizable pieces of each day. More interesting, perhaps,

TABLE 2.—*Reported leisure activities of the average day and month*

[Percent of men reporting each characteristic]

Leisure activities	Group I (N=27)	Group II (N=20)	Total group (N=47)
Passive pursuits:			
Amusements (TV, radio, cards, etc.)	89	75	83
Reading (newspapers, books, etc.)	59	55	57
Cultural activities (concerts, theater)	11	10	11
Resting (sunbathing, napping)	22	50	34
Active pursuits:			
Manual expressive (gardening, woodwork, etc.)	52	40	47
Artistic (painting, writing poetry, etc.)	11	15	13
Physical activities (exercise, sports, walking, etc.)	33	15	26
Visiting friends	15	25	19
Traveling	11	10	11

is the fact that approximately three-quarters of the group had additional, more active and expressive occupations, too (the familiar gardening, woodworking, amateur carpentering, etc., and for a few, the studied development of physical activities such as hiking, swimming, calisthenics). The stereotypic pastimes of old age, napping, sunning, sitting in the park, were reported by a third of the group. Reported activities did not vary with chronological age within the group studied.

Just how solitary or social were the men's leisure activities is difficult to judge. The fact that almost all of the sample (92 percent) had some immediate family member(s) available suggests that many of the things described above were done in a family setting. The wife was often mentioned as sharing these activities. Extrafamily socializing, however, was not prominent (table 3). Pursuits such as participation in clubs or religious-social activities or more informal socializing with friends on a regular or frequent basis characterized only about a quarter of the group; half the group reported virtually no social participation beyond the family. Only partly does this seem to reflect a social retreat in old age, since similar minimal social activity was characteristic of 34 percent of these men

in earlier adult years. Fifty-five percent of the group described closely similar pictures of social participation for middle and old age; 30 percent of the group retreated in social participation over the years, and 15 percent expanded their involvements outside the family. Substantial reduction in extrafamilial social participation occurred primarily in the age group 70 years and older (11 out of 14). This was not associated, however, with health status (group I and group II) or with widowed status. Changes in types of roles or responsibilities in activities outside the family may well have changed over the years. Our ratings catch only the regularity and frequency of reported social participation.

The family, not the wider social relationships, appeared to be the focus of most of the day-to-day interests and concerns of these men. Our data bore out this point in several ways. One indication was in the functions which the elderly men fulfilled as family members. Townsend's study (1957) of family life of older people of the working class of East London points out that the "old mom" has useful and satisfying functions to fulfill in the lives of her children, as grandmother, helper to her daughters, etc. Not so the old man. He is virtually without comparable sig-

TABLE 3.—*Social relationships of healthy aged men*

[Percent of men with reported characteristic]

Social relationships	Group I (N=27)	Group II (N=20)	Total group (N=47)
Social activity outside family:			
Involved in little interaction	48	50	49
Some or regular socializing but not a prominent part of daily living	30	15	23
Highly involved in frequent and varied social interactions	22	35	28
Age of persons with whom social interactions are primarily involved (including family and outside family):			
Primarily elderly	33	50	40
Own and younger generations	59	40	51
Primarily younger generations	8	10	9

nificant functions. But in the present study, the picture was quite different. The men of our sample assumed active housekeeping roles, sharing many household chores and responsibilities with their wives. Sixty-two percent described regular and substantial and traditionally feminine housekeeping functions (cleaning, laundering, cooking, dishwashing). Errands (chauffeuring for shopping, transporting packages and messages, etc.) and chores of "fixing" around the house, his own and his children's, were described by 60 percent of the sample. Of the 33 men who had grandchildren, 45 percent described frequent babysitting, entertaining and chauffeuring grandchildren. For men in our culture these activities may not be peculiar to old age; however, whether new or continuations of old patterns, they supply meaningful family functions for the older man.

The age circles in which these men showed the greatest participation and commitment (table 3) also point to the importance of family ties. The man's interpersonal relationships were coded in terms of the age of the persons involved, whether age peers or members of the younger generation. Forty percent of the group moved almost exclusively among persons their own age, predominantly their near relatives. For about half the group, the central circles of interaction involved both generations. Here the younger generation was comprised of the man's children and grandchildren. Four men, less than 10 percent, appeared to be cut off from their age peers and to find their associations primarily among younger people.

The Tone of Time

The feeling tone with which these physically healthy men were living old age varied considerably. For some, life was filled with hopelessness and emptiness.

"An old man is a helpless man. It's as natural as birth that people should avoid you. Memory becomes bad. Nobody cares about you."

"I haven't got a thing to do and I can't stand it. I want to occupy my mind. . . . I got a lot of aggravation for no reason. . . . I can't stand it. I'm not happy."

"I feel I'm a forgotten man. I don't exist anymore. . . . I don't feel old. . . . I'm just living out my life."

Others presented a stoical position of accepting the inevitability of old age:

"You know you're getting old. You have to put your mind to it and take it as it comes. You can't get out of it. Take it gracefully."

For others there were major fulfillments and satisfactions:

"I go home with my cup overflowing. There are so many opportunities to do things for people. These are the happiest days of my life."

"I do what I want to, when I want to, and don't have to pinch pennies. I don't think there is anything I long for. I enjoy things."

"I've never found time on my hands. It's just so many things that I want to do that I haven't found time to do. I've got stacks of good books around that I want to read and I want to study."

None of these lives was so simple as to be fully represented by the single theme of affect which for analytical purposes was imposed on them (table 4). However, using the dominant theme for classification, 28 percent of the group in general found time and life burdensome; 25 percent showed more variation in feelings, were less hopeless and unhappy, but nevertheless manifested much dissatisfaction with old age; 47 percent expressed strong satisfactions in their current lives. Thus, although ill-health has been shown to contribute significantly to feelings of dissatisfaction and rejection (Thompson and Streib, 1958), good health is not necessarily accompanied by good affective state. Studies of populations, unselected for health, such as the New York study of 500 people over 60 years of age (Kutner et al., 1956), report distributions

TABLE 4.—*The nature of time in old age*

[Percent of men with reported characteristic]

Time	Group I (N=27)	Group II (N=20)	Total group (N=47)
Time as leisure or full of responsibilities:			
Responsibilities..................................	37	20	30
Leisure..	63	80	70
Tone of time:			
Satisfaction and interest in time now....................	52	40	47
Elements of enjoyment, but significant ambivalence, dissatisfaction, regret.................................	22	30	25
Time is burdensome.................................	26	30	28
Goal characteristics:			
Maintains goals and a future.........................	81	70	77
Excludes future and goal striving.....................	19	30	23

very similar to the present findings on roughly comparable variables. On indices of morale (based on answers to a series of questions such as "things just keep getting worse and worse for me as I get older"), the New York sample splits approximately equally in thirds, as high, medium, and low in morale. In our study, as in the New York study, increasing chronological age after 65 did not systematically increase the number of persons expressing hopeless despair.

Family Relationships

The aged family is not as familiar in research as the young family, and it is only through work on the latter that most concepts of family interactions have been developed. Especially is this the case in analyzing parent-child relationships. The evolution of these roles beyond the adolescent years through the life cycle has not been filled in by research. Similarly, husband-wife relationships through the lifespan have not been studied extensively. Very little is known about how compatibility and understanding within the family and how family roles change with age or about the determinants of relationships in the old family. The meaning of the picture presented by the men in this sample suffers,

therefore, from a lack of reference points in data from other research.

Based on the subject's reports and those of his informant, husband-wife rapport in this study was rated as (a) good and improved in old age, (b) continuing compatible or workable (including a considerable range), (c) continuing poor, or (d) deteriorated in old age from either compatible or poor earlier relationships (table 5). About a third of the men were rated as having poor and often deteriorating relationships with their wives. Among the two-thirds described as compatible, there was a broad range, from satisfying relationships to mere ragged compatibility. (Unreliability of coding prevented a finer breakdown of these categories.) Whereas eight families were rated as showing deteriorating relationships in old age, only one was rated as improving. In the one-third of cases in which relationships were clearly poor, the expectation existed, however, that these couples would continue to live together. One may speculate that the difficulties and insecurities (financial and personal) are too great to risk separation in old age.

Relationships between aged father and children, examined in similar terms, showed the following characteristics: compatible

TABLE 5.—*Family relationships*

[Percent of men with specified family relationship]

Relationship	Group I	Group II	Total group
Husband-wife relationships:	(N=21)	(N=11)	(N=32)
Good and improved in old age	0	9	3
Continued compatible or workable	57	73	63
Continued poor	10	9	9
Deterioration in old age	33	9	25
(No wife in old age)[1]	(6)	(9)	(15)
Father-child relationships:	(N=24)	(N=15)	(N=39)
Continued good or improved	37	40	38
Distant, respectful	21	27	23
Mixed good and poor	13	27	18
Conflict, rejection in old age	29	6	21
(Number of men without children)	(3)	(5)	(8)
Grandfather-grandchild relationships:	(N=20)	(N=14)	(N=34)
High involvement	50	36	44
Peripheral involvement	40	43	41
Conflict	10	21	15
(Number of men without grandchildren)	(7)	(6)	(13)
Father-child status relationships:	(N=24)	(N=15)	(N=39)
Father in authority and status roles	17	7	13
Reversal of father-child authority and status roles	21	26	23
Mutual dependency between father and child	17	7	13
Peerlike relationship	17	7	13
Father and child autonomous, independent of each other	21	40	28
Power struggles between father and child	8	7	8
(Not codable)	0	6	2
(Number of men without children)	(3)	(5)	(8)

[1] Includes number of widowers and men who have been separated from their wives for many years, and 1 man who had never married.

feelings, ranging from close to distant but respectful, characterized 6 percent of the father-child relationships. In 21 percent of the cases, relationships were thoroughly conflictful and rejective. In 18 percent of the families, relationships varied widely with different children in the family. In these gross characteristics, relationships between generations did not reflect greater strain than relationships between elderly husbands and wives.

How similar are relationships between parents and between parents and child within the same family? Our sample shrinks considerably in making this analysis, since some men were widowed, others childless. Of 30 families in which the comparison was possible, in 17 families in which parent relationships were rated as compatible, 15 showed good father-child relationships, 2 showed conflict between father and children. In 13 families in which parental relationships were characterized as poor, father-child relationships were good in 6 families and poor in 7 families.

Father-child relationships were analyzed, also, with respect to the kinds of roles and statuses vis-a-vis each other, for it was apparent that the compatibilities and incompatibilities noted above rested upon quite varied father-child roles. One kind of intergenerational compatibility was founded upon mutual respect of children and father for one another in a peerlike relationship. The children had grown up to the father (in independence, authority, etc.) but without replacing him, and without the father's suffering devastating losses in his status with his children, regardless of other status changes in his life. This kind of mutual respect, evolved through a lifetime and maintained in old age, is illustrated in the following father and son's reports. The father (No. 35) spoke of his children:

"With my youngest, even with my older boy, too, we were never like father and children. . . . We were pals, see. Even my daughter, too, very close attached. . . . They knew my bad times and they all know the bright times. . . . Nothing was secret in my home. . . . My own children will benefit from it or my grandchildren, so I have personal satisfaction."

The son said of his father:

"He has always striven to give us the maximum that was in his power and has always tried to instill in us a certain importance that our everyday life has with other fellow human beings. I try to instill that same thing in my daughter. We think that he is a very well-integrated person. . . . It was his favorite pastime to pile all of his children into the Model T and take us for a ride. We would have picnics. . . . We make it a practice to plow in on them about every second Sunday for dinner. We stayed pretty close. . . . He will voice his opinion. . . . It's more or less in an advisory capacity. . . . it doesn't necessarily follow. . . . When any of us do have a small degree of success, he gets a great deal of pleasure out of it."

This pattern characterized five of the families.

Just as status equality was dominant in these families, status difference was accented in others ($N=9$) in which traditional father-and-child roles were reversed, the father being in the dependent role and the child assuming the role of advisor or authority figure. Such reversals were accepted in some families; resented in others. Several kinds of father dependency and feelings about it are illustrated in three cases:

Father (No. 10) said of his children:

"They never call me up. . . . I tell them many times, 'Why don't you call me up sometimes? If I go to see you, I got to go all over . . . and you got to go once to see me.' In a year's time, he will never come to see me. . . . She comes here to see grandpop, otherwise, she wouldn't come. . . . My daughter-in-law, you know, is very nice to me. She comes, she kisses me . . . I like my children, and my children like me. . . . Every 5 years, they make a party in a hall—my birthday, every 5 years. Sometimes I get mad, you know, I say I'd like to die, my daughter or son-in-law makes me so angry. . . . Sometimes if things are not right in the house, I give her hell sometimes, too."

His daughter summed up the 30 years since his retirement in which he has lived with her:

"He's gotten better as he's grown older. . . . he was very, very ignorant, illiterate when he was younger, selfish, self-centered. . . . I civilized him. . . . I just fought back. . . . I always stepped on him since he came to live with me, I kept him in line. . . . When he tried to dictate to me, I am very cruel in a way, I'd say, 'Look, Pop, either you live here like I like it, or you pack up and move out.' . . . I educated him. 'Pop, you don't spit out in the street and let the wind blow it away, you spit in your handkerchief. Pop, you don't stand there and blow your nose in the street . . . if you don't stop that I won't walk in the street with you.' . . . When he was a young man he was far from clean, changed his shirt once a month and went to the bathhouse once a month and got his bath. . . . 'Remember, Pop, if you want respect you must give respect.' "

While relationships were not always smooth in this household, they were not primarily conflictful.

Another father (No. 26) had little to say about his personal relations with his children, only that he considered them variably successful and that he must hear from the children every few days if he is not to worry. But his daughter showed considerable resentment. She assessed her parents critically.

"The role is in reverse. I seem to be the one; they run to me and tell me their irritations and stories and I would have to stop and make it peaceful again. They are like two old children. . . . My sister wants him to go to New York, but my mother wouldn't budge. [The other children] they are constant visitors. They are devoted to my mother. She has always been the focal or vital point in our family. My parents have everything. They live in a very nice apartment, and their children are devoted to them in every sense. I help them along. I slave and I don't have to do it, but I help them achieve some little things that they want, but they are not unhappy. They don't count their blessings. I keep telling them you're living golden years and you don't have to worry about it. . . . you should travel and go about and be close companions, but they continue to act like two bad children. . . . As I told Mother and Dad, if you were modern people you would probably get away from each other, but you live together and you are just like cats and dogs. . . . I love my father and mother, but I sometimes think they are a burden because they wear me out mentally, and yet I could go there and do little things. . . . They feel that they are out of their children's lives. They don't get enough letters and all of that."

Dependency weaning, of a positive sort, is illustrated in a son's (No. 16) description of the hand he took in his father's adjustment following the mother's death. To curb his father's growing dependence upon him, the son embarked on a rehabilitation program, developing his father's interests and self-confidence.

"I think that on insistence from me he started taking an interest in outside activities. He probably told you about his activities at the athletic club. I got him started there. It was absolutely new. He had never done anything like it before. . . . He caught on and went right ahead. Where there were other things [classes in current events, music appreciation], he went on. [Before that] it was more or less of a desire just to be near me. . . . He stayed around the office . . . made lunches for me . . . I couldn't devote as much time as I would have liked. . . ."

There were five families in which the role of father appeared to be relatively unaltered from younger years: the father tended to remain adviser, counselor, authority figure. This relationship did not exist, however, as "purely" as the role reversals just described, and tended to exist where relationships and contacts were not especially close.

There were parents and children who were mutually dependent in very particular ways, where this dependency seemed to hold the status balance (five subjects). For example, father provided house and care for grandchildren; his children provided the family group to live in. Other fathers and children were relatively independent of one another (11 subjects), some warm, others resentful in feelings toward each other. Still other families (three subjects) showed unresolved status and power struggles, such as the father's attempts to use his money as a controlling device (loans, property, wills) without necessarily winning thereby.

Our data distinguish some of the dimensions of intergenerational relationships. There is need for much more research if we are to understand family interactions in the later years.

Daily Functioning

As these elderly men discussed the day-to-day events and issues in their current living, strong contrasts appeared in the level of planning, complexity, and variations characteristic of their daily activities. Ignoring the specific content of activities and interactions, an attempt was made to analyze the aspect of purposefulness and complexity in daily living (table 6). Daily behavior with a high degree of planning, variation, and complexity characterized 42 percent of the group. Mr. W. was rated in this category. He and his wife had worked out a partnership in housekeeping. This was woven into a round of social activities, some of which were shared by husband and wife, some were independent. Heavy involvement in several Golden Age Clubs, presidency of one, occasional evening pinochle gatherings, active neighboring, much visiting with relatives filled most days. Long trips with his wife gave him a view of the world unavailable to him when he had worked long hours on his job.

Only 11 percent of the men were rated as living extremely routine lives, dictated mainly by necessary chores. This extreme is illustrated in the following typical daily routine for Mr. C. He gets up in the morning, walks down the street for the paper, gets his own breakfast, reads or walks or occasionally goes to see a friend, waits for evening, starts the supper before his daughter arrives home from work, maybe listens to

TABLE 6.—*Quality of current living*

[Percent of men with reported characteristic]

Current living	Group I (N=27)	Group II (N=20)	Total group (N=47)
A. Complexity of daily living:			
Chores, routines as necessity requires; no initiative......	0	25	11
Chores, amusements, puttering; some initiative, some absorption, planning not prominent...............	52	40	47
New, many, complex activities; initiative, planning, ingenuity......................................	48	35	42
B. Summary scores on daily functioning:			
Highly adequate functioning:			
5–6..	29	35	32
7–8..	19	0	11
9–10...	19	15	17
11–12..	14	25	19
Inadequate functioning: 13–14......................	19	25	21

the radio, goes to bed early. A middle category, living that is not highly organized, planned or complex, but with some variations, characterized approximately half of the group.

One further summary rating of daily functioning was derived, reflecting the man's purposeful and meaningful activities and interpersonal relationships. The following variables, weighted equally, contributed to the score: organization of daily behavior, maintenance of goals, interpersonal relationships, social initiative and participation outside the family (table 6). The possible range of scores was from 15, indicating inadequate functioning, to 5, reflecting highly effective functioning. Twenty-one percent of the men were in the category of extremely inadequate behavior, 32 percent in the category of highly adequate functioning. It is apparent that the relative homogeneity of health in the sample did not bring with it a similar picture of homogeneity and well-being in personal-social functioning.

Thus far the data presented have been descriptive of a medically select group of elderly men, with reference, where possible, to findings in the literature on the less healthy aged. In the following discussions we will examine relationships within our data, considering attitudes, activities, and interpersonal behavior in old age in relation to differences in life history settings, and differences in present environmental circumstances.

Functioning in Old Age and Life History Characteristics

A man's national-cultural origin, his educational attainments, and his occupational career shape the setting of his life in broad and basic respects. How or whether these backgrounds provide individuals with differing adaptabilities in old age is not known.

Our sample had within it 20 foreign-born subjects and 27 native-born subjects. This background factor seems to make a difference in the man's responses to old age. As a group, the foreign-born men were rated as functioning less well than the native born. They showed up consistently and significantly [1] as less adequate in each of the following respects: their daily schedules were more limited and routine, their activities tended to be thoroughly passive; more often

---

[1] Differences are reported on chi-Squares and *t*-tests where the probability level is 0.05 or better.

they maintained no future perspectives; they expressed greater dissatisfaction and unhappiness with present living. No differences in family relationships or in amount of social contacts appeared between the groups. (The special features of the foreign-born and native-born men of this sample studied must be recognized. They differed in ethnic background: 75 percent of the foreign-born men and 19 percent of the native-born were Jewish. The groups were similar, however, in educational and occupational backgrounds.) One possible explanation of the differences in the adaptation of the foreign born and native born is that the foreign-born men have probably experienced greater personal and social changes and discontinuities in their lives than have the men born into the culture in which they now live as old men. Such discontinuities might be the handicapping factor in adjustment in old age. This interpretation of foreign-native differences is supported in closer inspection of the subcultures in our sample. Men leading the most routine and discontented existence are those men in the foreign-born group who had little formal education outside Jewish religious school attendance and who as very young boys had been taken into their fathers' trades or had been forced by poverty to begin work very early; in other words, they were the men for whom the personal social world appeared to have changed in many extreme ways from early adulthood to old age and appeared to be quite different from the culture of their adult children.

Differences in educational background and functioning in old age were examined. support (Jones, 1959; von Mering and Weniger, 1959), that the educated man and the professional man are better able to draw upon interests and personal resources to make old age more livable than is the uneducated. Our data failed to show such differences. Educational background made no significant difference in any of the measures of attitudes and behavior discussed in the preceding pages or in the ratings of subjects' behavior and reputations during their 2-week stay on the ward. (Comparisons between professional and nonprofessional workers also revealed no differences.) In many respects, old age appears to have resulted in very similar ways of living for men of all educational backgrounds. There was similarity in the actual content of their daily activities (those reported in table 2). Also, men of more education did not appear to fare better in what may be called morale. In only one respect did educational factors relate clearly to present adaptations. There was a significant association between education and the elderly man's relationships with his children. Conflict and feelings of rejection were more frequent between the less-educated men and their children. Inspection of the individual families suggests that discrepancies in educational level of parent and child, rather than low education, per se, characterized the families for whom conflict was accentuated.

Assuming as we have that considerable adaptability and striving are required to find involvements and satisfactions in old age, one might expect relationships between earlier patterns of striving and present modes of coping in old age. Work as a central issue in the lives of men affords an area in which one can sample life patterns of achieving and striving. Data were obtained on the kind of commitment the man had had to his work (whether it was only a means to a living or provided also a gratification in itself), and on the amount of movement "upward" in his work career (independent of the social status value of his occupation).

The nature of past commitment to work was not related to the man's present functioning in old age. This is not to say that the transition to retirement may not have been felt differently by men who were losing a major source of gratification and those who were not. But the majority of these men were well past the transitional stage, and whatever initial differences there may have been were not apparent later in retirement.

Men characterized as upwardly mobile in their work careers, however, showed different adaptions in old age from men who showed no upward attainments in their occupations. The men who had been successful in moving upward had the more complex and varied daily living patterns in old age. The upwardly mobile men also enjoyed better relationships with their children in old age. There were no differences in tone of present time for men who had been successful and those who had not been successful in their careers.

In summing up the contributions of social psychological variables of life history, the present data suggest that education and occupational level have little predictive value for social functioning in old age, as measured here. Work career success interpreted as evidence of adaptability and striving is somewhat predictive of greater adaptability in old age. Extensive cultural "displacement" from conditions of early adulthood and large cultural differences between aged parent and grown children tend to be handicapping in certain adjustments in old age.

The Present Environment and Adjustments in Old Age

The effects of current environmental circumstances upon the aged man's functioning were explored. Environment was evaluated in terms of the ways in which it provides the individual with resources and supports or imposes strains or deprivations. Within this framework we have analyzed the process of retiring, the restriction in income, the characteristics of aged man's personal associates, and the degree of disintegration of the group of personally significant persons in the man's adult life.

Loss of job and job income can be conceptualized as environmental deprivation, although one may not automatically assume that retirement means "loss" to the individual. We attempted to define the event of retirement in terms of its psychological meaning for the man at the time retirement occurred. From the recollections of the subjects and their informants, the meaning of the transition from employment to retirement was determined (p. 262). Men who had been in control of the decision to retire or not to retire were not regarded as deprived. Men who had been retired by compulsory age-limit policies, but feeling no personal incapacity necessitating retiring, were considered deprived. Men were regarded as deprived, also, who had experienced mixed pressures in leaving the job, usually the convergence of feelings of decline, feelings of not wanting to "give up," and pressures from family or employer.

Among these three groups of men who had met the end of employment differently, there were now differences in current functioning—in organization of daily behavior, relationships with children and grandchildren, and feelings of satisfaction in present living. In each instance, the men who had been in control of the retirement decision fared best. Those who had arrived at retirement through a feeling of personal decline mixed with other pressures fared least well. In the characteristics of their present adaptation the "pure" compulsory retirement group appeared to be more like the undeprived group than the group with mixed pressures.

The relationship between current functioning and economic deprivation could be explored only in a very limited fashion in this study. Income, particularly past income, was very difficult to ascertain. An estimate of present income was used in analyses of relationships between economic status and behavioral characteristics. Few associations appeared. However, patterns of daily living that were restricted and routine, and conflict and rejection in relationships with children were significantly more frequent in the lowest income group (less than $2,000).

Hypothesizing that a range of ages of persons in the immediate environment (children, younger and older adults) contributes to the well-being of the aged, we examined the age circles in which the men moved. The subjects were classified in one of three categories: living mainly in a circle of age peers, living mainly with the younger generation, living across two or three generations. This variable did not in any way differentiate the subjects on qualities of social functioning and attitudes.

The most significant environmental variable in the aged man's functioning was the presence or loss of persons in significant close relationships. By the time a man has reached 65 years of age, the probability is high that he will have suffered losses among family and friends through deaths and various kinds of displacements. Mr. Q. in our sample was very fortunate in this regard; the structure of his personal social environment had remained almost intact. His wife was living and his relationship with her was a satisfying one—similarly for his grown children and other relatives and close friends. His only real loss of persons was a loss of touch with his former work associates, which was of little importance to him.

On the other hand, Mr. A. had few intimates left in his environment. His wife was dead, he had no children; his relatives lived several hundred miles away and ties with them were weak. Since his retirement, he had had no contact with former work associates. Mr. P. had some of the characteristics of each of the other men described. His wife, with whom there had been a very close relationship which virtually excluded anyone else, had died a few years ago. His children, though near at hand, were unwilling to attempt to develop a close relationship with their father. After 3 years of widowhood, Mr. P. had remarried, but only a distant companionship existed with his second wife. He, like Mr. A., lived in an environment in which he had no close personal ties. Each of these men faced different problems of living in old age.

Men with pronounced losses or lacks in personal ties and supports, men with important losses but with some available supports, and men with very few losses were compared in their current modes of living and their attitudes toward life (table 7). The impact of personal losses was clearly reflected in their current responses to life. Less organized and more routine-bound daily behavior, the absence of goals, and feelings of unhappiness and uselessness occurred significantly more frequently among the men who had sustained extensive losses. Differences in the men's abilities to relate to others during the 2 weeks of residence on the ward were also associated with differences in environmental losses. Ratings made by the nursing personnel showed lower ratings in sociability on the ward, more negative ratings in mood (depressed or irritable), and more frequent ratings of "very old" and "senile" for men with marked environmental deficits.

The theme of each of the environmental conditions studied has been one of depriva-

TABLE 7.—*Environmental loss and measures of attitudes and behavior*

Measure	Environmental loss			X^2
	Minimal	Some	Much	
Organization, purposefulness in daily behavior:				
Routine..................................	0	2	3	} **14.19
Some planning and variation..............	6	7	9	
Complex organization.....................	11	9	0	
Tone of time:				
Hopeless.................................	13	8	1	} **17.465
Ambivalent..............................	3	6	3	
Satisfied.................................	1	4	8	
Goal striving:				
Present..................................	17	14	5	} **12.03
Absent...................................	0	4	7	
Sociability on ward:				
Good....................................	13	11	2	} **10.575
Poor....................................	4	7	10	
Mood on ward:				
Good....................................	12	9	1	} **11.06
Poor....................................	5	9	11	

(Summary score of daily functioning)..($r = +0.81$***)

**Significant at the 0.01 level.
***Significant at the 0.001 level.

tion or limitation by cutting down the supports or resources which the individual can count on in his environment. There has been a consistent association of these more deprived circumstances with more routinized living, with less involvement and with greater dissatisfaction and hopelessness.

SUMMARY AND DISCUSSION

Changes that take place in the individual as he grows older have been investigated with greatest fidelity in their biological aspects and in certain psychological areas, such as sensory and perceptual processes and psychomotor skills. In these investigations, the individual has been dealt with as an entity in himself, and youth-to-age has been the primary context in which changing functions have been interpreted. In almost all these characteristics, however, variability in old age is well recognized. Variables and conditions loosely labeled "social" are

known to be related to many aging processes.

At the present stage of research, the observed relationships between biological manifestations of aging (such as physical health, particular pathologies, longevity, etc.) and the social and cultural conditions (such as occupations, marital status, educational attainment) are only associations or correlations; the direction of influence and the interaction of influences have not been established.

The social psychological variables that have been of concern to us in this study have included a range of factors and conditions; some external to the individual (social environmental factors); some personal (his goals and attitudes); and some midway between person and environment (the interpersonal relationships in which he is involved). We have posed (1) a correlational problem: what kind of social organism is correlated with the physically healthy aged organism, and (2) a problem of environmental antecedents or influences; how are certain life history variables and contemporaneous settings associated with variable functioning in aged persons?

On our first question the data indicated that the characteristic of good physical health did not greatly narrow the range of personal-social well-being in old age. No differences were found between subgroups of health, groups I and II. Both hopeless resignation and creative involvement occurred in our sample. Some men had withdrawn to routines and self-centeredness; others were engaged in varied and absorbing activities.

In our analysis of age-related experiences and adjustments of these men, we attempted to refine characterizations of the process of retirement to include its sharp or gradual quality and the nature of the decision process bringing about retirement. In these analyses the reports of the informants added materially to the self-reports of the subjects. Whether the decision to retire was controlled by the man himself, or completely controlled institutionally, or a resolution of conflicting internal and external pressures, different consequences seemed to result. The man who had arrived at retirement through conflicting pressures seemed, some years after retiring, to adapt least well in old age.

Through informant and self-reports, we attempted, also, to identify dimensions of relationships within the older family, an area of research in which there is little information. In the group as a whole, relationships between elderly father and children differed little in general level of compatibility from relationships between elderly husbands and wives. Status relationships between fathers and children showed wide variations. In only a very small number of families was the role of father one of authority figure or elder statesman.

In our investigation of environmental antecedents of functioning in old age, the familiar sociological groupings of educational and occupational levels were not related to differentiated patterns of functioning. The lack of association in this sample between education and occupation and functioning in old age is interesting in a number of ways. By working only with a physically healthy group, we have ruled out possible associations between social class variables and adjustment stemming from correlations between social class and health factors. At the height of the subjects' adult careers, the "ways of life" most assuredly differed for the accountant or lawyer and the railway brakeman or garment worker. At age 70, however, the elements of day-to-day activities as well as the attitudes about being old showed little difference. Probably this "leveling" results partly from the tendency of these men to drop their specializations, to find similar hobbies and use common recreations afforded by the culture, and to engage in many household "maintenance" activities. Inner resourcefulness in finding sustaining involvements was by no means the sole property of the more educated among these men. Attitudes, too, did not differ among these subgroups.

We would not conclude from our data that life history factors do not enter into the problems and integrations of the aged—rather that they enter in a more complicated way as they combine with particular, present circumstances in which the aged persons live. (We will return to this point later.)

Factors of the immediate environment were found to be very closely related to the aged persons' behavior and attitudes. As the environment showed qualities of deprivation or displacement (in loss of intimate persons, loss of income, in cultural displacement), the attitudes and behaviors of the aged showed more deteriorative qualities. Losses of significant persons were especially associated with deteriorated functioning. Degree of loss (or lack) in the total structure of psychological supports in the environment—more than the loss in any one particular area—was critical for functioning.

It was suggested earlier that the apparent close tie between environment and functioning in old age is somewhat analogous to the close interdependency in early childhood of the state of the person and the immediate environment. The apparent strong interdependency in old age may have several explanations. The aged person may have less adequate defenses against stresses. On the other hand, many of the environmental changes (such as the irreversible losses suffered by the individual) are overwhelming in nature and his reactions generally can be seen as in keeping with stimulus conditions. These speculations refer only to the negative aspects of the close relationship between person and environment in old age. More understanding should be obtained on the restorative influences of environmental variables upon behavior and psychological well-being in old age.

In light of the findings on the effects of the immediate environment, the question of life history influences might be reexamined. It seems probable that different life settings (group or family culture, education, etc.) build up, selectively and specifically, different strengths and vulnerabilities in the individual, also that different settings of earlier adult years make the occurrence of certain environmental circumstances in old age more or less likely. For example, one may speculate that limited education would make cultural changes less well understood and less easily adapted to. For aged persons living in cultural surroundings greatly different from those of their early life, limited education might increase the felt stresses in the changed setting. A family pattern through youth and middle age, in which indulgence in symptoms of illness is fostered, might lay the groundwork for particular kinds of responses to physical decline in old age. Cultural differences in size of family and cohesiveness of family might affect the frequency of occurrence of isolation and loneliness in old age of persons of different class or ethnic origins. Thus, in specific and forceful ways, social-cultural backgrounds may interact with environmental circumstances in old age and influence the behavioral characteristics of the aged.

The methodology of the present study is like other social psychological studies of aging in that its primary data source is the self-reports of the aged. It differs from many other studies by adding to these reports the accounts of intimate informants and observations of the subjects during their residence at the research hospital. The double source of data provides a check on the aged person's self-assessments and aids materially in interpreting the data. Subjects and informants generally gave similar factual descriptions, but interpretation of the impact of experiences and the character of adaptations gained much from the availability of self and other's perceptions. It was found, too, that certain topics were more subject than others to biased, defensive reporting by the aged (past failures, difficulties in the transition to retirement, present economic circumstances, nature of authority, and dependency with grown children).

The general success of the self-reports from these subjects should not be generalized uncritically in gerontological research without due recognition of the select nature of this group, and of the built-in double-checks on the data obtained. These men were thoroughly aware of the multiple sources of data being obtained on them in the project as a whole. Even in the present group, the self-reports of at least two of the subjects were internally highly contradictory and confused.

The knowledge we seek regarding old age is usually knowledge concerning change; yet we obtain only present status data. In the present study we attempted to meet this problem by asking the subject for comparisons between present and past. This is not ideal for obvious reasons. Here the outside perspectives of the informants again gave some greater assurance of validity of data.

Among the most interesting and critical data needed on the functioning of aged persons are data on the nature of interpersonal interactions: What roles does the aged individual take with his peers and with younger adults? How, in concrete form, does the older person attempt to control others, to maintain his independence, to accept or manipulate his dependence on them? What is the interplay between the psychological and the "mechanical" aspects of behavior, such as the elder person's more limited locomotion, restrictions placed on him in the use of a car, visual and auditory dysfunctions, etc.?

The interviews provide provocative case material but not systematic findings on these questions. This would seem a much needed next step in research. However, investigation of interactions of aged and the "other" is not amenable to interview study. Data and methodology in this area present especially challenging problems in gerontology.

Behavior and attitudes in this paper have been viewed in the contexts of the subjects' good health and different social environments. The subjects' social responses and their environmental circumstances in relation to perceptual and cognitive functioning, and cerebral circulation and metabolism and psychiatric qualities are examined in the next chapter.

BIBLIOGRAPHY

CUMMING, E., DEAN, L., NEWELL, D., and McCAFFREY, I. 1960. "Disengagement—a tentative theory of aging." *Sociometry, 23, 23–35.*

DUNHAM, H. 1956. "Sociological aspects of mental disorders in later life," J. Kaplan (Ed.). *Medical Disorders of Later Life.* Stanford University Press, Stanford, Calif., 157–177.

GRANICK, S. 1957. "Personality adjustment of the aged in retirement communities," *Geriatrics,* 12, 381–385.

HENRY, W. 1959. "Personality development in adulthood and old age." *J. of Projective Techniques, 43,* 383–390.

JONES, H. 1959. "Human health relative to age, place and time," J. Birren (Ed.), *Handbook of Aging and the Individual: Psychological and Biological Aspects.* University of Chicago Press, Chicago, Ill., 336–363.

KOLB, L. 1956. "The mental hospitalization of the aged—is it being overdone?" *Amer. J. Psychiat., 112, 627–636.*

KUTNER, B., FANSHEL, D., TOGO, A., and LANGNER, T. 1956. *Five Hundred Over Sixty,* Russell Sage Foundation, New York.

STREIB, G., THOMPSON, W., and SUCHMAN, E. 1958. "The Cornell study of occupational retirement." *J. of Soc. Issues, 14,* 3–17.

THOMPSON, W., and STREIB, G. 1958. "Situational determinants: health and economic deprivation in retirement." *J. of Soc. Issues, 14,* 18–34.

TOWNSEND, P. 1957. *The Family Life of Old People: An Inquiry in East London.* Free Press, Glencoe, Ill., 284 pp.

VON MERING, O., and WENIGER, F. 1959. "Social-cultural background of the aging individual." J. Birren (Ed.). *Handbook of Aging and the Individual: Psychological and Biological Aspects.* University of Chicago Press, Chicago, Ill., pp. 279–335.

WALDMAN, A. 1959. "Living arrangements and mental disorders among the aged." *Amer. J. of Orthopsychiatry, 19,* 708–712.

WEINBERG, J. 1956. "Personal and social adjustment." J. Anderson (Ed.). *Psychological Aspects of Aging.* American Psychological Association, Washington, D.C., pp. 17–20.

ZBOROWSKI, M. 1952. "Cultural components in attitudes toward pain." *J. of Soc. Issues, 8,* 16–30.

CHAPTER 15

Interdisciplinary Relationships: Interrelations of Physiological, Psychological, and Psychiatric Findings, in Healthy Elderly Men

by James E. Birren, Robert N. Butler,
Samuel W. Greenhouse, Louis Sokoloff,
and Marian R. Yarrow

The investigation of human aging belongs to many different disciplines, and its history shows each pursuing its problems in relative independence from the problems of the other. It is generally accepted, however, that aging characteristics are probably rooted in interdependent processes, an understanding of which might be furthered by an approach from an interdisciplinary point of view.

The research reported here brings together data from medicine, physiology, psychology (experimental, clinical, and social), and psychiatry. Within the restricted range of medical and environmental variables imposed by the sample selection, a series of hypotheses and questions which require cross-disciplinary conceptualizations and data have been investigated.

We have also pursued a broad empirical approach, made possible by the large number of different observations of the same individuals. That is, intercorrelations were run between variables from each of the disciplines with variables from each of the other disciplines. Such an approach, the examination of relationships among virtually all measured factors, has as its rationale the hope of uncovering unsuspected associations which might suggest future research. In analyzing these data, we have not attempted to discuss or offer explanations for every intercorrelation, but we have speculated on ideas suggested by these statistical explorations. Concepts and methods of analysis that have been used by each of the disciplines and reported in preceding chapters are not described again in this chapter except as special features of methodology or variations of analyses introduced when cross-disciplinary purposes are involved. References to individual chapters are given for details of methodology.

The interdisciplinary data are organized in terms of increasing complexity of functions. We begin with an examination of physiological and medical interrelationships and progress to relations between physiology and psychological processes. Then we have examined physiological and psychological characteristics in relation to the highly integrative behaviors involved in the functioning of the aged individual as a social being.

RELATIONS WITH CHRONOLOGICAL AGE

One variable of common interest to all disciplines was chronological age. Previous discussions have largely treated the present sample as though the subjects were all of the same age. While for many purposes it is justified to regard the sample as homogeneously "old," some attention should be given to the within sample variation in age. It should be pointed out that of the 47 men, 38 were in the single decade of 65 to 74 years, not nearly as broad a distribution of ages as might be inferred from the range of 26 years between the youngest and oldest member (65 to 91 years). Thus, a failure to find many relations with chronological age in the present sample should not be used as evidence that there are indeed few such relations with chronological age in the population over 65.

Of considerable significance in interpreting the results relating to age is the fact that the two groups separated on the basis of medical criteria were not significantly different in mean age. Thus, obtained differences in groups I and II for many of the variables of the study are not artifactually the result of an age difference.

None of the variables representing the major findings of the study showed a significant relation (1 percent level) with chronological age within group I (table 1). Clearly within group I, variation in chrono-

TABLE 1.—*Selected correlations of variables with chronological age within sample*

Variables	Group I	Group II	Total group
E.E.G.			
1. Modal frequency	* 0. 42	−0. 03	−0. 06
5. Percent time 8 cycles	−. 18	* . 52	. 22
Physiology			
6. CMRO$_2$	−. 10	−. 44	* −. 31
8. CVR	. 28	. 41	** . 39
9. MABP	. 10	. 29	* . 30
45. Arterial O$_2$ saturation	* . 40	−. 10	−. 20
Psychiatry			
14. Total age related checklist (number of O's)	−. 05	* −. 49	* −. 29
Psychology			
23. Principal component I, "verbal"	−. 19	** −. 59	** −. 42
27. Principal component V, "set"	−. 34	−. 23	* −. 29
Projective psychology			
33. Sum of projective ratings	. 30	** . 76	** . 58
Medical			
34. Protein bound iodine	−. 29	−. 37	* −. 33
39. Measured vital capacity	−. 31	** −. 69	** −. 50
40. Measured breathing capacity	−. 31	** −. 59	** −. 43

* Significant at the 0.05 level.
** Significant at the 0.01 level.

logical age was not significant. In group II, however, a few correlations appeared to be significant. Of the physiological measurements, only measured breathing capacity and vital capacity were significant at the 1 percent level of confidence. These remained significant for the total group; cerebral vascular resistance also was significant at the 1 percent level for the total group. From the total physiological and medical points of view there was thus very little within sample relation to chronological age; what did occur was primarily the result of the contribution of group II subjects. This implies that the correlation of physiological measurements and chronological age will be small in healthy individuals. It further implies that when impairments in health develop, they have consequences for the magnitude of correlations of bodily functions and chronological age; perhaps the impairing quality of disease is itself a function of chronological age.

The same pattern of within sample correlations with chronological age was found for the psychological as for the physiological measurements; i.e., no significant correlations in group I and a limited number of significant correlations for group II. Those psychological correlations with age which appeared seem primarily involved with "stored information" and a verbal communication type of performance. Thus, some aspect of higher thought processes seems to be related to chronological age in the less healthy, again as a possible correlate of health impairments which, if they develop, as suggested above, develop in a manner related to the chronological age of the individual.

Within sample variation in chronological age is not regarded as of importance in the present study. When correlations occurred, they were significant only for group II, and consequently for the total group, leading to the suggestion that there. may be an interaction between chronological age and the rate of development of health impairments once initiated.

In terms of relative importance for persons in the age range over 65, health status is more significant in determining various aspects of functioning than the unspecified consequences of advanced chronological age. Such a statement, however, tends to obscure the fact that there is an interaction between chronological age and the incidence of chronic disease of later life, an interaction which may hold considerable general behavioral and physiological significance for future research.

PHYSIOLOGICAL-MEDICAL-EEG COMPARISONS

Louis Sokoloff and Walter D. Obrist

Evidence was presented in chapters 6 and 7 to indicate that cerebral circulatory, metabolic, and electroencephalographic functions in the aged are to a major degree influenced, if not actually limited, by the state of health of the individual. In the optimally healthy aged subjects (group I), cerebral blood flow and oxygen consumption were not statistically significantly different from the values observed in normal subjects five decades younger, and although there were significant changes in some electroencephalographic parameters, these changes were rather minimal. It was not until recognizable objective signs of disease appeared that the impact of failing health on these functions became clearly apparent. Thus, it was in the asymptomatic disease group (group II), and mainly the arteriosclerotic subjects within that group, that significant declines in cerebral blood flow and cerebral venous oxygen tension were first observed and definite hanges in the electroencephalogram occurred.

The categorization of the subjects into groups according to their health status was accomplished chiefly on the basis of categorical variables which reflected the presence or absence of pathognomonic signs of disease, for example, the presence or absence of abnormalities in the electrocardiogram, appearance of calcifications of the cerebral vessels in the skull X-rays, organic heart murmurs, neurological signs of Parkinsonism, etc. Because they were categorical, these variables could not be included in the product-moment correlation matrix, which, therefore, lacked representation of a large segment of obviously relevant clinical data.

On the basis of the preceding relationships, it might reasonably have been expected that similar associations would be reflected in product-moment correlations between the physiological and the quantitative medical variables. From an examination of the multidisciplinary correlation matrix, it is apparent that this was not obviously so. Of 360 correlation coefficients determined between 12 cerebral circulatory, metabolic, and electroencephalographic variables and 10 medical variables in both groups I and II, individually and combined, only 27 were statistically significant at less than the 5-percent level of confidence. This incidence is hardly more than might be expected by chance alone, despite the fact that there are included a number of automatic significant correlations between variables which represent measurements of essentially the same or related functions by different methods. The seven significant correlations between mean arterial blood pressure (MABP) or cerebral vascular resistance (CVR), which is calculated from MABP and cerebral blood flow (CBF), and the daily averages of systolic and diastolic blood pressure are

examples of this type; indeed, 5 of the 9 significant correlations at the 0.01 level of confidence are included in this group. In the remaining statistically significant correlations, no consistently meaningful pattern could be observed.

The quantitative medical variables which were included in the correlation matrix appeared, therefore, to be relatively unrelated to cerebral blood flow, metabolism, and electrical activity, probably because they reflected bodily processes which neither directly nor indirectly would be likely to influence or vary with the cerebral functions (Lassen, 1959) except, perhaps, in the presence of rather marked degrees of pathological change. In other words, while the cerebral functions and medical measurements vary within the physiological range, they would not be related to each other; it is only when one deviates so far from normal as to limit the other, or both are independently limited by a third influence introduced by disease, that significant correlations between them could be expected. The range of pathological change was, however, sharply restricted in this series of subjects by the stringent selection process designed to exclude it. Indeed, even the asymptomatic disease subjects (group II) were by almost any standard remarkably healthy for their age, a situation which undoubtedly greatly lessened the likelihood of finding significant correlations between the cerebral physiological and medical variables studied.

There is one area of intercorrelation between the EEG and medical variables which lends some support to observations previously reported in the literature. Obrist and his co-workers have observed an inverse relationship between blood pressure and the incidence of EEG slow wave abnormalities in aged psychiatric patients (Obrist, Busse, and Henry, 1961). This

TABLE 2.—*Correlations between EEG and average daily blood pressure*

EEG measurement	Average daily systolic blood pressure		Average daily diastolic blood pressure	
	Group I	Group II	Group I	Group II
Peak occipital frequency....................	0.07	0.23	−0.11	0.31
Percent-time slow (1–7 cps.).................	−.06	*−.53	.10	−.30
Percent-time alpha (8–12 cps.)...............	−.06	.23	−.11	.18
Percent-time fast (13–30 cps.)...............	*.46	−.23	*.49	.06

*Significant at the 0.05 level.

relationship was found only in cases with clinical evidence of cardiovascular disease; it did not appear in the absence of such disorders (Obrist and Henry, 1958). From the correlation coefficients between average daily blood pressure and the EEG variables presented in table 2, it can be seen that there was a tendency in these studies also for blood pressure to be negatively related to slow EEG activity in the subjects with asymptomatic disease (group II). The correlation coefficient between average daily systolic blood pressure and percent-time slow activity observed in this group equalled —0.53 and was statistically significant at the 0.05 level. In the healthy subjects in group I, however, no such correlation was observed. Since the chief distinction between group I and group II was the greater degree of arteriosclerotic disease in the latter, it would appear that, as in the previous studies cited, cardiovascular disease was an important factor contributing to the inverse correlation between blood pressure and EEG slowing in elderly people. These results might be interpreted as indicating that in the presence of cardiovascular disease, increased blood pressure protects against slowing of the EEG. In the present study, positive significant correlations were also observed between percent-time fast activity and average daily systolic and diastolic blood pressures in the healthy subjects

(group I). Such a result has not been previously reported and requires further investigation. As regards the relationship between the cerebral circulatory and metabolic variables on the one hand and the electroencephalographic variables on the other, evidence was reviewed in chapter 7 which strongly suggested that alterations in EEG pattern occur in states of impaired cerebral circulation and metabolism. Circulatory disturbances capable of producing clinical signs of cerebral anoxia or ischemia are associated with a slowing of frequencies in the EEG, notably an increased number of waves in the theta and delta bands (1–7 cps). There is also evidence in the literature (see ch. 7) to suggest a slight increase of slow activity in the EEG records of average, nonhospitalized, elderly subjects, manifested primarily by a shift in alpha frequency to 8 or 9 cps. There has been considerable speculation concerning the possibility of whether these changes in the EEG might not reflect the effects of cerebral circulatory insufficiency or metabolic impairments. Although in both groups I and II as a whole, there were no statistically significant changes in cerebral oxygen consumption and only a moderate decline in cerebral blood flow in group II, it was still considered possible that such a relationship between cerebral circulatory or metabolic and electroencephalographic functions might be observed in individual

TABLE 3.—*Product-moment correlations between EEG frequency measurements and cerebral metabolic variables* [1]

EEG measurement	Cerebral circulation and metabolism					
	$CMRO_2$	CBF	CVR	MABP	VpO_2	CMR_G
Peak occipital frequency:						
Group I..................	0. 00	0. 02	0. 02	−0. 19	−0. 05	−0. 05
Group II.................	−. 10	. 35	−. 11	. 29	. 41	−. 08
Total..................	. 00	. 21	−. 20	−. 13	. 20	−. 06
Percent-time slow (1–7 cps):						
Group I..................	. 14	−. 01	−. 07	. 01	. 20	*. 43
Group II.................	−. 04	−. 45	. 13	−. 31	−. 38	. 01
Total..................	. 04	−. 19	. 10	. 00	−. 09	. 26
Percent-time alpha (8–12 cps):						
Group I..................	−. 28	−. 15	. 25	. 35	. 12	−. 20
Group II.................	. 15	. 15	. 02	. 06	−. 03	−. 07
Total..................	−. 09	−. 04	. 12	. 11	. 04	−. 14
Percent-time fast (13–30 cps):						
Group I..................	. 01	. 05	−. 01	−. 04	−. 17	. 25
Group II.................	. 27	. 28	−. 23	−. 05	. 03	−. 19
Total..................	. 12	. 18	−. 17	−. 15	−. 03	. 08
Percent-time 8 cycle activity:						
Group I..................	−. 13	−. 07	. 07	. 23	. 11	. 11
Group II.................	−. 01	−. 25	. 30	−. 02	−. 22	−. 11
Total..................	−. 11	−. 21	*. 30	. 21	−. 10	. 02

[1] A description of the variables may be found in chs. 6 and 7.
*Significant at the 0.05 level.

product-moment correlations. The correlation coefficients obtained in groups I and II, both separately and combined, are presented in table 3. Of the 90 correlations, only two are significant at the 0.05 level; i.e., cerebral glucose consumption (CMR_G) versus percent-time slow activity, and cerebrovascular resistance versus percent-time 8 cycles, a finding most likely attributable to chance. In fact, the positive correlation between cerebral glucose consumption and slow activity is contrary to the prediction of greater slowing of the EEG with lower cerebral metabolic rates. This lack of findings may also reflect the narrow range of pathological change in this select group of healthy old subjects. It is likely that the EEG is influenced by circulatory and metabolic factors only when pathological processes intervene to produce cerebral vascular insufficiency and anoxia. Although there was evidence of such processes in the arteriosclerotic subjects in group II (ch. 6), the decrease in blood flow was, nevertheless, still of insufficient magnitude to limit the cerebral oxygen consumption or influence the EEG. Indeed, in a separate study on aged psychiatric patients with more advanced degrees of cardiovascular disease, coefficients of correlation of 0.6 and higher were observed between cerebral oxygen consumption and EEG variables; these findings will be presented in a separate report.

I-288

PSYCHOPHYSIOLOGICAL RELATIONS

James E. Birren

Perhaps the most basic question to be raised about the relations of physiological and psychological aspects of aging is whether psychological functions are related to the individual life span. This question may be subdivided into two questions: (*a*) are there psychophysiological changes of aging characteristic of the species, and (*b*) are there individual patterns of psychological aging related to measurable aspects of physiology. Not only are changes in cognitive and psychomotor capacities important when viewed as part of a potential complex of age changes characteristic of the species, but they are also of significance in the maintenance of the individual's skills and personal and social adjustment.

Chapter 8 reported cognitive differences between groups I and II which represent distinctions in health. Since psychological differences appear within this very narrow range of variation in health, the question arises whether the psychological and physiological variables are equally correlated in the healthy and the less healthy groups. The answer to this question provides a partial test of the hypothesis that as long as physiological variables remain within "normal" limits they provide a necessary basis for functioning but not a sufficient or determining condition for cognition The discontinuity hypothesis is that individual differences in psychological functions remain largely autonomous of somatic functions until critical or limiting levels are reached; e.g., as a consequence of disease or trauma, after which a new set of relationships holds. A simultaneous hypothesis should also be kept in mind, the hypothesis of a genetically based species pattern of psychophysiological aging. The hypothesis of a genetically based pattern of aging does not necessarily deny

concomitant exogenous aging of even larger practical significance, nor does it imply anything about its ultimate modifiability.

With these considerations in mind, the correlations between 22 physiological and 9 psychological variables, representing cognitive and speed factors, were analyzed separately for groups I and II (table 4). In this analysis not all the psychological and physiological variables were independent measures.

There were 198 possible correlations between the psychological and physiological measurements in both groups I and II. In group I, only five correlations were at or beyond the 5 percent level of significance. In group II there were 26 correlations significant at the same level (table 4). The significant correlations which occur involve relatively few physiological variables. Over half of the physiological variables had no relationship with psychological variables. In contrast, two variables, $CMRO_2$ and vital capacity, each had eight correlations with psychological variables, all but one of these being in group II. This differential pattern of psychophysiological correlations in groups I and II does offer support for the discontinuity hypothesis; i.e., that psychological functions are related to physiological variables when the latter lie in an abnormal range as in disease.

The largest component, Principal Component I, in the psychological measurements, was identified as the general intellective factor underlying the WAIS and other tests. It was interpreted as measuring stored information, largely verbal; e.g., as distinguished from more labile perceptual functions. This component was highly related to a group of personality tests scored in terms of "how well the man programed his

TABLE 4.—*Correlations between psychological and physiological variables: for groups I and II and total groups* [1]

	Psychological variables											
	23 Component I—Verbal achievement			24 Component II—Enumeration			25 Component III—Flexibility of set			26 Component IV—Speed		
Physiological variables	I	II	All	I	II	All	I	II	All	I	II	All
1. E.E.G. modal frequency	—26	27	10	—13	17	03	28	—30	00	26	—02	10
2. E.E.G. percent time slow Δ	11	—04	—01	05	23	09	—12	*47	06	—09	—09	—09
3. E.E.G. percent time fast α	26	—31	04	—14	—37	—22	—28	—06	—18	19	05	12
4. E.E.G. percent time β	—10	19	08	16	14	16	13	08	14	—07	04	—01
5. E.E.G. precent time at 8 cycles	24	—27	—09	—03	—24	—13	—41	11	—21	—12	—06	—10
6. Cerebral metabolic rate	01	*55	27	—05	*—55	—27	—03	18	08	—36	—17	—25
7. Cerebral blood flow	—06	17	13	—15	—24	—17	—10	—13	—07	—23	25	01
8. Cerebral vascular resistance	—04	—08	—23	—03	15	03	—01	—27	—16	20	14	14
9. Mean arterial blood pressure	—18	02	—25	—29	07	—04	—33	*—51	**—41	—10	*49	26
10. VPO₂	—16	—19	—08	—27	27	01	—27	—29	—26	00	*57	*35
11. Glucose consumption	—03	28	09	—36	—25	—31	—34	—04	—20	—13	—51	—33
34. Protein bound iodine	—15	13	00	03	28	13	—04	13	09	10	—25	—06
35. Total cholesterol	*—40	12	—19	—25	11	—08	19	19	15	—15	00	—07
36. Basal metabolic rate	—25	23	—11	11	09	09	20	**—58	—10	27	28	26
37. Pulse rate, daily average	—17	—10	—07	13	31	21	01	—01	03	14	10	12
38. Weight-height ratio	38	02	*33	03	—27	—05	—16	17	02	13	—08	03
39. Vital capacity, measured	19	*58	**39	13	06	11	18	00	13	14	*—46	—12
40. Breathing capacity, measured	00	42	25	—04	—08	—04	—13	39	12	14	—26	00
41. Systolic blood pressure, daily average	—31	—06	—29	—16	09	—05	—14	*—46	*—34	05	*44	23
42. Diastolic blood pressure, daily average	07	13	02	—22	03	—11	—16	—32	—27	—06	*51	25
43. Pulse pressure, daily average	—32	03	—25	—08	13	00	—14	—38	*—30	00	12	05
45. Arterial oxygen saturation	—12	*49	—01	—22	—04	—17	—09	—06	—10	23	—16	07

I-290

Psychological variables

Physiological variables	Component V—Concept formation (27)			Level of aspiration (29)			Draw-a-Person test (30)			Homonyms number (31)			Homonyms percent (32)		
	I	II	All	I	II	All	I	II	All	I	II	All	I	II	All
1. E.E.G. modal frequency	—10	12	02	06	07	10	—10	06	01	—21	04	—05	—27	13	—15
2. E.E.G. percent time slow Δ	05	—10	—02	—29	—06	—19	17	09	12	07	05	03	21	—18	13
3. E.E.G. percent time fast α	—01	—08	—02	14	—19	—03	—06	*—54	—23	02	—18	—04	06	—03	—06
4. E.E.G. percent time β	—25	34	—05	08	—13	03	—10	—01	—03	11	24	19	15	09	—21
5. E.E.G. percent time at 8 cycles	06	—08	—04	02	—18	—13	—02	—31	—17	12	—21	—06	14	—07	25
6. Cerebral metabolic rate	**49	33	**43	17	**78	**54	03	41	22	01	**71	*31	09	21	—05
7. Cerebral blood flow	25	—15	17	33	23	*31	—05	—07	—01	—24	17	—02	—03	—05	—25
8. Cerebral vascular resistance	—34	13	—21	—25	—38	—38	—15	—20	—21	09	—24	—13	—08	41	**52
9. Mean arterial blood pressure	—34	—09	—22	—08	—23	—29	**—49	—35	*—38	—29	—20	—29	—30	33	**56
10. VPO₂	04	*—55	—23	07	*—49	—26	18	—33	—07	—31	—40	—28	—17	—08	—20
11. Glucose consumption	17	22	18	04	48	29	—15	06	—05	—10	27	05	13	04	04
34. Protein bound iodine	—05	—06	—04	—12	10	02	16	15	16	—13	15	—01	02	—01	—09
35. Total cholesterol	—24	—04	—18	—04	05	01	—22	37	05	—20	27	—02	*—43	—41	03
36. Basal metabolic rate	—19	—18	—20	—11	—15	—13	—07	*—45	—20	—18	—18	—19	—12	15	10
37. Pulse rate, daily average	—07	—03	—02	—08	—26	—13	—05	—21	—09	—16	—09	—09	19	12	—15
38. Weight-height ratio	08	—08	07	—02	23	17	34	26	*33	15	09	18	34	—19	*—31
39. Vital capacity, measured	09	28	18	36	**64	**50	27	**58	**40	17	**62	*36	16	14	—17
40. Breathing capacity, measured	—07	—19	—03	32	46	**38	—01	54	20	—09	35	11	04	—19	**—42
41. Systolic blood pressure, daily average	—27	—01	—20	02	—27	—22	—19	*—54	**—38	—30	—39	**—38	—01	29	**45
42. Diastolic blood pressure, daily average	—24	—05	—19	11	—12	—06	03	—25	—12	—04	—13	—11	25	*51	*30
43. Pulse pressure, daily average	—18	09	—12	02	—04	—07	—22	—34	*—30	—25	—24	*—29	—08	09	*33
45. Arterial oxygen saturation	—36	15	—26	—26	17	—10	—12	26	—03	—26	30	—14	—14	33	18

¹ Decimal points omitted.
*Significant at the 0.05 level.
**Significant at the 0.01 level.

thinking and behavior." The correlation was remarkably high, −0.87, between the general intellectual component and a sum of performance ratings of the Draw-A-Person, Homonyms and other tests. (See ch. 12 for a description of the latter items.) The above correlation holds for both groups I and II, i.e., −0.89 and −0.83, respectively. Since the correlation does not change significantly for the combined groups, one may not regard the high correlation as the adventitious result of increased variance of the total group by the combination of two groups of unequal variance.

Since the question has been much raised whether general intelligence changes with age, it was thought important to compare this component with the physiological measurements. Few of the physiological variables correlated with the general intellective factor. Surprisingly absent from the correlations are the EEG measurements, which also failed to show a correlation with the speed factor. Since the EEG has been widely discussed in relation to age, showing some significant changes, it was rather expected that it would show a relation with the cognitive measurements. Possibly EEG correlations with cognitive functioning may not appear until more gross brain damage is present than existed in the present sample.

The cerebral metabolic rate ($CMRO_2$) and the general intellective factor showed a correlation but only in group II, 0.55. There appears to be a slight tendency for group II subjects to have a lower cerebral metabolic rate than group I subjects and there is a distinct possibility that the lowered metabolic rate is associated with lowered intellective functioning. The lack of such a relationship between $CMRO_2$ and the general intellective factor in group I is of considerable importance because of the fact

that the psychological measurements are about equally highly correlated among themselves in group I as in group II, implying high reliability of measurement as well as similarity of measured function. Thus, group I subjects show a dispersion of reliably measured individual differences of general intelligence as in group II, and yet these measurements are unrelated to the $CMRO_2$ in group I. It is possible that the cognitive differences measured in group I subjects are related to the cerebral metabolic rate but the change in the latter has not proceeded to a measurable extent.

While the tendency for the sparsely occurring significant correlations to appear in group II and not in group I has been offered as supportive evidence for the hypothesis that psychological functions are largely autonomous of somatic functions until limiting levels of disease are reached, this interpretation must be reconciled with the finding of chapter 10 that in a number of mental speed measurements the maximally healthy and the asymptomatic disease groups were equally slow (slower than young controls). The "speed" factor, component IV, shows correlations (*all* in group II) with VPO_2, 0.57; glucose consumption, −0.51; diastolic blood pressure, 0.51; mean arterial blood pressure, 0.49; vital capacity, −0.46; and systolic blood pressure, 0.44. In all of these correlations, with the exception of VPO_2, the direction of the relationship is that of a lower level of physiological function being associated with psychomotor slowness. The higher level of VPO_2 (in group II) may reflect a lower extraction of oxygen from the blood by the cerebral tissues, and the correlation may also lie in the direction of lower physiological function associated with a slowing of behavior. In the above correlations with blood pressure, slow performance is related to elevated blood pressure. These results are difficult to interpret. It was expected that since both groups were equally slow compared with young subjects, any physiological basis for the change would be equally seen in the two groups. One interpretation is that the changes in speed are early manifestations of underlying physiological changes or *disease states* that remain unmeasured in these subjects. However, the bases for the decline in speed in the healthy aged remain essentially undemonstrated.

Component III was interpreted as a measure of the ability to shift set or response expectancies rapidly. In group II this component was related only to mean arterial blood pressure, basal metabolic rate and systolic blood pressure (all three highly interrelated measures); in group I it was only related to percent time at eight cycles in the EEG. The meaning of these isolated correlations is doubtful. The ability to form alternative points of view rather rapidly is a prerequisite to concept formation and developing an abstract approach to problem solving. It is surprising for us that such a component did not relate more closely to other measurements.

These considerations clearly point to the need to probe further into the physiological as well as the environmental basis for late life decline in psychomotor speed and in mental ability shown by some individuals or alternatively to search for the bases for the maintenance of high level capacities.

PHYSIOLOGICAL - PSYCHOLOGICAL-PSYCHIATRIC INTERRELATIONSHIPS

Robert N. Butler and Seymour Perlin

One of the prominent issues in the psychiatric evaluation of the aged is that of unraveling the contributions of various kinds of changes (physiological, psychological, and environmental) to manifest behavior, both adaptive and pathological. Specifically the question is to what extent maladaptive features and indications of decline are a function of disease, personality, social adversity, and/or of processes of aging itself.

Certain properties of the aged, such as intellective, perceptual, and psychomotor declines, are currently attributed to aging. To what extent are these declines the consequences of, or to what extent are they reinforced by, the presence of other factors in the aged such as sensory defects, disordered mental functioning and social deprivations? Of special interest is the examination of a subsample of the subjects evaluated psychiatrically as showing senile manifestations (see ch. 11). It is reasonable to suppose that in elderly subjects exhibiting pathological behavior, the influence of morbid states would likely be modifiable.

With these issues our major concern,[1] associations between physiological and psychological variables described in the preceding sections and psychiatric data were examined. The following psychiatric assessments were used:

Senile quality; depressive trends; Age Relevant Checklist of symptoms; ratings of impaired recent memory; measures of retention; overall adaptation rating; and self-reports of "declines" and reactions to declines, from which were derived scores of morale and adaptability. (See ch. 11 for definitions.)

---

[1] It was of interest, methodologically, to compare mental status assessments made in the psychiatric interviews and on psychological tests. There was substantial agreement, correlations ranging from 0.69 to 0.89 between WAIS derived psychiatric mental status scores and corresponding full WAIS scores obtained by psychologists. See app. C, chapter 11.

Psychiatric and Physiological Variables

Several past reports have related electroencephalographic changes to severity of intellectual impairments (McAdam and Robinson, 1956; Weiner and Schuster, 1956). In the present sample, in which intellectual changes were minimal, no relationships were found between psychiatric appraisal of intellectual decline (Age Relevant Checklist, item 1) and either clinically evaluated encephalograms or such measures of electrical activity as peak occipital frequency and mean percentage slow waves (table 5). Electroencephalographic measures, and their clinical interpretations, were unrelated to senile manifestations. Psychiatric study of the nine subjects in the sample who were clinically rated as having abnormal encephalograms showed no common characteristics. In this connection it should be noted that in contrast to previous reports (Silverman, Busse, and Barnes, 1955) where one-third of elderly community subjects were found to have temporal lobe abnormalities, such abnormalities were found in only 9 percent of the present sample. EEG measures were related to psychiatric ratings of morale and adaptation in group II (table 5). The observed associations which seem to be plausible were: the greater the self-reported decreases (conceptualized as relating to morale), the lower the peak occipital frequency ($r = -0.59$); and the greater the adaptive capacity, the less percent Time Slow Waves ($r = -0.57$) (generally held to be associated with increased pathology). There were no associations, however, between clinically abnormal encephalograms and depression. The meaning of these abnormalities is not established but they are suggestive of organic pathology. Our subjects with temporal lobe abnormalities did not show any distinguishing psychiatric symptoms, with the exception of the 92-year-old subject who did demonstrate senile manifestations.

Medical data (such as cholesterol level, protein-bound iodine, mean arterial blood pressure, basal metabolism, and history of smoking) were not related to the psychiatric variables, with one exception involving Senile Quality. Senile Quality was significantly related to arteriosclerosis: 6 out of 10 arteriosclerotics were diagnosed Senile Quality, whereas 5 out of 37 nonarteriosclerotics were similarly diagnosed. However, the possibility of early undiagnosed arteriosclerotic changes cannot be entirely ruled out in any group of subjects since it is known that arteriosclerosis has selective organ-system effects, that cerebral arteriosclerosis may occur in the absence of other organ changes (Alpers, Forster, and Herbut, 1948), and that the localization of arteriosclerosis in selective areas of the brain can occur.

Cerebral physiological measures of CBF and $CMRO_2$ were related to certain psychiatric variables (table 5). Senile Quality was significantly associated with lower $CMRO_2$ and CBF values on the entire sample. The Age Relevant Checklist (high scores reflect deterioration) was significantly related to $CMRO_2$ in group II only. Impaired recent memory and retention were not related to cerebral physiological measures. Morale and adaptation showed moderate associations with $CMRO_2$ and CBF, although depression was not related to these measures. We were interested in the question of whether certain forms of senility, as represented in our Senile Quality assessment, reflected prodromal manifestations of Chronic Brain Syndrome. Abnormally reduced cerebral blood flow and metabolic rate and electroencephalic changes were found in hospitalized Chronic Brain Syndrome patients. (See ch. 6 and 7.) Neuropathological evidence has been reported

TABLE 5.—*Relations of psychiatric variables and physiological measurements*

[Total sample] [1]

	CBF	$CMRO_2$	Glucose	VPO_2	CVR	EEG	
						Modal frequency	Percent time slow
Depression (mild) [2]	N.S.	N.S.	N.S.	N.S.	N.S.	N.S.	N.S.
Senile quality [2]	(***)	$*r=0.52$ (Gr. II)	N.S.	N.S.	N.S.	N.S.	N.S.
Age relevant checklist	N.S.		N.S.	N.S.	N.S.		N.S.
Impaired recent memory [2]	N.S.	N.S.	N.S.	N.S.	N.S.	N.S.	N.S.
Overall adaptation	N.S.	N.S.	N.S.	N.S.	N.S.	N.S.	N.S.
Morale: Self-Rep. Decr.	$*r=-0.35$	$*r=-0.37$	N.S.	N.S.	N.S.	$**r=-0.59$ (Gr. II)	N.S.
Adaptability:							
Percent reactions	N.S.	N.S.	N.S.	N.S.	N.S.	N.S.	
Decreases							$**r=-0.57$ (Gr. II)
Percent Comp. and Acc. reactions	N.S.	$**r=0.44$	N.S.	$**r=-0.47$	N.S.	N.S.	N.S.

[1] Unless indicated otherwise.
[2] *t*-test.

* Significant at the 0.05 level.
** Significant at the 0.01 level.
*** Significant at the 0.001 level.

N.S. = Not significant.

in the literature for at least two Chronic Brain Syndromes: one associated with arteriosclerosis, the other with senile brain disease (i.e., primary neuronal degeneration) (APA Diagnostic and Statistical Manual, 1952). It is not yet established whether the cerebral circulatory, metabolic, and electroencephalographic abnormalities occur in both forms of Chronic Brain Syndrome.

Attention is drawn to one cluster of six Senile Quality subjects with low oxygen consumption associated with evidence of vascular disease; i.e., arteriosclerosis, and to another subgroup of five who maintained adequate oxygen consumption and did not show substantial vascular changes. The first cluster showed the more severe senile manifestations and somewhat longer histories of such changes. Its members exhibited many of the signs (but not all) characteristic of the Chronic Brain Syndrome; they were found to have abnormally low cerebral oxygen uptake comparable to that found in hospitalized Chronic Brain Syndrome cases. It seems reasonable to view provisionally these subjects as early, ambulatory, Chronic Brain Syndrome cases.

An analysis was made to determine the relation between arteriosclerosis and $CMRO_2$. The latter was dichotomized at the median, between 3.0 and 3.1. The data were suggestive of a relation between arteriosclerosis and low $CMRO_2$. As a result it seems probable that arteriosclerosis explains the cerebral physiological changes in this group.

The possibility of an alternative nonvascular pathway to senility was considered. Might Senile Quality not reflect primary neuronal degeneration possibly related to the Chronic Brain Syndrome associated with senile brain disease? Venous oxygen tension was examined since its increase, in the presence of adequate blood flow, would be suggestive of a primary reduction in utilization of oxygen by the brain. There were no differences, however, between the Senile Quality subjects with low-oxygen uptake and those with normal oxygen uptake with respect to VPO_2. Since the latter is also influenced by other factors (e.g., hyperventilation) and since the number of cases under study was so small, no conclusions can be drawn for or against the possibility of a nonvascular senile quality. The possibility of a "functional senility," which could be explained on the basis of disuse or extinction of intellectual abilities possibly mediated by social adversity and isolation, cannot be ruled out either.

In a companion study of 10 carefully selected and studied patients hospitalized with diagnosed Chronic Brain Syndrome with cerebral arteriosclerosis [2] (Butler, Dastur, Lane, Perlin, and Sokoloff, 1963), abnormal reductions were found in both blood flow and oxygen utilization (see ch. 6), confirming the findings of Freyhan, Woodford, and Kety (1951). However, independent evaluations led to separation of the 10 Chronic Brain Syndrome cases into 7 "confused" and 3 "paranoid"; the "paranoid" had normal cerebral physiological findings.

Table 6 presents the mean cerebral oxygen metabolic rates of a spectrum of populations: the present sample, with emphasis on the Senile Quality and non-Senile Quality groups, a normal young sample, and a hospitalized Chronic Brain Syndrome group. The CBF measurements were done in the same laboratory and the measurements of the hospitalized and normal young

[2] We are indebted to Dr. Edward D. Griffin, of St. Elizabeths Hospital, Washington, D.C., and to Drs. Isadore Tuerck and Albert Kurland, of Spring Grove State Hospital, Catonsville, Md., for their cooperation in obtaining subjects for this study; and to Dr. William Pollin for his careful selection evaluation.

TABLE 6.—*Mean values of cerebral oxygen metabolic rate in various groupings of aged subjects*

Groupings [1]	Number	CMRO$_2$
Normal young.............	15	3.5
Non-Senile Quality.......	33	3.3
Senile Quality...........	11	3.0
Extreme Senile Quality (CBS without psychosis).	2	2.7
CBS with arteriosclerosis with psychosis........	10	2.7
"Paranoid" CBS........	3	3.4
"Confused" CBS........	7	2.4
Presenile dementia........	1	2.4
Normal healthy aged, group I..............	28	3.3

[1] CBS = Chronic brain syndrome.

groups were made over the same period as the present aged sample. The table indicates the general tendency for impaired mental status to accompany reduced cerebral oxygen uptake in keeping with the findings in other organic brain disorders in individuals of different ages (Sokoloff, 1960).

The early recognition and separation of forms of senility would make research in this field more plausible as well as indicate changes in clinical management. Investigation of the early stages of a disorder is likely to contribute to knowledge of pathogenesis. However, followup of this population and extension into other populations are required both to substantiate these findings and to test the thesis that "Senile Quality" includes the early stages of the Chronic Brain Syndromes of the aged. There may be several possible pathways towards reduced cerebral oxygen consumption and senile manifestations, perhaps eventually culminating in the Chronic Brain Syndromes of the aged. These pathways may reflect the traditional etiologic divisions of the Chronic Brain Syndromes of the aged, that associated with senile brain disease and that associated with arteriosclerosis.

Psychiatric and Psychological Variables

Psychiatric evaluation revealed that the healthy aged were subject to personality and psychoneurotic disorders, including depression, which are manifestly similar to those occurring in the young. No correlations were found between these disorders and cerebral physiological and electroencephalographic variables. However, there was a suggestive relationship between depression and systolic, but not diastolic, blood pressure. Associations between blood pressure elevation and depression have been reported in younger subjects as well. It is concluded that functional psychiatric disorders occur in old age as well as in earlier periods which, within this study, were not associated with cerebrovascular disease or aging per se.

Cognitive, perceptual, and psychomotor measurements were significantly related to psychiatric evaluations. There were differences between the Senile Quality and the non-Senile Quality groups on an impressive variety of tests and subtests of cognitive functioning (table 7). The Senile Quality subjects uniformly do less well. While it may be argued that evaluation of senile manifestations is based upon decline in intellectual function and thus a relationship to tested decline would be expected and therefore circular, it is our opinion that "Senile Quality" reflects a morbid state and not normal aging, and that it is therefore more appropriate to compare the non-Senile Quality aged to young samples in the study of age-specific effects.

The psychiatric Age Relevant Checklist, characterizing the degree of "deteriorative" and "regressive" behavior manifested by the subject, was related to tested cognitive functioning, Principal Component I

TABLE 7.—*Psychological test scores: Effects of depression and Senile Quality on WAIS subtests*

Tests	No psychiatric diagnosis and no Senile Quality (N=15) (Mean)	Senile Quality only (N=5) (Mean)	Depression only (N=7) (Mean)	Depression with Senile Quality (N=6) (Mean)	Significance of Senile Quality effect	Significance of depression effect
WAIS Subtests						
Information....................	12.40	10.00	12.00	8.50	(*)	N.S.
Comprehension.................	12.73	10.80	10.86	9.17	N.S.	N.S.
Arithmetic....................	12.27	10.20	11.57	8.00	(*)	N.S.
Similarities...................	9.13	6.60	9.29	5.17	(*)	N.S.
Digit Span....................	9.07	7.20	9.29	7.17	(*)	N.S.
Vocabulary....................	11.87	8.00	11.86	8.33	N.S.	N.S.
Digit Symbol..................	5.80	5.20	6.86	4.17	N.S.	N.S.
Picture Completion............	8.67	4.40	7.86	6.17	(***)	N.S.
Block Design..................	7.33	4.20	7.29	5.33	(*)	N.S.
Picture Arrangement...........	6.20	3.00	6.71	4.17	(**)	N.S.
Object Assembly...............	7.00	6.00	6.71	6.33	N.S.	N.S.
Verbal total................	68.60	52.80	65.86	46.33	(**)	N.S.
Performance total...........	35.73	22.80	35.57	30.17	(*)	N.S.
Total WAIS..............	104.33	75.60	101.43	76.50	....	....
Mill Hill Alpha and Beta[1]........	28.07	20.40	28.43	19.00	(**)	N.S.
Verbal Fluency[1]...............	28.67	17.40	[3] 34.29	22.20	(*)	N.S.
Speed Copy Words[1].............	30.47	22.20	[3] 33.86	27.20	N.S.	N.S.
X Reaction Time[1].............	.213	[2] .230	[3] .254	.270	N.S.	(*)
Raven Matrices[1]...............	26.80	17.60	24.71	22.83	N.S.	N.S.

[1] Described in ch. 8, this volume.
[2] Number of subjects with relevant data: 4.
[3] Number of subjects with relevant data: 5.
* Significant at the 0.05 level.
** Significant at the 0.01 level.
*** Significant at the 0.001 level.

Note: Tests for interaction effects proved to be not significant.

(r= −0.59). Also impaired recent memory and test scores of retention, possibly indicative of organic mental disorder, were significantly related to Principal Component I and to WAIS scores (table 8). These findings are but a further reflection of the association of senile manifestations and impoverishment of intellectual functioning.

In interpreting psychological test performance, the role of depression cannot be excluded. Depression did not relate to selected psychological test scores as did Senile Quality (table 7), but there was a significant relationship of depressive trends with Principal Component I, the general intellective factor (table 8). The MMPI depression scale also correlated (r= −0.29) with Principal Component I.

There were significant associations between psychomotor speed to psychiatric evaluations. Impairment expressed in scores on the Age Relevant Checklist, recent memory, and overall adaptation, was related to slow reaction time.

Depression was related to both measures of speed (reaction time, Principal Compoment IV, table 8). The nondepressed subjects had a mean reaction time of 0.21 second; the young sample had 0.18 second, and the depressed had 0.25 second. MMPI depression scale also correlated with mean reaction time but in group II only ($r = +0.52$). This finding of a relationship between speed and depression is particularly striking in view of the fact that the depressions observed in this sample were mild and that clinical retardation was not notable. Therefore it would seem important in studies of the relation of speed and aging to control for the effects of depression (and probably motivation). Even if slowing of speed is a function of aging, slowing is also a function of depression, a common occurence in the aged. When slowing becomes an impairment, the possibility of modifiability

through the treatment of depression warrants consideration in contrast to a view of unalterability in the aging process.

The associations between depression and mean reaction time contrast with the relative absence of a relation between depression and cognitive and perceptual tests (which were associated with Senile Quality). The possibility that depression of greater severity might affect cognitive and perceptual test performance is not, of course, ruled out and, in fact, is likely. Similarly, with advancing senility speed of response would probably be more markedly slowed. But in the early stages the differential effect of depression upon psychomotor speed and intellectual tests may be useful diagnostically.

The question arises as to whether hearing loss interacts with depression on response

TABLE 8.—*Psychiatric variables and psychological measurements*

(Total group)[1]

Variables	Principal component I	Principal component IV	WAIS		Reaction time	Total projective rating	Dep. Scale MMPI
			Verb.	Perf.			
Depression [2]	(*)	N.S.	N.S.	N.S.	(*)	(*)	(*)
Senile Quality [2]	$r = 0.59$ $p < 0.01$	(Gr. I) (*)	} (***)	(**)	N.S.	(***)	N.S.
Age Relevant Checklist	$r = 0.59**$	N.S.	N.S.	N.S.	$r = 0.55***$	$r = 0.61**$	N.S.
Impaired Recent Memory	$r = 0.67***$	N.S.	$r = 0.59***$	$r = 0.55***$	$r = 0.45**$	N.S.	N.S.
Retention	$r = 0.76***$ (Gr. II)	N.S.	$r = 0.44*$ (Gr. II)	N.S.	N.S.	N.S.	N.S.
Overall adaptation	N.S.	N.S.	N.S.	N.S.	$r = 0.50***$	N.S.	N.S.
Morale: Self-Rep. Decr.	N.S.	$r = 0.36*$	N.S.	N.S.	N.S.	N.S.	$r = 0.29*$
Adaptability: Percent Reactions. Decreases	} N.S.	N.S.	N.S.	N.S.	N.S.	$r = 0.33*$	N.S.
Persent Comp and Acc. Reactions	N.S.	N.S.	N.S.	N.S.	N.S.	$r = 0.34*$	N.S.

[1] Unless indicated otherwise.
[2] Depression and Senile Quality could and did coexist; findings were therefore reported in terms of pure depression and pure "Senile Quality". (See tables 3 and 4.)
* Significant at the 0.05 level.
** Significant at the 0.01 level.
*** Significant at the 0.001 level.

N.S. = Not significant.

TABLE 9.—*The relation of auditory acuity and depression to reaction time*

Diagnostic category	Group I		Group II	
	Subjects	Mean reaction time	Subjects	Mean reaction time
No decrease auditory acuity—no depression.............	11	0.21	12	0.22
Decrease auditory acuity—no depression.................	7	.21	3	.26
No decrease auditory acuity—depression.................	8	.24	2	.30
Decrease auditory acuity—depression....................	0	....	2	.33
Total................................	26	....	19	....

Analysis of variance

Source	d.f.	F
Depressive trend	1	* 5.263
Auditory acuity decrease.................................	1	1.524
Interaction	1	*** 19.476

* Significant at the 0.05 level.
*** Significant at the 0.001 level.

speed. Decreased audition per se did not affect speed but interacted with health (group II), and especially depression, to reinforce slowing (table 9).

Obersteiner (1874) reported lengthened reaction times in psychotic patients, and Hunt and Cofer (1944) indicate that "all investigators agree that the average reaction time for every diagnostic group is larger than that for groups of normal individuals. Patients with 'organic' disorders apparently react more slowly than those with 'functional' disorders, but this can hardly be considered an established fact." Also, "Intra-individual variability, as measured by the standard deviation of reaction times from a single subject, is increased in all the diagnostic groups." Surprisingly it is difficult to find definitive studies of the relationship of reaction time to depression in younger people (Huston and Serf, 1952; Jastrow, 1892; Wells and Kelly, 1922–23).

Mechanisms underlying the relationship between speed and depression are still unknown. The question may be raised whether an increase in reaction time, as a reflection of central nervous change, predisposes to a depressive response. The occurrence of a relationship between depression and reaction time in the young would suggest that even if this were at times true, factors other than or in addition to "aging" are operating.

As a result of these interdisciplinary explorations, it is concluded that many more factors must be considered in the psychiatric evaluation of the elderly person than is often necessary in the young. Moreover, it is important to discover and recognize those factors which are not necessarily inevitably or unalterably part of the aging process but are subject to preventive and therapeutic measures.

RELATIONSHIPS WITH SOCIAL PSYCHOLOGICAL DATA

Marian R. Yarrow

The principal social psychological interests in the interdisciplinary explorations concerned (a) the influence of current environment upon functioning as reflected in the measures of physiology, psychology, and psychiatry, and (b) the associations between daily purposive behavior and the more molecular physiological, cognitive, and psychomotor measures and the psychiatric assessments. Environment was measured in terms of the availability of supports and the amount of loss suffered by the aged person in his personal environment, particularly losses of significant persons through deaths and separations. Assessments of daily functioning took into account the planful and goal-directed aspects of behavior, the general affective state of the individual and the nature of social interactions.

The significance of contemporaneous environmental deficits in the daily adaptations of these elderly men was emphasized in chapter 14. In the present analyses (table 10), a similar trend involving more functional relations was observed. Men who had sustained marked environmental loss tended toward less adequate functioning on tests of cognitive and psychomotor performance and on some of the psychiatric measures. Loss was unrelated to measures of cerebral physiology. Men characterized in psychiatric evaluations as manifesting depressive trends were more often those who had experienced severe contemporaneous losses. They were more likely to give self-reports emphasizing decreases with age. There is some circularity in the latter measurement since social factors were among the subjects' reported declines and gains. On the other side of the coin, psychiatric ratings of adaptability, i.e., the restitutive or compensatory processes in response to aging, related nega-

TABLE 10.—*Relationships with environmental deficit* [1]

	Environmental deficit		
	Group I ($N=27$)	Group II ($N=20$)	Total ($N=47$)
Psychiatric variables:			
Age-relevant checklist	0.25	0.32	* 0.28
Depressive trends	$t=-1.82$	* $t=-2.17$	* $t=-2.33$
MMPI Depression score	.14	.06	.10
Ratio of declines to total changes with age	.11	** .64	* .34
Adaptability	.16	** .59	* .36
Cognitive and psychomotor variables:			
Principal Component I (general intellective factor)	* −.43	−.19	* −.29
"Programming" score on projective tests	.39	.34	* .33
Principal component IV (mental speed timing)	* .42	.22	.31
Mean Reaction time	** .49	.30	** .35
Cerebral physiological variables:			
CBF	−.09	.05	−.02
$CMRO_2$	−.21	−.22	−.21
CVR	.06	.06	.02
VPO_2	.36	.24	.29
Glucose consumption	.08	.20	.14

[1] Product moment correlations are reported unless identified differently.

* Significant at the 0.05 level.
** Significant at the 0.01 level.

tively to environmental deficits. The dichotomous classification of Senile Quality was not related to loss, but the amount of deteriorative behavior as rated on the Age Relevant Checklist was associated with severity of environmental loss.

The relationships between cognitive and psychomotor capacities and the life situation of the aged subjects followed a similar pattern of association between poor functioning and deprived circumstances. An explanation of these associations may possibly lie in the relation between losses and the individual's affective state. The effect of losses upon cognitive and psychomotor behaviors may be mediated through the depressive state of the individual since losses are related to depressive trends and the latter are related to poorer scores on the general intellective factor and on tests involving speed of response (table 8). The correlations between environmental loss and slower reaction time and mental speed are consistent with the associations reported in chapter 14 between extreme environmental deficits and a generally lower order of functioning in daily behavior (more routine activity, less goal-directed behavior, more social withdrawal).

It is concluded that loss or disintegration of the group in which the individual's identity is rooted has consequences for the aged person, potentially influencing a very broad range of his behavior and motivations. Response to loss is not uniform from subject to subject, although the pattern of correlations yields a consistent picture of directional influence. At least two research issues are opened by these data: what are the bases of differences in ability to cope with losses in old age, and what kinds of substitutive environments are psychologically most sustaining for the aged.

The ability of the aged person to live independently, effectively, and with a sense of satisfaction is probably the ultimate objective of the elderly individual and of society. The routes by which this objective is achieved or by which the individual fails to achieve this objective are undoubtedly varied and involve multiple interdependencies. In interpreting associations between effective daily behavior and measures from other disciplines (table 11), the interactive effects of a number of variables in this study can be taken into account.

Effective daily functioning was related to cognitive and psychomotor test performance, better test scores being associated with more adequate functioning. The meaning of this relationship by itself is not clear. If, however, one regards decline in cognitive processes as reflective of disease (group II was significantly lower than group I, p. 149), less adequate daily functioning may be regarded as a consequence of disease, mediated by reduced cognitive functioning. The role of environmental deprivation, too, enters as a modifying condition in the association between cognitive performance and daily behavior. The effects of environmental deprivation (which is related to both cognition and daily behavior) must be mediated through some change in the organism, such as changed motivations. There is some evidence for depression as the mediating process (depression is related to environmental loss and to less adequate social functioning) (tables 10, 11).

The slowing of the older person, since it occurred equally in group I and group II subjects, may tentatively be regarded as a genetically based manifestation of senescence, though subject to the additive effects of disease, auditory loss, and depression and environmental deprivation. The present relationship between slowing and less adequate daily functioning may reflect an organism that for multiple reasons is less able to mobilize behavior effectively.

TABLE 11.—*Correlations of selected variables with the social functioning measure* [1]

	Social functioning		
	Group I (N=27)	Group II (N=20)	Total sample (N=47)
Psychiatric variables:			
Age-relevant checklist	0. 08	0. 34	0. 14
Depressive trend	$t=.30$ N.S.	$*t=-2.19$	$t=1.00$ N.S.
MMPI depression score	*. 44	*. 48	**. 45
Rates of declines to total changes with age	*. 45	**. 60	***. 51
Adaptability	. 23	**. 62	**. 40
Cognitive and psychomotor variables:			
Principal component I (general intellective factor)	*—. 40	—. 28	*—. 35
"Programming" score on projective tests	. 31	**. 59	**. 43
Principal component IV (mental speed timing)	. 29	. 34	*. 31
Mean reaction time	. 31	. 37	*. 34
Cerebral physiological variables:			
CBF	*—. 47	—. 22	*—. 38
$CMRO_2$	*—. 47	***—. 74	***—. 61
CVR	*. 44	. 30	*. 36
VPO_2	—. 02	. 45	. 23
Glucose consumption	*—. 44	—. 16	*—. 30

[1] Product moment correlations are reported unless identified differently.
  * Significant at the 0.05 level.
  ** Significant at the 0.01 level.
  *** Significant at the 0.001 level.

The appraisal of daily behavior was not related to psychiatric ratings of behavior signs stereotypically regarded as characteristic of old age (Age Relevant Checklist) or to ratings of Senile Quality. For example, two of the men rated Senile Quality were in neurophysiological respects not unlike hospitalized chronic brain syndrome cases. Yet, they were living independently and getting along reasonably well in the urban community. Diagnosis of lifelong personality pathology (kind of pathology varied) were not related to daily functioning. The man's self-image, as reported to the psychiatrists, as a person undergoing many declining changes was associated with poorer daily functioning. The latter finding may suggest that seeing oneself in the image of old age reinforces a tendency toward withdrawal. The association between daily behavior and psychiatric ratings of adaptations to age changes is primarily a measure of consistency between assessments from the points of view of two disciplines.

The predominant discrepancy between the appraisal of behavior which viewed the man in his social environment and the psychiatric appraisals which focused more upon pathology and mechanisms of adaptation points to the significant role of modifying factors which reduce relationships between senescent characteristics and the ability to function in a complex social environment. Again, one such modifying factor is the availability of a supportive environment. Interpersonal environmental factors may add to or lessen the difficulty of the man in coping with declines—memory losses, difficulties in concentration, etc. Hence, no high or direct relation appears between small or moderate declines and the ability to carry on effectively. Also, differing adjustments to old age undoubtedly depend upon long standing personality characteristics. The subjects of this study did not provide material for this kind of analysis except on a case study basis. As pointed out earlier (p. 185), while some lifelong personality tendencies made adjustment to old age more difficult (for example, the paranoid reaction), others, such as tendencies toward compulsivity and schizoid tendencies, were very effective in coping with problems in old age. Daily living, by the compulsive, was carried out with highly elaborated scheduling, systematic and detailed planning of activities. The schizoid types, with their general attitude of detachment, appeared to be more insulated from the effects of tragedies around them and to be more absorbed in philosophical introspections. In such instances, "pathology" would be compatible with good present functioning. The extent to which different personalities were represented in our sample would tend to reduce correlations between daily behavior and specific declining functions.

The presence of minimal disease in some of the subjects of this study was related to a variety of specific cerebral physiological and psychological measures. Consistent with this apparent influence of disease were the significant associations found between daily behavior and measures of cerebral blood flow, oxygen consumption, glucose utilization, and vascular resistance. Again the underlying mechanisms are obscure. It is possible that there is a close relation between central nervous systems and social functioning in the aged. One might expect that as social behavior represents highly integrative functions of the organism, these functions would be "damaged" when cerebral defects arise. However, the line of influence may be via the effects of cerebral physiology upon other processes which bear a more immediate relation to daily behavior. Replication of these findings would be extremely important in investiga-

tions with methods sensitive to the timing of multiple changes in the organism.

Of the biological and psychological processes and conditions of environment that have been tapped, none contributes so strongly in contrast to the others as to be considered the key or vital factor. The picture is, instead, one of factors reinforcing or cancelling out the effects of others in a manner far too complex to be neatly disentangled or to have relative contributions accurately weighted. One of the demands upon future research will be the clearer separation of the additive consequences of independent processes, as well as the identification of clusters of interacting variables.

Various health, environmental and personality factors may be limit-setting for the individual. Whether a variable exercises a limiting effect on the individual depends upon the intensity of the variable or a combination of variables and the individual characteristics of the host and his social environment. For example, for the isolated institutionalized aged a small increment in opportunities for social interaction may have a considerable influence upon the person. The same variable for healthy community-resident aged may have little effect. On the other hand, if older persons with optimum health and social psychological supports are studied, perhaps senescent changes will be seen more prominently.

From the literature and from the data of this study one discerns at least the influences of (1) environmental loss and deprivation, (2) disease, and (3) a genetically based pattern of senescent changes. These three factors interact with the physical and personality subtrate of the individual. How important particular influences appear depends not only on the sample of subjects, as has been pointed out, but also on the sample of measurements.

There was clear evidence in the present study for the role of disease and social deprivation on the social and psychological well-being of the individual. Degradation of behavior with advancing age, sometimes called "senility," within this study seems more the product of antecedents of disease and social deprivation than a genetically based pattern of senescence.

REFERENCES

ALPERS, B. J., FORSTER, F. M., and HERBUT, P. A. Retinal, cerebral, and systemic arteriosclerosis. A histopathologic study. *Arch. Neurol. and Psychiat.*, 440–456, *60*, 1948.

AMERICAN PSYCHIATRIC ASSOCIATION. *Mental Disorders, Diagnostic and Statistical Manual,* Washington, D.C., 1952.

BIRREN, J. E., RIEGEL, K. F., and MORRISON, D. F. Age differences in response speed as a function of controlled variations of stimulus conditions: evidence of a general speed factor. *Gerontologia,* 1–18, *6*, 1962.

BUTLER, R. N., DASTUR, D. K., LANE, M. H., PERLIN, S., and SOKOLOFF, L. Relationships of senile manifestations and chronic brain syndromes to cerebral circulation and metabolism. In preparation.

CHOWN, SHEILA, M. Age and the rigidities. *J. Gerontol.*, 353–362, *16*, 1961.

FREYHAN, F. A., WOODFORD, R. B., and KETY, S. S. Cerebral blood flow and metabolism in psychoses of senility. *J. Nerv. and Ment. Dis.*, 449–456, *113*, 1951.

HUNT, J. MC V. and COFER, C. N. Psychological deficit. In *Personality and the Behavior Disorders,* ch. 32, pp. 993–995, J. Mc V. Hunt, Ed. The Ronald Press, New York, 1944.

HUSTON, P. E., and SERF, RITA. Psychopathology of schizophrenia and depression. I. Effect of amytal and amphetamine sulfate on level and maintenance of attention. *Amer. J. Psychiat.,* 131–138, *109*, 1952.

JASTROW, J. Reaction-time in the sane. In *A Dictionary of Psychological Medicine*, p. 1069, D. H. Tuke, Ed. Blakiston, Son & Co., Philadelphia, 1892.

LASSEN, N. A. Cerebral blood flow and oxygen consumption in man. *Physiol. Rev.*, 133–238, *39*, 1959.

MCADAM, W., and ROBINSON, R. A. Senile intellectual deterioration and the electroencephalogram: a quantitative correlation. *J. Ment. Sci.,* 819–825, *102*, 1956.

OBRIST, W. D., BUSSE, E. W., and HENRY, C. E. Relation of electroencephalogram to blood pressure in elderly persons. *Neurology*, 151–158, *11*, 1961.

———, and HENRY, C. E. Electroencephalographic findings in aged psychiatric patients. *J. Nerv. and Ment. Dis.*, 254–267, *126*, 1958.

SILVERMAN, A. J., BUSSE, E. W., and BARNES, R. M. Studies in the process of aging: electroencephalographic findings in 400 elderly subjects. *EEG Clin. Neurophysiol.*, 67–74, *7*, 1955.

SOKOLOFF, L. The metabolism of the central nervous system in vivo. *Handbook of Physiology.* Vol. III, pp. 1843–1864, J. Field, Ed., Sect. I. Amer. Physiol. Soc. Washington, D.C., 1960.

WEINER, H., and SCHUSTER, D. B. The electroencephalogram in dementia. Some preliminary observations and correlations. *EEG Clin. Neurophysiol.*, 479–488, *8*, 1956.

WELLS, F. L., and KELLY, C. M. The simple reaction in psychosis. *Amer. J. Psychiat.*, 53–59, *2*, 1922–1923.

CHAPTER 16

Summary and Interpretations

by James E. Birren, Robert N. Butler,
Samuel W. Greenhouse, Louis Sokoloff,
and Marian R. Yarrow

The present studies were undertaken to observe the normal aging process in man, or at the least, an approximation thereof. Although this was not a longitudinal study, the major interest was in the effects of the passage of time or chronological aging. Factors of health were, therefore, of prime consideration. Numerous diseases occur with such frequency and are so closely associated with advancing age that they are not only difficult to distinguish from the effects of old age but are considered by many to represent an integral part of the aging process. For the purposes of the present studies, the optimistic attitude was adopted that pathological changes which are occasionally observed in younger individuals and which occur frequently but not uniformly in aged individuals of the species reflect the influence of disease rather than that of normal aging. If such extraneous factors could be eliminated, as one might hope will ultimately be accomplished by the advances of medical science, then one could examine the changes induced in the organism by aging per se. This was the philosophical point of view behind the design of the studies reported here. An effort was made, therefore, to obtain as healthy a group of aged individuals as was reasonably possible.

Health has been defined by the World Health Organization as "a state of complete physical, mental, and social well-being and not merely the absence of disease or infirmity" (WHO, 1946). Such a definition represents an ideal since measurements do not allow us to be sure when one is in a state of complete well-being. In order to approach this ideal these studies were limited to the relatively few subjects who met the rigorous health standards adopted for this project. Of an undetermined but large group of volunteers of elderly men functioning normally in their communities, all but a few were excluded on the basis of health criteria. Most were rejected on the basis of a simple medical history or preliminary medical examination in the field. The relatively few who were admitted to the National Institute of Mental Health were subjected to an extraordinarily comprehensive series of medical, laboratory, and X-ray examinations.

It became clear that to achieve the original ideal of acquiring a group of elderly subjects as healthy as can be obtained during young adulthood, an impractically large group of subjects would have to be screened. A compromise, more of principle than of substance, was made. Accepted subjects were classified into two groups: group I consisted of those individuals without any observed evidence of disease, or questionable evidence of minimal disease, or definite evidence of truly trivial disease (i.e., partial deafness, cataracts, varicose veins, benign prostatic hypertrophy); group II subjects were characterized by definite evidence of diseases having more serious implications but of such minimal degree as to be asymptomatic and, perhaps, unlikely to be revealed by routine medical examinations less comprehensive than those employed in these studies.

Although methods of medical examination are still insufficiently precise and the need for subjective evaluation is still great, there is little reason to doubt that the rigorous selection process used here resulted in a group of elderly men remarkably free from disease. This freedom from disease was not only from types deemed likely to affect the nervous system but from all types. Similarly, even allowing for possible overlap, there is little doubt that group I as a whole was healthier than group II, particularly in regard to vascular disease. The results of the research lend support to the validity of the medical classification, for in numerous areas group I differed little if at all from healthy young subjects and surpassed the levels of group II subjects whose functions were more closely in accord with those previously reported in the literature for presumably healthy old men.

Comprehensive medical studies of groups I and II subjects in comparison with healthy young control subjects revealed few significant age-specific differences in quantitative variables. One notable exception was the decreased serum albumin with advancing age, which may be a promising lead in studying the fundamental biological processes of aging. Data on pulmonary function, on the other hand, illustrate the interaction between aging and disease.

The existence of survival characteristics in this population are suggested by several provocative findings: increased blood pressure in the presence of arteriosclerosis, reflecting increased cardiac work; the lack of differences between smokers and nonsmokers in a wide spectrum of physiological measurements; the unusually high incidence of chronic smokers, and the elevated serum cholesterol levels correlating neither with age nor manifest disease.

Studies of the cerebral circulation and metabolism failed to confirm any relationships between these functions and chronological age or duration of life per se. In the optimally healthy elderly subjects (group I), cerebral blood flow and oxygen consumption did not differ significantly from the values observed in a group of normal young subjects approximately five decades younger (mean age=21 years). In the elderly men in group II, who differed from those of group I only in that they exhibited clear evidence of mild asymptomatic disease, chiefly vascular in type, there was a statistically significant decline in cerebral blood flow of approximately 10 to 16 percent. Cerebral oxygen consumption also tended to be reduced but not to a statistically significant degree. All the changes in cerebral circulation and oxygen utilization in group II could be accounted for by the results obtained in the arteriosclerosis subjects within that group. Hypertensive subjects without arteriosclerosis were normal with regard to these functions. Cerebral venous oxygen tension, which reflects the oxygen tension in the cerebral tissues, tended to be lower in all the aged subjects, but only in the arteriosclerotic subjects was the decline sufficient to be statistically significant.

This finding suggests the existence of cerebral circulatory insufficiency and hypoxia even in the presence of such minimal degrees of arteriosclerosis. In fact, the reductions in cerebral blood flow and cerebral venous oxygen tension in the arteriosclerotic subjects were essentially the same as those observed in a group of hospitalized patients with chronic brain syndrome and psychosis;

the only difference between these groups was the significant reduction in cerebral oxygen consumption in the patients with chronic brain syndrome. When looked at in their entirety, these results suggest that decreases in cerebral blood flow and oxygen consumption are not the consequences of chronological aging per se but rather of arteriosclerosis which causes first a relative cerebral circulatory insufficiency and hypoxia and then ultimately, perhaps, after secondary tissue damage ensues, a reduction in cerebral metabolic rate.

One puzzling observation is worthy of further consideration. Although cerebral oxygen consumption was not significantly altered in the elderly subjects of group I or group II, cerebral glucose utilization was significantly reduced in both. Except in hypoglycemia the rate of cerebral oxygen consumption and glucose utilization always vary together, and it would indeed be surprising if the far less precise measurement of glucose utilization would be the more sensitive indicator of a change in cerebral metabolic rate with age. Normally, a slightly greater amount of glucose is utilized by the brain than can be accounted for by the cerebral oxygen consumption, assuming the complete oxidation of the glucose to carbon dioxide and water. The fate of the excess glucose is still unknown. It is possible that there is in the aged a subtle change in cerebral metabolism which involves the pathways of this extra glucose utilization and is, therefore, not reflected in the oxygen metabolism of the brain. Further speculation about this possibility is, however, unwarranted until the finding of the divergence between cerebral oxygen consumption and glucose utilization in the aged is confirmed by other studies.

In contrast to the cerebral circulatory and metabolic findings, the EEG differed significantly from young adults, not only in the asymptomatic disease group (group II) but even in the healthy subjects (group I). The changes were chiefly a shift to slower activities in the frequency spectrum. Thus the mean peak frequency in group I was 9 cps., a full cycle slower than previously observed in young adults, and the entire spectrum, especially the major frequencies, appeared to have shifted to the slow side. The changes in the subjects in group II were essentially of the same type but to a somewhat greater degree. For example, 8 cycle activity was statistically significantly greater and individual peak frequencies significantly slower in group II than in group I. The arteriosclerotic subjects within group II revealed similar, slightly more significant trends. The incidence of clinically normal EEGs in both groups was 81 percent, which is comparable to figures reported for young adults. In contract to previous aging studies, only 9 percent of the subjects exhibited temporal lobe foci. There were no differences between groups I and II with respect to incidence or type of abnormality.

The EEG findings in these studies suggest that the electrical activity of the brain undergoes change with age, regardless of whether detectable physical disease is present or not. It is difficult to interpret the age changes in the EEG, since features of the EEG are not highly correlated with other variables. Health status, particularly cardiovascular disease, is however, an important factor influencing brain potentials.

Intercorrelations among the medical, cerebral circulatory, metabolic, and EEG variables revealed few statistically significant correlations not attributable to chance and contributed little of substantive value to the understanding of the nature of the relationships among these variables. There was suggestive evidence that the presence of disease enhanced the significance of these intercorrelations which indicated that these variables were not directly related to each other but varied in a deteriorative direction together when pathological processes were present. One significant correlation tended to confirm previous observations in the literature; namely, a negative relationship between blood pressure and percent slow EEG activity in group II but not in group I. This finding suggests that increased blood pressure exerts a protective effect on the electrical activity of the brain when vascular disease is present.

When the results of the cerebral circulatory and metabolic and the EEG studies are examined as a whole, they suggest that the brain does undergo change as a consequence of chronological aging per se, more clearly manifested in its electrical activity than in its circulation and metabolism. However, when arteriosclerosis is present, the pathological change in the vascular system becomes the pacemaker of the decline in functions of the brain with age.

In cognitive and psychomotor processes, elderly men selected for good health were shown to function more adequately than men unselected for health. One may be impressed by the results showing a considerable independence of the intellectual and perceptual measurements from the physiological measurements in the total group of these relatively healthy elderly men. One may note however, that there was a significantly larger number of significant cognitive-physiological correlations in group II, the somewhat less healthy subjects, than in group I. This suggests that moderate disease of the sort found in certain of the present subjects results in an increased dependency of psychological capacities upon physiological status.

Two major contrasting findings were obtained in the mental test data with regard to health and age. In verbal intelligence the present subjects were significantly superior to young adults, whereas several perceptual or psychomotor measures showed significantly lower performance than would be expected of a group of young adults. Verbal abilities were related to health differences, the less healthy subjects were significantly lower than group I subjects. This led to the view that the less healthy subjects had lost some superiority from a previously higher level of verbal achievement as a consequence of disease. In group II, the correlation between the general intellective factor, which embraces verbal ability, and the cerebral metabolic rate $CMRO_2$ was 0.55. Further, the correlation between a simple summation of 23 cognitive and psychomotor measurements with the $CMRO_2$ was 0.68 in group II, whereas in both of these instances the correlation in group I was not significantly different from zero; i.e., 0.01 and -0.03, respectively.

Both groups of subjects showed the reduced auditory acuity for high frequencies previously found as characteristic of late life. By contrast, two-click discrimination was the same in group I as in young subjects but was less acute in group II. Absolute judgment of the number of clicks in a train or series of clicks differed with age but not between groups I and II. The span for recall of digits presented to one ear was to some extent age related, but the age difference in recall of simultaneously presented series of digits to the two ears was larger. The aged appear to have more difficulty in simultaneously monitoring two auditory channels compared with monitoring a single channel. The disruption of speech by delayed speech feedback showed little or no relation with age. These auditory and auditory memory measurements thus show a differential pattern with respect to age and health perhaps reflecting to different extents peripheral and central influences of disease and aging. Analysis of the correlation of auditory acuity and reaction time suggests that there may be a common element beyond that correlation which might be expected to arise from interference with the hearing of a stimulus to which a response is to be made.

When the psychomotor speed of the healthy (group I) and less healthy (group II) were compared it was found that the two groups did not differ although both groups were significantly slower than young adults. The inference may be drawn from this pattern of age and health related differences that a large part of the presumed intellectual changes (loss of stored information) is the result of cortical damage or loss of neurons associated with vascular impairment of cerebral circulation, with consequent hypoxia and reduced metabolism. However, the slowing of behavior with age requires a different interpretation.

It is significant that the psychomotor slowing was not related to a particular sensory modality; responses were slow to both auditory and visual stimuli. Furthermore, the slowing was not a function of the particular muscle groups; finger, jaw, foot, and speech reactions have all been shown to be involved. Also, both simple and complex sensory stimuli evoked slower responses in the older subject; complex stimuli involving most associative activity were responded to the most slowly. Recent work supports the view that the speed of response in the aged has more of the character of a general process than in young subjects, thus the slowing is not likely the consequence of damages to limited areas of the cerebral cortex. While relatively simple reflexes may be slower with advanced age, the differences in time are small compared with the time differences found in voluntary activity. While the psychomotor slowing and the segmented nature of psychomotor performance shown

by some aged individuals could conceivably result from loss of cells in the cerebellum, this does not appear to be a sufficient explanation. The reason is that so many kinds of behavior, such as verbal associations and mental arithmetic, show a slowing with age, implying longer latencies in the nonmotor components of mental or psychomotor skills. Evidence for a widespread simultaneous slowing of perceptual, associative and psychomotor functions gives rise to the suggestion that there is associated with advancing age a lowering of subliminal cortical excitation. Such a phenomenon might have been viewed as a result of reduced cerebral metabolic rate were it not for the fact that the present results showed little change in mean cerebral metabolic rate and also that slowing was equal in the healthy and less healthy aged subjects. A diffuse lowering of cortical excitability with age might arise from a lowering of activity of the brain stem reticular formation. Such a change in the brain stem could be a normal accompaniment of aging or in turn could result from a local reduction in blood flow and subsequently in metabolism; since the tissue volume is small, the changes might not be sufficiently large to be reflected in total blood flow or metabolic rate. It appears conservative to expect that further research will show changes of a punctate or specific character occurring with age as a consequence of local changes in specialized cells and cellular organizations and perhaps having rather special vulnerabilities.

These oversimplified views must be qualified in the face of present evidence even before the expected particularization which will come about by additional work. For one thing, the reaction time measurements were found to be related to the severity of environmental deficits as well as to depressive trends. Because of the widespread observation of psychomotor slowing with age, including lower mammals, it seems necessary to regard the slowing as occurring independent of any personality disposition or environmental loss but modulated or potentiated by such factors. The correlation between reaction time and blood pressure adds a further element in a group of relations that appear with advancing age between disease, environmental changes or losses, personality dispositions, and the regulation of behavior and physiological functions by the nervous system. The interrelations with age of short term memory, attention and the generalized slowing of behavior would appear to be a fruitful basic behavioral area to be investigated in a context of physiological and behavioral measurements.

Compared with the prevailing medical and psychiatric view of the aged, both social psychological and psychiatric interview evaluation revealed these men as a whole to be vigorous, candid, interesting, and deeply involved in everyday living. In marked contradiction to the usual stereotypes of "rigidity" and of "second childhood," these individuals generally demonstrated mental flexibility and alertness. They continued to be constructive in their living; they were resourceful and optimistic. The group was not uniform, however. Some individuals showed maladaptive patterns of withdrawal and depression. Some showed evidence of mental decline.

The healthy aged were found to have disorders, evolving from personality and life experience, which appear similar to those affecting the young. These disorders, including depression, do not seem to be dependent upon either cerebrovascular disease, insofar as present methods can detect it, or chronological age, per se. Nor did educational and occupational background relate to measured patterns of attitudes and behavior in this group, which included a wide range of background characteristics.

Factors of the immediate social psychological environment, however, were found to be very closely related to the aged person's behavior and attitudes. As the environment showed qualities of deprivation or displacement of the person (in loss of intimate persons, loss of income, in cultural displacement), the attitudes and behaviors of the aged showed more deteriorative qualities. Losses of significant persons were especially associated with deteriorative functioning. All the men described changes with advancing age including social psychological, physical, personality-affective, and cognitive changes. Such changes were not uniformly viewed as losses or unalterable. Adaptations to changes ranged from acceptance of physical decreases to compensations for social psychological losses; maladaptions ranged from depressive withdrawal to paranoid isolation.

The importance of the individual's personality in determining the nature of his response to losses and disruptions was apparent. Effective use of insight, involving accurate perception of the changed circumstances of old age and appropriate behavioral modification, was a comman occurrence. Other adaptive patterns included the use of activity to the extent of extreme counterphobic maneuvers in which the aged person undertook excessive, at times personally dangerous, activities to demonstrate his youthfulness, his prowess, and his fearlessness before aging and death. Denial of aging changes was found to be a useful reparative measure against depression.

It was of considerable interest that psychiatrically evaluated depression was significantly associated with mean reaction time. This finding is consonant with most writings reporting relationships between depression and psychomotor and physiological retardation. However, there was no relationship between depression and cerebral circulatory, metabolic, or electrical measurements. High mean blood pressure, decreased audition, and environmental deprivation also interacted and significantly correlated with mean reaction time. Therefore, the important question arises as to the extent to which the psychomotor slowing in older persons can be explained solely as a consequence of aging of the central nervous system.

In some of the subjects, early manifestations of mental decline, referred to as Senile Quality, were observed. These characteristics involved intellectual functions and feelings, namely, decreased comprehension, memory, attention and set, and reduced emotional responsiveness. The mean chronological age was not significantly different for the Senile Quality and the normal aging individuals.

There is some evidence to support the belief that cerebral arteriosclerosis with consequent reduction in cerebral blood flow and oxygen consumption is one pathway in the formation of manifestations of senility, perhaps prodromal to the development of the organic brain disorder. However, senile manifestations could not be totally explained in this way. There were individuals with early senile manifestations who did not have diagnosed atherosclerosis or evidence of cerebral circulatory or metabolic changes. We are left with the realization that both senility and atherosclerosis are fairly common occurrences in old age and that they may not, in fact, bear any essential pathogenic relationship to each other. It would seem reasonable to conclude, however, that when atherosclerosis does occur with sufficient intensity, cerebral circulation and metabolism are affected and senile manifestations may be produced. Other antecedents and correlates of senility may include social psychological and other experiential phenomena.

The relation between reductions in cerebral circulation and metabolism and poorer day-to-day functioning registers another link between disease state and the picture of aging. The correlations between cerebral physiology and behavior may not reflect a direct influence of one on the other. One might hypothesize that as cerebral defects develop, a number of functions (cognitive, perceptual and others) are affected which more directly affect the aged person.

Continued clarification of the many factors contributing to the manifest picture of aging is important for research, prevention, and treatment. Since it is reasonable to suppose that effects intrinsic to aging are less likely to be subject to modification than are the causes and effects of morbid states, it is important to recognize those factors which are presently or potentially subject to intervention. Arteriosclerosis, slowing in psychomotor speed, and deteriorative aspects of the social environment were particularly prominent factors in this study in the interdependencies among variables. Their importance merits further study.

When one is faced with the broad range of behavioral and neural changes of aging, it is difficult to keep the details in balanced emphasis. In discussing the present results one would like to retain the surety surrounding the study of isolated variables, yet there is equally the scientific motivation to consider the survival and behavior of the organism as an integrated phenomenon. The interrelatedness of the manifestations of aging remains a tentative matter, yet certain features of this study stand out with implications for the future population of older persons and for research. It is apparent that if individuals retain their health with advancing age they are remarkably "young." Disease appears to impress its effects upon the organism in diffuse ways not properly viewed as the result of aging in the sense of the unfolding of a genetic pattern of change characteristic of the species. With the promise of medical advances in the control of the now common metabolic diseases of later life, more individuals will be seen who are old in years but functionally young by present standards. Implied in this optimistic picture of a healthy, better educated future aged population is the need for increased study of interpersonal relations and the environmental elements in optimum personality development over the life span. There will be a greater need for understanding of the social psychological variables in human adaptability in proportion to the advances in control of disease.

With the anticipated increased control of now prevalent diseases, particularly vascular, specific brain syndromes and functional disorders will be approached with greater specificity of research.

In the results there were a number of changes which appeared to be related to age rather than to differences in health. Such changes could be the result of changes in the central nervous system not the consequences of or dependent upon generally recognized systemic disease but inherent in the rather specialized nature of brain tissue and its organization. Furthermore, findings of this study lead to the suspicion that psychological reactions to the loss of friends and other environmental supports may amplify if not initiate changes in the older nervous system and thereby the rest of the organism. While it is easy to express the view that the involution of the older nervous system may be advanced or retarded by nonphysical-chemical variables, its demonstration remains for future research. Such matters can be pursued more effectively as we obtain a clearer picture of the aging nervous system within itself and in relation to the rest of the organism and its social environment. The behavioral and neural changes of aging remain a provocative set of relations to study.

REFERENCE

WORLD HEALTH ORGANIZATION. Constitution of the World Health Organization. Public Health Reports 1268–77, *61,* 1946.

Index of Names

Subject Index

Activities, leisure, 265
Adaptation:
    case illustrations, 180–3;
    cerebral physiology, 294–5;
    defined, 177;
    E.E.G., 294–5;
    high-low, 179;
    individual, 211–2;
    ratings, 202–3;
    senile quality, 183
Adaptive patterns:
    counterphobia, 175–6, 178–9;
    denial of aging, 175–6, 178–9, 183;
    individual, 211–2;
    insight, 176;
    psychopathology, value of, 175–6, 178–9
Addition rate:
    age differences, 103;
    description, 100–1;
    results, 104
Age, correlations within sample, 284–5
Age related checklist, 200, 284
Aging, defined, 1
Albumin, serum, 22, 40–1;
    age correlation, 40–1
Alpha 1 globulin, serum, 22, 40–1;
    age correlation, 41
Alpha 2 globulin, serum, 22, 40–1
Arithmetic alternation rate:
    description, 101;
    results, 104
Arteriosclerosis, role of, 310
Arteriovenous glucose difference:
    age effects, 62, 64;
    chronic brain syndrome, 69;
    disease effects, 65, 67;
    vascular disease, 68–9
Arteriovenous oxygen difference:
    age effects, 62, 64;
    chronic brain syndrome, 67, 69;
    disease effects, 65, 67;
    vascular disease, 68–9
Audiogram, 113–5
Audition:
    click perception, 115–22;
    delayed speech feedback, 132–6;
    depression, 300;
    diotic and dichotic digit spans, 122–32;
    discussion of results, 137–8;
    frequency sensitivity, 113–5;
    group differences, 113–5;
    intercorrelations, 134, 136–7

Auditory perception, defined, 111
Background of study, 1–3
Basal metabolic rate, psychological correlates, 290–1
Behavioral changes in aged, possible basis for, 315
Beta 1 and 2 globulin, serum, 22, 40–1;
    age correlation, 41
Blood CO_2 tension:
    age effects, 63;
    chronic brain syndrome, 71;
    disease effects, 66–7;
    pulmonary function, 48;
    vascular disease, 67, 70–1
Blood CO_2 content:
    age effects, 63;
    chronic brain syndrome, 71;
    disease effects, 66;
    vascular disease, 67, 70–1
Blood glucose concentration:
    age effects, 63;
    chronic brain syndrome, 71;
    disease effects, 66;
    psychological correlates, 290–1;
    vascular disease, 67, 70–1
Blood oxygen content:
    age effects, 63;
    chronic brain syndrome, 71;
    disease effects, 66;
    psychological correlates, 290–1;
    vascular disease, 67, 70–1
Blood oxygen saturation:
    age effects, 63, 284;
    chronic brain syndrome, 71;
    disease effects, 66–7;
    pulmonary function, 48;
    smoking, 49;
    vascular disease, 67, 70–1
Blood oxygen tension, cerebral venous:
    age effects, 62, 64, 72–3;
    chronic brain syndrome, 67, 69;
    disease effects, 65, 67, 72–3;
    pulmonary function, 48;
    vascular disease, 45–6, 67–9, 72–3
Blood pH:
    age effects, 63;
    chronic brain syndrome, 71;
    disease effects, 66;
    vascular disease, 67, 70–1
Blood pressure, 24, 42–4;
    cerebral blood flow, 42–4;
    depression, 44;
    E.E.G., 43, 287;
    smoking, 49;
    psychological correlates, 290–1

Breathing capacity, maximum, 23, 46–7;
    age correlation, 284;
    psychological correlates, 290–1;
    smoking, 49
Card sorting speed, description, 100;
    results, 104
Cerebral blood flow:
    age effects, 62, 64, 72–3;
    blood pressure, 42–4;
    cerebral vasculature calcification, 45–6;
    chronic brain syndrome, 67, 69;
    correlation with E.E.G. findings, 286–8;
    correlations with medical findings, 285–6;
    correlations with psychiatric variables, 295;
    disease effects, 65, 67, 72–3;
    environmental deficit, 301;
    psychological correlates, 290–1;
    retinal blood vessels, 44–5;
    smoking, 49;
    social functioning, 303
Cerebral circulation, refs., 59;
    discussion, 72–4;
    methods, 60–1;
    psychiatry, correlation, 294–5
Cerebral circulatory insufficiency, 310
Cerebral glucose utilization:
    age effects, 62, 64, 73–4;
    chronic brain syndrome, 69;
    correlation with E.E.G., 288;
    correlation with psychiatric variables, 295;
    disease effects, 65, 67;
    environmental deficit, 301;
    psychological correlates, 290–1;
    social functioning, 303;
    vascular disease, 68–9
Cerebral oxygen consumption, 310–1;
    age effects, 62, 64, 72–3, 284;
    chronic brain syndrome, 67, 69, 73;
    correlation with E.E.G. findings, 286–8;
    correlation with medical findings, 285–6;
    correlation with psychiatric variables, 295–29;
    discussion, 72–4;
    disease effects, 65, 67, 72–3;
    environmental deficit, 301;
    methods, 60–1;
    senile quality, 297;
    smoking, 49;
    social functioning, 303;
    vascular disease, 67–69
Cerebral physiology, adaptation, 294–5;
    relations to social functioning, 303–4
Cerebral R. Q.:
    age effects, 62, 64;
    chronic brain syndrome, 69;
    disease effects, 65, 67;
    vascular disease, 68–9
Cerebral vascular resistance:
    age effects, 62, 69, 284;
    cerebral vascular calcification, 456;
    chronic brain syndrome, 69;

Cerebral vascular resistance—Continued
    correlation with E.E.G., 288;
    correlation with psychiatric variables, **295**;
    disease effects, 65, 67;
    environmental deficit, **301**;
    psychological correlates, 290–1;
    social functioning, 303;
    vascular disease, 67–9
Cerebral vasculature, calcification, 45–6;
    cerebral blood flow, 45–6;
    cerebral vascular resistance, **45–6**;
    venous oxygen tension, 45–6
Changes, self reported, 169–72;
    reactions, 171–2, 174;
    significance, 186;
    social functioning correlation, 303;
    types, 169–1, 173, 209–10
Cholesterol, total, serum, 22, 39–0;
    age correlation, 40;
    psychological correlates, 290–1;
    smoking, 49
Chronic brain syndrome:
    blood constituents, 67, 69, 71;
    cerebral circulation and metabolism, **67, 69,**
        71, 294, 296–7;
    diagnosis, 169;
    discussion of effects, 73
Click perception, 115–22;
    response time, 120, 122;
    threshold, 116
Cognitive organization, 97–8
Communication, projective tests, 217–8
Computer utilization, 31–2
Concept evaluation, methods, 195–8
Concept formation, see principal component V
Copy Speed Test:
    age differences, 103;
    depression, 298;
    description, 101;
    results, 104;
    senile quality, 298
Counterphobia, 175–6
Creatinine, serum, 22, 39–40
Current living:
    groups I, II, differences, 272;
    quality of, 272
Daily functioning, 271–6:
    adequacy in, 272;
    ages of persons in immediate environment, 275;
    cerebral physiological variables, 302–4;
    cognitive and psychomotor variables, 302–4;
    degree of disease. 304;
    economic deprivation, 275;
    educational background, 273;
    environmental deficits, 275–6, 303;
    ethnic background, 272–3;
    occupational status, 273;
    past commitment to work, 273–4;
    personality characteristics, 303–4;
    physical health, 272;

Maladaptive patterns, 176–7:
   exacerbation of psychopathology, 176–9;
   identity crisis, 176–9;
   individual, 211–2;
   new psychopathology, 176–9;
   psychological isolation, 176–9
Mean arterial blood pressure:
   age effects, 62, 64, 284;
   chronic brain syndrome, 69;
   correlation with E.E.G., 288;
   disease effects, 65, 67;
   E.E.G., 288;
   smoking, 49;
   vascular disease, 67, 68, 69
Mean cerebral venous pressure:
   age effects, 62, 64;
   chronic brain syndrome, 69;
   disease effects, 65, 67;
   vascular disease, 68, 69
Medical criteria, 15–6:
   arteriosclerotic subgroup, 37–8;
   findings in group I, 15;
   findings in group II, 17
Medical evaluation:
   blood pressure, 24;
   electrocardiograms, 23;
   height and weight, 23;
   hematological, 21–2;
   history, 20–1;
   methods, 18–9;
   neurological examination, 21;
   physical examination, 21;
   pulmonary function, 23;
   schedule, 19–20;
   urine, 21;
   X-rays, 23
Memory, physiological relations, 295;
Mental status, methods, 193–5, 201, 213;
Mill Hill Test:
   depression, 298;
   senile quality, 298
Mirror Tracing, description, 102:
   age trend, 106;
   results, 104
MMPI:
   adaptability, 299;
   correlation with environmental deficit, 301;
   depression, 256, 294, 299;
   group, I, II, differences, 254–6;
   memory, 299;
   method of administering, 253;
   morale, 299;
   profile, 255;
   scale description, 253;
   senile quality, 299
Morale, 177–183:
   cerebral physiology, 294–5;
   E.E.G., 294–5;
   individual, 211–2
Multidisciplinary research, problems, 33–4;

National Association of Retired Civil Service Employees, 7, 13;
Perception:
   central and peripheral factors, 111–2
Perception of Line Difference Test, description, 101:
   age difference in speed, 103;
   results, 104
Principal components:
   analysis, 146;
   correlation, 149;
   group differences, 149;
   interpretations, 150–3;
   measures, 147;
   subject scores, 148
Principal component I (general factor, verbal achievement), 289–92:
   age correlation, 284;
   cerebral physiological correlations, 290;
   E.E.G., correlations, 290;
   environmental deficit, 301;
   medical variables, correlations, 290;
   psychiatric correlations, 299;
   social functioning, 303
Principal component II, enumeration:
   physiological correlations, 290
Principal component III, flexibility of set:
   physiological correlations, 290
Principal component IV, speed:
   physiological correlations, 290;
   psychiatric correlations, 299;
   social functioning, 303
Principal component V, concept formation:
   age correlations, 284;
   physiological correlations, 291
Projective ratings:
   adaptability, 299;
   age correlation, 284;
   depression, 299;
   environmental deficit, 301;
   memory, 299;
   morale, 299;
   senile quality, 299
Protein-bound iodine serum, 22, 39–42:
   age correlations, 42, 284;
   psychological correlates, 290–1
Proverbs, selections, 222, 246:
   correlation with, Weigl, Homonyms, 233;
   group I, II, differences, 225
   rating of, 232–3;
   senile quality, 227
Psychiatric view of aged, 314;
Psychiatry:
   adaptive patterns, 172–83, 178–9;
   case illustrations, 180–3;
   diagnosis, 162–4, 180–3, 204–5;
   E.E.G., 294–5;
   impairments, cognitive, 169, 206–8;
   individual, 204–5;
   interview, 193–8

Psychiatry—Continued
  maladaptive patterns, 176–7, 178–9;
  methods, 161–2; 193–203;
  methods of aging, literature, 159–60;
  psychopathology, 162–4, 180–3, 204–5;
  reaction to change, 169–72;
  representativeness of sample, 184;
  senile manifestations, 164–9;
  social functioning, 303
Psychopathology:
  age factor, 163, 169, 186;
  physiological correlates, 297;
  value of, 175–6
Psychological data reduction, 98–9;
Psychological factors, background, 97–8;
Psychological measurements:
  intercorrelations, variables, 144–6;
  interpretation of results, 106–7;
  list, 99;
  principal component analysis, 146–50;
  relation to health, 106
Psychological measures, see principal components, tests;
Psychological performance: physiological correlates, 289–93:
  health, 312
Psychological testing of aged, methods, 218–9;
Psychological test performance:
  age differences, interpretations, 153–5;
  groups I and II, 102–4
Psychomotor speed, age, 312;
Psychophysiological relations:
  group I and II, 289
Pulmonary function:
  clinical status, 45–6;
  correlations, 49;
  CO_2 tension, 48;
  hemoglobin, 48;
  maximum breathing capacity, 23, 46;
  methodology, 46;
  oxygen saturation, 48;
  pH, 48
Pulse pressure, see blood pressure;
Pulse rate: smoking, 49:
  psychological correlates, 290–1
Ratings, of behavior at institute, 262:
  environmental deficits, 275
Raven Progressive Matrices Test, description, 99–100:
  age deficit, 103;
  depression, 298;
  results, 104;
  senile quality, 298
Reaction time:
  adaptability, 299;
  age differences, 103–6;
  audition, 300;
  depression, 298–300;
  environmental deficit, 301;
  measurements, 101–2;

Reaction time—Continued
  memory, 299;
  morale, 299;
  results, 104;
  senile quality, 298–9;
  social functioning, 303
Retinal vasculature:
  blood pressure, 44–5;
  cerebral blood flow, 44–5;
  cerebral vascular resistance, 44–5;
  funduscopic findings, 44–5
Retirement:
  types of, 264
Retiring, social process of, 263–5;
Right bundle branch block, 51–2;
Rorschach Test, description, 223–4;
  group I, II, differences 225;
  scores, 235, 239;
  senile quality, 234
Sample, see subjects;
Self-reports and those of others, 278–9;
Senile manifestations, basis for, 315;
Senile quality, 164–9, 229–30:
  adaptation, 183;
  case illustration, 182;
  characteristics, 168;
  cognitive functioning, 315;
  Draw-a-Person Score, 226–8;
  Homonyms, 226, 228, 232;
  Level of Aspiration, 226–8;
  Personality Test Variables, 224–6;
  Proverbs, 227, 233;
  Rorschach, 227, 234;
  Sentence Completion, 227, 233;
  Sum of Ratings, 226, 228;
  Tests, 167;
  Thematic Apperception Test, 227, 229;
  Weigl, 227, 233
Senile quality correlations:
  arteriosclerosis, 294, 296;
  cerebral physiology, 294–7;
  medicine, 294;
  Tests, 298
Sentence Completion Test, description, 222–3, 247–9:
  group I, II, differences, 225;
  senile quality, 227, 233;
  subject scores, 239
Smoking, chronic:
  physiological correlates, 48–50
Social environment effects on functioning, 314;
Social environment: nature of, 259–261:
  old age and childhood, 261
Social functioning, see daily functioning;
Social psychological changes, discussion, 276–9;
Social psychological data:
  collection and analysis, 262–3
Social psychological variables, summary, 276–9;
Social relationships, 266–7:
  group I, II, differences, 266

BIOMEDICAL and BEHAVIORAL CHARACTERISTICS – PART II

CHAPTER 1

Introduction

by Samuel Granick and Robert D. Patterson

If our society is to contribute to a healthy and dignified old age, we will need to understand better than we do today the effects of the thousands of variables that act upon man as he moves through the trajectory of his life cycle.

One of the original objectives of this project was to seek a way of exploring and defining "normal human aging." The investigators chose an approach to the problem which would control to a significant extent the variables of medical and mental disease since these states may obscure and distort the nature and quality of the normal aging processes. The results of the first phase of this investigation of the biological and behavioral functioning of a group of elderly individuals who were living in the community, free of significant physical and mental pathology, are described and discussed in the volume entitled *Human Aging: A Biological and Behavioral Study* (Birren et al., 1963).

The study has now become a longitudinal one. The initially healthy men have been followed as they moved from an average age of 71 to 81 years. The average followup interval was 11.1 years. The significantly greater-than-expected survival rate and high level of emotional health observed were confirmatory of the Roman adage *mens sana in corpore sano*.

There is a mild "population explosion" of the elderly, in both absolute and relative terms. By the year 2000 there may be 30 million people over 65. Furthermore, if disease prevention advances as have other areas of medicine in recent decades, the aged of the future may be functionally healthier than today's aged—indeed more like the men in this study.

Our results may, accordingly, provide some insight into what the future aged population may be in a position to do with their time and energy. It might not be too utopian to anticipate that our social structure could move to provide means and opportunities for individuals to be able to live and function constructively, happily, and dynamically during the latter decades of their lives.

AIMS AND PERSPECTIVES

Original Investigation

The aim of the first phase of the study was to describe as fully as possible the aging process by studying individuals who were free of physical disease and major psychological disability. The plan was analogous to obtaining a pure culture in bacteriology in order to discover its unique characteristics free of extraneous elements.

As might be expected, this orientation was the product of an earlier evolution of a few investigators' interests. It evolved from questions which were raised about the relationships between cerebral physiological changes and their mental and behavioral correlates. Considerations of the state of scientific knowledge in these areas at the time led to the realization that research in aging had focussed mainly on limited aspects of the human organism. Only minor attention had "been given to matters of congruence and dependencies of the simultaneous changes in individuals as they grow older. Systems of integration and control in aging, whether at the biochemical, psychological, or social level, have yet to be elucidated by research." (Birren et al., 1963.) A determination soon developed to study how aging manifests itself in the whole person. The undertaking thus became broadly interdisciplinary, combining the efforts of 22 investigators and their coworkers. The areas represented included the following: medicine, cerebral physiology, electroencephalography, audiology, psychology (cognitive, psychomotor, and personality), social psychology, and psychiatry. Each specialty was encouraged to pursue its own questions with respect to the functioning of the aged individual.

A basic aim was that the disciplines interrelate so that the data could be presented both in the context of specialty areas and in the context of the other aspects of the organism's functioning. A major part of the group effort was directed toward the blending of the data to produce concepts and sharpen issues which might help define the nature and process of normal aging. This was a team effort in the best sense of the word: for 5 years during the first phase a continuous research seminar was conducted to explore the directions and implications of the data and prepare an interdisciplinary report.

The project began in 1955 as an intramural activity of the National Institute of Mental Health (NIMH), in Bethesda, Md. This provided effective financial support, adequate space, equipment, and personnel. Virtually all of the investigators were employed at NIMH, thus facilitating communication, cooperation, and integration in their efforts.

Followup

The reports of the original investigation do not suggest that it was planned as a longitudinal study. However, it became a longitudinal study in 1961–62 when a 5-year followup was conducted, before the major report of the first phase was published. Subjects were relocated and invited to return to the Clinical Center at the National Institutes of Health for reexamination.

The second followup, which constitutes the subject of this report, was carried out during 1967–68. It was conducted by new team members at the Philadelphia Geriatric Center, Philadelphia, Pa. The original research team had scattered and it was not possible to arrange for the work to be done at the NIMH. Since many of the subjects lived in Philadelphia and the Philadelphia Geriatric Center was able and willing to provide the necessary space and facilities, the change of location was accepted as the most favorable compromise available.

For both followup studies a careful effort was made to replicate the original procedures. As might be expected, the replication was only approximate. During the 1961 followup, personnel were generally the same as during the initial study. These original investigators were able to arrange for the procedures to follow quite closely those used in 1956–57.

The change of location from NIH to the Philadelphia Geriatric Center required special efforts in order to arange for procedures to be as close as possible to those used in the original study. In addition to an examination of reports of the first study, several conferences were held with the original investigators to discuss methodology. They provided specific guidance for each examination and for the various laboratory studies.

The original battery of examinations could not be administered completely in the followup studies. Some of the subjects could not tolerate or cooperate fully on all of the tests. An example is the cerebral blood flow studies. At the second followup, subjects were asked but not pressured to have these studies repeated. Since this involved venous and arterial punctures which some of them had earlier experienced as unpleasant and stressful, the majority declined to participate again in that part of the study. We were successful, however, in assembling a sizable and varied array of data which reflect the functioning of the survivors over an 11-year period. Table 1 lists the tests administered and the types of data collected during each of the three studies.

TABLE 1.—*Examination batteries*

Examination or test	Period of study		
	1956	1961	1967
Medicine and Physiology:			
Medical history	X	X	X
Physical examination with complete neurological	X	X	X
Hematology[1]	X	X	X
Blood chemistry[1]	X	X	X
Urinalysis	X	X	X
Chest X-ray	X	X	X
Skull X-ray	X	X	X
Electrocardiogram	X	X	X
Electroencephalogram	X	X	X
Pulmonary Function Studies	X	X	X
Cerebral Blood Flow Studies	X	X	
Audiometric examination	X		X
Click Perception Tests	X		
Delayed Auditory Feedback Tests	X		
Psychological:			
Addition rate	X	X	X
Arithmetic alternation rate	X	X	X
Draw-a-Person	X	X	X
Emotional Projection Test	X		
Family Scene	X		X
Homonyms	X	X	
Learning	X		
Level of Aspiration	X	X	
Minnesota Multiphasic Personality Inventory	X		
Mirror tracing	X		
Perception of line difference	X	X	
Raven Progressive Matrices	X	X	X
Reaction time	X	X	
Rorschach	X	X	
Sentence Completion Test	X		X
Speed of card sorting	X	X	
Speed of copying digits	X	X	X
Speed of copying words	X		X
Stroop Test	X		X
Thematic Apperception Test	X		
Wechsler Adult Intelligence Scale	X	X	X
Weigl Color Sorting	X	X	
Wisconsin Card Sorting	X	X	
Word fluency	X		
Social psychological (interview):			
Family history (or interval history)	X		X
Educational history	X		
Occupational history	X		
Retirement planning and activities	X	X	X
Marital history	X	X	X
Living arrangements	X	X	X
Use of time	X	X	X
Social relations and interaction	X	X	X
Attitudes toward life	X	X	X
Goals and aspirations	X	X	
Critical turning points in life	X	X	X
Significant losses	X	X	X
Observed physical and mental changes in aging	X	X	X
Psychiatric (interviews):			
History of psychiatric contact	X	X	X
Personal-social history (or interval history)	X	X	X
Psychiatric Symptom Check List	X	X	X
Mental status evaluation	X		X
Assessment of attitudes about:			
futurity	X	X	X
death	X	X	X
self	X	X	X
aging	X	X	X

[1] See ch. 3 for details.

Aims of Followup

The central aim of both followup studies was similar to that of the original investigation. The appearance of diseases, however, necessitated special care in delineating apparently age-related changes. The longitudinal data also offered the following new opportunities: (1) **To observe** the longitudinal effects of aging on a variety of biological and behavioral dimensions; (2) to clarify the interrelationships among these dimensions with respect to aging; (3) to relate physical and behavioral factors to later developments in old age as well as to survival or death; (4) to describe adaptive responses to aging in both physically healthy and unhealthy individuals; and (5) to observe through time the personal reactions to advancing age in such areas as self-concept, view of the environment, and orientation to time.

Relation to Other Longitudinal Studies

At the time this investigation was started, longitudinal studies of aging were conspicuous by their absence. References often appeared in the literature to their potential value in enabling researchers to clarify the process and speed of normal aging. Some followup studies were available in groups of subjects tested in early or middle-adult life, such as those reported by Owens (1959, 1966), and by Bayley and Oden (1955). These were limited in scope, since they focused mainly on intellectual functions, and offered little that could be applied with confidence beyond age 65. More recently the work of Jarvik and her associates (1962, 1963), dealing with the intellectual performance of aged twins, as well as the reports of Kleemeier (1962) and of Berkowitz and Green (1963), also devoted to intelligence, are more cogent to the problem of tracing the longitudinal patterns of functioning in the aged. Interdisciplinary studies are represented by the work of Riegel, Riegel and Meyer (1967), and the Duke University investigation led by Ewald Busse (Busse, 1967; Pal-

more, 1969) which focussed on the interrelationships among factors, such as intelligence, attitudes, personality functioning and health status, as individuals move from the middle years into the later decades of life.

The present study is closest in aims and methods to the Duke University investigation because intensive behavioral examinations were performed along with medical and physiological studies. The present study initially controlled more stringently for physical health. Thus our subjects are not a representative sample of the aged population, whereas the sample studied at Duke University is probably more nearly representative of the area in North Carolina in which they reside. These two studies complement each other, and where their findings are similar, their validity may merit much confidence.

A comprehensive report of the 1961 followup was never prepared. However, some aspects of the work have been reported (Butler, 1967; Botwinick and Birren, 1965; Birren, 1964; and Libow, 1967).

The Sample

The ideal population which the initial researchers wished to study was the physically healthy, socially independent aged.

Practical aspects of the investigation led to a decision to seek volunteer men, 65 years or older who met the following criteria: (1) Had no symptomatic physical diseases, (2) resided in the community, and (3) were not psychotic. Restriction of the sample to men was made because the research literature on aging reports predominantly on males, thus providing comparison groups, and because of the simplification of research administration it permitted.

Subjects were drawn from men who responded to an appeal for vounteers for a study of the healthy aged. Publicity was released through two organizations: The Home for the Jewish Aged (now named the Philadelphia Geriatric Center) in Philadelphia, and through the Association of Retired Civil Employees in Washington, D.C. The health of volunteers was assessed at three points. Upon application, men were screened for freedom from medical diseases. Upon arrival at the NIH Clinical Center, they were again screened to be sure they were free of clinical medical disease or psychosis. After passing this examination they were accepted for 2 weeks of intensive research studies. Medical data collected during the studies made it evident that the goal of a sample of totally healthy subjects had to be compromised slightly. Therefore, two subgroups of the men were formed on the basis of the absence (group I) or presence (group II) of asymptomatic subclinical disease states (see medical studies reviewed below). A few subjects who were discovered to have clinical medical diseases during the full-study procedure were rejected from the regular study and placed in group III.

The final sample consisted of 47 men, 65 years or older, with a median age of 71 and a range from 65 to 91 years. (See table 2.)

TABLE 2.—*Age of subjects*

Age	Group I [1]	Group II [1]	Total
65 to 69 _____	11	7	18
70 to 74 _____	12	8	20
75 and over _____	4	5	9
Total _____	27	20	47
Mean age _____	70.8	72.4	71.5

[1] Groups I and II refer to medically differentiated groups. Group I meets all the medical criteria set by the research. Group II represents a subclinical or asymptomatic disease group.

Cultural and Racial Backgrounds

All subjects lived in urban environments at the time of the study, and, in most

cases, for long periods previously. Twenty of the men were born in foreign countries, having migrated in childhood or early youth. In regard to religious background, 20 of the subjects were Jewish, 23 were Protestant, and four were Catholic. The foreign-born included a much larger proportion of Jewish than non-Jewish men (75 and 25 percent, respectively). (See table 3.) Forty-six subjects were white and one was Negro.

TABLE 3.—*Cultural backgrounds*

Background	Group I (N=27)	Group II (N=20)	Total (N=47)
Origin:			
Foreign born _____	11	9	20
Native born _____	16	11	27
Religion:			
Jewish ____ _____	9	11	20
Protestant _____	16	7	23
Catholic _____	2	2	4
Education:			
Grade school or less _____	11	9	20
Some high school or high school graduate _____	7	4	11
Some college or college graduate _____	9	7	16
Occupation:			
Professional _____	5	6	11
Business, managerial _____	6	4	10
Clerical _____	10	0	10
Skilled and semiskilled _____	6	10	16

There was an extremely wide range of educational background in the sample, from men with college degrees to men with almost no formal education. Educational level of the aged is difficult to assess in terms of our present educational structure. Keeping in mind this reservation about the reliability of educational achievement, it appeared that the mean education (9.5 years) of the sample was about 1 year greater than the average for men of similar ages in the United States.

The sample included men from many classifications of occupation, overrepresenting the higher status white-collar occupations and underrepresenting the lower status manual occupations. Twenty-three percent of the men had been professionals during their work careers; 21 percent had been business entrepreneurs or managers; 21 percent had been clerical workers; and 35 percent had been skilled or semiskilled workers.

Work Status

At the time of the first study, 32 of the 47 men were fully retired. They had been retired for an average of 7 years, several for as long as 30 years. Ten of the men were in semiretired status. Five were currently employed in their major occupation.

Marital Status and Living Arrangements

The majority of the men were living in intact families at the time of admission to the study, 31 in their own households with their wives, six in the households of relatives. Seven were living alone in apartments or rooming houses. Three were living in the Home for the Jewish Aged, having been very recently admitted. Thirty-two of the men were married or remarried; 14 were widowed, divorced, or separated; and one had never married.

FOLLOWUP EXPERIENCE

The followup efforts proceeded with surprisingly few problems in contacting the survivors and in gaining their cooperation for reexaminations. We were impressed with the interest of the men in the investigation and their desire to be part of it. Many were pleased to be making what they regarded as a socially constructive contribution to science. Most spoke with pleasure about their 2-week stay at the NIH Clinical Center during the first study. They felt well treated and had not minded the inconveniences and occasional discomforts which some of the examinations produced. A particular source of pleasure for them was their sense of pride at being in close contact with scientists and other personnel connected with the project. During the third study it was evident that the special efforts by the original investigators to make the subjects comfortable, treat them with dignity and high regard, provide them with diversions, and encourage them to feel they were participating in an important endeavor, stimulated in the men a sense of pleasant identification with the investigators.

A further product of the good will of the subjects was the favorable attitude toward the project which was generated in their relatives. This proved valuable in efforts to locate and reinvolve the men for the second followup. It was especially valuable when trying to obtain information on the deceased subjects from their families. Wives, children, brothers, and sisters often referred to the sense of pleasure and satisfaction which the men had felt about the project. Families willingly went to considerable effort in some cases to cooperate with us.

During the present followup, special efforts were made to maintain the men's feelings of contributing to an important scientific study. Considerable time and effort were invested in providing comfortable accommodations for subjects who traveled from outside the local area. For local subjects appointments were arranged to suit their convenience and transportation was provided. At the conclusion of the original investigation, as well as after the followup studies, letters of thanks and commendation were sent to the subjects. A token honorarium was also provided. In addition, at the conclusion of the second followup, a luncheon party was arranged for the available subjects and their guests. Speeches, photographs, and small gifts were part of the occasion, and a general feeling of good will was the prevailing mood. Most of the men communicated their sense of satisfaction in having participated in what they regarded as an important effort. They also mentioned their readiness to cooperate with a fourth round of examinations.

Table 4 shows the status of subjects in relation to study participation at each phase. One of the participants (No. 26) was quite ill and could not come to the examination center. He was able to cooperate somewhat when visited at a nursing home by the psychological examiner and a psychiatrist. The examinations, however, were very incomplete and the data from only a few of the psychological tests were useful. Another subject (No. 22), who had been eliminated from the first study (placed in group III) because of a diagnosis of polycythemia vera, had been added to the followup group, but included only to a limited extent in the analyses and discussions. He had heard about the third study through a friend, and requested to be included. Individual investigators have used the data about him where they felt it was appropriate and where inclusion would not influence survivor-nonsurvivor comparisons. Of the four men who dropped out of the study, two were unable to cooperate because of family involvements, and the other two refused without offering reasons.

Time has allowed selective factors to operate upon the original group. Half the men have died. Based on life tables (National Center for Health Statistics, 1964), 14 men would have been expected to live 11 years or more, whereas 23 men actually survived. The difference is statistically significant ($p = 0.05$).

Although survivors were initially younger than nonsurvivors, there was no significant interaction between age and survival. (See table 5.) The extreme age of one subject (11 years older than the next oldest subject) caused a t test to be significant. With the oldest subject removed, it is not significant.

TABLE 4.—*Participant status and study time*

Study	Participated	Dead	Dropped out	Percent survivors participating
	N	N	N	
1st (t₁)	47	--	10	74
2d (t₂)	29	8	4	82
3d (t₃)	[1] 19 (20)	24		

[1] See text.

TABLE 5.—*Age of subjects at first study and survival*

Age	Alive	Dead	Total	Statistic
65 to 69	11	6	17	$X^2 = 3.63$ df $= 2$
				$0.20 > p > 0.10$
70 to 74	10	12	22	
75 and over	2	6	8	
Total	23	24	47	
Mean age	70.0	73.2	71.6	

The X^2 test result is presented because in contrast to the t test it is not affected by the extreme score in the sample.

Among demographic factors, foreign birth was adversely related to survival. (See table 6.) Jewish subjects survived in significantly less proportion than non-Jewish. This appears to be an artifact which came about because most foreign-born subjects were Jewish and most American-born were non-Jewish. Foreign-born subjects were as healthy as American-born subjects. Physical health, therefore, does not account for the difference in survival. A possible explanation is that the greater personal and social changes and discontinuities in the lives of the immigrants caused them to have poorer social functioning scores (Yarrow, Blank, Quinn, Youmans, and Stein, 1963) and also led to their earlier deaths.

Being married was significantly associated with survival (p=0.025). This statistic may reflect the more general effects of psychological losses on survival (see ch. 6, Youmans and Yarrow). Educational level, occupation before retirement, and current income, however, were not related to survival.

Survivors Restudied

Table 7 shows the characteristics of the survivors who participated in the third study. They were 10 years older than the original sample. Their mean age did not increase by 11 years even though that was the mean followup period because deaths of older men reduced the mean age of the survivors. They were more often married, American-born, and Protestant or Catholic than were persons in the original study. Most still lived within the community rather than in institutional settings.

Nine individuals dropped out at one or both of the followup studies. At the second study almost all men who did not return were committed to other responsibilities such as taking care of ill wife (in three instances) or to work which they said they could not leave for the week required. At the third study several men did not want to "get involved" with what they saw as a major undertaking. Dropouts did not appear to differ remarkably from subjects who continued participation. Their mean age was close to that of the entire group (70.5 years), and they came in representative proportions from medical groups I and II. They did show trends toward having lower WAIS IQs and lower morale.

REVIEW OF PREVIOUSLY PUBLISHED RESULTS

The following sections, presented in near-outline form, constitute a summary of the results of the original investigation based on the reports of Birren and his co-workers (1963).

TABLE 6.—*Nativity, religion, and survival*

Nativity and religion	Alive	Dead	Total		
Foreign born:					
Jewish	3	12	15	$X^2=4.28$	df=1
Protestant and Catholic	2	3	5	p<0.05	
Total	5	15	20		
Native born:					
Jewish	2	3	5	$X^2=4.04$	df=1
Protestant and Catholic	16	6	22	p<0.05	
Total	18	9	27		

TABLE 7.—*Age and social-cultural characteristics of participants in third study*

Characteristic	Number
Age:	
75 to 79	7
80 to 84	9
85 to 89	3
Mean: 81 years	
Marital status:	
Married	14
Widowed	4
Divorced	1
Origin:	
Foreign born	3
Native born	16
Religion:	
Jewish	4
Protestant and Catholic	15
Retirement status:	
Semiretired	3
Retired	16
Residence:	
Private home	11
Apartment	4
Home for aged	3
Nursing home	1

Medicine

For purposes of the medical studies, disease was defined as pathological processes occurring occasionally in the young and not universally in the aged (Libow, 1963; Lane and Vates, 1963). Aging was in contrast defined as a progression of adult changes characteristic of the species and which should occur in all individuals if they live long enough.

At the first study, after all the medical data were collected, subjects were divided into two groups: Group I composed of 27 men who represented the optimally healthy aged who had only insignificant and asymptomatic abnormalities such as X-ray evidence of osteoarthritis, senile cataracts, and minimal conduction defects in the electrocardiogram; and group II composed of 20 men who showed definite evidence of diseases with more serious implications though they were completely asymptomatic. This group contained men with diastolic blood pressures of 90 to 94 millimeters of mercury, elevation of blood pressure during the cerebral blood flow studies, and a mild case of gout.

Group II contained also a subgroup of 10 men who showed signs of arteriosclerosis. The evidence for this included historical, physical, or electrocardiographic evidence suggestive of arteriosclerotic heart disease; chest X-ray evidence of calcification of the thoracic aorta with or without tortuosity, and/or widening; historical and/or physical evidence of interference with peripheral circulation.

Differences between the optimally healthy (group I) and younger men in general were considered as probably representing age-related changes. When differences between young and old occurred only in comparisons using group II men, the changes were interpreted as probably being disease related rather than age related.

Among blood studies, serum albumin was lower in both groups than in young controls. This was interpreted as an age-related metabolic change. Similarly serum alpha two globulins and beta globulins were elevated. None of the standard hematologic indices were different from young controls except for the sedimentation rate, which was increased, probably because of the reduced serum albumin. The protein bound iodine (PBI) correlated negatively with age over the age range of the subjects. The decrease with age appeared to be due to a true decrease in circulating thyroid hormone.

Diastolic blood pressures in both groups and systolic blood pressures in group I resembled those of young adults more closely than values for the aged in previous studies. Mean systolic blood pressure in group II subjects was higher than in young adults, a finding similar to other studies of old people. Only in group II was there a significant increase of systolic and diastolic blood pressure with age. This appeared, therefore, to be associated with arteriosclerosis.

A high proportion of men showed some minimal retinal arteriosclerosis. Its presence was not correlated with cerebral blood flow, cerebral vascular resistance, or other indications of cerebral vascular arteriosclerosis. Calcification of the internal carotid artery siphon was correlated with reduced cerebral blood flow and reduced cerebral venous oxygen tension.

Among pulmonary functions there were aged-related reductions in maximum breathing capacity and timed vital capacity, as well as reductions that appeared to be due to undetected pulmonary pathology. Arterial oxygen saturation was equally reduced in both groups which suggested an age-related change.

No relationship was found between smoking and any medical factors. The reason for this negative finding was unclear but was felt possibly to be attributable to selection and survival biases.

The men's electrocardiograms confirmed and extended into an older age group an earlier finding of a shift of the QRS axis with age. No shift of the T axis with age was seen. Right bundle branch block which was seen in five subjects did not appear to be evidence of coronary artery disease. It was noted that "Our evidence strongly suggests that with the approach of an era in which arteriosclerosis and other diseases occurring frequently with increasing age may be reversible and/or preventable, the present picture of human aging, with its behavioral and central nervous system changes may be markedly altered."

Cerebral Circulation and Metabolism

Cerebral blood flow was measured by the nitrous oxide method. There were no significant differences in the cerebral circulation and metabolism between optimally healthy men (group I) and normal young subjects (Dastur, Lane, Hansen, Kety, Butler, Perlin, and Sokoloff, 1963).

Arteriosclerotic cerebrovascular changes appeared to be responsible for all of the decrease of cerebral blood flow and oxygen consumption among group II subjects. Men with asymptomatic arteriosclerosis had cerebral blood flows 16 to 20 percent below that of normal young adults.

A further comparison group of patients hospitalized with chronic brain syndrome with psychosis had cerebral blood flows as low but no lower than group II subjects with arteriosclerosis.

Arteriosclerosis reduced cerebral blood flow leading to anoxia and ischemia which caused the brain to extract more oxygen from the blood. It was speculated that such chronic anoxia led to eventual loss of ability by the brain tissue to extract or utilize oxygen from the blood to maintain metabolic and mental functions. Failure to extract oxygen from the blood was observed in patients with chronic brain syndrome and psychosis.

While cerebral blood flow was not as sensitive an indicator of brain changes in aging as cognitive and perceptual tests or electroencephalograms, when cerebral blood flow was impaired it appeared to be the pacemaker of deteriorative brain changes which were reflected in the other measures.

Electroencephalography

The incidence of clinically normal electroencephalograms (EEG) was 81 percent (Obrist, 1963), which was comparable to figures reported for young people. In contrast to other aging studies, only 9 percent of the men in the present study had temporal lobe foci. Groups I and II did not differ with respect to incidence or type of abnormality.

Frequency analysis gave a mean spectrum with a peak frequency of 9 cps (cycles per second), which was a full cycle slower than previously found in young adults. The entire spectrum, especially the major frequencies, appeared to have shifted to the slow side.

Group II (subclinical disease subjects) showed significantly more 8-cps activity than group I (healthy subjects), although other points along the spectrum did not differ appreciably. This was associated with slower individual peak frequencies in group II, which was the major EEG difference between the two groups. A subgroup of 12 cases with arteriosclerosis revealed similar, slightly more significant trends.

It was concluded that the EEG undergoes changes with age, even in the absence of any detectable physical disease. Because the group with subclinical pathology had slower tracings, it was suggested that health status, particularly cardiovascular disease, is an important factor influencing brain potentials.

Auditory Perception

A series of experiments on age changes in auditory processes was conducted in order to differentiate "sensory" and "perceptual" processes and to see how such measures related to physiological, psychiatric, sociological, and psychological measures (Weiss, 1963). To "sense" meant to recognize that a message or stimulus had been received. To "perceive" meant, that in addition to sensing, the organism was aware of the more complex information conveyed by the stimulus—for example, recognition of the meaning of a word.

On clinical testing, group I men showed hearing loss (compared to young subjects) especially in the upper frequency range which was within the expected range of normal for their ages. Group II contained several men with severe hearing loss.

A complex series of tests involving discrimination between a single sound or two or more sounds (clicks) in rapid succession was used to study individually the relationship of changes in sensation and perception to age. Both showed decrements with age. Changes in sensation and perception did not necessarily occur together.

Digit recall tests indicated that ability to store sensory as well as perceptual data declined with age, but again the two were not necessarily related to each other in a single subject. Older subjects also had more difficulty monitoring two information channels (via the two ears) than did younger subjects.

Mental Abilities and Psychomotor Responses

In general the performance of the subjects compared more favorably with test results of young subjects than did the aged in previous studies (Botwinick and Birren 1963; Birren, Botwinick, Weiss, and Morrison 1963). But changes with age were found and these were regarded as especially significant. A prominent age-related change was loss of speed in test performance.

In figure 1 the mean Wechsler Adult Intelligence Scale (WAIS) subtest and total scores of groups I and II have been plotted in relation to the mean of the young standardization group. The subtests with verbal content tend to be high, both relatively and absolutely, in comparison with the subtests which involve the manipulation of nonverbal symbols and materials.

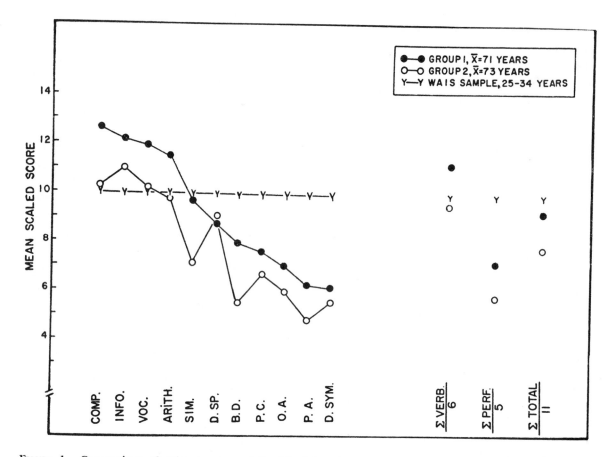

FIGURE 1.—Comparison of subtest scores of the Wechsler Adult Intelligence Scale for three groups of subjects: young adult standardization group and groups I and II of the present study. The expected mean value for young adults (25–34 years) is 10 on each subtest.

Using results from 32 tests which measured a wide range of abilities, an attempt was made to develop a parsimonious description of the results. The method chosen involved an analysis of the intercorrelations of the 32-test scores by the Hotelling Principal Component method. Five principal components which accounted for 58 percent of the total variance were extracted. Component I, which accounted for 30 percent of the total variance, was given the descriptive labels "stored information" or "general intellectual achievement." Tests high in this component included the WAIS subtests of general information, verbal similarities, and vocabulary. Component II appeared to be a measure of speed of assimilation of numbers and rapidity of associated response. Speed of addition and card sorting were high on this component. Component III seemed to measure some aspect of ability to maintain a decision set versus flexibility. The WAIS Object Assembly test and the Line Difference test (judging which of two lines is longer while disregarding other differences) were high on this component. Component IV was called speed of association and reasoning. It seemed to measure the balance between a disposition to rapid responses and reasoning. Component V was related to concept formation and stimulus orientation. Task vigilance and attention were important.

Group II subjects tended generally to have lower psychological performance than subjects of group I. Health differences in the range studied thus presumably make a difference in psychological functioning. These psychological differences were most apparent in verbal abilities or general achievement level. Groups I and II were, thus, different in performance on principal component I. The problem of interpretation of the results involved the issue of whether the lower scores of group II were a result of: (a) a failure to gain information over the adult years, (b) a loss of information, or (c) a sampling artifact. The interpretation regarded as most probable was that the lower values of group II reflected a late-life loss of information. The illnesses observed in group II would presumably not be prevalent during the early- and middle-adult years when they would be expected to show an increase in score above that for young adults.

On perceptual and manipulative types of tests the older subjects were in general lower in performance than young subjects. Comparable control subjects, however, were not available for all comparisons. For available data, the age difference was greater than the differences between groups I and II. Older subjects tend to have sensory limitations and are also slow in responses. In many situations where the task requires operation on or manipulation of symbolic materials, it is not clear whether the slower output and errors result from the necessity to take additional time to perceive the pertinent information or whether the older organism is less "activated" or "energized." In this study both groups I and II were slower than young subjects but did not differ significantly from each other. This pointed up the puzzling impression that age is a more relevant factor in speed measures, and

health in verbal measures. Why this is so is regarded as an important question for further investigation.

Personality Measurements

A total of 11 tests was administered, six of the "projective type" (such as TAT, Rorschach, and Sentence Completion), two involving mainly verbal manipulations (Homonyms and Proverbs), and three calling essentially for "performance" rather than "verbal" responses (Draw-a-Person, Weigl Card Sorting, and Level of Aspirations). The responses were scored and analyzed in terms of their formal characteristics rather than in the usual "clinical" fashion (Singer, 1963). Weightings were made in relation to the following qualities: how well the individual was able to wait for and comprehend instructions; how many appropriate and varied associations he was able to call up for use in a situation; how well he had adhered to the task goal, keeping his thoughts directed without drift and without perseverations; how well he ordered the sequence of his thoughts; how appropriately he limited the amount of his productions; and how appropriately he terminated his responses.

The subjects judged to be the most healthy (group I) responded generally in a fashion which did not differ in quality from what is expected from younger groups of adequately functioning individuals. Planning ability was found to be adequate. Instructions were correctly perceived and good ability was shown to wait until the total set of instructions was given. Responses given were to the point, with satisfactory breadth of content which was free of perseveration and redundancy. Their range of associations was wide and they were able to discuss various nuances about their ideas. In addition, termination of the test responses was proper and in line with the overall plan of their reactions. Some of the content, however, was age related and reflected the interests and attitudes of elderly people.

The group II subjects performed somewhat less adequately than those in group I but not to a statistically significant degree. An analysis which compared the subjects rated as showing Senile Quality with those rated as nonsenile revealed that the former group was significantly less effective in their responses. The Senile Quality group often started their responses poorly, and falsely anticipated the directions. They were impulsive in their reactions and displayed limited understanding. They were also more literal and personal in an inappropriate fashion, failing to respond to the proper intent of the problem at hand. Planning was loose, associations were restricted in range, verbal expressions were primitive in content, perseveration was evident, and termination of responses was loose or lacking in planning.

Minnesota Multiphasic Personality Inventory

The men had a significantly elevated mean depression (D) scale (Kornetsky, 1963). There was a significant association between the D scale scores and clinically rated depression. The general pattern of responses was mildly different from the general population but similar to what is found in groups of individuals with higher than average intelligence. Elevation of the masculinity-femininity (Mf) scale, as well as most of the other scores, characterizes this pattern.

Psychiatry

Twenty-eight percent of the men had psychoneuroses and 62 percent presented functional psychopathology (Perlin and Butler, 1963). Mild reactive depression was the most common diagnosis (19 per-

cent). Modifications of psychopathology, including exacerbation and amelioration, had occurred with advancing age. The psychopathology found was not associated with serious impairments.

Eleven men (23 percent) exhibiting a Senile Quality showed the following characteristics: decreased comprehension, memory, attention, and set as well as reduced emotional responsiveness. It was postulated that some of these individuals had an early stage of chronic brain syndrome. Men with Senile Quality were not older than the other men.

The importance of chronological age per se as an overriding factor in the psychiatric disorders of the aging appeared questionable; the significance of other factors, including personality, psychosocial disruptions and losses, diseases and the like, was emphasized.

Efforts were directed toward further defining the aging experience of an individual, in terms of intrinsic and environmental changes, and reactions to them. Quantification was achieved through content analysis of the men's reports of types of changes they experienced with aging and their responses to them. Physical changes were most frequently mentioned, with personality-affective, social-psychological, and cognitive changes following in a descending order of frequency.

The changes were often viewed as positive. Indeed, one-third of the subjects reported all of their personality-affective changes as positive. The changes were not uniformly viewed as inevitable and unalterable by the aged subjects. There was a relationship between the kind of change and the mode of reaction reported. Acceptance was the most frequently reported reaction to physical diseases; compensation was most common with social-psychological decreases; and both were seen as responses to cognitive and personality-affective decreases.

An identity crisis associated with aging occurred in 28 percent of the men. Psychological isolation and depression were seen as especially maladaptive patterns.

In contrast to other age groups where diagnosis is reasonably predictive of adaptation, in the aged the discrepancy between diagnosis and adaptation seemed to be much greater, suggesting a need for revision in assessment and diagnosis in dealing with the aged. The importance of relating the effect of an aged person's adaptive patterns to his morale was emphasized.

Social Psychology

Concern was directed to three areas: (a) The nature of the aged person's social environment, (b) his adaptation to his changed physical and social circumstances, and (c) the relationship between certain environmental and behavioral variables (Yarrow, Blank, Quinn, Youmans, and Stein 1963).

For half of the men retirement had been a gradual process and for the other half it was abrupt. Retirement was either purely forced or purely voluntary for half of the men while it was a mixture for the other half. Only a small number (13 percent) described having made plans for retirement beforehand.

Daily activities of three-quarters of the men involved some active or expressive behavior such as gardening, woodworking, and swimming. Socializing was limited almost entirely to the immediate family for half of the subjects and was not great for the others. Ninety-two percent of the men had immediate family members available. Social interactions were most often with people of their own age group. In contrast

to earlier reports that old men were without significant social roles, 62 percent of these men assumed active roles in housekeeping which are traditionally feminine. Nearly half of those with grandchildren did babysitting.

Outlook on life was rated. About one-fourth found time and life burdensome. One-fourth were more hopeful but dissatisfied, and half expressed strong satisfaction with their current lives.

The quality of family relationships was examined. About one-third of the men had poor (and often deteriorating) relationships with their wives. Two-thirds had compatible relationships which actually varied over a wide range. Relationships with their children showed a broadly similar pattern. These included a wide range of types of relationships varying from mutual respect of children and father for one another in a peerlike relationship to dependency of father upon children.

Daily activities of 42 percent of the men were varied, complex, and highly planned. Only 11 percent led extremely routine lives. Foreign-born subjects functioned less well than native-born subjects on several measures. This was attributed to the extreme social changes and discontinuities in the lives of the immigrants which handicapped their adjustment in old age. Educational and occupational level had little predictive value for social functioning. Work career success was somewhat predictive of greater adaptation in old age.

The immediate environment had profound influences upon the men's behavior and attitudes. The amount of losses of close relationships had the most significant influence. More losses were associated with less satisfaction with life, less organized daily behavior, less goal striving, less sociability on the study ward, and poor mood. Men who retired almost purely voluntarily

adjusted best, with purely compulsory retirees next, while men with mixed reasons
for retiring adjusted most poorly. Mixed
reasons for retiring were associated with
ambivalent feelings about being retired,
which, in turn seemed to be a causal factor
for their poor social functioning. Restricted and routine living patterns were
more frequent in men with the lowest incomes.

Differences between men of varying occupations and social status became smaller
in old age. They dropped their specializations as they retired. Inner resourcefulness
and attitudes did not significantly vary
with these characteristics.

Interdisciplinary Relationships

The uncovering of unsuspected relationships between variables in different
disciplines was a major aim of the interdisciplinary studies (Birren, Butler, Greenhouse, Sokoloff, and Yarrow, 1963). Thus
a large number of intercorrelations of variables from different disciplines were computed.

Correlations with chronological age
were virtually absent among Group I men.
There were, however, significant correlations with age among group II men. These
included percent-time 8-cycle-per-second
waves on the EEG; psychiatric Age Related Checklist score; general intellectual
achievement (psychology Principal Component I); the sum of projective test ratings; and pulmonary vital capacity and
breathing capacity. Health status thus appeared to be more important than chronological age in determining various aspects
of functioning. Such a statement, however, tends to obscure the fact that chronic
diseases are more frequent with advancing
age—a fact of major importance in the
study of aging.

Medical and cerebral physiologic varia-

bles were rarely significantly correlated.
Significant correlations would be expected
only when one function varied from normal enough to affect the other, or when
both were affected by a third factor which
might be introduced by disease. Since the
subjects of this study were markedly
healthy for their ages, the range of pathological changes was sharply restricted and
this lessened the likelihood of any correlations between cerebral physiological and
medical variables.

Confirmation was found for an earlier
observation of a negative relationship between average diastolic blood pressure and
percent-time slow waves of the EEG among
subjects with cardiovascular disease. This
was interpreted as indicating that in the
presence of cardiovascular disease, increased blood pressure protects against
slowing of the EEG. Such slowing has
been associated with cerebral ischemia and
anoxia. For the first time a correlation
was found between higher blood pressure
and greater percent-time fast activity
among very healthy subjects (group I).

Characteristics of the EEG were not correlated with cerebral circulatory variables.
This, like the interrelation of medical and
cerebral physiological variables, was interpreted as indicating that in the men
studied cerebral circulatory abnormalities
were not marked enough to be reflected in
EEG changes. A companion study of patients with more advanced cardiovascular
disease, however, showed definite relationships between EEG and cerebral circulatory variables.

Correlations between 22 physiological
variables and nine psychological variables
(including the Principal Component Analysis elements) were computed. In group I
there were five significant correlations
while in group II there were 26 significant
correlations. This was interpreted as sup-

porting the "discontinuity hypothesis" which states that individual differences in psychological functioning remain largely autonomous of somatic functions until critical or limiting levels are reached; e.g., as a consequence of disease and trauma, psychological functions show a significant relationship to physiological reactions.

Few of the physiological factors correlated with the general intellectual factor (Principal Component I). The cerebral metabolic rate of oxygen correlated only in group II. EEG measures were not correlated with the general intellectual factor although a significant correlation had been expected on the basis of earlier reports. It was speculated that EEG correlations with cognitive functions may not appear unless more gross brain damage is present (discontinuity hypothesis).

Subjects of both groups I and II showed lower speed factor measurements (Principal Component IV), which suggested slowness was largely autonomous of somatic functions. However, this had to be reconciled with a finding of six physiological variables significantly correlated with the speed factor. All were in the direction of slowness increasing with poorer physiologic function. The factors were cerebral venous pressure of oxygen and glucose consumption; diastolic blood pressure; mean arterial blood pressure; vital capacity; and systolic blood pressure. One interpretation was that the changes in speed were early manifestations of underlying physiological changes or *disease states* that remained unmeasured in these subjects. An alternative was that slowness is an inherent part of aging which may be more marked in the presence of disease.

An attempt was made to unravel the contributions of various kinds of changes (physiological, psychological, and environmental) to adaptive and pathological behavior. Contrary to findings in earlier studies, EEG measures were unrelated to senile manifestations. However, morale (self-reported positive or negative changes with aging) correlated with peak occipital frequency, and better adaptation correlated with less percent-time slow waves on the EEG. This suggested that organic pathology underlay the correlations but the meaning of the changes was uncertain. Temporal lobe EEG abnormalities were not associated with any characteristic psychopathology.

Senile Quality was correlated with the presence of arteriosclerosis. No other medical and psychiatric variables were correlated. Because arteriosclerosis (identified anywhere in the body) was associated with a lower cerebral metabolic rate of oxygen and both were correlated with presence of Senile Quality, it suggested that Senile Quality represented a change due to cerebrovascular disease. Companion studies of patients with chronic brain syndrome and marked vascular disease further supported the impression. No support was found for an alternative explanation that primary neuronal degeneration without cerebral circulatory deficiency caused the senile changes and reduced brain metabolic rates.

Senile Quality subjects uniformly performed less well on psychological tests involving cognitive, perceptual, and psychomotor skills.

Depressed subjects scored less well on the general intellectual factor (Principal Component I) though not significantly less well on any specific test. Their reaction times were slower than other subjects even though retardation was not clinically observable. A very significant interaction effect of depression and reduced auditory acuity on the reaction time was seen. The meaning of these relationships was uncertain.

Interdisciplinary correlations were used to explore how psychosocial functioning was influenced by other variables. The relation between more contemporaneous losses and poorer psychosocial functioning has already been emphasized. Parallels were found in the correlation of psychosocial losses with less adequate functioning on tests of cognitive and psychomotor performance, more frequent diagnoses of depression, and less adaptability.

The presence of Senile Quality was not related to losses, but deteriorative behavior rated with the Age Relevant Checklist was associated with severity of environmental losses. It was speculated that the relation between losses and all of the other factors mentioned may be mediated by depressive states.

Social functioning was significantly correlated with several variables including: general intellectual factor (Principal Component I); mean reaction time; two measures of depression; adaptation; and several of the cerebral physiologic measures. All were in the expected direction with better social functioning associated with better psychological, psychiatric, and physiologic functioning.

Ratings of psychopathologic features were relatively little related to social functioning. This reflected the large modifying role of environmental supports in determining the impact of psychiatric characteristics on social functioning.

Of the biological and psychological processes and conditions that were tapped, none contributed so strongly in contrast to the others as to be considered the key or vital factor. The picture was, instead, one of factors reinforcing or canceling out the effects of the others in a manner far too complex to be neatly disentangled.

REFERENCES

BAYLEY, NANCY, and ODEN, MELITA H. The maintenance of intellectual ability in gifted adults. *J. Geront.*, 10: 91–107, 1955.

BERKOWITZ, B., and GREEN, R. F. Changes in intellect with age: I. longitudinal study of Wechsler Bellevue sources. *J. Genetic Psychol.*, 103: 3–21, 1963.

BIRREN, J. E. A neural basis of personal adjustment in aging. In: Hanson, P. F. ed. *Age With a Future.* Munksgaard: Copenhagen, 1964.

——, BOTWINICK, J.; WEISS, A. D.; and MORRISON, D. F. Interrelations of mental and perceptual tests given to healthy elderly men. In: Birren, J. E., et al., eds. *Human-Aging: A Biological and Behavioral Study.* Washington, D.C.: U.S. Government Printing Office, 1963.

——, BUTLER, R. N.; GREENHOUSE, S. W.; SOKOLOFF, L.; and YARROW, MARIAN R. Interdisciplinary relationships: interrelations of physiological, psychological, and psychiatric findings in healthy elderly men. In: Birren J. E., et al., eds. *Human Aging: A Biological and Behavioral Study.* Washington, D.C.: U.S. Government Printing Office, 1963.

BOTWINICK, J., and BIRREN, J. E. A followup study of card-sorting performance in elderly men. *J. Geront.* 20: 208–210, 1965.

BUSSE, E. W. Therapeutic Implications of Basic Research with the Aged. *The Institute of the Pennsylvania Hospital Strecker Monograph Series IV.* Nutley, N.J.: Roche Laboratories, 1967.

BUTLER, R. N. Aspects of survival and adaptation in human aging. *Amer. J. Psychiat.*, 123: 1233–1243, 1967.

DASTUR, D. K.; LANE, M. H.; HANSEN, D. B.; KETY, S. S.; BUTLER, R. N.; PERLIN, S.; and SOKOLOFF, L. Effects of aging on cerebral circulation and metabolism in men. In: Birren, J. E., et al., eds. *Human Aging: A Biological and Behavioral Study.* Washington, D.C.: U.S. Government Printing Office, 1963.

JARVIK, LISSY; KALMANN, F. J.; and FALEK, A. Intelligence changes in aged twins. *J. Geront.* 17: 289–294, 1962.

——, and FALEK, A. Intellectual ability and survival in the aged. *J. Geront.*, 18: 173–176, 1963.

KLEEMEIER, R. W. Intellectual change in the senium. *Proceedings of the Social Statistics Section of the American Statistical Association,* 1962. pp. 290–295.

KORNETSKY, C. Minnesota Multiphasic Personality Inventory: results obtained from a population of aged men. In: Birren, J. E., et al., eds. *Human Aging: A Biological and Behavioral Study.* Washington, D.C.: U.S. Government Printing Office, 1963.

LANE, M. H., and VATES, T. S., JR. Medical selection, evaluation, and classification of subjects. In: Birren, J. E., et al., eds. *Human Aging: A Biological and Behavioral Study.* Washington, D.C.; U.S. Government Printing Office, 1963.

LIBOW, L. S. Medical investigation of the process of aging. In: Birren, J. E., et al., eds. *Human Aging: A Biological and Behavioral Study.* Washington, D.C.: U.S. Government Printing Office, 1963.

———. Study of medical aspects of retirement, including interdisciplinary correlation of 5- and 10-year followup of NIMH study of human aging. Presented at the National Institute of Child Health and Human Development Workshop meeting on "Health and Retirement," December 11–12, 1967, New Orleans, La. To be published as a National Institutes of Health Monograph.

National Center for Health Statistics. U.S. Life Tables: 1959–61. Vol. 1, No. 1, U.S. Department of Health, Education, and Welfare. Washington, D.C., 1964.

OBRIST, W. D. The electroencephalogram of healthy aged males. In: Birren, J. E., et al., eds. *Human Aging: A Biological and Behavioral Study.* Washington, D.C.: U.S. Government Printing Office, 1963.

OWENS, W. A., JR. Is age kinder to the intellectually more able? *J. Geront.,* 14: 334–339, 1959.

———. Age and mental abilities: a second adult followup. *J. Educ. Psychol.,* 51: 311–325, 1966.

PALMORE, E. B. Physical, mental, and social factors in predicting longevity. *Gerontologist,* 9: 103–108, 1969.

PERLIN, S., and BUTLER, R. N. Psychiatric aspects of adaptation to the aging experience. In: Birren, J. E., et al., eds. *Human Aging: A Biological and Behavioral Study.* Washington, D.C.: U.S. Government Printing Office, 1963.

RIEGEL, K. F.; RIEGEL, RUTH M.; and MEYER, G. A study of the dropout rates in longitudinal research on aging and the prediction of death. *J. Personality and Soc. Psychol.,* 5: 342–348, 1967.

SINGER, MARGARET T. Personality measurements in the aged. In: Birren, J. E., et al., eds. *Human Aging: A Biological and Behavioral Study.* Washington, D.C.: U.S. Government Printing Office, 1963.

WEISS, A. D. Auditory perception in relation to age. In: Birren, J. E., et al., eds. *Human Aging: A Biological and Behavioral Study.* Washington, D.C.: U.S. Government Printing Office, 1963.

YARROW, MARIAN R.; BLANK, P.; QUINN, OLIVE W.; YOUMANS, E. G.; and STEIN, JOHANNA. Social psychological characteristics of old age. In: Birren, J. E., et al., eds. *Human Aging: A Biological and Behavioral Study.* Washington, D.C.: U.S. Government Printing Office, 1963.

CHAPTER 2

Medical Factors in Survival and Mortality of the Healthy Elderly

by Leslie S. Libow

INTRODUCTION

What are the measurable factors in the healthy elderly, which antedate, predict, and perhaps contribute to the development of disease and mortality? What are the changes which are not related to the occurrence of disease, but rather are associated with the pattern of aging? This 11-year longitudinal study of relatively healthy elderly men, with a mean age of 71 years at the beginning of this investigation, has been directed toward these questions. The medical findings of the initial study have been presented in our previous monograph (Birren, Butler, Greenhouse, Sokoloff, and Yarrow, 1963).

The major prospective studies such as those at Framingham (Kannel, LeBauer, Dawber, and McNamara, 1967) and Tecumseh (Epstein, Ostrander, Johnson, Payne, Haynes, Keller, and Francis, 1965) focused on entire communities and delineated factors contributing to the development of vascular disease. The subjects were randomly distributed for various characteristics. They were mainly middle aged, though older subjects, too, were studied.

The present study, by contrast, has focused on a "selected" group of 47 community resident elderly men, chosen for their good health. Generally excluded from the study at its inception were factors such as significant obesity and hypertension. This group is not representative of the average older population. Perhaps because of this, certain factors which precede and contribute to disease in the elderly may have had an opportunity to more clearly express their effects.

Several such factors, some expected and others surprising, have been revealed in this study. This chapter focuses on factors in mortality in general, and specifically on factors in mortality from coronary heart disease and cancer of the gastrointestinal tract.

SUBJECT MATERIAL

The medical selection, evaluation, and classification of subjects has been completely described previously (Lane and Vates, 1963). In the original study in 1956, these volunteer subjects were screened in their home communities and then at the National Institutes of Health and 47 men were finally accepted as healthy. They were then further subdivided into two groups. Group I, with 27 subjects, was the "optimally" healthy, with no apparent

Table 1.—Mean blood pressure by age groups [1]

Age group	N [2]	Group I Systolic B.P. (mm. Hg)	Group I Diastolic B.P. (mm. Hg)	N	Group II Systolic B.P. (mm. Hg)	Group II Diastolic B.P. (mm. Hg)	N	Total Systolic B.P. (mm. Hg)	Total Diastolic B.P. (mm. Hg)
65 to 69	10	130	77	7	129	75	17	130	76
70 to 74	13	124	74	10	146	79	23	134	76
75 to 79	3	121	67	2	155	86	5	135	74
80 to 84	1	146	91	0	---	--	1	146	91
85 to 89	0	---	--	0	---	--	0	---	--
90 to 94	0	---	--	1	125	75	1	125	75

[1] Libow, 1963. [2] N = number of subjects.

significant disease, and particularly, no vascular disease. The problems typical of this group consisted of factors such as benign prostate hypertrophy, minimal deafness, varicose veins, and in several subjects, right bundle branch block on electrocardiogram. This electrocardiographic abnormality occurred in the absence of any other evidence of cardiac, pulmonary, or pulmonary embolic disease. Group II, with 20 subjects, was the more typically "average" healthy aged, with some significant but generally asymptomatic disease, particularly cardiovascular. Some subjects had findings such as minimal cardiomegaly on chest X-ray, ECG abnormalities, and in nine subjects, elevated mean arterial blood pressures (MABP). The MABP determinations were obtained during cerebral physiologic studies via a catheter in the femoral artery. These nine subjects had pressures more than three standard deviations above the mean pressure 84±23 mm. Hg) of the control subjects age 20 years. Three of these nine subjects had clinical systolic and diastolic pressures which can be considered as elevated, though not impressively for their age; i.e., 164/92, 157/92, and 155/91 mm. Hg. The distribution of the clinical blood pressures for all subjects and the mean blood pressures for both groups are presented in tables 1 and 2.

Within group II was a subgroup termed

Table 2.—Mean blood pressure of these healthy elderly men at the initial study

	Mean systolic B.P. ±S.D. (mm. Hg)	Mean diastolic B.P. ±S.D. (mm. Hg)
Group I (N=27) ---	127±10	75±5
Group II (N=20) --	[1] 140±18	78±5

[1] Significantly different from group I, at the 0.01 level.

"arteriosclerotic" because these subjects demonstrated significant, multisystem, generally asymptomatic evidence of arteriosclerosis, based on medical evaluation, chest X-ray, electrocardiogram, and the state of the retinal and peripheral vasculature. Several of these subjects had evidence suggesting coronary heart disease.

By the 5-year followup, eight subjects had died. Twenty-nine of the 39 survivors were restudied at the NIH.

By the time of the 11-year followup, 24 subjects had died, and 23 were still living. Eighteen were restudied at the Philadelphia Geriatric Center. One survivor was discovered after the preparation of this chapter and is not included in its analyses.

METHODS

The medical, chemical, and physiological methods employed in the original study have been described previously (Lane and Vates, 1963; Libow, 1963). The followup studies employed the same methodology to the extent possible. The studies repeated were as follows: comprehensive medical evaluation, complete blood count, urinalysis, blood urea nitrogen, creatinine, fasting blood sugar, protein bound iodine, serum cholesterol, electrocardiogram, and chest and skull X-rays.

Since the 11-year studies were centered at the Philadelphia Geriatric Center, these examinations and interviews were not performed by the original investigators who were, however, able to supply consultative guidance for the procedures to be followed and for the interpretation of the data.

RESULTS

Those factors which relate to mortality at the 5- and 11-year followup are listed in table 3. The specific figures and the statistical results as well as significance levels are presented in tables 4 through 18. All data presented, unless otherwise specified, are values obtained from these volunteers at the initial study in 1956. Comparisons are then made between the survivor and deceased groups at the 5- and 11-year followup, utilizing the original data.

TABLE 3.—*Factors which relate significantly[1] to mortality: 5- and 11-year followup*

Factor	11 years	5 years
Chronic cigarette smoking	+[2]	+
Systolic blood pressure	+	+
Diastolic blood pressure	−	"+"[3]
Mean arterial blood pressure	−	+
"Arteriosclerotics"	+	+
Weight[4]	+	+
Age	−	+

[1] Significance refers to a "p" value of at least 0.05; specific data and significance levels are presented in tables which follow.
[2] + refers to statistically significant factor; − refers to lack of significance.
[3] Approaches statistical significance; 0.10>p>0.05.
[4] A negative relationship; i.e., lighter weight relates to greater mortality.

Chronic Cigarette Smoking

The mean duration of smoking, at the initial study in 1956, was 47.2 years. Fifteen subjects smoked more than 20 cigarettes per day and four subjects smoked 10 to 20 cigarettes per day.

Cigarette smoking related significantly to mortality at the 5- and 11-year study (table 4). Those who discontinued smoking had done so between 3 and 25 years prior to the study, and after an average smoking duration of 30 years. Those who discontinued smoking had a mortality rate almost identical with those who had never smoked (table 5).

Blood Pressure

Systolic Blood Pressure. The systolic blood pressure relates significantly to mortality at the 5- and 11-year followup (tables 6 and 8).

TABLE 4.—*Chronic cigarette smoking and mortality: 5- and 11-year followup*

	Nonchronic smokers[1]	Chronic smokers[2]	Total
5-YEAR FOLLOWUP			
Died	1	7	8
Survived	19	12	31
Total	20	19	39

chi square = 4.26
df = 1
p = ≤ 0.05

11-YEAR FOLLOWUP			
Died	6	13	19
Survived	13	6	19
Total	19	19	38

chi square = 3.789
df = 1
0.10>p>0.05

[1] Nonchronic smokers are those who never smoked cigarettes (11 subjects) and those who stopped smoking cigarettes prior to study (9 subjects). Cigar and pipe smokers (8 subjects) are excluded from these analyses.
[2] Continued to smoke cigarettes up to time of the initiation of this study in 1956. Followup studies revealed no changes of smoking habits in survivors.

TABLE 5.—*Effect of discontinuing cigarette smoking on survival and mortality at 5- and 11-year followup*

	Survived	Died	Total
5-YEAR FOLLOWUP			
Never smoked cigarettes ___	10	1	11
Discontinued smoking cigarettes _____	9	0	9
Chronic cigarette smokers _	12	7	19
Total _____	31	8	[1] 39

chi square = 6.310
df = 2
significance: p = ≤ 0.05

	Survived	Died	Total
11-YEAR FOLLOWUP			
Never smoked cigarettes ___	7	3	10
Discontinued smoking cigarettes _____	6	3	9
Chronic cigarette smoking _	6	13	19
Total _____	19	19	[2] 38

chi square = 5.179
df = 2
significance: $0.10 > p > 0.05$

[1] Of 47 subjects, 8 are cigar and pipe smokers and are not included in this data.

[2] At the 11-year study, 1 subject's whereabouts were unknown; thus, 38 rather than 39 subjects.

Diastolic Blood Pressure. The diastolic blood pressure approaches a significant relationship to mortality at the 11-year study (table 8).

Mean Arterial Blood Pressure (MABP). The MABP relates significantly to mortality at 11 years (table 8).

As stated previously, only three of the 47 subjects could be considered as clinically hypertensive, and even these values are but minimally "elevated" for this age. The remaining subjects had pressures

TABLE 6.—*Systolic blood pressure and weight measured at initial study and relationship to mortality at 5-year followup*

	N [1]	Systolic B.P. [2] (mm. Hg)	Weight (Kg.)
Died _____	8	144	60.4
Survived _____	39	130	69.9
significance:		t = 2.39 $p \leq 0.05$	2.46 $p \leq 0.05$

[1] N = number of subjects.
[2] B.P. = blood pressure.

TABLE 7.—*Weights obtained in 1956 appearing as a continuum in relation to longevity*

	N [1]	Weight in 1956 (Kg.)
Died by 5-year followup ____	8	60.4
Died between 5- and 11-year followup _____	16	66.0
Alive at 11-year followup __	[2] 20	71.0
Total _____	44	---

significance: $p \leq 0.05$

[1] N = number of subjects.
[2] Data not available on 3 subjects.

which were well within any standard of normal, particularly for this age group (tables 1 and 2).

"Arteriosclerotics"

As described in the methodology section, a subgroup of group II, termed "arteriosclerotics," demonstrated significant, relatively asymptomatic evidence of generalized arteriosclerosis. The relationship of this subgroup category with mortality was very significant at 5 and 11 years (table 9).

TABLE 8.—*Certain factors [1] relating to mortality at 11-year followup*

	N [2]	Systolic B.P. [3] (mm. Hg)	Weight (Kg.)	MABP [4] (mm. Hg)	Diastolic B.P. [3] (mm. Hg)
Died _____	24	138	64.1	[5] 105	78
Survived _____	22	126	[5] 71.0	[5] 95	[5] 74
t _____	--	2.87	2.55	2.23	1.09
p _____	--	0.01	0.02	0.05	$0.10 > p > .05$

[1] Data obtained at initial study in 1956.
[2] N = number of subjects.
[3] B.P. = blood pressure.
[4] MABP = mean arterial blood pressure.
[5] Data available on 20 subjects.

TABLE 9.—*Relationship of subgroup of "arteriosclerotics" to mortality at 5- and 11-year followup*

5-YEAR FOLLOWUP

	Nonarteriosclerotic	Arteriosclerotic	Total
Died _____	3	5	8
Survived __	34	5	˙39
Total __	37	10	47

chi square=7.04
df=1
significance: 0.005>p>0.001

11-YEAR FOLLOWUP

Died _____	15	9	24
Survived __	22	0	22
Total __	37	9	[1]46

chi square=8.01
df=1
significance: p≤0.005

[1] 46 subjects, rather than 47; whereabouts of 1 subject were unknown.

Weight

Contrary to expectations, mortality at the 5- and 11-year followup related significantly to a lighter weight at the time of the original study (tables 6 and 8). Furthermore, a continuum of weight obtained in 1956 and longevity is apparent (table 7). Those who had died by the 5-year followup had the lightest weight (60.4 kg.), those who had died between 5 and 11 years had an intermediate weight (66.0 kg.), and those alive at the 11-year followup had the heaviest weight (71.0 kg.).

The chronic cigarette smokers weigh significantly less than the nonsmokers (65.7 vs. 72.8 Kg.; $p \leq 0.05$). Even when "holding constant" the effect of cigarette smoking on weight and mortality, there remains a consistent relationship of lighter weight to mortality.

The weight and height of the entire group of 47 subjects did not differ appreciably from the figures for larger populations at this age (Master, Lasser, and Beckman, 1960; *Statistical Bulletin: Metropolitan Life Insurance Company*, 1959). When controlling for the effects of height

by utilizing a weight-over-height ratio, the relationship remains the same. That is, a lower ratio is significantly related to a greater mortality.

Age

For this group of subjects, mean age 71 years at the outset of this investigation, age was of borderline significance as a factor in mortality at the time of the 11-year study, as it had not been a significant factor at the 5-year study (see p. 7 for discussion).

Calcification of the Internal Carotid Artery "Siphon" [1]

The skull X-rays of 42 subjects were classified into "intimal," "medial," or "absent" calcification of the carotid artery siphon. The differentiation followed somewhat the method of Lindbom (1950) for calcification of the arteries of the lower extremities. These groupings were then compared as to cerebral physiological measurements (Dastur, Lane, Hansen, Kety, Butler, Perlin, and Sokoloff, 1963).

Figures 1 and 2 demonstrate the appearance of "medial" and "intimal" calcifications in lateral views. Note the linear and continuous appearance of the medial calcification and the "fleck like" discontinuous appearance of the intimal calcification.

The intimal calcification is related to a significantly lower cerebral blood flow than the medial calcification (table 10).

[1] The carotid "siphon" is an angiographic term denoting the internal carotid artery in its intracranial course through the carotid canal and the cavernous sinus up to the point immediately prior to joining the Circle of Willis. Calcification of the siphon is often seen on plain skull films. The skull X-rays were interpreted and classified by Dr. G. DiChiro, Head, Section on Neuroradiology, National Institute of Neurological Diseases and Stroke, Bethesda, Md.

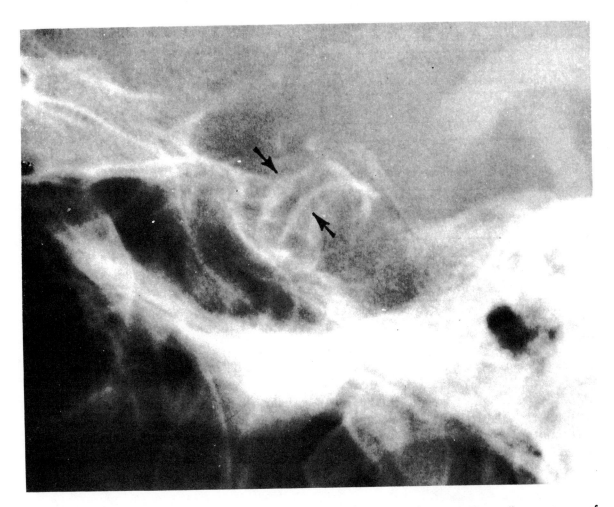

FIGURE 1.—X-ray of skull in lateral position. Arrows indicate the "linear continuous" appearance of calcium in the walls of the carotid artery "siphon." In this case, the entire course of the vessel is outlined. This is representative of medial-type calcification.

The "medial" group has an apparent increased mortality in contrast to the "intimal" group (table 11). However, this increased mortality was not statistically significant. These relationships and the details of the radiologic criteria are re-

TABLE 10.—*Cerebral circulation* [1] *in healthy elderly subjects with intimal or medial calcification of the carotid artery siphon*

Grouping of subjects	N [2]	Age (years)	MABP (mm. Hg)	CBF (ml./100 g./min.)	CVR (mm. Hg) (ml./100 g./min.)
Absent calcification _____	10	71.3±1.3	93.1±2.0	56.9±3.5	1.6±0.1
Medial calcification _____	9	71.6±1.8	99.3±4.8	60.6±3.8	1.6±0.1
Intimal calcification _____	20	72.0±1.3	101.2±2.8	[3] 52.5±2.0	1.8±0.1

[1] All values are means ± standard errors.
[2] Size of groupings. Three subjects with bilateral calcification of the "siphon" are not included in these data; thus, N=39 rather than 42. (See table 11.)
[3] Statistically significantly different from the group with medial calcification (p=0.05).

FIGURE 2.—X-ray of skull in lateral position. Arrow indicates the "fleck like" appearance of calcium within the sella turcica. This is representative of intimal-type calcification.

TABLE 11.—*Relationship of calcification of carotid artery siphon to mortality*[1] *at 5-and 11-year followup*

Grouping of subjects	N [2]	5-year followup			11-year followup		
		Survived	Died	Mortality Rate percent	Survived	Died	Mortality Rate percent
Absent calcification _____	12	11	1	8.3	8	4	33.0
Medial calcification _____	10	6	4	40.0	3	7	70.0
Intimal calcification _____	20	16	4	20.0	12	8	40.0

[1] The mortality rates among the 3 groupings are not statistically significantly different, though the "medial" classification has a consistently greater mortality rate.
[2] Number of subjects: 42 had X-rays and cerebral physiological studies.

ported more fully elsewhere (Libow, 1967; DiChiro and Libow, 1970).

Right Bundle Branch Block (RBBB) and Lack of Relationship to Mortality

At the initial study, five subjects had complete RBBB and three subjects had incomplete RBBB patterns on their electrocardiograms. None had histories of cardiac, pulmonary, or pulmonary embolic disease. There was no significant relationship between RBBB pattern and mortality. The serum cholesterol of the subjects with RBBB was not significantly different from that of the subjects without RBBB.

Apparent Coronary Heart Disease (CHD) as a Cause of Death

Nine subjects died from apparent CHD by the time of the 11-year study. The source of the clinical information leading to this diagnosis is presented in table 12. Five of these nine sources are death certificates, with two of the five being listed, additionally, as "sudden deaths." Death certificates are reported as being only 80 percent accurate in the diagnosis of coronary heart disease (Beadenkopf, Abrams, Daoud, and Marks, 1963).

CHD and Serum Cholesterol

The serum cholesterol of this group of nine subjects who died from apparent CHD was significantly greater in 1956 than that of the surviving subjects (261 vs. 225 mg%) (table 13).

CHD and Chronic Cigarette Smoking

Chronic cigarette smoking was significantly related to mortality from apparent CHD (table 14). There was no relationship of cigar and pipe smoking to mortality.

CHD and Systolic, Diastolic, and Mean Arterial Blood Pressure

There was no significant relationship between death from apparent CHD and the systolic, diastolic, or mean arterial blood pressure.

TABLE 13.—Relationship of serum cholesterol to mortality from apparent coronary heart disease at 11-year followup

	N [1]	Serum cholesterol (mg%)
Died from CHD	9	261
Survivors	20	225
		t = 2.20 significance: p = 0.05

[1] N = number of subjects.

TABLE 12.—Coronary heart disease as cause of death: Clinical information and its source

Subject number	Clinical information	Source
1	Substernal pain leading to shock and sudden death.	Hospital record and death certificate.
10	Congestive heart failure, arteriosclerotic heart disease, auricular arrhythmia, cardiomegaly by X-ray.	Hospital record.
16	"Coronary occlusion"	Death certificate.
25	"Sudden death; coronary occlusion"	Death certificate.
36	3 acute coronary occlusions	Physicians' reports.
38	Bilateral bundle branch block and Stokes-Adams syndrome.	Hospital record.
39	Extensive myocardial fibrosis; plaques in left and right coronary artery.	Autopsy.
52	"Sudden death; coronary occlusion"	Death certificate.
57	"Coronary occlusion"	Death certificate.

TABLE 14.—*Relationship of chronic cigarette smoking to death from apparent coronary heart disease at 11-year followup*

Incidence of cigarette smoking in survivors and in those who died from CHD

	Never smoked	chronic cigarette smokers	Total
Died from CHD ____	0	6	[1]6
Survived _____	7	6	[2]13
Total _____	7	12	19

the Fisher [3] exact p value is ≤0.05

[1] Of 9 subjects who died from apparent CHD, 3 had stopped smoking and are omitted from the analysis.

[2] Of 22 who survived, 6 had stopped smoking and are omitted from the analysis. Three others were cigar and pipe smokers and they, too, are omitted from the analysis.

[3] Siegel, 1956.

CHD and Weight

There was no relationship between weight and death from apparent CHD.

Cancer of the Gastrointestinal Tract and Serum Albumin

Seven subjects died from cancer by the time of the 11-year study. All had cancer of the gastrointestinal tract. The location of the cancer, the date of death, and in some cases the date of diagnosis, are listed in table 15.

The serum albumin, measured chemically (Rutstein, Ingenito, and Reynolds, 1954), was significantly lower in the group to die subsequently of cancer of the gastrointestinal tract than in the group of survivors (table 16). When measured electrophoretically, the albumin differences exist in the same direction, but are not statistically significant (table 16).

There was no relationship between weight in 1956 and the development of cancer.

TABLE 15.—*Mortality due to carcinoma*

Subject number	Source of information	Anatomical location	Date of death [1]
3	Death certificate _____	Rectum _____	1958
31	Physician's report _____	Colon _____	1959
30	Death certificate and physician's report.	Colon and stomach _____	1960 (1960)
2	Hospital record and physician's report.	Colon _____	1961 (1960)
28	Hospital record _____	Stomach _____	1964
19	Death certificate _____	Colon _____	1965
53	Autopsy _____	Colon _____	1967 (1966)

[1] Parentheses indicate known year of diagnosis of carcinoma.

TABLE 16.—*Serum albumin in apparently healthy elderly subjects and ensuing death from cancer of the gastrointestinal tract*

Method	N [2]	Died from cancer	N	Survivors without cancer
Chemical [1] Serum albumin (g%) --	7	3.30	19	3.54
		t=2.43 df=24 p=0.05		
Electrophoretic [3] Serum albumin (g%) --	5	3.03	19	3.26
		t=1.49 df=22 p=not significant		

[1] Chemical method of Rutstein, Ingenito, and Reynolds (1954).

[2] N=number of subjects.

[3] Filter paper electrophoretic method.

Causes of Death

Information as to apparent cause of death is available for all 24 deceased subjects. This information was obtained as follows: death certificates (11 cases), hospital records (six cases), physician reports (four cases), and autopsies (three cases). Of the 24 subjects, further substantiation was achieved through data sources such as the 5-year followup, hospital records (two cases), death certificates (five cases), physician reports (two cases), and questionnaires completed by families (13 cases).

The distribution of the major causes of death is listed in table 17.

Changes in Survivors at the 11-Year Followup Study

The survivors have been restudied and the findings compared with those of 1956. Changes in survivors are shown in tables 18 and 19.

Of the 18 survivors restudied (table 18), three had developed malignancies and seven others were taking medications for various conditions. The remaining eight subjects revealed the expected moderate changes of the late seventies and early eighties, without specific significant disease.

As shown in table 19, the following measurements reveal no significant changes over the 11 years, from mean age 71 to 82: hemoglobin, serum cholesterol, blood urea nitrogen, systolic blood pressure, diastolic blood pressure, creatinine, and protein bound iodine. The erythrocyte sedimenta-

tion rate and the fasting blood sugar significantly increased during this time interval.

DISCUSSION

This 11-year study of 47 originally healthy elderly men has revealed several factors which precede, correlate with, and perhaps contribute to the development of disease and mortality. The relative lack of significant obesity and hypertension, as well as the excellent general health of these subjects, has allowed a freer expression of certain disease factors, unhampered by the extremes of blood pressure and weight and by the multiple disease states so usual in the elderly.

Certain factors, of known significance in midlife, have been shown to be of significance even in the decade from 70 to 80 years.

Certain other factors have been quite surprising. Lighter weight has been shown to relate to increased mortality. Diminished serum albumin has been found to precede cancer of the gastrointestinal tract.

Systolic Blood Pressure

A significant relationship has been found between systolic blood pressure and general mortality at the 5- and 11-year study. No such relationship has been found between systolic pressure and death from apparent CHD.

By contrast, the Framingham study data reveal a significant relationship of general mortality to systolic blood pressure up to

TABLE 17.—*Apparent Causes of Death*

Cause	N [1]	Percent	Expected percent [2]
Coronary heart disease	9	38	39
Cerebrovascular accident	1	4	17
Malignancy	7	29	19
Miscellaneous [3]	7	29	25
Total	24	100	100

[1] N = number of subjects.
[2] From *Vital Statistics of the United States*, 1966, vol. II—Mortality (1968).
[3] Pulmonary embolus (N=3), surgical complications (N=2), cold exposure (N=1), generalized arteriosclerosis (N=1).

age 69, and no relationship at ages 70 to 74. However, at ages 70 to 74, there is a significant relationship between systolic pressure and death specifically from CHD (The Framingham Study, 1968, secs. 19 and 20).

TABLE 18.—*Medical status of subjects at 1967 followup study*

Subject number	Significant disease of central nervous system [1]	Significant disease of cardiovascular system	Other significant diseases	Explanation of abnormalities	Health ratings [3]
6	X [2]	X	O	Chronic brain syndrome (CBS); Peripheral vascular disease (PVD), mild EKG abnormality (ST and T wave changes).	III
7	O	O	O	Healthy _____	I
9	O	X	X	EKG abnormality (interventricular conduction defect) PVD (mild); Cancer of sigmoid colon, 1960.	III
14	O	O	O	Healthy _____	I
15	O	X	O	PVD (mild) _____	II
18	X	O	X	CBS and transient ischemic attack (TIA); emphysema.	III
20	O	O	O	Healthy _____	I
27	O	O	O	Healthy _____	I
42	O	X	O	Calcific aortic stenosis; hypertension; EKG abnormality (ST and T wave changes).	III
47	O	X	O	PVD (mild) _____	II
51	X	X	O	CBS and TIA and PVD (mild) ____	III
54	O	X	O	PVD (mild) _____	II
55	O	O	O	Healthy _____	I
56	O	O	X	Cancer of rectum, 1961; possible metastases to lung _____	III
58	O	X	O	EKG abnormalities (T wave changes and left axis deviation).	II
59	O	O	O	Healthy _____	I
23	X	X	O	CBS and TIA; EKG abnormality (left ventricular hypertrophy); hypertension.	III
8	O	O	X	Cancer of jaw, 1967 _____	III

[1] Including disease of the cerebrovascular system.
[2] X indicates presence of disease.
[3] I=Healthy; II=Mild abnormalities; III=Significant abnormalities of one or more systems.

TABLE 19.—*Changes in survivors* [1]

Parameter	1956 Mean ± S.D.	1967 Mean ± S.D.	Significance of difference P
Hemoglobin g% _____	14.8± 1.0	15.1 ± 0.0	N.S.
E.S.R.[2] mm./1st hr. _____	16.9±12.1	27.1±13.0	0.01
Cholesterol mg% _____	233.0±32.0	199.0±52.0	N.S.
BUN [3] mg% _____	18.0± 3.4	19.0± 7.5	N.S.
FBS [4] mg% _____	75.0± 6.0	85.0± 8.0	0.05
Creatinine mg% _____	1.1± 0.14	1.1± 0.11	N.S.
PBI [5] mg% _____	5.2± 1.1	6.1± 0.7	N.S.
Systolic B.P. mm./Hg _____	122.0±11.0	128.0±19.0	N.S.
Diastolic B.P. mm./Hg _____	73.0± 5.0	76.0± 8.0	N.S.

[1] Excluded from the group of the 18 survivors who were restudied are 10 subjects, 7 taking medications and 3 others with cancer.
[2] E.S.R.=Erythrocyte sedimentation rate.
[3] BUN = Blood urea nitrogen.
[4] FBS = Fasting blood sugar.
[5] PBI = Protein bound iodine.

Insurance data, too, reveal an increasing general mortality rate for each small increase in level of systolic or diastolic pressure. This effect diminished with each increase of age (*Statistical Bulletin*, July 1960).

Reports of decreased morbidity and mortality following treatment of hypertensives often do not contain conclusions pertinent to subjects beyond 60 years (Farmer, Gifford, Hines, 1963; Hodge, McQueen, and Smirk, 1961). One study has reported a diminished mortality associated with the lowering of blood pressure in elderly subjects (Priddle, Liu, Breithaupt, and Grant, 1968).

The exact mechanism behind this correlation of systolic pressure and mortality is uncertain. Rather than the systolic pressure contributing to mortality via cardiovascular effects, it is possible that both the systolic pressure and the mortality reflect a third factor, that of arteriosclerosis. It is generally believed, for instance, that elevations of systolic pressure often result from decreased elasticity of the aorta due to arteriosclerosis.

On the other hand, it may be that the level of systolic pressure, itself, exerts adverse effects. The blood pressures in the original study and the lack of increased pressure in the survivors (table 18) would hardly warrant treatment by our present criteria. However, it may be that even these pressures need lowering. This question appears to deserve further study.

Chronic Cigarette Smoking

Chronic cigarette smoking has been found to relate significantly to general mortality at the 5- and 11-year study. Also, death from apparent CHD is related to chronic cigarette smoking.

The well-known lethal effects of chronic cigarette smoking are greatest in midlife and decline with increasing age (*U.S. Public Health Service Review*, 1968). In the Framingham study, risks of every manifestation of CHD, but especially fatal attacks, were significantly increased in heavy cigarette smokers (Kannel, Castelli, and McNamara, 1967). The exception was the 70- to 74-year-old male group, which in contrast to our subjects, did not show a significant relationship of chronic cigarette smoking and mortality from CHD (The Framingham Study, sec. 20, 1968).

The mechanism by which cigarettes take their toll on mortality in general and on CHD specifically is not clear. The Framingham group has postulated some acute effect, superimposed on the background of chronic smoking and not via an atherosclerotic mechanism. They advance the idea of release of catecholamines, triggering lethal attacks (Kannel, Castelli, and McNamara, 1967). Supporting a chronic vascular mechanism rather than an acute effect is a study of over 1,000 autopsies which reveals a relationship of increased atherosclerosis to chronic cigarette smoking (Auerbach, Hammond, and Garfinkel, 1965).

Our subjects who stopped smoking after approximately 40 years of the habit have a mortality rate almost identical to the nonsmokers. A similar reversal has been noted in the studies of somewhat younger subjects in several epidemiological studies (Doyle, Dawber, Kannel, Kindh, and Kahn, 1964; Doll and Hill, 1964). This makes it seem likely that the mortality factor in smoking is an acute one and quite reversible upon discontinuance of smoking. This is hardly the definition of atherosclerosis or almost any other chronic effect.

Weight

Unexpectedly, general mortality was significantly related to a lighter antecedent weight. In general, increasing weight at all ages relates to increasing mortality (*Statistical Bulletin,* February 1960; *Statistical Bulletin,* March 1960; *Statistical Bulletin,* April 1960). In the Framingham study the CHD which related to overweight was due to angina pectoris or sudden death, not to myocardial infarction (Kannel, Castelli, McNamara, 1967). For subjects 70 to 74 years, there was no significant association between death from CHD and overweight (The Framingham Study, sec. 20, 1968). Similarly, there was no relationship in this study between weight and mortality from apparent CHD.

In one major longitudinal study, no relationship was found between CHD and obesity (Keys, Taylor, Blackburn, Brozek, and Anderson, 1963). Stamler (1967) has suggested that the increase in CHD in overweight persons, shown in most studies, may be the result of the frequent accompaniment of obesity by factors such as hypertension and diabetes mellitus, and that "pure" obesity may be unrelated to a proneness to CHD. Even if Stamler is correct, this still leaves the significant relationship of mortality and lighter weight unexplained.

The absence of very overweight men and the absence of hypertensives may have allowed this unusual relationship to be revealed. Cigarette smoking has somewhat influenced this relationship since smokers weigh less than nonsmokers, though not significantly. Similarly, the "arteriosclerotics" weigh less than the nonarteriosclerotics, though the reason is obscure. However, even when the effects of cigarette smoking and arteriosclerosis on mortality are held "statistically constant" (effects somewhat excluded via matching of subjects), the lighter weight continues to relate to mortality. The group developing cancer did not weigh less than the other subjects in the original study. The heights of these subjects have been shown to have no influence on the mortality-lighter weight relationship. The mean weight of our subjects is similar to that reported for much larger populations of elderly men (Master, Lasser, and Beckman, 1960; *Statistical Bulletin,* 1959). One possible mechanism for this relationship is presented later in this chapter.

The relationship of lighter weight and increased mortality in our group of elderly men is apparently supported by the data of the Build and Blood Pressure Study (Society of Actuaries, 1959). The study shows that for men of short height (63 to 66 inches—the average height of our subjects) who were issued life insurance policies between ages 50 and 69 (the upper age limit of the data in their study), there is, indeed, an increased mortality at moderately lighter weights. This relationship does not exist for men ages 20 to 49 nor for women at any age or height. There is also, as is well known, an increased mortality for markedly overweight men and women at all ages and heights.

Calcification of the Carotid Artery Siphon

The finding of a significantly lower cerebral blood flow in the group with "intimal" type calcification is consistent with the expected physiological effects of disease of the intima; i.e., atherosclerosis. This physiological finding appears to substantiate this somewhat uncertain radiographic classification.

The higher mortality rate for the "medial" group is inconsistent with the expected mortality effect of intimal disease.

The value of this new radiographic-physiologic correlation in helping to further differentiate the cerebral vascular diseases of the elderly remains to be proven.

Right Bundle Branch Block

In the initial study we reported on the

apparent benign nature of Right Bundle Branch Block (RBBB). There was no significant history of coronary heart disease, pulmonary disease, or pulmonary embolic disease in the five subjects with complete RBBB or in the three subjects with incomplete RBBB. There was no significant difference in serum cholesterol between the group with RBBB and the other volunteer subjects. The followup study fails to reveal any significant relationship of this electrocardiographic finding and mortality.

Prior reports show an increasing incidence of RBBB with age (Johnson, Averill, and Lamb, 1959). A report of 281 patients with RBBB concluded that the significance depended entirely on accompanying demonstrable heart disease (Shreenivas, Messer, Johnson and White, 1950).

The cause of RBBB remains obscure, but coronary heart disease does not appear likely. With increasing age there are changes in connective tissue as well as increasing opportunities for nonspecific inflammatory diseases to affect the right bundle, without significantly affecting cardiac function and survival.

Serum Cholesterol and Death From CHD

There is little doubt of the relationship of serum cholesterol to the development of CHD in middle-aged men (Kannel, Dawber, Cohen, and McNamara, 1965; Keys, Taylor, Blackburn, Brozek, Anderson, and Whiter, 1963; Stamler, 1967). The Framingham data show a similar relationship in men ages 70 to 74 (The Framingham Study, sec. 20, 1968). The Framingham data separate middle-aged men into the following categories of serum cholesterol: "normal" = below 225 mg%, "borderline" = between 225 mg% and 259 mg%, "abnormal" = above 260 mg%. The borderline group has approxi-

mately 50 percent more CHD than the normal group.

It is striking that our subjects who died of apparent CHD had a mean serum cholesterol of 261 mg%, so very similar to the values of the Framingham study (Kannel, Dawber, Cohen, and McNamara, 1965) and other studies (Keys, Taylor, Blackburn, Brozek, Anderson, and Whiter, 1963; Chapman and Massey, 1964). This appears to substantiate, somewhat, our classification of death from CHD.

Cancer of the Gastrointestinal Tract and Serum Albumin

In our study, a diminished level of serum albumin appears predictive of the development of cancer of the gastrointestinal tract. These subjects were in apparent excellent health at the time the serum albumin was measured. Over the next several years, cancer of the gastrointestinal tract became obvious and led to death.

It is well known that clinically obvious gastrointestinal cancer is commonly associated with reduced serum albumin (Meindok, 1967).

All cancers, not just gastrointestinal cancers, may be associated with diminished serum albumin. The mechanism of decrease appears to be a diminished synthesis by the liver, rather than an increased catabolism or change in plasma volume or distribution of albumin (Steinfeld, 1965).

For gastrointestinal malignancies, specifically, loss via the gastrointestinal tract into the stool appears to be an additional mechanism (Sum, Hoffman, and Webster, 1964; Jarnum and Schwartz, 1960; Diamant and Volberg, 1963).

Whether the cancer of the gastrointestinal tract was already present at the time of the initial study is difficult to say. If so, then the level of serum albumin could prove to be a useful screening device. For example, of our 47 subjects, 16 had serum albumin of 3.3 g% or less. Six of the 16 (37 percent) went on to develop cancer of the gastrointestinal tract. Only one subject with cancer of the gastrointestinal tract had a serum albumin of over 3.3 gm% (i.e., 3.8 g%). There was no relationship between serum albumin levels and mortality from all other major causes.

Alternately, and less likely, the metabolic state leading to a lower serum albumin in the healthy elderly may also predispose to the development of gastrointestinal malignancy. In the original study the entire group of 47 subjects had a significantly lower serum albumin compared to a group of young controls (3.27 g% vs. 3.81 g%) (Libow, 1963). What is not at all apparent are the factors in common which exist between the normally decreased albumin in later life and the development of the most frequent malignancy of later life.

Changes in Survivors

Comparing these elderly survivors with themselves, 11 years earlier, is an uncertain effort, but provides some information as to the effects of time on certain medical measurement. By excluding those with cancer and those taking medications, we are left with eight subjects for comparison. These eight have acquired the frailties of later life. However, certain tentative conclusions may still be drawn about "age related" rather than "disease related" changes in these survivors.

Of particular note is the lack of increase of systolic and diastolic pressure over the 11-year period. Reports of increases with age (Master, Lasser, and Jaffe, 1957) probably arise from cross-sectional rather than longitudinal studies.

The increased erythrocyte sedimentation rate with age appears to continue a trend noted in our initial study.

The increase in fasting blood sugar, though still very much within the normal range, may be another reflection of the "diabetic type" glucose tolerance curve noted in a high percentage of healthy elderly (Andres, 1967).

The medical status of the 18 survivors restudied at the 11-year followup was presented in table 19. Six subjects were found to be quite healthy, four subjects had evidence of mild disease, and eight subjects had significant disease of one or more systems.

Possible Mechanism Relating Changes in Protein, Weight, and Mortality

The decreased serum albumin in this entire group of elderly volunteers, as compared to young controls, noted in the original study (Libow, 1963), and the unexpected relationship of lighter weight to increased mortality suggest a subtle negative balance of calories and proteins with advancing age. Data from animal studies provide evidence to both substantiate and negate a theory of diminished protein synthesis with age (Barrows, 1969). One study of male and female mice revealed a 14-percent decrease, with age, of total body nitrogen and weight, only in the males. These males also had a very significantly greater mortality rate (Sobel, Hrubant, and Hewlett, 1968).

One mechanism to explain these changes would be a decrease in thyroid hormone. The primary mechanism of action of thyroxine appears to be an increase in the incorporation of amino acids into protein (Sokoloff and Kaufman, 1959; Sokoloff, 1964). Protein bound iodine (PBI) did not decrease with age in this longitudinal study nor in cross-sectional studies of men between the ages of 18 and 94 years

(Gaffney, Gregerman, Yiengst, and Shock, 1960). With age, however, there does appear to be a decreased synthesis of thyroxine (Gaffney, Gregerman, and Shock, 1960), and a decreased basal oxygen consumption (Shock and Yiengst, 1955). This diminished thyroxine synthesis is not reflected in the PBI levels because the overall thyroxine binding ability does not decrease with age (Braverman, Dawber, and Ingbar, 1966). A decreased synthesis of thyroid hormone would lead to a decreased protein synthesis, a decreased oxygen consumption, and perhaps to a decreased weight secondary to diminished tissue synthesis. These changes may, in turn, relate to mortality.

SUMMARY

An 11-year longitudinal study of originally healthy elderly men had revealed several factors which precede and correlate with disease and mortality. Study of the survivors reveals the effect of "age" on several clinical measurements.

Chronic cigarette smoking of 47 years average duration correlates with mortality in general, and also with mortality from apparent coronary heart disease specifically. Those who stopped smoking had done so between 3 and 25 years prior to the study, and after an average duration of 30 years of smoking. This group which discontinued smoking have survival rates almost identical with nonsmokers, suggesting reversibility of the effect of cigarette smoking on mortality.

The systolic blood pressure and mean arterial blood pressure correlate with mortality. The diastolic blood pressure has only a suggestive relationship to mortality. These significant correlations occur within a range of systolic pressure ordinarily considered normal for this age or any age. Though the pressure itself may have an adverse effect on survival, it is suggested that the relationship of pressure and mortality are not cause and effect but may reflect the mortality effects of a third factor; i.e., atherosclerosis. This latter factor, when affecting the aorta and large vessels, is known to produce a somewhat elevated systolic pressure.

Unexpectedly, an antecedent lighter weight relates significantly to ensuing mortality.

Calcification of the "siphon" of the carotid artery, as seen on routine skull X-ray, has been classified into "intimal" and "medial" type calcification. The intimal group has a significantly lower cerebral blood flow than the medial group, as might be expected if the intimal calcification truly reflects atherosclerosis of the intima. This sign may prove useful in helping to differentiate the cerebrovascular syndromes of the elderly.

Right Bundle Branch Block is apparently a benign and not infrequent electrocardiographic finding in the elderly. It does not relate to mortality or coronary heart disease.

Mortality from apparent coronary heart disease relates significantly to antecedent higher serum cholesterol levels and to chronic cigarette smoking.

A subtle, though significant, reduction in serum albumin appears to precede the development of clinically evident cancer of the gastrointestinal tract. This may prove to be a useful "screening" test for cancer of the gastro-intestinal tract.

The survivors reveal no change in systolic, diastolic, or mean arterial blood pressure over the 11-year period. Prior reports of an increasing blood pressure over this age range may reflect the cross-sectional rather than longitudinal nature of those studies.

The survivors show no change over 11

years in the following additional "parameters": hemoglobin, serum cholesterol, blood urea nitrogen, creatinine, and protein bound iodine.

The survivors do show a significant increase in erythrocyte sedimentation rate and fasting blood sugar over the 11-year study period.

An attempt is made to relate the significantly diminished serum albumin of this entire group at the start of the study with the unexpected relationship of lighter weight and increased mortality. Because the primary mode of action of thyroxine appears to be a stimulation of amino acid incorporation into protein, and because thyroxine production is apparently decreased in later life, a diminished thyroxine effect is suggested as a possible mediator of this negative protein and caloric balance.

ACKNOWLEDGMENTS

The author wishes to express his appreciation to Dr. John Bartko of the Office of Biometry, National Institute of Mental Health, Section on Theoretical Statistics and Mathematics, for his biostatistical consultative guidance.

To Mrs. Annie Randall of the Office of Biometry, National Institute of Mental Health, Section on Theoretical Statistics and Mathematics, for her expert technical analyses.

To Dr. Henry Altschuler of the Philadelphia Geriatric Center for performing laboratory tests at the 11-year followup.

To Dr. Charles Harris of the Philadelphia Geriatric Center for performing the medical examinations at the 11-year followup.

To the entire staff of the Philadelphia Geriatric Center for their care in obtaining the necessary data, over the many years of the followup study.

To Mrs. Carmel Garner for her invaluable secretarial assistance.

REFERENCES

ANDRES, R. Relation of physiologic changes in aging to medical changes of disease in the aged. *Mayo Clin. Proc.*, 42: 764–784, 1967.

AUERBACH, O.; HAMMOND, E. C.; and GARFINKEL, L. Smoking in relation to atherosclerosis of the coronary arteries. *New Eng. J. Med.*, 273: 775–779, 1965.

BARROWS, C. H., JR. The effect of age on protein synthesis. *8th Intl. Cong. Gerontol. Proc.* 1:179–182, 1969.

BEADENKOFF, W. G., ABRAMS, M.; DAOUD, A.; and MARKS, R. L. An assessment of certain medical aspects of death certificate data for epidemiologic study of arteriosclerotic heart disease. *J. Chronic Dis.*,16: 249–262, 1963.

BIRREN, J. E.; BUTLER, R. N.; GREENHOUSE, S. W; SOKOLOFF, L.; and YARROW, M. R. *Human Aging: a Biological and Behavioral Study*, Washington, D.C.: U.S. Government Printing Office, 1963. 328 pp.

BRAVERMAN, L. E.; DAWBER, M. A.; and INGBAR, S. H. Observations concerning the binding of thyroid hormones in sera of normal subjects of varying ages. *J. Clin. Invest.*, 45: 1273–1279, 1966.

Build and Blood Pressure Study. Volume I. Society of Actuaries: Chicago Ill.: The Society, 1969. 268 pp.

CHAPMAN, J. M., and MASSEY, F. J. The interrelationship of serum cholesterol, hypertension, body weight, and risk of coronary disease. Results of the first 10-year followup in the Los Angeles heart study. *J. Chronic Dis.*, 17: 933–949, 1964.

DASTUR, D. K.; LANE, M. H.; HANSEN, D. B.; KETY, S. S.; BUTLER, R N.; PERLIN, S.; and SOKOLOFF, L. Effects of aging on cerebral circulation and metabolism in man. In: Birren, J. E.; Butler, R. N.; Greenhouse, S. W.; Sokoloff, L.; and Yarrow, M. R., eds. *Human Aging: A Biological and Behavioral Study*. Washington, D.C.: U.S. Government Printing Office, 1963. Chapter 6.

DIAMANT, M. E., and VOLBERG, L. S. Plasma protein loss associated with carcinoma of the colon. *Amer. J. Dig. Dis.*, 8: 877–881, 1963.

DICHIRO, G., and LIBOW, L. S. Carotid siphon calcification and cerebral blood flow in the healthy aged male. *Radiology*, 99:103–107, 1971.

DOLL, R., and HILL, A. B. Mortality in relation to smoking: 10 years observations of British doctors. *Brit Med. J.*, 1: 1399–1410, 1964.

——, ——. Mortality in relation to smoking: 10 years observations of British doctors. *Brit. Med. J.*, 1: 1460–1467, 1964.

DOYLE, J. T.; DAWBER, T. R.; KANNEL, W. B.; KINCH, S. H.; and KAHN, H. A. The relationship of cigarette smoking to coronary heart disease. *J. Amer. Med. Assn.,* 190: 886–890, 1964.

EPSTEIN, F. H.; OSTRANDER, L. D., JR.; JOHNSON, B. C.; PAYNE, M. W.; HYANES, M. S.; KELLER, J. B.; and FRANCIS, T., JR. Epidemiological studies of cardiovascular disease in a total community—Tecumseh, Mich. *Ann. Intern. Med.,* 62: 1170–1187, 1965.

FARMER, R. G.; GIFFORD, R. W., JR.; and HINES, E. A. Effect of medical treatment of severe hypertension. A followup study of 161 patients with groups 3 and 4 hypertension. *Brit. Med. J.,* 1, 1–6, 1963.

The Framingham Study. An Epidemiological Investigation of Cardiovascular Disease. Incidence of death by sex, age, and level of characteristic at examination for 22 characteristics. Washington, D.C.: U.S. Government Printing Office, 1968. Section 19.

The Framingham Study. An Epidemiological Investigation of Cardiovascular Disease. Incidence of death from coronary heart disease by sex, age, and level of characteristic at examination for 22 characteristics. Washington, D.C.: U.S. Government Printing Office, 1968. Section 20.

GAFFNEY, G. W.; GREGERMAN, R. I.; YIENGST, M. J.; and SHOCK, N. W. Serum protein bound iodine concentration in blood of euthyroid men aged 18–94 years *J. Geront.,* 15: 234–241, 1960.

GAFFNEY, G. W.; GREGERMAN, R. I.; and SHOCK, N. W. Relationship of age to the thyroided accumulation, renal excretion and distribution of radio iodide in euthyroid man. *J. Clin. Endocr.,* 22: 784–794, 1962.

GREGERMAN, R. I.; GAFFNEY, G. W.; and SHOCK, N. W. Thyroxine turnover in euthyroid man with special reference to changes with age. *J. Clin. Invest.,* 41: 2065–2074, 1962.

HODGE, J. W.; McQUEEN, E. G., and SMIRK, F. H. Results of hypotensive therapy in arterial hypertension. *Brit. Med. J.,* 1: 1–6, 1961.

JARNUM, S., and SCHWARTZ, M. Hypoalbuminemia in gastric carcinoma. *Gastroenterology,* 38: 769–776, 1960.

JOHNSON, R. L.; AVERILL, K. H.; and LAMB, L. E. Electrocardiographic findings in 63,375 asymptomatic individuals. Part VI: Right bundle branch block. The First International Symposium on Cardiology in Aviation. 1954. pp. 271–278.

KANNEL, W. B.; CASTELLI, W. P.; and McNAMARA, P. M. The coronary profile: 12-year followup in the Framingham Study. *J. Occup. Med.,* 9: 611–619, 1967.

——, DAWBER, T. R.; COHEN, M. E.; and McNAMARA, P. M. Vascular disease of the brain-epidemiologic aspects. *Amer. J. Public Health,* 55: 1355–1366, 1965.

——, LEBAUER, E. J.; DAWBER, T. R.; and McNAMARA, P. M. Relationship of body weight to

development of coronary heart disease. The Framingham Study. *Circulation,* 35: 734–744, 1967.

KEYS, A.; TAYLOR, H. L.; BLACKBURN, H.; BROZEK, J.; ANDERSON, J. T.; and WHITER, H. H. Coronary heart disease among Minnesota business and professional men followed 15 years. *Circulation,* 28: 381–395, 1963.

LANE, M. H.; and VATES, T. S., JR. Medical selection, evaluation, and classification of subjects. In: Biren, J. E.; Butler, R. N.; Greenhouse, S. W.; Sokoloff, L.; and Yarrow, M. R., eds. *Human Aging: A Biological and Behavioral Study.* Washington, D.C.: U.S. Government Printing Office, 1963. Chapter 3.

LIBOW, L. S. Medical investigation of the processes of aging. In: Biren, J. E.; Butler, R. N.; Greenhouse, S. W.; Sokoloff, L.; and Yarrow, M. R., eds. *Human Aging: A Biological and Behavioral Study.* Washington, D.C.: U.S. Government Printing Office, 1963. Chapter 5.

——. Study of the medical aspects of health and retirement, including interdisciplinary correlation of 5- and 10-year followup of NIMH study of Human Aging. Presented at NICHD workshop meeting on Health and Retirement, December 11 and 12, 1967, New Orleans, La. Photocopy.

To be published as NIH monograph.

LINDBOM, A. Arteriosclerosis and arterial thromboses in the lower limb. A roentgenological study. A monograph. *Acta Radiol.,* Supp. 80. 1950.

MASTER, A. M.; LASSER, R. P.; and JAFFE, H. E. Blood pressure in apparently healthy aged, 65–106 years. *Proc. Soc. Exp. Biol. Med.,* 94: 463–467, 1957.

——, ——, and BECKMAN, G. Tables of average weight and height of Americans aged 65 to 94 years. *J. Amer. Med. Assn.,* 172: 658–662, 1960.

MEINDOK, H. Diagnostic significance of hypoalbunimemia. *J. Amer. Ger. Soc.,* 15: 1067–1071, 1967.

Metropolitan Life Insurance Company. New weight and height standards. *Statistical Bulletin,* 40 (November–December): 1–4, 1959.

——. Mortality among overweight men. *Statistical Bulletin,* 41 (February): 6–10, 1960.

——. Mortality among overweight women. *Statistical Bulletin,* 41 (March): 1–4, 1960.

——. Overweights benefit from weight reduction. *Statistical Bulletin,* 41 (April): 1–13, 1960.

——. Blood pressure level and mortality among men. *Statistical Bulletin,* 41 (July): 1–4, 1960.

National Center for Health Statistics. *Vital Statistics of the United States.* 1966. Volume II, Mortality, Part A. Washington, D.C.: U.S. Government Printing Office, 1968. Tables 1–8.

PRIDDLE, W. W.; LIU, S. F.; BREITHAUPT, D. J.; and GRANT, P. G. Amelioration of high blood pressure in the elderly. *J. Amer. Ger. Soc.,* 16: 887–892, 1968.

RUTSTEIN, D. D.; INGENITO, E. F.; and REYNOLDS, W. E. The determination of albumin in human blood plasma and serum. A method based on the interaction of albumin with anionic dye—2 (4-HydrozyaBenzeneazo) Benzoic Acid. *J. Clin. Invest.,* 33: 211–221, 1954.

SHOCK, N. W., and YIENGST, M. J. Age changes in basal respiratory measurements and metabolism in males. *J. Geront.,* 10: 31–40, 1955.

SHREENIVAS, MESSER, A. L.; JOHNSON, R. P.; and WHITE, P. D. Prognoses in bundle-branch block; factors influencing the survival period in right bundle-branch block. *Amer. Heart J.,* 40: 891–902, 1950.

SIEGEL, S. *Nonparametric Statistics,* New York: McGraw-Hill, 1956. pp. 96–104.

SOBEL, H.; HRUBANT, H. E.; and HEWLETT, M. J. Changes of the body composition of C57BL/6aa mice with age. *J. Geront.,* 23: 387–389, 1968.

SOKOLOFF, L. The action of thyroid hormones on protein synthesis, as studied in isolated preparations and in the whole rat. In: Proceedings of the Second International Congress of Endocrinology, Part I, London, 1964. Excerpta Medical International Congress Series, No. 83, Amsterdam: Excerpta Medica Foundation, 1964. pp. 87–94.

—— and KAUFMAN, S. Effects of thyroxine on amino acid incorporation into protein. *Science,* 129: 569–570, 1959.

STAMLER, J. *Lectures on Preventive Cardiology.* Grune and Stratton, Inc.: New York, London, 1967. pp. 1–434.

STEINFELD, J. L. Albumin synthesis and degradation in patients with cancer. *Nat. Cancer Conference Proc.,* 5: 401–409, 1965.

SUM, P. T.; HOFFMAN, N. M.; and WEBSTER, M. D. Protein-losing gastroenteropathy in patients with gastrointestinal cancer. *Canad. J. Surg.,* 1: 105, 1964.

U.S. PUBLIC HEALTH SERVICE The health consequences of smoking. *U.S. Public Health Service Review.* Washington, D.C.: U.S. Government Printing Office, 1968 Revised.

CHAPTER 3

Cerebral Circulatory and Electroencephalographic Changes in Elderly Men

by Leslie S. Libow, Walter D. Obrist, and Louis Sokoloff

INTRODUCTION

This study provides the unique opportunity to determine changes over an 11-year period in some cerebral circulatory and electroencephalographic (EEG) functions occurring in elderly men, whose mean age was 71 years at the start of the study.

Our initial study in 1956 divided the volunteers into two major groupings. Group I, the optimally healthy aged, were as free of significant disease (particularly vascular disease) as was clinically possible. Group II, the more typical elderly, had some asymptomatic, minimal disease. The "arteriosclerotic" subgroup within group II was composed of subjects with apparent multisystem arteriosclerosis.

There was no decrease in cerebral blood flow (CBF) in group I compared to controls of mean age 20 years. There was a decrease in CBF only in the "arteriosclerotic" subgroup within group II.

The finding of a normal CBF with a decreased internal jugular venous oxygen tension (JVPO$_2$) and a normal cerebral oxygen consumption (CMRO$_2$) in groups I and II, together with a decreased CMRO$_2$ in a separate group of chronic brain syndrome patients, leads to the following conclusions (Dastur et al., 1963). First, decreased CBF is not a reflection of age, per se, but rather a reflection of arteriosclerosis. Second, a decreased CBF leads to a diminished JVPO$_2$ (taken to reflect the O$_2$ environment of the cerebral tissue) and, finally, in the chronic brain syndrome subgroup, a diminished CMRO$_2$ occurs.

The initial EEG study (Obrist, 1963) revealed 19 percent abnormal tracings, an incidence comparable to that of young adults. However, the mean peak occipital frequency was nine cycles per second, one full cycle slower than in young controls. This slowing was more evident in group II than in group I, and even more significant in the arteriosclerotic subgroup. It was concluded that the EEG undergoes slowing with age and that this slowing is accentuated in the presence of vascular disease.

Only in group II, the group with a

greater degree of arteriosclerosis, was there a significant negative correlation between systolic blood pressure and percent-time slow EEG activity, suggesting that in the presence of vascular disease, increased blood pressure protects against EEG slowing.

By contrast, only in group I was there a significant positive correlation between blood pressure (systolic and diastolic) and percent-time fast EEG activity. The meaning of this new relationship, however, was unclear.

The present study focused on two main questions. What changes occured over the 11-year period in the survivors? What relationship existed between the initial findings and the subsequent development of mental decline, chronic brain syndrome, and/or mortality?

METHODS

Subjects and Procedures

Of the original 47 subjects, 23 survived and eight volunteered for repeat cerebral circulatory studies. Seven of these eight were in group I. Of the eight survivors restudied, four were taking medications. These medications were assumed not to affect the cerebral circulation. The general health of the subjects was good. However, the many frailties accumulated over the ensuing 11 years certainly no longer qualified the group as "healthy elderly."

The initial and followup cerebral circulatory studies were performed by two different investigators at two different laboratories.[1] Thus, it is with some uncertainty that the data are compared. Nevertheless, the same methods were employed, and certain conclusions may be warranted, particularly because the findings are in the direction consistent with known pathophysiologic changes.

The procedures used were described in the initial study (Dastur, et al., 1963).

The CBF and related variables were measured by the Kety-Schmidt nitrous oxide (N_2O) technique (Kety and Schmidt, 1948). The mean arterial blood pressure (MABP) was measured by means of an air-damped mercury manometer connected by plastic tubing to a needle in the femoral artery. The mean internal jugular venous pressure (MJVP) was measured with a Statham strain gauge pressure transducer. The cerebral vascular resistance (CVR) was calculated from the values for CBF and MABP. The O_2 and CO_2 contents and cerebral oxygen consumption were measured, but the results are not presented. Unlike the N_2O technique, which was measured by exactly the same method and probably with the same precision and accuracy as in the previous study, the measurements of O_2 and CO_2 are far more sensitive to fine procedural differences, and the spread of data due to analytical errors can vary considerably from laboratory to laboratory. Therefore, because of the small size of the sample, we have great reservations about comparing the differences in metabolic measurements of the group, and even more so, in individuals.

Electroencephalograms were obtained in 19 of the 24 survivors, utilizing electrode placements and montages that were similar to the earlier examination.[2] Because the two tests were carried out at different laboratories and employed different recording procedures, they were sufficiently dissimilar to preclude direct quantitative comparisons. In addition, no control was

[1] We are indebted to Dr. H. A. Shenkin of the Episcopal Hospital of Philadelphia for performing the cerebral physiological studies in 1967.

[2] Sincere thanks are expressed to Dr. Daniel Silverman, Albert Einstein Medical Center, for providing the EEG recordings in the 11-year followup study.

exercised over the drug intake of the subjects in the second test, with the result that some of the EEG alterations could be attributed to the effects of medication. Only gross comparisons of the initial and 11-year followup tracings were therefore attempted. These consisted of noting large changes in dominant frequency (greater than 0.5 cycle per second) and the presence or absence of focal disturbances.

RESULTS AND DISCUSSION

The individual measurements and comparison of some cerebral circulatory functions (CBF, CVR, MABP) studied initially and 11 years later, are presented in table 1.

Cerebral Circulatory Changes

The CBF significantly decreased over the 11-year period (1956: 56.0 (ml./100 g./min.); 1967: 44.2 (ml./100 g./min.); p= 0.05). The CVR significantly increased over the 11-year period (1956: 1.7 (mmHg/ml./100 g./min.) ; 1967: 2.3 (mmHg/ml./100 g./min.); p=0.02). The MABP did not change significantly (1956: 95.1 (mmHg) ; 1967: 99.8 (mmHg). These changes are similar qualitatively and quantitatively to

those already seen in the arteriosclerotic subgroup of group II in the original studies and are fully consistent with the development and progression of cerebral vascular disease during the 11-year interim.

Mortality, Survival, and Development of Chronic Brain Syndrome (CBS) as Related to Initial Cerebral Circulatory and Metabolic Functions

There was no correlation between mortality at the time of the 11-year study and any of the following cerebral circulatory or metabolic values obtained in 1956: CBF, CVR, A–VO$_2$ (arteriovenous oxygen difference), CMRO$_2$, CMR$_G$ (cerebral glucose utilization), and JVPO$_2$. There was a significant and positive relationship between mortality and mean arterial blood pressure (table 2).

There was no relationship between the internal jugular venous oxygen tension in 1956 and the later development of mental decline.

To our knowledge, this is the only attempt to study cerebral circulatory function longitudinally over such an extensive time period. Unfortunately, the influence of time on the investigators and the sub-

TABLE 1.—*Comparison of initial and followup cerebral circulatory functions in 8 subjects*

Subject number	Age		MABP (mm Hg)		CBF (ml./100 g./min.)		CVR (mmHg/ml./100 g./min.)	
	1956	1967	1956	1967	1956	1967	1956	1967
7 _____	67	78	101	99	58	45	1.6	2.2
8 _____	71	82	112	113	40	42	2.5	2.7
15 _____	75	86	98	111	63	38	1.5	2.9
47 _____	65	76	79	104	73	61	1.0	1.7
51 _____	71	82	96	90	66	38	1.3	2.4
54 _____	72	83	93	89	50	37	1.8	2.4
55 _____	65	76	86	98	56	38	1.5	2.6
59 _____	74	85	96	94	42	55	2.2	1.7
Mean ____	70	81	95.1	99.8	56.0	[1] 44.2	1.7	[2] 2.3
S.E. _____	--	--	3.5	3.2	4.1	3.4	0.17	0.15

[1] Significantly different from the 1956 mean, at the 0.05 level.
[2] Significantly different from the 1956 mean, at the 0.02 level.

TABLE 2.—*Relationship of initial cerebral circulatory and metabolic findings to survival and mortality at 11-year followup*

	Nonsurvivors	Survivors	t	Significance level
CBF (ml./100 g./min.)	55.34	55.92	−0.170	N.S.
CVR (mmHg/ml./100 g./min.)	1.86	1.69	1.613	N.S.
MABP (mmHg)	[1](22) 106.0	[2](20) 95.0	2.23	0.05
JVPO$_2$ (mmHg)	35.73	35.68	0.43	N.S.
Arterial O$_2$ Saturation (%)	97.27	96.90	0.586	N.S.
pCO$_2$ (mmHg)	50.82	50.79	0.022	N.S.
CMRO$_2$ (ml./100 g./min.)	3.27	3.32	0.347	N.S.
CMR$_G$ (mg./100 g./min.)	4.61	4.33	0.625	N.S.

[1] Parentheses indicate number of subjects studied. The number of nonsurvivors ranges between 21 and 23 for all variables.

[2] The number of survivors ranges between 18 and 20 for all variables.

jects has prevented as exhaustive a study as was originally performed.

The decline in CBF over this 11-year period of later life is not surprising. All eight subjects, seven of whom were in group I, lacked evidence of significant arteriosclerosis in 1956. Their health status has, of course, changed over the 11 years, and at the followup they would all be classified into group II. It is not unreasonable to assume an increasingly significant arteriosclerosis over this period, followed by a diminished CBF. Our followup data do not exclude the possibility that the CMRO$_2$ declined initially and led to a secondary decline in CBF. However, our initial study strongly suggests that the CBF decrease precedes the CMRO$_2$ decrease in the aging process, and that the impairment of metabolism is secondary to a prolonged period of cerebral hypoxia (Sokoloff, 1966).

The increased CVR without accompanying increased MABP is consistent with the diminished CBF. The elevated CVR, without elevated MABP, probably reflects cerebral arteriosclerosis.

The lack of changes in MABP is consistent with the lack of changes in clinically measured systolic and diastolic pressures.

The JVPO$_2$ in 1956, taken to reflect the O$_2$ environment within the cerebral tissue, did not correlate with the ensuing changes (decline) in survivors in several measurements of mental functions; i.e., chronic brain syndrome, CBS signs, and senile quality. This suggests that the O$_2$ environment of cerebral tissue, if reflected adequately in the JVPO$_2$, is not a sensitive or specific enough indicator of forthcoming mental decline.

The lack of relationship of any of the cerebral circulatory or metabolic measurements obtained in 1956 with mortality is not surprising since only one death was due to a cerebrovasculer accident. Nine deaths were due to arteriosclerotic heart disease, seven to cancer, and eight to various other noncerebral diseases.

Relationship of Initial EEG Measurements to 11-Year Survival

Previous reports have suggested that the EEG is a reasonably good predictor of survival or death in aged psychiatric patients who have a high incidence of organic brain disease (Obrist and Henry, 1958; Pampiglione and Post, 1958; McAdam and Robinson, 1962; Cahan and Yeager, 1966). The present study offered an opportunity to examine this possibility in a group of elderly subjects who were initially selected on the basis of good health. Using EEG measurements obtained at the original examination, comparisons were made between two groups: 24 [3] survivors at the 11-year followup, and 24 subjects who died during the interval.

Table 3 presents such a comparison for the major EEG variables: peak (dominant) occipital frequency, and percentage of time occupied by activity in the slow (1 to 7 cycles per second), alpha (8 to 12 cycles per second), and fast (13 to 30 cycles per second) frequency bands. It is evident from the lack of statistically significant differences that none of the EEG variables is a good predictor of 11-year outcome. However, two minor trends are apparent: (1) Subjects who died tended to have lower peak occipital frequencies than the survivors, which is consistent with the earlier observation that the less healthy subjects had significantly lower frequencies; and (2) percent-time fast activity tended to be higher in the deceased group. The latter finding is consistent with the previously obtained positive correlation between fast activity and systolic blood pressure. The sys-

tolic blood pressure was significantly higher in the deceased group (see ch. 2).

In an additional analysis, survivorship was examined in relation to EEG abnormalities assessed by clinical standards. Five subjects showed mild temporal lobe foci on the initial test, all consisting of episodic theta activity confined to the anterior temporal region. Four of the subjects survived (Nos. 8, 15, 22, 27) and the fifth case (No. 32) died of acute pneumonia following exposure to cold. It would appear that these mild temporal dysrhythmias bear little relationship to mortality, a conclusion that is consistent with the clinically silent nature of such foci (Kooi et al., 1964; Busse and Obrist, 1965). Four subjects, on the other hand, revealed diffuse slow activity in their initial recordings. Three of them died (Nos. 25, 30, 36), two with heart disease and one with cancer; the fourth (No. 8) remained in relatively good health. Although an association of diffuse slowing with death might be expected on the basis of the psychiatric studies cited above, this type of abnormality is obviously too rare in the present sample to permit a firm conclusion.

As discussed in the original report from this study (Obrist, 1963), EEG variables are poorly correlated with physical and mental status in the presence of good

---

[3] The medical and cerebral circulatory studies utilized data of 23 survivors and 24 deceased. The EEG study includes a 24th survivor excluded from the initial study by other investigators.

TABLE 3.—*Comparison of survivors and nonsurvivors at 11-year followup utilizing initial EEG measurements* [1]

EEG variable	Mean and S.D.		t test of difference
	Survivors [2] (N = 24)	Nonsurvivors (N = 24)	
Peak occipital frequency _____	9.25 ± 0.91	8.91 ± 0.65	1.46
Percent time			
Slow (1 to 7 cps.) _____	12.8 ± 8.6	12.0 ± 5.6	0.35
Alpha (8 to 12 cps.) _____	63.1 ± 20.3	60.1 ± 18.4	0.51
Fast (13 to 30 cps.) _____	10.5 ± 6.9	15.5 ± 10.9	1.84

[1] None of the differences between survivors and nonsurvivors is statistically significant.
[2] Survivors include 23 subjects from groups I and II of the initial study and subject number 22 from group III (Lane and Vates, 1963). (The Group III subject is not included in the cerebral circulatory data.)

health. It is only when pathological processes intervene to impose some limitation on cerebral physiologic or metabolic function that a relationship might be expected (Obrist et al., 1963; Obrist, 1964). In view of the apparent lack of CNS involvement in most cases of death (only one subject, No. 35, died of a direct brain insult; i.e., stroke), it is perhaps not surprising that the EEG measurements failed to predict death or survival in the present series.

Repeat EEG's: 11-Year Followup Study

Five subjects revealed a slowing of the dominant occipital rhythm to approximately 8 cycles per second; of these, four had changes between 0.5 and 1.0 cycle per second over the previous recordings (Nos. 8, 20, 22, 54), and one underwent a decrease in frequency of 1.5 cycles per second (No. 6). A sixth subject (No. 51) showed diffuse theta activity (5 to 7 cycles per second), not present in the first tracing. Since the literature suggests that such slowing is associated with mental and physical deterioration (Obrist et al., 1962; Otomo, 1966), careful attention was paid to signs of intellectual and/or neurological deficit. Only the two cases with the greatest EEG alteration (Nos. 6, 51) showed clear impairment; both were diagnosed as having chronic brain syndrome and had a neurological history suggestive of cerebral vascular disease. The remaining four subjects continued to function well, without gross mental or physical changes from the previous examination.

With respect to focal EEG disturbances, three of four survivors (Nos. 8, 15, 22) retained the mild anterior temporal focus noted in the first recording. Neither the severity (abundance and frequency of the waves) nor the topography of the foci appeared to change. In the fourth case (No. 27), the original focal abnormality was ap-

parent only during hyperventilation. This was not observed on the recent test, possibly because the subject exerted less effort in overbreathing.

Two cases developed a new EEG focus. In contrast to the other subjects whose slowing was confined to the anterior temporal area, both of these new foci involved larger areas of the hemisphere and were maximal in the midtemporal region. In one case (No. 23), delta activity of moderate severity was found on the left side, and in the other (No. 18), a left-sided theta rhythm occurred that was accentuated by drowsiness. It is interesting that these two subjects were also considered to have chronic brain syndrome, one of whom (No. 18) had a history of stroke without residual neurological signs. The three subjects who retained the more restricted anterior temporal focus showed little evidence of gross mental or physical deterioration. These findings suggest that a distinction should be made between asymptomatic anterior temporal slowing, which is commonly found in this age group (Busse and Obrist, 1963), and foci involving the midtemporal or Sylvian regions, which frequently accompany a vascular accident (Bruens et al., 1960).

The fact that all four cases of chronic brain syndrome manifested obvious EEG disturbances supports previous claims that the EEG may have diagnostic value in aged psychiatric patients (Frey and Sjögren, 1959; Obrist and Busse, 1965). The failure of EEG to predict survival in this sample or to correlate with lesser degrees of mental and physical impairment argues for its limited usefulness in the elderly non-ill population. Although it might be concluded that only pronounced serial EEG changes have clinical significance, it should be remembered that more subtle alterations could not be evaluated in the present study due to inter-test differences in methodology. Carefully controlled longitudinal studies now under way (Obrist et al., 1966; Wang et al., 1970) should provide more definitive information.

Relationship of CBF, EEG, and Clinical Events in Individual Cases Over an 11-Year Period

For the eight survivors who had repeat cerebral blood flow studies, an integration of all measured cerebral functions is presented in table 4. Of the four survivors who developed chronic brain syndrome by the time of the 11-year followup, only one subject (No. 51) had repeat cerebral circulatory studies. His CBF had greatly decreased (1956, CBF = 66 ml./100 g./min.; 1967, CBF = 38 ml./100 g./min.). In addition to CBS, his history suggested transient ischemic attacks. His EEG revealed diffuse theta activity (5 to 7 cycles per second) not present in 1956. However, two other subjects whose CBF decreased by a somewhat similar magnitude did not have evidence of CBS, transient ischemic attacks, or EEG changes (No. 15: 1956, CBF = 63 ml./100 g./min.; 1967, CBF = 38 ml./100 g./min.) (No. 55: 1956, CBF = 56 ml./100 g./min.; 1967, CBF = 38 ml./100 g./min.).

Of five survivors whose EEG's in 1967 revealed significant slowing compared to 1956 recording, three had repeat cerebral circulatory studies. The CBF in all three of these subjects was 43 ml./100 g./min. or lower (Nos. 8, 51, 54). The subject (No. 47) with the highest CBF in 1967 (60.6 ml./100 g./min.) also had the highest EEG frequency in his completely normal tracing in 1967.

The one subject whose CBF showed considerable improvement (No. 59: 1956, CBF = 42 ml./100 g./min.; 1967, CBF = 55 ml./100 g./min.) had excellent mental function in 1956 and 1967 and no EEG changes.

CONCLUSION

Cerebral circulatory studies of the same elderly subjects, conducted initially and 11 years later, reveal a decreased CBF and increased CVR, and an unchanged MABP. These changes appear consistent with the expected effects of cerebral arteriosclerosis.

Comparison of survivors and the non-survivors by utilizing the initial cerebral circulatory and metabolic data obtained in 1956 reveals no significant relationship of mortality to CBF, CVR, $CMRO_2$, $A-VO_2$,

TABLE 4.—*Integration of cerebral function measurements obtained at 11-year followup*

Subject number	CBF [1] (ml./100 g./min.)	CVR [1] (mmHg/ml./100 g./min.)	MABP [1] (mmHg)	EEG Slowing in 1967	CBS [2]	TIA [3]
7	−13	+0.6	−2	---- [4]	----	----
8	+2	+0.2	+1	X [5]	----	----
15	−25	+1.4	+13	----	----	----
47	−12	+0.7	+25	----	----	----
51	−28	+1.1	−6	X [6]	X	X
54	−13	+0.6	−4	X	----	----
55	−18	+1.1	+12	----	----	----
59	+13	−0.5	−2	----	----	----

[1] Change from 1956 to 1967; (+) = increase; (−) = decrease. For individual values, see table 1.
[2] CBS = chronic brain syndrome.
[3] TIA = transient ischemic attacks.
[4] -- represents absence of characteristic.
[5] X represents presence of characteristic.
[6] Diffuse theta activity (5 to 7 cycles per second) not present in first tracing.

or JVPO$_2$. Only the MABP related significantly and positively to mortality.

The initial electroencephalographic records revealed a trend toward lower peak occipital frequencies and higher percentage fast activity in subjects who died by the time of the 11-year followup. Mild temporal foci observed on the initial examination were not related to mortality. The four survivors who developed chronic brain syndrome all had obvious EEG changes consisting of an increase in slow activity.

REFERENCES

BRUENS, J. H.; GASTAUT, H.; and GIOVE, G. Electroencephalographic study of the signs of chronic vascular insufficiency of the Sylvian region in aged people. *Electroenceph. Clin. Neurophysiol.*, 12: 283–295, 1960.

BUSSE, E. W., and OBRIST, W. D. Significance of focal electroencephalographic changes in the elderly. *Postgrad. Med.*, 34: 179–182, 1963.

——, ——. Presenescent electroencephalographic changes in normal subjects. *J. Geront.*, 20: 315–320, 1965.

CAHAN, R. B., and YEAGER, C. L. Admission EEG as a predictor of mortality and discharge for aged state hospital patients. *J. Geront.*, 21: 248–256, 1966.

DASTUR, D. K., ET AL. Effects of aging on cerebral circulation and metabolism in man. In: Birren, J. E., et al., eds. *Human Aging: A Biological and Behavioral Study*. Washington, D.C.: U.S. Government Printing Office, 1963.

FREY, T. S., and SJOGREN, H. The electroencephalogram in elderly persons suffering from neuropsychiatric disorders. *Acta Psychiat. Scand.*, 34: 438–450, 1959.

KETY, S. S., and SCHMIDT, C. F. The nitrous oxide method for the quantitative determination of cerebral blood flow: theory, procedure, and normal values. *J. Clin. Invest.*, 27: 476–483, 1948.

KOOI, K. A., ET AL. Electroencephalographic patterns of the temporal region in normal adults. *Neurology*, 14: 1029–1035, 1964.

LANE, M. H., and VATES, T. S., JR. Medical selection, evaluation and classification of subjects. In: Birren, J. E., et al., eds. *Human Aging: A Biological and Behavioral Study*. Washington, D.C.: U.S. Government Printing Office, 1963.

McADAM, W., and ROBINSON, R. A. Diagnostic and prognostic value of the electroencephalogram in geriatric psychiatry. In: Blumenthal, H. T., ed. *Medical and Clinical Aspects of Aging*. New York: Columbia University Press, 1962. pp. 557–564.

OBRIST, W. D. Cerebral ischemia and the senescent electroencephalogram. In: Simonson, E. and McGavak, T. A., eds. *Cerebral Ischemia*. Springfield, Ill.: Charles C Thomas, 1964. pp. 71–98.

——. The electroencephalogram of healthy aged males. In: Birren, J. E., et al., eds. *Human Aging: A Biological and Behavioral Study*. Washington, D.C.: U.S. Government Printing Office, 1963.

——, and BUSSE, E. W. The electroencephalogram in old age. In: Wilson, W. P., ed. *Applications of Electroencephalography in Psychiatry*. Durham, N.C.: Duke University Press, 1965. pp. 185–205.

——, and HENRY, C. E. Electroencephalographic findings in aged psychiatric patients. *J. Nerv. Ment. Dis.*, 126: 254–267, 1958.

——, HENRY, C. E.; and JUSTISS, W. S. Longitudinal changes in the senescent EEG: a 15-year study. *Proceedings of the Seventh International Congress on Gerontology*, 1966. pp. 35–38.

——, ET AL. Relation of the electroencephalogram to intellectual function in senescence. *J. Geront.*, 17:197–206, 1962.

——, ET AL. Relation of EEG to cerebral blood flow and metabolism in old age. *Electroenceph. Clin. Neurophysiol.*, 15: 610–619, 1963.

OTOMO, E. Electroencephalography in old age: Dominant alpha pattern. *Electroenceph. Clin. Neurophysiol.*, 21: 489–491, 1966.

PAMPIGLIONE, G., and POST, F. The value of electroencephalographic examinations in psychiatric disorders of old age. *Geriatrics*, 13: 725–732, 1958.

SOKOLOFF, L. Cerebral circulatory and metabolic changes associated with aging. *Res. Publ. Assoc. Nerv. Ment. Dis.*, 41: 237–254, 1966.

WANG, H. S.; OBRIST, W. D.; and BUSSE, E. W. Neurophysiological correlates of the intellectual function of elderly persons living in the community. *Amer. J. Psychiat.*, 126: 1205–1212, 1970.

Psychological Test Functioning

by Samuel Granick

Orientation

In the original study, psychological testing was administered to explore the nature and quality of cognitive, perceptual, and personality functioning in the group of healthy aged S's. Our followup effort cannot have the same general purpose since the intervening time of more than a decade has modified the medical status of most of the surviving men. Relatively few of them are now free of significant physical pathology, so that the group no longer can be characterized as "healthy aged S's." The reexamination, however, offers us a unique opportunity to observe the effects of time, combined with various other factors (such as illness, normal physiological aging, added experiences in some areas and reduced experiences in other areas of functioning) on the psychological performance levels of those who survived. We can attempt also to gain further awareness of the mental and personality potentials of the aged individuals who remain healthy, as compared to those who experience progressively more severe physical disability. By this means it may prove possible, in addition, to learn some things about the effects of medical problems on the psychological functioning of people who have been accustomed to enjoying good health. Another area which the followup enables us to examine is the matter of the delineation of psychological test performance patterns or factors which are associated with survival. A retrospective comparison, therefore, of the original test scores made in 1956 of those who were still living during 1967–68 with the test scores of the men who had died during the intervening period should prove to be instructive.

Choice of Test Battery

The extensiveness as well as the intensiveness of the psychological examinations of the original investigation could not be duplicated in the 1967 followup study. Practical considerations involving limitations of resources, time, and opportunity for conferring with several of the original group of investigators made it unfeasible to try to include some of these tests in the 1967 followup battery. A particular stumbling block was the problem of duplicating equipment, testing environment, and specific procedures for some parts of the examination, such as those involving auditory perception, reaction time, and learning. An additional important factor was the problem of the extent to which we could expect the S's to maintain their interest and motivation to participate in and cooperate with the procedures. They were more than 10 years older and generally less healthy and energetic than at the time of the original study. Keeping appointments for the psychological testing (and, of course, the other phases of the followup study)—much of it in the midst of winter and often during inclement weather—was a strain and much unlike the ease and comfort with which such things were handled in 1956 when the S's were housed on the research ward of the Clinical Center at the National Institutes of Health.

The various considerations involved in carrying out the entire followup study program led to the decision to limit psychological testing to two sessions of no more than two hours each. In selecting the tests for the followup study, we chose those which could be most readily administered within the time limits in a fashion which would approximate the procedures followed in 1956. We also attempted to choose a wide enough range of tests so as to touch on most of the psychological areas covered by the original study. The listing in table 1 of the first chapter presents a comparison of the sets of tests employed in the original study and in the two followup examinations, in 1961 and in 1967.

Description of Tests Used

The *Wechsler Adult Intelligence Scale (WAIS)* is so well known and widely used as to require no detailed description herein. All 11 subtests were administered, following the directions provided in the test manual (Wechsler, 1955). The scores used in our data analysis are the scaled scores uncorrected for age, as was the case in the original investigation.

The *Raven Progressive Matrices* is a nonverbal test requiring the subject to grasp relationships among geometrical figures and designs. It calls for "immediate capacity for observation and clear thinking" and assesses "a person's capacity for intellectual activity" (Raven, 1954). There are 60 prob-

lems in the test, divided equally into five sets, which increase progressively in difficulty. The number of correct answers given by the subject represents his score.

Addition Rate consists of a series of problems calling for the addition of seven one-digit numbers which the subject is asked to complete during a period of 2 minutes. The score is obtained by multiplying the number of digits added per second by the fraction 6/7.

Arithmetic Alternation Rate involves alternation of subtraction and addition for a column of seven numbers, the first one being a double digit, and the others single digits. A 2-minute period was allowed for the several problems presented. Scoring is based on the number of alternation operations per second multiplied by the fraction 6/7.

Speed of Copying Digits calls for copying a series of 96 digits printed on a single page, the time required for this task being recorded. The score for this test is the number of digits copied per second.

Speed of Copying Words requires the subject to copy words from a list on a single page as quickly as he can manage during a 2-minute period. The number copied represents the score.

The Draw-a-Person Test calls for each subject to draw the picture of a human figure as best he can. He is further encouraged to draw a "complete person" if he asks about it or draws only a head. After completing it he is asked to indicate the sex of the figure and then requested to draw a second person; but this time to make it of the opposite sex from the first one. On occasion, some of our subjects behaved self-consciously and with resistance because of strong insecurity about their abilities in this area. Some reassurance and encouragement was then given, which was in each instance sufficient to enable the individual to proceed. Only the male figure was scored for the present report. The system developed and described by Goodenough (1926) was used and the total number of points achieved represents the score.

The Family Scene is a TAT-like picture developed and standardized by Neugarten and Gutman (1958), which serves as a stimulus for projecting attitudes and feelings about aged parental figures and young adult children in a family setting. The subject first is directed to make up a story about what he imagines may be going on in the setting pictured. Then he is asked to describe his perception of the way in which each member of the family pictured may be feeling about and interacting with every other member. Responses were rated for quality on a scale of five, ranging from one, representing the elaboration of a central theme, involving variety of content and clear-role identification, to five, representing pointless card description, impoverished content, and confusion.

The Sentence Completion Test had been developed for the original study by Singer (1963) and consists of 28 items aimed at stimulating expressions of attitudes and feelings about such matters as various aspects of aging, parts of the body, family members, emotional expression, and health. Emphasis in the construction of the test was on minimizing tendencies toward perseveration of response by the subject so as "to enhance the formal as well as content analysis of responses." Of particular interest in the evaluation of the responses is the differentiation between those men who can function flexibly, shift their sets readily, and provide varied responses, from those who are functioning less adequately in these areas of their personality makeup. Scoring, accordingly, is for the total array of responses, and is carried out on a scale of five, ranging from

one, the best responses, wherein "variety in answers and differing length of answer" are presented, to five, responses which show the "subject confused about the task demands," or using confused language. The present report does not include a content analysis of the responses to the test.

Generally, the testing appears to have sampled cognitive and perceptual aspects of the men's psychological functioning. Those tests which are associated with affective and social reaction (Draw-a-Person, Family Scene, and Sentence Completion) were not analyzed for these areas essentially, but rather for quality of intellectual control, self-expression, and organization of ideas. It would have been possible, of course, to deal with additional personality factors of the men as revealed through these tests, such as affective control, social adaptability, defense mechanisms, and levels of security, tension, and anxiety, but this was not the approach of the original study. On the other hand, these factors are covered quite extensively and in depth through other phases of the investigation; namely, in the psychiatric and social psychological chapters of this volume.

Test Administration

The conditions and procedures for the examinations of the S's have been described in an earlier chapter of this volume. The psychological test battery was administered without much difficulty because of the cooperative orientation of most of the S's. Despite the many frustrating features of some of the tests for most of the men, particularly such features as the drawings, the arithmetic alternations, and some parts of the Raven Progressive Matrices, encouragement from the examiner generally produced conscientious application. No significant problems of communication were encountered, except in the cases of two men who were physically debilitated and located in nursing homes. Even here, however, they tried to cooperate and seemed to be performing to the best of their abilities. Generally the men were quite good natured about the procedures and did not slacken their effort in dealing with those aspects of the testing they regarded as simple or childish. They felt pleased with the examiner's attention and interest in them. Moreover, they were happy to be spending their time on what they regarded as a good and valuable scientific program. On the whole, they carried over to the present examination the esprit de corps they are reported to have demonstrated during the original study.

RESULTS

Previous vs. Present Functioning

Advanced aging is associated with considerable decline in cognitive and perceptual functioning in the research reports of most investigators (Botwinick, 1967). This is a fairly consistent finding both in cross-sectional and longitudinal studies. Not all aspects of cognition and perception decline, of course. Some, in fact, even increase somewhat in effectiveness, such as vocabulary and verbal tasks dependent upon stored memory. Most functions, however, especially those related to nonverbal problem solving under time pressure, and requiring flexibility of approach and reactions, tend to be exceedingly difficult for the aged to handle and are performed much below the levels younger adults achieve.

The testing of the total group of 47 S's in the first phase of the present investigation demonstrated this pattern quite clearly in a group of healthy aged men of average and above average mental endowments (Birren, et al., 1963, chs. 8 and 10). A

very important feature of the results was the apparently significant negative effect which even relatively mild, asymptomatic physical defects (particularly of the cardiovascular system) can have on cognitive and perceptual functioning. The difference in mental functioning found between the group of aged S's who were evaluated as totally free of physical disease (group I) and those who were showing some asymptomatic arteriosclerosis (group II) were not extensive, but yet sufficiently evident to be regarded as significant. They appeared to suggest that the latter group of S's were reflecting a loss of some of their stored information or some decline in their ability to use this information efficiently. Thus, health status would appear to be a crucial element in the mental functional effectiveness of the aged. It would seem also that for individuals of advanced age the margin of defense against the deleterious effects of even mild physical pathology is thin.

Our followup data offer us an opportunity to gain further objective evidence on the effects which time and decreased physical capacity might exert on the cognitive and perceptual abilities of elderly individuals. The surviving S's who were reexamined continued, by and large, to be a moderately healthy group, but they were far less so than during the original investigation, as noted in chapter 2. Table 1 contains a comparative analysis of their performance on the various tests at the time of the original study, 1956, and more than 11 years later, in 1967.[1]

---

[1] It would have been advantageous to present a comparative description between the original study and the two followup examinations, in line with the reports in the medical, psychiatric, and social psychological chapters. Unfortunately the data from the 1961 study were not available to the writer at the time of the preparation of this volume. Wherever feasible, the results of the 1961 study will be noted, however, on the basis of both pub-

TABLE 1.—*Comparison of test scores*

Test	Mean (1956)	t	Mean (1967)
WAIS:			
Information	13.1	0.71	13.0
Comprehension	13.0	−.25	13.2
Arithmetic	12.0	1.67	10.9
Similarities	10.2	−1.70	11.6
Digit span	9.4	.27	9.2
Vocabulary	12.8	[1] −2.55	14.1
Digit symbol	6.7	1.56	6.0
Picture completion	7.9	−1.51	8.8
Block design	8.3	.20	8.2
Picture arrangement	6.4	[1] −2.14	7.7
Object assembly	7.2	1.63	6.7
Draw-a-Person	24.2	[1] 2.05	21.4
Sentence Completion (Rating) [2]	1.6	[1] −2.17	2.0
Family Scene (Rating) [2]	1.9	−1.79	2.5
Raven	29.4	−.31	29.6
Addition Rate	.93	[3] 2.89	.80
Arithmetic Alternation Rate	.36	[3] 3.08	.28
Speed of Copying Digits	1.07	1.62	.93
Speed of Copying Words	34.95	[3] 6.85	29.11

[1] Significant at 0.05 level of confidence.
[2] The lower the score, the better the performance.
[3] Significant at 0.01 level of confidence.

The results indicate quite clearly that the intellectual capabilities of our S's held up fairly well as they moved into more advanced old age (mean age = 81.2; S.D. = 3.3). The average total Verbal and Performance Scores on the WAIS are considerably above the average reported for the Kansas City old-age sample used in the standardization study of the scale (Dopplet and Wallace, 1955). For the 75-years-and-over male S's of this sample the Verbal mean was 42.68 and the Performance mean was 22.58, whereas the means for our S's on the 1967 examination were 71.9 and 37.4, respectively. These mean scores of our S's are also higher than the average of the younger aged samples of the standardization population such as the 60-to-64- and the 65-to-69-year-old groups. Our results confirm the findings of the original study with the total group of 47 S's and demonstrate the relatively high residual mental capabilities of our group of aged men. It should be noted also that over the

lished and unpublished materials which are at hand.

11-year period the achievement of the surviving S's remained stable on the two sections of the WAIS (1956 Verbal and Performance means being 70.4 and 36.9, respectively), reflecting their basically high intellectual endowment and the maintenance of their functional effectiveness.

A report by Birren (1964) provides the total WAIS scores of 29 S's who were tested for the 1961 followup study. Of these S's, 17 were among those also retested in 1967, thus enabling us to compare their general intelligence scores at three different time periods. Scores achieved by the same S's on the Raven Progressive Matrices and Speed of Copying Digits Tests were also made available to the writer. Table 2 offers the means for these data along with t test comparisons.

The results for the WAIS total scores are somewhat puzzling since what appeared to be a deterioration of functioning in 1961 was only, it seems, a temporary lapse of intellectual effectiveness. Thus, the performance level of the S's in 1967 is quite significantly above their 1961 scores

TABLE 2.—*Test scores at 3 time periods*

Testing period	Tests and means		
	WAIS total (N=17)	Raven (N=16)	Copying Digits (N=17)
1956 (1) ----------------------	108.59	31.00	1.08
1961 (2) ----------------------	100.47	26.31	1.12
1967 (3) ----------------------	110.35	29.63	.99
t (1 to 2) ----------------------	[1] 5.56	1.88	−.51
t (1 to 3) ----------------------	−.56	.59	1.03
t (2 to 3) ----------------------	[1] −3.37	−1.40	[2] 2.13

[1] Significant at 0.01 level of confidence.
[2] Significant at 0.05 level of confidence.

and even a little higher than they had scored originally in 1956. No obvious reason for this pattern presents itself. We are inclined to speculate, however, on the possibility of higher motivation during the 1967 followup examinations to prove themselves as still having capabilities. Perhaps also they may have tended to respond with greater effort to the third examination, which was administered by a female, than to the other two (particularly the second), which were conducted at a different location and by male examiners.

Seven of the S's scored seven or more points higher in 1967 than they did in 1956, and 12 of the 17 S's were 10 or more points above their 1961 scores. Only three of the 17 S's had notably lower scores for the third-testing period than for the 1956 examination. These same S's were somewhat higher in their scores in 1961 than in 1967, but also a good deal below their performances of 1956. It is of interest that these three S's are among the four individuals listed in table 3 in chapter 5 as having Chronic Brain Syndrome.

The likelihood that the group of S's surviving in 1967 had retained their intellectual effectiveness is supported also by results on the Raven Progressive Matrices Test. The scores for all three periods are quite close. Here again, the 1961 mean score is below the other two (but not to a statistically significant degree), supporting the possibility that the S's did not extend themselves or were not able at the time to perform at their best levels on the intelligence tests. What seems most important to note is that the declines of 1961 were probably temporary lapses of intellectual effectiveness rather than indications of mental deterioration.

The Speed of Copying Digits Test, on the other hand, does show the more traditional pattern of functioning of the aged. Our S's performed on a par with their 1956 scores at the 5-year followup. After the passage of 11 years, however, a mild but statistically significant decline seems to have occurred. It appears likely that the reduced ability to respond with speed as the individual moves into advanced aging is the operative factor in this instance.

Despite the generally good quality functioning of the surviving group of S's, a pattern of decline of mental powers associated with aging is evident in the results of the 1967 followup. Similar to what is reported in the original study, there is a striking difference between functioning on the verbal as compared to the performance tests, the latter being far more difficult for the aged than for young adult S's. This is particularly evident in the fact that our S's scored only about half as well on the performance as on the verbal subtests of the WAIS. Thus, the verbal subtests are on a par generally with the scores of young adults but the performance subtests are handled much less adequately. Other tests in our battery, such as the Raven Progressive Matrices and Speed of Copying Digits, also show lower levels of performance for our S's than for young groups, as was the case in the original investigation in 1956 (Birren, et al., 1963).

The 11-year timespan between the two sets of measures also reflects some significant erosion of other perceptual and cognitive capabilities in our S's. Two of the five tests in which a statistically reliable decline is noted involve some visual motor coordination (Draw-a-Person and Speed of Copying Words). Two others (Addition and Alternation Rate) also involve writing, but it is minimal. Probably the essential elements here are speed and flexibility of adaptation. The remaining test (Sentence Completion) may also have a relationship to the factor of flexibility, a trait which is widely reported to decrease with advanced aging.

Further evidence of decreased capacity in our S's over the 11-year timespan is reflected in results on the additional five tests in which there is a moderately lowered performance level (but nonsignificant statistically) for the 1967 examination. Three of these tests (Digit Symbol Substitution, Object Assembly, and Speed of Copying Digits) call for working under the pressure of time and also exercising some motor coordination. For the other two tests (Arithmetic and Family Scene), the main factor is probably flexibility of reaction, similar to what is involved in the Sentence Completion task.

In all, therefore, our S's seem to have experienced the kinds of difficulties in their cognitive and perceptual functioning which tend to handicap the aged generally. On the other hand, the decline in performance is far from extensive or uni-

form. On the total of 19 tests, five were performed at about an equal level over the 11-year timespan; on two (Similarities and Picture Completion) a moderate (but statistically nonsignificant) improvement is evident; and on two (Vocabulary and Picture Arrangement) the S's scored significantly above their 1956 levels. Abstraction ability, flexibility of adaptation, and working under time pressure are called for in one or another of these tests, similar to what is involved in the tests which proved more difficult for our S's in the followup study. It may thus be inferred that the S's retained a substantial proportion of their capabilities along these lines. The most consistent loss of capacity, on the other hand, appears to be in the area of psychomotor coordination, especially when speed of performance is an essential factor. This finding fits the pattern of reported results of numerous research investigations over the past 50 years or more, and lends support to the supposition that loss in this area is related to the normal aging process of the human organism rather than to such psychological factors as motivation, experience, and education.

Survivors vs. Nonsurvivors

The relationship between survival in the aged and the nature and quality of psychological functioning is of considerable importance in providing insights into the aging process. A body of evidence is accumulating which associates quality intellectual functioning with longevity in elderly S's. Kleemeier (1961) was, perhaps, the first to recognize that a sharp or extensive decline in cognitive and perceptual functioning may signal the approach of death in the individual. The reports by Berkowitz and Green (1963) and Berkowitz (1965) partially support this idea, but their results also touch on the issue of a possible relationship between initial ability and survival. They note differences in rate of intellectual decline on retesting after 9 years for survivors as opposed to nonsurvivors with respect to IQ. No comparisons, however, were made between S's of varying intellectual levels with respect to their longevity. This matter is discussed by Jarvik and Falek (1963), who note that the survivors in their longitudinal study of twins tended to be of relatively higher intelligence at initial testing than those whose lifespans were shorter. A significant relationship between intelligence (especially as measured by the performance score on the Wechsler Bellvue Scale) and longevity was also reported by Riegel, Riegel, and Meyer (1967) for their group of 380 elderly men and women who had been tested and followed by them for an extended time period. They noted, in addition, that the S's who survived longest tended to be superior to the others in such factors as health, physical and social activities, and psychosocial attitudes. These findings appear to be replicated and extended in the research reported by Palmore (1969; 1969a) on a sample of 268 S's. Intelligence test functioning, particularly on the performance subtests of the WAIS, was found to correlate to a fairly high extent with longevity. When combined with the factors of physical functioning, reported work satisfaction, and actuarial life expectancy, an effective formula appeared available for predicting longevity in the general aged population represented by the total sample. Palmore also developed prediction formulas for six subgroups of aged S's and in three of these, intellectual functioning was one of the factors. In analyzing his data further he noted that the psychosocial measures of "work satisfaction" and "overall happiness" (taken together, they may be re-

garded as an estimate of morale) are among the most significant factors in the prediction or estimation of the number of remaining years of life for aged individuals.

Attention was given in all of the studies cited above to the matter of physical health and its relationship both to psychological functioning and survival. Our data from the 1956 examinations of the 47 S's, however, are particularly relevant to this feature since, unlike the other investigations, the orientation of this study was not toward the assembly of a random or broad type of sample. The sample of S's selected was limited to individuals of demonstrably good physical health. Their psychological test performances, thus, provide us with a picture of their psychological reactions which can be regarded as relatively free of the influence which physical factors may generally have on the functioning of the aged. Decline in capabilities over what they might have shown in their earlier years might then be related to the result of the normal aging process. Moreover, a comparison of the test performances in 1956 between those who survived and those who were deceased by the time of our followup study in 1967 would be expected to provide some indications of the kinds of psychological functions which may be sensitive to the relatively early approach of death.

In table 3 we offer a comparison between survivors and nonsurvivors regarding their scores on a variety of the cognitive and perceptual tests administered during the original investigation in 1956 (Birren, et al., 1963, chs. 8 and 9). Scores on these tests, along with a group of others of this nature, making a total of 32 tests, were intercorrelated in the original study, and analyzed by the Hotelling Principal Component Method. Standardized scores were then derived for each subject summarizing his performance on the tests represented in each of the five-principal components which the analysis produced. We compared the survivors and nonsurvivors on these scores, as presented in table 4.

Another group of psychological tests administered in the original study fall into the general category of personality tests. The scores developed by Singer (1963) for most of these tests may be regarded as measuring the intellectual functioning of the subjects, in part. They are also considered by her to be ratings of "how well the aged person was able to wait for and comprehend instructions;. how many appropriate and varied associations he was able to call on for use in the situation; how well he adhered to the task goal, keeping his thoughts directed without drift from the task goal and without perseveration; how well he ordered the sequence of his thoughts; how appropriately he limited the amount of verbalizing; and how appropriately he terminated his responses." In addition, we have the raw scores on the

TABLE 3.—*Comparison of survivors and nonsurvivors on cognitive and perceptual tests*

Test	Survivors		t	Nonsurvivors	
	Number	Mean		Number	Mean
WAIS Verbal	23	70.4	[1] 3.00	24	56.0
WAIS:					
Performance	23	36.9	[1] 2.98	24	29.4
Information	23	13.1	[1] 2.77	24	10.4
Comprehension	23	13.0	[2] 2.53	24	10.3
Arithmetic	23	12.0	1.97	24	9.9
Similarities	23	10.2	[1] 2.74	24	7.2
Digit Span	23	9.4	.98	24	8.7
Vocabulary	23	12.8	[1] 3.07	24	9.5
Digit symbol substitution	23	6.7	[2] 2.14	24	5.3
Picture completion	23	7.9	1.62	24	6.8
Block design	23	8.3	[1] 3.27	24	5.7
Picture arrangement	23	6.4	1.73	24	5.3
Object assembly	23	7.2	1.97	24	5.7
Raven Progressive Matrices	23	29.4	[1] 3.79	24	20.6
Wisconsin Card Sorting (number of concepts)	22	4.1	[2] 2.12	23	2.3
Mill Hill Vocabulary	23	29.5	[1] 2.78	24	23.0
Mean Reaction Time	22	.22	−1.17	23	.24
Speed of Copying Digits	23	1.1	[2] 2.02	24	.9
Speed of Copying Words	23	34.3	[1] 2.81	23	26.8
Verbal Fluency	23	19.2	1.92	22	14.4
Speed of Addition	23	.9	.70	21	.8
Speed of Alternation	23	.3	0.13	21	.3

[1] Significant at 0.01 level of confidence.
[2] Significant at 0.05 level of confidence.

TABLE 4.—*Comparison of survivors and nonsurvivors on principal component standardized scores*

Principal component	Survivors (N=23) mean	t	Nonsurvivors (N=24) mean
I. Stored information achievement	0.45	[1] 3.34	−0.43
II. Enumeration speed	.12	.76	−.11
III. Flexibility in set	.29	1.90	−.24
IV. Speed of association and reasoning	.09	.58	−.08
V. Concept formation or stimulus orientation	.14	.64	−.04

[1] Significant at 0.01 level of confidence.

Minnesota Multiphasic Personality Inventory (MMPI) as presented by Kornetsky (Birren, et al. 1963, ch. 13). The comparisons made for these various test scores and ratings between the survivors and the deceased S's are offered in table 5.

The substantial number of significant differences between the scores in tables 3, 4, and 5 suggests quite strongly that the two groups varied considerably from each other, both in their intellectual as well as in their general personality functioning. It is striking that the surviving group showed itself to be superior to the nonsurvivors in virtually every area tested and in a remarkably consistent fashion.

The Principal Component scores in table 4 appear to sum up quite well the essential difference in cognitive and perceptual functioning between the two groups. Survival over the 11-year timespan

seems, thus, associated with higher intellectual capabilities, particularly with respect to the effective use of stored information. Although not statistically significant, Principal Component III, representing flexibility in mind set and actions, also favors the surviving group to a considerable extent. This would appear to be related to what is demonstrated, in part, by the results with some of the personality tests, particularly the Rorschach. Thus, the surviving group showed in the early testing a greater freedom of ideational flow and imaginativeness than the group of S's who were deceased by the time of the followup in 1967.

Attention is drawn, in addition, to the significantly higher quality of functioning on the part of the survivors on tests involving motor coordination, both where speed of performance is a factor (Digit

TABLE 5.—*Survivors versus nonsurvivors on personality test scores*

Test	Survivors		t	Nonsurvivors	
	Number	Mean		Number	Mean
Level of Aspiration Index	23	1.55	−0.50	23	1.78
Level of Aspiration Performance	23	70.78	1.93	23	61.74
Weigl Color-Form Sorting	23	2.48	−1.20	23	3.00
Draw-a-Person (score)	23	22.74	[1] 2.21	23	16.65
Draw-a-Person (rating) [2]	23	4.04	[1] −2.56	23	6.00
Rorschach (rating) [2]	21	2.57	[3] −3.23	22	4.36
Proverbs	23	3.74	−1.65	23	4.91
Homonyms (number)	23	26.30	[1] 2.14	23	21.61
Homonyms (percent)	23	74.91	1.87	23	63.17
Sentence Completion (rating) [2]	23	1.70	−.26	23	1.78
Emotional Projection (rating) [2]	23	2.39	−1.56	23	3.17
Family Scene (rating) [2]	23	1.87	−1.53	23	2.48
Problem Situation (rating) [2]	23	1.43	−1.78	23	1.87
TAT (rating) [2]	23	2.05	−1.53	23	2.57
Sum of Ratings (personality measures) [2]	23	32.61	[3] −2.86	23	44.43
MMPI scales:					
Hypochondriasis (Hs)	20	13.90	−1.05	21	15.33
Depression (D)	20	20.75	−1.95	21	23.81
Hysteria (Hy)	20	19.95	−.08	21	20.10
Psychopathic Deviate (Pd)	20	21.15	.60	21	20.29
Paranoia (Pa)	20	9.35	.81	21	8.67
Psychasthenia (Pt)	20	24.40	−.21	21	24.76
Schizophrenia (Sc)	20	24.75	−.25	21	25.19
Hypomania (Ma)	20	18.85	.74	21	17.90
Social I. E. (Si)	18	25.79	[1] −2.22	19	31.84

[1] Significant at 0.05 level of confidence.
[2] The lower the rating the better the quality of performance.
[3] Significant at 0.01 level of confidence.

Symbol Substitution and Speed of Copying Words), and where it is not (Draw-a-Person), as well as on the nonverbal tests generally (WAIS Performance and Raven Progressive Matrices). These tests, as noted earlier in this chapter, are associated with functions which appear to decline normally with old age. Thus, the probability is suggested that aging had proceeded further in the nonsurvivors than in the survivors at the time of the initial testing in 1956 despite their closeness in chronological age. In this regard, the fact that a significantly greater proportion of S's from group II than from group I (70 percent as compared to 37 percent; $X^2 = 5.02$; $p < 0.05$) make up the nonsurvivors reflects the apparent negative effects of even relatively mild physical pathology on the psychological functioning of the aged.

Still another array of important differences between the two groups of S's is evident in their scores on the MMPI scales. The nonsurvivors showed a relatively greater inclination than the survivors toward withdrawal from social contacts. In addition, a substantial but not statistically significant difference along the same direction is shown with respect to responses to the Hypochondriasis and the Depression scales. The survivors would, thus, seem to have had a more favorable outlook toward themselves as well as on the environment than did the deceased group. These results appear generally in line with what Palmore (1969) and others have reported with respect to the relatively high correlation between longevity and measures of morale.

A possible relationship suggests itself between our findings and a cultural factor, in view of the relative absence of foreign-born S's among the survivors as compared to their substantial representation in the original study (about 43 percent; see ch.

1). The general consistency of the direction of the results, however, would seem to argue against this. Relatively culture-fair tests such as Digit Symbol Substitution, Block Design, and Raven Progressive Matrices show the same pattern of superiority of the survivors over the nonsurvivors as culture influenced tests, such as Information, Comprehension, Similarities, and Vocabulary. Moreover, if culture were a significant factor we would expect significant differences favoring the surviving group on the other tests in the battery in which such matters as grasp, organization, and expression of verbal concepts are involved. This is not the case in several instances such as on the following tests listed in table 5: Sentence Completion, Proverbs, TAT, Family Scene, and Emotional Projection.

SUMMARY AND IMPLICATIONS

The followup psychological study on the group of healthy aged men 11 years after the original investigation has enabled us to carry through two kinds of exploration: (1) An evaluation of the effects of the time interval on the performance and functioning of those subjects who survived; and (2) a comparative analysis of the test performance and reactions, at the time of the original study, of the survivors and those who were deceased at the time the followup was undertaken. The following results were obtained:

1. The pattern of decline of cognitive and perceptual capabilities generally associated with advanced aging is present in the performance of the surviving S's. It is, however, neither extensive nor consistent. Most of the decreases in level of functioning are small and not statistically significant. The significant erosion of abilities involved tests calling for one or more of such factors as visual motor coordina-

tion, speed of responsiveness, and flexibility of adaptation.

2. On the other hand, there is also abundant evidence that the S's continued to function quite well intellectually as compared to the aged population generally. There were a number of tests in which no decline in performance was evident. On a few others there was a noticeable improvement in functioning, two of the increases in performance being at a statistically significant level. The S's generally showed high-quality verbal abilities and use of stored information. They also showed high-residual capabilities in abstraction, and despite the observed decline in effectiveness, they did succeed in performing quite well at times under time pressure and where flexibility of adaptation are called for.

3. The outstanding and most consistent features of decline in functioning shown by the S's were in the area of psychomotor coordination, especially when speed of performance is an essential factor. Since this finding fits the pattern of reported research results over the past 50 years or more, it strengthens the supposition that decline in psychomotor coordination represents part of the normal aging process of the human organism.

4. Available data from the 1961 followup study of the S's who had survived to that date indicate a considerable decline in intellectual functioning as measured by the WAIS. For the group of S's retested in 1967, on the other hand, this decline was not sustained. No definitive explanation for this rather puzzling and unexpected result presents itself. It appears to be an important finding, however, which is worthy of further investigation. Some possible reasons for the inconsistent performance may be the following: (a) Aged S's, particularly those of advanced old age, may be normally inconsistent in their performance to a far greater extent than younger S's; (b) the S's may have had a greater desire during the third examination to excel or present their best performance in order to demonstrate that they were still capable despite their advanced age; (c) differences in the testing conditions for the third examination may have evoked greater motivation to excel—particularly since the psychometrist for this examination was a female, whereas a male had conducted the testing during the previous two studies; (d) possible differences may have existed in the extent of stimulation, patience, and encouragement of the S's exercised by the examiners during each of three periods of the investigation. In any event, evidence that the 1961 performance was probably a temporary lapse of intellectual functioning is provided by results on the Raven Progressive Matrices Test in which no significant decline in achievement occurred for the two followup studies. On the other hand, a gradual age-related decline did show up on the Speed of Copying Digits Test, where a small but significant difference is evident between the second and third testing. It seems likely that the speed factor is involved here and that the S's are at the start of what may be a more definitive decline in their capabilities.

5. Of the 47 men who were the S's for the original investigation in 1956, 24 were deceased by the time of our followup in 1967, and 23 were still living. A comparison of these two groups regarding their psychological test performances in 1956 produced a fair number of significant differences between them, indicating that they varied considerably from each other in both their intellectual and general personality functioning.

6. The surviving group showed itself to have been superior to the deceased group

of S's in 1956 in virtually every area of functioning tested and in a remarkably consistent fashion.

7. In the cognitive and perceptual areas, the surviving group demonstrated higher intellectual capabilities than the non-survivors, particularly with respect to the effective use of stored information. This was true for the verbal as well as the non-verbal tests and also for tasks involving motor coordination and working under the pressure of time.

8. The survivors were also superior to the nonsurvivors on cognitive and percept-ual tests involving flexibility of mind set and actions (Principal Component III) but this was not achieved on a statistically significant level. On several of the per-sonality tests, however, such as the Rors-chach, Homonyms, and Problem Situation, the survivors did demonstrate fairly clear-cut superiority over the deceased S's in their reactivity. They displayed this super-iority, particularly, in their greater idea-tional freedom, imaginativeness, and organization of ideas.

9. Evidence from the personality testing (particularly the MMPI) indicated that the survivors had somewhat higher general morale and sense of well-being than the nonsurvivors. Particularly significant also is the response pattern of the latter group which suggests that, in contrast to the survivors, they tended toward withdrawal from social contacts. (See ch. 6 for related results based on other measures.)

10. The comparison between survivors and nonsurvivors essentially substantiates the findings by Jarvik and Falek (1963), Riegel, Riegel, and Meyer (1967), and Palmore (1969; 1969a) indicating that longevity is associated with high morale and sense of satisfaction with oneself and the environment, above average intelli-gence, high-quality intellectual function-ing, and the maintenance of good physical health.

11. Thus, the probability seems reason-able that a substantial drop in elderly S's on standardized psychological tests or measures of personal-social adequacy and in intellectual effectiveness may be a signal that death is not far off. This is related to the hypothesis advanced by Kleemeier (1961), and our results provide indirect partial support to the implications of his data.

12. In considering the total pattern of the data from our investigation, one is struck by the remarkably high quality of mental functioning of our surviving S's at present despite their fairly advanced age. Their performances remain, to a con-siderable extent, close to what they were more than a decade earlier. Declines, of course, are evident but what stands out are the residual capabilities of the S's. This is a matter which has received relatively limited attention in gerontological re-search reports. Yet, from both a practical and theoretical standpoint in understand-ing and dealing with advanced aging, it is crucial to consider the resources which the individual possesses, along with his po-tential for both reinforcing and extending them. Reports by Birren and Morrison (1961) and by Granick and Friedman (1966, 1967) suggest that the aged may be getting less credit than they deserve for the extent of their intellectual, percep-tual, and personality strengths and capa-bilities. Botwinick's (1967) summary of the research literature in maturity and old-age demonstrates that such is the case with respect to the acquisition by the elderly of new knowledge, concepts, and skills. All of this seems to fit the pattern of functioning of the original 47 S's of this investigation, and particularly the S's who were available for the 1967 followup study.

They offer us a basis for a somewhat more optimistic approach to old age than has been the case generally.

ACKNOWLEDGMENTS

Grateful acknowledgment is made to Dr. James E. Birren for help with the planning of the data gathering for this chapter, and for his reactions to a preliminary version of the chapter. Thanks are due to Mrs. Audrey Granick for the psychological testing of the subjects and to Miss Barbara Wolf for her work on the statistical analysis. Dr. John Bartko and Mrs. Annie T. Randall, NIMH Section on Theoretical Statistics and Mathematics, were very helpful in providing data from the original study.

REFERENCES

BERKOWITZ, B. Changes in intellect with age: IV. Changes in achievement survival in older people. *J. Genetic Psychol.*, 107, 3–14, 1965.

BERKOWITZ, B., and GREEN, R. F. Changes in intellect with age: I. Longitudinal study of Wechsler Bellevue sources. *J. Genetic Psychol.*, 103, 3–21, 1963.

BIRREN, JAMES E. Neural basis of personal adjustment in aging. In: Hanson, P.F. ed. *Age With a Future.* Copenhagen: Munksgaard, 1964. pp. 48–59.

BIRREN, JAMES E.; BUTLER, ROBERT N.; GREENHOUSE, SAMUEL W.; SOKOLOFF, LOUIS; and YARROW, MARIAN R., eds. *Human Aging: A Biological and Behavioral Study.* Washington, D.C.: U.S. Government Printing Office, 1963. 328 pp.

BIRREN, JAMES E., and MORRISON, DONALD F. Analysis of the WAIS subtests in relation to age and education. *J. Gerontology*, 16, 363–369, 1961.

BOTWINICK, JACK. *Cognitive Processes in Maturity and Old Age.* New York: Springer, 1967. 212 pp.

DOPPELT, JEROME E., and WALLACE, WIMBURN, L. Standardization of the Wechsler Adult Intelligence Scale for older persons. *J. Abnorm. Soc. Psychol.*, 51, 312–330, 1955.

GOODENOUGH, FLORENCE L. *Measurement of Intelligence by Drawings.* Yonkers-on-Hudson, N.Y.: World Book Co., 1926. 177 pp.

GRANICK, SAMUEL, and FRIEDMAN, ALFRED S. Residual Capacities in Aged Subjects. Paper presented at annual meeting of American Psychological Association, Division 20, New York City, September 1966.

GRANICK, SAMUEL, and FRIEDMAN, ALFRED S. The effect of education on the decline of psychometric test performance with age. *J. Gerontology*, 22, 191–195, 1967.

JARVIK, LISSY, and FALEK, A. Intellectual ability and survival in the aged. *J. Gerontology*, 18, 173–176, 1963.

KLEEMEIER, ROBERT W. Intellectual changes in the senile or death and the I.Q. Presidential address, Division on Maturity and Old Age, American Psychological Association, New York, September 1961. (Mimeograph)

NEUGERTEN, BERNICE L., and GUTMAN, D.L. Age-sex roles and personality in middle age: a thematic apperception study. *Psychol. Monogr.*, 72 (17): 1–33, 1958.

PALMORE, E.B. Physical, mental, and social factors in predicting longevity. *The Gerontologist*, 9: 103–108, 1969.

PALMORE, ERDMAN B. Predicting longevity: A followup controlling for age. *The Gerontologist*, 9, 247–250, 1969a.

RAVEN, J. C. *Guide to Using Progressive Matrices (1938).* Beverly Hills, Calif.: Western Psychological Services, 1954.

RIEGEL, KLAUS F.; RIEGEL, RUTH M; and MEYER, GUNTHER. A study of the dropout rates in longitudinal research on aging and the prediction of death. *J. Personality and Soc. Psychol.*, 5, 342–348, 1967.

SINGER, MARGARET T. Personality measurement in the aged. In: Birren, James E.; Butler, Robert N.; Greenhouse, Samuel W.; Sokoloff, Louis; and Yarrow, Marian R., eds. *Human Aging: A Biological and Behavioral Study.* Washington, D.C.: U.S. Government Printing Office, 1963. 328 pp.

WECHSLER, DAVID. *Manual for the Wechsler Adult Intelligence Scale.* New York: The Psychological Corporation, 1955. 110 pp.

CHAPTER 5

Psychiatric Aspects of Adaptation, Survival, and Death

by Robert D. Patterson, Leo C. Freeman, and Robert N. Butler

Psychiatrists have too infrequently studied mentally healthy people. A more thorough knowledge of them will give perspective in evaluating the "pathology" we see in patients and guide our thinking in efforts toward more effective preventive mental health programs. This research is an attempt to supplement the scant empirical data about the late phases of normal lives by researchers familiar with psychopathology and organic diseases.

The multidisciplinary approach of the Human Aging project should be complemented with a comprehensive view of the psychological lives of the men. This includes their intrapsychic lives; their responses to existential questions about the meaning of life and death; the influence of physical factors on mental function; the role of interpersonal relationships in their lives and the influence of past experiences on their current behavior.

Previous reports based on these men have tried to contribute to these aims. Chapter II in *Human Aging: A Biological and Behavioral Study* (Perlin and Butler, 1963) endeavored to describe and quantify behavior which was then examined in relation to adaptation as well as to many physical and social-psychological variables. Another paper examined experiences and reactions of the men to aging changes (Werner, Perlin, and Butler, 1961). Still another brought together data from all disciplines which was of special importance to psychiatrists (Butler, 1963a). At the 5-year followup (Butler, 1967), the stable and changing elements of intrapsychic life were emphasized with special reference to adaptive psychopathology. Also, factors related to survival or nonsurvival were examined.

In this chapter many observations from previous phases will be updated. The contribution of the life history and changes over time—especially the 11 years that we have documented as thoroughly as we could—are the special concern of this phase.

PURPOSES OF FOLLOWUP

Psychiatric followup had two broad aims: (1) To further understand normal psychological development in late life which can serve as data for therapeutic and social planning; and (2) to test specific hypotheses. A group of hypotheses involved prediction of the effects of individual psychological features upon survival. Also, we hypothesized that as a group the survivors would maintain a high level of adaptation because of the favorable physical, social, psychological, and psychiatric characteristics they exhibited at the time of the first study. Wherever specific predictions were made at the first study, we have endeavored to examine the outcome. Conclusions drawn at the first study were reexamined in the light of the followup data. For example, the concept of adaptive psychopathology was examined for applicability at the followup studies.

METHODS

Sample

The men studied constituted neither a random sample of aging American men nor a unique group of prominent or especially creative men. They were men who responded to a special limited appeal for volunteers for a study of the healthy aged living in the community. (For details of sample characteristics, see chapter 1.) They were generally alert, engaging, and had a great interest in understanding themselves psychologically. A few men spontaneously mentioned that they volunteered because they wanted to show others how successful aging could be.

The initial study included 47 men. At the second study 5 years later, 39 of the men were still living and 29 of these were restudied. At the third study 11 years after the first, 23 men were surviving and 18 of these were restudied. The dropouts who are discussed more fully in chapter 1 did not differ significantly from those who continued participation. They did tend, however, toward having lower morale (measured at the first study) than other subjects.

At the third study, one subject (No. 26) could not leave a nursing home in a place distant from the study because of physical illness and mental confusion. Because of limitations of the researchers' abilities to arrange a standard interview, only one unstructured interview was obtained. He had developed a mild chronic brain syndrome, was well adapted to the nursing home, and was not depressed. Since his data are incomplete, he is treated as not restudied. Atttempts to reinvolve the other unrestudied subjects (all of whom were reached by phone) revealed no other institutionalized or severely deteriorated men.

One man (Lehigh, No. 22)[1] from group III (symptomatic disease group previously excluded from reports) has been added to the followup group. He had been eliminated from the first study because he had polycythemia vera. Through a friend he heard about the third study and asked to be included. He has been included except where his data would bias survivor-nonsurvivor comparisons.

It appears that a feeling of working with the researchers contributed to the men's sense of competence and usefulness. We believe that this attitude of collaboration also contributed to the richness of the data. One man (Murray, No. 7) said that participating in the first phase of the study helped him become reinvolved in life after a major setback had occurred in his retirement plans. Many experienced participating in the study and visiting the NIH Clinical Center as special privileges for which only a select few could qualify. While they enjoyed the third-round studies at the Philadelphia Geriatric Center, they did not feel the aura there that they had associated with the Clinical Center. Thus the study itself probably became a factor in the men's lives which tended to increase their sense of self-esteem, physical health,

---

[1] Pseudonyms are used throughout.

and usefulness. We do not believe this potential bias invalidates the kinds of conclusions drawn from the study.

A semistructured interview technique was used. At the first study, a comprehensive life history was obtained and subjects were asked about a wide range of physical and emotional experiences believed to be related to aging during three 1½- to 2-hour interviews. (For details of interview protocol see Perlin and Butler., 1963, p. 195.) At the second and third studies, an interval life history was obtained and an abbreviated form of the original sequence of questions about aging experiences was asked. A specially designed mental status test (see Glossary)[2] was administered at the first and third studies. Diagnoses were applied as defined in the American Psychiatric Association Diagnostic and Statistical Manual of Mental Disorders (1952).

The dispersal of members of the original research team and their involvement in new responsibilities, with the consequent need to introduce new members at the third study, presented important methodological problems. At the third study, interviews were conducted by one of us (L.C.F.) who had not seen the subjects before. In an attempt to achieve uniformity of clinical ratings, the investigator (R.N.B.) involved at all three study times discussed his techniques with the new investigators. One of us (R.D.P.) attempted to verify comparability of ratings through the use of tape recordings and interview transcripts collected at each study. When ratings did not appear to be comparable, the data were not used except where noted in the depression section.

A distinction between group I (optimally physically healthy) and group II (asymptomatically diseased) was significant in relation to many variables across different disciplines at the first study. However, the two groups were not significantly different on any psychiatric variables. At followup studies, the original group distinctions were no longer appropriate because health status had changed with time.

RESULTS

Psychiatric variables measured at the first study are shown with their subsequent relation to survival in table 1. A high level of adaptation and a better mental status were significantly related to survival.

Adaptation was defined as a global appraisal of the individual's adjustment to his current situation irrespective of the adaptive techniques. High adaptation was characterized by resourcefulness in meeting needs and obtaining satisfaction from life, by high self-esteem, and an absence of self-defeating behavior.

We do not know how adaptation and survival are related. Direct effects of gross maladaptive behavior such as self-neglect do not appear to have been important factors. Because adaptation and Organic Mental Decline were associated, there is the possibility that early organic deterioration affected both adaptation and survival. However, even among subjects without detectable Organic Mental Decline, higher adaptation was associated with survival ($t = 2.92$, d.f. $= 33$, $p = 0.01$).

Separation of the Mental Status test scores into four quartiles reveals that 10 out of 11 men in the highest quartile survived. Low performance was not as closely related to nonsurvival (seven of 11 died).

Other factors which psychiatrists hypothesize might be significantly related to survival are also shown in table 1. Since adaptation was a global, clinical judgment,

---

[2] All clinical ratings and measuring scales are defined in the Glossary on p. 94.

TABLE 1.—*Psychiatric factors related to survival and nonsurvival* [1] (N=47)

Factor	Number of subjects or mean score of subjects		Statistical test and significance
	Survivors	Nonsurvivors	
Adaptation:			
Excellent	13	5	$\chi^2=6.67$ df=2 p=0.05
Fair	5	8	
Poor	5	11	
Mental Status test score [2], by Quartiles:	$\overline{X}$ 145	123	t=2.82 df=42 p=$<$0.01
1 (highest)	10	1	
2	5	6	
3	4	7	
4 (lowest)	4	7	
Organic Mental Decline (formerly Senile Quality):			
Present	3	8	$\chi^2=2.78$ df=1 N.S.
Absent	20	16	
Number of Chronic Brain Syndrome signs:			
0	6	3	
1	9	6	$\chi^2=6.15$ df=3 N.S.
2	7	8	
3 or more	1	7	
Functional diagnosis (any):			
Present	14	15	$\chi^2=0.03$ df=1 N.S.
Absent	9	9	
Depression	3	6	
Schizoid Personality	4	0	
Obsessive compulsive or compulsive personality	6	3	
Number of symptoms	$\overline{X}$ 2.0	2.2	$\chi^2=2.04$ [3] df=4 N.S.
Morale index	$\overline{X}$ 70.1	56.1	t=1.40 df=44 N.S.
Denial of aging changes:			
Present	7	10	$\chi^2=0.25$ df=1 N.S.
Absent	16	14	
Attitudes about death:			
Denial	5	2	
Normal	14	14	$\chi^2=2.6$ df=2 N.S.
Fear	4	8	
Activity-Passivity:			
Average passivity	11	11	
Passive-dependency	2	7	$\chi^2=3.76$ df=2 N.S.
Counterphobia	10	6	
Functional breakdown:			
Predicted	2	4	$\chi^2=0.14$ df=1 N.S.
Not predicted	21	20	
Identity crisis:			
Present	4	9	$\chi^2=1.47$ df=1 N.S.
Absent	19	15	
Age relevant checklist score	$\overline{X}$ 22.1	27.0	t=1.14 df=45 N.S.

[1] See Glossary for definition of terms.
[2] Scores of 3 subjects not available.
[3] 5 frequency classes were used for the test.

it may be assumed that many of the discrete behaviors measured were contributory to the more general adaptation score which was highly related to survival. The trends among the measures are frequently in the direction anticipated from this assumption. None reach the usual level for statistical significance, however. Among these are Organic Mental Decline (called Senile Quality in our earlier studies), number of chronic brain syndrome diagnostic signs, diagnosis of depression, Morale

Index, attitudes about death, Predicted Functional Breakdown, Identity Crisis, and Age Relevant Checklist score (see Glossary for definitions of terms).

Thus, two measures of organic mental impairment (Organic Mental Decline and chronic brain syndrome signs) were not significantly related to survival. This might have occurred because mild degrees of organic impairment in healthy men are truly unrelated to survival. That marked organic mental changes influence survival is well known (Roth, 1955). We believe a more parsimonious explanation is that significant differences were not found because of the small size of our sample. For both Organic Mental Decline and chronic brain syndrome signs there is a substantial trend in the direction of fewer survivors among those with organic signs.

There is almost no difference between the survivors and nonsurvivors in the number of symptoms or functional diagnoses they had. That functional psychopathology had no adverse effect on survival is consistent with the findings at the first study that current psychiatric nosology is not invariably predictive of adaptation and that sometimes—but not always—psychopathology had adaptive value (and presumably survival value) in old age. Five types of psychopathology that were sometimes adaptive were: obsessive-compulsive, schizoid, passive dependent personalities, counter-phobia, and denial. Survival was more frequent in the presence of each of these features, with the exceptions of passive dependency and one of two measures of denial (denial of aging changes) (see table 1). These trends are pointed out because they are generally consistent with the larger body of data presented earlier (Perlin and Butler, 1963, ch. 11; Butler, 1967) that indicates the occasional usefulness of psychopathology in old age.

Characteristics of Survivors

Because of the tendency toward survival of subjects who were better adapted and had fewer organic changes, the survivors were healthier on almost all psychiatric measures at the first study than were the nonsurvivors. Thus the "elite" who survive into advanced old age have emerged as the study continued. A comparison of adaptation scores shows that 72 percent of the 18 subjects with the best adaptation survived, 38 percent of the 13 subjects with medium scores survived, and 31 percent of the 16 subjects with the poorest adaptation survived.

Table 2 summarizes changes in some characteristics which will be discussed below.

TABLE 2.—*Changes in psychiatric status among survivors at followup*

Category of change	Number of subjects	Percent
Adaptation (N=19):		
Improved	4	21
Declined	2	11
Organic mental changes (N=19):		
Disappeared	1	5
Appeared	6	32
Mental status test score (N=19):		
Improved	6	32
Declined	12	63
Fear of death (N=19):		
Increased	0	0
Decreased	1	5
Persistent	3	16
None	15	79
Lived longer than self-predicted at first study (N=24):		
Yes	8	33
No	9	38
No data	7	29

Adaptive Psychopathology

At the first and second studies, it appeared that schizoid and obsessive-compulsive traits sometimes contributed to good adaption in old age. Six men with these diagnoses who were followed for 11 years continued to be well adapted. We had thought that these modes of adaptation might prove to be fragile but our concern was not justified. In all six men the pathological traits had been present throughout adulthood. Although in no instance was major maladjustment in adulthood attributable to the psychopathology, the men's histories suggest that the schizoid and obsessional traits limited their interpersonal satisfactions and work achievement.

The adaptive value of obsessive-compulsive features became even more clear as the men grew older and many had less varied daily lives which they tended to fill with routines and almost ritualized behavior.

Mr. Gottleib's (No. 20) obsessional tendency made him quite satisfied clipping newspaper articles every day to send to his children even though he suspected they might not read them.

Denial also was found to make a durable contribution to adaptation. Insight was the highest level of adaptation but denial often served as a less sophisticated means of defense. The seven men originally rated as denying aging changes showed no detrimental effects of this during followup. Examples of adaptive use of denial will be given in connection with specific life concerns (see pp. 86–87 and next section).

At the first study, passive dependency was found to be adaptive under the special circumstances of living in an institution or an especially protective family setting. These were not the circumstances in which most of the passive-dependent men lived. Its lack of adaptive value for them is suggested by their mean adaptation score (2.8) which was significantly lower than other subjects (1.8; $X^2 = 10.6$, d.f. = 2, $p < 0.01$). Therefore it is not surprising that only two of nine passive-dependent men survived (neither of the survivors was hospitalized and both were less than

optimally adapted.) Passive dependency may contribute to survival through facilitating adaptation when organic brain changes or physical disease requires the patient to accept extensive personal care. The data do not permit a test of this hypothesis, however.

New Successes in Old Age

The stereotype which visualizes old age as inevitably a period of depressing declines was earlier refuted in an elaborate content analysis of the subjects' reported experiences of the aging process (Werner, Perlin, and Butler, 1961). The analysis showed that the men frequently reported favorable changes as they aged, especially in the social-emotional sphere of their lives. Longitudinal study has permitted us to see the unfolding of lives in which there was an exhilarating new sense of success starting in old age in two subjects. These examples further deny the stereotype of inevitable decline. Both are also examples of men who denied aging changes.

We believe that because nothing in the experiences of these men is inherently unusual (such as a Grandma Moses discovering her talent for painting in old age), these examples have encouraging implications for social and therapeutic planning for large numbers of aged people.

Mr. Settles (No. 19) had not completed high school because he was about to flunk. Instead, he took a business course and worked for a few years as an accountant. Later he owned a retail coal business but had to close it after 18 years when the coal industry declined. He then worked as a guard in a factory for 12 years.

He had a satisfying marriage. They had eight children who were successful except for one child who contacted polio at age 2 and was a semi-invalid until his death at age 26.

At 67 he was forced to retire because of his age. After 3 months of idleness he took a job as a doorman at a fashionable mens' club. He enjoyed the job and took pride in his remarkable ability to learn the names of the members who came to the club.

At the second study, when he was 75, he was

alert and in excellent spirits. The most important recent event for him had been "getting a promotion." "I'm cashier and office man at a very important club—a very wealthy men's club. I come in contact with lawyers, doctors, manufacturers, presidents of banks—the influential people in town. Men with names you read in the paper and society columns—and I come in contact with them."

He worked six nights a week and regularly enjoyed walking 1½ miles in getting to work. He planned to work a few years more before retiring again. Several times he had enjoyed long vacation trips and would have taken more but for his wife's disinterest. Five years after the second study he died of carcinoma of the colon.

Mr. Tudor (No. 27) considered himself "a person who missed the boat in his early years." After much difficulty deciding what kind of work he wanted to do, he attended law school at night to obtain a degree. After a few years of practicing law he stopped because he said he found himself having to defend clients in ways that he felt were morally objectionable. He then worked as a personnel counselor at a rehabilitation center for a few years. He left that because he did not like the "institutional politics" involved. He then tried to to sell investments but because he was not aggressive enough he could not earn a good living.

He continued to live with his parents until they both had died, when he was about 50. At age 55 he married for the first time. He said it was very hard to adjust to married life after being single for so long. He described himself as having been a favorite child of his parents and thus unused to sharing and helping out as he needed in marriage. He had sexual difficulties involving premature ejaculations before and after he married. Because his sperm count was low, they were unable to have children. At first his wife had wanted to have children. Later they both felt it was best that they had not had children so late in life because they believed a child with older than normal parents would not be normal emotionally.

He became more aware of troubles in his life as he read psychology and met friends who were in psychoanalysis. He became concerned that he changed jobs so many times and seemed to lack self-confidence. He described having felt miserable when clients would not accept his advice. He felt even worse seeing his wife go off to work each day while he was "sort of lying down on the job." After his wife had started in psychoanalysis and he saw her benefit from it, he began his own 2½-year psychoanalysis at age 60. After treatment he was more successful in his work than he had ever been in his life and he was able to participate in his marriage with fewer inhibitions. He attributed the growth in his personal and professional life to his treatment.

At age 76 he had begun a daily exercise program at a gymnasium at his doctor's suggestion.

He enjoyed it so much and felt it did him so much good that he said, "I've become a regular fanatic on physical fitness." The exercises made him feel better and he quoted his wife as saying that he was "easier to live with" since he started exercises.

The study followed him to age 78. At that age he thoroughly enjoyed working almost full time as an investment counselor and salesman. He said he was working as hard as ever in his life. He had a sense of helping his many older clients get more out of their investments from his counseling. He felt that his relationship with his wife had continued to grow emotionally closer over the years.

Changes in Mental Abilities

Men who showed signs of organic mental changes were more likely to die during the followup 11 years than their peers, and those who survived showed surprisingly small declines in mental ability. Upon readministration of the Mental Status test at the third study, six men achieved higher test scores than they did at the first study. One man showed no change and 12 declined. The overall decline of performance between study one and study three did not quite reach statistical significance $(0.10 > p > 0.05)$ (see table 3).

Interrelation of Organic and Psychosocial Factors

A continued interest in using the mind as a satisfying instrument in an environment where there was some sense of purpose appeared to substantially influence the mens' level of mental performance. Our findings are consistent with the idea that the physiological state of the brain sets upper limits on possible mental performance and that psychosocial factors superimpose their influence (Rothschild, 1945). A crucial question is how large an influence therapeutic manipulations of the environment can play. Manipulations of the environment of severely impaired aged suggest that the influence can be substan-

TABLE 3.—*Amount of change in Mental Status test performance over 11 years in relation to other variables*

Subject number and name	age t₃	Change of test score t₁ to t₃	Rank of test score t₃	Chronic Brain Syndrome t₃	Organic Mental Decline t₃	CBS signs t₁	t₃	Arteriosclerosis[1] t₃	Adaptation t₁	t₂	t₃	Depressive trend t₃	Hypochondriasis	Thinking ability[2] (self rating) t₃
6 Crabtree	84	->24	19	X	X	2	4	X	1	1	3	X	—	D
51 Dooley	81	-24	9	X	X	0	4	X	1	1	1	—	X	D
18 Everett	78	-17	13	X	X	1	2	—	2	2	1	—	X	D
28 Smith	85	-16	18	X	X	3	4	X	3	3	2	—	—	A
58 Moran	81	-15	12	—	X	1	3	—	1	2	2	X	X	D
56 Bryant	80	-15	7	—	—	1	0	—	3	3	1	—	X	N
42 McLure	79	-12	15	—	—	2	0	—	1	2	1	X	—	A
54 Lewis	83	-11	5	—	X	2	0	X	1	1	1	—	—	D
15 Hyatt	87	-8	10	—	—	2	1	—	1	2	1	—	—	D
8 Wozny	83	-6	16	—	—	0	0	—	1	1	1	—	—	N
47 Jones	76	-4	3	—	—	1	0	X	3	1	1	—	—	D
20 Gottlieb	85	-2	8	—	X	2	3	—	2	2	2	X	X	D
9 Dixon	79	0	17	—	X	1	4	X	3	3	3	X	—	N
59 Ginsburg	84	+1	4	—	—	0	0	—	1	1	1	—	—	D
27 Tudor	77	+2	6	—	—	1	0	—	2	2	1	X	—	N
55 Postik	75	+7	1	—	—	0	0	—	2	—	1	X	—	N
7 Murray	79	+10	11	—	—	2	0	—	3	—	1	X	—	N
22 Lehigh	81	+11	2	—	—	0	0	—	—	1	1	X	—	N
14 Rhine	80	+16	14	—	—	0	0	—	1	1	1	—	—	N

[1] Means arteriosclerosis other than cerebral arteriosclerosis.
[2] N=no impairment; A=ambiguous or no data; D=clearly stated decline.

II-70

tial (Goldfarb, 1953; Kahana and Kahana, 1971).

All six of the men whose Mental Status test performance improved had lively interests in maintaining their mental abilities and lived in environments where keeping their minds active was meaningful. Their favorable psychosocial status is reflected in measurements made by the social psychologists (see ch. 6). They had suffered fewer psychosocial losses (see Glossary), were more often married, had more satisfaction with their retirement, and were more active rather than passive than the average of the other survivors. (All differences were trends which do not reach statistical significance—which is not surprising with such a small sample.)

Their improvement on the test may have been due to better psychosocial conditions in their lives at the time of the third study which facilitated better performance on mental function testing. Another possible cause is an accumulation of new knowledge. It is possible that both mechanisms operated.

Mr. Rhine (No. 14) is the most dramatic example of a man with a great investment and success in maintaining his intellectual abilities. He lived in a favorable psychosocial situation.

At 80 he had the greatest improvement in his mental status test of anyone in the study. He was also the subject with the most pride—shown in a charming way. When asked what his greatest fault was, he replied that he had none.

Throughout life he took great pride in his physical agility (discussed in detail in the following section). His narcissistic investment in maintaining his physical and mental abilities was still a major goal in his life. Among activities that kept him active intellectually were selling advertisements for a local paper; playing pinochle and cards; "learning from" an older friend who was "more dynamic" than himself; singing in a group each week; and "sometimes doing three things at once such as watching television, listening to the radio, and reading the paper."

He had had no major losses, had a warm and satisfying relationship with his wife, and had many friends. He approached his Mental Status test at the third study in the same spirit he had approached racing, pole vaulting, and discus throwing in athletic contests up to the age 75.

Other men showed the influence of organic brain changes setting upper limits on their intellectual performance. Mr. Everett (No. 18), 78, who is discussed in detail below in this section, suffered moderate intellectual decline despite a wish to maintain his mental abilities and a favorable psychosocial environment.

The most unfavorable combination of the organic and psychosocial influences on performance is seen in Mr. Crabtree (No. 6). The extreme difficulty of differentiating organic mental decline from depression, except by longitudinal observations, is also shown.

Mr. Crabtree (No. 6), 84, declined more in intellectual performance than any other man in the group. He refused to try to answer more than the first few questions on the Mental Status test when he realized how poorly he was doing. A diagnosis of moderately severe chronic brain syndrome was made.

He had suffered extreme psychological losses since the start of the study. His wife died; he was alienated from his children, and he was living in a nursing home. He was depressed and saw no purpose to living.

At the first study he was felt to have Organic Mental Decline and did not reveal depression. At the second study, to the surprise of the investigators, he no longer showed any signs of Organic Mental Decline. The explanation for the apparent change was then reconstructed. He was for the first time able to verbalize how depressed and upset he was by his wife's confinement to a nursing home where she was slowly dying of a brain tumor. Although the "facts" about his wife's illness were known at the first study, it was not recognized that it was depression that caused what looked like organic signs. It may be that again at the third study his depression was the major factor in his decline.

Five subjects never showed any clinically evaluated signs of even the mild organic mental changes commonly associated with aging. The mental status of all subjects was so good that the remote memory, orientation, and recent memory subtests did not discriminate among subjects. As a group, subjects did as well on the information subtest at the third study as at the first.

Organic Changes

At the first and second studies, only one man (subject No. 10) was given the diagnosis of chronic brain syndrome. At the third study, four men were given the diagnosis. One was Mr. Crabtree (No. 6), described above. Few guidelines are available to indicate what amount of organic impairment should be the criterion for a diagnosis of chronic brain syndrome—much less for the use of qualifying words like mild or severe. A 10-item Mental Status Questionnaire has been standardized against psychiatrists' diagnoses among institutionalized aged (Kahn, 1960). We chose 10 as nearly identical questions as possible from the Mental Status test used in this study. On the basis of this comparison we would have diagnosed only Mr. Crabtree (No. 6) and subject No. 10, who did not survive to the third study, as having chronic brain syndromes (moderately severe). We have accepted a less severe deterioration as criterion and diagnosed mild chronic brain syndrome in three additional survivors (see table 3).

Late Course of Organic Mental Decline

Followup provided some answers to the question posed at the first study: What happens later to men who show early signs of Organic Mental Decline? The mild degrees of decline observed at the first study affected survival. Only three of the initial 11 men with Organic Mental Decline survived for 11 years. This trend, although strong, is not statistically significant. Aside from early death, at least three possible later courses of Organic Mental Decline were recognized: progression of symptoms, arrest at a plateau, or disappearance of symptoms. All three types were seen. There were two instances of progression to chronic brain syndrome; one of no change (plateau), and two in which the symptoms disappeared. Mr. Crabtree (No. 6) was unique in showing disappearance of symptoms at the second study but a chronic brain syndrome at the third study. Mr. Murray (No. 7) was one of those in whom symptoms disappeared. He was depressed when he showed organic signs and is our second example of a failure to differentiate between depression and organic decline. The appearance of organic signs during depression has been called "pseudo-dementia" (Post, 1965, p. 86).

We regretably do not have data on possible preterminal mental declines among the men who died. Such preterminal changes have been observed in institutionalized persons (Lieberman, 1965).

Memory difficulty was not a major concern of any subject although very mild difficulty with memory was clinically apparent in a majority. Half of the men *said* there had been a decline in their abilities to remember over recent years. Included among them were three men who improved on their Mental Status tests. The seeming conflict may be explained on the basis that the Mental Status test did not measure small but clinically and self-recognizable changes in memory. It is remarkable that in these instances small declines in memory ability occurred while general intellectual ability improved (see ch. 4).

Subjects who experienced declines in their memories developed styles of conversation that effectively avoided the types of things they could not recall. Mr. Gottleib (No. 20) told about his son's participation in World War II, but could not recall the date of the war at all. Several men used note pads and calendars with notes on them as special reminders which they would not have used when their memories were better. Three men who became garrulous were quite aware of it as well as of its effect on others, and made efforts to curb it. Mr. Gottleib (No. 20) asked the help of the interviewer in curbing his garrulity. His sensitiveness in this matter grew out of a lifelong tendency to be concerned that others might be critical of his behavior.

Self-Monitoring

Aged people often come to the attention of social agencies when they are unable to adapt their life-styles to declining mental capacities. Protective service programs for the aged have been developed in large measure to meet this need when there are no kith or kin to help. The adaptive processes used by these subjects when they suffered mental decline were examined to learn how these changes were reacted to by men who generally showed a high level of adaptability.

One problem in old age that leads to requests for psychiatric help concerns the old person who has deteriorated mentally but refuses to give up responsibilities that he or she can no longer handle. Such a problem did not occur in any of the men in this study. These men generally succeeded in maintaining or withdrawing from activities as their mental capacities dictated. They accomplished this through insightful self-monitoring of their mental capacities which they used to guide their behavior.

Of 17 subjects, 14 demonstrated the reliability of their self-monitoring of intellectual functions when asked if their abilities to think had changed. Those who had declined were about as likely to recognize their true state as were those who had not declined. Among 10 subjects who had de-

clined in Mental Status test performance, the self-assessment of eight agreed, and among seven subjects whose Mental Status test performance had not declined, the self-assessment of six agreed (r–0.606; p<0.05)[3] (see table 3).

The following are examples of successful self-monitoring.

Mr. Settles (No. 19) stopped driving a car when he reached 74 although he continued to go to work daily. "I thought the pace was too fast for me. My reflexes might not be fast enough. I feel that by stopping before I had an accident that I was doing the right thing. I have good vision and I feel of course that my reflexes are as good as they should be for my age. I just didn't want to take any chances."

Mr. Dooley (No. 51), an 81-year-old divorced man, experienced a modest Organic Mental Decline. During the 11 years of the study, he ended extensive volunteer work in a hospital and later moved into a home for the aged where he was relieved of many personal responsibilities.

At 77, Mr. Tudor (No. 27) had experienced no decline. He was enjoying "working harder than ever" as an investment counselor. He had no plans for retiring and wanted to "go on as long as I can."

Judging from the uniformly favorable experience of those who kept active in work or avocational activities, we suspect that perhaps half of the men could have had even more successful lives in their later years had they been prepared upon retirement to take up a substantial part of their new free time with some special interest—whether an exciting hobby or part-time paid or volunteer work. We have come to believe that the availability of postretirement counseling may be of equal or even more importance than preretirement counseling because it is so difficult

---

[3] Two subjects gave ambiguous answers about changes in their thinking abilities.

for workers to anticipate what problems retirement will present.

In two instances subjects voluntarily offered the thought that their reduction of responsibilities had not been well matched to the high level of mental capacity they maintained. They said that in retrospect they might have been wise to plan more demanding activities for their later years. For example, at the third study when Mr. Gottlieb (No. 20) was asked if his retirement had been smooth, he replied "Yes, too smooth. Probably I should have planned for more things to do."

Organic Mental Decline did not invariably lead to a decline of adaptation. Only two men at the third study had declined in adaptation; one was the subject (Mr. Crabtree, No. 6) who had suffered great psychosocial losses and had deteriorated most among the group, and the second was a man (Mr. Moran, No. 58) whose decrease was small and probably not related to organic changes (see table 3). These observations are meant as a refinement of the observation made at the first study that there was a positive correlation between Organic Mental Decline and lower adaptation.

The following is a biographical sketch based on observations made during more than a decade in the life of a man who experienced a mild stroke and a mental decline greater than three-fourths of the subjects. Longitudinal study afforded an unusual opportunity to observe the development of organic changes and his adaptation to them. He shows more clearly than any other subject the effective use of self-monitoring and active compensation to maintain optimal adaptation despite organic decline. An ability to relinquish responsibilities without conflict when necessary is clearly shown. He also demonstrates the adaptive value of recognizing the concept of the life cycle.

Mr. Everett (No. 18) was a 66-year-old college graduate who taught in a public school system for 36 years. He was married and had two children. He had always been meticulous and agreeable, a follower rather than a leader, and a person who planned ahead.

At the first study, the children at school were more wearing on his "nerves" and he was more irritable with them than in earlier years. He was torn between retiring, which he could do, or going on another year, which he had been asked to do. Remembering names was harder for him. To compensate for this deficit, he "religiously" called the name and looked at the face of each child as he took the roll for each of his classes. He found it much more trouble to learn his son's new phone number than it would have been in earlier years. He put the number on a card to have it handy.

In contrast, his wife, who was 10 years younger, continued to attend concerts after he stopped. Of his reduced social activities and responsibilities, he said, "you begin to look after yourself a little bit more as you get older."

At the time of the second study he was 70 and had retired. As to his thinking ability, he said, "I'm not as alert as I was." Asked at another point if he felt he had increased wisdom, he quipped, "Yes, I'm weaker—and wiser."

His trouble recalling names had become worse in the last year of teaching. As the method of calling the roll each day became inadequate, he added writing the name of each student on the blackboard at the side of the room. In this way he could unobtrusively look at the names before calling on a student when necessary.

Gradually he turned over to his son and wife the responsibilities for several rental properties he owned. He spoke of making plans for "when I get more disabled" (apparently meaning mental or physical) without evident anxiety or depression. Giving up responsibility did not appear to be connected with any conflict or loss of self-esteem.

Also, at the second study he said he knew he had arteriosclerosis because a doctor had told him. Another doctor tried to tell him it was "nothing to worry about," but he declined to accept the chance for denial of his condition, instead accepting it realistically. He told the interviewer, "Both my parents died of strokes."

Irritability and fatigue which troubled him at the first study were not a concern at the second, apparently because after retirement, these feelings were less often stimulated. He admitted being lonely sometimes.

A hospital near his home and rental properties planned to buy several blocks of buildings, including all of his properties, for new construction. "I'm going to have an upheaval," he said. He would have to move from the house he had lived in almost all of his life—a home his father had built. The rental properties he depended on for part of his income would be sold and he would need to acquire new ones with the help of his son who is a real estate agent. As soon as he could, he got authoritative information about when to expect the rebuilding. "I didn't grieve about it at all because you can't take anything away with you and you can't keep anything always," he said.

After the second study, he had a cerebral thrombosis. He was confused in the hospital for 3 days, but recovered without paralysis. He felt his memory was "somewhat worse" after the stroke.

At the time of the third study he was 78. Mental status retesting showed a decline greater than three-fourths of the other subjects.

In telling about his illness, he called it a cerebral thrombosis and made clear that the use of the technical name served to avoid the more emotion-laden name of stroke. It appeared this brush with death finally called for some denial about his arteriosclerosis.

In the interview, he was slow and careful in answering questions and had some difficulty reconstructing the chronology of events over the past 10 years. The deficit was more marked at the beginning of the interview when he was under the stress of being questioned by a person unfamiliar to him. Such deterioration of behavior under stress in organic brain conditions was first called "catastrophic reactions" by Goldstein (1939).

There were many fewer demands on his mental capacity than 12 years earlier. He was not teaching. He had quit his work on a settlement house board, but still went to its annual meetings. His wife and son took responsibility for the rental properties. The hospital had bought his house as expected. He and his wife moved well in advance of the reconstruction to a new apartment which they enjoyed very much. His son had handled the real estate problems and bought new rental property which he managed for his father.

He had a strong sense of having a legacy in his children and grandchildren—and a pleasure and pride in seeing how far they went in life. This made his own decline and eventual death lessen in importance. Of his son, he said, "Oh. He has gone further than I ever went." When asked how long he would like to live, he said "Long enough to see my grandchildren get a good start in life."

One year after the third study, Mr. Everett died of pulmonary emphysema.

We believe that the examples given demonstrate a process quite different from the one hypothesized by disengagement theory (Cumming and Henry, 1961). They stated that "Disengagement is an inevi-table process in which many of the relationships between a person and other members of society are severed, and those remaining are altered in quality. Disengagement is a culture-free concept, but the form it takes will always be culture-bound."

The self-monitoring and behavioral modifications we observed represent a process of being attuned to both inner (psychological and physiological) reality and outer (social and cultural) reality. The end result for these men was by no means always a disengagement from social participation. (See ch. 6 for further discussion.)

Relation of Physical and Mental Health

Surviving subjects had been in good health except for acute illnesses and none had any incapacitating chronic medical disease even at the time of the third study. Without exception, the men easily acknowledged objective evidence of physical decline. Reduced energy was experienced by 80 percent and was the most common change reported. A majority of the men noticed an increased tendency to nap when not active during the day. Sensitivity to cold, reduced hearing or vision, dizzy spells, impotence, and tremors were each mentioned by a few subjects. These are common in old people, are associated with its common diseases, and may not be attributable to the process of aging per se. What interests us are the psychodynamic and psychosocial reactions to them.

Physical declines and illnesses were taken in stride by three-fourths of the men. They had come to terms with the expectation of physical problems to such a degree that they often described their bodies with a matter-of-factness suggestive of a description of a machine that was showing signs of wearing out. There was no sense of hopelessness in their acceptance and no instances of panic about physical deterioration. Men who had not fully come to terms with the physical declines were experiencing what they saw as discouraging increases in physical difficulties.

We had observed the psychological role of acceptance of age-related changes in the first study (Werner, Perlin, and Butler, 1961). It is most interesting to see how enduring this complex psychological process proved to be. This was an active realistic acceptance and not a passive resignation.

Attitudes

Subjects' attitudes about their health ranged from intense interest in physical culture and pride in good health to intense preoccupation with illness.

Mr. Rhine (No. 14) was a most marked example of intense pride in physical health. During adolescence in Germany he became intensely interested in physical culture and devoted hours to exercises. At least two determinants of his intense interest are known. He was born in a city that changed countries over the years. He was ridiculed and physically attacked by fellow students because he was alternately considered German while he lived in France and French when he lived in Germany. Additionally he spent most of his childhood in the German culture when health clubs were very popular. His interest continued with no evidence of abatement at 80 years of age. At 75 he participated for the last time in an athletic contest and told with pride how he took a prize in competition with other men in the "over sixty" class. On his 77th birthday, he had his wife photograph him walking on his hands, and submitted the picture to a newspaper which published it. He continued daily exercises and attributed his good health to physical culture. His body was a major source of pleasure and self-esteem for him.

The new interest in physical fitness shown by Mr. Tudor (No. 27) is a much less extreme example (see p. 69).

The largest number of subjects were intermediate in their concern about health.

Typical was Mr. Lewis (No. 54), 83, who said he was hesitant to walk distances he would have gone 10 years earlier. He attributed this largely to being out of practice. A year earlier he fainted on the street and injured his shoulder, which necessitated his wearing a sling for 2 weeks. Even so he thought little about his health and visualized death as "just passing out." Such an unemotional approach to illness was typical of Mr. Lewis and was one facet of his general repression of feeling within his schizoid personality.

Although Mr. Murray (No. 7) had a routine of doing a few calisthenics each morning to keep himself in shape, he was not preoccupied with his health.

Hypochondriasis

A few men had a morbid concern with physical illnesses.

A marked preoccupation with illness was a life-long concern of Mr. Bryant (No. 56). He developed hypochondriacal symptoms in his adolescence following an appendectomy with a wound infection. His symptoms apparently were intense over the next 15 years. He had two surgical procedures to relieve adhesions with no success. He continued to have "pain" from his adhesions.

He thought he might die from his "bowels becoming completely stopped up some day," and enjoyed telling about his trials with illnesses and with incompetent and unscrupulous doctors. Talk about his illness was an important mechanism for approaching or keeping emotional distance from others. He skillfully used his symptoms for secondary gains.

At the second study, the researchers (L.S.L. and R.N.B.) diagnosed a gastrointestinal malignancy. Surgery was done at the National Cancer Institute with excellent clinical results and a 7-year follow-up to date. He adjusted well to being informed of his diagnosis and the necessity for surgery. After the crisis he returned to his routine hypochondriasis.

Of the original 47 men, 12 were rated as hypochondriacal at one or more studies. Seven of these men survived to the time of the third study. Subjects were rated as hypochondriacal when they showed even minimal overconcern about their health or exaggerated trifling symptoms. Instances of complaints about organs in which no disease at all could be identified were uncommon.

In four instances, hypochondriasis seemed due in part to a diffusion of concern about health from appropriate areas of health concern. Included here are three men whose wives were chronically ill. The men's hypochondriasis seemed to reflect an increased concern for their own health which was a generalization of their intense awareness of their wives' symptoms. Their symptoms did not simulate the illnesses of their wives, however. The fourth man in this group had a reason to be fearful that he had prostatic cancer. However, he showed a diffuse concern with his health.

Mr. Jones (No. 47) sensibly feared he had prostatic cancer because he knew he was receiving hormone treatment appropriate for that, but his doctor had not made a positive diagnosis. While he minimized his fears of having cancer, he was mildly depressed and showed a new generalized concern about his health. He was distressed that the hormone treatment made him impotent and caused slight breast enlargement. He said, "Physically the body pulls the mind down." An occasional twinge of pain in a strained leg muscle, some sleeplessness, flatulence, and a poor memory seemed to be threatening signs of deterioration at that time. When cancer was ruled out by diagnostic tests, his hypochondriasis and depression were relieved. Five years later, at the third study, the very slight changes in his memory were no longer threatening to him.

As is well known, there is a strong tendency for hypochondriasis to be associated with depression. Five of the seven hypochondriacal men were also depressed. In several instances over the 11 years, the two symptoms appeared and disappeared together. Of the two men who were hypochondriacal but never depressed, Mr. Everett (No. 18) showed the symptom to a very mild degree; and cause is unknown. In Mr. Bryant (No. 56), hypochondriasis was a major defensive personality feature which had assumed functions beyond response to current life situations.

The mild concern with physical illness so regularly associated with similar mild depression is quite different in severity from the classical delusions of physical decay associated with psychotic depressions. Secondary gain through the use of illnesses to control others was marked only in Mr. Bryant (No. 56).

The case of Mr. Moran (No. 58) suggests that hypochondriasis symbolizes deterioration and helplessness in depression. He had the most intense hypochondriacal symptom of any man in the study. He was one of those with a chronically ill wife. He developed an unshakable conviction, contrary to objective findings, that because one of his testicles was out of place it was causing him pain when he walked and that it caused his penis to shrink. In the two studies before he developed the symptom, he showed no tendency to be hypochondriacal. He gave a history of healthy sexual development and behavior. He took pride in continued sexual potency at the time of the first two studies. At the third study, when he showed the symptom, he was also depressed for the first time. It appeared that both symptoms resulted from a sense of no longer being useful and being doomed to steady decline such as he saw so vividly in his wife. He had become sexually impotent and his complaint of his penis' shrinking seemed to symbolize a general sense of impotence.

There was a trend—and it was only that—for hypochondriasis to be associated with greater Psychosocial Losses. This suggests the interpretation that disintegration of the subjects' psychosocial lives led to a fear of the same thing happening to their bodies, a fear which was expressed in hypochondriasis.

We compared the functions of hypochondriasis among these men to the range of functions seen commonly in patients of all ages (table 4). The mild hypochondriasis seen in these men often symbolized a sense of deterioration and/or represented a displacement of anxiety from some area of greater concern. Such areas of greater concern were deteriorating psychosocial

TABLE 4.—*Psychic functions of hypochondriasis in persons of all ages*

1. To symbolize and make concrete one's sense of defectiveness or deterioration.
2. To serve as a ticket to interaction with caretakers (or punishers), doctors, nurses, etc.
3. To displace anxiety from areas of greater concern.
4. To serve as part of identification with a deceased loved one through similar symptoms.
5. To serve as punishment for guilt.
6. To avoid or inhibit unwanted behavior or interactions.
7. To punish others.
8. To regulate (usually reduce) interpersonal intimacy.

life, including illness with impending death of the wife; and possible cancer. Among the survivors, only Mr. Bryant (No. 56, p. 76) showed marked "use" of the other functions of hypochondriasis. Over many years he had come to use hypochondriasis for almost all of its possible functions. His constant suffering with pains atoned for guilt, justified his dependence on doctors, and permitted him to avoid unpleasant social situations. An example of the latter is his saying at the start of one of the interviews that he would talk willingly unless his pains became severe, in which case he would have to break off the interview. Thus his hypochondriasis was a ready escape mechanism in case of any unpleasantness during the interview. He probably used his hypochondriasis in all of these ways unconsciously.

We have the impression that symbolizing deterioration and displacing anxiety as seen commonly among these men were less seriously maladaptive than some of the other functions indicated in the table. For example, hypochondriacal symptoms used as self-punishment or as a regulator of interpersonal intimacy are relatively more seriously maladaptive.

Reactions to Illnesses

Illnesses played an increasing, though still small, role in the lives of the men as they aged. Two subjects had carcinomas surgically removed, four had prostatectomies for benign prostatic hypertrophy, and one or probably two had cerebral thromboses without major sequelae. Subjects generally had a clear understanding of their illnesses, sought medical treatment, and followed recommendations in an intelligent way. Thus physicians' efforts to explain diseases and treatments were a great benefit to these men. Explanations relieved anxiety, assured proper follow-

through of treatment, and showed an appropriate respect for the old person's intelligence.

Nonetheless, denial, here as in other areas of their lives, was a frequent and usually adaptive mechanism. Many subjects denied some of the implications of their illnesses. Three men denied the potentially incapacitating or fatal implications. Mr. Wozny (No. 8), who underwent apparently successful surgery to remove a mouth cancer, actively excluded from his awareness thoughts that he might still have a cancer that could cause a painful illness (see p. 87). The other two men had fainted while walking. They saw doctors for diagnosis and treatment, but excluded from awareness anxiety about possible serious consequences from future attacks.

Active mastery and emphasis on intelligent, voluntary activity helped several subjects overcome a sense of passive helplessness in the face of physical illness.

The lifelong hypomanic character of Mr. Wozny (No. 8), a retired steel mill worker, was evident at the first and second studies. He had always been oriented toward action. He had been accident prone and got into fights easily until near the time of his retirement. At the third study he was no longer hypomanic, but neither was he depressed. In his twenties he drank heavily but he "decided" to control his intake and did so with success.

At the time of his hospitalization for surgery for mouth cancer, his wife expected him to be a difficult patient—especially unwilling to stay in bed as directed. He took pride in describing how he *actively* complied and stayed in bed as directed. He may have felt so bad that he wanted to stay in bed some of the time after the surgery. However, his explanation that he actively decided to collaborate with the doctors also seems true. His behavior suggests an unconscious motivation to be such a good patient that he deserved to be spared from his potentially fatal illness (Ross, 1969).

At 68, Mr. Postek (No. 55) took pride in his response to a physical crisis which faced him when he was 350 miles from home. He developed acute urinary retention due to benign prostatic hypertrophy. He was at an engineers' survey camp where he was teaching. The local doctor placed an indwelling urethral catheter attached to a bottle to catch the urine so he could drive himself home alone and avoid the need for someone to bring his car home for him. He was proud of having used his engineering skill to repair the catheter system with plastic tape when it broke during the trip. When he got home, he promptly obtained the necessary surgery. His delight at mastery over a frightening illness was expressed in his humorous retelling of experiences during his trip home "tied to a bottle." He further mastered his experience by explaining his surgery in engineering terms for his friends—"They did a cotton cover job just south of the naval base almost to the penal colony."

Relationships of Husbands and Wives

In successful marriages there was a wide variation in complementary roles. In one marriage the husband was fatherly and protective of "his girl" while in another the husband was dependent and intensively mothered by his wife. The complementary quality of the need and satisfaction patterns of the two people seemed to be an essential element in their good adjustment.

Chronically incapacitating illnesses of their wives were a major source of stress for the men. During followup, five men's wives were severely incapacitated for long periods. Two of these wives died during the study. The necessity for profound shifts in the complementary roles when their wives became ill may in part explain the stress they experienced.

For four of the men, taking care of their wives became a major new responsibility. Three men evolved a new and satisfying caretaker relationship with their wives. One man complained bitterly about having to care for his wife, but did take care of her. Three features of this new caretaking were personal deprivation in order to care for another person; development of a new facet of personality which was expressed as a desire to care for another person; and the complementary development of the wife's need for care when the

husband's purposes in life needed renewing (such as at retirement). Each of these elements is to some degree represented in each of the men described.

Mr. Murray (No. 7), who was 79 at the third study, had moved to the West late in his career and made plans for satisfying part-time work after retirement. His wife became a chronic invalid and insisted that they return East for her medical care. They had not been emotionally close over the years. He particularly disliked her sharp tongue. He felt that extensive travel with his work had acted to preserve their marriage.

At the first study he was depressed by his wife's incapacitation and the disruption of his retirement plans. He overcame his depression by making care of his wife a major, new, and satisfying goal in life. He took care of her at home even when she became bedridden, although it was not a financial necessity. The emergence of a strong, maternal quality in his personality was a new development at that time. He amazed himself with how he was able to tolerate the new intimacy and occasional hostility that developed in caring for his wife. He cared for her for 5 years before her death.

He said, "With her death I lost a purpose in my life." Being without a major goal after her death appeared to be a crisis in his life even 2 years afterward. He filled his days with routine activities around his home and was not depressed.

The wife of Mr. Moran (No. 58) suffered a series of depressions with brief psychiatric hospitalizations over a 15-year period. By the time of the third study she had not been hospitalized for several years. Her hearing was very poor and she was doing only minimal household and cooking duties either because of chronic depression or organic mental changes or both. He tried to be supportive of her and relieve her of some responsibilities. It appeared that his intimate observance of her old-age decline contributed to his sense of fatalism about his own future and to his depression at the third study.

Mr. Lewis (No. 54) was a well-adapted schizoid, a former professor of political science. His wife had lost one leg in an accident in childhood. In the years before the third study, she developed instability in her walking. Mr. Lewis found that he needed to stay home much more in order to protect her from falling and help her with household chores. Her need for him probably complemented a desire of his to stay home more as he felt less accepted and less able to talk authoritatively with former colleagues at work.

Mr. Dixon (No. 9) adapted to his wife's illness only with much anxiety and profuse expressions of resentment at his situation.

He had been very dependent on mothering

women. His first wife died 4 years before the first study. He was angry that she "died when I needed her most." After a miserable year alone he tried to improve his situation by remarriage to a woman who could take care of him. Ironically, a short time after the marriage she developed diabetes which caused several sudden crises and hospitalizations.

The fears he expressed for his wife in large measure were a projection of his fears about his own health and helplessness. He made a point of how his second wife could never take care of herself because she was so uneducated—although she lived alone all of her adult life while he had had a miserable time alone for 1 year after his wife died. He described his wife as so ill that it seemed she must be bedridden, despite the fact that she was actually able to carry on household work, although impaired intellectually and subject to diabetic crises. He was hypochondriacal and during the interview left a listener confused for a few moments as to whether he was describing his own or his wife's illnesses.

After the third study he and his wife were admitted to a home for the aged where he was always anxious and often explosively emotional. He was devoted to his wife's needs until her death less than a year later. He then went to live with his daughter, later moving to another old age home when he came to feel that his daughter's kindness was motivated by her interest in a more generous inheritance.

There were other shifts of husband-wife roles not related to illnesses.

Mr. Gottleib (No. 20) retired several years before his wife, who was younger. He took over much of the housework while she was still employed, but had to give it up and find new activities again when she retired and reclaimed her usual duties. Among his new activities was clipping newspaper articles for his children (see pp. 68 and 88)

Husbands made positive efforts to overlook or minimize the faults of their wives (except for Mr. Dixon, No. 9). This attitude appeared to reflect a reluctance to criticize the other person in a partnership in which they had invested much of their lives and so on which their futures depended so heavily. Criticisms, when voiced, centered upon puritanical attitudes about sex, hypercriticism, and excessive neatness.

Sexual Life

A decrease in the number of sexually active men found in other studies (New-man and Nichols, 1960) was seen in these men. Among the married men who were studied all three times, there was a 37-percent drop in the number of those sexually active. At the first study, 80 percent of these married men were active (12 out of 15), and at the third study, 43 percent (six of 14) were sexually active. One unmarried man was sexually active at the time of the first study but not at the third. His girlfriend had died. Newman's study reported 25 percent still active in a group of married men and women who were over 75 and thus comparable in age to the present study. Five men who ceased sexual activity, but whose wives were still with them, attributed their behavior primarily to impotence. One man said his sexual activity was satisfactory until he underwent a suprapubic prostatectomy. Another man attributed his impotence to the effects of bilateral hernia repairs which caused testicular atrophy. The remaining three men cited no specific cause for their impotence. It is doubtful that prostatic surgery or the hernia repair caused impotence on a physiologic basis (Finkle, 1968). Finkle has shown that attitudes of the man and wife about sex have a profound influence on the retention of potency following prostate surgery.

Frequency of relations among those who were active ranged from once a week to once in 6 months.

Two men said they reduced their frequency of sexual relations because of a fear of causing themselves heart attacks. Cultural and psychoanalytic studies have revealed a symbolic association among ideas of death, violence, and sex. For example, the French use the expression *petit morte* (little death) for sexual relations. Occasional sudden death associated with sexual relations and due to cardiac disease has been described (Massie, 1969).

A decline in sexual interest was reported in almost all subjects. None reported an increase. Among many of the men, and evidently their wives as well, a decline of sexual interest and pleasure accompanied a declining frequency of relations for several years before cessation.

This decline in the importance of sexual activity probably reached a natural culmination in the impotence of some of the men. Such impotence probably represents a mixture of psychic and physical factors. Only one man was greatly disturbed by the occurrence of impotence. Mr. Moran (No. 58), described above, became greatly preoccupied with his impotence and with the idea that his penis was "shrinking." This concern seemed to unconsciously symbolize a general sense of impotence that he felt.

In retrospect, we wish we had expanded our investigation into the men's feelings and personal reactions toward their wives. We would like to have learned about possible effects of the anticipation of loss of one's spouse on their marriages, which might extend the findings of Neugarten (1968) in which she described the "rehearsal for widowhood" in middle-aged women. There is need for exploration of the interpersonal meaning of sex in the life of old people. Most studies in the literature have emphasized desire, potency, and performance but not the interpersonal context.

Depression

Depression was the most common psychiatric symptom. Of the 19 survivors (53 percent) 10 had reactive depression at one or more of the three study times (see table 5). All of the depressions were mild and none required psychiatric treatment. At two successive studies, three of the 19 men were depressed. Judged on their histories,

TABLE 5.—*Ten instances of depressive trend or psychoneurotic depression among 19 survivors*

Subject number and name	Study time		
	1	2	3
6 Crabtree			X
7 Murray	X		
9 Dixon	X	X	X
23 Smith	X	X	
42 McClure		X	X
47 Jones	X	X	X
55 Postek			X
56 Bryant		X	
58 Moran			X
59 Ginsburg			X

two of these had been mildly depressed during most of the intervening period. One man was mildly depressed continuously over the 11 years.

Depression was rated at two levels of severity. These were diagnosable psychoneurotic depressive reaction and depression too mild to warrant a diagnosis which was called Depressive Trend.[4]

Depression was associated with interpersonal conflicts and losses in four instances, with a sense of physical and/or psychosocial deterioration in four instances, and with a depressing life review (see below) in three instances.

There was no relationship between the amount of mental decline during followup and the incidence of depression (see table 3). These data amplify the finding in the first study that there were no simple relationships between depression and psychological test performance. There was a relationship to the general intellectual factor (Principal Component I of a Hotelling Principal Component Analysis) and to reaction time (see Birren, et al., 1963, p. 298).

Age-specific prevalence rates for psycho-

[4] In two instances ratings of depression at the third study were changed (one from diagnosis to trend and the other the reverse) on the basis of comparison with previous studies and the ratings made then.

neurotic depressive reaction were calculated using data from survivors and nonsurvivors (table 6). There is no significant increase in the rate with age. We believe this indicates that depression is not inherently more frequent as men age. Under less favorable physical and psychosocial conditions depression is probably more frequent with increasing age (Post, 1965).

A relationship between depression and higher systolic blood pressure which was seen at the first study was not present at the third study. The small sample size involved makes speculation about the meaning of the finding inappropriate.

Depression is generally described as an emotional state which occurs when there is an acute decrease in a person's self-esteem. Psychodynamic explanations of how this comes about constitute two types: through self-reproaches (superego attacks), or through one's feeling powerless to achieve important goals. The latter mechanism has been emphasized as the predominant one in depressions in old people. Busse (1955) described depression in the normal aged (that is, persons not referred for psychiatric illness) as predominantly due to a "recognition of weakness and an inability to obtain necessary narcissistic supplies or defend against threats to security." Guilt was an uncommon cause of depression among his normal aged subjects. Similarly, the old person's losses of resources such as physical health, family, and economic and social power

have been emphasized as causes of clinical depressions (Goldfarb, 1967). These resources provided security and sustained self-esteem through affording opportunities to demonstrate competence.

Bibring (1953) has elegantly outlined a theory of depression (at any age) as a result of a sense of helplessness and powerlessness. Most depressions among our subjects, too, were understandable in this way. In the main we agree with Bibring's contention that anger when present is a response in addition to the basic sense of hopelessness. An example is Mr. Dixon (No. 9).

He was frankly angry at both his wives for failing to care for him (his first wife died and the second became ill and dependent on him). Anger was a response in addition to depression when he felt in danger without a woman to care for him.

There were a few instances among the subjects, however, where guilt and self-reproach seemed to be a primary factor in depression.

Bibring outlined ways in which depression may be resolved: (1) When a goal which seemed unreachable again appears within reach; (2) when the goal is sufficiently modified to become reachable; (3) when the goal is abandoned; (4) when self-esteem is recovered sufficiently through other means, with or without change in the unreachable goal; or (5) when a defense is erected against the depressing feeling (such as in apathy or mania).

Among our subjects all of these methods

TABLE 6.—*Prevalence of psychoneurotic depressive reaction by age* [1] *(N=48)*

| Age | Depression | | Percent | |
	Present	Absent		
65 to 69 _____	3	13	19	$\chi^2=1.64$ df$=4$ N.S.
70 to 74 _____	6	30	12	
75 to 79 _____	4	25	14	
80 to 84 _____	3	9	25	
85 to 89 _____	0	4	0	

[1] Ratings from all 3 study times are combined.

were observed, even including one instance of increased hypomania as a response to retirement (Mr. Wozny, No. 8).

Knowledge of what constitutes successful and unsuccessful methods of resolution of depression would be most useful in treatment. The following are examples of successful attempts to solve the problems presented in depressions.

Mr. Murray's (No. 7) caring for his invalid wife for 5 years until her death has been described above (p. 79). Hopelessness about achieving his original retirement plans was caused by his wife's illness. He solved the problem of his depression through giving up his original retirement goals and instead making care of his wife a major new goal in life.

Mr. Smith (No. 23), a retired plumbing inspector, who was 74 at the first study, had lived with his mother, brothers, and sister for 25 years after his wife died. Two years before the first study his mother died. At that time he was moderately depressed. His depression seemed to grow from a recognition of how much he had been dependent on her and a sense of bodily deterioration with age which had been heightened by recent minor illnesses. He was classified as having a passive-dependent trend, and functional breakdown was predicted.

Eleven years later he continued to live with his siblings. He was not depressed. His self-esteem was supported by his status as the oldest brother in the house in a secure domestic arrangement where his dependency needs were met. Also, he was treated as a friend and respected when he went almost daily to the office where he had formerly been employed. He maintained a self-reassuring facade of going there to "work" answering the telephone, but his mild organic brain syndrome made significant contributions unlikely.

Life Review

We conceive of the life review as a naturally occurring, universal mental process characterized by the progressive return to consciousness of past experiences. Particularly it is the resurgence of unresolved conflicts; simultaneously, and normally, these revived experiences and conflicts can be surveyed and reintegrated. Presumably this process is prompted by the realization of approaching dissolution and death, and the inability to maintain one's

sence of personal invulnerability. It is further shaped by contemporaneous experiences and its nature and outcome are affected by the lifelong unfolding of character. The resurgence of unresolved conflicts may lead to constructive resolution or depression (Butler, 1963b).

These men often indicated that they had reviewed or were still reviewing their lives. Subjects who reviewed their lives without becoming depressed sometimes had attitudes that approached that described by Erikson (1959, p. 98) as typical of successful accomplishments of the last phase of life. He described an attitude of "acceptance of one's own and only life cycle and of the people who have become significant to it as something that had to be and that, by necessity, permitted no substitutions." Most of the men implicitly understood and accepted the fact that life has phases, each of which has its challenges and special satisfactions—and indeed they had found both in old age. Only a few men were envious of the "advantages" of younger people. Contrary to Erikson's observation, they were often less than fully confident that their lives had to have been the way they were. Rather, there was often a hint of a defense of life as it was lived. Old conflicts and unfulfilled wishes were not erased, but were under control with a resultant sense of mastery. Mr. Gottleib (No. 20) is an example of these points.

He was 85 at the third study. His life review appeared to have been mostly an internal dialogue. He was a mildly obsessive former stockroom clerk who had three children and a successful marriage. He described himself as never having a plan in life—"I just drifted along." At the third study he indicated that questions at the first study about his life goals had made him think about that aspect of himself. He seemed to resolve the issue for himself with only a slight doubt remaining which was typical of his obsessional personality. "Every person should have a plan but I don't feel unhappy because I did not have. I've had much happiness. If I had a plan I might be happier or with some other plan I might have been less happy."

He said he had no regrets about not becoming a foreman and reminded himself how pleased he always was that he did not have all the worries that a foreman did.

Erikson has described an intellectual process in which there is no attempt to change the life cycle by adding new chapters, so to speak. There was suggestive evidence that the men gradually approached this attitude as they reached advanced old age. When under 80, the men seemed more likely to be involved in life review with attempts to actively achieve goals not put aside. However, the number of subjects is too small to draw positive conclusions. In no subject did the urge for continued activity approach a panic about completing life tasks. Mr. Jones (No. 47) gives the clearest evidence of the active type of response to the life review. In his seventies he successfully pursued life goals largely set aside at the close of his adolescence. He experienced some depression which we associated with his life review.

Mr. Jones (No. 47), a former small business operator, was unique in the group because he suffered a schizophrenic-like psychotic episode in his late adolescence which required brief hospitalization and was followed by a full social recovery.

He was first seen at age 65 when he was about to retire. He was mildly depressed. As to his success at being the kind of person he wanted to be, he said "In some respects, yes. But I certainly haven't accomplished the things I wanted to accomplish." In his adolescence and twenties, he had goals: "Yes. Yes. I did. Well, every kid has ambitions to be prominent, to be somebody important. . . . I felt people should do something to bring our political institutions up to our social achievements, if you want to save the human race from destroying itself with tools it has developed." In response to a question about how well he had lived up to his ideals, he said, "Well, I think I was influenced largely by my mother who was a very strong woman with middle class ideals, and she influenced me to get along in the world. You know what I mean? Make money. In trying to do that I neglected the field I should have been going into; the field probably would have been a college professor or something of the sort. So I tried

business. I wouldn't say I was a howling success at it, but I did all right." A career in political life might also have suited him well, he felt. These goals were "pretty tough—almost impossible to attain," he said. At the third study, when he was 76, he had returned to work fulltime as treasurer of a retired persons' association where he had responsibility for managing their substantial investment capital. His position made him a natural advisor for the association's members about their insurance and investment problems. He was not depressed. His new job, started 5 years after retirement, represented a step toward accomplishment of some of the goals he had laid aside but not forgotten after adolescence. In his new job he was working for a social cause. He had even successfully lobbied in the State legislature to pass a bill benefiting retired persons.

Loss of a significant person through death was not a frequent cause of depression among survivors, primarily because only two men lost their wives during followup. Similarly, economic hardship did not contribute to depression.

Institutionalization

Three widowers who entered institutional homes during the followup accurately predicted their ability to adjust in an institution. None of the survivors were institutionalized or anticipated it soon at the time of the first study. Since each subject had been asked at the beginning to predict his adjustment if he entered a home, these three were studied. Two (Dooley, No. 51, and Bryant, No. 56) predicted their adjustment would be "fair" and "fair to good," adding that they might not like it but they would "get along,"— "make the best of it'.' On entering old age homes, these two made good adjustments. The third man (Crabtree, No. 6), when asked if he ever planned to enter a home, said, "No . . . my feeling is that I would not be my own boss any more. I won't give up being the boss as long as I can possibly hold on to it." He predicted his adjustment would be poor and that he would become depressed—a prediction which proved completely correct 9 years later. The relationship between an independent personality such as Mr. Crabtree's and difficulty in adjustment to institutional life has been reported (Perlin, 1958).

Death

Death is an event for which most of the subjects were well prepared even at the beginning of the study. Most had established psychological patterns with regard to death which were stable over the 11 years. Most had already made burial and related plans when first seen. At the third study, definite plans for disposition of their bodies at death had been made by 17 of the 18 men from whom data were available. The exception, Mr. Murray (No. 7), whose plans were indefinite, could not decide between burial and cremation because he was disturbed by "being reduced to nothing" eventually either way. Most subjects had also written wills and made plans for the future of their wives if they survived them.

The adaptive capacity of many of the men was challenged by their living longer than they had predicted they would 11 years earlier. Almost half of the 17 survivors from whom data were available had outlived the age at which they had predicted they would die. These eight men had collectively lived 23 man-years beyond their expectations. Three had lived longer than they said they wanted to live 11 years earlier.[5] Most among those restudied 11 years later were pleased that they had lived so long. One man called his life "a kind of dividend now." Two men who were depressed had contrasting views that "there is nothing left in life to do but die" and experienced a feeling of "being finished."

Ratings of subjects' Fears of Death (see

---

[5] Seven of the 24 survivors were not asked either question or did not respond directly to it.

Glossary) changed little during the 11 years. Four men were afraid of death at the first study. Three of them were still afraid at the third study and one was no longer afraid. No subjects developed Fear of Death during followup. The stability of attitudes about death suggests they are rooted in early experiences. The following is an example in which the cause can be partially traced.

Mr. Gottleib's (No. 20) wife commented that he always disliked conversations in which death was mentioned. During the first 14 years of his life, his father was an undertaker in a small rural village. He said, "That left impressions on me . . . it gave me reason to think more often of death and things that attended it than if you were just in a family where perhaps it might only occur once or maybe never in your childhood . . . it sort of dramatized it." He recalls his father embalming bodies in a barn where there were ice chests to keep them. "I seem to have recollections of different men who came with a pole. . . . They measured the one who had died and they brought the length of the corpse so my father could order a casket." He never helped his father with the work. It appears that childhood experiences and fantasies related to his father's work probably acted as trauma which prevented healthy acceptance of ideas about death and activated anxiety whenever death was discussed, even when he was 85 years old.

Religious beliefs such as belief in immortality were little related to attitudes about death. The majority of the men's adaptive responses to the approach of death did not involve religious principles for support. Their responses to questions about how much they thought of death, how they visualized dying, and their preparations for death rarely mentioned religious ideas. Their religious beliefs changed little during followup. Our findings are consistent with an earlier study which indicated that religious feelings do not characteristically increase in old age and that there is less strict adherence to religious dogma (Busse, 1955). Among our subjects, a few men seemed less sure of the existence of immortality at the third study. About one-third of them said they believed in immortality. Only one man (Dooley, No. 51) relied heavily on his religious convictions in his adaptation to the approach of death. For him, religious work had been a major part of his life throughout adulthood.

Adaptive Responses to the Approach of Death

Insight was the most frequent adaptive device. Subjects saw death as a biological necessity. Most had a sense of completeness about the life cycle they had experienced. Pride in having a legacy (Butler, 1968) was shown by the great emotional investment of the men in their children, grandchildren, and great-grandchildren. All but one subject had children and all but two had grandchildren or persons who filled these roles (such as adopted children or wives' children from previous marriages). Those without grandchildren wished they had them. One subject (Rhine, No. 14) spoke with pleasure about becoming a father and grandfather simultaneously when he married his second wife. A sense that their children and grandchildren would carry on the things which they valued seemed to become more salient with time. One subject spoke of his emotional investment in his grandchildren as greater than it ever was in his children.

A frequent adaptive characteristic was to attempt active mastery of the problem of death. Writing a will, discussing problems the family would face after one's death, and arranging burial were some of the limited number of opportunities for active mastery which the subjects could and did take in preparation for the essentially passive experience of death.

Three subjects seemed to actively make death their servant through investing in ownership of large numbers of grave plots (40 in one instance and 20 in another),

thus turning something unpleasant (dying) into something pleasant (making money as a result of death).

Sometimes activity during the passive experience of death was emphasized in intellectualizations or humor. One subject (Murray, No. 7) brought a book with him at the third study which described death as a very active process. "Do you know that at death there is a great deal of activity going on in our bodies? All the different elements in our bodies—the material, the vegetable, and the mineral—go into their respective parts. This book has helped me a lot."

Humorous references to activity, when in fact there is none, included speaking of death as "kicking off" and of "pushing up daisies" from a grave. One man joked that he "would warm up a harp" in Heaven for his wife if he died before she did. One man and his wife liked to remind each other jokingly of an aunt who seemed to underestimate her capacity to hold on to life. She used to say "Well, I won't have to do so and so again (such as paint the house) because I won't live that long." But she lived on and had to do many of the things over and over again.

Among defenses against anxiety surrounding death, denial was prominent. An example is Mr. Rhine (No. 14), the physical culture faddist whose boyish enthusiasm for maintaining good health led him to deny that people ever die except truly accidentally.

He said his sister "was never sick a day in her life"—but she had died 1½ years earlier. He attributed her death to "letting her diabetes go too long" his mother's death to improper surgery, and his wife's death to eating food improperly with a new set of false teeth.

A marked increase in denial of fear of death occurred in Mr. Wozny (No. 8), the man who had surgery for carcinoma of the mouth 1 year before the third study.

At the first study his denial took the form of abbreviated answers to questions.

I: Do you think about death?
S: About death?
I: Uh, hum.
S: No. I got no reason to.
I: Do you fear death?
S: No.
I: Would you welcome death?
S: If you're going to die you don't know. It's either that way or you are going to lay there you don't know.

After his surgery, denial was more forceful.

I: Were you afraid that you had cancer before you went to the hospital?
S: Was I afraid of—what?
I: Did you have some fear that it would turn out to be cancer?
S: Wasn't afraid of nothing! I don't let nothing worry me.
I: Lots of people are afraid of cancer, you know, when they get on in years.
S: I don't. I don't. I don't. It don't bother me. I don't worry about *anything*. I ain't got no worries . . . .

The operation "took a lot out of" him, he said.

I: Well I guess maybe you had some thought that you might get sick and die.
S: No. No. I didn't get nothing! . . .
I: How did you feel when they told you it was cancer?
S: Didn't bother me. No.
I: I guess you had seen other people have cancer?
S: Not up till then.
I: Nobody in your own age group?
S: No. No. (Pause.) My brother died—he had cancer of the bladder. He died 1 year ago . . . .
I: You don't think much about dying, death?
S: No, no, no, no, no.
I: How do you see it—as a kind of suffering?
S: I wouldn't know. Tell you, I go to bed at night and say my prayers. If I get up in the morning, all right, and if I don't I won't know *nothing* 'bout it and I won't worry about it.

Mr. Wozny's denial was adaptive. It protected him from an unpleasant reality and yet had no important liabilities. His successful use of denial lay in using it selectively, for example, denying that one might become an invalid and have a painful death, but not denying that one must see the doctor regularly in order to avoid complications of an illness.

DISCUSSION

The first phase of our study suggested answers to many questions about what is intrinsic to the aging process. Conclusions were inferences about a process from a still picture, however. Now we have a motion picture—a longitudinal study. Through repeated measurements of many variables, it has become possible to see the process of aging with a reliability no single set of measurements could reveal. Also, measurements and predictions from 11 years ago now stand beside outcomes with no question of retrospective bias.

A largely optimistic picture of old age emerges. Life for a majority of the men was characterized by vitality, interest, and enjoyment during most of old age. Their lives typically did not gradually deteriorate over a long period. Thus their often mentioned fear of slowly deteriorating, mentally or physically, before death, did not occur frequently. Only one-third of the men who died had organic mental changes at the study before their deaths. The increased proportion of men with organic mental decline at the third study indicates that long survivors are more likely to experience some organic decline. The men recognized that some decline of mental abilities was a not improbable occurrence in their stage of life and so they were probably more prepared to accept and/or compensate for such changes than are people in other stages of life. This is a specific example of the general principle that adaptive challenges are responded to most effectively if they come in the phase of life in which they are most anticipated. For example, loss of parents is best adapted to if it comes after adolescence; and dying is most easily accepted in old age. In reference to normal developmental events, Neugarten has called this "being on time" (1969).

To a large extent the successful aging of these men can be attributed to four resources: Good health; financial security; families; and personal adaptability. These resources are frequently lacking in the aged general population: one-third of noninstitutionalized people over 65 have a chronic disease so severe that it limits their activities, and one-third live on incomes below the poverty line. Psychiatric patients even more frequently lack these resources (Lowenthal and Berkman, 1967). Provision of these resources or suitable substitutes for them must be a primary concern of any public health approach to the mental health problems of the aged. These men demonstrate that, with resources, old age can be a satisfying part of the life cycle.

Because in most instances the men in our study had these resources, it is possible to give some answers to the question: what is helpful in addition?

One aspect is having goals until the end of life. This could involve modifying goals to fit the needs of old age or possibly finding new ones. Knowledge of changes during old age in the goals of successful men should be very useful. In this study there were men who did not succeed in maintaining goals. For instance, Mr. Murray had no satisfying purpose in life when his goal of caring for his wife ended with her death. Mr. Gottlieb busied himself with semi-purposeful clipping of newspapers for his children, and Mr. Dooley could no longer be active in church work as he had during all of his adult life.

Other men maintained goals. Several had a goal of continued work. These men enjoyed their work which continued to be an important part of their self-images. For them, working demonstrated their industry, competence, and youthfulness. In two men who were still working extensively at the third study, there was a suggestion that without work they would find it difficult to maintain self-esteem. People who derive their self-esteem largely from the work they do may increasingly encounter difficulty since retirement ages are continuing to drop and our culture is becoming less work- and more leisure-oriented.

For other men, enjoying recreational activities was the major goal. Some men traveled. However, since travel usually depended upon the continued stamina and interest of both husband and wife, it was relatively easily interrupted. Visiting with friends and neighbors, reading, gardening, and doing chores around the house were especially frequent major satisfactions for the oldest men. Some of them seemed satisfied with very little organized activity in life. We suspect that in part this reflects the influence of what Bühler (1968) has described as a normal "regression to predominant need satisfaction" in advanced old age. By this she means an ending of pursuits not related to basic needs such as food, protection, and human contact. This may in part be due to the men's inability to find larger meaningful goals in old age.

Preretirement and postretirement counseling about the development of goals and interests would have been helpful. A transitional period of part-time work preferably in the same job would have eased the adjustment. An additional benefit from such an arrangement would be the opportunity for the retiring person to teach his younger colleagues what to expect and how to plan for retirement.

The high reliability of the men's self-monitoring of their mental abilities suggests that employers could rely more heavily upon mutual agreement about the best time for retirement. There is no doubt that many of the men in the study could have worked full time to a more advanced age than they did. The high level of intellectual function so many of them retained into advanced old age suggests that "getting senile" is only an occasional valid reason for retirement. Obsolescence of the old person's skills, his boredom with his work, and the pressure of young people to fill his place in the work hierarchy also were factors for these men.

New socially and personally useful roles need to be developed for the growing numbers of men and women who have many years to live in retirement.

Leisure activities for the aged need to become a more important part of general social planning. The minority of the men who attended social clubs and senior citizen centers appeared to enjoy them. Efforts should be made to make such facilities appeal to the widest possible range of social, economic, and personality types.

Our understanding of adaptive psychopathology has gained from longitudinal study. It has supported the impression gained during the first study that obsessive and schizoid personalities as well as the mechanisms of denial and counterphobia can make durable contributions to adaptation. This impression suggests that a new appreciation of the value of these types of adaptive behavior is needed. This probably applies to all ages—not just old age.

A concern with what is adaptive or maladaptive rather than with what is "psychopathological" alone may be especially important as mental health professionals work more in community-oriented settings where insight as a means of cure may less often be a reasonable goal. Nonetheless, insight was the most common way of resolving problems among our subjects. Their experience suggests that insight may not *always* be the ideal means of adaptation.

It is surprising that adaptation, even in the narrow range of this sample, was significantly related to survival. Initially good physical health may have permitted the relationship to be detectable. Anecdotes about people who died because of overwhelming troubles in their lives have anticipated such a scientific finding. We know that patients hospitalized for psychiatric illnesses have increased death rates. Relationships between less dramatic psychiatric factors and survival rate are also known. Bereaved relatives (spouses, siblings, and children) are known to have an increased death rate during the first year after the death (Rees and Lutkins, 1967). Further, a measure of work satisfaction was found to be as good a predictor of survival as life expectancy tables among men 60 to 69 years old (Palmore, 1969).

In considering the meaning of the relationship between psychological factors and increased death rate, two hypotheses which are not mutually exclusive are:

1. Biological condition
   - Psychological condition.
   - Increased death rate.

2. Psychological condition ⟶ Biological condition ⟶ Increased death rate.

By Hypothesis 1 we mean that biological factors can influence both adaptation and survival. Organic mental decline is an example of such a sequence. Its presence was associated with early death and with poor adaptation. By Hypothesis 2 we mean that a psychological state such as poor adaptation or low-job satisfaction can lead to physical diseases and an increased death rate. In the instance of bereaved families, the causal sequence is surely in the direction of Hypothesis 2. Understanding of the relative contributions (since both probably are to some degree true) of these two hypotheses toward survival could have substantial importance for social planning. It is possible that greater knowledge of psychosomatic relationships and genetics will reveal what physical factors mediate the relationship of adaptation and other psychiatric factors to fatal diseases. It appears that our society in general plans for the aged as though biological state were primary and psychological factors only secondary in the causal sequence. For example, massive funds are used to treat medical diseases and provide nursing homes to care for the physically ill while little attention is given to the part emotional factors play in causing the physical illnesses. Our society's choice between the hypotheses may be correct, but scientific proof is needed.

Prolonging life without regard to its quality is a dubious goal at best. We may find that maintenance of a meaningful life and maintenance of life itself are *very* closely related.

Our emphasis on the subjects' frequently active responses to challenges might appear to be in conflict with earlier inferences from projective test data that with increasing age men tend toward more passive and less active responses to challenges (Neugarten and Gutmann, 1968; Gut-

mann, 1969). The apparent difference may be due to sample selection. Men with active mastery orientations may have been more likely to volunteer for the NIH study, while subjects in the studies referred to were sought out by the researchers and might have included more passive men. Further, the subjects in those studies appeared to be younger than our subjects. We observed a tendency for passive-dependent men to survive less long and for counterphobic (active) men to survive longer than expected. Thus, selective survival of more active, mastery-oriented men may partly explain the contrasting findings.

The richly detailed and insightfully told life histories of these men quickly dispel any listener's prejudices that old people are uninteresting. This suggests that life histories of old people should be utilized more as a means of interesting students in the problems of old age. A unique feature of such nearly complete life histories is the chance they afford to trace the changing influence of psychopathology, physical factors, and adaptive modes during the whole life cycle. For example, a person interested in adolescent psychoses can gain new perspective from the history of Mr. Jones who was able to tell about the influence of his adolescent idealism, love affair, and psychosis on the next 50 years of his life. Our culture probably underestimates the capacity of old people to pass on wisdom about life. This may occur because we are so impressed with how rapidly technical knowledge grows obsolete. The lives of these men suggest, as does the work of writers and dramatists, that there are unchanging truths about life.

Differentiating between timeless wisdom and the prejudices of a person who lived in a specific culture and period in it is not a goal of this chapter. Nonetheless it is interesting to note what events the men picked as especially important to them. These included positive childhood experiences with parents, as well as negative ones such as loss of parents and poverty. They often emphasized how greatly the level of their aspirations during adolescence and early adulthood influenced their education and the course of their adult lives. It appeared that almost all of the men would have set their aspirations higher rather than lower if they had another opportunity. Marrying and having children emerged as extremely important to all of the men. Having a wife and/or children provided social and physical security for many, especially in old age. Having children and grandchildren was a major way of satisfying the wish to leave a legacy. Many of the men mentioned stock investment opportunities that they had missed which still distressed them years later. Retirement was a major event in their lives and was associated with both positive and negative changes.

An appraisal of the events these men chose as significant suggests that mental health planners should place great importance upon helping young persons achieve the maturational step of forming a secondary family. It also appears evident that there are special social planning needs of persons who do not have families to rely upon. This situation may become even more crucial if, as birth rates drop, more couples are childless.

Today, psychiatric treatment in geriatrics deals largely with organic brain syndrome and its associated behavioral problems. Less severe disorders do not receive treatment because of negative attitudes toward treatment on the part of patients and therapists and because of potential patients' inabilities to afford treatment.

There may be profound shifts in this situation in the future. A way may be found to prevent arteriosclerotic brain disease; then, if increasing affluence and medical insurance plans allow old people to afford preventive care and if mental health professionals turn greater attention to promotion of preventive mental health, millions of old people may live to advanced age with well-preserved intellect and mental health.

On the other hand, if no prevention of arteriosclerosis is achieved, if medical care delivery does not improve, and if problems of preventive mental health are not solved, then millions of the elderly may find old age the worst time of their lives.

SUMMARY

1. Survival was significantly related to the level of adaptation and Mental Status test scores of the men. No conclusive evidence is available to explain what factors mediate the relationship. Among other factors which showed a trend toward association with survival were: absence of Organic Mental Decline; fewer organic brain syndrome signs; high morale; counterphobic rather than passive-dependent behavior; and presence of certain adaptive psychopathology and defenses. As a group, neither functional psychiatric diagnoses nor psychiatric symptoms influenced survival.

2. The men had a largely optimistic view of old age. For the majority, their lives had been characterized by vitality, interest, and enjoyment. Their optimism was realistic. Most of the men were fortunate in having adequate income, relatively good health, available families, and personal adaptability. A few achieved their greatest sense of self-satisfaction in their old age.

3. Mental ability measured with the Men-

tal Status test did not change significantly over the 11 years. Changes in ability, both up and down, appeared to be related to two general factors: the physiological state of the brain, and the person's desire to maintain or increase his mental capacity which in turn depended to a large degree on his psychosocial environment.

Eight of the 11 men who had organic mental changes at the first study have died.

4. The men were resourceful in compensating for organic declines and usually adapted to the mild changes without distress or depression. Almost all of the men were aware of any declines in mental ability they were undergoing.

5. There were two cases of "pseudo-dementia"—organic signs seen in depression which disappear when the depression is relieved.

6. Certain psychopathological features made durable contributions to adaptation. Schizoid and obsessive-compulsive personalities were associated with adequate or even excellent adaptation. Denial (used selectively) and counterphobia were similarly adaptive defense mechanisms. This finding suggests that psychopathology and defenses must always be evaluated with regard to their influence upon adaptation.

7. Depression was the most common psychiatric symptom. The prevalence rate of psychoneurotic depressive reaction was 14 percent. It did not increase with age. A wide range of precipitating factors were identifiable. The men were resourceful in resolving the problems that caused their depressions. None required psychiatric treatment. Mild transient hypochondriasis was frequent and served a wide range of psychic functions, especially at times of stress.

8. Intelligent *active* response to illness was a favored adaptive method. Denial of possible future chronic incapacitation and pain was common. Denial of the need for diagnosis and treatment was minimal.

9. The number of sexually active men declined as did the sexual interest of most. The insufficiency of interpersonal and psychodynamic data about sexual life in old age in this and other studies was noted.

10. Maintenance of meaningful goals throughout old age was important to life satisfaction. Subjects accomplished this, for example, through continued work, recreational activities, and caring for people such as an ill wife, or things, such as a house.

11. Dying was an event for which most of the men were well prepared from the beginning of the study. Here, too, active responses of preparation were satisfying to the men. Also adaptive were recognition of the life cycle including death, a sense of leaving a legacy, and denial.

ACKNOWLEDGMENTS

The authors wish to express their thanks to the following people for their generous help. Dr. Thomas E. Anderson, Chief, Section on the Mental Health of the Aging, NIMH; Mrs. Marie L. Blank, social worker in the Section; Dr. Peter L. Putnam, of the NIMH Center for Epidemiologic Studies; and Mrs. Victoria Fries, graduate student, Departments of Sociology and Human Development, University of Chicago, all offered valuable criticism. Dr. Diane Wilkins, as a COSTEP student at the NIMH, contributed ideas from her study of the marriages of the men. Mrs. Sara Blumberg of the Philadelphia Geriatric Center provided valuable longitudinal data analogous to "waiting room observations" used in child psychiatry. Drs. John J. Bartko and Samual Granick directed statistical procedures. Mrs. Annie T. Randall, also of the Biometry Branch, performed statistical tests and assisted us in locating hard-to-find stores of data.

REFERENCES

AMERICAN PSYCHIATRIC ASSOCIATION. *Diagnostic and Statistical Manual of Mental Disorders.* Washington, D.C.: the Association, 1968.

BIBRING, E. The mechanism of depression. In: Greenacre, P., ed. *Affective Disorders.* New York: International Universities Press, 1953.

BIRREN, J. E., ET AL. *Human Aging: A Biological and Behavioral Study.* Washington, D.C.: U.S. Government Printing Office, 1963.

BÜHLER, CHARLOTTE. The course of human life as a psychological problem. *Human Development,* 11: 184–200, 1968.

BUSSE, E. W., ET AL. Studies of the process of aging. X: the strengths and weaknesses of psychic functioning in the aged. *Amer. J. Psychiat.,* 111: 896–901, 1955.

BUTLER, R. N. The facade of chronological age: an interpretive summary. *Amer. J. Psychiat.,* 119: 721–728, 1963a.

BUTLER, R. N. The life review: an interpretation of reminiscence in the aged. *Psychiatry,* 26: 65–76, 1963b.

BUTLER, R. N. Aspects of survival and adaptation in human aging. *Amer. J. Psychiat.,* 123: 1233–1243, 1967.

BUTLER, R. N. Toward a psychiatry of the life cycle: implications of socio-psychologic studies of the aging process for the psychotherapeutic situation. In: Simon, A., and Epstein, L. J., eds. *Aging in Modern Society.* Psychiatric Research Report #23. Washington, D.C.: The American Psychiatric Association, 1968. pp. 233–248.

CUMMING, ELAINE, and HENRY, W. E. *Growing Old: The Process of Disengagement.* New York: Basic Books, Inc., 1961.

ERIKSON, E. H. Growth and crises of the healthy personality. *Psychological Issues,* 1: 1–171, 1959.

FINKLE, A. L. Sex after prostatectomy: most patients retain their potency after prostatectomy. *Med. Aspects of Human Sexuality,* 2 (3) : 40–41, 1968.

GOLDFARB, A. I. Geriatric psychiatry. In: Freedman, A. M.; Kaplan H. I.; and Kaplan, H. S., eds. *Comprehensive Textbook of Psychiatry.* Baltimore: Williams and Wilkins, 1967.

GOLDFARB, A. I., and TURNER, HELEN. Psychotherapy of aged persons: II. utilization and effectiveness of "brief" therapy. *Amer. J. Psychiat,* 109: 916–921, 1953.

GOLDSTEIN, K. *A Holistic Approach to Biology Derived from Pathological Data in Man.* Boston: Beacon Press, 1963.

GUTMANN, D. L. *The Country of Old Men: Cultural Studies in the Psychology of Later Life.* Ann Arbor: Institute of Gerontology, University of Michigan-Wayne State University, 1969.

KAHANA, EVA, and KAHANA, B. The therapeutic potential of age segregated and age integrated patient environments for elderly psychiatric patients. *Arch. of Gen. Psychiat.* 23: 20–29, 1970.

KAHN, R. L., ET AL. Brief objective measures for the determination of mental status in the aged. *Amer. J. Psychiat.,* 117: 326–328, 1960.

LIEBERMAN, M. A. Psychological correlates of impending death: some preliminary observations. *J. of Gerontology,* 20: 181–190, 1965.

LOWENTHAL, MARJORIE F.; BERKMAN, P. L.; and associates. *Aging and Mental Disorder in San Francisco.* San Francisco: Jossey-Bass, Inc., 1967.

MASSIE, E., ET AL. Sudden death during coitus—fact or fiction. *Med. Aspects of Human Sexuality,* 3 (6) : 22–26, 1969.

NEUGARTEN, BERNICE L. The awareness of middle age. In: Neugarten, Bernice L., ed. *Middle Age and Aging: A Reader in Social Psychology.* Chicago: University of Chicago Press, 1968.

NEUGARTEN, BERNICE L. Dynamics of transition of middle age to old age. Paper presented at the Boston Gerontologic Society meeting, December 6, 1969. To be published in *J. of Geriatric Psychiatry.*

NEUGARTEN, BERNICE L., and GUTMANN, D. L. Age-sex roles and personality in middle age: a thematic apperception study. In: Neugarten, Bernice L., ed. *Middle Age and Aging: A Reader in Social Psychology.* Chicago: University of Chicago Press, 1968.

NEWMAN, G., and NICHOLS, C. R. Sexual activities and attitudes in older persons. *J.A.M.A.,* 173: 33–35, May 7, 1960.

PALMORE, E. B. Physical, mental, and social factors in predicting longevity. *Gerontologist,* 9: 103–108, 1969.

PERLIN, S. Psychiatric screening in a home for the aged. *Geriatrics,* 13: 747–751, 1958.

PERLIN, S., and BUTLER, R. N. Psychiatric aspects of adaptation to the aging experience. In: Birren, J. E., et al., eds. *Human Aging: A Biological and Behavioral Study.* Washington, D.C.: U. S. Government Printing Office, 1963.

POST, F. *The Clinical Psychiatry of Late Life.* Oxford: Pergamon Press, Inc., 1965.

REES, W. D., and LUTKINS, SYLVIA G. Mortality of bereavement. *British Med. J.,* 4: 13–16, 1967.

ROSS, ELIZABETH K. *On Death and Dying.* New York: MacMillan Company, 1969.

ROTH, M. The natural history of mental disorders in old age. *J. Ment. Sci.,* 101: 281–301, 1955.

ROTHSCHILD, D. Senile psychoses and psychoses with cerebral arteriosclerosis. In: Kaplan, O. J., ed. *Mental Disorders in Later Life.* Stanford: Stanford University Press, 1945.

WERNER, MARTHA; PERLIN, S.; and BUTLER, R. N. Self perceived changes in community-resident aged: "aging-image" and adaptation. *Archives of General Psychiatry*, 4: 501–508, 1961.

GLOSSARY

Adaptation: A global appraisal of the individual's adjustment to his current situation. Psychopathological traits were not by themselves considered evidence of maladjustment. High adaptation was characterized by resourcefulness in meeting needs and obtaining satisfaction from life, by high self-esteem and an absence of self-defeating behavior. Scale used: 1 = excellent—very good; 2 = good; 3 = fair—poor.

Age relevant checklist: Consisted of 34 personality and behavior characteristics noted in the literature as related to aging. An example is the degree of preoccupation with the past which was rated on a six-point scale. The checklist has been reproduced. (Perlin and Butler, 1963, p. 200.)

Chronic Brain Syndrome: Marked organic mental impairment. The five diagnostic signs given in the American Psychiatric Association *Diagnostic and Statistical Manual* (1968) were used as criteria. They are impaired orientation, memory, intellectual function, judgment, and lability of affect.

Death, fear of: Each subject was rated as having a normal concern about death, a fear of death, or a denial of fear of death. The second category represented an explicit statement of fear.

Denial of aging changes: Minimization and/or direct refusal to "see" such changes within oneself which were obvious to others.

Identity crisis: A sense of inner conflict among one's goals, accomplishments, and behavior which was new in the aging period.

Mental Status Test: A quantitative test similar in form to that which is commonly asked in psychiatric interviews to evaluate orientation, memory, judgment, and cognitive abilities. Seven of the 14 subtests were abbreviations of subtests from the WAIS. The test has been reproduced (Perlin and Butler, 1963, p. 193).

Morale index: A measure of the subject's self-evaluation. It was intended to obtain some measure of what is seen as positive in the aging experience by the aged themselves. It was derived from a content analysis of the first study interviews. The figure is the percentage of personality or affective changes which were reported as positive in old age.

Organic Mental Decline: A clinical impression of mild decline in the mental status and in the function of the subject rather than a rating based on specific signs or symptoms. The changes included cognitive dysfunctions such as recent memory loss and impaired comprehension; inappropriate behavior related to these deficits, such as going to appointments at the wrong times and losing the point when answering questions; and disturbances of affect, such as flatness and emotional incontinence.

When changes were more severe, a diagnosis of chronic brain syndrome was added.

Organic Mental Decline had been called "Senile Quality" in earlier publications of this study, but that term was discarded because of its implication that such a decline is characteristic of the aged and because the term is commonly loosely used.

Psychosocial Losses: A rating made by the social psychologists. The degree of loss or lack of personally significant people in the subject's environment was assessed on a seven-point scale.

Symptoms: Were enumerated using a checklist of 23 items. Inquiry about each symptom was made during the interviews. Typical symptoms were hypochondriacal ideas, depression, compulsions, nightmares, and hallucinatory experiences. The list has been reproduced. (Perlin and Butler, 1963, p. 201.)

CHAPTER 6

Aging and Social Adaptation: A Longitudinal Study of Healthy Old Men

by E. Grant Youmans and Marian Yarrow

Old age has become an increasingly extended period of time in the life cycle. For many persons it may cover a quarter of a century—a period in life longer than the formative years of growth and development. Just as every phase of the life course has important changes, so old age is marked with changes in the individual's physical and psychological capacities and also in his social circumstances and opportunities. Almost inevitably the aged person is faced with limitations of one kind or another, and with the need to develop substitutions and reorganizations in his mode of living. How the individual adapts to the changes or anticipated changes undoubtedly reflects his developmental experiences as well as the requirements imposed by his immediate life situation.

Since many of the conditions of old age, both medical and environmental, have changed in the past few decades, behavior in old age may reflect these changes. It is especially important to investigate the behavioral side of old age within known medical and social contexts to ascertain the features of behavior as age progresses. The present analyses are concerned with continuities and changes in social behavior and attitudes over the aging period studied here, and with factors associated with deteriorative and integrative processes. We have asked: (*a*) In what respects were the individual's responses and manner of coping consistent or changing over the years? (*b*) What conditions or experiences influenced behavior and attitudes in the later years? (*c*) Were there distinguishable behavior characteristics in 1956 between the men who survived to 1967 and the men who did not survive?

Materials and Methods

Aspects of behavior assumed to be indicative of the nature of the individual's involvements in the affairs of living were studied. These were:

(*a*) the organization of the subject's daily activities. The regular activities in which the subject engaged were rated in terms of the extent to which they were structured, planned, and varied, by the subject's own making.

(*b*) the subject's current outlook on life. Expressed feeelings of satisfaction, interest, contentment, and enjoyment in living were rated.

(*c*) the degree of passivity characteristic of the subject. The ordinary engagements of everyday living were judged on the passivity or activity involved.

(d) the subject's social interactions. Appraisal was made in terms of the amount of interaction beyond the immediate family group, and also in terms of the degree to which social interaction came as the result of the subject's own initiative or was engineered and aided by others.

The individual's environment was assessed in regard to personal-social deficits. These were defined as losses of persons who, in earlier adult years, had been the subject's primary intimate group. These were losses over which the person had little or no control: deaths of persons close to him, mentally or physically incapacitating illnesses of spouse, and departures of children or friends.

The data were obtained through interviews with the subject. The interview consisted of open-ended questions in which the man was asked to describe concrete details of his activities, for example, to give an account of the events of the preceding day and week. Similar probes were used for each subject to obtain reasonably equal coverage of areas relevant to the analysis dimensions. (For more details, see description of questions in *Human Aging*, Yarrow et al. (1963), pp. 262–263.) The behavioral dimensions were rated on five-point scales. Environmental deficit was rated on a seven-point scale. High-scale points represent the favorable ends of the behavior and attitude dimensions; high-scale score on environmental loss represents much loss.

To insure against general "halo" effects in the coding of the interview responses, the protocol was dealt with in the following manner: Three subdocuments were created. The first included only the responses describing the man's regular affairs of living; this was rated for degree of organization of behavior. The second document enumerated only the subject's activities, to permit a rating on the passivity-activity dimension. The third document included only the subject's descriptions of his social interactions outside his family. Each of these documents was rated without knowledge of the subject and without reference to the total interview protocol. Ratings of the subject's current outlook were based on the entire interview. Ratings of environmental deficit depended mainly upon specific sources within the interview, although the total interview was available. Coding was done by pairs of coders, rating independently. Coders were not familiar with the subject's ratings at other time periods. Correlations between the two raters range from 0.80 to 0.98.

FINDINGS

Continuity and Change Over Time

A first question asked of the data is a longitudinal one: What were the changes and continuities in observable behavior, in characteristics that reflect the man's general state of well-being and determine the kind of stimulus he is to others around him?

In 1956 these men, then mainly in the decade of 65 to 75 years of age, were faring reasonably well both in attitudes and behavior (Birren, et al., 1963, pp. 266–272). Half of the group were genuinely involved in social contacts beyond the immediate family circle; half were rated satisfied and interested in life; only about a fourth were finding life burdensome. Only 11 percent of the group carried on at the level of chores and routines, while 42 percent had new, complex, absorbing activities to report. Was the picture for the group sustained in the next 11 years and did individuals tend to retain their particular adaptations as they grew older? For answers to these questions, let us look first at the group profiles on four indexes of behavior as the men appeared in 1956, 1961, and 1967 (fig. 1). The three sets of bar graphs in the left portion of the figure represent the survivors and are comparisons of the same men at each measurement period. On the right is the

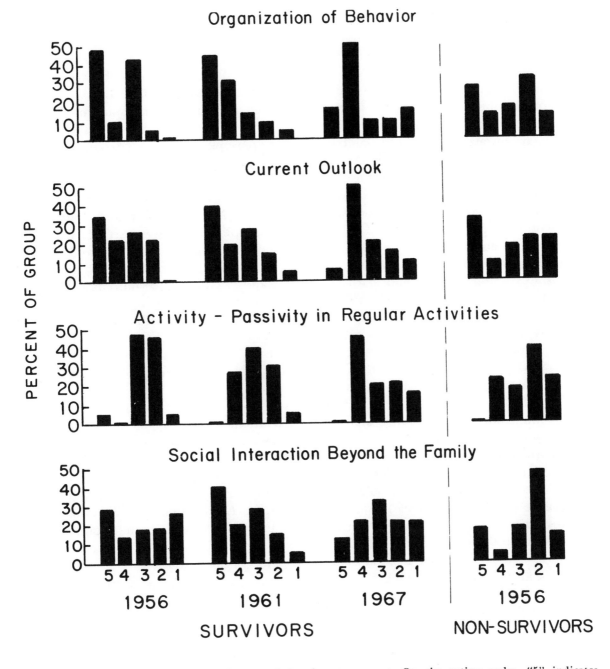

FIGURE 1.—Ratings of behavior at three periods of measurement. On the rating scales, "5" indicates the favorable score (complexity in behavior, satisfaction in outlook, high-activity level, many social interactions); "1" is the least favorable score. Each bar represents the percent of subjects at each category of the scale.

picture of the men who did not survive to 1967. Ratings of "5" on the graphs are indicative of the desirable end of the scales.

The profiles of the survivor group were generally similar on the three time-spaced measurements. Whatever differences occurred did not indicate systematic progressive shifts in the group as a whole toward the less favorable characteristics. That is, the group did not move toward less complexity in daily behavior, or toward a more discouraged outlook on life, or toward passivity, or toward narrowed social contacts. The "t" tests of change in the individual's ratings from 1956 to the last available rating on each subject showed no significant changes. Correlations of subjects' scores in 1956 with corresponding scores in 1961 and again in the 1967 expressed relatively strong associations between status at one period and status at the next (the range of r's is 0.56 to 0.75; $N = 24$). (One variable was an exception: The passivity-activity ratings in 1956, though significantly related to passivity ratings in 1961 ($r = 0.58$), had little relation to assessments of this dimension in 1967 ($r = 0.24$). We will return to consider this in the context of a later analysis question.)

In many instances, the interview protocols in 1967 echoed the subject's responses 11 years before. Mr. Dooley[1] is an example of a man whose earlier report and his followup record carried similar themes. In 1956 he described his daily routine as follows: "I read a book some time back and it was "Try Giving Yourself Away." I tried it and I thought it was very worthwhile . . . . I've been giving my time to a hospital . . . . I go downtown every day . . . at 10 I start going from room to room doing what I can to help patients—cheering them up . . . running

errands—whatever their problem, I try to help them out . . . . I'm active in church work—I go out to do church work in the evening . . . aside from that I'm not very busy . . . . I give 7 days a week in the hospital unless something prevents me from it."

In 1967, he said: "Time passes very quickly . . . . I think my life is fuller than other older people's. Lots of them don't go to church or take an interest in anything . . . . I'm fairly successful as an older person. Feel I've accomplished a lot . . . . I see death approaching because I'm an old man. Am not afraid."

Sameness over the years is equally apparent in Mr. Dixon's record, although for him life is far less satisfying. In 1956 he said, "I retired about a year and a half ago . . . . And I have too much time on my hands . . . . On certain days I have nothing ahead; I get up and have my dinner and go to the library . . . . Then I take a little walk . . . . Then I watch television . . . . I have very few telephone calls from my children. They have their life."

In 1967: "Time goes too slow. Can't sleep at night. Worry about my wife and money . . . . To me the days are all the same . . . . I want to go into the Home because my wife would have no one to care for her if I died . . . . (Lonely?) Oh yes, sure. In the house I got nobody to talk to. My wife doesn't understand . . . . I can't go and leave my wife too much. Also, lots of housework!"

For a few of the men, 11 years of time brought marked behavioral decline and withdrawal. Mr. Crabtree was such a man. In 1956 he told the interviewer: "I'm happy around here . . . . I'm happy that I can go around and do the things that I do. I'm not a youngster . . . . I get up at let's say seven or seven thirty. Then I go

---

[1] The same pseudonyms are used as in ch. 5.

back to bed and read the paper or watch television. Then if I have an appointment somewhere . . . I go. One day I have a meeting of the Golden Age Club. So, Monday afternoon I wouldn't give up for no money in the world; I have to go to that meeting. Every day I go see my wife (in a private nursing home) . . . . Saturday night I go to a dance. Sunday night most of the time I go to another dance. Monday we have a card game in the house."

In 1967 he had "given up." "Have no friends . . . . Time, lots of time . . . . (Life as an older person) is bad, all bad . . . . Want to leave here (nursing home) . . . . Nothing to do, just sleep . . . . No good here . . . . Now I'm old, can't get around."

Granted the basic continuity in behavior with advancing age, these men did change as they grew older. The nature of change becomes more apparent in further examinations of the men's functioning. The interrelations among the measures provide some answers.

Interrelations of Functioning

The several aspects of social functioning indexed here are conceptually distinct and functionally separable dimensions of social response: how competent or organized was daily behavior, how much were social interactions maintained outside the immediate family, how passive or active were the man's activities, and how optimistic or unhappy was his view of life?

In the initial measurement of these men (see table 1), there was appreciable interrelation among the four sets of scores (a range of correlations from 0.24 to 0.64). In 1967, intercorrelations among the four measures were generally higher; the range was from 0.58 to 0.78. The contrast between the two periods appears especially in the quality of passivity: In 1967, the

correlation with outlook on life was 0.58; with social interaction, 0.78; and with organization of behavior, 0.76. The corresponding coefficients in 1956 for the survivor group were 0.26, 0.24, and 0.36. The consistent trend in the measures toward greater interdependency suggests a changing state of affairs as aging progresses. Perhaps in later years, maintenance of social functioning or decline of social functioning becomes more nearly all or none within the individual than in earlier years.

This interpretation seems most clearly applicable to the passivity aspect. We are inclined to interpret the amount of passivity or activity in the man's way of life in 1956 as a long-time habit or a matter of choice, but independent of his morale and involvements. In the later years, passivity seemed more likely to be "forced," and part and parcel of a generally less favorable state in the individual. Thus, Mr. Moran, at age 81, explained, "I'm putting up with life [said cheerfully] . . . . I started to age when I was 71 years old. Before then I could do anything. Now I'm slowed down."

To gather further evidence relating to the apparent increased interdependencies in functioning, we turned to measures obtained by other investigators in the project. A psychiatric index of adaptation and WAIS scores (total verbal and total performance scores) (see descriptions on pp. 50–51) was correlated with each of the social psychological indices and with each other. That the systematic changes noted in the social psychological measures appeared also in these correlations is evident in table 1. Thus, the quite general changes over time toward increased interrelatedness of functions give further support to the interpretation of greater vulnerability in the later years.

One might ask, how much would the men be able to withstand in 1967? Would

TABLE 1.—*Interdependencies of functioning in aged men*

(Correlations below the diagonal are on measurements in 1956; values for the men who survived to 1967 are the upper entry; values for those who did not survive are the lower entry (boldface type). Correlations above the diagonal are measurements in 1967.

		1	2	3	4	5	6	7
1	Organization of Behavior	--	75	69	76	43	76	28
2	Outlook	61 **60**	--	69	58	69	57	15
3	Social interaction	58 **30**	58 **64**	--	78	40	60	21
4	Activity—passivity	36 **54**	26 **32**	24 **49**	--	35	64	27
5	Adaptability	12 **52**	26 **47**	20 **40**	−18 **27**	--	66	15
6	WAIS Verbal Score	58 **39**	28 **26**	24 **13**	37 **13**	03 **37**	--	64
7	WAIS Performance Score	38 **15**	14 **10**	03 **−08**	23 **06**	−13 **26**	67 **27**	--

NOTE.—All scales set with high scores are indicative of favorable status. One subject who was interviewed died the following week. He is, therefore, in the "survivor" group in these analyses and in the "non-survivor" group in the other reports. Survivors total 24; nonsurvivors, 23. An r of 0.41 is required for a p value of 0.05.

those who "looked good" across the measurement spectrum show a quick collapse of their *total* structure of behavior and attitudes in the face of assaults and stressful encounters, psychological or physical in nature—more so than in the earlier years?

Bearing on this issue is a comparison of the men's responses to environmental stresses in 1956 and in 1967. In the initial study, a depleted intimate social environment, associated most often with the death of spouse, was significantly related to the deteriorative aspects of functioning (Yarrow et al., *Human Aging*, p. 276). This association appeared not only within the data gathered by the social psychological interviews; environmental loss was significantly related to the psychiatric assessments of depressive trends and adaptability and similarly to measures of cognitive functions and reaction time Birren et al., 1963, p. 301).

If vulnerability is greater in the later stages of old age, one should expect higher associations between environmental assaults and deteriorative functioning in the 1967 than in the 1956 data (table 2). To a remarkably consistent degree, the magnitudes of association support this line of reasoning. The stresses of loss made the more severe inroads on behavior and outlook in later years studied. This is apparent as one examines dimensions one at a time, and in the fact that deteriorative trends within the individual were likely to occur simultaneously across the entire spectrum of measurements.

Where the aged man succeeded in maintaining himself in the face of losses, he seemed to do so being well aware of the hard effort that was needed if he was to succeed. Mr. Murray expressed this awareness: "Yes, you need people and I am trying to keep in touch, . . . trying to get in touch again . . . . I see many people, and always speak. Even speak to people I've never seen on the street or bus . . . . I'm not very happy about it (his life). What is it all about? . . .

There's no incentive or interest as there was when younger . . . . All old people can do is live day to day . . . . There's not as much energy. I've felt this more since my wife's death."

Thus, each of the clues in the data contributes consistently to characterize the change that is occurring: Men in the later measurement years appeared more often to present either a generally "good" or a generally "poor" behavioral status. They were less likely than in earlier years to maintain good functioning in some respects along with poor functioning in others.

1956 Characteristics of Survivors and Non-survivors

Ordinarily medical factors are investigated as predictive variables in survivorship. In the present data it was possible to view environmental and behavioral factors in a similar fashion: were there differences in 1956 between those men who survived to 1967 and those who did not? The status of the two groups in 1956 is compared in table 3. Ratings on behavioral organization distinguished between the groups; the survivors were carrying on more organized and complex living than the men in the nonsurvivor group. On other behavioral dimensions, too, the direction of difference favored the survivor

group; survivors showed more social interaction, were more active, and more satisfied in outlook when they were studied in 1956 than were the men who did not survive to 1967.

Inspection of the profile of these ratings on each of the subjects also revealed a difference between the survivors and non-survivors. Of the 23 nonsurvivors, 10 had unfavorable ratings on four or more of the social psychological measures, but only two of the 24 survivors showed similar clustering at the negative poles on the 1956 ratings [2].

Comparison of survivors and nonsurvivors revealed a significant difference (table 3) in the extent to which they were alone, the sole living member of an intimate group of earlier years. Severe deficits in personal environment were found significantly more often in the group of nonsurvivors than among the survivors.

Reasoning that the nonsurvivors might in 1956 already be exhibiting the high interdependency of functioning that was found in the survivors in 1967, and that greater independency of functioning is a survival characteristic, intercorrelations within the survivor and nonsurvivor

[2] These data include one more subject as a survivor than do other disciplines because the subject involved died after social psychological data were collected but before other studies were completed.

TABLE 2.—*Relations between environmental losses and behavioral characteristic of aged men*

Behavioral characteristic	Product-moment correlations			
	1956		1961	1967
	Survivors	Nonsurvivors		
Organization of Behavior	−0.54	−0.50	−0.51	−0.71
Outlook	−.59	−.58	−.18	−.88
Social interaction	−.26	−.31	−.36	−.50
Activity–passivity	.17	−.25	−.27	−.35
Adaptability	−.29	−.36	----	−.56
WAIS Verbal Score	−.33	−.39	......	−.62
WAIS Performance Score	−.13	−.09	----	.15

NOTE.—High-scale scores on attitude and behavior are indicative of favorable status; high-scale score on environmental loss is indicative of much loss.

TABLE 3.—*Mean ratings on behavioral and environmental variables*

	1956 status			1967 status (N=20)
	Survivors (N=24)	Nonsurvivors (N=23)	t	
Organization of Behavior	3.96	3.09	[1] 2.38	3.32
Outlook on life	2.67	2.04	1.54	2.55
Social interaction	3.04	2.65	.91	2.65
Activity—passivity	2.54	2.43	.40	2.80
Environmental loss	2.58	4.13	[1] 2.98	3.32

[1] Significant at the 0.05 level.

groups were compared (table 1). There was, however, no clear confirmation of these expectations.

In summary, nonsurvivors were to some degree distinguishable, as a group, from survivors in terms of behavioral status and environmental conditions. However, individual variability was considerable in both groups.

SUMMARY AND DISCUSSION

This study provides longitudinal data on the social adaptations of a group of men over an 11-year period in old age. The elderly men gave evidence of a high degree of stability in their activities, relationships, and general outlook on life. As a group, there was no general tendency for the men to withdraw from their social environments. This finding is relevant to the "disengagement" theory proposed by Cumming and Henry (1961) which suggests that withdrawal by the aging person is a normal aging process. Indeed, a few of the subjects showed such disengagement, but it was far from the general trend. Conditions instrumental in producing this behavior need to be studied more thoroughly before it is possible to draw conclusions about the significance of disengagement in the course of growing old. This theory has stimulated much research and comment. Most investigators (Brehm, 1968; Carp, 1968; Glenn and Grimes, 1968; Havighurst, 1961; Kapnick, 1968; Klee-

meier, 1964; Kutner, 1962; Maddox, 1964; Neugarten, 1964; Palmore, 1968; Prasid, 1964; Rose and Peterson, 1965; Shanas, 1968a, 1968b; Williams and Wirths, 1965; Youmans, 1969), however, have indicated the need for refinement and modifications in the theory.

Although the men in this sample maintained a high degree of involvement in living, the framework of stability in their functioning appeared to contain several elements of change. Deaths and departures of family members and close friends had deteriorative influences which seemed to be more devastating as the men grew older. Also, different aspects of the individual's behavior and attitude tended to become more closely interrelated. This was interpreted as a generalized fragility, as possibly having the effect of increasing the man's vulnerability to critical events as aging advanced. Many of the men in this study who continued to maintain their involvement in living did so with greater expenditures of effort. An intact and supportive intimate social environment was one important social psychological factor in resisting assaults in old age and thus a significant factor in survival.

A comparison of the 11-year survivors with the nonsurvivors on their original rating showed the survivors to have suffered fewer psychosocial losses and to have scored significantly higher on Organization of Behavior. Thus, nonsurvivors were distinguishable from survivors, to some extent, in their social psychological functioning.

Research efforts in social gerontology have not given a great deal of attention to theory. Social gerontologists have been concerned with the practical issues and problems confronting old persons. Philibert (1965) and Kastenbaum (1965) maintain that a comprehensive theoretical framework is needed to facilitate the collection of integrated knowledge about human aging and to provide a meaningful guide for the development of social policies and programs for the aged. Developmental studies of the same subjects, over periods of time at various stages in the life cycle, can provide faithful assessments of changes occurring with age, which will aid in the development of comprehensive theory and programs for the aged.

ACKNOWLEDGMENTS

This study was partially supported by PHS Research Grant No. MH 15075 from the National Institute of Mental Health to Samuel Granick of the Philadelphia Geriatric Center. Many colleagues contributed to this study. We wish especially to acknowledge the collaboration of Paul Blank, Harriet Murphy, Olive W. Quinn, and Johanna Stein, who assisted in the 1957 and 1962 phases of the study; to Samuel Granick and Helen Sutton for fieldwork in the 1967 phase; to James Copp and William Kenkel for helpful suggestions; and to Frances Polen for assistance during the entire project.

REFERENCES

BIRREN, J. E., ET AL., eds. *Human Aging: A Biological and Behavioral Study.* Washington, D.C.: U.S. Government Printing Office, 1963.

BREHM, H. P. Sociology and aging: Orientation and research, *Gerontologist,* 8: 24–31, 1968.

CARP, F. M. Some components of disengagement. *J. Geront.,* 23: 383–386, 1968.

CUMMINGS, E. and HENRY, W. E. *Growing Old.* New York: Basic Books, 1961.

GLENN, N. D., and GRIMES, M. Aging, voting, and political interest. *Am. Soc. Review,* 33: 563–575, 1968.

HAVIGHURST, R. J. Successful aging. *Gerontologist,* 1: 8–13, 1961.

KAPNICK, P. L., GOODMAN, J. S., and CORNWELL, E. E., JR. Political behavior in the aged: Some new data. *J. Geront.,* 23: 305–310, 1968.

KASTENBAUM, R. Theories of human aging: The search for a conceptual framework. *J. of Social Issues,* 21: 13–36, 1965.

KLEEMEIER, R. W. Leisure and disengagement in retirement. *Gerontologist,* 4: 180–184, 1964.

KUTNER, B. The social nature of aging. *Gerontologist,* 2: 5–8, 1962.

MADDOX, G. L., JR. Disengagement theory: A critical evaluation. *Gerontologist,* 4:Pt. I, 80–82, 1964.

NEUGARTEN, B. L. *Personality in Middle and Late Life: Empirical Studies.* New York: Atherton Press, 1964.

PALMORE, E. B. The effects of aging on activities and attitudes. *Gerontologist,* 8: 259–263, 1968.

PHILIBERT, J. A. J. The emergence of social gerontology. *J. of Social Issues,* 21: 4–12, 1965.

PRASID, S. B. The retirement postulate of the disengagement theory. *Gerontologist,* 4: 20–23, 1964

ROSE, A. M., and PETERSON, W. A. *Older People and Their Social World.* Philadelphia: F. A. Davis, 1965.

SHANAS, E. A note on restriction of life space: Attitudes of age cohorts. *J. of Health and Soc. Behavior,* 9: 86–89, 1968 (a) .

SHANAS, E.; TOWNSEND, P.; WEDDERBUM, D.; FRIIS, H.; MILHOJ, P.: and STEHOUWER, M. *Old People in Three Industrial Societies.* New York: Atherton Press, 1968.

WILLIAMS, R. H., and WIRTHS, C. G. *Lives Through the Years.* New York: Atherton Press, 1965.

YARROW, MARIAN R., ET AL. Social and psychological characteristics of old age. In: Birren, J. E., ET AL., eds. *Human Aging: A Biological and Behavioral Study.* Washington, D.C.: U.S. Government Printing Office, 1963.

YOUMANS, E. G. Some perspectives on disengagement theory. *Gerontologist,* 4: 254–258, 1969.

CHAPTER 7

Survival Among Healthy Old Men: A Multivariate Analysis

by John J. Bartko and Robert D. Patterson

The study of factors relating to survival or nonsurvival at the 5- and 11-year follow-up periods has been an important theme throughout the preceding chapters. This chapter is an attempt to fulfill a need for an interdisciplinary examination of these factors, and an attempt to assess their relative contributions toward survival. Analyses were performed on a set of variables as well as subsets of behavioral and physical variables alone.

In particular, the role of social and psychological influences in survival was of concern because so little is known about them. The finding that men who had greater psychosocial losses survived less frequently than those with fewer losses stimulated our interest to explore similar relationships more fully (see ch. 6).

The multidisciplinary nature of the data required a statistical multivariate analysis. Multivariate analysis is generally considered to include those techniques concerned with the analysis of multiple measurements made on individuals. The measurements are generally assumed to be intercorrelated. The specific multivariate technique applied to analyzing a set of data depends, of course, on the question one wishes to ask of the data.

In this chapter a linear discriminant function was used to obtain the risk, or probability, of a subject's not surviving 11 years after the first study.

VARIABLES

Fifteen variables (table 1) were used. The selection process for the variables was essentially as follows. An arbitrary numerical limit for variables was set at one-third the number of subjects (47); hence, there are 14 variables allocated among the disciplines. The 15th variable, actuarial prediction, was "universal" in nature; i.e., without reference to a particular discipline.

The variables were submitted by the investigators representing the disciplines of medicine, psychiatry, cerebral physiology, electroencepholography, and experimental, clinical, and social psychology. The variables were selected on the basis of their analyses as those most highly related to survivorship. In a few instances where variables were about equal in this regard, the variable of greatest theoretical interest was selected.

The variables, their measurement scales, and discipline membership are described in the appendix of this chapter. In some

TABLE 1.—*Variables used in multivariate study*

Behavioral variables	Physical variables
1. Adaptation.	1. Actuarial prediction at $\hat{t}_1$.
2. Mental Status Test.	2. Average systolic blood pressure.
3. Organization of Behavior.	3. Cerebral metabolic rate oxygen.
4. Psychosocial Losses.	4. Chronic cigarette smoking.[1]
5. Raven Progressive Matrices Test.	5. Electroencephalogram modal frequency.
6. Rorschach.	6. Groups I, II (health status) .
7. Speed of Copying Words.	7. Weight.
8. WAIS vocabulary subtest.	

[1] Coded 0 for pure nonsmokers, persons who stopped smoking, and cigar and pipe smokers. Coded 1 for chronic cigarette smokers.

areas there was a dearth of candidates for consideration; e.g., EEG, while for others; e.g., psychology, there was a plethora of possibilities. Data reduction techniques were not used since it was felt important to use variables which other investigators could measure directly as opposed to linear functions of variables; e.g., factor scores.

The variables selected are only a very small proportion of the more than 600 measurements made on the subjects at their initial examination. Since the total 600 x 600 correlation matrix of variables was not an input feature of the multivariate technique, no statistical assurance is given that the variables selected were the "best" statistical subset (in the multivariate sense) from the 600 available. There may be other variables whose performance is better than those presented below. However, the results which follow are quite good. Further, while not passing through a statistical multivariate sieve, the 600 variables have passed through 11 years of statistical as well as clinical analyses. Many univariate analyses as well as smaller scaled crossdisciplinary multivariate studies have been performed. Hence the variables selected have a sound clinical and statistical foundation. They represent the best judgment of the investigators, most of whom were participants in the initial as well as the followup examination.

METHODS AND RESULTS

The classical linear discriminant function (LDF) for two groups is a weighted linear function of multivariate variables. The coefficients of the LDF are derived following the criterion of maximal separation (distance) between the groups (Fisher, 1936). Associated with the LDF is a classification problem. Given a sample object on which measurements are made, an LDF value is obtained. It is a single value; namely, the sum of weighted measurements made on the object. If this LDF or single measure is greater than some value (usually zero), then the sample object is classified into, let us say, the first group, otherwise the second.

Classical Approach

We have applied this technique to the 47 subjects of whom 23 were survivors (S) at the 11-year followup, and 24 were nonsurvivors ($\overline{S}$). The discriminant analysis program that was utilized operated in a stepwise fashion on the 15 variables. The variables with a significant contribution at $p \leq 0.05$ or better were included in the linear discriminant function (LDF). They were Organization of Behavior (Behavior or Behv) and Smoking. The LDF obtained was:

$$LDF = -2.88 + 1.07(Behv) - 1.60(Smok).$$

To illustrate the use of the LDF, suppose

a subject were a nonsmoker (0) and had a Behavior rating of 5; his LDF value is then $-2.88 + 1.07(5) - 1.60(0) = 2.47$. This subject in the classical sense would be classified as a survivor (S), because for this particular LDF (equation 1) the boundary value is zero with the mean LDF for survivors positive while the mean LDF for nonsurvivors is negative.

The classical assignment matrix appears in table 2. The variables Behavior and Smoking yield the same classification matrix, four misclassifications out of the 23 survivors (S) and five misclassifications out of the 24 nonsurvivors ($\bar{S}$), as did all the variables when included in the LDF.

Our main interest is not in illustrating the use of the LDF for classification purposes, but rather in the use of the LDF to study the quantitative nature of the dependence of risk (probability) of not surviving 11 years on Behavior and Smoking.

Risk Approach: All Variables

We wish to stress the approach to finding the probability, or risk of not surviving 11 years.

The classification process using an LDF assigns an individual to a group depending on his value of the LDF. Greater certainty in assignment is felt the farther the LDF value is from the decision value or dividing point. There are intermediate values about which one might feel uncertain; i.e., values in the region of overlap

TABLE 2.—*Linear Discriminant Function: Behavior and smoking variables*

	Classical LDF [1] classification		
	S	$\bar{S}$	
Actual number:			
Survivors (S)	19	4	23
Nonsurvivors ($\bar{S}$)	5	19	24

[1] LDF = Linear Discriminant Function.
LDF = $-2.88 + 1.07$ (Behv) ** -1.60 (Smok) *

*p < 0.05.
**p < 0.01.

of populations; hence one might be tempted in consequence to construct a doubtful region; i.e., one in which no judgment or group assignment is made. This mode of thinking can be formalized by asking not for a classification procedure but for the probability of belonging to a population. Such a technique is a natural outgrowth of a desire to know the risk of not surviving rather than the assignment of a subject to a class of survivors or nonsurvivors. This probability or risk is termed the posterior probability. In order to find this posterior probability or risk of not surviving 11 years (P), we use Bayes' theorem, (Parzen, 1960),

$$P = pf(\bar{S}; x_1 \ldots x_k) / [pf(\bar{S}; x_1 \ldots x_k) + (1-p) f(S; x_1 \ldots x_k)] \quad (2)$$

where p is the prior or unconditional probability of becoming a nonsurvivor. The functions $f(\bar{S}; x_1 \ldots x_k)$ and $f(S; x_1 \ldots x_k)$ represent the k-variate frequency distributions of those subjects who would not survive ($\bar{S}$) and those who would (S).

In alternate form, P can be written as

$$P = 1/[1 + ([1-p]/p) f(S; x_1 \ldots x_k) / f(\bar{S}; x_1 \ldots x_k)]. \quad (3)$$

If the frequency distributions f(S) and f(S) are multivariate normal with different means but with the same variances and covariances, then

$$(1-p)/(p)f(S)/f(S) = [(1-p)/p] \exp(LDF)$$
$$= [(1-p)/p] e^{LDF} \quad (4)$$

where "e" represents the base of the natural logarithm and LDF represents the linear discriminant function. Further details can be found, for example, in Anderson (1958).

The main limitation of the use of (4) is the assumption of multivariate normality. The consequences regarding estimated risk of using the multivariate normal assumption when departures from the assumption occur has been investigated by Truett et al., (1967). The results they obtained and our results are quite good even though the assumption of multivariate normality may not be entirely tenable.[1]

In table 3 the risk of not surviving is computed for each of the 47 subjects using

$$P = 1/[1 + ([1-p]/p) e^{LDF}] \quad (5)$$

where $p = 24/47$, $(1-p) = 23/74$ and the LDF is $-2.88 + 1.07(Behv) - 1.60(Smok)$, from equation (1).

Table 3 was constructed to illustrate the relative contributions of Smoking and Organization of Behavior to the discriminant equation.

Since smoking was coded as a (0,1) variable and Behavior was a 5-point scale variable, it was possible to group the sub-

---

[1] A weaker condition is sufficient, namely, that the linear compound, i.e., the LDF, of variables be univariate normal. The results (table 3) and the histogram plot of the LDF (not presented), while showing gaps, did not indicate skewness, and therefore tended to uphold the reasonableness of the assumption. A fit by an iterative maximum liklihood approach (also not presented) agreed very closely with the results of table 3.

jects by their Smoking and Behavior values. Organization of Behavior was devised to measure the degree of planning, variation, and complexity of the person's daily activities (see appendix for details). All of the combinations were represented except for a smoker with a Behavior rating of 1 (table 3). The risk of not surviving for 11 years depends very heavily upon the Organization of Behavior.

As an illustration of the use of the Risk of Not Surviving column, consider a nonsmoker with a Behavior rating of 4, his LDF value is $-2.88 + 1.07(4) - 1.60(0) = 1.40$, with a risk value via equation (5) of 0.208.

Note the higher risk in general for the smokers and higher risk for subjects with low Behavior scores. A nonsmoker with a 1 (least organized) on the Behavior scale has an 86-percent chance of not surviving, while another nonsmoker with a 5 (most organized) has an 8-percent chance of not surviving. The risk for smokers exceeds that for nonsmokers for all levels of Behavior rating. The difference in risk ranges from 0.10 (Behavior rating of 1) to 0.36 (Behavior ratings 3 and 4). For smokers,

TABLE 3.—*Risk of not surviving: Smoking and Behavior variables* (N = 47)

	Behavior rating	Observed no. survivors (S)	Observed no. non-survivors ($\bar{S}$)	Total at risk	Risk [1] of not surviving	Expected no. non-survivors	Comments
Nonsmokers ____	1	0	1	1	0.866	0.866	
	2	0	7	7	.689	4.823	
	3	8	1	9	.432	3.888	one $\bar{S}$ called a S.
	4	4	1	5	.208	1.040	one $\bar{S}$ called a S.
	5	5	1	6	.083	.498	one $\bar{S}$ called a S.
Total ____	--	17	11	28	----	11.115	
Smokers _____	1	0	0	0	.970	----	
	2	1	5	6	.916	5.496	one S called a $\bar{S}$.
	3	1	4	5	.791	3.955	one S called a $\bar{S}$.
	4	2	2	4	.565	2.260	two $\bar{S}$ called S.
	5	2	2	4	.309	1.236	two S called S.
Total ____	--	6	13	19	----	12.947	Total of 9 mis-classifications.
Total ____	--	23	24	47	----	24.062	

[1] Risk $= 1/[1 + (23/24) e^{LDF}]$: LDF from equation (1).

the risk of not surviving is less than 0.5 only for the case in which the Behavior rating is most favorable; i.e., a 5.

The number of subjects in each class is shown as well as the number misclassified. There is good agreement between the number of observed and expected non-survivors (24 vs. 24.06).

The last column (Comments) of table 3 can be compared to the misclassification entries of table 2. Of the 23 survivors, four were misclassified as nonsurvivors (on variables Behavior and Smoking). When all of the variables were run through the discriminant analysis program, the classification matrix remained the same but two subjects switched survivor-nonsurvivor classifications. One of these became correctly classified because with the inclusion of the other variables, his profile coincided very closely with those of other survivors. The subject who became misclassified when all variables were used was a pure nonsmoker and had a rating of 4 on Behavior; i.e., he was a good survival risk. He was, however, at least one standard deviation away from the means of the survivor group on EEG, Raven, Rorschach, and Speed of Copying Words variables in the direction of the nonsurvivor group means profile.

Of the 24 nonsurvivors, five subjects were misclassified (tables 2 and 3) as survivors when the two variables Behavior and Smoking were used. When all of the variables were used, the classification matrix remained unchanged, with the same five subjects misclassified.

Risk Approach: Behavioral Variables

Table 4 presents the classical LDF classification table for all subjects on the Behavioral variables alone. The only variables of statistical significance entering the

TABLE 4.—*Linear discriminant function: Behavior and mental status variables*

| | Classical LDF [1] classification | | |
	S	S̄	
Actual number:			
Survivors (S)	16	7	23
Nonsurvivors (S̄)	7	17	24

[1] LDF = Linear Discriminant Function.
LDF = −6.40 + 0.76 (Behv) ** + 0.03 (Ment) *.

*p < 0.05 (Ment = Mental Status Test).
**p < 0.01.

LDF were Behavior and the Mental Status (Ment) score. The LDF obtained was:

$$LDF = -6.40 + 0.76(Behv) + 0.03(Ment).$$

The LDF, equation (6), was utilized as discussed above. The risk values were obtained using an equation of the form of equation (5). Figure 1 illustrates the risk values. The Behavior measure is numbered 1 through 5 on the chart. The abscissa is the Mental Status Score and the ordinate is the Risk of Not Surviving.

The contributions of Mental Status and Organization of Behavior to the risk prediction give a unique opportunity to speculate about the role of organic mental factors versus social and emotional factors in survival.

The Mental Status Test score appeared to reflect two major influences: (1) The degree of any organic mental decline, and (2) lifelong intelligence prior to any organic decline.

Organization of Behavior reflected the subject's social and emotional state. Those with higher scores were more involved with others, better adapted, had higher morale, and fewer psychosocial losses. These factors might have an effect upon survival. However, Behavior was also associated with Organic Mental Decline and this could be the reason for its association with greater survival.

The effect of organic mental changes

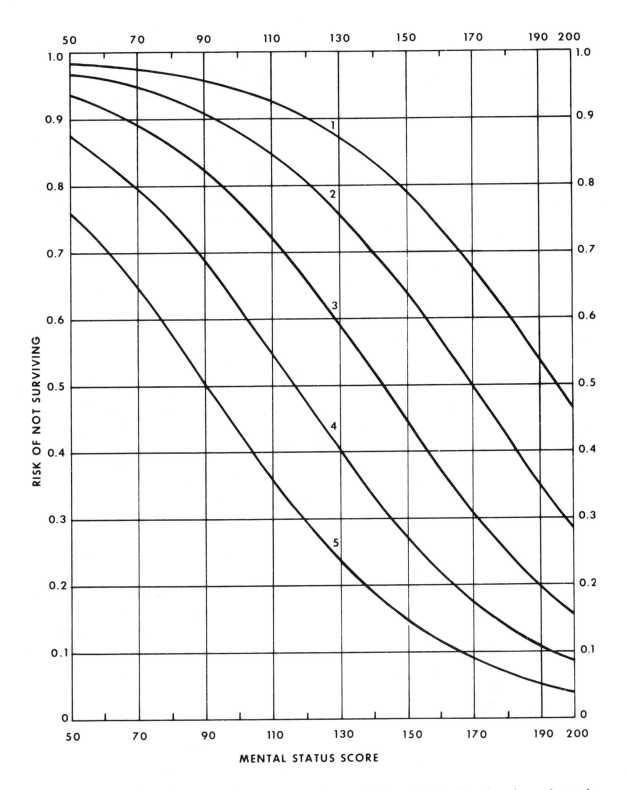

FIGURE 1.—Relationship of Mental Status Score and Organization of Behavior (numbers along the curves) to the risk of not surviving.

on Behavior is to some extent controlled if we compare two subjects with the same Mental Status score and differing Behavior scores. In figure 1 we can compare two men each with a Mental Status score of 133 (the mean of the group). If one man had a Behavior score of 1 (poorest), his risk of not surviving would be 0.86 while if the other man's Behavior were structured, varied, and involved self-initiated activities (score 5), his risk of not surviving would be 0.22. With the organic state of the brain partially controlled by the constant Mental Status score, it seems that the impressive difference in probability of survival may in part be due to social-emotional factors.

The figure also demonstrates the strong relationship between mental ability (in this instance measured by the Mental Status Test) and the risk of not surviving which was discussed in chapters 4 and 5. A person with a Mental Status score of 55 (the lowest in this study) had between an 0.98 and 0.74 risk of not surviving, depending upon his Organization of Behavior score. In contrast, with a score of 182 (the highest score in the study), the risk of not surviving was between 0.59 and 0.06.

In a manner similar to that employed in table 3 the expected number of non-survivors was found to be 24.2. This is quite good agreement with the actual number of 24.

Risk Approach: Physical Variables

An analysis was performed using the physical variables alone. Average systolic blood pressure (ASBP) was the first variable (via the stepwise LDF program) to enter and weight (Wt) was second. The LDF obtained was

$$LDF = 1.85 - 0.05 \,(ASBP) + 0.07(Wt) \qquad (7)$$

Note that the coefficient on weight is positive. The LDF is positive for the survivor group mean and negative for the nonsurvivor group. The positive coefficient on weight is in keeping with the fact that the survivors were heavier than the nonsurvivors. This is contrary to what one would expect from a sample of young men, in whom greater weight is associated with shorter survival. Unlike a random sample, however, none of the men in this study were obese. Lighter weight and earlier death may have been associated because of catabolic processes, as discussed in chapter 2.

Table 5 presents the LDF classification table.

Following previous discussions and using equations (5) and (7), risk values were obtained. Figure 2 illustrates the risk values. Weight ranges from 45 to 90 Kg. and appears above the curves of the chart. The abscissa represents average systolic blood pressure and the ordinate represents the Risk of Not Surviving.

In a manner similar to that employed in table 3 the expected number of nonsurvivors was found to be 23.5. This is quite good agreement with the actual number of 24.

Figure 2 presents the same data using the risk approach. The figure may be interpreted in a manner similar to figure 1. It shows the substantial influence of

TABLE 5.—*Linear Discriminant Function: Blood pressure and weight variables*

	Classical LDF [1] classification		
	S	S̄	
Actual number:			
Survivors (S)	17	6	23
Nonsurvivors (S̄)	9	15	24

[1] LDF = Linear Discriminant Function.
LDF = 1.85 − 0.05 (ASBP) ** + 0.07 (Wt.) *.

*$p < 0.05$ (Wt. = Weight).
**$p < 0.01$ (ASBP = Average Systolic Blood Pressure).

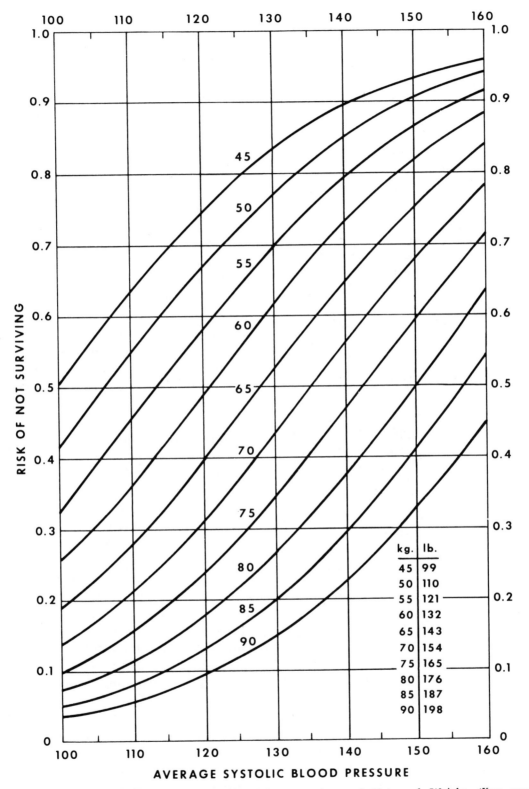

FIGURE 2.—Relationship of Average Systolic Blood Pressure (mm. of Hg) and Weight (Kg.; numbers along the curves) to the risk of not surviving.

weight upon survival even for constant blood pressure values. If a man with a blood pressure of 133 (the mean for the group) weighed 45 Kg., his risk of not surviving would be 0.86, while if he were heavier and weighed 90 Kg., his risk of not surviving would be 0.16; i.e., his probability of surviving would be substantially greater. A similar interrelationship of weight, blood pressure, and survival has been reported by The Society of Actuaries (1959) (for discussion see ch. 2).

The range of values for weight and blood pressure presented in the figure corresponds to the range of values actually observed in the study. There is no justification for generalizing that obese old men (with weights greater than those shown in the figure) would also have small risks of not surviving. Indeed obese men in general have higher mortality rates than the nonobese.

A substantial association between level of systolic blood pressure (all values which are normal for aged men) and risk of not surviving is also shown. This finding is consistent with other studies discussed in chapter 2.

Since weight was associated with survival, it was hypothesized that the physical appearance in 1956 of the 11-year survivors and nonsurvivors might be a distinguishing feature. Those who were nearer death might appear "older." They might look thinner, have more wrinkled skin, more stooped posture, or even have characteristically different facies. Front and side view photographs of 40 of the 47 men dressed only in shorts and shoes were available. Therefore it was possible to have two judges try to discriminate the survivors from nonsurvivors using only the photographs as the basis for classification. The judges were a physician-internist and a nurse who work extensively with geriatric patients. They were not able to discriminate better than chance. The negative result emphasizes the subtlety of any relationship between physical appearances and survival among healthy men. It also suggests, reassuringly, that a picture is not as good as "600" variables in predicting survival.

DISCUSSION

Since the subjects of this study were in very good physical health and were at least free of psychotic mental disease, it may seem remarkable that measurements made on them should contribute much to prediction of whether or not they would live 11 years. Perhaps even more surprising is the fact that the measurements in most instances did not indicate the presence of the diseases from which the subjects died. The relationship between the variables and 11-year survival is more remote than the connection we recognize between a terminal illness and death. The results urge us to examine factors associated with eventual death which are not diseases in the usual sense.

Inferences about the meaning of the association between Organization of Behavior and the risk of not surviving must be made cautiously because it is significantly correlated with many other physiological, social, and psychological factors. It was also significantly correlated with the age of the subjects at the first study ($r = -0.46$). However this cannot totally account for the high predictability of survival because the actuarial variable (which is directly related to age) was not a good discriminator.

Greater Organization of Behavior may be associated with survival because the men with the most complex behavior anticipated crises and actively planned effective responses which minimized the detrimental effects of the events. This might be most easily identified with regard to medical illnesses: high-scoring men might be more alert to early signs of illness and get the needed care, thus avoiding potentially fatal developments. In the emotional area the higher scoring men might, for example, be able to avoid or minimize some depressions by well-organized behavior. Some evidence (Roth and Kay, 1956) suggests that this may be life prolonging since depression increases the risk of dying. Unfortunately, detailed data are not available from this study for testing this hypothesis.

An alternate hypothesis to explain the association of Behavior with survival seems the more plausible to us. It is that the central nervous system influences other organs through neuronal and hormonal controls that affect development of fatal conditions. Selye (1970) has explored the organism's pathological and sometimes fatal hormonal responses to stress. The characteristics of the hormonal responses during stress in old men may be related to the organization of their routine behavior and to their intelligence.

Would a deliberate change in the level of organization of a person's behavior have an influence on his survival? Are there some organically impaired individuals for whom greater complexity of activities would be detrimental? We do not know. Answers to these questions would be of immediate use to those concerned with the health of the aged.

The association of higher intellectual ability (here measured by the Mental Status Test) with greater survival might have the same explanation as suggested for Behavior. The more intelligent men might have a greater likelihood of surviving because they were able to more effectively cope with life-threatening situations than were the less intelligent men.

On the other hand, low-intellectual functioning is associated with Organic Mental Decline and this, like the more severe impairment of chronic brain syndrome, is associated with lower survival. In this instance the association of low intelligence and earlier death may be primarily due to the underlying organic disease which is often generalized arteriosclerosis.

Other associations between social-emotional states and death are known. We recognize them in accidental deaths and suicides. There has been speculation that the extreme emotional state (i.e., a curse placed on the victim) in Voodoo death leads to death through cardiovascular collapse (Cannon, 1942). Among the aged, numerous studies have shown an association between the moving of institutionalized persons from one living area to another and increased death rates (Blenkner, 1967). A study by Rees and Lutkins (1967) found an increased risk of death in the year following the loss of a family member. This finding is supported by the association of the degree of psychosocial losses with survival reported in chapter 6.

In summary, little is known about how social and emotional conditions lead to death, except in the instances of death from physical violence such as accidents and suicide. However, our results suggest an association between psychological and social influences that determines the complexity of one's daily behavior and survival.

Whether social and psychological influences act through the central nervous system to influence survival or whether physiological states of the central nervous system affect behaviors of the types measured here, it appears that in either case the central nervous system is a sensitive indicator of conditions which bear on prediction of survival.

The association between cigarette smoking and survival may have as yet unrecognized social and mental health implications for the aged. Grannis (1970) has gone so far as to suggest that the excess number of aged females in the United States population may be entirely accounted for by the excess deaths among smokers who have more frequently been males. He reports that the increased sex ratio among the aged has developed during the past 75 years, a period during which cigarette smoking among males became widespread. This suggests that to an important degree the high frequency of widowhood in our society is traceable to cigarette smoking among men. In turn, the frequency of widowhood has a significant impact on the satisfactions and mental health of aged women.

Palmore (1969) used a regression analysis to predict longevity. Using data from the Duke University longitudinal aging study, he found actuarial prediction of age of death to be the most significant variable. In the risk approach presented here, actuarial prediction was not among the best predictors. There was no significant difference between the actuarial prediction of age of death for the survivors and nonsurvivors; hence it does not serve as a discriminator. Further, for our selected group of healthy men the actuarial or life expectancy tables were not strictly applicable since the tables cover a broad spectrum of aged men in terms of health, environmental conditions, etc. To illustrate, only 14 of the 47 men had life expectancies of 11 or more years according to the life tables, while in fact 23 men survived 11 or more years ($x^2 = 8.2$; $p < 0.01$).

There is also a fundamental difference in the kind of questions being asked in the two approaches. Our study sought to discover physical and psychological factors which maximally *differentiated* a group of aged healthy male survivors from a comparable group of nonsurvivors. The risk approach used here asks not for a specific death age but for the probability of an old man's surviving 11 years. The results indicate that his Behavior and Smoking ratings, among others, are good predictors of risk and that his age is not. However, when a regression analysis is carried out as Palmore has done, the question becomes: at what age will the man die? The actuarial prediction of the man's age of death then becomes overwhelmingly the best predictor.

SUMMARY

1. The dependence of the 11-year probability of nonsurvival on a set of 15 variables has been investigated using discriminant functions. Quite good results were obtained as assessed by the agreement of the theoretical risk function (expected number of nonsurvivors) with the actual number of nonsurvivors.

2. Two of the variables used as discriminators were as good as all of the variables taken together. They were a social psychological variable which measured the degree of organization and complexity of a subject's daily behavior and the presence or absence of cigarette smoking. The two variables correctly classified about 80 percent of both survivors and nonsurvivors. Further, in terms of a risk analysis, the greater the subject's Organization of Behavior score, the lower was his risk of not surviving. Smokers had a much higher risk of not surviving.

3. When the analysis was restricted to behavioral variables alone, Organization of Behavior and Mental Status Test score were the two significant variables. Higher

Mental Status scores were associated with a lower risk of not surviving.

4. When physical variables alone were used for risk prediction, average systolic blood pressure and weight were the significant ones. Lower blood pressure, even though in the normal range, and *greater* weight (also in the normal range) were associated with lower risk of not surviving.

5. How long healthy old men will survive is moderately predictable. Measurements of physical and behavioral variables within the normal range may be used as predictors. It appears that some social and psychological influences may be remote but important factors in causal sequences leading to death.

ACKNOWLEDGMENTS

The authors wish to express their appreciation to Mr. Robert R. Rawlings and Mr. Nils B. Mattsson of the National Institute of Mental Health, Computer System Branch, for computer services and assistance.

To Dr. Samuel W. Greenhouse for many helpful comments, suggestions, and discussions.

To Dr. Morton Kramer for many helpful comments and suggestions.

To Drs. Robert N. Butler, Samuel Granick, Leslie S. Libow, Louis Sokoloff, and Marion R. Yarrow for their comments and suggestions.

To Dr. Leslie S. Libow for making arrangements for the photograph analysis and Mrs. Anna A. Heineman and Dr. Antonio Y. deLeon who judged the photographs.

To Mrs. Annie Randall for her assistance with data preparation and various statistical tasks.

To Miss Kathleen Potter for her secretarial assistance.

REFERENCES

ANDERSON, T. W. *An Introduction to Multivariate Statistical Analysis*. New York: John Wiley & Sons, 1958.

BIRREN, J. E., ET AL., eds. *Human Aging: A Biological and Behavioral Study*. Washington, D.C.: U.S. Government Printing Office, 1963.

BLENKNER, MARGARET. Environmental change and the aging individual, *Geront.*, 7: 101–105, 1967.

CANNON, W. B. Voodoo death. *Amer. Anthrop.*, 44: 169–181, 1942.

FISHER, R. A. The use of multiple measurements in taxonomic problems. *Annals of Eugenics*, 7: 179–188, 1936.

GRANNIS, G. F. Demographic perturbations secondary to cigarette smoking. *J. of Geront.*, 25: 55–63, 1970.

PALMORE, E. B. Physical, mental, and social factors in predicting longevity. *Geront.*, 9: 103–108, 1969.

PARZEN, E. *Modern Probability Theory and Its Applications*. New York: John Wiley & Sons, 1960. 119 pp.

REES, W. D., and LUTKINS, S. G. Mortality of bereavement. *Brit. Med. J.*, 4: 13–16, 1967.

ROTH, M., and KAY, D. W. K. Affective disorders arising in the senium II. *J. Ment. Sci.*, 102: 141–150, 1956.

SELYE, H. Stress and aging. *Journal of the American Geriatrics Society*, 18: 660–681, 1970.

Society of Actuaries. *Build and Blood Pressure Study, Vol. 1*. Society of Actuaries: Chicago, Ill., 1959. Table 112.

TRUETT, J.; CORNFIELD, J.; and KANNEL, W. A multivariate analysis of the risk of coronary heart disease in Framingham. *J. of Chronic Dis.*, 20: 511–524, 1967.

APPENDIX

Description of Variables

Variables are described briefly here and in more detail in the preceding chapters and in Birren, et al., (1963) .

Actuarial life expectancy was determined for each subject using 1959–61 life tables (National Center for Health Statistics, 1964) .[1]

Medical Variables

Average systolic blood pressure was the mean of the daily auscultatory blood pressures obtained during the subjects's stay at the NIH Clinical Center.

Chronic cigarette smoking placed all men in one of two groups designated 0 or 1. A "nonsmoker" was designated zero and defined as anyone who did not smoke cigarettes. This included those who had stopped smoking prior to the study and those who smoked cigars and pipes. The classification was made on the basis of published survival risk figures (The Surgeon General's Advisory Committee on Smoking and Health, 1964)[2] and on the survival experience of the men in this study.

Weight was the average morning weight in kilograms during the man's stay at the Clinical Center.

Group refers to group I: the extremely physically healthy subjects, and group II: the asymptomatic disease group.

Cerebral Physiologic Variables

Cerebral metabolic rate of oxygen (ml./100 gm./min.) was calculated from direct measurements of cerebral arterial and venous oxygen concentrations and blood flow.

Modal occipital frequency of the electroencephalogram was obtained from a frequency analysis of the waking EEG's in relaxed subjects.

Clinical and Experimental Psychology Variables

WAIS vocabulary subtest required subjects to de-

fine words. A higher score indicated better function.

Rorschach score was not the usual measure of personality factors but an especially developed scale to measure organization and appropriateness of responses of the type which may change when people become "senile." A higher score indicated poorer function.

Speed of Copying Words is the number of words copied correctly during a 2-minute period.

Raven Progressive Matrices is a nonverbal test of mental abilities.

Social Psychology Variables

Psychosocial Losses was a measure of the loss or lack of personally significant people in the man's environment. A higher score indicated more intense loss.

Organization of Behavior was obtained from interview data and was intended to measure the level of planning, complexity, and variation characteristic of the men's daily lives. The following 5-point scale was used:

1 = Activities are few. These are chores, routines, as necessity requires. Little variation.

2 = Predominantly routines but some little "puttering" or attempt to break through routine and chores.

3 = Sporadic or spotty attempts at planned activities and absorptions. Some slight direction, mainly things to fill in.

4 = Structured and planned, some variation but not elaborate. Some "direction" to activities.

5 = Many activities. Structured, planned, varied, involved, new, complex, self-initiated activities and involvement.

Psychiatric Variables

Adaptations was a global appraisal of the individual's adjustment to his current situation. A higher score indicated poor adaptation.

The Mental Status Test measured mental abilities and organic mental impairment. A higher score indicated better function.

---

[1] Life tables 1959–61, vol. I No. 1, Public Health Service Publication No. 1252.

[2] Smoking and Health: Report of the Advisory Committee to the Surgeon General of the Public Health Service. U.S. Government Printing Office, 1964.

CHAPTER 8

Reflections on Human Aging

by *James E. Birren, Robert N. Butler, Samuel W. Greenhouse, Louis Sokoloff, and Marian Yarrow*

In this followup study the original investigators, who first conceived, organized, and executed the initial studies of this aged population, have the opportunity to reflect from a vantage of 14 years upon the usefulness, successes, failings, and overall contributions of this program to the problems of human aging. An examination of this kind can provide lessons, not only for the participants in this research, but also for others who may contemplate studies of a similar nature.

The Evolution of the Research

The original goals of the study were a product of their time and of the unique opportunities afforded by the structural organization of the National Institute of Mental Health for the pursuit of interdisciplinary investigations. It is almost axiomatic that an institution such as the NIMH would be populated by a staff whose focus was primarily on behavior and the function of the nervous system. The heavy emphasis in the research on basic and higher nervous functions reflects, for better or for worse, the areas of interest and expertise of the investigators.

At the time the research was being planned, there were two prevalent notions regarding the influences of aging on the nervous system. One was that speed of perception and response and certain intellectual functions were specifically and irreversibly impaired by the aging process. The other was that chronological aging was accompanied by progressive declines in the rates of cerebral blood flow and energy metabolism; it was undetermined which was the antecedent and which the secondary change. These notions were supported by considerable masses of data, but in most cases these were acquired from research on elderly patients who were institutionalized or hospitalized and, therefore, not representative of the truly normal aged. There remained the possibility that changes in cerebral physiology and intellectual functions were not characteristic of the normal aging process but were more a reflection of one or more of the numerous infirmities that so frequently accompany old age. The initial formulation of the project was directed, therefore, to these questions: Were changes in reaction time, intelligence, cerebral circulation, and in metabolism manifestations of the aging process per se or were they consequences of the diseases which occur with such high incidence in old age? Which was the primary change—vascular insufficiency and reduced cerebral blood flow leading to cerebral tissue hypoxia and secondary impairment of metabolism and function or conversely, a primary parenchymal reduction in metabolism followed by secondary cerebral circulatory adjustment to the reduced metabolic demand? Finally, since changes in reaction time and intellectual functions and in cerebral circulation and metabolism reflected alterations in CNS functions, were there related decrements in these functions? Implicit in these questions was the assumption that the diseases prevalent in the elderly were not in fact an inextricable part of the normal aging process but true pathological disease states to which the elderly were peculiarly vulnerable. As healthy a group of elderly subjects as possible, therefore, was chosen for comparison with normal young subjects. Recruitment was conducted only among the normal aged living and functioning in the community, and among these, selection was limited to those who met rigid physical and psychiatric criteria of normality. Logistical problems imposed restrictions in addition to those dictated by the design for normal healthy aged men. The rigid criteria for health were not easily fulfilled. The cooperative efforts of the Philadelphia Home for the Jewish Aged and the Washington Chapter of the National Association of Retired Civil Service Employees aided greatly in the recruitment process. However, these sources of subjects led to various kinds of sampling biases; there was, for example, a heavy representation of foreign-born Jewish males in the sample.

While homogeneity of the group on the health criteria and the nonrepresentativeness of sample were not inconsistent with the relatively simple and modest goals with which the project began, they were soon outgrown as the project developed. Other disciplines in the NIMH, in addition to physiology, medicine, and cognitive and perceptual psychology, became involved: Psychiatry, clinical psychology, social psychology, and electroencephalography were enlisted in rapid succession. The unpardonable sin was committed of including statistical expertise after the fact. By the time these other disciplines were incorporated into the program, the machinery for recruitment of the sample had been established, and there was little opportunity to alter or influence the nature of the sample.

Limitation of Sample

The restricted sample was far from ideal; for some of the disciplines the objectives had to be suited to the available sample, rather than the other way around. From the vantage of hindsight, it appears that these shortcomings might well have been avoided. It would seem now that a larger and broader sample—including wider representation of ethnic, social, economic, and educational groups, sex, and even health status—might have led to a better understanding not only of the normal process of aging per se but also of the patterns of change in ordinary aging individuals. As it turned out, the subjects were actually an elite group in regard to health, hardly representative of the average aging population. This point is very important and we hope not to be misinterpreted as meaning that our sample is not representative of any population. If we were to apply the same rigid criteria of selection in the entire population of aged over 65 living in the community, we would be left with a residue population of very healthy aged which our sample represents. But our point is that this residue population is elite and, with regard to health, quite above the usually considered normal, healthy aged living in the community. All of these restrictions on the scope of the sample imposed limits on our extrapolations to the average aged, and forcefully emphasized the importance of full multidisciplinary participation in the planning of a design.

Because the initial design emphasized intensive, comprehensive study of the individual subject, sample size was limited. If the study were now being planned, the investigators would aim for some number considerably in excess of the 47 men with which we began—even if it meant giving up some of the measurements received by each subject. A small sample imposes obvious problems, such as the limited cross classifications that can be formed for analysis of the data and the unreliability of statistical estimates. The smallness of sample gave rise to difficulties in the followup study in determining the significance of sets of characteristics measured at one time for predicting end points occurring at a future time. Thus, analysis of measurements made in 1956–58 for significance in survival during the next 10 years had to be limited to a few variables from each of the various disciplines. Although such a procedure may be as logically sound, if not intuitively better, than cranking in some 580 measurements because one had available a sample of, say, 1,000, the impression remains that a larger number of variables than the 14 used in these analyses would have been desirable had several hundred subjects been available.

Even at the very inception of this project, the investigators were agreed on obtaining a group of aged deliberately selected for excellent health. A random community sample, undifferentiated for health, was never seriously considered. However, a purposively selected sample, extremely homogeneous in regard to good health, has some drawbacks. Had the net been widened to include subjects with more common health ailments, the roles of health and disease might have been seen more clearly. As is pointed out elsewhere, the study sample was happenstance with regard to characteristics of ethnic background, socioeconomic status, etc. Ideally, one might attempt to set up a population listing of aged persons living in a community stratified by census tract or block, select strata, and sample at random from within each stratum. Such a sampling procedure would have enabled us not only to obtain a heterogeneous group with regard to the factors already listed, but would also have resulted in the inclusion of a broader range of the health spectrum more characteristic of the average aged population.

Age Selection

In any research study of the aged and of the aging process, the question always arises as to the minimum age of the group. It has been customary to put this limit at age 65. In our view, this limit is reasonable for a cross-sectional study. In a longitudinal study, however, we feel that another age group, say between 55 and 60, would be desirable for a number of reasons. Differences in the generations may exist in both health and social variables and it is only through successive sampling of different decades that generation differences can be distinguished from the effects of aging. Aside from rather obvious substantive reasons for this conviction, such as whether changes in physiological or psychological processes might not be more severe in this earlier 10-year interval, there are other more formal reasons. In our case, the availability of a group with an average age of 60 would have made possible a comparison of measurements 10 years later with a similar aged group measured initially. This would have enabled us to compare one average 70-year-old group with another 10 years later, thereby providing a check on the consistency of the same measurement methods.

Advantages of Homogeneity of Health

Emphasis on health served well certain basic study objectives; namely, to isolate influences closely associated with chronological age when age was relatively uncontaminated by the diseases and infirmities so common in the elderly. This search led to the unexpected finding that aging need not result in declines in cerebral blood flow and metabolic rate. In the optimally healthy men (group I), these functions were not different from the levels observed in normal subjects 50 years younger. In the slightly less healthy group (group II), the cerebral blood flow was reduced, but the change was almost entirely accounted for by the subjects within that group who exhibited signs of developing arteriosclerosis. Cerebral oxygen consumption had not yet been affected in these subjects and, therefore, there was evidence of a relative cerebral hypoxia confirmed by reduced levels of oxygen tension in the cerebral venous blood. The results of other measurements were similar though less absolute. Some changes in the EEG, particularly a slowing of the peak frequency and decrements in psychomotor performance, were observed in group I subjects, but these were markedly less than previously observed in more representative aged subjects and significantly less than in the group II subjects, particularly those in the arteriosclerotic subgroup. These results clearly implicated health as a major determinant of aging in the nervous system. Contrary to previous beliefs, it was now apparent that reductions in cerebral blood flow and metabolic rate were not inevitable consequences of chronological age per se, and that when they occurred they were the effects of vascular disease which impaired the cerebral circulation, leading first to tissue hypoxia and eventually to all its secondary deteriorative effects. The decrements in response speed and other nonverbal intellectual functions and the slight changes in the EEG observed in the optimally healthy subjects suggested that there might be some purely age-related changes, but it was clear that when disease, such as arteriosclerosis, intervened, it became the pacemaker of the changes in the brain, which superficially appeared as aging.

Purists have raised the question of whether healthy old age, as defined by criteria as rigorous as ours, actually exists and whether, in fact, it is possible to select an elderly group that is free of arteriosclerosis. It is, indeed, likely that we were not 100 percent successful in accomplishing that. However, we were successful in minimizing or controlling the influences of health and of discriminating between even small degrees of disease. Despite the fact that the classification between groups I and II was established on the basis of clinical grounds completely independent of the research data, almost all of the disciplines observed significant differences in their research results between the two groups. Furthermore, the mortality statistics obtained in the followup study add additional support to the validity of the original discrimination. Of the 27 members of group I, 17 survived the 11 years between the original and followup studies, whereas only six of the 20 in group II survived. None of the nine subjects placed in group II because of evidence of arteriosclerosis, even minimal, survived the 11-year followup.

Thus it appears that our preoccupation with health in the original design of the project led, perhaps unexpectedly, to the clearer definition of the role of disease in the aging of the nervous system. The full implications of these results are yet to be realized and are dependent on developments in the health field. If one assumes, as it is now becoming more fashionable to do, that arteriosclerosis is not an inextricable part of the aging process and is, in fact, a true disease, ultimately susceptible to control, cure, or prevention, then one can conceive of a situation in which chronological aging may proceed unencumbered by this blight. One might then expect a lengthening of the lifespan and a reduction in mortality and morbidity in what is currently considered old age. In addition, the results of these studies suggest that the functioning of the CNS and the social and psychological behavior dependent on it would be more effectively preserved.

Focus on the Central Nervous System

The initial decision to focus on the efficiency of the nervous system, both physiologically and psychologically, in a healthy group of older men, unfortunately, but almost necessarily, excluded from consideration many other potentially valuable explorations. Aging is not confined to the nervous system; the aging of the whole organism is a representation of the changes in all its organ systems. The relative influence of the various organ systems on the overall pattern of aging may vary from one individual to another. Other organ systems were examined in the present study, but only to exclude disease. The research design did not include protocols for the systematic study of the effects of normal aging on such vital organs and functions as the endocrines, metabo-

lism, heart, kidney, and lungs, skeletomuscular system, etc. An excellent opportunity to assess the influence of chronological aging per se on these systems and to relate them to the level of psychological and social performance of the individual as a whole was, unfortunately, lost.

Hazards of Longitudinal Studies

The effort to integrate and assimilate the results of the initial and followup studies into a picture of aging derived from the program as a whole has illuminated a special problem to which longitudinal studies are especially vulnerable. The followup studies had several purposes. One was to identify the specific variables in the original studies which might serve as predictors of the subsequent course of aging and survival. Another, and perhaps even more important, purpose was to examine longitudinally in the same subjects the effects of continued aging in this segment of the lifespan. The changes induced in the individuals by an added decade of life were to be evaluated.

These research goals were not easily achieved. In the interim, the interests, viewpoints, and conceptualizations of the original investigators had changed. Many of the original investigators were not available to carry out the measurements made in the followup studies. Hence, discontinuities in viewpoints and methodology intervened. Such a situation always presents a hazard in data analysis and interpretation. The seriousness varies with the nature of the methodology and the precision of the techniques used, which make possible the detection of aberrant measurements. For example, discontinuities in technique required the elimination of cerebral metabolic rate in the followup studies. Serious limitations were imposed on the choice of the EEG measurements that could be used for comparison.

Predictor Variables

Survival and mortality are variables unaffected by continuity of measurement, and they led to, in some respects, disappointing and, in other respects, fascinating and enlightening results. Disappointment was associated with the failure of any of the cerebral physiological measurements of the initial studies to provide any objective basis for prediction of viability during the succeeding 11 years of life. As described above, health status, particularly the presence of arteriosclerosis, was an effective prognosticator of mortality.

It is intriguing that two other variables in combination gave almost complete prognostic reliability—smoking and the organization of behavior. In view of recently developing knowledge of the pernicious influences of cigarette smoking, it is not surprising that this variable was found to be so significantly involved in determining viability in old age. However, the finding of the relationship of survival or death to organization of behavior is fascinating and should serve to stimulate further investigation. Organization of behavior included an assssessment of the individual's day-to-day coping with living, that is, his maintenance of organized, planful living, and of gratifying pursuits in his pattern of living. Disruption of this functional integrity is apparently an indicator of insidious erosion of survivability. What it is within the complex that comprises the assessment is probably worthy of further study and identification.

Problems of Methods in Behavioral Investigation

What we have learned in this study about the physical and social environments with which these aged subjects coped on a daily basis was learned indirectly. Our source of information was primarily self-assessing interviews, with all of the limitations that reside in this kind of data. Yet what was obtained with these relatively crude indicators led to a number of interesting discoveries. Environment and daily coping not only related to each other, but these measures showed significant associations with a range of tested functions, including a differentiation between survivors and nonsurvivors in 1967. One might find a suggestion in these findings: How much more valuable and enlightening might be the data from direct observational measures of the man in his environment. Systematic observational data on aged persons is hardly visible in the research literature (in contrast to psychological studies of the early developmental periods in the life cycle). It would seem desirable to bend research efforts somewhat more toward these approaches, and to rely less exclusively on the interview with the aged.

A second note on the interaction of measurement methods and theory, on at least one broad dimension—variously labeled as morale, depressive trend, and outlook on life—two disciplines made independent assessments of the subjects. One should expect very close agreement among these measures, for conceptually they overlap. When sizable disagreement occurred on a fair number of the subjects, did this indicate a serious sampling problem to which investigators of aged subjects should be especially alert? Namely, is the subject's morale state particularly unstable and much determined by the specific test or interview situation? Does one need to avoid a single-situation sampling? This is certainly a methods question for subjects of any kind and age; it may be even more relevant for aged subjects. The hypothesis is that the immediate configuration of factors (physical and social) may have a stronger governing influence on the aged than on younger persons who are more in control and command of self and destiny.

Since careful phenomenological, indepth, prospective studies of the elderly are rare, it would have been most advantageous had we been able to follow our subjects on a continuing basis. We could have learned much about the evolution of grief and depression and, hopefully, about the elements in the psychosocial environment that help in their resolution.

Still another reflection on the methods and points of view with which we began: the predictive value of the traditional psychiatric nosology had to be questioned as a result of this work. Symptomatology, such as obsessive-compulsive behavior and impairing in earlier years, proved to be adaptive in old age. That depression may simulate organic states further indicated the need for psychiatry to reconsider its theories and its practices with respect to the elderly, who constitute one-fourth of all annual admissions to our public mental hospitals.

Evidences of cognitive decrements combined with high levels of functional adaptation demonstrated the value of other supportive factors—social circumstances, family life, medical status, finances—to continued survival in the community rather than in an institution. It is necessary to distinguish between test findings and their clinical consequences.

To the psychiatrist, both the initial and the continuing impression was of the vitality and psychic durability of the group studied. This view was in sharp contrast to the customary one of the inevitable decline of the aged.

Moreover, the elderly, like the young, suffer anxiety, grieve, become perplexed and depressed. Age and organic brain damage are important, but of perhaps greater importance to morale and to the genesis of psychopathology in old age are losses.

From a number of sources in the data of the followup study, when compared with the earlier data, there was a hint of changes in these men that fell between the measurements. A change could be detected toward an increasing delicacy of the individual's maintained integration as a person. This integration appeared to be more "brittle" or "fragile," the whole to be more easily shattered if any part of it were disturbed or disrupted. Hints in the social psychological analyses appeared in the higher interrelatedness of measures in the followup as compared with 1956, and in the greater disruptive effect of environmental losses upon functioning at the later time period. A test of the hypothesis of fragility requires other than the present data. Again, more direct, continuing observation of aging persons would provide firmer bases for interpretation. This aspect of the changing organism not only has theoretical relevance in gerontology, but relevance in the programs and social management of the aged.

Objectives in Aging Research

After a long and complex program of research has been completed, one always raises the questions: Was it worthwhile? What was accomplished? An answer to these questions forces us to consider the general issue of the scientific purposes of studying the aged or the aging process. One hears objections to studying aging—One can't prevent aging. Is one interested in controlling aging?

In our view, there are four major significant objectives in research on aging. The first is to explore and understand the mechanisms of the aging process itself. By this we mean those fundamental anatomical, physiological, chemical, psychological, and social processes, more or less common for all members of the species, that change with chronological age and become determinants in the performance and function of the organism as a whole. The study of mechanisms of the aging process can result in fundamental knowledge which may have broader implications for developmental processes at all ages.

This understanding of the mechanisms of aging is not merely an end in itself, but provides a substantive basis for the second objective—to intervene in the aging process and retard its rate. The prevention of aging may not be a feasible or necessarily a desirable objective. The retardation of the aging process, which is theoretically possible and attainable, may have salutary consequences for the human race in that it may extend useful and fruitful living within the limits of the theoretical lifespan. The most important consideration is the quality of existence in the years prior to death. If these years could be made free from the usual deleterious effects of senility, the time of death is immaterial.

A third objective of research on aging is to examine certain phenomena that are common to individuals at all ages, but which occur with higher frequency and in exaggerated form in the aged. These phenomena usually take the form of disease states, but it is a truism in medical research that normal functioning is often best elucidated by the study of pathology. Also, there are diseases and emotional problems that occur at any age but are most common in the aged—hypertension,

arterosclerosis, diabetes, cancer, isolation, grief, irritability, response to stimulation, feeling of uselessness.

Lastly, even if one failed in all other objectives, there still remains the worthy goal of improving the quality of life of the aged. It is here, perhaps, that one can be most optimistic about the results, if the problems can be clearly defined.

Given the inexorable march of time with all its physical consequences, there are many things that can be done to ameliorate the considerable problems faced by the aged in our society today. These require recognition of the differences between the effects of chronological age and the effects of the processes of aging within the individual and the effects of his environment. For example, in evaluating infirmities of age, it is important to distinguish between those changes attributable to time and those resulting from disease. The latter can often be managed effectively by appropriate and specific medical means. However, in many cases this would require a complete reorientation in thinking about the diseases associated with aging. Senility is often a diagnosis indiscriminately inflicted upon the aged, when in fact it may be a manifestation of depression not too dissimilar from that observed in earlier life. Grief caused by personal loss is often cruelly disregarded in the aged and attributed to senile changes, when in fact it can be just as effectively managed in the aged as in the young. Isolation, which society so often imposes on the old, produces syndromes no different from what we already know to be the consequences of isolation in the young.

The so-called communication gap, so glamorized and of so much concern when considered in regard to relations between youth and the middle aged, is a far more significant and destructive influence in the relationship between the aged and the rest of the population.

These are examples of phenomena that could be studied and understood, with the knowledge gained thereby applied to alleviate the problems of the aged. As a result, one could expect to improve the value and quality of life. Conditions such as these can only grow in importance with the increasing representation of the aging in our national population.

Our studies have addressed themselves to some of these objectives. Certainly we attempted to distinguish between true mechanisms of aging in the nervous system and the impact of disease. We sought to define truly time-related decrements in physiological, psychological, and behavioral performance. We attempted to separate and identify environmental and physical factors in the processes of change associated with aging. We tried to characterize the organicity and functionality of some of the psychiatric aberrations of the aged. We tried to identify some of the prognostic signs that appear to be related to increased chances of survival. We did not attempt to study diseases and disease-related problems. We did not touch on those aged people most in need of alleviating treatment. We did, however, show the distinct possibility of aged people leading a good life.

One of the contributions of this study is to help form a more realistic concept of man himself in old age. This can be of direct benefit to society; its institutions and expectations concerning the aged can be more realistically based on research information. Enough older persons survive to old age with the adaptive capacity to exercise choice and to experience contentment to provide us with a cultural expectation. While research must continue on why changes do occur, what has been learned has helped to replace unrealistic folklore with a basis for thinking more rationally about old age. To the extent that we can identify with the men of this study, we can look forward more confidently to growing old.

Despite the intensity of this research program and the efforts of many investigators for many years, these studies represent only a beginning and achieve only a minute scratch on the surface of a major medical-social problem that can only grow in enormity.

CHAPTER 9

Summary and Conclusions

by Samuel Granick and Robert D. Patterson

The primary aim of the Human Aging study has been the delineation of those biomedical and behavioral changes in elderly individuals which can be attributed to normal aging. Two additional goals were to study people's characteristic experiences associated with adjustment to aging, and to identify factors related to longevity and survival. Our investigation has had a developmental orientation because it has sought to contribute to an understanding of the evolution of the normal physiological and psychological processes of old age. It represents an attempt to achieve the kinds of insights and concepts about the nature of the latter part of the life cycle which the considerable research on fetal life, childhood, and adolescence has accomplished for the early phases of human growth. We believe this study demonstrates the feasibility of developmental studies in gerontology, reflecting the positive features of this approach, along with the pitfalls and shortcomings involved. Some issues of experimental design are discussed in Chapter 8, Reflections on Human Aging.

Research Problems and Procedure

A predominant theme of research reports describes aging as inherently a period of rapid declines with marked "senile" changes, particularly for those beyond the age of 70. Essentially, the picture presented is pessimistic. This pessimism appears to parallel the tendency of current day society to expect little more than problems from the aged and to disregard their social, cultural, economic, political, and artistic potentials.

The original organizers of the present investigation considered the possibility that this conception might be a grossly exaggerated picture of the involution which occurs during old age. They noted that most information on the functioning of older adults had been derived from ill and institutionalized subjects. Only limited success had been achieved in separating the effects of physical and mental pathologies from those of aging per se. It was hypothesized that the healthy individual of advanced age might retain a very substantial proportion of the capabilities he had developed in his earlier years and that he might, furthermore, be able to acquire new ideas and skills quite effectively. Moreover, medical progress in the control and elimination of deteriorative diseases could then be expected to enable increasingly larger numbers of elderly individuals to function vigorously, creatively, and effectively within the community.

The research procedure of this investigation involved the selection of an optimally healthy community resident group of subjects whose biological and behavioral functioning could be studied intensively along multidisciplinary lines. Practical considerations made it necessary to limit the study to males. It was accepted also that the ideal of assembling a group of *completely* healthy elderly was not practical. Consequently, after all medical studies were completed, the 47 subjects were subdivided into two groups with respect to their medical status: group I, consisting of 27 subjects who were free of any significant physical symptoms or evidence of disease; and group II, with 20 essentially healthy subjects who were free of symptoms but who had mild asymptomatic abnormalities which were most frequently related to arteriosclerosis. Over 600 characteristics were measured or rated regarding each individual during the first study. Extensive statistical and descriptive analyses were carried out within each of the disciplines as well as with respect to interrelationships among the disciplines. We have summarized the major previously published findings in chapter 1.

The original plan of the investigation did not call for a longitudinal study, but the value of such a procedure became evident shortly after the conclusion of the initial examinations. Accordingly, a 5-year followup study was conducted in 1961, at the NIH Clinical Center. Of the 39 surviving subjects, 29 were willing and able to return for the second round of study.

The 11-year followup in 1967, which is reported in detail in the preceding chapters, required a change of location to the Philadelphia Geriatric Center because the original research team had disbanded. Unlike the circumstances of the previous two studies, several new members joined the research team and played major roles in gathering and analyzing the data. At this point, there were 23 survivors, 19 of whom participated. Considerable effort was invested in duplicating the original examinations. Some abbreviations in the procedures were necessary because of the more limited tolerance of most of the subjects, and because of the impossibility of working out suitable duplications of a few of the original tests. It was possible, however, to include the major elements from the various disciplines which were represented in the initial investigation.

Age-Related Changes

At the time of the first study it was possible to identify a number of changes which were regarded as age-related in contrast to changes which seemed primarily a product of disease. Those which appear to be most significant are outlined in table 1. It is impressive that so few variables showed changes with age. In many ways, the subjects functioned on a par with much younger adults, and showed little of the deficit and deterioration generally associated with aging.

The number of age-related changes undoubtedly would have been greater if more variables had been measured—especially under stressful conditions. For example, measurement of maximum functional capacities of the heart and kidneys under physiological stress might have revealed other age-related changes, as might careful study of psychological functions under controlled psychological stresses.

Another condition which limited the identification of age-related changes in some instances was the absence of standards for normal adults with which to compare our results. This situation was most common in psychiatry and social psychol-

TABLE 1.—*Age-related changes in healthy men*

Study area	Type and direction of change
Medicine	Erythrocyte sedimentation rate elevated.
	Serum albumin lower.
	Beta globulin elevated.
	Serum alpha 2 globulin elevated.
	Maximal breathing capacity reduced.
	Timed vital capacity reduced.
	Arterial O_2 saturation reduced.
	QRS axis in EKG shifted.
Cerebral physiology:	
Circulation	No changes.
EEG	Entire wave frequency spectrum, especially the major frequencies, slower.
Audiology	Hearing in upper frequency range reduced.
	Capacity of the auditory sensory data storage system reduced.
	Capacity of the auditory perceptual system reduced.
Psychology:	
Intellectual and Psychomotor	Speed of responses to auditory stimuli reduced.
	Nonverbal intelligence scores lower.
	Concept formation slower and reduced in amount.
	Speed of Copying Digits lower.
	Speed of word fluency lower.
	Speed of perception lower.
Personality	No age-related differences in formal characteristics of responses.
	Content of projective tests somewhat age related.
	Depression score on MMPI higher.
Psychiatry	Certain psychopathological traits became adaptive during old age.
	Self reports about changes in the following areas:
	Physical—predominantly less favorable.
	Cognitive—predominantly less effective.
	Personality-affective—predominantly favorable.
	Social-psychological—predominantly less satisfactory.
	Depression sometimes masqueraded as organic brain syndrome.
	Psychological preparation for death occurred, including life review.
	Discrepancy between diagnosis and adaptation greater than in younger groups.
Social Psychology	Social roles and status changed.
	Psychosocial losses increased.
	"Leveling" of social status between men of different occupations upon retirement.
	Adaptive capacities under stress decreased.
	Dependence of social functioning upon immediate environment increased.

ogy. For example because of the absence of a strictly comparable study in younger adults, it could not be determined precisely if the incidence of depression was age-related.

It seems likely that *small* changes in innumerable biological and psychological functions occur with age, but these changes were often smaller than our capacity for accurate measurement.

Changes in Survivors

The 11-year followup study permitted evaluation of the effects of continued aging upon the survivors. Of the 47 subjects,

23 survived, and 24 died. The average age of the survivors was 81 years.

Contacting the survivors and arranging for their followup examinations was a process surprisingly free of difficulties. Most of the subjects and their families were exceedingly interested in the project and eager to cooperate. Even families of deceased subjects were very willing to help us assemble information on the causes of death. The survivors often expressed feelings of satisfaction about being a part of what they regarded as an important scientific effort. We suspect that participation in the study had some positive influences on the mental health and psychological functioning of the men.

Major changes found in the survivors over the 11-year followup are summarized in table 2. The results in all areas show a remarkably limited amount of change. Almost all changes are in the direction of decline, but few are severe.

Increased intercorrelations among measurements in the social psychology area were noted at the third study (see ch. 6). The relative independence of different aspects of functioning which was characteristic in the earlier period was much less evident when the men were older. This finding suggests that a problem in one area of life was much more likely to spill over and affect the other aspects of functioning during the later years.

The physical health of the subjects declined during the followup, but the picture had many positive elements. In terms of functional assessment, only one man was incapacitated (by an organic brain syndrome), and two widowers lived in homes for the aged primarily because of the convenience for them. The remainder lived in the community and managed their affairs adequately. Medically, 10 subjects were classified as being healthy or showing only minor abnormalities. Eight men had significant abnormalities, most often cardiovascular disease. No significant increase in blood pressure was evident in the healthy group, but they did manifest significant increases in erythrocyte sedimentation rate and in fasting blood sugar.

The eight subjects who had repeat cerebral blood flow studies had reduced blood flow and increased cerebral vascular resistance. These changes can probably be attributed to arteriosclerosis. New electroencephalographic abnormalities occurred in the four subjects who had developed chronic brain syndrome. Few other electroencephalographic changes were noted in the remaining subjects.

On psychological tests, the survivors improved somewhat with respect to verbal functioning. With respect to performance

TABLE 2.—*Changes in survivors after 11 years*

Study area	Type and direction of change
Medicine	Almost 1/2 had significant diseases. Erythrocyte sedimentation rate increased in healthy subjects. Fasting blood sugar increased in healthy subjects.
Cerebral Physiology: Circulation	Cerebral blood flow decreased. Cerebral vascular resistance increased.
EEG	8 subjects showed some type of EEG change. No systematic changes in the group, but 5 subjects showed slowing of the dominant occipital rhythm. Changes found in all 4 cases of chronic brain syndrome.
Psychology	Vocabulary improved. Picture Arrangement improved. Speed of Addition declined. Speed of Arithmetic Alternation declined. Speed of Copying Words declined. Quality of Draw-a-Person declined. Quality of sentence completions declined.
Psychiatry	Trend toward more organic mental changes. Self-monitoring of intellectual and physical capacities more prominent. "Energy" decreased (self-reports). Sexual interest declined.
Social Psychology	Losses in social environment increased. Vulnerability to failure at coping with stressful events increased. "Energy" decreased (self-reports).

on nonverbal psychological tests, decline is characteristic in the aged, particularly on tests calling for visual motor coordination, flexibility of adaptation, and speed of reaction. The men in this study showed such a decline when compared to young adults, but they performed relatively well when compared to other groups of aged. Generally they maintained their cognitive status quite well. Tests involving flexibility of adaptation and abstraction showed some decline over the 11-year period, but this finding was not consistent. In some instances performance in these areas was quite good. On the whole, the data suggest that declines in the areas of speed, psychomotor functioning, flexibility, and abstraction are probably age-related.

The psychiatric and social psychological followup studies both found the subjects reporting decreases in energy. This did not, however, prevent them from being active and involved in a variety of interests. There were no significant group changes in the complexity of organization of daily behavior, the amount of passivity, and outlook on life.

Organic mental declines were more evident than in the past but still mild or absent in most subjects. As they grew older, it became clearer that most of the men were quite aware of their organic mental changes, and tended to carefully regulate their activities to fit their intellectual capacities. At least one-third of the survivors lived longer than they predicted that they would 11 years earlier. Psychological losses continued to increase and had profound effects upon their outlook on life.

In summary, the changes observed between the first and the followup study suggest that a gradual erosion of capacities ensued in the men with the passage of time, often in the form of re-duced reserve capacities. Such erosion may be inherent in or normal for the aging process. Examples are found in the areas of reduced energy and general physical status; less effective cognitive functioning, particularly when flexibility of adaptation is involved; lower speed of motor and intellectual responsiveness; and greater vulnerability to breakdown under psychosocial stresses.

Survivor-Nonsurvivor Comparisons

Since almost equal numbers of subjects were survivors and nonsurvivors in the 11 years following the first study, comparison between the two groups regarding their initial examination characteristics was feasible. We wanted to know: in what other ways might they represent two separate populations? What elements of biological and behavioral functioning are associated with survival? Our data offered the opportunity for at least partial answers to these and related questions. Table 3 summarizes the significant differences between the two groups on a variety of the measures.

A remarkably consistent picture emerges, showing the survivors to have been superior to the nonsurvivors in every area in which a statistically significant difference is found. The fact that only a few of the group II subjects are among the survivors (6 out of the original 20, or 30 percent) indicates that even asymptomatic disease (which was most often mild arteriosclerosis) is significant with respect to longevity. Thus, groups I and II do indeed seem to have been different from each other in important ways associated with survival, even though relatively few differences were found between them at the time of the original study. The specific differences may be useful, along with other factors, in the development of a

TABLE 3.—*Significant differences between survivors and nonsurvivors*
[Initial measurements]

Study	Factor	Direction for survivors
Medicine	Health Status (groups I and II)	Healthier.
	Systolic Blood Pressure	Lower.
	Diastolic Blood Pressure	Lower.
	Mean Arterial Blood Pressure	Lower.
	Weight	Heavier.
	Arteriosclerosis	Less.
	Chronic Cigarette Smoking	Less.
	Serum Cholesterol in those who died from Coronary Heart Disease.	Lower.
	Serum Albumin in those who died from Carcinoma	Higher.
Cerebral Physiology:		
Circulation	None	
EEG	None, but a tendency shown with respect to:	
	Peak Occipital Frequency	Higher.
	Percentage Fast Activity	Lower.
Psychology:		
Intellectual and	WAIS Verbal scale	Higher.
Psychomotor	WAIS Performance scale	Higher.
	WAIS subtests:	
	Vocabulary	Higher.
	Information	Higher.
	Comprehension	Higher.
	Similarities	Higher.
	Digit Symbol Substitution	Higher.
	Block Design	Higher.
	Speed of Copying Digits	Higher.
	Speed of Copying Words	Higher.
	Principal Component I (Stored Information)	Higher.
Personality	Draw-a-Person	Higher.
	Rorschach	Higher.
	Homonyms	Higher.
	MMPI–Si Scale (Social Involvement)	Higher.
Psychiatry	Adaptation	Better.
	Mental Status	Higher.
Social Psychology	Organization of Behavior	Higher.
	Environmental Loss	Lower.

means for predicting survival in old people. These elements in the individual's biological and behavioral functioning may also prove effective as early indications of serious pathology, and show the way toward the continued maintenance of good physical and mental health in the aged.

The mean age for the survivors, at the time of the original study in 1956, was 70 years, and for the nonsurvivors 73 years. The difference is statistically significant when a *t* test is applied, because of the extreme age of one subject who was more than 11 years older than the second oldest individual.[1] If the oldest subject is not counted with the deceased group, the average age is reduced to 72 and the age difference between the groups becomes nonsignificant.

In the medical area there was an unexpected finding that men who died of carcinomas had serum albumin lower than the other subjects. The albumin was

[1] This man, incidentally, died at the age of 103 at the time the followup study began. Part of the examination was administered to him, but since he died before most of it could be completed, he has been grouped with the deceased subjects in all but the social psychological analyses.

measured between 2 and 11 years prior to their deaths; all of the carcinomas happened to be in the gastrointestinal tract. If the finding is substantiated by future studies, it could prove useful for diagnostic purposes or in the study of the causes of cancers.

Also, unexpectedly, men with higher weights (but not obesity) survived more frequently than men with lower weights.

Chronic cigarette smoking was found to be significantly associated with mortality at both the 5- and 11-year followup studies. It is of interest that this difference between the survivors and nonsurvivors manifested itself so clearly even during the first followup despite the lack of apparent physiological differences between the smokers and nonsmokers in the original investigation.

It is surprising that measures of cerebral physiology did not have the sensitivity shown by several of the other examination procedures to distinguish between long- and short-term survivors. There are no statistically significant differences between the groups on any of the measures of cerebral physiology. In the electroencephalograms, however, there was a tendency for the nonsurvivors to have lower peak occipital frequencies and higher percentage fast activity.

The various psychological measurements provide a substantial number of differences between survivors and nonsurvivors. That the nonsurvivors performed significantly less well on the WAIS Verbal scale and its subtests than the survivors seems particularly noteworthy since, in general, the aged maintain these skills relatively well. This finding suggests an early element of decline of functioning which may be an indication that death is not far off.

As with the verbal-cognitive tests, the survivors were significantly above the level of functioning of the nonsurvivors on the performance-type intellectual and perceptual tests. Included in this group of tests are the WAIS Performance, including several of its subtests, the Speed of Copying Digits and Words, and the Draw-a-Person test from among the group of personality measures.

The Rorschach and Homonyms tests also showed distinct differences between the surviving and the nonsurviving groups. These tests tapped features of mental functioning such as the exercise of imagination, organization of ideas, integration of multiple aspects of a situation, identification of relationships, and production of varied concepts spontaneously in response to a stimulus.

The survivors reported themselves more involved in social relationships (MMPI Social Involvement scale). This factor may be associated with the difference between the two groups on the social-psychological measure of environmental loss, a factor noted earlier and below as having a profound influence on their behavior as well as survival.

On the psychiatric examination, survivors had higher Mental Status Scores (related, of course, to the intelligence test results described above). Adaptation, which measured resourcefulness in meeting needs and obtaining satisfactions as well as self-esteem, was also higher among survivors.

Organization of Behavior, a social-psychological measure which was intended to measure the amount of planning and complexity of typical daily activities, and Environmental Loss were both rated more favorably among the survivors.

A stepwise linear discriminant function analysis was carried out in order to assess the contributions of the various measures to prediction of survival. A set of 15 variables was suggested by the investigators from the various disciplines. These variables were intended to represent the best predictors from among the large number available.

Organization of behavior and cigarette smoking together were found to be as good discriminators as all 15 variables together. They classified 80 percent of both survivors and nonsurvivors correctly. Thus, the survivors who had the most organized daily behavior and were nonsmokers had the greatest probability of surviving.

When the analysis was restricted to behavioral variables alone, the combination of Organization of Behavior and Mental Status was the most discriminating for survivorship. The results were interpreted as suggesting that psychological factors had an important effect upon survival. When, on the other hand, the physical variables alone were considered, mean systolic blood pressure and weight were the significant discriminators. Lower blood pressure, even within the normal range, and greater weight (also within the normal range) were associated with survival.

Implications for Longevity and the Quality of Old Age in the Future

Aging has been conceptualized as a process of accumulating defects which eventually become so numerous that the organism can no longer function and it dies. Indeed, many people have acquired four, five, or more chronic diseases by the time they reach advanced old age. That they die from these diseases seems a natural outcome of this accumulation of defects.

At the time of the original examinations in 1956, these men were distinctly different from the aged generally. They were virtually totally free of physical diseases. Their medical data profiles would, in many instances, have been almost indistinguishable from those of young men— if their ages and photographs had been omitted. Despite their impressive state of health and functioning, they have been surviving only a little longer than men of average health. This points to the probable importance of genetic determinents of the lifespan.

In countries where average longevity is low, it is easy to identify factors which could be changed to increase longevity; e.g., control of infectious diseases, improved diet, and accident prevention. Among the men in this study, it is much harder to identify such factors, and the contribution of any of them to increasing longevity is likely to be modest.

On the other hand, our data encourage considerable optimism about the potential quality of life within the probable relatively fixed genetic limits on longevity. The demonstration by the study subjects of their capacity to lead satisfying and effective lives into quite old age suggests the same may be possible for many more elderly.

On the basis of this investigation, four areas seem potentially most likely to make substantial contributions to the quality of life in old age and to longevity. They appear to be the areas where application of our present knowledge will be most useful. They are also the areas where future research appears most likely to be beneficial.

The first area is prevention or treatment of arteriosclerosis. Its effects underlie many of the debilitating conditions of old age.

Second is the prevention of cigarette smoking or the avoidance of its harmful influences, even among those who are already healthy old smokers.

A third area involves reduction of the detrimental effects of psychosocial losses.

Governments and other organizations will probably be increasingly required to provide some of the services which nuclear families have traditionally provided, because modern families are smaller and they often become geographically dispersed. Changes in cultural practices, even though they would be difficult to bring about and would require much time, might be very important. Examples include encouraging marriages between men and women of more nearly equal ages, and instituting practices that foster healthy compensations for grief and the restoration of psychosocial losses. Early treatment of illnesses related to losses should be improved.

A fourth area is that of helping the aged sustain effective life goals. Maintenance of life goals has a significant positive influence upon the retention of intelligence, organization of daily behavior, morale, and adaptation. Whether or not the aged will have satisfying goals can be influenced by many elements of a society. Such influences include economic, business, and labor union policies with regard to employment and retirement practices for the aged, and city and institutional planning to make possible the attainment of varied goals within the limits of the physical and emotional requirements of the aged.

PSYCHOANALYSIS and AGING

Failures in Transformation; and the Psychopathology of Later Life

When social life fails to provide the trustworthy collective representations that older persons can fashion into transforming objects, they may revive early modes of managing and expressing narcissism. Thus, they may idealize their own wishes, reviving the grandiose self and its adolescent demands—to be all-containing, male and female, omnipotential. Conversely, they may seek for some idealized, all-providing parental figure. Men in later life may become, in effect, their own children and express their self-concern through the passive mode, demanding the right to be cared for; while older women may express egocentricity through the active mode, through insisting on the right to be in total charge of their chosen domain. For both sexes, the heightened self-concern can take the form of pettiness, irritability, and hypochondria. The digestion, the bowel movements, the articulation of the limbs—all these can become a source of fascination to the older person, if not to his audience. Obsessive reminiscence is another possibility, as the older person, unable to dramatize his present depleted state, idealizes his past. This perspective is often escalated into a world view: The present, that belongs to the young, is full of corruption; only the past knew virtue.

Unfortunately, the self is re-invested precisely at the time when it is most prone to suffer losses in the cosmetic, physical, sexual, existential, and social spheres; and these losses are likely to be experienced by the egocentric elder as personal defeats and insults, rather than natural (if painful) decrements. Too often, the sense of insult is warded off through desperate means. The idealization of the omnipotential, illusioned self is maintained through hypomanic denial of the blemish and/or through paranoid projection of imperfection (or of the responsibility for imperfection) onto others. The alcoholism that proliferates in later life often plays the same function of buttressing denial and of filling the drinker with a temporary, hectic sense of his own omnipotence. Profound depression can result when these quasi-psychotic defenses fail.

Unfortunately, modern psychiatry focuses on the losses of the older person, which are irreversible. Thus, the current emphasis is on medicating the pain of irretrievable loss. Practitioners might do better to treat the heightened but potentially reversible narcissism that renders these losses so poignant, so insulting, and so destructive. The emphasis should not be on resignation and adjustment to object loss; rather, it should be on guiding the patient toward forming new and narcissism-transforming objects, the cultural abstractions that cannot be lost and that are appropriate to the postparental season of life.

Threats to the Aging Male

What is true for narcissism is also true for the other great relational capacities released by the phasing out of parenthood. While many men accomplish the transition to a more bimodal phrasing of their sexuality and find therein an expansion of self, other men, much like adolescents, are frightened by the emergence of a new side to their sexual nature. This is particularly true in a society which, like ours, puts particular value on an uncompromised machismo. Accordingly, we predict that midlife psychopathology, particularly in those men who have become troubled for the first time in the middle years, would be formed around these problematic issues having to do with threats from the "feminine" side of self.

This tentative formulation is borne out by preliminary work. A review of the cases followed in the short-term psychotherapy project of the Tavistock Clinic, London (Malan 1963) indicates a significant shift, occurring after age 40, in the nature of presenting complaints and diagnostic formulations. The younger Tavistock patients are mainly troubled by oedipal issues, having to do with the inhibition of "masculine" sexual and aggressive strivings. The typical diagnostic formulation for men under 40 presents them as victims of an unresolved struggle with a domineering father. The crippling guilt and anxiety that are aroused by this struggle lead the younger man to inhibit the aggressive and sexual strivings that have compromised the relationship with the father. A fair number of younger patients become impotent or homosexual in order to deny the "manly" but guilt-provoking urges. However, table 3 indicates that there is a decided shift, beginning around age 35, both in the presenting complaint and diagnostic conception. Older patients are less apt to complain of a castrating father than of a domineering and smothering mother. By the same token, the feared quality of aggression is no longer discovered in the self but is complained of in the wife as an external threat—at least half the older men present with a complaint about an overbearing wife.

The inner life problems of the older Tavistock patient are not focused around genital and aggressive needs but around the internal, "feminine" ones; older

Table 3

Tavistock Brief Psychotherapy Sample: Distribution of Male Patients by Diagnosis and Presenting Complaints

Age	Focus of Problem: Dominant Oedipal Father	Oedipal Diagnosis: Guilt with Father Inhibits Sex and Aggression	Guilt (Oedipal) Leads to Impotence as Symptom	Homosexual Issues Based on Oedipal Guilt	Symptom: Loss of Achievement Drive	Pre-Genital Diagnosis: Inability to Express Needs	Dominant Wife Seen as Problem	Focus of Problem: Dominant Mother
Under 20 Years		2[1]		1				
20+ Years	3	5	2	3				1 WC
30+ Years	1	2	2				? WC[3]	1
35+ Years				1		1	1 WC	1
40+ Years		2	3	2	1	2	2	1
45+ Years		1			?[2]	1	1	2
50+ Years		1			1		1	1

1. Entries are not independent: The same individual may be noted more than once.
2. Question marks infer possible, but not definite example.
3. WC = working class
   N = 21; 13 cases under age 35; 8 over age 35

men, much more than younger men, are troubled by their wish to depend on others, to get out of the rat race, or to cry. Clearly, where younger men are troubled by the pressure from "masculine" and phallic issues that demand to be lived out, older men coming for psychotherapy are more often troubled by unmet "feminine" and pregenital demands.

These tentative results conform to the diagnostic impressions that we receive from older male patients studied at the Institute of Psychiatry, Northwestern University Medical School. Typically, the men are from 45 to 60 years old, reasonably established as regards love and work, and without prior history of significant mental illness. In the majority of cases, we find that the psychiatric crisis is closely associated with midlife changes in the wife. During his earlier years, the husband can externalize and live out the discrepant, "feminine" side of his own nature through indulging and sponsoring his wife's femininity. But as women become more assertive and eschew the more submissive role toward men, the aging husband loses this "projective ecology." He begins to sense—usually with some discomfort—that so-called feminine traits are a feature of his own internal landscape and not exclusive to his wife.

The older traditionalist who faces a newly "liberated" wife can find other, circumscribed religious arenas in which to live out his growing passive-dependent tendencies. His dealings with God are usually private, and in any case God's omnipotence justifies quite completely the abasement of a mere human. The aging traditionalist can thus indulge the bisexuality of later life without shame, and he need not make some final choice between the active and passive, the "masculine" and "feminine" sides of his nature.

But the patients that we have studied are more profoundly damaged at the outset of their lives and are offered less opportunity to build compensatory psychosocial ecologies or "life structures," to use Levinson's term (1977), in their postparental years. Neurotic symptoms or disturbed behavior are predictable results. Typically, these men were strongly identified, as children, with a mother who was viewed as omnicompetent. The father was weak or out of the picture. He could not be idealized and internalized to provide some compensating version of specifically masculine strengths or virtues. The son admires the mother and identifies with her, but at the same time he may unconsciously hate her for having castrated the father. In his earlier years, the son tends to deny the maternal identification (and his father's fate) through hard work and counterdependence. He may marry a relatively docile woman who will live out, for him, the "womanly" aspect that he is denying in himself. However, postparental developments pose dual threats: On the one hand, the patient is troubled by a revival of the earlier feminine identification, the reappearance of his sexual bimodality; and on the other hand, his wife has "come out of the closet," has declared her own autonomy, and is no longer willing to be a metaphor of the femininity that he is denying in himself. Thus, changes in himself and in his wife confront him with his own closeted self; and the wife seems to be castrating him as the mother once emasculated the father. Further-more, the now relatively independent wife is seen as a defector. She provokes a forced separation from the maternal figure of the sort that the patient has never been able to tolerate or achieve on his own. The wife's growth confronts the man with his own dependency at the same time that it cuts him off from the kinds of support that meet (and thereby legitimize) these needs.

The Older Male: Defensive Coping

The various symptoms and acting-out behaviors that we see clinically represent desperate attempts to deny sexual bimodality, to seek new but disguised sources of oral supply, or to re-externalize the feminine and needful aspect of the self. For example, alcoholism, a syndrome that typically intensi-fies in the middle life of men, serves these multiple functions very well. It is an ideal vehicle for externalizing the ambivalence around active and passive modalities. On the one hand, as McClelland and his associates (1972) have shown, strong drink is instant machismo. Because it releases inhibitions on aggression, it is confounded, as "firewater," or "Dutch courage," with the energies that it sponsors, to become a liquid metaphor of male power. On the other hand, drinking is an oral activity, a recapitulation of infantile sucking in which the individual takes in a liquid that has analgesic, soothing (as well as stimulating) qualities. Within the course of the same drinking bout, the alco-holic is both a god and a helpless infant. He starts the evening by claiming that he can "lick anybody in the house," but ends it impotent, like an infant, unable to walk and submerged in his own mess. Under the cover story, "It's the liquor talking," the alcohlic has been permitted to externalize—and enjoy—both aspects of his troubling duality without having to take personal responsibility for either of them.

Psychosomatic symptoms, even including the heart attacks that proliferate in later life, may also support these midlife re-externalizations. In effect, the ailing man brings his troubling passive needs to the one major institution in our society that recognizes and even insists on a dependent stance—the hospital. By becoming a patient, the middle-age man says, "It is not *I*, but my diseased organs that ask for help. My spirit is still willing; but my heart, liver, or stomach is weak." In effect then, psychosomatic illness also serves, at great price, to restore the *status quo ante*; the damaged organ takes on the role of the weak, dependent, feminine entity that was once played by the wife. The damaged aspect of self is re-externalized onto the damaged, "castrated" organ, rather than the "damaged" wife.

Other, perhaps more strongly defended, men may emphasize the denial rather than the covert expression of their emerging proclivities. Though more research is required, these may be the "type A" men (described by Friedman and Rosenman 1974) who, out of a desperate need to refute the changes in their psyches and their bodies, drive themselves through overwork to a premature heart attack. Significantly, the type A characteristics no longer predict coronary disease after age 50. The correlations between character and coronaries weaken at about the point when these driven, masculine, protesting men begin to accept the duality of their own nature.

Other men of this persuasion may escalate their machismo, heap chips on their shoulders, and hunt for antagonists, particularly oppressive authorities. Again, they deny certain passive wishes and simultaneously project the responsibility for these onto the objects of such wishes. They accuse their boss of requiring from them the submission they themselves secretly desire.

The increasingly frequent middle-age divorce, where an older man leaves his wife of 20 years and marries a young wife, is relevant here. The usual interpretation is that the aging, divorced male seeks to renew virility via a new sexual partner. However, in many such cases, the aim is not primarily to enhance potency but to re-externalize passive features of the personality. Just as some men seek to externalize their unfolding passivity via alcoholism or psychosomatic illness, others try to recreate a lost *status quo ante* and to relocate their feminine side in a new external vessel by discarding this now autonomous wife in favor of a still dependent, still adoring, younger woman. Through her, the older man hopes to both live out and cordon off the discrepant, questionable aspect of his own nature.

Personality Theory in Old Age

There is no satisfactory personality theory which is applied to the entire lifespan. The Freudian theory emphasizes, and quite profitably, the early portion. The differing but stimulating views of numerous theorists, including Adler, Horney, Jung, Sullivan, and others have had an impact upon psychoanalytic thinking. However, for many of us interested in the latter part of the lifespan, Erikson's "The Eight Stages of Man" provides a useful basis for thought and investigation (1959).

As elaborated on in other chapters of this publication, the eight stages in the life cycle, as delineated by Erikson, are represented by a choice or crisis for the expanding ego. As one moves from the identity-versus-confusion problem of adolescence into young adulthood, the focus shifts to intimacy versus isolation, that is, the ability to merge one's self with the self of another. Adulthood, the next stage, is concerned with generativity versus self-absorption (investment in the product of one's own creation and identification with the future), and the late adulthood stage is concerned with the crisis of ego integrity versus disgust and despair (the view that one's life has been the product of one's own making, that it could not be a different one, and that it has been a meaningful life).

To demonstrate that there are frequent if not consistent personality changes in old people that come about as the result of aging, it would be necessary to demonstrate that there exists an orderly sequential pattern of changes of personality traits that alter behavior in old age. Repeated cross-sectional studies often show variable results, although certain investigators or research teams are more consistent in their findings. The failure to demonstrate consistent personality changes accompanying aging is in part accounted for by the use of research instruments which are of unproved reliability or validity, particularly when applied to older persons. It appears that aging per se does not independently alter personality. Rather, the passing of time, the biological status of the individual, and the type, degree, and the time of the event in the life cycle all influence personality and behavior. The psychoanalyst can and should make a significant contribution to understanding personality and behavior in late life. The psychoanalytic method is ideal for observing the relationship between biological and social factors and their effect upon the older person. The psychoanalytic setting permits the evaluation of antecedent events. If personality theory is to progress, the psychoanalyst has a unique contribution to make.

The psychosocial approach to the study of personality has traditionally focused on so-called personality traits. That psychophysiological disposition underlies traits is accepted, but the measure of the trait is how the individual responds in a social or interpersonal situation. This approach permits the use of standardized tests.

Psychoanalysis and psychodynamics add another dimension, as such studies are concerned with the events within the individual, the feelings within the individual, and the cause and consequences of anxiety, guilt, hostility, depression, etc. Although the distinction is not sharp in these two approaches to the study of personality, both have particular value for the study of personality in old age.

Personality and developmental theories of aging are complicated by the fact that, as humans pass through their life experiences, they become increasingly different rather than similar. Infants at 6 months of age are more similar than children at age 12. This divergence continues throughout the lifespan as a response to a large array of possible learning and living experiences. Perhaps this divergence phenomenon reverses in extreme old age, as very old people show considerable similarity in certain characteristics, but this may result from the fact that they are a biologically elite group and that very old people are usually treated by society in a relatively uniform manner, that is, protected and respected.

Personality traits are theoretically the result of various combinations of endogenous and exogenous factors. In late middle life, the menopause in women is the most commonly recognized physiological alteration associated with personality change and various psychiatric disorders. A wide variety of biological age changes has been identified, but their often subtle impact upon personality and psychic well-being has been given relatively little attention (Busse

1977). This lack of attention in part is attributed to the fact that these age changes and the onset of chronic diseases and disabilities do not interfere with the capacity to work until relatively late in life. They do, however, influence many other spheres of living, including sexual behavior and recreational or leisure time activities. Included in the significant biological alterations associated with aging are presbycusis, presbyopia, declines in muscle mass and strength and reaction times, significant changes within the endocrine and nervous systems (neuronal loss), decline of gustatory sensation, loss of teeth, and numerous other system, organ, and cellular changes (Busse 1978).

Neugarten and associates (1964) published a study of personality in middle and late life. Eight empirical approaches were used, each focusing on a personality theory. A study of Erikson's theory of ego development concluded that Erikson's model of personality in assessing adult personality was relatively successful, as it was concluded "the hypothesized interdependence of ego dimensions and their proposed hierarchical order has some validity." However, it appears that adulthood is more homogeneous than the theory indicates. This study included a model of personality based on psychoanalytic and ego concepts. The study found that personalities maintained their characteristics in middle and late life, and personality changes or disintegration were not related to age per se but to losses, particularly those involving health and social support systems. Neugarten believes there are sex differences in certain personality traits in late life. Men are more affiliative; that is, they ally themselves with groups of men in male group identity. Males are more nurturant, as their patterns of response are more affected by the supplies from their environment, yet they are more responsive in their stimuli, for example, in their eating and drinking patterns. In contrast, women become more individualistic, in effect, egocentric, and more aggressive.

Increasing cautiousness or conservatism is often associated with advancing age. Several reports deal with this subject, but perhaps the most enlightening is that of Botwinick (1966). Botwinick used groups of young adult volunteers as well as older subjects and paid attention to the influence of education and socioeconomic factors. He used a questionnaire of 24 life situations, 12 of which had been previously used by other investigators. He considered not only the age of the participants but also the age of the central character in the life situation or life problem that was presented. In responding, the subjects had a choice of two alternatives. One alternative was rewarding but risky, and the other alternative was less rewarding but safer. The overall results were that elderly subjects were more cautious in their decisions than younger subjects, and neither sex nor education was related to the cautiousness. Moreover, Botwinick found that both young and old adults were less cautious when solving problems of the aged than they were when solving problems of younger adults. It appears that cautiousness increases with advancing age, but the degree of the cautiousness is influenced by the type of problem and its time of placement in the lifespan.

A recent study by Okun, Siegler, and George (1978) suggests that cautiousness is not strictly an age effect but is a "multidimensional construct." These reported differences can be attributed to the cohort influence.

According to Birren and Renner (1977), there is no pressure on the field of psychology to produce a unifying theory or to explain how behavior is organized over time. They view the psychology of aging as predominantly a problem and data-oriented area of research. Baltes and Willis (1977) reach many conclusions, including "all existing theories (of psychological aging and development) are of the prototheoretical kind and are incomplete."

The psychological theories that appear are often the extension of personality and developmental theories into middle and late life. Personality theories usually consider the innate human needs and forces that motivate thought and behavior and the modification of these biologically based energies by the experiences of living in a physical and social environment.

Schaie (1977-78) recently advanced what he calls "a stage theory of adult cognitive development." His tentative scheme involves four possible cognitive stages. These sequential stages are denoted as acquisitive (1-childhood and 2-adolescence), achieving (young adulthood), responsible and executive (middle age), and reintegrative (old age). He postulates two overlapping cognitive patterns during middle life—a "responsible" component and "executive" abilities; neither can be judged by common psychometric testing. He suggests that during the lifespan there is a transition from "what should I know" through "how should I use what I know" to "why should I know" phase of life. Schaie believes that new strategies and techniques will have to be developed to fully test a stage theory and that alterations in the theory will emerge.

Kalish and Knudtson (1976) recommend the extension of the *concept (theory) of attachment* common in infant and child psychology to a lifetime conceptual scheme for understanding relationships and involvements of older people. They further state that the *concept (theory) of disengagement* is not functional and that it should be eliminated. Attachment is a relationship established and maintained by social bonds and is distinguished from social contacts. Elderly people lose significant early objects of attachment. New attachments are often much weaker and frequently not mutual, therefore vulnerable. Kalish and Knudtson argue that an appreciation and understanding of attachments will provide a better approach to explaining the psychological changes in elderly people. Relevant to the attachment concept is the finding by Lowenthal and Haven (1968) that, more than any other single factor, having a confidant appeared to discriminate between elderly persons who were institutionalized and those who could remain in the community.

Figure 1

Etiological Diagnosis (Some examples)	Diagnostic Categories From a Developmental Structuralist Approach	Symptom-Cluster Diagnosis (Some examples)
	1. Ego Defects	
Birth injury Encephalitis Vascular Disease, etc.	A. Basic physical organic integrity of mental apparatus (perception, integration, motor, memory, regulation, judgment, etc.)	Minimal brain dysfunction Senile Psychosis, etc.
	B. Structural psychological defects and defects in ego functions	
Partial Genetic Bases of Schizophrenia	(1) Reality testing, organization of perception and thought, and capacity for human affective engagement	Schizophrenic Disorders
	(2) Perception and regulation of affect	Manic-Depressive Disorders, etc.
	(3) Integration of affect and thought	
	(4) Defect in integration and organization and/or differentiation of self- and object representations	Borderline Disorders
	2. Major Constrictions and Alterations in Ego Structure	Severe Character Disorders
	A. Limitation of experience of feelings and/or thoughts in major life areas (love, work, play)	
	B. Alterations and limitations in pleasure orientation	
	C. Major externalizations of internal events, e.g., conflicts, feelings, thoughts	
	D. Limitations in internalizations necessary for regulation of impulses, affect (mood), and thought	
	E. Impairments in self-esteem regulation	
	F. Limited tendencies toward fragmentation of self-object differentiation	
	3. Moderate versions of 2, above	Moderate Character Disorders

Figure 1, *Cont'd*

Etiological Diagnosis (Some examples)	Diagnostic Categories from a Developmental Structuralist Approach	Symptom-Cluster Diagnosis (Some examples)
	4. *Encapsulated Disorders*	
	A. Neurotic symptom formations	Symptom Neuroses
	(1) Limitations and alterations in experience of areas of thought (hysterical repression, phobic displacements, etc.)	Conversion Reactions Phobias
	(2) Limitations and alterations in experience of affects and feelings (e.g., obsessional isolation, depressive turning of feelings against the self, etc.)	Depressive Reactions Compulsive Syndromes
	B. Neurotic encapsulated character formations	Neurotic Obsessional or Hysterical Character
	(1) Encapsulated limitation of experience of feelings, thoughts, in major life areas (love, work, play)	Neurotic Sexual Disorders
	(2) Encapsulated alterations and limitations in pleasure orientation	
	(3) Encapsulated major externalizations of internal events (e.g., conflicts, feelings, thoughts)	
	(4) Encapsulated limitations in internalizations necessary for regulation of impulses, affect (mood), and thought	
	(5) Encapsulated impairments in self-esteem regulation	Neurotic Narcissistic Disorders
	5. *Basically Intact Flexible Ego Structures*	
	A. With phase-specific developmental conflicts	
	B. With phase-specific developmentally expected patterns of adaptation, including adaptive regressions	
	C. Intact, flexible, developmentally appropriate ego structure	
Phase-Appropriate Stress Situations		

The Aging Body

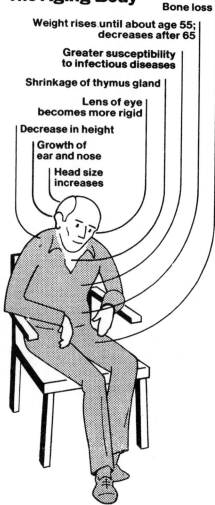

Bone loss

Weight rises until about age 55; decreases after 65

Greater susceptibility to infectious diseases

Shrinkage of thymus gland

Lens of eye becomes more rigid

Decrease in height

Growth of ear and nose

Head size increases

Index of Names

Subject Index

PSYCHOACTIVE DRUG USE – PART III

THE AGING PROCESS AND PSYCHOACTIVE DRUG
USE IN CLINICAL TREATMENT

Barrie Piland

INTRODUCTION

With the growing size of the elderly population, and the enactment of Medicare legislation
in 1965, increasing attention has been paid
to health care among the elderly. The relatively slow development of geriatric medicine
as a specialization, however, underscores the
need to closely examine the unique physiological changes associated with old age in order
to provide the best and most appropriate medical care possible. In no instance is that
more true than in the case of psychiatric care,
especially when psychoactive drugs are used
as a form of treatment. The potential for
inappropriate use of psychoactive drugs
among elderly patients rests on two primary
bases: 1) diagnoses of psychiatric symptoms
that fail to take into account the unique physiological, psychological, and sociological characteristics of the older person may lead to
improper use of psychoactive drugs; and 2)
even when diagnoses are appropriate, the
prescribing of psychoactive drugs may not
adequately take into account the interaction
between the drug and the altered metabolic
capacities of the older person.

This chapter presents a description of some
of the major physiologic and psychologic
changes which accompany the aging process
and affect the employment of psychoactive
(psychotropic) agents in the geriatric population. It provides a review of current therapeutic uses and utilization of psychoactive
drugs in the treatment of mental illnesses or
emotional disturbances occurring in the elderly. It also reviews some physical changes

that contribute to emotional problems in the
aged.

A major focus is on the differences in psychoactive drug dosages required by the elderly
population relative to younger age groups.
Some important drug interaction effects are
also reviewed. It is beyond the scope of this
paper to discuss modes of therapy which are
employed either concurrently with or alternative to psychoactive drug use.

The substantive portion of the paper is organized into three sections. The first section
presents a discussion of how the aging process can alter the body's ability to process
and utilize various psychoactive drugs. The
second section is devoted to the use of psychoactive agents in the treatment of anxiety,
insomnia, depression, and physiologically
based psychosis in the elderly. The third
section provides a summary.

THE AGING PROCESS AND DRUG USE

The aging process produces alterations in
the human system which affect the absorption,
transport, tissue localization, metabolism, and
excretion of drugs. These physiologic changes
do not occur uniformly in persons of the same
chronologic age; they vary according to the
number and severity of chronic diseases and
pathological processes present in each individual (Salzman and Shader 1974). Therefore,
both biologic and chronologic age are important considerations when administering drugs
to the elderly person (Lenhart 1976). In
addition, previous use of a variety of drugs

may cause a predisposition to adverse drug reactions over a long lifetime. Because of the above factors, response to treatment with drugs actually becomes more diverse with increasing age (Lamy 1974). Despite the heterogeneity found in the elderly population, however, certain changes are predictable in kind, if not in degree, and have their effects on the quantity and duration of drug available at the receptor site (Holloway 1974).

The central nervous system, which serves as the receptor site for psychotropic agents, is known to be the most sensitive in terms of age-related altered responses to drug agents. In addition to the accumulation of pigment, decreases in nitrogen and phosphorous, and increases in sulfur and lipids, the aging brain undergoes a loss of neurons which varies according to phylogenetic area. Resultant disturbances in interaction and balance among the various cerebral centers lead to deterioration in integrated brain functions. This unequal rate of neuron loss is primarily responsible for the altered reactivity and sensitivity of the aged brain. Paradoxical or abnormal reactions to drugs stem from an impaired central nervous system. It is known, for instance, that in elderly patients the action of stimulants is lessened whereas the action of depressants is enhanced (Holloway 1974; Lamy 1974; Bender 1974; Salzman et al. 1976; Salzman and Shader 1974).

The sedative effect of many psychotropic agents is also more pronounced in older than in younger persons. This is probably due to increased central nervous system sensitivity, to decreased brain capacity, or both (Salzman and Shader 1974). When fewer active cells are present to act as receptors, the dose per milligram of active tissue is increased, presenting difficulties in determining the amount of drug being absorbed and utilized (Lenhart 1976). The aging central nervous system is also especially vulnerable to cerebral hypoxia resulting from hypotension and vascular disease (Holloway 1974). Oxygen consumption, a measure of cerebral metabolism, decreases with age and is probably the result of arteriosclerosis (Salzman and Shader 1974). With increasing age there is an accompanying decrease in total systemic perfusion. A reduction in cerebral blood flow occurs normally with aging but is quite pronounced in the cerebral arteriosclerotic individual (Holloway 1974). A wide variation in the clinical effect of psychotropic drugs stems from alterations in cerebral metabolism (Salzman and Shader 1974).

Venous congestion in elderly patients, due to reduced cardiac reserves, reduced cardiac output, and frequently diminished vascular elasticity associated with local atherosclerosis, serves to increase the circulation time of drugs, thus impairing their distribution and often delaying their excretion. Diminished cardiac output causes blood flow redistribution to the cerebral and coronary circulation at the expense of peripheral flow to the kidney and liver (Lenhart 1976; Salzman and Shader 1974; Baker 1974; Bender 1974).

A diminished arterial flow can hamper absorption of orally administered agents by reducing the number of available active cells, thus causing a reduction in the size of the absorbing surface. It also reduces the availability of enzymes necessary for maintaining transport mechanisms in the gastrointestinal tract. In this manner passive absorption across the intestinal epithelial membrane is reduced (Stotsky 1970; Bender 1974). Other factors related to the aging process also interfere with absorption. The reduction in mainly intracellular fluid volume, due to generalized loss of body weight, may alter absorption because of the accompanying increased sodium and decreased potassium levels (Lenhart 1976). The diminished acidity of gastric juice affects the degree of solubility and state of ionization of drugs, and a slowed stomach emptying time influences the rate at which drugs absorbed mainly from the intestine are made available to the duodenum (Holloway 1974; Lamy 1974).

Drug action is also affected by changes in blood components. Serum albumin levels frequently decline in the elderly so that protein-bound drugs are forced to compete for binding sites. This increases the ratio of free to bound drugs and results in enhanced drug toxicity. Both benzodiazepine antianxiety agents and tricyclic antidepressants are enhanced in this manner (Salzman and Shader 1974; Salzman et al. 1976; Lamy 1974).

Aging is accompanied by the replacement of functional tissue by fat, varying in increase from 18 to 36 percent in men and from 33 to 48 percent in women from age 18 to 35 years old. Psychotropic agents, which are mainly highly lipid soluble compounds, tend to be drawn by and subsequently to become localized in body fats. As mentioned above, central nervous system tissue increases in lipids with aging. Storage of lipid soluble drugs results either in their decreased intensity or increased duration of effect before they slowly return to circulation (Holloway 1974; Lenhart 1976; Stotsky 1970).

Unlike drugs of low lipid solubility, which are promptly excreted through a kidney with healthy glomerular filtration, the highly lipid soluble agents must be reabsorbed by the renal tubule and then converted to less lipid soluble metabolites (Bender 1974). Most psychotropic agents are converted to water-soluble compounds, often in the form of a glucuronide or sulfate conjugate, before excretion by the kidneys or other organs (Friedel and Raskind 1976). The rate at which this process occurs is another major determinant of the duration of activity such drugs have through the regulation of the serum or plasma level of these agents (Stotsky 1970). This biotransformation procedure is centered in the microsomal fraction of the liver cells and is dependent upon the level of enzyme activity in this area. Evidence strongly suggests that there is a varying reduction in microsomal metabolism with increasing age. Either because of a decrease in the rate of synthesis or because of an alteration in enzyme structure, the activities of several circulating enzymes, such as cholinesterase, are diminished (Lamy 1974; Lenhart 1976).

The aging kidney experiences reductions in renal blood flow, glomerular filtration, and tubular secretory capacity. The functional decrement may range from 20 percent to 50 percent in relatively healthy older persons, and only a few persons 70 years and older are without some degree of renal pathology. Diminished hepatic and renal function can each prolong the plasma half-life of drugs with a resultant increasing risk of drug toxicity and drug interactions (Lamy and Vestal 1976; Bender 1974; Lamy 1974).

Homeostatic capability declines with increasing age. The adjustments of secondary systems and their effect on drug activity are diminished and only a small change is needed to create disequilibrium in one or several processes. The aged population's impaired capacity to handle orthostatic stress, for example, can be further taxed by the administration of phenothiazines and antidepressants. Postural hypotension is very often the result (Bender 1974; Baker 1974; Holloway 1974). Abnormal chain or paradoxical drug reactions can stem from an impaired reserve capacity of tissues that are less able to withstand temperature changes as well as fluid and electrolyte loss (Lenhart 1976; Baker 1974).

Generally, the combined effects of aging on the various systemic functions act to slow down or impair the body's processing of psychotropic drugs; accordingly, these agents have a prolonged action time before they are eliminated from the system, although the degree of variation differs among individuals. Also, the wastage of muscle tissue and subsequent fat substitution which accompanies aging results in a decrease in total body volume. Both factors indicate the necessity for

lower dosage levels (Hall 1975; Baker 1974; Freeman 1974).

Finally, the practice of polypharmacy in treating elderly patients is common and is brought about by multiple pathologic conditions occurring with a myriad of symptoms. However, this practice may invite an increase in adverse drug reactions as well as decreased compliance (Davison 1975).

In summary, changes in the central nervous system, arterial and venous flow, blood components, the ratio of functional tissue to fat, renal flow, and homeostatic capability can have significant effects on the metabolism and elimination of drugs in elderly patients. The specific nature of the effects those factors may have will depend upon the characteristics of individual drugs, drug groups, and drug combinations.

DRUG TREATMENT OF EMOTIONAL DISTURBANCES OR MENTAL ILLNESS

DRUG TREATMENT OF ANXIETY

Anxiety is a common reaction to the various problems and dilemmas accompanying the aging process and may coexist with feelings of depression. Anxiety may be manifested in hypochondriasis or it may be the cause of agitated or hostile, aggressive behavior. A chronically anxious state can add to the severity of depression, insomnia, and behavioral reactions as well as have a worsening effect upon concurrent physical disease states (Lifshitz and Kline 1970).

Antianxiety agents, such as minor tranquilizers or anxiolytics are a group of chemically heterogeneous compounds that produce similar clinical effects and that possess, in varying degrees and frequently in combination, anxiety-relieving, sedative, and skeletal muscle-relaxant properties (Fann et al. 1976; Markoff et al. 1974). It should be noted that hypnotics, or sleep-producing agents, are to a considerable degree interchangeable with antianxiety agents in their effect, depending on dosage level. They share the pharmacological property of central nervous system depression whereby progressively larger doses, the amount varying from agent to agent, can lead to drowsiness, sleep, and finally a coma state (Greenblatt and Shader 1974a).

Although not ideal agents, the benzodiazepine derivatives are considered the most effective of all currently available anxiolytics (i.e., anxiety-reducing agents) for both young and old patients and have replaced barbiturates and the propanediols (e.g., meprobamate and tybamate) as the antianxiety agents of choice. Chlordiazepoxide (Librium), diazepam (Valium), and oxazepam (Serax) are the most frequently used benzodiazepines (Markoff et al. 1974; Greenblatt and Shader 1974b; Salzman et al. 1976). Each of the derivatives possesses, in varying degrees, anticonvulsant, sedative-hypnotic, anxiolytic, and muscle-relaxant effects (Ayd 1975). They have moderate addiction potential, and overdoses usually do not result in serious poisoning. When used to treat anxiety they are less apt to cause undesired drowsiness than equivalent doses of either barbiturates or meprobamate (Greenblatt and Shader 1974a). However, elderly persons are more susceptible to their sedative side effects (Salzman et al. 1976). Another advantage of the benzodiazepine derivatives is that, unlike barbiturates, they do not alter the blood levels of concomitantly administered tricyclic agents, which are sometimes needed during initial treatment of endogenous depression (Shader 1976). Certain side effects that accompany central nervous system depression are more dangerous for elderly persons. Muscle weakness and ataxia are especially threatening to a population more predisposed to falls. Dysarthria (difficulties in speech articulation) may also occur. Older persons are also more vulnerable to a paradoxical reaction associated with the use of Librium, sometimes referred to as "Librium rage." As the name suggest, irritability and hostility are somehow increased (Lenhart 1976; Appleton 1976). Diazepam may have the strongest antidepressant effect of these agents, at least for elderly males with mild anxious depressions (Salzman et al. 1976; Fann and Wheless 1975). Fairly recent findings about oxazepam suggest that it may offer unique benefits to the elderly population. It, unlike chlordiazepoxide and diazepam, is rapidly biotransformed to an inactive product, and because it does not accumulate and build up toxic effects, it is the more appropriate drug choice for chronic therapy (Greenblatt and Shader 1974a; Merlis and Koepke 1975).

The use of antihistamines, such as hydroxyzine (Vistaril, Atarax), as either antianxiety agents or as hypnotics, particularly in elderly patients, is inadvisable. These agents, metabolized by the liver, have anticholinergic effects that can produce the already described symptoms of atropine-like toxicity. Their nonspecific sedative effects are only a secondary pharmacologic property (Greenblatt and Shader 1975; Greenblatt and Miller 1974; Modell 1974). The propanediols, such as meprobamate (Miltown) and tybamate (Tybatran), are another group with questionable efficacy and safety in the control of anxiety. Meprobamate usage can easily lead to addiction, and overdoses can cause serious poisoning (Greenblatt and Shader 1974b).

Barbiturates are a poor drug choice when an antianxiety effect is needed. Their efficacy in this area is highly variable and often inadequate as their effect is to produce a general central nervous system depression which has little focus on anxiety (Greenblatt and Shader 1974a).

DRUG TREATMENT OF INSOMNIA

Insomnia, a very common complaint of elderly patients, is typified by symptoms such as increased time required to fall asleep, frequent nightly awakenings, increased frequency of dreaming, lighter sleep, and an increase in total bed time with an accompanying decrease in total sleep time. Findings of all-night electroencephalographic recordings support the notion that stages of deep sleep diminish steadily in their intensity with advancing age (Amin 1976). Oxazepam, because of characteristics described earlier, is thought by some to be helpful for complaints centering around restlessness at night and/or early morning awakening; it is rapidly absorbed and has a relatively short duration of action. Use of oxazepam is contraindicated in cases where patients have been chronic barbiturate or other soporific users since previous experience with those drugs diminishes the effectiveness of ordinary doses of oxazepam (Ayd 1975). Dosage levels are best administered in accordance with the tolerance of each individual patient.

Barbiturates have serious limitations when used as hypnotics for elderly patients. Habituation and addiction can easily occur at doses only slightly higher than prescribed, and intentional or unintentional overdose can easily cause deep coma and death. Through possible depression of folic acid and vitamin B-12 levels, they may cause depression, toxic psychosis, and apparent dementia. Their use is contraindicated during pneumonias or cerebrovascular episodes due to their depressant effect on vital brainstem centers. Their tendency to accumulate and produce toxic delirium makes them a poor choice for patients with impaired renal function (Greenblatt and Shader 1974a; Morrant 1975; Dawson-Butterworth 1970). All barbiturates, but especially phenobarbital, accelerate liver microsomal metabolism of drugs (such as certain of the antipsychotic phenothiazines, the tricyclic antidepressants, warfarin, coumarin, and diphenylhydantoin), resulting in a lowering of their clinical effects (Fann 1976; Ayd 1975).

The piperidinedione hypnotics, glutethimide (Doriden) and methyprylon (Noludar), are similar to barbiturates in chemical structure and should also be avoided; glutethimide is likely to cause cerebellar signs and osteomalacia due to vitamin D deficiency, as well as being extremely difficult to treat in overdose situations (Morrant 1975; Dawson-Butterworth 1970). It also accelerates liver microsomal metabolism, and addiction can easily occur (Greenblatt and Miller 1974). Barbiturates, glutethimide, and methyprylon are potent REM depressors, and withdrawal may lead to REM rebound with intensified insomnia and nightmares. REM rebound in elderly patients is particularly undesirable, since anginal attacks and cardiac arrhythmias, as well as confusional episodes with vivid hallucinations, occur with greater frequency during REM sleep. Patients experiencing REM rebound symptoms may return to drug use as a source of relief and in this manner build up dependency (Modell 1974; Amin 1976; Greenblatt and Miller 1974).

The quinazolone derivative methaqualone (Quaalude) also causes intense REM depression, as well as physiological addiction when administered in essentially therapeutic doses. Lately it has been recognized as a drug possessing strong abuse potential, and there is some evidence that it accelerates liver microsomal metabolism (Fann and Wheless 1975; Modell 1974; Greenblatt and Miller 1974).

Chloral hydrate, predecessor to the barbiturates and in use for over a century, does not appear to depress REM sleep, although some reports are conflicting. It acts fairly quickly with rapid metabolism in the liver as well as other tissues; therefore, it is only contraindicated in cases where renal or hepatic disease are marked and in patients with severe cardiac disease. This and other chloral derivatives are seldom abused or utilized in cases of intentional overdose, possibly because of their gastric irritant properties. These are the only hypnotics that can cause protein-binding displacement, leading to an increased concentration of the pharmacologically active unbound faction of the displaced drug. This results in a transient potentiation of the other protein-bound drugs. When a chloral derivative is concomitantly administered with warfarin or bishydroxycoumarin, transient excessive hypothrombinemia can occur. Similar interactions with drugs such as diphenylhydantoin, phenylbutazone, or imipramine could potentially occur but are as yet inadequately documented (de Groot 1974; Morrant 1975; Modell 1974; Greenblatt and Miller 1974).

The benzodiazepine flurazepam has little effect on REM sleep, and like chloral hydrate, only minimally accelerates liver microsomal metabolism. In terms of abuse and overdos-

age it may be the least hazardous of all the hypnotics. It does produce a reduction in slow-wave sleep, however. Insomnia associated with hyperthyroidism and uremia is accompanied by a reduction in slow-wave sleep, and flurazepam may further complicate this type of insomnia. It is possible that flurazepam could produce cumulative or residual clinical effects. Its major metabolite, which possesses significant central nervous system depressant activity, accumulates significantly and remains in the blood for several days after drug therapy termination (Amin 1976; Greenblatt and Miller 1974).

DRUG TREATMENT OF DEPRESSION

Depression, when appearing in older persons, shares many characteristics of the illness experienced by younger persons. In both old and young, depression has an episodic nature, a tendency to remit, and a potential for favorable immediate outcome (Prange 1973; Epstein 1976), although depression may vary in severity and duration. In cases of situational or reactive depression, a person may be responding to a temporary loss or rejection; the failure of the depressive syndrome to spontaneously remit after a year or more can be an indication of pathology (Greenblatt and Shader 1975). In cases of endogenous depression, the onset of depression may occur without obvious cause or sufficient basis to explain the severity of symptoms (Greenblatt and Shader 1975).

Depression in elderly patients is often misdiagnosed. Incontinence, confusion, disorientation, and apathy are symptoms in both senility and depression (Fann and Wheless 1975). Undernutrition, which can result from a depressed, apathetic state, is often the cause of a confusional state (Epstein 1976). A worsening depression can produce signs of retardation, memory defect, and cognitive impairment. Moderate to severe depressions, with minimal organic brain disease, are often misdiagnosed as chronic brain disease accompanying either cerebral arteriosclerosis or senile brain disease (Fann and Wheless 1975; Epstein 1976).

Depression in elderly patients may be unrecognized as well as misdiagnosed. The clinical picture for these patients more typically lacks the dramatic presentation of a younger depressed person. An air of apathy, inertia, introversion, self-deprecation, and unwillingness to communicate are often regarded as normal behavior for an elderly person. Even when depression is identified it is often thought of as a normal or realistic response to the physical and emotional stresses accompanying aging (Hodkinson 1975). Endogenous or manic-depressive disorders coinciding with chronic physical illness can be overlooked and left untreated in this manner (Epstein 1976).

Approximately 20 percent of the population 65 years and older suffers from some form of psychiatric disorder, and it is important to realize that functional disorders, whether precursors to chronic brain disease or not, predominate in those over age 70. The greater incidence of depression with advancing age is not surprising. The aged population suffers the loss or diminution of occupation, income, status, health, and loved ones at a time in life when adapting and coping abilities are also diminished due to cerebrophysiologic changes. Sociopsychologic changes which accompany advancing years constitute a more frequent exposure to depression-precipitating circumstances. The elderly person is called on to cope when recuperative ability, resilience, energy, and general homeostatic capacity are reduced. Reactive depressions to illness, bereavement, and other losses are common, but many older persons also have had a history of recurring depressive episodes throughout their life. Also, latent or existent neurotic conditions can be aggravated by old age (Fann and Wheless 1975).

From the above, it can be concluded that the depressed older individual can have a variety of symptoms emanating from a wide range of conditions and circumstances. Prompt treatment can be essential for elderly persons because the illness may be severe, prolonged, and likely to recur. The risk of suicide is considerable, and attempts by elderly. persons are often successful (Young 1972).

Treatment of depresion in elderly persons is generically similar to treatment of younger patients. Antidepressant drugs are the major treatment choice for moderate and severe depressions. Accurate diagnosis is essential for appropriate treatment choice. Endogenous depression may be manifest on a constant basis or it may be only one phase of a "bipolar" affective (manic-depressive) disease; psychomotor agitation and hyposomnia are characteristic of the former, while psychomotor retardation and hypersomnia characterize the latter (Greenblatt and Shader 1975; Shader 1976). Middle-aged or elderly patients with endogenous depression may have one or more of the following characteristics: prolonged or severe symptoms; a history of depressive episodes; a family history of similar symptomatology; no obvious precipitating cause; anorexia or weight loss; early morning awakening; and sexual disinterest or dysfunction (Greenblatt and Shader 1975). Prompt and energetic treatment of endogenously de-

pressed elderly patients is particularly imperative because the condition can last for 2 years or longer. It is also accompanied by a high suicide risk, potential malnutrition, and subsequent permanent memory impairment and the incurring of an acute confusional state (Kral 1976).

The tricyclic antidepressants currently are the preferred drug agents for treatment of endogenous depression, followed by the generally less effective and more toxic monoamine oxidase (MAO) inhibitors (Young 1972; Greenblatt and Shader 1975; Lifshitz and Kline 1970; Fann and Wheless 1975; Fann 1976; Markoff et al. 1974; Medical Letter on Drugs and Therapeutics 1975). The tricyclics have, since their introduction in 1958, retired the MAO inhibitors to a fairly minor role (Fann and Wheless 1975; Frazier 1976; Fann 1976). The tricyclics act to block the neuronal uptake into presynaptic nerve endings, thus having direct action on sympathomimetic amines in the brain (e.g., norepinephrine) and indirect action on catecholamine-releasing substances (e.g., tyramine). Although both the tricyclics and MAO inhibitors specifically act on the biology of amines, the former has little inhibitory effect on monoamine oxidase (Frazier 1976). A wide variety of tricyclics are currently available in the United States. Some are nonsedating, such as protriptyline, imipramine, desipramine, and nortriptyline, and are more appropriate for treating retarded or withdrawn depressions characterized by hypoactivity and hypomentation. Those with a sedative effect, such as amitriptyline or doxepin, are more therapeutically appropriate for treating agitated or hyperactive depressive states (Fann and Wheless 1975; Fann 1976; Hollister 1976). With the exception of protriptyline, which acts as a stimulating drug, all possess anxiolytic properties which are of great help when endogenous depression is accompanied by anxiety. Excepting the more potent protriptyline and nortriptyline, all possess about equal potency on a milligram basis and a narrower, barely threefold, dose range, compared to the larger ranges of other psychotropic drugs (Prange 1973). There is considerable lag time, usually from 1 to several weeks, before tricyclic antidepressants attain a sufficient blood level for therapeutic results (Fann 1976; Greenblatt and Shader 1975; Fann et al. 1976). The lag time can be interpreted as a serious drawback in the treatment of extremely depressed, strongly suicidal patients (Fann 1976; Hollister 1976). Attempts to shorten this period through simultaneous administration of stimulant compounds or thyroid hormones and androgenic agents, as well as parenteral administration (i.e., of amitriptyline and imipramine), are either considered not promising for a routine practice or evidence is indeterminate concerning their effectiveness.

It is generally recommended that dosage levels of tricyclic antidepressants begin at a lower level and increase at a more gradual rate when administered to elderly persons (Fann 1976). However, a strictly rigid adherence to this recommendation could sometimes prevent older patients from receiving a sufficiently high, yet still tolerated therapeutic level (Prange 1973). Genetic differences in the ability to concentrate tricyclics do exist and it is wise to routinely monitor patient blood levels (Frazier 1976). Prescription amounts of tricyclics should never exceed roughly a week's supply at one time, as overdoses are often fatal. Elderly patients deemed suicidal or forgetful should not be allowed to self-administer these agents (Hollister 1976; Schmidt 1974). The affinity of tricyclics for tissue and plasma proteins makes them nearly impossible to dialyze in emergency situations (Frazier 1976).

The potential side effects of the tricyclics are numerous. They, along with all antipsychotic agents as well as antiparkinsonian drugs, possess anticholinergic properties which can produce atropine-like effects, among these a central anticholinergic confusional reaction which occurs more commonly in elderly patients. Symptoms are a marked disturbance of short-term memory, disorientation, impaired attention, anxiety, and visual and auditory hallucination (Davis 1974; Hollister 1976). This deliriform psychotic state is often mistakenly interpreted as an increase in psychiatric symptoms, and dosage levels are elevated still further (Fann 1976). The elderly, due to a diminution of liver metabolism rates, are particularly vulnerable to peripheral anticholinergic effects as well (Prange 1973). A dry mouth, often considered the least dangerous atropine effect, can cause problems with dentures, can increase the wearing away of the gingiva and natural teeth, and if severe enough can cause acute parotitis. Another effect, the inhibition of bowel motility, can lead to constipation, followed by fecal impaction and paralytic ileus. Micturition can easily develop into acute retention of the urine, and both urinary and bowel problems can worsen anxiety in compulsive patients. Paralysis of visual accommodation can aggravate unsuspected and untreated cases of narrow-angle glaucoma. These drugs are particularly hazardous in patients with a history of seizures, urinary retention, prostatic hypertrophy, increased intraocular pressure, narrow-angle glaucoma, or intestinal obstruction (Greenblatt and Shader 1975; Fann 1976; Morrant 1975; Schmidt 1974; Hodkinson 1975). Mydriasis as well as tachycardia can

also occur (Medical Letter on Drugs and Therapeutics 1975). Dryness of the mouth, along with two other common side effects, drowsiness and blurred vision, seems to wear off relatively soon after treatment initiation (Schmidt 1974). It is worth mentioning that the sedating antidepressants as well as the antipsychotics can indirectly cause bronchopneumonia in elderly patients by causing upright motionless daytime dozing with resultant decrease in respiratory efficiency (Morrant 1975).

When tricyclics are first administered they also exert a hypotensive effect, causing a danger of orthostatic hypotensive episodes which can easily lead to falls and subsequent injuries in frail older patients. Particularly when cerebral or myocardial ischemia is present, a sudden drop in blood pressure can produce serious infarctive lesions (Young 1972; Fann 1976; Morrant 1975). Great caution must be used in administering tricyclics to such patients, and especially to those with a history of arrhythmias. Tricyclics are known to produce changes in the EKG, such as a lengthened Q-T interval and the production of prominent U-waves. Thus ventricular repolarization is prolonged and the falling of a ventricular premature contraction on this extended period may set off ventricular tachyarrhythmias. Evidence exists that death from arrhythmias can occur in overdose situations involving patients with cardiac disease. The use of these drugs only rarely precipitates congestive heart failure and cardiomyopathy. All patients with any preexisting cardiac disease or abnormalities should be given a base-line electrocardiogram before tricyclic administration is begun and elderly patients in particular should be carefully screened (Lutz and Wayne 1976; Hollister 1976). Parkinsonian syndrome manifestations such as tremor or akathisia (inability to sit still) can develop on high dosage levels of tricyclics. The best treatment is to lower the dosage level (Morrant 1975; Prange 1973). All major side effects of the tricyclics can be relieved by terminating their use (Schmidt 1974).

Patients on tricyclics who are taking antihypertensives such as guanethidine (Ismelin) and bethanidine, which block the adrenergic neuron, will experience a reversal of the antihypertensive effect 12 hours or more after tricyclic administration (Morrant 1975; Davis et al. 1973; Fann 1976; Fann 1973; Greenblatt and Shader 1975). The norepinephrine pump in the adrenogenic neuron membrane is blocked by the tricyclics so that guanethidine is not carried to its active site within the neuron. Although all tricyclics at least partially antagonize this agent, some evidence suggests that doxepin may do so only minimally. Because the antihypertensive agent methyldopa (Aldomet) does not utilize the norepinephrine pump for transport to the neuron, its activity is not affected by the tricyclic compounds (De Groot 1974; Prange 1973; Greenblatt and Shader 1975).

The activity of tricyclics is potentiated by thyroid hormone and by the enzyme inhibitor methylphenidate, the latter inhibiting microsomal enzymes and thereby slowing tricyclic metabolism with a resultant rise in tricyclic blood levels. Recently these combinations have been used to enhance the effect of tricyclics, but their efficacy and safety is still questionable. Secobarbital induces enzymes, with a resultant lowering of tricyclic blood levels. Major tranquilizers and estrogens also inhibit metabolism. Results from studies on how tricyclic drugs alter the metabolism of other agents are contradictory and inconclusive (Shader 1976; Greenblatt and Shader 1975; Frazier 1976). However, pertaining to their effects on absorption, it is known that by reducing gastrointestinal motility they delay or reduce the absorption of phenylbutazone and levadopa. Both the tricyclics and the antipsychotic agents called phenothiazines increase their own absorption by decreasing gut motility. Through their slowdown of the gastric emptying process they may, in turn, enhance the absorption of digoxin (Hall 1975; MacLennan 1974; Greenblatt and Shader 1975).

It should be noted that in the case of severely agitated or markedly paranoid depressed patients, or those with suspected schizophrenia, it may be necessary to treat with a tricyclic and an antipsychotic drug combination (Schmidt 1974). One of the phenothiazines, thioxanthenes, or butyrophenones is appropriate but must be used with extreme caution due to the combined anitcholinergic properties of these drugs (Fann and Wheless 1975; Kral 1976; Schmidt 1974). Amitriptyline and perphenazine are the most commonly prescribed combination for this purpose (Shader 1976).

The MAO inhibitors, e.g., isocarboxazid, pargyline, phenelzine, and trancylcypromine, although seldom the initial treatment choice for elderly patients, are sometimes successful in severe depressions where treatment with tricyclics has failed to gain desired results (Fann 1976; Frazier 1976; Webb 1971; Kline 1974). These agents increase norepinephrine at the receptor site by blocking its intracellular degradation (Appleton 1976). The correlation between a decrease in MAO levels and antidepressant effects as well as the finding that brain MAO activity increases with age are indicators of the efficacy these drugs possess for certain elderly patients (Fann

and Wheless 1975; Fann et al. 1976; Nies et al. 1973).

The changeover from a tricyclic to an MAO inhibitor should be made only after a 10- to 14-day drug-free interval (Prange 1973; Webb 1971; Schmidt 1974). Concurrent use of the two drug classes is not recommended, although there is some dispute over the reliability of evidence supporting their enhancement of each other's toxicity. However, hyperpyretic crises (high fevers), severe convulsions, and death have been reported as a result of this combination (Greenblatt and Shader 1975; Schmidt 1974; Medical Letter on Drugs and Therapeutics 1975). A lag time before onset of therapeutic action also seems to occur with these agents--although its existence is not uniformly accepted. Patients displaying psychomotor retardation particularly benefit from these drugs. However, immediately after treatment onset, the anxiety of a more agitated patient may either be increased or go unrelieved (Fann 1976; Markoff 1974; Kral 1976).

The potential side effects and the necessary precautions involved with the administering of MAO inhibitors are numerous. Among the possible side effects are anxiety, agitation, manic symptoms, worsening of psychotic episodes, constipation, edema, nausea, diarrhea, abdominal pain, weakness, drowsiness, tachycardia, blurred vision, impotence, chills, and headaches (Fann and Wheless 1975). These agents may block cardiovascular response, increasing the exercise tolerance of patients with angina pectoris and myocardial insufficiency to the point, if unwarned, of risking myocardial infarction (Webb 1971). Hypotension is also a frequent problem, and use of these drugs can lead to hepatocellular damage as well (Appleton 1976; Medical Letter on Drugs and Therapeutics 1975; Webb 1971; Kral 1976).

MAO inhibitors offer further disadvantages. They are interactively toxic with numerous other drugs and with certain foodstuffs as well. They potentiate the action of anesthetics, barbiturates, adrenal corticosteroids, ganglion-blocking agents, morphine, atropine, and 4-amino-quinoline compounds. The antidepressant and hypotensive effects of MAO inhibitors are, in turn, potentiated by diuretics (Fann and Wheless 1975). The use of sympathomimetic amines, which are common ingredients of over-the-counter cold and sinus drugs as well as analgesics, is contraindicated. MAO inhibitors potentiate pressor amines so that a severe to fatal hypertensive crisis can occur. Another such pressor agent, tyramine, which releases endogenous sympathetic amines, is also potentiated. It is found in a wide range of foods whose consumption is contraindicated, such as cheese, chicken liver, avocado, meat extracts, beer, sherry, or Chianti (Lifshitz 1970; Throne 1974; Fann 1973). Older persons, besides having a greater likelihood of being somewhat hypertense, are apt to have a more difficult time remembering and observing all the precautions and restrictions that accompany therapy with MAO inhibitors (Young 1972). Also it is more likely that elderly patients will be taking one or more of the contraindicated medications (Lifshitz and Kline 1970). A further complication is that, unlike the tricyclics, side effects occurring with MAO inhibitor therapy may be long lasting, and harmful interactions with other drugs or foodstuffs are still possible as long as 2 weeks after treatment termination (Medical Letter on Drugs and Therapeutics 1975; Appleton 1976).

Clinically derived estimates of the incidence of mania in the aged population vary considerably. One study estimates that this disorder comprises only 0.6 percent of the functional disorders found in this population while another refers to recurrent manic or manic-depressive episodes as a syndrome frequently encountered in this age group (Prange 1973; Davis et al. 1973).

Lithium carbonate has been used since 1949 in the treatment of cyclic affective disorders and the consensus seems to be that it is prophylactic in recurrent bipolar depressions for both manic and depressive phases (Young 1972; Medical Letter on Drugs and Therapeutics 1975; Davis et al. 1973; Markoff 1974; Schmidt 1974). However, there is a diversity of opinion regarding its effectiveness in treating acute mania attacks (Markoff 1974; Young 1972; Davis et al. 1973; Appleton 1976). Its successful treatment of the depressed phase may often require the concomitant administration of a tricyclic drug (Shader 1976; Hollister 1976; Frazier 1976). Here, too, there is conjecture about its efficacy in the actual treatment of acute depressive episodes (Appleton 1976; Schmidt 1974). Some evidence points to the usefulness of lithium as a prophylactic for endogenous depressions (Fann 1976).

Two major contraindications to the long-term, prophylactic use of lithium are the presence of renal disease and cardiac insufficiency, which occur with great frequency in elderly patients (Young 1972). Rapid salt depletion during lithium treatment can cause gastrointestinal, central nervous system, and neuromuscular toxicity. Therefore, diuretic therapy, required for several concurrent conditions occurring in elderly patients, is contraindicated. The half-life of lithium is considerably longer in elderly patients, so

that smaller dosage levels are sufficient to build up an adequate therapeutic blood level. Lithium toxicity and an accompanying confusional syndrome can occur at lower blood levels in the elderly patient. Careful and continuous monitoring of blood levels is particularly important when the outpatient is elderly as the earlier signs of toxicity can be passed off by family and neighbors as lapses to be expected with old age (Fann 1976; Schmidt 1974; Davis et al. 1973; Fann 1973).

Finally, the use of stimulant compounds as antidepressants has not met with great success, and these are especially dangerous when administered to elderly patients. Their cardiovascular effects, including increased blood pressure and tachycardia, are particularly dangerous in cases where cardiovascular function is compromised and there is an increased vulnerability to cerebrovascular accidents. Generally, their mood-elevating effect is quite often followed by a depression which is more severe than the original one (Fann and Wheless 1975).

TREATMENT OF PHYSIOLOGICALLY
BASED PSYCHOSES

A broad, heterogeneous group of psychotic conditions, consisting of varying psychopathologies, are known to occur in the aged population (Friedel and Raskind 1976). Organic brain syndrome manifestations, for example, appear in approximately 16 percent of persons aged 65 and over. There are two forms of the disease. Senile psychosis, or dementia, is causally related to organic disease of the nerve cells. Arteriosclerotic psychosis, or dementia, is associated with focal indications of cerebrovascular disease.

The latter condition is present in about one-third of the organic brain syndromes which occur in elderly persons. It acts as a major contributor to pathologic conditions in only 10 percent of the above (Hollister 1975; Fann 1976). Unlike senile psychosis, cerebral arteriosclerosis often occurs before age 65. It is only infrequently found in patients younger than age 55. The condition produces pathological changes in the form of small infarcts. These can appear as glial proliferation with only patches of scarring, or a number of small pseudocysts can be produced which give a Swiss cheese appearance to a "brain slice" (Hollister 1975). Onset is said to be more abrupt than senile psychosis, although headaches, dizziness, and fainting spells are often part of the patient's history in the months preceding onset (Prien 1972). An increase in stressful conditions may cause a sudden appearance of symptoms. The illness fluctuates in severity, sometimes changing in a matter of hours, and is accompanied by emotional lability and/or epileptiform seizures and also sleep disturbances. Its variability is probably due to changes in circulation. Since insight usually remains intact, the patient is often acutely depressed or anxious about his mental deterioration. As the illness worsens, the more subtle or complex aspects of personality tend to be destroyed and memory, intellectual function, and judgment-making ability progressively decline. About 20 percent of cases develop paranoid syndromes. Death, usually a result of cerebrovascular accident, myocardial infarction, or infection, may not occur until years after disease onset and several periods of improvement and decline (Fann et al. 1974; Prien 1972; Fann 1976; Whanger 1973).

Senile dementia normally occurs in the seventh to ninth decades and strikes women more frequently than men (Fann 1976). Two types of nerve cell lesion can occur: senile plaques, or clusters of enlarged, abnormal nerve fibers and synaptic endings, and the neurofibrillary tangles of Alzheimer, made up of twisted intraneuronal fibers (Hollister 1975). The latter is most often associated with presenile, i.e., before 60, dementia (Prien 1972). The etiology of senile dementia is unknown (Hollister 1975). Vague feelings of anxiety and depression frequently precede its onset, which is often insidious and marked by a progressive loss of memory for recent events. Depression tends to fluctuate and then disappear as the dementing process takes hold. Memory failure is accompanied by intellectual impairment, disorientation, and poor judgment (Prien 1972). The early stages may be somewhat indistinguishable from the normal aging process. However, deterioration subsequently proves to be more rapid and profound and is accompanied by higher mortality (Fann 1976). Unsteady gait, muscular weakness, fatigue, and speech disturbance may develop. Paranoid reactions may occur in 15 to 20 percent of cases. Prognosis is usually poor. Diffuse pathological changes occur over a number of years, leading to a total disorganization and degradation of behavior which requires institutional care. Heart failure or pneumonia are common cause of death (Prien 1972; Fann 1976).

A combination of these syndromes occurs in over 20 percent of cases. Paranoid behavior manifests in 35 percent of patients with dual pathologies. It should be noted that the patient's psychological makeup determines the nature of any secondary reaction to mental impairment accompanying either of these conditions. Depression or agitation, withdrawal, strong persecutory and expansive reactions, or the absence of any marked response are all possible behavioral patterns (Fann et al. 1974; Whanger 1973; Prien 1972).

Schizophrenia is another form of psychosis which occurs in elderly patients. Some patients may have been ill for several years preceding old age and are episodic psychotics, whereas onset in others occurs after age 65 (Davis 1974; Davis et al. 1973). The illness can be either functional or organic so that the later occurring type, often called late paraphrenia, can develop either as a consequence of organic brain syndrome in predisposed persons, or can occur independent of such deterioration. With this illness, an intact personality with well-organized paranoid delusions is frequently accompanied by symptoms of passivity or by classic auditory hallucinations, much like the clinical description of early onset schizophrenia (Fann 1976; Fann et al. 1974; Young 1972). Cases of schizophrenia developing after age 60 and independent of dementia comprise only 5 percent of all schizophrenic illness. Evidence suggests a possible hereditary predisposition. Patients are often healthy and able to ward off dementia. However, if the schizophrenic condition is left untreated, a prolonged course can be anticipated (Whanger 1973).

The treatment of psychoses in elderly patients involves use of the same antipsychotic agents commonly administered to younger patients. Numerous double blind studies offer sound evidence of their efficacy in treating geriatric patients (Davis et al. 1973; Davis 1974). However, starting doses should be reduced by one-third to one-half the amount given to young patients and dosage buildup should be more gradual (Prien and Caffey 1974). These agents are helpful in relieving symptoms such as agitation, violent and irrational behavior, and typical perceptual disturbances. They do not, however, alter the course of any underlying organic disorder. Their effect is achieved mainly through blockage of central adrenergic and dopaminergic synapses, resulting in a decrease in membrane excitability (De Groot 1974; Eisdorfer 1975).

The phenothiazine derivatives are by far the most commonly administered antipsychotic agents for relief of chronic brain syndrome and schizophrenic symptoms occurring in elderly persons (Prien 1972; Fann 1976; Friedel and Raskind 1976; Schmidt 1974; De Groot 1974). Although they exhibit a diversity of pharmacologic actions, they almost all share the ability to exert a calming effect without severely impairing motor function or forcing sleep on the patient. This is probably because their chief locus of action is the subcortical brain (Eisdorfer 1975). Exceptions are thioridazine and chlorpromazine which can produce drowsiness (Prien 1972). These agents are classified by chemical structure into three side chains; aliphatic derivatives, such as chlorpromazine (Thorazine); piperidine derivatives, such as thioridazine (Mellaril); and piperazine derivatives such as trifluoperazine (Stelazine) (Greenblattt and Shader 1974b).

Numerous side effects can accompany the use of these agents. All initially produce a degree of orthostatic hypotension (drop in blood pressure on standing up). But this effect is particularly strong with chlorpromazine and thioridazine. They are also more likely to provoke seizures and thioridazine, in high doses, can cause irreversible retinal damage stemming from segmentary retinopathy. Other possible dose-related side effects are jaundice, agranulocytosis, dermatitis, and photosensitivity. Epilepsy and mental depression may become potentiated, a drop in body temperature can occur, sometimes causing hypothermia in elderly patients, and cerebral anoxia may be exaggerated. These agents can also suppress thyroid function (Lamy 1974; Markoff et al. 1974; Holloway 1974; Greenblatt and Shader 1974b). Their possession of anticholinergic properties and resultant atropine-like symptoms are similar to the tricyclic antidepressants. Elderly organic brain syndrome patients are particularly vulnerable to the confusional state which can result from central nervous system toxicity (Friedel and Raskind 1976). Rare side effects, such as hepatic toxicity and blood dyscrasias, occur with greater frequency in elderly patients (Prien 1972; Webb 1971). Like the tricyclic antidepressants, phenothiazines are capable of producing a cardiomyopathy that is especially dangerous to patients with heart disease. Electrocardiographic abnormalities of a nonspecific, reversible, and perhaps benign nature, are produced by several of the phenothiazines. These alterations are disproportionately high with thioridazine. Cases of cardiac toxicity have been associated most often with this drug, and to a lesser degree with chlorpromazine. Excessive dosage levels of thioridazine have been suspected of causing supraventricular arrhythmias, conduction defects, and ventricular arrhythmias (Friedel and Raskind 1976; Prien 1972; Lutz 1976).

All antipsychotic agents can produce extrapyramidal side effects. Acutely or early in treatment, parkinsonism, acute dystonias, akinesias, and akathesias can occur. Later in treatment (usually years after initiation of therapy, but can also be a matter of months), tardive dyskinesia can develop. Half of patients over age 60 experience extrapyramidal side effects, and 90 percent occur during the first 10 weeks of treatment (Holloway

1974). They probably stem from blockage of dopamine receptor sites in the basal ganglia (Greenblatt and Shader 1974b). Thioridazine seems to cause relatively fewer of these symptoms. The piperazine derivatives are the most potent and activating phenothiazines, and also the most likely to cause extrapyramidal symptoms, in particular akathisia (Prien 1972). Patients with this condition feel unable to sit or stand still. Their motor restlessness is frequently mistaken for psychotic agitation, and dosage levels are increased when they should be lowered (Medical Letter on Drugs and Therapeutics 1975). Chlorpromazine, although particularly effective in controlling agitation and hyperactivity, incurs a greater risk of parkinsonian reactions such as tremors, muscle weakness, and rigidity (Prien 1972). This syndrome, the most commonly experienced extrapyramidal side effect in elderly patients, can occur in a mild form or else can be clinically indistinguishable from either postencephalitic or idiopathic parkinsonism. Antiparkinsonian medicines have often been administered to elderly users of antipsychotics as a prophylactic measure. This practice is unwise due to the combined anticholinergic action of these agents. Not all patients will develop this condition, and the surfacing of symptoms can serve as a guide for dosage mediation. When this condition emerges, drug dosage can be lowered and/or antiparkinsonian agents administered. Continued need of all medication should be reviewed periodically.

Tardive dyskinesia appears in a significant proportion of older patients, especially women, and most often emerges after years of treatment with antipsychotics. Sometimes it appears only after drug treatment has been withdrawn or drastically reduced. The condition consists of buccal-facial-mandibular and buccal-lingual movements along with involuntary choreiform limb and occasionally trunk movements. It can persist indefinitely or gradually remit, but does not progressively worsen after drug withdrawal or minimal dose administration. The etiology of this appears to be a denervation sensitization of dopramine receptor sites. Elderly persons with a history of treated psychosis are especially at risk because they may have received high doses over long periods of time. Persons with brain damage are also more vulnerable. Drug holidays are strongly recommended during long-term use of antipsychotics along with lowered doses of these agents as a way to minimize the build-up of these symptoms and to check for their presence (Fann 1976; Eisdorfer 1975; Medical Letter on Drugs and Therapeutics 1975). Elderly patients on these drugs over long periods of time should be examined regularly, especially the tongue area because this is usually the first sign of dys-kinetic movement.

It should be noted that the combining of vari-ous phenothiazines, such as the more potent piperazine derivatives with one of the aliphat-ics, has shown no convincing evidence of increased efficacy or lowered side effects. However, total dosage may be reduced in this manner. Certain other combinations of pheno-thiazines are contraindicated and may actually cancel therapeutic effects. When phenobar-bital is administered with a phenothiazine, it acts to accelerate its metabolism, resulting in a lowered serum level of the phenothiazine and a lessening of its clinical effect. Pheno-thiazines administered with tricyclic antide-pressants tend to bring about increased blood levels of both these agents. Although anti-cholinergic complications are increased by this combination, there is a possibility that their combined antagonistic dopaminergic prop-erties act to reduce extrapyramidal symptoms. Phenothiazines act in the same way as tricyclic antidepressants to block the action of certain antihypertensive agents (Fann 1973; Salzman et al. 1975).

Finally, it should be mentioned that long-acting injectable forms of fluphenazine, either the enanthate or decanoate ester, are cur-rently available in the United States. Flu-phenazine is one of the piperazines. Their advantage is that they need to be administered only once every 3 or 4 weeks so that, when necessary, there can be greater control over medication intake. This could be beneficial in the management of elderly outpatients who live alone. Their dosage level should be about half that administered to younger pa-tients. Drugs given in this manner are able to exert an antipsychotic effect at lower dos-age levels over equivalent periods of time. Their overall efficacy, however, is still open to debate. A high incidence of dystonic and depressant side effects has been reported along with a high incidence of extrapyramidal reactions with the enanthete form (Arie 1973; Prien and Caffey 1974).

SUMMARY

This paper reviews 1) some of the major phys-iologic changes attendant upon the aging proc-ess, that occur in varying degrees and affect an elderly person's ability to metabolize psy-choactive drugs, and 2) the efficacy of psy-choactive drug treatment of such emotional disturbances or mental illnesses as anxiety, insomnia, depression, and physiologically based psychosis found among aged persons.

The aging process produces physiologic alter-ations that affect the absorption, transport, tissue localization, metabolism, and excretion of drugs. There appear to be wide variations in the extent of these changes among the elderly; they vary according to the number and severity of chronic diseases and patho-logical processes present in the specific indi-vidual. The central nervous system is the most sensitive organ in terms of age-related response to psychoactive drugs. Changes in the various aging body systems that alter the central nervous system, the arterial and venous flow, blood components, renal flow, functional tissue, and homeostatic capability have significant effect on the ability of the elderly to metabolize and eliminate psychoac-tive drugs. Accurate diagnosis and prescrib-ing require that the patient's drug history and biologic and chronologic age be taken into account.

In drug treatment of anxiety in the elderly, the benzodiazepine derivatives (minor tran-quilizers)--although not ideal agents--are considered the most effective of currently available anxiety-reducing agents. Depending on dosage level, the hypnotics are interchange-able to a large degree with the anxiolytics. Barbiturates are a poor choice as anxiolytics, and antihistamines are inadvisable.

In the treatment of insomnia, the use of the benzodiazepine derivatives (oxazepam and flur-azepam), barbiturates, the piperidinedione hypnotics, and the quinazalone derivatives (methaqualone and chlorohydrate) were re-viewed. Particular caution in relation to bar-biturates, the piperidinedione hypnotics, and methaqualone was indicated, due to their REM depression characteristics, addictive potential, and tendency to accelerate liver microsomal metabolism.

Depression in the aged has characteristics common to that occurring in younger persons, and its treatment with antidepressant drugs is similar. However, diagnosis of depression in elderly patients requires special care, since many symptoms of depression are also charac-teristic of senility or the general difficulties of old age. The efficacy, actions, and side effects of the tricyclic antidepressants, mono-amine oxidase (MAO inhibitors), lithium car-bonate, and stimulants are reviewed. In general, it is recommended that dosages begin at lower levels and increase at a more gradual rate for the elderly than for younger persons, in order to prevent undesirable side effects.

Drug treatment of physiologically based psy-chosis, such as organic brain syndrome, and some schizophrenias, in the elderly is similar to that of younger persons, with the exception of dosage levels. Recommended beginning dosage levels of antipsychotic agents are one-half to two-thirds that of younger persons. The phenothiazine derivatives are the most commonly used agents and have the ability to have a calming effect, without severely impairing motor function or making patients sleepy. Nevertheless numerous side effects accompany their use. The long-acting piperazine, fluphenazine, has the advantage of requiring administration only once every 3 or 4 weeks, thus allowing greater control over the medication. Its overall efficacy remains in doubt however.

The use of psychoactive drugs in the treatment of emotional disturbance and mental illness in the elderly requires accurate diagnosis and both physician and patient awareness of the necessity to titrate dosages and the duration of administration according to the person's biologic and chronologic needs.

REFERENCES

Amin, M.M. Drug treatment of insomnia in old age. Psychopharmacological Bulletin, 12:52-54, 1976.

Appleton, W.S. Third psychoactive drug usage guide. Diseases of the Nervous System, 37:39-51, 1976.

Arie, T. Dementia in the elderly: Management. British Medical Journal, 4:602-604, 1973.

Ayd, F.J. Oxazepam: An overview. Diseases of the Nervous System, 36:14-16, 1975.

Baker, H.M. Drug therapy in geriatrics. Journal of the Indiana State Medical Association, 67: 171-174, 1974.

Bender, A.D. Pharmacodynamic principles of drug therapy in the aged. Journal of the American Geriatrics Society, 22:296-303, 1974.

Davis, J.M. Use of psychotropic drugs in geriatric patients. Journal of Geriatric Psychiatry, 7:145-159, 1974.

Davis, J.M.; Fann, W.E.; El-Yosef, M.K.; and Janowsky, D.S. Clinical problems in treating the aged with psychotropic drugs. In: Eisdorfer, C., and Fann, W.E., eds. Psychopharmacology and Aging. New York: Plenum Press, 1973.

Davison, W. Pitfalls to avoid in prescribing drugs for the elderly. Geriatrics, 30:157-158, 1975.

Dawson-Butterworth, K. The chemopsychotherapeutics of geriatric sedation. Journal of the American Geriatrics Society, 18:97-114, 1970.

De Groot, M.H.L. The clinical use of psychotherapeutic drugs in the elderly. Drugs, 8:132-138, 1974.

Eisdorfer, C. Observations on the psychopharmacology of the aged. Journal of the American Geriatrics Society, 23:53-57, 1975.

Epstein, L.J. Depression in the elderly. Journal of Gerontology, 31:278-282, 1976.

Fann, W.E. Interactions of psychotropic drugs in the elderly. Postgraduate Medicine, 3:182-186, 1973.

Fann, W.E. Pharmacotherapy in older depressed patients. Journal of Gerontology, 31:304-310, 1976.

Fann, W.E.; Carver, E.F.; and Richmann, B.W. Psychopharmacological treatment of disorders of senescence. North Carolina Medical Journal, 35:672-677, 1974.

Fann, W.E., and Wheless, J.C. Depression in elderly patients. Southern Medical Journal, 68: 468-473, 1975.

Fann, W.E.; Wheless, J.C.; and Richmann, B.W. Treating the aged with psychotropic drugs. The Gerontologist, 16:322-328, 1976.

Frazier, S.H. Changing patterns in the management of depression. Diseases of the Nervous System, 37:25-29, 1976.

Freeman, J.T. Some principles of medication in geriatrics. Journal of the American Geriatrics Society, 22:289-295, 1974.

Friedel, R.O., and Raskind, M.A. Psychopharmacology of Aging. Seattle: University of Washington, 1976.

Greenblatt, D.J., and Miller, R.R. Rational use of psychotropic drugs. I. Hypnotics. American Journal of Hospital Pharmacy, 31:990-995, 1974.

Greenblatt, D.J., and Shader, R.I. Rational use of psychotropic drugs. II. Antianxiety agents. Journal of the Maine Medical Association, 65:225-229, 1974a.

Greenblatt, D.J., and Shader, R.I. Rational use of psychotropic drugs. III. Major tranquilizers. American Journal of Hospital Therapy, 31:1226-1231, 1974b.

Greenblatt, D.J., and Shader, R.I. Rational use of psychotropic drugs. IV. Antidepressants. American Journal of Hospital Emergency, 32:59-64, 1975.

Hall, M.R.P. Use of drugs in elderly patient. New York State Journal of Medicine, 75:67-71, 1975.

Hodkinson, H.M. Psychological medicine--the elderly mind. British Medical Journal, 2:23-25, 1975.

Hollister, L.E. Drugs for mental disorders of old age. Journal of the American Medical Association, 234:195-198, 1975.

Hollister, L.E. Clinical use of tricyclic antidepressants. Diseases of the Nervous System, 37:17-21, 1976.

Holloway, D.A. Drug problems in the geriatric patient. Drug Intelligence and the Clinical Pharmacy, 8:632-642, 1974.

Kline, N.S. Antidepressant medications. Journal of the American Medical Association, 227:1158-1159, 1974.

Kral, V.A. An overview of psychopharmacology of old age. Psychopharmacological Bulletin, 12:51-52, 1976a.

Kral, V.A. Somatic therapies in older depressed patients. Journal of Gerontology, 31:311-313, 1976b.

Lamy, P.P. Geriatric drug therapy. Clinical Medicine, 81:52-57, 1974.

Lamy, P.P., and Vestal, R.E. Drug prescribing for the elderly. Hospital Practice, 111-118, 1976.

Lenhart, D.G. The use of medications in the elderly population. Nursing Clinics of North America, 11:135-143, 1976.

Lifshitz, K., and Kline, N.S. Psychopharmacology in geriatrics. In: Clark, W.G., and Del Guidice, J., eds. Principles of Psychopharmacology. New York: Academic Press, 1970.

Lutz, E.G., and Wayne, M.D. Cardiotoxic effects of psychotropic drugs. The Journal of the Medical Society of New Jersey, 73:105-112, 1976.

MacLennan, W.J. Drug interactions. Gerontologic Clinics, 16:18-23, 1974.

Markoff, R.A.; Kinzie, J.D.; Botticelli, M.G.; and Bolian, G.C. A simplified guide to the rational use of psychotropic drugs. Hawaii Medical Journal, 33:201-206, 1974.

Medical Letter on Drugs and Therapeutics. Antidepressant drugs. Medical Letter on Drugs and Therapeutics, 17:54-64, 1975.

Merlis, S., and Keopke, H.H. The use of oxazepam in elderly patients. Diseases of the Nervous System, 36:27-29, 1975.

Modell, W. Updating the sleeping pill. Geriatrics, 29:126-132, 1974.

Morrant, J.C.A. Neurological syndromes associated with antipsychotic drug use. Archives of General Psychiatry, 28:463-467, 1973.

Morrant, J.C.A. Medicines and mental illness in old age. Canadian Psychiatric Association Journal, 20:309-312, 1975.

Nies, A.; Robinson, D.S.; Davis, J.M.; and Ravaris, C.L. Changes in monoamine oxidase with aging. In: Eisdorfer, C., and Fann, W.E., eds. Psychopharmacology and Aging. New York: Plenum Press, 1973.

Prange, A.J. The use of antidepressant in the elderly patient. In: Eisdorfer, C., and Fann, W.E., eds. Psychopharmacology and Aging. New York: Plenum Press, 1973.

Prien, R.F. Chronic Organic Brain Syndrome--A Review of the Therapeutic Literature with Special Emphasis on Chemotherapy. Washington, D.C.: Veterans Administration, 1972.

Prien, R.F., and Caffey, E.M. Guidelines for Antipsychotic Drug Use. Research Report No. 95, Perry Point, Md.: Veterans Administration, 1974.

Salzman, C., and Shader, R.I. Psychopharmacology in the aged. Journal of Geriatric Psychiatry, 7:165-184, 1974.

Salzman, C.; Shader, R.I.; Bessel, A.; and van der Kolk, B.A. Clinical psychopharamcology and the elderly patient. New York State Journal of Medicine, 76:71-77, 1976.

Salzman, C.; Shader, R.I.; and Hartmats, J.S. Response of the elderly to psychotropic drugs: Predictable or idiosyncratic? Psychopharmacological Bulletin, 11:48-50, 1975.

Schmidt, C.W. Psychiatric problems of the aged. Journal of the American Society, 22:355-359, 1974.

Shader, R.I. Problems of polypharmacy in depression. Diseases of the Nervous System, 37:30-36, 1976.

Stotsky, B. Use of psychopharmacologic agents for geriatric patients. In: Shader, R.I., and Di Mascio, A., eds. Clinical Handbook of Psychopharmacology. New York: Science House, 1970.

Throne, M.L. The use of psychotropic agents in heart disease. Journal of the Medical Association of Georgia, 63:280-281, 1974.

Webb, W.L. The use of psychopharmacological drugs in the aged. Geriatrics, 26:95-103, 1971.

Whanger, A.D. Paranoid syndromes of the senium. In: Eisdorfer, C., and Fann, W.E., eds. Psychopharmacology and Aging. New York: Plenum Press, 1973.

Young, J.P.R. Acute psychiatric disturbances in the elderly and their treatment. British Journal of Clinical Practice, 26:513-516, 1972.

PATTERNS OF PSYCHOACTIVE DRUG USE AMONG
THE ELDERLY

Robert Prentice

INTRODUCTION

In 1970, people 65 years of age and over represented about 10 percent of the total U.S. population, and that figure is expected to climb to over 11 percent in the year 2000. By way of contrast, people 65 and over constituted only about 4 percent of the population in 1900 (American Health Care Association 1975). A large share of that increase can be attributed to improved health care in the earlier years, enabling more people to live into old age.

Older people as a group, however, still suffer from a highly disproportionate share of chronic illnesses (Manard 1975) and, largely as a result, they receive more medications than other age groups. While people 65 and over represent 10 percent of the total population, they receive over 25 percent of all prescriptions written (U.S. Senate Special Committee on Aging 1973).

An increasing share of all prescriptions is accounted for by psychoactive drugs, especially since the introduction of tranquilizers in the mid-1950s. In 1970, 214 million prescriptions for major and minor tranquilizers, antidepressants, stimulants, sedatives, and hypnotics were filled in American drugstores, representing 17 percent of all prescriptions filled (Parry et al. 1973). Nearly a third of the adult population indicated that they had used at least one prescription or over-the-counter psychoactive drug in a 1-year period (Parry et al. 1973).

As yet, there have been very few systematic attempts to explore the extent to which older people use psychoactive drugs. In 1967, a DHEW Task Force on Prescription Drugs assembled a Master Drug List, ranking the prescription drugs used most frequently by persons 65 years of age and over. Of the 21 most widely used drugs, 8 were psychoactive drugs (DHEW 1968). That study was conducted 10 years ago, and little work of a comparable nature has been done since then. Both the absence of data and the need for additional research were cited in the report of the Conference on Drug Use and the Elderly (1975), sponsored by the National Institute on Drug Abuse and the National Institute for Drug Programs. Against that background, then, it is the purpose of this paper to draw together the currently available data on patterns of psychoactive drug use among the elderly as an initial effort in what is hoped will be an ongoing research direction.

It is important to make clear at the outset that the discussion of psychoactive drug use patterns among the elderly is based solely on data from surveys and case studies. Prevalence rates for particular drugs are not assessed in relation to the advisability of using those drugs for specific conditions experienced by elderly patients. The presentation and discussion of data should therefore be taken only as an attempt to profile the extent to which older people use psychoactive drugs. Whether or not that drug use is appropriate, even in cases where prevalence rates are comparatively high, is contingent upon more detailed analyses of the relationship between drug use, diagnoses, and the physiological and social characteristics of aged persons.

It is also important to specify the types of drugs being considered in this report. Although the term "psychoactive" may refer to both licit and illicit drugs, it was determined that illicit drugs are beyond the scope of this paper. Accordingly, throughout the remainder of the discussion, the term psychoactive drugs is taken to be synonymous with legally prescribed or legally purchased over-the-counter psychoactive drugs. As a general guide to the drugs being considered, a classification system, taken from Parry et al. (1973) is provided in table 1.

There are some difficulties in the task at hand. Few studies have attempted to measure the nature and extent of psychoactive drug use among the elderly. Among the studies that do exist, the data are often not directly comparable. There is variation, for example, in the classification of psychoactive drugs. In one study, sedatives are combined with minor tranquilizers, in another they are grouped with hypnotics, and in another they are treated as a separate class. There are also discrepancies between studies in terms of what constitutes the "older population." Among the studies cited in this report, the oldest age categories represented range from "50 and over" to "65 and over."

There are also differences in terms of methodological strategies pursued and data sources utilized. In the case of prescription psychoactive drugs, for example, some studies use prescription orders based on physicians' records, some focus exclusively on drugs actually administered, and others are concerned with reported use based on direct interviews. In an ideal situation, the different data sources could be considered as merely separate components in a comprehensive data base, from which fruitful comparisons could be made. However, the general paucity of studies frustrates that potential and makes comparisons extremely difficult.

Given the variations among studies, and the lack of information in general, it is very difficult to present the data in a synthetic and comparative fashion; accordingly, the style of presentation will tend to rely on serial discussions of individual studies, with integrating comments when appropriate.

The following section focuses on prescription psychoactive drugs. Data on patterns of use among the elderly are presented in two parts: The first part summarizes studies on psychoactive drug use in the general elderly population; the second part reviews studies conducted among institutionalized populations. Following the presentation of data on patterns of prescription psychoactive drug use, there is a review of studies on noncompliance, improper prescribing, and drug-related illness and death.

The next section focuses on over-the-counter (OTC) psychoactive drugs. Data are presented on the extent of OTC psychoactive drug use among the elderly.

The final section summarizes the findings cited in this report. In addition, suggestions are made for future directions of research efforts.

PRESCRIPTION PSYCHOACTIVE DRUGS

Psychoactive drugs are prescribed for a variety of reasons, not all of which are directly related to diagnoses for psychiatric illnesses. Balter and Levine (1969) have indicated that most psychoactive drugs are prescribed by general practitioners and internists, and only a third of all prescriptions for antidepressants and major tranquilizers--usually prescribed for psychiatric disorders--are written by psychiatrist and neurologists. Parry et al. (1973) found that 85 percent of the people in their survey who reported use of a prescription psychoactive drug had never seen a psychiatrist. Psychoactive drugs are also prescribed in a variety of contexts, including doctors' offices, outpatient clinics, general hospitals, nursing homes, and psychiatric wards.

The apparent far-reaching use of prescription psychoactive drugs raises several issues that need to be examined. A prerequisite for any further discussion, of course, is a basic knowledge of the extent to which people use particular drugs, in what contexts, and for what purposes. It is also important to know whether people use those drugs properly and, if not, why misuse occurs. "Misuse" here refers to inappropriate use of prescription psychoactive drugs, resulting either from the patient's failure to comply with proper directions for the use of a medication or from improper prescribing on the part of a physician. If misuse does occur, it is important to know how widespread it is, what the reasons for it are, and whether it involves harmful consequences.

The discussion of prescription psychoactive drug use among the elderly that follows is presented with those issues in mind. However, the paucity of available data makes it very difficult to address those issues directly. Accordingly, the purpose of this section is to provide relevant information to the extent possible, and to point out the limitations of the data in relation to the issues under

TABLE 1.—Classification of psychoactive drugs

Type of Class	Examples: Generic Names	Examples: Trade Names
Prescription Drugs		
Major tranquilizers		
Phenothiazine derivatives	Chlorpromazine, thioridazine	Thorazine, Mellaril
Butyrophenones	Haloperidol	Haldol
Thioxanthenes	Thiothixene, chlorprothixene	Navane, Taractan
Minor tranquilizers		
Substituted diols	Meprobamate, tybamate	Equanil, Miltown, Tybatran
Benzodiazepines	Chlordiazepoxide, diazepam, oxazepam	Librium, Valium, Serax
Miscellaneous	Hydroxyzine, buclizine	Atarax, Softran
Antidepressants		
Tricyclics	Imipramine, amitriptyline	Tofranil, Elavil
Monoamine oxidase inhibitors	Isocarboxazid, phenelzine	Marplan, Nardil
Other	Methylphenidate, combination of amitriptyline and perphenazine	Ritalin, Triavil, Etrafon
Stimulants		
Amphetamines	Detroamphetamine (and combinations), methamphetamine	Dexedrine, Dexamyl, Desoxyn
Others	Deanol, pentylenetetrazol (and combinations)	Deaner, Metrazol
Sedatives		
Barbiturates (long-acting and intermediate-acting)	Phenobarbital, butabarbital	Eskabarb, Butisol
Others	Bromisovalum	Bromural
Hypnotics		
Barbiturates (short-acting)	Secobarbital, pentobarbital	Seconal, Nembutal
Others	Glutethimide, ethchlorvynol	Doriden, Placidyl
Over the Counter		
Stimulants	Caffeine	No-Doz, Vivarin, No-Nod
Tranquilizers	Scopolamine and/or methapyrilene	Cope, Compoz
Sleeping pills	Scopolamine and/or methapyrilene	Sleep-Eze, Mr. Sleep, Sominex, Nytol

consideration. Some suggestions for further research are offered in the final section.

PATTERNS OF PSYCHOACTIVE DRUG USE AMONG THE ELDERLY

The studies to be discussed presently are grouped into two general types. The first group consists of studies that address patterns of prescription psychoactive drug use in the general elderly population. The second group focuses specifically on the elderly residing in institutional settings.

General Population

One of the best available data sources on prescription drugs is the National Disease and Therapeutic Index (NDTI 1975a,b). Prescription data from the NDTI are based on a survey of U.S. physicians who are asked to fill out forms on a quarterly basis, detailing drug orders for patients during a 48-hour period. The NDTI, unfortunately, is a private data source, available on a subscription basis only; accordingly, permission must be received before data can be published.

While the NDTI is a comprehensive data source, time and cost factors have restricted this analysis to a presentation of data on the proportion of selected prescription psychoactive drug orders issued to the elderly. Table 2 summarizes the findings. It is important to emphasize here that the number represents appearances, and not prescriptions or people. Appearances are the number of times a particular drug is recorded in the NDTI survey; it is a broader category than prescriptions, since it also includes hospital orders, physician samples, direct dispensing, nursing home orders, etc. Appearances also differ from the number of people receiving drug orders, since some people may receive more than one order.

If it is kept in mind that people 65 years of age and over constitute 10 percent of the total U.S. population, it can be seen that, with the exception of the stimulants and Stelazine (a major tranquilizer) older people receive a highly disproportionate number of orders for the prescription psychoactive drugs sampled. In fact, again with the exception of the stimulants and Stelazine, older people receive at least one-fifth of all orders for the sampled drugs; in the case of Thorazine (a major tranquilizer), the sedatives, the nonbarbiturate hypnotics, and three out of four of the barbiturate hypnotics, older people receive over one-fourth of all drug orders. While data on Mellaril (another major tranquilizer) are not presented, evidence (cited elsewhere in this monograph) suggests that use

patterns in respect to age do not differ substantially from Thorazine, and, in fact, Mellaril may even be used more extensively by older people.

Of the most widely used individual prescription psychoactive drugs sampled, older people receive 21.2 percent of all orders for Valium (minor tranquilizer), 23.4 percent of all orders for Librium (minor tranquilizer), 30.4 percent of all orders for Dalmane (nonbarbiturate hypnotic), 21.1 percent of all orders for Elavil (antidepressant), and 27.1 percent of all orders for phenobarbital (sedative). Older people receive the most highly disproportionate percentage of drug orders for Butisol Sodium (sedative), for which nearly half of all orders are issued to people 65 and over, and Doriden, Placidyl, and Amytal (hypnotics), for which approximately a third of all orders are issued to people 65 and over.

It is also apparent from the data presented that, for the drugs sampled, it is not uncommon for women to receive two out of every three drug orders issued. That general pattern appears to hold true among people 65 and over as well, with a few exceptions. The gap closes substantially when looking at barbiturate hypnotics, and in the case of Tuinal, older men actually receive more drug orders than older women. In the case of Elavil, an antidepressant, all women receive a little more than three out of every four drug orders, but older women receive a more highly disproportionate number in comparison to older men. The analysis takes into account the fact that women constitute a greater proportion of the population 65 years of age and over than they do in the population as a whole.

Approaching the issue of psychoactive drug use patterns from another direction, Parry et al. (1973) interviewed a national household sample of 2,552 persons, ranging in age from 18 to 74. The interviews, conducted in late 1970 and early 1971, consisted of a series of questions related to the respondents' drug use during a 1-year period preceding the interview. A validity study conducted prior to the national survey indicated that the results may tend to underestimate prevalence rates by a few percentage points.

It is important to point out two features of the survey that restrict its scope when considered in the present context. First, since the sample was based on adults in households, it does not include those who were residing in institutions at the time of the survey; thus, the data should be regarded as reflecting only psychoactive drug use patterns in the noninstitutionalized population. Second, no

TABLE 2.—Number and percentage of appearances of selected prescription psychoactive drugs by age group and sex, NDTI, 1975 (Number in thousands)

Drug Class and Name	All Ages						65 Years and Over					
	Male		Female		Total		Male		Female		Total	
	Number	%	Number	%	Number	%	Number	%	Number	%	Number	%
Major tranquilizers												
Thorazine	1,714	38.9	2,688	61.1	4,402	100	384	3.7	777	17.7	1,161	26.4
Stelazine	880	35.3	1,611	64.7	2,491	100	92	3.7	196	7.9	288	11.6
Minor tranquilizers												
Valium	10,959	35.7	19,729	64.3	30,688	100	2,229	7.3	4,267	13.9	6,496	21.2
Librium	2,464	36.0	4,378	64.0	6,842	100	538	7.9	1,060	15.5	1,598	23.4
Antidepressants												
Elavil	1,514	22.2	5,319	77.8	6,833	100	246	3.6	1,197	17.5	1,443	21.1
Tofranil	1,151	32.6	2,383	67.4	3,533	100	195	5.5	498	14.1	693	19.6
Stimulants												
Biphetamine	121	17.0	590	83.0	711	100	N.A.	N.A.	8	1.1	N.A.	N.A.
Dexedrine	225	48.2	274	51.8	529	100	18	3.4	7	1.3	25	4.7
Sedatives												
Phenobarbital	2,163	40.2	3,222	59.8	5,285	100	456	8.5	1,004	18.6	1,460	27.1
Butisol sodium	343	27.4	910	72.6	1,253	100	141	11.3	411	32.8	552	44.1
Barbiturate hypnotics												
Seconal	1,139	35.5	2,072	64.5	3,211	100	318	9.9	381	11.9	669	21.8
Nembutal	848	33.4	1,690	66.6	2,538	100	268	10.6	473	18.6	741	29.2
Tuinal	451	40.6	661	59.4	1,112	100	153	13.8	143	12.9	296	26.7
Amytal	159	32.6	329	67.4	488	100	66	13.5	92	18.9	158	32.4
Nonbarbiturate hypnotics												
Dalmane	3,303	36.7	5,698	63.3	9,001	100	937	10.4	1,802	20.0	2,739	30.4
Placidyl	494	35.3	906	64.7	1,400	100	130	9.3	333	23.8	463	3.1
Doriden	431	41.8	600	58.2	1,031	100	156	15.1	210	20.4	366	35.5
Quaalude	171	48.6	181	51.4	352	100	46	13.1	50	14.2	96	27.3

How to read the table: In 1975, Thorazine (a major tranquilizer) appeared in the NDTI a total of 4,402 times; 1,714 (38.9 percent) of those drug orders were issued to males, and 2,688 (61.1 percent) were issued to females. A total of 1,161 of those orders for Thorazine were issued to people over 65 years of age and over, constituting 26.4 percent of all appearances; 384 (8.7 percent of all appearances) were issued to older men, and 777 (17.9 percent of all appearances) were issued to older women.

persons 75 years of age or older were interviewed, thereby excluding over one-quarter of the population 60 and over.

As can be seen from table 3, roughly one-fifth (21 percent) of older men and one-third (32 percent) of older women indicated that they had used at least one prescription psychoactive drug in the last year. For older men, the prevalence of use was substantially higher than that of men in the other age groups; a similarly disproportionate percentage for older women would be evident if stimulants were excluded from consideration.

Minor tranquilizers/sedatives and hypnotics are the drugs of use most frequently cited by both older men and older women. Substantially more older women (25 percent) than older men (11 percent), however, indicated use of minor tranquilizers/sedatives. For both older men and older women, the use of minor tranquilizers/sedatives and hypnotics is more prevalent than in any other age group.

In addition to measuring prevalence rates, the survey attempted to determine levels of use of prescription psychoactive drugs. Table 4 distinguishes between "use" and "high level of use," by age group. "High level of use" is defined as a maximum pattern which involves regular daily use for at least 2 months.

While the reported data do not reveal level of use by specific class of drug, it can be seen that, for all prescription psychoactive drugs taken together, 9 percent of all those in the age group 60-74, or roughly one-third (32 percent) of those who had used a drug during the past year, indicated a high level of use. When comparing those figures with the 30-44 and 45-59 age groups, it appears that, while a larger percentage of older people may be using prescription psychoactive drugs, they are less likely to be using them at a high level.

The survey by Parry et al. (1973) also attempted to relate other demographic factors--geographic region, Index of Social Position (ISP), and education--to prevalence rate and level of use of prescription psychoactive drugs; unfortunately, the reported data did not correlate those factors with age. Among all persons in the survey, however, those living in the western States tended to show a somewhat higher prevalence rate, and they tended more often to use drugs at a high level. ISP (based on the standard Hollingshead scoring) and education appeared to have little effect on prevalence rates; however, those persons with lower ISP and education ratings showed some tendency to use drugs

at a high level more often. It cannot be discerned from the reported data whether, or to what extent, those tendencies hold true for the age group 60-74.

Abelson and Atkinson (1975) provide some additional data which give an indication of the extent to which recent use of prescription psychoactive drugs is also the first use (table 5). Their study was based on interviews with a national household sample of 3,071 adults and 952 youths, conducted between November 1974 and March 1975. It should be pointed out that the primary focus of the study was on illicit drug use, a phenomenon associated predominantly with younger age groups; accordingly, data on prescription drug use among older people (defined broadly as "50 and over") was a peripheral aspect of the study.

The data suggest that those in the age group 50 and over (as compared with adults of all ages) are more likely to have reported use of a sedative within the past year and less likely to have reported use of a stimulant, while reported use of tranquilizers (major and minor combined) is roughly the same between the two groups. Particularly interesting, however, is the indication that, for both groups, approximately two-thirds of those who used sedatives and one-half of those who used tranquilizers within the past year did so for the first time.

Guttman (1977) specified some characteristics of elderly users of prescription drugs. In a Washington, D.C., household sample of 447 persons aged 65 and over, with an average age of 71.9 years and a male/female ratio of 59.6 percent to 40.4 percent, he found that 13.6 percent of the respondents in the survey used sedatives/tranquilizers daily, and 1.1 percent indicated daily use of antidepressants. Roughly half (50.7 percent) of those who used psychoactive drugs on a daily basis reported that they could not perform their regular daily activities without their medication; 28.6 percent indicated that their health was the main reason for using psychoactive drugs; and 38.6 percent reported taking several kinds of drugs in combination. He also found that, with a statistically significant difference, users of prescription psychoactive drugs tended to be younger and native born, while nonusers tended to be older and foreign born.

In summary, it appears that the elderly receive a disproportionately high number of orders for the tranquilizers, sedatives, hypnotics, and antidepressants sampled from the NDTI, while the number of stimulants ordered for the elderly appears to be proportionately low. The hypnotics and sedatives appear to

TABLE 3.—Use of prescription psychoactive drugs during past year by drug class and by sex and age

| Drug Class and Sex | Percentage Using in Past Year Among Age Groups | | | | |
	18-29	30-44	45-59	60-74	All Ages
Major tranquilizer					
Men	*	1	1	*	1
Women	1	2	2	2	2
Minor tranquilizer/sedative					
Men	5	7	9	11	8
Women	12	21	22	25	20
Antidepressant					
Men	+	2	1	4	2
Women	2	2	2	2	2
Stimulant					
Men	1	2	2	1	2
Women	10	11	6	3	8
Hypnotic					
Men	1	1	2	7	3
Women	3	3	4	8	4
All psychoactive drugs					
Used any during past year					
Men	6	12	14	21	13
Women	23	32	31	32	29

*Less than 0.5 percent
+No cases
Past year refers to 1969-1970

SOURCE: Parry et al. (1973)

TABLE 4.—Users in past year (1969-1970) and high-level users of prescription psychoactive drugs by age group

| Age Group | Among All Persons in Each Age Group | | Among Users in Each Age Group |
	Percent Using	Percent Using at High Level	Percent Using at High Level
18-29	15	5	31
30-44	24	10	39
45-59	23	10	42
60-74	27	9	32

TABLE 5.—Medical experience with prescription psychoactive drugs during 1974 (percent)

	Any	Sedatives	Tranquilizers	Stimulants
50 years and over				
Used in past year	*	15	14	1
First used in past year	15	10	7	1
All adults 18 years and over				
Used in past year	*	10	15	3
First used in past year	15	7	8	2

*Not available

SOURCE: Abelson and Atkinson (1975)

be the classes of psychoactive drugs most disproportionately issued to the elderly. Women in general are more likely than men to receive orders for psychoactive drugs, and that pattern tends to hold true for the older population.

In terms of the percentages of the older population who use prescription psychoactive drugs, approximately one-fifth of older men and one-third of older women reported use of at least one drug during a 1-year period. The highest prevalence of use occurred in the combined classes minor tranquilizers/sedatives (11 percent of older men and 25 percent of older women), followed by hynotics, (7 percent of older men and 8 percent of older women); comparatively lower prevalence rates were reported for stimulants, major tranquilizers, and antidepressants. A greater proportion of both older men and women reported use of minor tranquilizers/sedatives and hypnotics than did those in other age groups.

Among the elderly who use prescription psychoactive drugs, one-third reported a high level of use (regular daily use for at least 2 months). Two-thirds of those who reported use of sedatives and one-half of those who reported use of tranquilizers in a 1-year period indicated that it was their first use of those drugs (age group 50 and over).

Institutionalized Populations

Although the functions of psychoactive drug use among the elderly residing in institutions and those in the general population may differ substantially, it is nevertheless desirable to include use data for the institutionalized elderly in order to provide a more comprehensive profile of psychoactive drug use in various contexts. Unfortunately, it is necessary, at the present time, to rely on data from individual case studies. Even those studies are sparse, and useful data were found only in relation to nursing home residents and psychiatric inpatients; accordingly, the data presented on patterns of prescription psychoactive drug use among institutionalized elderly populations are limited in both scope and generalizability. The data are too scanty to be regarded as anything but preliminary indications of use patterns; they should not be regarded as representative.

Nursing home residents. In 1970, nearly three-quarters (72.4 percent) of the older population living in institutions were in nursing homes and related facilities (Manard 1975). It has been estimated that slightly more than 5 percent of the population 65 years of age and over are in nursing homes or related facilities on any given day, and that approximately 20 percent of the older persons can expect to spend some time in nursing homes during their lifetime (U.S. Senate Special Committee on Aging 1975). The nature and extent of psychoactive drug use within nursing homes, then, can affect a potentially significant segment of the older population.

In terms of the psychoactive drugs most frequently prescribed in nursing homes, some preliminary data are provided in a General Accounting Office audit of Medicaid payments for prescription drugs in nursing homes in Illinois, New Jersey, and Ohio (U.S. Senate Special Committee on Aging 1973). The audit, commissioned by the Subcommittee on Long-Term Care of the U.S. Senate Special Committee on Aging, covers the periods of January, April, July, and October of 1970. Table 6 presents the GAO data on prescribing

TABLE 6.—The 10 drugs most prescribed in nursing homes in three States in 1970, by number of prescriptions paid for by Medicaid

Rank	Drug Name and Class	Number of Prescriptions	Percent of All Prescriptions
1	Thorazine (major tranquilizer)	23,126	3.5
2	Darvon compound (analgesic)	21,436	3.2
3	Mellaril (major tranquilizer)	17,977	2.7
4	Phenobarbital (sedative)	9,663	1.4
5	Chloral hydrate (hypnotic)	8,264	1.2
6	Doriden (sedative)	7,802	1.1
7	Librium (minor tranquilizer)	7,259	1.1
8	Aspirin and Bufferin (analgesics)	6,875	1.0
9	Nembutal (hypnotic)	6,133	0.9
10	Valium (minor tranquilizers)	5,308	0.8

NOTES: Total number of prescriptions was 657,882.
   Sample covers January, April, July, and October of 1970 in the States of Illinois, New Jersey, and Ohio.
   Drug classes used here conform with categories used elsewhere in this monograph rather than those in the original.

SOURCE: U.S. Senate Special Committe on Aging (1973, p. 247).

patterns among the elderly poor in nursing homes.

Of the 10 most frequently prescribed individual drugs in the GAO audit, 8 were psychoactive drugs. The first and third most frequently prescribed drugs--and the two most frequently prescribed psychoactive drugs--were Thorazine and Mellaril (both major tranquilizers) which, taken together, accounted for 7 percent of the total number of prescriptions.[1] The sedatives phenobarbital and Doriden ranked 4th and 6th, the hypnotics chloral hydrate and Nembutal ranked 5th and 9th, and the minor tranquilizers Librium and Valium ranked 7th and 10th.

The most notable deviation from the NDTI data in table 2 on drug orders for the older population taken as a whole is the proportionately higher number of prescriptions for major tranquilizers in nursing homes. That observation is supported by the NDTI data supplement, "Leading Drugs Used in Nursing Homes" (NDTI 1975), which shows that, from July 1974 through July 1975, tranquilizers (both major and minor) were the most frequently ordered drug class in nursing homes, with Mellaril and Thorazine, respectively, being the most frequently ordered tranquilizers. In terms of the percentage of older people residing in nursing homes who receive prescriptions for psychoactive drugs, there are a few studies which report relevant data. Ingman et al. (1975) conducted a study of the patterns of prescribing and administering of drugs among the elderly in a long-term care institution in Connecticut. Drug orders for 2 different dates 10 months apart were recorded for each of 131 patients (ages not given) residing in 3 areas of the 300-bed facility. These included an area primarily for severely brain-damaged persons; an area for ambulatory and more self-sufficient residents; and an extended care unit for the maximally disabled and patients recently discharged from hospitals.

Table 7 summarizes their data on the number and percentage of patients with prescriptions for psychoactive drugs. Over one-third (34.4 percent) of the patients had prescriptions

[1]The figure cited here differs from that discussed in the text of the subcommittee report. The subcommittee chose to focus on percentages calculated from total drug costs, which distorts actual prescription patterns by injecting the added factor of variable costs between different drugs. Percentages and ranks discussed here are based on the actual numbers of prescriptions.

TABLE 7.—Number and percentage of 131 nursing home patients with prescriptions for psychoactive drugs, by drug class

Drug Class	Patients with Prescriptions for			
	One Drug	Two Drugs	Three Drugs	Totals
Major tranquilizers				
Number	39	5	1	45
Percent	29.8	3.8	0.8	34.4
Minor tranquilizers				
Number	25	1	0	26
Percent	19.1	0.8	0	19.9
Antidepressants				
Number	13	1	0	14
Percent	9.9	0.8	0	10.7
Hypnotics				
Number	30	2	1	33
Percent	22.9	1.5	0.8	25.2

SOURCE: Ingman et al. (1975)

for major tranquilizers, one-quarter (25.2 percent) had prescriptions for hypnotics, one-fifth (19.9 percent) had prescription for minor tranquilizers, and one-tenth (10.7 percent) had prescriptions for antidepressants. More patients (4.6 percent) had prescriptions for two or three major tranquilizers than for any other class of psychoactive drug.

Beardsley et al. (1975) conducted a study of drug use among 270 patients (ages not given) in five nursing homes in the Greater Minneapolis-St. Paul area. The nursing homes were selected to represent different geographic locations, sizes, and types of ownership. Data on drug use were collected by two pharmacists who used patients' charts, medication records, and nursing Kardex files. Cases of drug use were recorded only if a drug had been ordered by a physician and had been administered within the month prior to the review.

Among the 1,109 cases of drug use recorded (an average of 4.1 per patient), psychoactive drugs comprised 20.1 percent of the total. As can be seen from table 8, the psychoactive drug classes represented were sedative/hypnotics (9.1 percent), major tranquilizers (5.4 percent), minor tranquilizers (3.6 percent), and antidepressants (2.0 percent). Roughly a third of the patients were receiving sedative/hypnotics and tranquilizers, while about 8 percent were receiving antidepressants.

Beardsley et al. (1975) also reported data on the most frequently used individual drugs within each drug class. As can be seen from table 9, chloral hydrate was the most frequently prescribed hypnotic, issued to 12.2 percent of the patient population. Mellaril was the most frequently prescribed major tranquilizer, issued to 11.1 percent of the patient population. Valium was the most frequently prescribed minor tranquilizer, issued to 9.3 percent of the population. Tofranil was the most frequently prescribed antidepressant, issued to 2.2 percent of the patient population.

Published data on polypharmacy in nursing homes are scarce. Ingman et al. (1975) found that 4.6 percent of the nursing home residents in their study were simultaneously receiving more than one major tranquilizer, 2.3 percent were receiving more than one hypnotic, and fewer than 1 percent were receiving more than one minor tranquilizer or antidepressant. Beardsley et al. (1975) did not report polypharmacy data specific to psychoactive drugs, but for all drugs there was an average of 4.1 per patient, with a range from 0 to 15 per patient. They found the average number of drugs per patient to vary in relation to payment mechanism, with Medicare recipients receiving 3.5 drugs, Medicaid recipients receiving 4.2, and patients with private third party payments receiving 5.5. They also found some variation between nursing homes, ranging from a low average of 2.8 per patient to a high average of 4.5. It is not clear,

TABLE 8.—Number and percentage of psychoactive drugs prescribed in nursing homes, by class of drug

Drug Class	Number of Cases of Drug Use	Percent of Total Cases	Percent of Those Receiving Psycho-active Drugs
Major tranquilizers	60	5.4	22.2
Minor tranquilizers	40	3.6	14.8
Antidepressants	22	2.0	8.1
Hypnotics	101	9.1	37.4
TOTAL	223	20.1	

NOTES: Number of cases of drug use during the month prior to review was 1,109.

Because of polypharmacy, i.e., some patients receive more than one drug in a class, the figures in this column are approximations. However, these are good approximations because the number of patients who use more than one drug in a class is very small.

SOURCE: Adapted from Beardsley et al. (1975).

TABLE 9.—Individual psychoactive drugs most frequently prescribed in five nursing homes, by class of drug

Drug Class	Drug Name	Number of Cases of Drug Use	Percent of Patients Who Receive Drug
Major tranquilizer	Mellaril	30	11.1
Minor tranquilizer	Valium	25	9.3
Antidepressant	Tofranil	6	2.2
Hypnotic	Chloral hydrate	33	12.2

NOTES: The number of drug cases recorded is not the number of patients, as some patients received more than one drug.

SOURCE: Beardsley et al. (1975)

however, to what extent those patterns may hold true for psychoactive drugs.

It is difficult to make direct comparisons between the data of Ingman et al. (1975) and Beardsley et al. (1975). It is not clear, for example, to what extent their classification systems overlap. Beardsley et al. combined sedatives and hypnotics into one class, while Ingman et al. did not specify which class includes sedatives. Another difference surrounds the question of what constitutes a "drug case." Beardsley et al. recorded only those cases where drugs were actually administered, while Ingman et al. recorded drugs

prescribed. As Ingman et al. pointed out, 53 percent of all "neuroactive" drugs in their study (psychoactive drugs plus analgesics, skeletal muscle relaxants, antiparkinson drugs, and autonomic agents) were issued p.r.n. (pro re nata, or according to need) so there was substantial nurse discretion in administration; of the average 2.1 neuroactive drugs per patient prescribed, an average of 1.3 drugs was actually administered.

Those differences notwithstanding, it appears that major tranquilizers and hypnotics are the classes of psychoactive drugs most frequently prescribed in the nursing homes sampled. (Those findings are generally compatible with the GAO study cited earlier). The data of Beardsley et al. on drugs actually administered indicated that over one-third of the nursing home residents in their sample received hypnotics (and sedatives), and over one-fifth received major tranquilizers. The data of Ingman et al. on drugs prescribed, which may overestimate actual use because of p.r.n. orders, indicate that over one-third of nursing home residents in their sample were issued prescriptions for major tranquilizers, while one-quarter received prescriptions for hypnotics.

Psychiatric inpatients. Perhaps the most comprehensive reporting of data on elderly psychiatric patients is that derived from a survey of psychoactive drugs used in 12 Veterans Administration hospitals, conducted in February 1974 by Robert Prien and colleagues (Prien et al. 1976; Prien et al. 1975; Prien 1975). The survey was based on a sample of 2,682 patients 60 years of age and over, with 1,276 (48 percent) having a primary diagnosis of mental disorder, 197 (7 percent) having an associated diagnosis of mental disorder, and 1,209 (45 percent) having no diagnosis of mental disorder. The sample was predominantly male, with no more than 6 percent female in any diagnostic category. Diagnostic categories were obtained from patients' medical records. Drug information was derived from patients' medication orders, and included all drugs administered on the day of the survey.

Of all patients 37 percent received at least one major tranquilizer, minor tranquilizer, or antidepressant. The proportion of psychiatric patients who received at least one drug (56 percent) was substantially higher than that of the nonpsychiatric patients (16 percent). The patterns of use also differed between the two groups. Among the psychiatric patients, major tranquilizers accounted for 69 percent of all psychoactive drug orders, with antidepressants accounting for 17 percent and minor tranquilizers accounting for 14 percent. Among the nonpsychiatric patients, minor tranquilizers accounted for 52 percent of all psychoactive drug orders, followed by major tranquilizers (33 percent) and antidepressants (15 percent). Five drugs--thioridazine (Mellaril), chlorpromazine (Thorazine), diazepam (Valium), chlordiazepoxide (Librium), and amitriptyline (Elavil)--accounted for 63 percent of all psychoactive drug orders across diagnostic groups (Prien 1975).

Prien et al. (1975) reported data on the prevalence of psychoactive drug use, by diagnostic category, in the patient population with primary diagnoses of mental disorder. Of

those 1,276 patients, 718 were diagnosed as having organic brain syndrome, 362 were diagnosed as schizophrenic, and 196 had other mental disorders. Of schizophrenic patients, 70 percent received psychoactive drugs (the highest percentage), followed by those with other mental disorders (66 percent) and those with organic brain syndrome (55 percent). Table 10 summarizes the data on the proportion of psychiatric patients who received specific psychoactive drugs, by diagnostic category. Of the three drug classes represented, major tranquilizers were used most frequently, with 44 percent of the psychiatric patient population receiving at least one drug in that class. Antidepressants (11 percent) and minor tranquilizers (10 percent) were used less extensively. The highest rate of use of major tranquilizers was among schizophrenic patients (62 percent), while the highest rates of use of antidepressants and minor tranquilizers were among those with other mental disorders (30 percent and 15 percent, respectively). The most widely used major tranquilizers across diagnostic groups were thioridazine and chlorpromazine, which accounted for 61 percent of all orders for major tranquilizers; diazepam accounted for 53 percent of all orders for minor tranquilizers; and amitriptyline accounted for 37 percent of all orders for antidepressants (data not shown).

Laska et al. (1973), in their study of psychoactive drug use among schizophrenic patients in a State hospital, found patterns of use that were generally consistent with those in the survey by Prien et al. (1975). All drug information was taken from the hospital's Drug Monitoring System. Of the 587 schizophrenic patients 65 years of age and over, 70.5 percent were using major tranquilizers, 13.8 percent were using antidepressants, and 8.2 percent were using minor tranquilizers (table 11). The percentage of women who used psychoactive drugs was substantially higher than that of men in all three drug classes.

Prien et al. (1975) also reported data on the proportion and dosage of psychoactive drug use within different age categories of the psychiatric patient population. Table 12 summarizes their findings. Contrary to findings for the general population, it appears that both the percentage of psychiatric inpatients receiving a drug and the mean daily dose of the drug declined as age increased in all three drug classes examined.

Laska et al. (1973) found a similar pattern extended to a wider age range in their study of schizophrenic patients. Among patients over 20 years of age, there was a general tendency for both the percentage of patients

TABLE 10.—Percentage of psychiatric inpatients receiving psychoactive drugs, by diagnosis

Psychoactive Drugs*	Percentage of Those Diagnosed Who Receive Drug			
	Organic Brain Syndrome (N=718)	Schizophrenia (N=362)	Other Mental Disorders (N=196)	Total (N=1,276)
Major tranquilizers				
Thioridazine	15	20	15	17
Chlorpromazine	9	22	11	13
Trifluoperazine	2	8	4	4
Haloperidol	4	3	2	3
Others	9	17	13	12
Total receiving at least one major tranquilizer	36	62	41	44
Minor tranquilizers				
Diazepam	6	4	8	5
Chlordiazepoxide	3	2	5	3
Others	2	1	2	2
Total receiving at least one minor tranquilizer	10	7	15	10
Antidepressants				
Amitriptyline	3	2	15	4
Doxepin	1	2	6	2
Nortriptyline	2	2	4	2
Others	2	3	7	3
Total receiving at least one antidepressant	8	9	30	11

*Patients receiving more than one drug are listed under each drug.

SOURCE: Prien et al. (1975)

TABLE 11.—Percent of schizophrenic inpatients 65 years and over who received psychoactive drugs, by drug class

	N	Tranquilizers		Antidepressants
		Major	Minor	
Men	214	57.5	5.1	4.2
Women	373	78.0	9.9	19.3
Total	587	70.5	8.2	13.8

SOURCE: Laska et al. (1973)

TABLE 12.—Use of psychoactive drugs by psychiatric inpatients, by age

Psychoactive Drug Class and Dose	Age of Patient			
	60-65 (N=336)	66-75 (N=328)	Over 75 (N=612)	All Ages (N=1,276)
Major tranquilizers				
Percent of patients who receive drug	54	46	38	44
Mean daily dose (milligrams)[1]	310	255	152	229
Minor tranquilizers				
Percent of patients who receive drug	14	9	8	10
Mean daily dose (milligrams)[2]	45	44	33	40
Antidepressants				
Percent of patients who receive drug	18	13	7	11
Mean daily dose (milligrams)[3]	93	86	74	85

[1] Converted to equivalent doses of chlorpromazine.

[2] Converted to equivalent doses of chlordiazepoxide.

[3] All doses equivalent.

SOURCE: Prien (1975)

receiving a drug and the average daily dose per drug to decrease as age increased (table 13).

Prien et al. (1976) reported data on polypharmacy patterns in their sample of elderly psychiatric patients in Veterans Administration hospitals. Of the sample of 1,276, 18 percent received two or more psychoactive drugs; 21 percent of those with diagnoses of schizophrenia and other mental disorders and 15 percent of those with diagnoses of organic brain syndrome received multiple drug regimens. The most frequently prescribed combinations were: 1) a major tranquilizer and an antidepressant (23 percent of all polypharmacy prescriptions); 2) two major tranquilizers (21 percent); and 3) a major tranquilizer and a minor tranquilizer or sedative-hypnotic (21 percent). The proportion of patients receiving two or more psychoactive drugs decreased with age: 26 percent of the patients 60-65 years of age received two or more drugs; 20 percent of the patients 66-75 years of age received two or more drugs; and 12 percent of the patients over 75 received two or more drugs. Substantially more females (42 percent) received two or more psychoactive drugs than did males (17 percent), but the sample of females was so small (N=50) as to restrict the validity of generalization.

Fracchia et al. (1971) also reported polypharmacy data for a sample of 569 (137 male, 432 female) psychiatric patients 55 years of age and older in a State hospital. The most frequently prescribed combinations were: 1) a major tranquilizer and an antidepressant-stimulant (35 percent of all polypharmacy prescriptions); 2) a minor tranquilizer and an antidepressant-stimulant (17 percent); 3) a major tranquilizer with a major tranquilizer (16 percent); and 4) a major tranquilizer with a minor tranquilizer (10 percent). There was evidence to indicate that the use of major tranquilizers in combination tended to decrease with advancing age: 60 percent of the patients under the age of 65 received a major tranquilizer as part of a combination, as compared with fewer than 30 percent of those over the age of 75. The use of minor tranquilizers as part of a combination, on the other hand, increased with advancing age.

In summary, among the elderly psychiatric inpatient populations sampled, major tranquilizers were found to be used much more extensively than any other class of psychoactive drugs. Prien found that major tranquilizers accounted for 69 percent of all psychoactive drugs used by psychiatric patients and that 44 percent of the psychiatric patients were using at least one major tranquilizer (Prien 1975; Prien et al. 1975). Patients diagnosed as schizophrenic were most likely to receive major tranquilizers, with roughly two-thirds of schizophrenic patients in two separate studies using at least one drug in that class. Major tranquilizers were also most likely to be used in combination with other psychoactive drugs, most frequently with an antidepressant or another major tranquilizer.

Contrary to patterns found in the general population, use of prescription psychoactive drugs among the psychiatric inpatient populations sampled tended to decline with age. That trend tended to hold true for both the percentage of people using drugs and the average dose per drug, as well as polypharmacy rates.

NONCOMPLIANCE, IMPROPER
PRESCRIBING, AND DRUG-
RELATED ILLNESS AND DEATH

The data presented thus far have focused exclusively on patterns of prescription psychoactive drug use among the elderly. It is also important, on the other hand, to examine patterns of misuse. Data on two types of misuse--noncompliance and improper prescribing--are presented here, followed by a review of data on drug-related illness and death.

Noncompliance

We were unable to locate any studies that specifically addressed the extent of older people's noncompliance with prescriptions for psychoactive drugs. Other studies of noncompliance shed little light on this issue. What is presented here, then, is a brief review of studies that outline only the broadest parameters of noncompliance.

In a review of noncompliance studies, Hussar (1975) indicates that there has been a wide variation between studies in terms of the degree of noncompliance reported, with most ranging from one-third to one-half of the patients sampled. Steward and Cluff (1972) place the range at 25 percent to 59 percent.

For the most part, efforts to correlate demographic variables with noncompliance have failed to discover any significant relationships (Hussar et al. 1974). In a study of 154 general medical clinic patients, Davis (1968) found that demographic variables had no influence on either attitudinal or behavioral compliance. Boyd et al. (1974) found no significant relationship between noncompliance and sex, race, or education in a sample of 134 outpatients.

A few studies, on the other hand, have found that age has some effect on noncompliance,

TABLE 13.—Percent of schizophrenic inpatients receiving psychoactive drugs and average total daily dose, by age and by sex

Drug Class and Sex	Under 16	16-20	21-40	41-64	65 and Over	All Ages
PERCENT OF PATIENTS RECEIVING DRUGS						
Major tranquilizers						
Male	89.3	96.9	94.7	76.1	57.5	80.5
Female	94.4	91.7	96.9	95.2	78.0	91.4
Male and female	90.6	95.0	95.6	86.0	70.5	85.8
Minor tranquilizers						
Male	5.8	12.3	12.9	8.5	9.2	9.2
Female	8.3	22.2	17.6	11.3	12.3	12.3
Male and female	6.5	15.8	14.8	9.9	8.2	10.7
Antidepressants						
Male	24.3	21.5	14.6	9.1	11.4	11.4
Female	47.2	30.6	21.8	18.1	20.0	20.0
Male and female	30.2	24.8	17.5	13.8	13.8	15.6
AVERAGE TOTAL DAILY DOSE (Milligrams)						
Major tranquilizers (chlorpromazine standard)						
Male	257.8	506.0	544.4	346.5	125.4	388.0
Female	154.9	481.1	725.0	478.3	181.4	459.1
Male and female	230.0	497.8	619.2	422.2	164.8	425.9
Minor tranquilizers (chlordiazepoxide standard)						
Male	21.7	36.3	44.3	30.9	42.6	40.8
Female	25.0	43.4	50.9	37.3	21.9	38.1
Male and female	22.8	39.8	47.6	38.4	26.7	39.2
Antidepressants (all doses equivalent)						
Male	63.6	70.8	104.5	87.1	62.3	87.2
Female	60.3	90.4	102.7	88.0	65.5	84.5
Male and female'	62.3	79.4	103.6	87.7	65.2	85.5

SOURCE: Adapted from Laska et al. (1973).

although the results are not consistent. Latiolais and Berry (1969) conducted a study of 180 indigent outpatients at a university hospital; within the sample, 82 patients (45.5 percent) were 50 years of age and over, and 38 patients (21.1 percent) were 60 years of age and over. Of the 77 patients who were misusing their medications, Latiolais and Berry found that 59.8 percent were over 50 years of age and 28.6 percent were over 60 years of age; conversely, of 103 patients who correctly used their medications, 34.9 percent were over 50 years of age and 15.5 percent were over 60 years of age. In Chi-square tests used to determine whether the relationship between age and misuse was statistically significant, they found that, when the sample was divided into "over 50 years of age" and "under 50 years of age," the significance level was 0.1 percent; when the sample was similarly divided at 60 years of age, the significance level was 5 percent. Latiolais and Berry (1969) concluded that older people are more likely to misuse their medications.

Clinite and Kabat (1969), in a study of 30 men recently returned home after hospitalization at a Veterans Administration hospital, found contradictory results. Patients aged 71-80 had a lower rate of medication error (9.6 percent) than any other group; however, patients aged 81-90 had the highest rate (42.9 percent). Those in the age groups 41-50 (42.5 percent) and 51-60 (36.5 percent) had higher error rates than patients in the 61-70 age group (27.6 percent). The relationship between age and noncompliance, then, revealed no clear pattern.

In a study of 178 chronically ill, ambulatory clinic patients over the age of 60, Schwartz et al. (1962) found that 68 percent of those over 75 years of age made medication errors, as opposed to 57 percent of those in the age group 60-74; however, when finer age breakdowns were examined, the relationship between medication errors and increasing age was considerably less straightforward. In general, the studies cited are too inconsistent to make any conclusive statements about the relationship between age and noncompliance.

Hussar (1975) has suggested that, while relationships between noncompliance and demographic variables have not been consistently demonstrated, there are some patient-related factors that contribute to noncompliance. Specifically, he cites as being more likely to be noncompliers, patients with chronic illnesses requiring long-term therapy, patients who live alone, patients with psychiatric illnesses, and patients who receive several drugs requiring frequent administration. The elderly as a group have the highest

incidence of chronic illnesses, often live alone (especially women) after the death of a spouse, and receive a disproportionate share of prescription drugs. When it is also considered that patients with psychiatric illnesses may tend to have higher rates of medication errors (Willcox et al. 1965), there is at least a superficial basis for speculating that noncompliance rates among the elderly who receive prescriptions for psychoactive drugs may be comparatively high. As yet, however, there are no studies which verify that speculation.

In a related issue, Doyle and Hamm (1976) have reported data which suggest that tendencies toward self-medication may have some effect on the manner in which older people use prescription drugs. Their study, based on a sample of 405 persons 60 years of age and older residing in three Florida counties, indicated that older people sometimes decide for themselves how they will use their medications, especially in terms of discontinuing medications they do not like and generally determining the duration of medication use. Roughly 40 percent of the respondents indicated that they do not continue to take medications that they dislike; only 43.3 percent of the respondents reported that they took medications until their doctor told them to stop. While 18.8 percent stopped when their prescriptions ran out, 18.3 percent stopped when they felt better, and 3.8 percent stopped when they thought they should. When asked why they kept old prescriptions, a large majority (82.2 percent) did not answer the question; however, 12.8 percent responded that they might need them, and 2.4 percent said they had not thought about throwing them out. A comparatively small, though still significant, percentage of respondents said they did not believe that sharing of prescriptions is harmful (13.3 percent), while 12.6 percent indicated that they had shared, or would consider sharing, their prescriptions.

Improper Prescribing

The issue of improper prescribing of psychoactive drugs is one that deserves careful study--especially in the case of the elderly, who receive a disproportionate share of those drugs. That issue is underscored by an apparent lack of special vigilance on the part of the elderly, as indicated in the study by Doyle and Hamm (1976), who found that 71.6 percent of their sample did not discuss the prescription of one doctor with another doctor, 74.8 percent asked no questions (about content, side effects, or cost) when filling their prescriptions, and only 13.0 percent went to see their doctor to have their medications prescribed, while 30.3 percent simply called

TABLE 14.—Percentage of nonconformance to criteria for psychoactive drug prescriptions in five nursing homes

Drug and Class	Nursing Home				
	A	B	C	D	E
Thioridazine (major tranquilizer)	24.7	18.2	11.2	18.8	16.2
Chlordiazepoxide (minor tranquilizer)	5.0	13.3	5.0	16.0	2.5
Amitriptyline (antidepressant)	4.8	12.5	6.0	6.3	5.4
Chloral hydrate (hypnotic)	1.8	0.4	0.8	0.5	2.1

SOURCE: Adapted from Stewart et al. (1976).

their doctor and 30.5 percent had the pharmacist call the doctor.

Unfortunately, we were able to find only a few studies that dealt with improper prescribing of psychoactive drugs among the elderly, and their emphasis was primarily on psychiatric inpatients and nursing home residents. While they do not necessarily constitute a representative body of data, they do highlight the need for additional research.

A 1971 DHEW study of 75 nursing homes, cited in the report on drugs in nursing homes of the Subcommittee on Long-Term Care of the U.S. Senate Special Committee on Aging (U.S. Senate 1973) provides some background on the context of questionable prescribing and administering of drugs. While much of the information was reported in anecdotal form, some interesting findings were presented: two-thirds of the patients sampled had not been given physical exminations at admission, and of those who did receive physicals, less than one-third covered more than 3 of the 10 body systems; 40 percent of the patients had not been seen by a physician for over 3 months; only 18 percent of the patients had received revised treatment of medication orders within the past 30 days; and 35 percent of the patients receiving tranquilizers had not had their blood pressure recorded in over a year.

Beardsley et al. (1975), in a study of drug use patterns in five nursing homes, attempted to determine whether p.r.n. medications were justified. They analyzed patient charts in order to correlate recorded symptoms with prescribed drugs. They found

that 37 percent of tranquilizer p.r.n. orders and 35 percent of hypnotic p.r.n. orders were not justified by the patient charts. While it was not clear to what extent those nonjustifications could be attributed to improper prescribing or to improper recordkeeping, the results at least raise questions as to the appropriateness of the medication orders.

Stewart et al. (1976) attempted to measure the degree of nonconformance to drug use criteria of drugs prescribed in five nursing homes. A single drug was selected to represent a drug class, and standards for proper prescribing were based on a combination of professional expertise and professional literature. Their results for psychoactive drugs, expressed as percent nonconformance, are summarized in table 14. The authors suggested that the low percentage of nonconformance for chloral hydrate most likely reflects the small number of patients who received the drugs more than three times a week. The wide ranges of nonconformance rates for amitriptyline and chlordiazepoxide are ascribed to the small number of patients receiving those drugs in the five nursing homes. The most notable finding was the comparatively high rates of nonconformance for thioridazine (a major tranquilizer), the most frequently ordered psychoactive drug in nursing homes (NDTI 1975a,b).

In a study of 131 elderly nursing home patients, Ingman et al. (1975) found that patients with superior mental and physical abilities actually received more neuroactive substances (psychoactive drugs plus analgesics, skeletal muscle relaxants, antiparkinson drugs, and autonomic agents) than did

TABLE 15.—Percentage distribution of drug abuse mentions, by age and facility type

Facility	6-9	10-19	20-29	30-39	40-49	50 and Over	Total
Drug Abuse Warning Network							
Emergency rooms	*	20	43	20	11	6	100
Crisis centers	*	40	50	7	2	1	100
Medical examiners	*	8	43	20	13	16	100
Inpatient units	1	17	49	18	8	6	100
Total DAWN System	*	27	44	16	8	5	100
1970 U.S. Census	18	17	15	12	12	26	100

*Less than 0.5 percent.

SOURCE: Drug Abuse Warning Network (1974-1975)

patients with diminished mental and physical capacities. The differences were significant at the .05 level for both dimensions.

In a study of 53 female psychiatric inpatients aged 62-89, Barton and Hurst (1966) conducted a double-blind experiment in which an inert syrup was substituted for chlorpromazine. Patients were rated along seven dimensions by ward nurses, who did not know whether the patients were receiving chlorpromazine or the placebo. When the last week of chlorpromazine therapy was compared with the third week of placebo administration, five dimensions showed slight deterioration as measured by mean scores, while two dimensions showed no significant change. Ward nurses were unable to distinguish between patients receiving chlorpromazine and those receiving placebos. The results led the authors to conclude that 80 percent of the patients were receiving tranquilizers unnecessarily.

While the studies cited above cannot provide the basis for making generalizations about the magnitude or pattern of improper prescribing of psychoactive drugs to the elderly, they do provide at least some preliminary indications that the appropriateness of prescribing practices needs to be examined in greater depth and scope.

Drug-Related Illness and Death

Another issue that needs to be explored in relation to psychoactive drug use and the elderly is the extent to which that use may lead to drug-related illnesses or death. While we found no studies that estimate the propor-

tion of the elderly population so affected, there are some studies that provide information on hospital admissions and deaths resulting from abuse of drugs.

One source of information is the Drug Abuse Warning Network (DAWN 1974-1975), a nationwide system which continuously monitors drug abuse contact reports from selected hospital emergency rooms, hospital inpatient units, crisis centers, and medical examiners (coroners). Although the DAWN data do not show the percentages of older people who contact the monitored facilities as a result of abuse of psychoactive drugs, they do indicate general patterns related to age and types of drugs abused.

Based upon data on selected leading drugs for the period April 1974 to April 1975, it appears that nearly half of all drug mentions are related to abuse of prescription psychoactive drugs. Minor tranquilizers account for 19 percent of all drug abuse contact mentions, followed by barbiturate sedatives (10 percent), nonbarbiturate sedatives (7 percent), stimulants (6 percent), and psychostimulants (2 percent). The most frequently mentioned individual drug was diazepam, which accounted for 10 percent of all mentions.

People aged 50 and over (the oldest age category represented), who constitute 26 percent of the U.S. population, accounted for 5 percent of all mentions in the total DAWN system (see table 15). That was the lowest proportionate representation among all adult age groups. The relatively low frequency of contact may be partially explained by the fact that people aged 50 and over are much less likely to abuse illicit drugs, thereby reducing the overall likelihood that they would contact the monitored facilities. (Petersen and Thomas [1975], for example, found that during 1972 no persons aged 50 and over who contacted a Florida hospital for acute drug reactions had done so as a result of abuse of illicit drugs.)

The comparatively low frequency of contact, however, also appears to carry over into the prescription psychoactive drugs. While DAWN data do not provide correlations between age and all prescription psychoactive drugs, information on selected individual drugs may be used as a rough indicator. Diazepam—the most frequently mentioned drug of abuse in the DAWN system—may serve as a case in point: People aged 50 and over accounted for only 7 percent of all diazepam mentions. Figures for other individual drugs are similar: chlordiazepoxide (8 percent); oxazepam (7 percent); phenobarbital (8 percent); butabarbital (8 percent); flurazepam (14 percent); secobarbital (8 percent); and pentobarbital (16 percent). Thus, it appears that the frequency of contacts due to abuse of prescription psychoactive drugs, as well as for all drugs, is comparatively low among people aged 50 and over.

The largest proportion of mentions (16 percent) accounted for by people aged 50 and over come from medical examiners (see table 15). Nearly two-third (62 percent) of the medical examiner mentions for people aged 50 and over were attributed to suicide gestures or attempts, a figure that is nearly twice as high as that for any other age group. A majority of emergency room mentions (50 percent) and inpatient unit mentions (53 percent) for people aged 50 and over were attributed to suicide gestures or attempts, figures which were also higher than those for other age groups.

Thus, it appears that people aged 50 and over are less likely to contact any of the monitored facilities (including medical examiners) as a result of drug abuse than are other adults, but when they do make contact, the pattern reflects a disproportionately high rate of deaths and suicide gestures or attempts. The DAWN data do not indicate to what extent those deaths or suicide attempts can be directly attributed to prescription psychoactive drugs. (Benson and Brodie [1975] have suggested that the high rate of chronic physical and mental illness—especially depression caused by social factors—among the elderly contributes significantly to suicide attempts, and that prescription psychoactive drugs are often used as a means.)

Petersen and Thomas (1975), in a study of acute drug reaction admissions to a Florida hospital, provide some supplementary data to the DAWN system, although the data are not necessarily representative. Consistent with the DAWN data, they found that, while people aged 50 and over constituted 39.0 percent of the county population served by the hospital, they represented only 5.4 percent of all admissions for acute drug reactions. Among those people aged 50 and over who were admitted to the hospital for acute drug reaction, nearly two-thirds (61.7 percent) were white females. Admissions for older females exceeded their distribution in the county population, as did admissions for older blacks (male and female). Nearly half (49.0 percent) of all aged admissions were for abuse of sedatives (as opposed to 35.9 percent for all ages) and nearly a third (31.9 percent) were for abuse of tranquilizers (as opposed to 24.4 percent for all ages). Roughly a third (35.0 percent) of aged admissions were associated with suicide attempts, a figure that was generally consistent with that for all ages (33.7 percent). In comparable settings, the DAWN data indicate that suicide attempts or gestures accounted for 53 percent of inpatient unit mentions for people aged 50 and over, as opposed to 28 percent for all ages. Thus, the Petersen and Thomas data on suicide attempts deviate from the patterns reported in the DAWN system.

In summary, we found no data that indicate the proportion of the elderly population for which illness or death can be attributed to abuse of prescription psychoactive drugs. There is evidence, however, which suggests that older people are less likely than other adults to be admitted to hospitals or to die as a consequence of abusing drugs. The comparatively low percentages of older people who contact DAWN-monitored facilities as a result of abuse of selected prescription psychoactive drugs, especially when considered in conjunction with the NDTI data cited earlier, suggest the possibility that older people may be particularly responsible in their use of those drugs.

OVER-THE-COUNTER PSYCHOACTIVE DRUGS

The manner in which over-the-counter (OTC) drugs are acquired and used makes it more difficult to obtain data on the nature and extent of their use than for prescription drugs. There are, for example, no equivalents to physicians' records or patients' charts to serve as useful data sources. Even

TABLE 16.—Self-reported use of OTC psychoactive drugs during the past year, by age and by by sex

Drug Class and Sex	Percent by Age Groups			
	18-29	30-44	45-59	60-74
Stimulants				
Men	17	2	2	2
Women	8	1	*	*
Sleeping pills				
Men	8	4	3	7
Women	7	7	4	5
Tranquilizers				
Men	4	1	1	2
Women	11	6	3	2
All psychoactive OTC drugs				
Men				
Any use in past year	25	7	5	9
No use in past year	75	93	95	91
Total	100	100	100	100
Women				
Any use in past year	21	12	7	7
No use in past year	79	88	93	93
Total	100	100	100	100

*Less than 0.5 percent.

SOURCE: Parry et al. (1973)

pharmaceutical industry data, which can provide information on production and sales volume, cannot easily be correlated with user characteristics. Unlike prescription drugs, which are dispensed through a system involving the physician, pharmacist, and patient, consumers purchase and use OTC drugs in relative anonymity. The most likely source of information, then, appears to be the consumers themselves.

In the survey of national psychoactive drug use patterns by Parry et al. (1973), the interviews included questions related to use of OTC psychoactive drugs. Table 16 summarizes the findings on the percentages of men and women, by age group, who indicated use of OTC psychoactive drugs during a 1-year period preceding the interview. The classes of drugs represented are somewhat arbitrary since, as the authors pointed out, many of the tranquilizers used are advertised as having tranquilizing effects, but actually have the same ingredients as OTC sleeping pills.

In the 60-74 age group only 9 percent of men and 7 percent of women reported use of any OTC psychoactive drugs within the past year. OTC sleeping pills were the most commonly used drugs for both older men and women, although the percentages were relatively low (7 percent and 5 percent, respectively).

Unlike the patterns of prescription psychoactive drug use, the extent of use of OTC psychoactive drugs among older people is not disproportionately high. The highest prevalence rates for OTC drugs are in the age group 18-29.

The authors also reported data on OTC psychoactive drug use by geographic region, education, and Index of Social Position. They found use to be substantially higher in the West than in other regions of the country, and somewhat higher among those with more education and higher social position. Since those factors were not broken down by age group, however, it is not clear to what extent those patterns hold true for the age group 60-74.

Only 3 to 4 percent of people in all age groups indicated that they used both prescription and OTC psychoactive drugs.

SUMMARY AND CONCLUSIONS

Roughly a third (32 percent) of the elderly population (60-74 years of age) reported use of a prescription or over-the-counter psychoactive drug within a 1-year period. One-fifth (21 percent) of older men and one-third (32 percent) of older women reported use of a prescription psychoactive drug, while 9 percent of older men and 7 percent of older women reported use of an OTC psychoactive drug.

The most widely used classes of prescription psychoactive drugs among older men and women were minor tranquilizers/sedatives (11 percent of older men, 25 percent of older women) and hypnotics (7 percent of older men, 8 percent of older women), both of which were used by greater proportions of older men and women than other age groups. The most widely used class of OTC psychoactive drugs among older men and women was sleeping pills (7 percent of older men, 5 percent of older women) although, as was the case for all OTC classes, smaller percentages of older men and women used them than did those in the age group 18-20.

Older people (65 years of age and over) received disproportionately high percentages of orders for most prescription psychoactive drugs sampled from the NDTI, especially among the sedatives and hypnotics. As is the general case in relation to prescribing patterns by sex, older women received substantially more orders for psychoactive drugs than did older men.

The data cited on prescription psychoactive drug use among institutionalized elderly populations were inadequate for making general statements about national patterns of use. Among the studies reported, however, major tranquilizers and hypnotics were found to be the psychoactive drugs most widely used in nursing homes. Major tranquilizers were the psychoactive drugs most widely used among elderly psychiatric inpatients, especially among those diagnosed as schizophrenic; however, contrary to use patterns in the general population, both the percentage of people using psychoactive drugs and the dosage per drug,

as well as the prevalence of polypharmacy, tended to decline with increasing age.

Reported studies of noncompliance failed to establish any significant relationship between noncompliance and demographic variables. In general, however, the magnitude of noncompliance reported in various studies ranged from 25 percent to 59 percent of patients sampled. Data presented on the extent of improper prescribing practices were insufficient for generalization. Data on the percentages of older people who contact hospitals, crisis centers, and medical examiners (coroners) as a result of abuse of drugs indicate that older people are less likely to do so than are other adults, although when they do make contact, it is likely to be related to suicide attempts.

In general, the limited nature of most of the published studies cited in this report has made it impossible to present a comprehensive profile of psychoactive drug use among the elderly. To suggest that data are not available, however, is not to imply that data sources do not exist; on the contrary, the potential for research in the area of psychoactive drug use and the elderly is promising. The National Disease and Therapeutic Index, for example, is rich in unmined information. NDTI data could be broken down by age, sex, type of drug, diagnosis, and location of patient, constituting a comprehensive national sample of prescription psychoactive drug orders. A major drawback of the NDTI, unfortunately, is that it is a privately published data source, thereby restricting access and publication potential; it is also based on voluntary reporting, which may affect its representativeness. Physicians' records, pharmacists' records, and patient interviews are other sources of data that could be utilized for national or regional samples.

In terms of directions for further research, more information is needed on the nature and extent of psychoactive drug use among the elderly. The survey by Parry et al., for example, provided very useful data on national patterns of psychoactive drug use; however, it dealt with only the broadest classes of psychoactive drugs (combining minor tranquilizers and sedatives), and it did not survey the elderly living in institutional settings. Ideally, future research could provide more information on prescribing and use of individual drugs as well as drug classes, and correlate the data with diagnoses and location of the patient (nursing home, hospital, etc.). Such a profile could provide better insights into the reasons why older people use (or are issued) psychoactive drugs, in addition to providing more detailed information on patterns of use.

More information is also needed on the extent of, and reasons for, misuse of psychoactive drugs. The studies of noncompliance, for example, have not generally been comprehensive enough to develop an accurate picture of the extent to which older people make medication errors for prescription drugs in general, or for psychoactive drugs in particular. Another issue that deserves particular attention is the improper prescribing and administering of psychoactive drugs. Older people would appear to be especially vulnerable to improper prescribing since the physiological changes associated with aging can have a significant effect on the way in which drugs are metabolized (Piland 1977). In addition, there has been some suggestion that the prescribing and administering of drugs in nursing homes are often accomplished without adequate safeguards, and are sometimes carried out with the regimen of the home as a primary consideration (U.S. Senate 1973; Learoyd 1972). As a general principle, the disproportionate use of psychoactive drugs by the elderly should warrant a close examination of the appropriateness of that use.

As a final comment, it has been apparent throughout this report that the reliance on individual case studies has often led to situations where data were not comparable due to differences in methodology or categories employed. The development of a data base on psychoactive drug use and the elderly would seem to require some future efforts to insure greater consistency between studies.

REFERENCES

Abelson, H.I., and Atkinson, R.B. Public Experience with Psychoactive Substances. Response Analysis Corporation, 1975.

American Health Care Association. Long Term Care Facts. 1975.

Balter, M.B., and Levine, J. The nature and extent of psychotropic drugs usage in the United States. Psychopharmacological Bulletin, 5:3-14, 1969.

Barton, R., and Hurst, L. Unnecessary use of tranquilizers in elderly patients. British Journal of Psychiatry, 112:989-990, 1966.

Beardsley, R.; Heaton, A.; Kabat, H.; and Martilla, J. Patterns of Drug Use in Nursing Home Patients. Minneapolis, Minn.: University of Minnesota, College of Pharmacy, 1975.

Benson, R.A., and Brodie, D.C. Suicide by overdoses of medicines among the aged. Journal of the American Geriatrics Society, 23:304-308, 1975.

Boyd, J.R.; Covington, T.R.; Stanaszek, W.F.; and Coussons, R.T. Drug defaulting: Analysis of noncompliance patterns. American Journal of Hospital Pharmacy, 31:485-491, 1974.

Clinite, J.C., and Kabat, H.F. Errors during self-administration. Journal of American Pharmacological Association, NS9:450-452, 1969.

Conference on Drug Use and the Elderly. Sponsored by the National Institute on Drug Abuse and the National Institute for Drug Programs, June 12-13, 1975.

Davis, M. Physiologic, psychological, and demographic factors in patient compliance with doctors' orders. Medical Care, 6:115-122, 1968.

Department of Health, Education, and Welfare, Task Force on Prescription Drugs. The Drug Users. Washington, D.C.: U.S. Government Printing Office, 1968.

Doyle, J.P., and Hamm, B.M. Medication Use and Misuse Study Among Older Persons. Jacksonville, Fla.: The Cathedral Foundation of Jacksonville, Inc., 1976.

Drug Abuse Warning Network. Project DAWN III. Rockville, Md.: National Institute on Drug Abuse, 1974-1975.

Fracchia, J.; Sheppard, C.; and Merlis, S. Combination medications in psychiatric treatment: Patterns in a group of elderly hospital patients. Journal of American Geriatrics Society, 19:301-307, 1971.

Guttman, D. A Survey of Drug-Taking Behavior of the Elderly. Rockville, Md.: National Institute on Drug Abuse, 1977.

Hussar, D.A. Patient noncompliance. Journal of American Pharmacological Association, 15:183-190, 1975.

Hussar, D.A.; Boyd, J.R.; Covington, T.R.; Stanaszek, W.F.; and Cousson, R.T. Drug defaulting: Determinants of compliance. Part I. American Journal of Hospital Pharmacy, 31:362-367, 1974.

Ingman, S.R.; Lawson, I.R.; Pierpadi, P.G.; and Blake, P. A survey of the prescribing and administration of drugs in a long-term care institution for the elderly. Journal of American Geriatrics Society, 23:309-316, 1975.

Laska, E.; Varga, E.; Wanderling, J.; Simpson, G.; Logeman, G.W.; and Shah, B.V. Patterns of psychotropic drug use for schizophrenia. Diseases of the Nervous System, 1973.

Latiolais, C.J., and Berry, C.C. Misuse of prescription medication by outpatients. Drug Intelligence and Clinical Pharmacology, 3:270-277, 1969.

Learoyd, B.M. Psychotropic drugs and the elderly patient. Medical Journal of Australia, 1: 1131-1133, 1972.

Manard, B.B. Old Age Institutions. Lexington, Mass.: Lexington Books, 1975.

National Disease and Therapeutic Index. Ambler, Pa.: IMS, 1975a.

National Disease and Therapeutic Index. S.v., Leading drugs in nursing homes. Ambler, Pa.: IMS, 1975b.

Parry, H.J.; Balter, M.B.; Mellinger, G.D.; Cisin, I.H.; and Manheimber, D.I. National patterns of psychotherapeutic drug use. Archives of General Psychiatry, 28:769-783, 1973.

Petersen, D.M., and Thomas, C.W. Acute drug reactions among the elderly. Journal of Gerontology, 30:552-556, 1975.

Piland, N.F. The aging process and psychoactive drug use. SRI International, 1977.

Prien, R.F. A survey of psychoactive drug use in the aged at Veterans Administration hospitals. Aging, 2:143-154, 1975.

Prien, R.F.; Haber, P.A.; and Caffey, E.M. The use of psychoactive drug in elderly patients with psychiatric disorders: Survey conducted in 12 Veterans Administration hospitals. Journal of American Geriatrics Society, 23:104-112, 1975.

Prien, R.F.; Klett, C.J.; and Caffey, E.M. Polypharmacy in the psychiatric treatment of elderly hospitalized patients: A survey of 12 Veterans Administration hospitals. Diseases of the Nervous System, 37:333-336, 1976.

Schwartz, D.; Wang, M.; Zeitz, L.; and Goss, M.E.W. Medication errors made by elderly, chronically ill patients. American Journal of Public Health, 52:2018-2029, 1962.

Steward, R.B., and Cluff, L.E. A review of medication errors and compliance in ambulant patients. Clinical Pharmacology and Therapy, 13:463-468, 1972.

Stewart, J.E.; Kabat, H.; and Wertheimer, A.I. Drug usage review sample studies in long-term care facilities. American Journal of Hospital Pharmacy, 33:138-144, 1976.

U.S. Senate Special Committee on Aging, Subcommittee on Long-Term Care. Drugs in Nursing Homes: Misuse, High Costs, and Kickbacks. (Supporting Paper #2). Washington, D.C.: U.S. Government Printing Office, 1973.

U.S. Senate Special Committee on Aging, Subcommitte on Long-Term Care. Nursing Home Care in the United States: Failure in Public Policy. (Introductory Report). Washington, D.C.: U.S. Government Printing Office, 1975.

Willcox, D.R.C.; Gillan, R.; and Hare, E.H. Do psychiatric outpatients take their drugs? British Medical Journal, 2:790-792, 1965.

PSYCHOACTIVE DRUG MISUSE AMONG THE ELDERLY: A REVIEW OF PREVENTION AND TREATMENT PROGRAMS

James Gollub

INTRODUCTION

The elderly consume over 25 percent of all prescription drugs. An increasing proportion of these prescriptions is accounted for by psychoactive drugs, defined in this paper as major and minor tranquilizers, antidepressants, stimulants, sedatives, and hypnotics.

There is growing, though limited, evidence of intentional and nonintentional misuse of psychoactive drugs by the aged, often resulting in physical and social harm (Eisdorfer and Stotsky 1977). Sometimes faulty diagnosis and application by the physician is the causal factor, while in other cases the individual may make a deliberate choice to misuse a drug, or may simply make a mistake.

Recognition of this problem has led to the development of intervention programs both for more accurate diagnoses of symptoms arising from complex medical and psychosocial problems and as environmental supports that afford the older individual an alternative to the misuse of psychoactive drugs. Only a few programs have been identified which are directly concerned with drug misuse by the elderly; however, other existing service programs could provide the basis for expansion or modification of service components to deal with drug abuse among aged persons. This report provides overviews of 1) programs that monitor the diagnosis, prescription, and administration of psychoactive drugs, and 2) programs designed to intervene in psychoactive drug misuse among the elderly.

A survey of the literature on drug misuse among the elderly reveals that misuse occurs at any point in the continuum of health care. Ten factors conducive to the misapplication or misuse of psychoactive drugs among the elderly have been identified in this report and fall into two categories: those attributable to health professionals and those attributable to the elderly. Actions for which health professionals may be responsible include:

- Inaccurate diagnosis
- Inaccuracies in drug treatment
- Polypharmacy, including failure to consider drug interactions
- Deliberate overmedication of arbitrary medication (institutional patterns).

Misuse by elderly persons includes:

- Drug overdoses, due either to emotional disturbance or to error
- Misuse, due to behavior resulting from organic brain disease
- Use of multiple prescriptions without the physician's knowledge
- Overuse of prescriptions without the physician's knowledge, including improper use of automatic refills and telephone prescriptions
- Exchange of drugs between individuals
- Use of expired drugs

The conditions that contribute to the misuse of psychoactive drugs among the elderly have been the subject of intervention programs in medicine, pharmacy, psychiatry, nursing, social work, and other related areas.

METHOD

The information for this report was derived from an extensive survey of the literature in the field of health and social services, supplemented by interviews with, and materials from, researchers and service providers in the fields of gerontology, psychiatry, psychopharmacology, pharmacy, nursing, drug-abuse intervention, and social work.

The search for programs dealing with the misuse of psychoactive drugs among the elderly revealed that very few such programs exist. Most programs are not concerned specifically with the elderly as the sole or major client. Although there are social service programs which serve the elderly consumer--such as hospitals, nursing homes, pharmacies, clinics, and community mental health programs--these programs are not reviewed in this report. This report reviews programs directly relevant to the problem of psychoactive drug use among the elderly.

Intervention programs that address the problem of psychoactive drug misuses by the elderly fall into two categories which reflect the current policies of health care and social service providers. The first category of intervention programs, initiated by health care providers, deals with errors of diagnosis, prescription, and drug administration by the health professional. This category includes programs of medical and psychiatric diagnosis that ensure appropriate treatment of the aged as well as retroactive and continuous drug-consumption monitoring in inpatient and outpatient settings (including mental health centers, nursing facilities, and housing environments).

The second category consists of those programs specifically designed to permit intervention in, and treatment of, the problems of psychoactive and other drug misuse among the elderly. Programs addressing this problem include chemical dependency outreach, referral, treatment, and followup programs; acute- and chronic-care programs for alcoholics and drug users; drug education programs; peer counseling; and behavioral therapy. These programs are initiated by health care professionals, by social service agencies, and sometimes by concerned individuals.

PROGRAMS THAT MONITOR THE DIAGNOSIS, PRESCRIPTION, AND ADMINISTRATION OF PSYCHOACTIVE DRUGS

INTRODUCTION

The increased sensitivity to drugs among older persons, and the potential for altered effects when drugs are used in combination, are important reasons why drug users and drug regimens should be carefully scrutinized by medical personnel. Pharmaceutical researchers and physicians in recent years have focused on the related issues of diagnosis of disorders, accurate prescribing for the elderly, general control of monitoring of the prescription process, and patterns of use by specific client groups. Much of this focus has been aimed at developing improved monitoring tools for institutions and community pharmacies, and on increasing the knowledge of medical practitioners in the area of drugs and their applications to and use by the elderly. Efforts to develop programs of intervention and alternatives to psychoactive drug use by the aged include the following:

- Improved diagnostic procedures
- Improved physician knowledge of age-oriented prescribing of medications
- Alternative methods of administering drugs
- Computerized and manual evaluations of drug use and impact in institutions, in the community, and in training programs
- Increased involvement of pharmacists in drug monitoring

The following sections of this report provide overviews of programs in each category.

THE ROLE OF DIAGNOSTIC PROCEDURES AND PROGRAMS IN REDUCING PSYCHOACTIVE DRUG MISUSE

Accurate diagnosis in the treatment of the elderly is crucial to the reduction of drug misuse, either intentional or nonintentional. Changes that occur in the social life, physiologic structure, and psychosocial environment of the older person often produce symptoms deceptively similar to those of more serious disorders, such as organic brain syndrome (Fann et al. 1976). In some instances, the solution is as simple as recognizing that the presenting problem is nonpsychiatric and therefore does not require a prescription for psychoactive drugs. The physician who understands the symptomatology of disease and aging will be better able to determine when it is more appropriate to suggest a social worker than to prescribe a psychoactive drug (Hall 1973).

Conversely, failure to diagnose psychiatric disturbance can lead to faulty treatment and create new medical problems for the older person. Burville (1971) points out that mental problems are overlooked in up to 50 percent of any group of medical or surgical patients. The probability of nondiagnosis of mental disorder in the elderly patient, where an underlying mental disorder may be masked by a somatic complaint, is even higher (Mechanic 1972). Schuckit et al. (1975) also stress the need for accurate diagnostic criteria applicable to older populations. Using personal interviews and chart reviews, Schuckit et al. (1975) established the prevalence of unrecognized psychiatric disorders in elderly medical and surgical patients at a Veterans Administration hospital. They attempted to integrate present criteria for these disorders into their diagnostic procedure (Alexander 1972; Foley 1971) and identified major mental undiagnosed disorders in 24 percent of their study population. This identification of undiagnosed disorders suggests that there is great potential for improvement of medical treatment of the aging patient, with particular reference to the prescription of psychoactive medications.

The two programs discussed below provide examples of diagnostic services geared specifically toward the geriatric patients, which help reduce the likelihood of improper diagnoses. Services include clinical assessment from a multidisciplinary approach, education, and consultation with physicians, patients, and families.

The Philadelphia Geriatric Center

Psychological assessment of the elderly has been considered at length by members of the Philadelphia Geriatric Center, who have developed a program specifically oriented toward the clinical assessment of the older person for the purpose of determining appropriate treatment (Whelihan 1976). The Philadelphia Geriatric Center's Baer Consultation and Diagnostic Center uses a multidisciplinary approach and assesses function from biomedical, psychological, and social points of view. The diagnostic process includes a complete medical history and physical examination, medical laboratory and pulmonary function tests, X-ray and electrocardiograph studies, ophthalmological and audiometric examinations, neurological and EEG studies, social work and evaluation of activities of daily living, nutritional assessment, and psychological and psychiatric examinations. Computerized

tomography studies and brain scans are frequently performed.

The diagnostic procedures are followed by a team conference, where the findings of the various disciplines are analyzed and integrated to provide a picture of overall strengths and weaknesses. At a second conference, the client and his or her family receive a detailed verbal report. Reports from each discipline are then sent to the primary care physician; a shorter report in layman's language is forwarded to the client. A 6-month followup monitors progress.

The psychologists systematically evaluate cognitive, behavioral, and emotional functioning in the elderly client. Functional analysis of the person vis-a-vis the environment (Lawton 1970) and the administration of psychological tests designed specifically for the elderly client assure that all areas of functioning are considered. Incorporation of both neuropsychological and psychological assessment tests in a single diagnostic package increases corroboration of observations concerning behavioral symptoms and physiological damage, and it also enhances the probability of correct treatment, thus reducing the likelihood of inappropriate use of psychoactive drugs.

Southeast/Bayview Mental Health
Center, Geriatric Services Program

The Southeast/Bayview Mental Health Center, Geriatric Services Program, in San Francisco, California, also shows that evaluation and health service delivery media can play a critical role in ascertaining the specific mental and physical health needs of older adults before they are prematurely or inappropriately assigned to institutional settings.

The Geriatric Services Program uses a multidisciplinary service team of psychiatric social workers, psychiatrists, and a senior aide. A physician is available for consultation and medical assessment, when indicated. The program emphasizes prompt evaluation, treatment, and followup in the care of the elderly. Precrisis intervention is aimed at maintaining the elderly person at optimum functioning in his or her own home. Home services are a major mode of treatment, supplemented by day-hospitalization for those who require it.

Primary prevention, including education, consultation, and community organization services, focuses on the causative factors of mental illness in the elderly. Secondary prevention uses geriatric evaluation techniques to distinguish between irreversible chronic brain disease and acute reversible brain syndrome due to drug toxicity, electrolyte imbalance, infection, vitamin deficiency, endogenous depression, or malnutrition (all of which can cause an individual to manifest overt symptoms similar to those of chronic organic brain syndrome). The diagnosis of disorders other than chronic brain syndrome often enables older persons to be treated in their homes, thereby preventing institutionalization.

The immediate priorities of the program include:

● Distribution of Resources Handbook for Seniors

● Identification of residents in need of service and treatment by Geriatric Services staff; aggressive case finding, development of followup-care and after-care programs for the elderly in their own homes and care facilities; liaison with Napa State Hospital for evaluation of patients and their return to the community, where appropriate; and implementation of State-mandated continuing care services to track, link, monitor, and refer certain patients who have been discharged from crisis outpatient services.

THE ROLE OF PRESCRIPTION AND ADMINISTRATION CONTROLS IN REDUCING PSYCHOACTIVE DRUG MISUSE

After a specific mental disorder has been appropriately diagnosed, there still remains ample opportunity for misapplication of therapeutic treatment. The source of error in these cases is not related to selection of treatment, for there are fairly standard guidelines for the application of psychoactive drugs to the treatment of psychiatric disorders. The problem is related to the effect of the physiological changes that occur with age on the older person's sensitivity to and tolerance of specific drugs. The hazards that may be related to physiologic change are also compounded when a multiple drug regimen is used.

In response to the problems of drug/person compatibility, pharmacists and doctors have evolved guidelines for use in prescribing for the elderly. Among the examples of guidelines discussed below are the review of factors related to patient history, current mental and physical status, and actual amounts of drugs required for therapeutic results.

Lamy Approach

Lamy has developed procedures for reducing drug misuse in his own clinical practice. Lamy (1976) points out the hazard that drugs may pose to the aged, particularly certain psychoactive drugs such as the phenothiazines

and barbiturates, and suggests that many drug-induced illnesses are not detected because of their similarity to stereotypical aspects of old age such as forgetfulness, weakness, confusion, tremor, anorexia, and anxiety.

Lamy urges caution in geriatric prescribing based on physiological and pharmacological difference in treating the aged, and suggests a careful drug history and periodic review of drug consumption. He also states that the wise physician will not take for granted that the patient a) has the prescription filled, b) understands how to take the medicine, c) is taking no medication other than that which the physician has prescribed, d) continues to take the prescribed drug, and e) accurately reports intake and adverse reactions. Lamy proposes a systematic approach to prescribing for the geriatric patient, a system that would include careful diagnosis, record-keeping, and reevaluation of the treatment. He also believes that pharmacy records and drug labeling are important tools to insure proper use of prescribed drugs.

Hall Approach

Hall (1973) also recognized the need for extra caution when treating the elderly with pharmacologically active drugs and drew up a list of simple rules pertaining to drug use by the elderly. These rules constitute an informal program that, within the context of Lamy's more comprehensive process, might promote more careful prescription and use of psychoactive drugs among the aged (De Groot 1974). The program consists of six points:

● Knowledge of the pharmacological action of the drug, and how it is metabolized;

● Use of the lowest effective dose in the individual patient; in practice, this means that the dosage should always be titrated with patient response;

● Use of the minimum number of drugs necessary; since memory tends to deteriorate with age, patients may neglect to take their medications if drug regimens are too complex;

● Avoidance of the use of drugs to treat symptoms, seeking rather to treat the cause; mental disturbance in the elderly patient is often diagnosed as senile psychosis without adequate consideration of alternative diagnoses;

● Neither withholding medication because the patient is "too old" nor continuing to use a drug when its side effects are worse than the patient's original symptoms; and

- Use of a drug for no longer a period than is necessary.

Drug Spotlight Program

The Drug Spotlight Program is another informational program designed to improve pharmacists' and physicians' knowledge of drug qualities and interactions. Through the joint efforts of several national hospitals and medical, nursing, and pharmacy groups, a program of continuing education has been initiated that is aimed at helping pharmacy and therapeutic committees of local hospitals review and, when necessary, improve drug therapy. The Drug Spotlight Program was initiated by the American Society for Clinical Pharmacology and Therapeutics; participants include the American Academy of Family Physicians, the American College of Pharmacists, the American College of Surgeons, and many other professional organizations. The specific goals of the Drug Spotlight Program (Reilly 1972) are:

- To achieve maximally effective drug therapy;

- To reduce the incidence of serious adverse drug reactions; and

- To achieve the lowest cost for drug therapy compatible with maximum effectiveness and safety.

A national advisory committee selects four drug groups to be "spotlighted" during the coming year, and suggests that these drugs be the focus of study by local hospitals, pharmacies, and therapeutic committees. The activities of the Drug Spotlight Program also include publication of scientific papers and editorials on the subject of the target drugs.

ALTERNATIVE METHODS
OF DRUG ADMINISTRATION

Researchers in pharmacy and medicine have also initiated experimental programs that offer alternative approaches to the traditional patterns of drug administration, programs that may help avert specific types of drug misuse. In the two approaches described below, one emphasizes the value of teaching inpatients how to self-medicate in preparation for their release, while the other focuses on minimizing medication error by reducing drug dosages to once per day.

Libow and Mehl Approach

Libow and Mehl (1970) piloted a program using patient self-administration of therapeutic drugs to circumvent the problems a person encoun-

ters when he or she must adjust to self-administration of medications following release from a hospital or nursing home. In this program, 20 elderly, frail, chronically ill patients were given medications for self-administration while in the hospital. They were judged by nurses and staff to be in a "good" mental state, resembling that of the physically ill elderly who reside in the community. The subjects in this program had significant medical diseases. In some cases the disease was in the subacute phase; in others, it was quiescent. The test "medications" were placebos (sugar), which patients were told would increase "appetite and strength." The medicine was issued in the usual pharmacy vial with the usual label, accompanied by verbal instructions from the physician. The subjects were instructed when and how much to take of the medication. Every few days, the physician counted the remaining medications in each vial and questioned the patients about their general well-being, appetite, and strength.

Of the 20 patients self-administering their medicines, five made errors. In 588 opportunities, there were 14 errors (2.3 percent); 6 errors were made by one patient. The results show impressive abilities for self-administration of medication, although this was probably enhanced by the structure of the study. The study period was brief, and participation was stimulating for the patients. The approach permits the patient to "learn" the medication schedule while under the "teaching" direction of the hospital staff. The inabilities raise questions about realistic post-hospital medication planning, e.g., should diuretics be given parenterally or orally; should prescribed drugs be variously shaped rather than several white tablets; and what would be the most convenient schedule? The ultimate goals of this program are to free nursing time for other tasks, to reduce post-hospital morbidity caused by patients' medication errors, and reduce hospital costs.

Ayd Approach

Drug administration within the psychiatric institution has been explored by Frank Ayd, Jr. (1975), who suggests a program of once-a-day drug dosage as a means of reducing noncompliance, the hazards of polypharmacy, and the unnecessary use of psychoactive drugs by the aging patient. Ayd argues that the aging brain is particularly sensitive to psychopharmaceuticals and that it is likely that at least 20 percent of psychogeriatric admissions are precipitated by the adverse effects of psychoactive drugs (Learoyd 1972). Polypharmacy and the consequent complexity of drug schedules complicate administration and are a burden on nurses. Error is inevitable, increasing in frequency with the complexity of drug regimens.

Ayd suggests that the total daily dose of many drugs now prescribed in divided doses could be administered once or twice daily, in the morning and/or evening. This pattern of administration has several advantages: 1) a single dose is more convenient for both patient and staff than divided daily doses; 2) outpatients who self-medicate, and families who have to medicate patients, find a single daily dose convenient, easy to remember, and economical.

Ayd refutes the objection that single-dose administration may increase side effects. DiMascio and Shader (1969) address claims that a single dose may be less effective than divided doses: "While few studies have shown a clinical superiority of the daily or twice daily schedule over the multiple dose schedule, none have reported the reverse." While such a program has yet to be tested extensively, it represents another attempt to minimize the problems encountered by the elderly in their use of drugs.

MONITORING THE PRESCRIPTION AND USE OF DRUGS

Formalized methods for monitoring drug use have existed for a long time, particularly in institutional settings; however, the processes of prescribing, dispensing, administering, and taking drugs (Brodie 1971) have often been studied for their role in fiscal management of medical supplies, rather than as a mode for ensuring appropriate therapy for patients.

Pharmacists have long had the opportunity to informally monitor drug prescription--both by reviewing amounts and dosages in the dispensing area and by checking the appropriateness of drugs selected in the ward (Knoben 1976). In the case of the community pharmacist, a review of a patient's history of drug use when comprehensive drug profiles are available can be accomplished, although some studies indicate that profiles have not been adequately used in determining actual or potential drug interaction hazards (Nelson et al. 1976). If a drug is given in the hospital or nursing home, the nurse provides another review of drug and dosage prior to administration.

Utilization studies of specific drugs or classes of drugs have been conducted by pharmacy and therapeutics committees, either routinely or in response to a potential problem. The ongoing medical audit of care, normally carried out by hospital review committees, generally includes a review of the treatment regimen.

Methods for carrying out drug monitoring and utilization studies have become highly technical in recent years. Computers, and the use of remote terminals at pharmacies and clinics, have enabled programs to maintain updated medical and pharmacy records of many patients and customers, as well as to compare drugs in use for interactive potential and for indicators of overuse and expiration of prescriptions.

Innovative programs for monitoring drug prescription and use are discussed below and include computer monitoring programs, community monitoring programs, institutional monitoring programs, programs in training monitoring skills, and drug use evaluation programs. While these programs do not directly address the problem of drug misuse by the elderly, the problem is subsumed in their broad applicability.

Computer Monitoring and Utilization Programs

Computer drug utilization review (DUR) programs are a new dimension in monitoring institutional patterns of drug prescription and consumption. Computer systems are used most frequently in institutional studies because of the greater accessibility of both patient medication data and data-processing equipment. However, computer drug utilization systems have also been used in the community to identify patterns of drug prescription and use by community pharmacy clients and by outpatients in health maintenance organizations and medical clinics. Prospective review systems are located at the Los Angeles County-University of Southern California (LAC-USC); the Medical University of South Carolina, Family Practice Clinic MIIS System; the Drug Intake and Management System (DIMES) in Massachusetts; and Monitoring and Evaluation of Drug Interactions by a Pharmacy Oriented Reporting System (MEDIPHOR) at Stanford, California. Retrospective drug use systems (including the LAC-USC and MEDIPHOR systems) include the PAID program in North Carolina, the Columbia Medical Clinic in Maryland, and the New Haven Health Care Plan in Connecticut.

The purpose of the drug review and control processes mentioned above is "rational prescribing," which is described by the Task Force on Prescription Drugs as "...the right drug for the right patient at the right time" (Task Force on Prescription Drugs 1969).

The LAC-USC System

In 1967, medical professionals at the Los Angeles County-University of Southern California (LAC-USC) Medical Center published a description of the first computer system that combined on-line prescription processing and review procedures. The aims of this kind of system are to 1) prevent excessive dispensing of drugs with known abuse potential; 2) prevent harmful drug interactions by surveying the patient's drug record before a new prescription is processed; 3) insure and monitor the proper drug and dosage for intended clinical purpose; 4) study the drug usage patterns and correct inefficient expenditures of funds through redirecting purchases of specific drugs; and 5) implement inventory control. The use of this system to perform prospective and retrospective drug use review has been highly successful. Prospective utilization to prevent potentially harmful drug interactions revealed that 7 percent of outpatient prescriptions were potentially dangerous. The process has been used to improve prescription patterns for antibiotics and hypertensive medications. With the advent of the Professional Standards Review Organizations and Health Maintenance Organizations, it is probably that greater emphasis will be placed on the role of systems for prospective and retrospective monitoring of drug use.

Medical University of South Carolina, Family Practice Clinic Program

At the Medical University of South Carolina's Family Practice Clinic, a computer-based system to monitor outpatient drug use is part of a comprehensive medical record system (Braunstein and James 1976). The pharmacy subsystem has been under development and revision for approximately 3 years (Karig et al. 1974) and has been fully operational in the Family Practice Center for approximately 1 year. The system stores records of 6,000 patients using the Family Center facilities. The monitoring system assumes that 1) practice of medicine in the outpatient situation is based largely on pharmaceutical intervention in disease processes (i.e., drugs, not surgery) and 2) the physician in an outpatient setting cannot supervise the patient's drug therapy as closely as the physician in an inpatient setting.

The pharmacy system has four parts:

- The pharmacist at the computer terminal enters the new drug into the patient's profile. The profile displays patient status information (e.g., Medicaid), information on the interaction potential of the prescribed drug (Martin 1971), and educa-

tional information for the patient. The label for the medicine is printed at a terminal in clear English.

- The patient's history is displayed, including dates of drug renewals.

- A short sequence on the characteristics and use of drugs other than the new prescription appears.

- A warning of potential drug-drug interaction of the new prescription and any drugs the patient is currently taking is displayed.

The computer also produces a weekly report listing all patients who returned at an inappropriate interval for a renewal or who did not return at all. The computer completes drug searches, listing all patients with a history of using a particular drug and indicating those individuals currently using the drug in question, which is useful for large-scale drug utilization studies.

Members of the center may use any pharmacy in the area, because the pharmacists record prescription data on postcards and send it to the center for entry on the computer profile. The system increases communication between physician and pharmacist, and reduces misuse of drugs in cases where the physician and pharmacist can interact with the patient.

The DIMES System

A computerized drug-management system that is in the implementation phase in Massachusetts is the Drug Intake Management and Evaluation System, or DIMES (La Brie Associates 1976). This computer-based diagnostic, information-storage and retrieval system monitors the use of psychoactive drugs in both hospital and outpatient clinic settings.

The DIMES system is currently capable of monitoring 125 drugs (both psychoactive and medical) commonly prescribed to psychiatric patients. As the system is further refined, more drugs will be added. Using the system's stored information, the computer evaluates the following questions and prints out the answers.

- Do the symptoms match the diagnosis?

- Is the drug prescribed consistent with the symptoms and diagnosis?

- Is the drug within effective dose range and below maximum dose?

- Does the patient have any medical conditions for which the drug is contraindicated?

- Is the patient taking any other medical or psychoactive drugs that have potentially negative interactions with this drug?

- Is the drug available in a more cost-effective form?

- Are new symptoms that occur after medication side effects of the current medication?

- Does a review of the patient's symptom history indicate the changes should be made in the drug administration schedule?

- Does a review of the patient's drug intake record suggest that changes should be made in the drug schedule?

Patients' current information files are available at any time, and periodic reviews of their symptom histories and drug intake records are generated automatically (with the introduction of each set of current symptoms) when new entries are made. The system also accepts previously generated patient medication profiles, which enables the DIMES system to begin functioning with an active database.

The MEDIPHOR System

The MEDIPHOR system (Tatro et al. 1975) is a computer-based monitoring and reporting system developed at Stanford University to study drug interactions in hospitalized patients. It has recently been adapted to monitor in community settings as well. The system uses information entered at a central inpatient pharmacy to monitor drug use, creates patient medication profiles, and generates drug interaction reports. It also prints or displays patient medication profiles.

The community pharmacy component of the MEDIPHOR system is particularly relevant to the elderly psychoactive drug user. The community pharmacy involved in the development of the prototype of the MEDIPHOR system (MEDIPHOR-C) is located near Stanford University, and has a prescription volume of approximately 175 per day. The process is as follows:

- The patient enters the pharmacy with one or more prescriptions;

- Responding to a series of prompts on a CRT, the prescription information is entered by the pharmacist and relayed to the central computer;

- The central computer formats a prescription label from the information received and sends this information back to the pharmacy; and

- An interaction search is performed by the central computer, matching the newly prescribed drug(s) against the previously stored patient profile information. If potential drug interactions are found, a short message ("mini-alert") is relayed to the label printer in the pharmacy with the patient's name, the interacting drugs, and a short description of the anticipated interaction.

These "mini-alerts" are divided into two groups. Group A includes those interactions for which telephone notification of the prescribing physician is desirable before the medication is dispensed to the patient. Group B interactions, because of lesser immediacy and/or severity, do not require such notification. For both groups, a full interaction report is printed by computer and is sent to the prescribing physician the next day.

Community Monitoring Programs

The computer drug-monitoring systems discussed above are highly technical methods of managing large amounts of data and drug-related questions in a short period of time. At the present time, there are few pharmacies and community clinics that have access to, or can afford to purchase, the services of this type of monitoring system. The most common and the most economically feasible alternatives are manual monitoring systems. Critical factors in these systems include awareness of all facets of drug-drug interaction and drug/body chemistry/food interaction, as well as the behavioral correlates of drug abuse. As a response to the need for monitoring of drugs in the community, pharmacists have initiated new roles and technical assistance approaches to improve their capacity to perform their job well.

The DIAL System

A noncomputerized system for detecting potential drug interactions, the DIAL system (Drug Interaction Alert System) is a compact procedure that uses a flow chart and a cross-indexed list of drug interactions to enable the pharmacist to evaluate a given patient's potential for experiencing drug interaction effects from a new prescription (Fish and Cooper 1975).

The DIAL system requires the pharmacist, upon receiving a new prescription order, to obtain the patient medication profile, the Drug

Interaction Alert List, and the Drug Interaction Flow Chart. Following the steps of the flow chart, the pharmacist answers a series of questions. The first question asks if any of the ingredients on the new prescription appear on DIAL. The pharmacist checks the profile for any existing prescription for which there are possible interactive drugs. He then identifies the potential interactions between the old prescription and the new. If likely drug interactions are identified, the pharmacist checks to see if the physician has anticipated the interactions and has prescribed compensatory drugs. If not, the pharmacist contacts the physician. An alternate medication may be prescribed by the physician, or the original prescription may be issued with appropriate warnings to the patient. All drugs with known interaction potential being taken by the patient are noted in the patient profile.

DIAL has been used successfully in hospital, nursing home, and community settings. The system could easily be computerized for monitoring large volumes of patient drug use data. However, it lacks a patient profile system specifically oriented to the monitoring task. The DIAL system has several attractive features, particularly its economy. It also permits a recordkeeping process that can be adapted to aspects of drug consumption other than drug interactions.

Tennessee Medication Maintenance Program

A program in Tennessee demonstrates that the pharmacist can perform a significant role in the treatment and maintenance of mentally ill patients in the community (Evans 1976). The program's objective was to establish and operate a model medication maintenance service in a community pharmacy, using support from the Northeast Community Mental Health Center, and subsequently, to conduct a limited evaluation of the model program in 1) patient acceptance of location and pharmacist's role and 2) quality of care.

Problems such as medication noncompliance, drug side effects, drug interactions, and minor alterations in the patient's mental status were handled by the pharmacist. However, telephone consultations with the psychiatrist were also used, particularly in the case of an uncontrolled patient. These actions were followed by dispensation of medications, review of the patient's need for education regarding aspects of the drug therapy, entry of information into the patient's progress notes, necessary referrals to the Center, and scheduling of the patient's next appointment.

The program was well accepted by mental health professionals and some patients. The data showed an overall improvement in participating patients, and suggested that selected patients could be safely maintained by the community pharmacy as part of an outreach program.

A program of this kind, though not aimed at the elderly per se, has a high degree of relevance to psychoactive drug use problems among this group. It is apparent that any formerly institutionalized older person who desires to return to the community might respond positively to the maintenance services this kind of program offers.

Institutional Monitoring Programs

High levels of drug use occur in institutions as might be expected in an environment where people are experiencing health problems. Medications are often prescribed to alleviate pain and anxiety, or to control undesired behaviors, in amounts that may be very strong, or for lengths of time that go beyond the boundaries of therapeutic benefit. As a means of averting misuse of drugs under these circumstances, drug utilization reviews were mandated by law. However, the DUR process does not call for continual monitoring and review of medications for each patient, or even for frequent reviews of each patient's regimen. New monitoring processes have been devised to address this need. Community and institutional pharmacists have also found new roles in working in institutional settings and working with nurses and doctors to insure appropriate use of drugs.

Appalachian Regional Hospitals Program

In 1971, a study outlined by the Appalachian Regional Hospitals pharmacy staff was conducted at the Wise, Virginia, Regional Hospital (Solomon et al. 1974). The major goal of the study was to determine the pharmacist's ability to detect potential therapeutic problems by using a patient medication profile. It was assumed that 1) far more therapeutic problems will be detected by the pharmacist with, than without the use of a patient medication profile; 2) the incidence of therapeutic problems will be higher for new prescriptions than for refill prescriptions; 3) the overuse of medications will be the most common therapeutic problem; 4) prescriptions financed by a third-party payor will more commonly be overused than underused; 5) medications payed for directly by the patient will more commonly be underused than overused; 6) psychotherapeutic drugs will be overused more often than drugs in other classifications; and 7) the potential misuse of medications (either overutilization or underutilization) will be more prevalent among patients 65 years of age and over than among patients in other age groups.

The results of the study indicate that the use of medical profiles by the pharmacist enables him to detect potential therapeutic problems that otherwise would go undetected for extended periods of time. Since it is believed that self-medication errors in nonmonitored cases occur in between 25 percent and 59 percent of all users (Stewart and Cluff 1972), pharmacist intervention would appear to be a valuable monitoring service. Because of this high level of self-medication error and potential for intervention, there is serious reason to further consider the validity and need for legally mandated monitoring services in both ambulatory and long-term care facilities where they do not already exist.

California Regional
Medical Programs Area V

In 1972, the California Regional Medical Programs Area V funded a study to document potential contributions of pharmaceutical service providers to nursing facilities and extended care facilities. The objectives of the study were to demonstrate that 1) the application of clinical pharmacy practice in an extended care facility can improve the quality and cost-effectiveness of patient care through promotion of safe and rational use of drugs, and 2) expanded use of the community's existing pharmacy manpower can be integrated into quality health care services.

The study was implemented in four extended-care facilities. A clinical pharmacist was appointed by the University of Southern California School of Pharmacy to work in the experimental extended care facilities, spending a month at each facility. The responsibilities of the clinical pharmacist in the experimental extended-care facilities included the following:

- To obtain a drug history of each patient on admission and to maintain each patient's drug profile;

- To evaluate each patient's clinical response or lack of response to drug therapy, including adverse drug reactions, and to verify these reactions with the patient's physicians;

- To provide drug information to the staff of the extended care facility and the patient's physicians;

- To instruct discharged patients and their families in the proper use of medications;

- To participate in the extended-care facility's drug utilization review committee; and

- To consult with the staff on their systems of procurement, preparation, and distribution of drugs.

Results of the study indicated that the incidence of medication error and inappropriate drug use was reduced as was the incidence of adverse drug reactions and drug interactions.

The study improved the cost-effectiveness of patient care because of the fewer drug-induced complications and fewer inappropriate drugs. The overall savings was $80,000, excluding the cost of the pharmacist's services. The authors suggested that a reimbursement system would persuade the community pharmacist to provide clinical pharmacy services to patients in extended-care facilities. In July 1975, the California Department of Health began to reimburse pharmacists for the drug-monitoring services that the pharmacists are required to perform. This offers the pharmacist a significant incentive to provide comprehensive patient-oriented pharmacy services and thereby control and reduce the inappropriate use of psychoactive drugs.

Isabella Geriatric Center Programs

The Isabella Geriatric Center is an example of drug monitoring at different levels of institutional and parainstitutional care through one central organization. The ongoing services at Isabella also attest to the significance of the nurse and pharmacist in promoting proper use of drugs by the elderly. The Isabella Center has three levels of housing and service for the aged: congregate housing apartments (250 persons), intermediate nursing care (Home Health Related Facility), and a nursing home.

Pharmacy services to apartment residents are similar to community pharmacy dispensing, including patient profiles. When a "House" resident presents a new prescription or a refill request to the pharmacist, the profile is automatically examined. (As in community pharmacies, full supervision of drugs used in the apartment house area is impossible since residents are not required to use Isabella home medical staff.) Charge slips for medications provide the pharmacist with a daily accounting system used to review patients' charts and adjust profiles.

Services to the Health Related Facility are adapted to meet the needs of residents who require institutional care to maintain a certain level of independence. The nursing department may administer medications to this group.

However, since the State code allows self-administration of medication with the attending physician's written permission, the Isabella Center initiated a program of self-administration of medication 10 years ago. This program is considered by the staff to preserve individual dignity and a degree of independence that should be acknowledged and nurtured.

The pharmacy receives a social history of each new admission. This preintroduction serves as a guideline for future observations. The members of the pharmacy staff attempt to establish a personal relationship with each of the residents. Only 4 out of the Health Related Facility's 207 residents do not qualify for self-administering medications; these patients are served in a private consultation room and their prescriptions are filled while they wait. The self-administering residents have medication boxes with clearly marked use and location information. Each resident has a profile card indicating: 1) if any duplicate prescriptions have been noted; 2) if any drug interactions have been observed or anticipated due to the medication; 3) the label and date; 4) type of sleeping medication in use, if any; 5) synopsis of diagnosis, and how it is reflected in the medication selected; and 6) a notation to retrieve containers.

The Isabella Home Skilled Nursing Facility is for aged persons in need of continuing nursing supervision and medical care, primarily residents who can no longer manage in the intermediate facility. The system used to administer and monitor medications in the Skilled Nursing Facility is a modification of the traditional bulk-drug floor stock system. This modified system uses a specially designed cart with space for drugs, recordkeeping, and storage of order sheets and profiles. The profiles for each patient are reviewed every 30 days, although there is an automatic "stop order" time for prescriptions. The carts are replenished by the pharmacy with precounted medications. The doctor reviews the patient's chart on his rounds; the pharmacist checks the medication order sheet and records the information on the patient profile record.

The John Rawlings and
Associates Service Approach

John Rawlings and Associates is a pharmacy service firm that serves nursing homes. Rawlings and Frisk (1975) report on the model program they have applied in three nursing homes, using a centralized unit-dose delivery system based on the model developed by Beste

at Providence Hospital in Seattle. The system is characterized by pharmacy review of the physician's original order, a medication profile sheet, a 24-hour cabinet exchange system featuring individual patient drawers, and a nurse's medication record. The services program revolves around the pharmacy services committee, which was generated as a result of Federal regulations governing skilled nursing facilities. The basic activities are:

- Taking in orders from the attending physician and compiling a medication history and profile for a new patient;

- Dispensing drugs;

- Monitoring and evaluation of drug storage;

- Monitoring of drug regimens every 30 days, with notes on irregularities continuously entered into the patient profile;

- Interprofessional relationships (the nurse practitioner working under the supervision of a physician is allowed to alter the drug therapy of certain medication classes);

- Establishing an adverse drug reaction reporting procedure, including the use of phone calls and adverse reaction report forms, that keep the physician notified of conditions; and

- Provision of written quarterly reports of pharmacy services provided, as mandated by Federal regulations.

The pharmacist providing these services believes that the cost for the pharmacy service, the average number of medications taken by each patient, and the medication cost per patient have all been substantially reduced through the implementation of this model.

The Nursing Home
Demonstration Project (NHDP)

Responding to recent Federal regulations for nursing homes (which stipulate basic patient care and services, including expanded clinical pharmacy functions), Devenport and Kane (1976) developed a program of integrated patient care and education. The program uses a primary care team composed of a nurse practitioner, a social worker, a physician, and a clinical pharmacist.

The Department of Family and Community Medicine at the University of Utah College of Medicine established the Nursing Home Demonstration Project (NHDP), described by Kane et al. (1974).

Although all 13 homes involved in the project continued to obtain drug orders from their local pharmacies and the State hospital (for those patients followed by the community mental health centers), the NHDP clinical pharmacist was involved in five major areas of drug use: 1) initial drug review for each patient; 2) monitoring drug therapy; 3) providing drug information; 4) inservice education; and 5) patient counseling.

Each home was visited by the nurse practitioner and social worker at least once a week. The physician and pharmacist were consulted on problems of patient management. Therapeutic problems were discussed with the recommendations approved by the physician in the areas of 1) drugs of choice; 2) therapeutic efficacy; 3) bioavailability; 4) dosage; 5) contraindications; 6) potential drug interactions; and 7) adverse effects.

The Nursing Home Demonstration Project suggests that the Federal requirements for a pharmacist in nursing care facilities can be met, and that measurable improvements in the area of rational pharmacy and skill of nursing home staff can also be achieved.

Monitoring Training Programs and Materials

In the majority of cases, innovative monitoring schemes have been designed by researchers in pharmacy and public health. Concern for the monitoring of drug use as an integral component of health care has lead to the development of training workshops and explanatory manuals by pharmaceutical associations. These not only describe an appropriate protocol for monitoring the use of drugs, they also attempt to inculcate in pharmacists a sense of awareness concerning sources of drug abuse, the symptoms that may be produced by the particular problem, and the appropriate strategy to take regarding medication.

California Pharmaceutical
Association Monitoring Course

In the syllabus for a course on drug monitoring in long-term care facilities, the California Pharmaceutical Association (CPhA) identifies strategies for alleviating drug misuse. Steps to be taken include the following:

● View all patients as potential drug misusers. Compliance is unpredictable. The level of knowledge concerning drugs possessed by the patient should not be overestimated.

● Look for risk factors that may contribute to drug misuse: a) patient characteristics—physical, psychological, and social factors that affect the patient's ability to comply;

and b) patient perceptions and expectations—failure to comprehend the seriousness of the illness, the importance of therapy, consequences of noncompliance, and misuse of over-the-counter drugs.

● Disease characteristics: lack of symptoms makes proper treatment difficult.

● Characteristics of the drug regimen: inadequate instructions of drug labeling; complexity of multiple drug therapy; cost of the medications; and untoward effects (i.e., unpleasant taste or adverse effects). Also, there is a greater risk of noncompliance in treatments of long duration.

● Patient education can improve compliance.

● Maintain comprehensive patient records.

Recent legal precedents have established that both the physician and the pharmacist are responsible for informing the patient of the risks of the drug. Written instructions may be more effective than verbal warnings, since they accompany the medication and the patient. A patient should know: a) the name of the medication; b) the appearance of the medication; c) the general purpose of the medication; d) the method of administering it; e) the timing and frequency of administration; f) the maximum daily dose of the drug; g) how long to use the medication; h) pertinent side effects and cautions; i) early symptoms of serious adverse effects (without causing the patient undue concern and potential noncompliance); j) other drugs, food, or activities (such as driving) that should be avoided; and k) the proper storage and handling of the drug.

California Pharmaceutical Association
Long-Term Care Monitoring Workshops

Since January 1974, when the final regulations for Skilled Nursing Facilities (SNFs) were published in the Federal Register, there has been a significant effort by the California Pharmaceutical Association and the trade journal California Pharmacist to acquaint the pharmacist-provider with his/her expanding role. Their activities have included a series of workshops and a workbook on monitoring drug therapy in the long-term care patient with psychogenetic disorders.

The syllabus was written for the Department of Health, Education, and Welfare under a contract between the California Pharmaceutical Association and the Office of Long-Term Care, U.S. Public Health Service, Region IX. The workbook focuses on drug therapy for patients with psychogenetic disorders and discusses the tools and methods of effective drug regimen monitoring. The workbook reinforces the pharmacist's knowledge of the characteristics of major psychogenetic problems found in the long-term care patient (e.g., anxiety, endogenous depression, chronic brain syndrome, exogenous depression, and acute brain syndrome). The workbook also tests the pharmacist's knowledge of recommended dosages of particular psychoactive drugs, such as diazepam, chlordiazepoxide, haloperidol, flurazepam, amitriptyline, and phenobarbital. The learning objectives of the workbook also include improving the ability of pharmacists to recognize the normal limits and potential significance of abnormal findings, as relates to drug therapy, for a series of laboratory tests. There is information in several other areas, including recognizing commonly occurring and potentially injurious adverse effects of psychoactive drugs in aged long-term care patients, recognizing the mechanisms associated with acute brain syndrome in the elderly, the merits and disadvantages of the use of certain drugs as hypnotics, and the means of improving the quality (safety, efficacy, and compliance) of drug therapy in aging patients.

The workbook and the associated workshops attempt to increase the skill of pharmacists, thereby reducing the misuse of psychoactive drugs in the older patient. The issue of implementation remains, however, since monitoring processes are not common and have yet to be mandated.

Health Resources Administration

The Health Resources Administration of HEW has also funded research and training in monitoring drug therapy of the long-term care patient. A major contract with the American Pharmaceutical Association involved extensive pharmacy training for nurses (HSM 110-73-421 1975). The purpose of this project was to expand the quality and scope of training offered by State and local pharmaceutical associations and schools of pharmacy to personnel involved with pharmacy services in nursing homes, and to offer a curriculum to schools of pharmacy to provide similar training to student pharmacists. Sixty programs were carried out under the contract. Of the 2,127 participants, 95 percent were pharmacists. The project included the development of a drug monitoring approach and protocol. In addition, a workbook for pharmacists was written, "Monitoring Drug Therapy of the Long-Term Patient" (American Pharmaceutical Association 1975).

DRUG UTILIZATION EVALUATION PROGRAMS

Drug utilization studies are another way to observe and review drug prescriptions of patients in long-term care facilities. Where monitoring of drug use is an ongoing in-house activity performed by resident or consulting pharmacists, such studies are either mandated by the State or are part of an extended project to collect data on patterns of drug use. Examples of protocols for review of drug use and the gathering of data on patterns of drug use are described below.

Kabat, Martilla, and Stewart Protocol

Kabat et al. (1975) designed and evaluated drug utilization review protocols (format) to be used by review committees in conducting the medical care evaluation studies (commonly referred to as sample studies) required by Federal regulations. The protocols are designed to contain all the information necessary to help the long-term care facility perform drug utilization review sample studies and to explain, in detail, the criteria found on the abstract sheet.

The drug utilization review process, however, provides only a general view of drug use patterns in institutions and often fails to remedy inappropriate drug administration practices. The reasons for this are: a) a patient requiring individual scrutiny may be treated as part of the larger group of patients, whose medication requirements for the same drug may vary; and 2) the committee's norms, criteria, and standards may not be stringent enough to insure remedial action on the part of resident physicians and consultant pharmacists.

Review of drug use, which is mandatory in all skilled nursing facilities certified for participation in the Medicare and Medicaid programs, includes medical care evaluation studies to promote the most effective and efficient use of available health facilities and services.

A DUR Committee in a skilled nursing facility, studying the current use of a psychoactive drug to determine if medication errors of interactions with other drugs are being ignored, would first determine what constitutes proper use of the drug. The committee then would compare patient medication records with the criteria for proper use and examine any discrepancies. Problem areas might be identified, such as physicians' carelessness in prescribing, a pharmacist's oversight during the monthly regimen review, or failure to perform necessary laboratory tests. The committee could suggest corrective measures, such as educational programs for physicians and pharmacists. A followup study is performed to determine how effectively the problem has been dealt with and whether further investigation is required.

Bureau of Quality Assurance
Drug Evaluation Protocol

The Bureau of Quality Assurance of HEW's Public Health Service has published drug evaluation protocols, several of which concern the evaluation of psychoactive drug use. Medical appraisal norms (statistical measures of observed drug performance) are generated and medical care criteria are established.

Boston Collaborative
Drug Surveillance Program

The Boston Collaborative Drug Surveillance Program in operation in 23 hospitals, uses trained nurses and pharmacists to perform daily monitoring, recording, and compilation of data on drug use among hospitalized patients (Allen and Greenblatt 1975). Monitors conduct structured interviews with newly admitted patients, collecting vital statistics and a medication history. A medication sheet is used to record all prescribed medication, therapeutic indications for each drug, the date the drug is started, and its dose, route, and frequency of administration. Medication changes are recorded, as well as the total amount of the drug consumed and the observed effectiveness of the treatment. When a medication is discontinued because of drug interactions, a special form is completed.

The Boston Collaborative Drug Study Program processes information from each hospital once a month. The data have been the basis for 80 publications over the past 10 years on such subjects as patterns and factors influencing the toxicity of drugs, drug-attributed adverse reactions, and clinical factors affecting adverse drug reactions and interactions.

At some of the hospitals involved in the Collaborative Drug Surveillance Program, the information generated is used to effect changes in individual drug regimens. This is the case in the program at the Arizona Medical Center (Trinca et al. 1975). At this hospital, the pharmacist involved in drug monitoring provides a link between the prescribing physician and the Department of Pharmacology by presenting difficult management problems at pharmacology rounds attended by physicians and students. By this means, drug surveillance is an educational tool for both students and physicians.

The PAID Program

The PAID Program is an example of retrospective intervention through utilization review. Patients covered by the Title XIX Medicaid Program in North Carolina have had their drug consumption monitored through a program operated by the PAID Prescriptions Company (specialists in prescription drug claim-processing) under contract to the North Carolina Department of Social Services and modeled on a program in California (Yarborough and Laventuries 1974; Hull et al. 1975).

Six pharmacists and a physician from each of four geographical regions meet once a month to review computer printouts of drug purchases. Local physicians and pharmacists are informed of unnecessary and inefficient drug use by a letter of inquiry, and they receive copies of recipients' drug profiles. This system has brought about a reduction in costs to the State and Federal Governments. Although many factors are not reflected in the prescription claims data, potential therapeutic problems can be identified; for example, a computer printout of medications purchased by outpatients in the California program indicated that 7.5 percent of drugs taken by 42,000 patients could have caused adverse reactions resulting in medical problems.

In their article on the PAID Program, Hull et al. (1975) cite four types of drug problems that can be revealed by patient profiles: prescription and therapeutic duplication; over-utilization; drug interactions; and noncompliance. DUR committees have been able to identify problems in the first three of these areas, but noncompliance is apparently detectable only in hospital environments. The DUR committee has focused on drug reactions with anticoagulants because they are widely prescribed to Medicaid patients and interact with many other drugs, particularly barbiturates (Starr and Petrie 1972). The program has immense practical application for the evaluation of psychoactive drug use among older persons, and can effectively address some of the drug use problems that do not require an in-depth knowledge of the individual patient's physiologic characteristics.

SUMMARY

The five types of programs described in this section--improved diagnostic procedures, improved prescription controls, improved drug administration procedures, drug prescription monitoring, and drug utilization review--indicate a trend toward the development of more rational use of drugs, both psychoactive and nonpsychoactive. There still remains, however, a significant potential for abuse by the individual who does not comply with the drug regimen, even when it is correctly prescribed. This source of variance lies with the individual and must be addressed through other means, such as education or therapy, depending on the motivation for the particular pattern of use. The following section provides examples of how the processes of diagnosis, prescription, administration, and monitoring of drug use can be supplemented through interventive programs within the community and institutions.

PROGRAMS DESIGNED TO INTERVENE IN PSYCHOACTIVE DRUG MISUSE AMONG THE ELDERLY

Psychoactive drug misuse by the elderly has only recently been recognized as a significant public health problem. Because the incidence and prevalence of psychoactive drug misuse by the elderly are not yet well known, there have been relatively few policies designed to offer intervention or treatment for those affected. The previous section described a predominantly preventative approach, although monitoring procedures also are capable of detecting misuse situations. Careful control of psychoactive drug applications, through clinical and community health services, will continue to be of significance in reducing the future incidence of certain categories of psychoactive drug misuse. However, there remain unidentified numbers of older persons who are suffering from one or more physical and emotional complications that center on, or are related to, psychoactive drug use and who have not received the attention they may require.

This section focuses upon the efforts made by various social and public health organizations to design interventions that specifically address psychoactive drug misuse problems found among the elderly. There are very few of these programs at this time although the number seems to be growing concurrently with the growth in awareness of the problem. Many of the established programs are extensions of preexisting programs for the treatment of alcoholism and the elderly alcoholic. In such programs, the intervention generally focuses on what is thought to be the motivating variable in the abuse phenomenon--social isolation, limited economic resources, and possible lifelong pathology that is associated with addiction to alcohol. Other interventions, however, do not operate with the same assumptions, and often treat misuse of psychoactive

drugs by the elderly as an inadvertent response produced by lack of information, or some aspect of social pathology that may be experienced in later life. Many of the programs recently initiated do not propose any hypotheses concerning the misuse of psychoactive drugs by the elderly; rather, they are investigating the misuse problem while at the same time offering clinical corrective treatment and guidance, thus collecting data while rendering services.

This section presents brief descriptions of the objectives, therapeutic approaches, and activities of a number of established or recently developed programs. The programs discussed include outpatient facilities emphasizing outreach, referral followup and education; inpatient drug abuse treatment in hospital and nursing home settings; drug abuse components of mental health centers; education and counseling programs; peer counseling; and rational self-help therapy.

The first programs to be described are those operated in Minnesota. Minnesota was the first State to recognize that there were psychoactive drug misuse problems among the elderly. As part of the 1973 Governor's Bill for the Chemically Dependent chemical dependency intervention programs are offered to underserved populations, including blacks, Chicanos, women, adolescents, and the elderly.

Three programs have been initiated in Minnesota that offer a service component to the elderly with psychoactive drug misuse problems: the Hennepin County Alcohol and Drug Access and Intervention Unit (A.I.D.); the Ramsey County Senior Chemical Dependency; and the Ebenezer Society Intervention Plus programs. These programs, established independently from one another, follow similar models of service provision, centered upon processes of misuse identification, referral to (if needed) a detoxification center, participation in a mutual-assistance Alcoholics Anonymous model, and efforts to change lifestyle and drug consumption patterns.

The programs also include examples of referred treatment programs for those elderly requiring higher levels of intervention and/or medical supervision. Programs of this type include: the Northwestern Hospital Treatment Program for the Chemically Dependent; the Queen Nursing Home Alcohol Treatment Program, which treats psychoactive drug abusers; the Camellia House Nursing Home Treatment Program, which offers similar services; and the Bridgeway Center.

Other programs described vary in their interventive mode and organizational foundation. In Tennessee, a coordinated program investigating the drug phenomena, while offering treatment to the elderly, has been initiated by the Department of Mental Health and Mental Retardation and associated mental health centers. In Chicago, the Augustana Hospital offers health education, counseling, and a research program centering on drug use problems among the elderly. In New York State, the Broome County Drug Awareness Center has been the source of an extensive drug education program for the elderly, including a traveling "minicourse" for the aged designed to improve knowledge about drugs. The College of Pharmacy at the University of Minnesota has also designed a series of programs to be presented to the elderly in order to increase their knowledge of psychoactive drugs. In Florida, the THEE DOOR service organization offers a variety of centers and counseling programs for prevention of, and intervention in, psychoactive drug abuse situations among the elderly. The Institute for the Study of Aging in Florida has funded a program focusing on peer counseling in their Management of Drug Abuse Among the Elderly program. The University of Kentucky has initiated a research program to study drug use patterns in the elderly and the utility of rational behavior training in reducing chemical dependency. The National Institute on Drug Abuse is currently supporting the Center for Human Services, in their efforts to develop and disseminate educational material for the elderly.

PROGRAMS[1]

Hennepin County A.I.D. (Minnesota)

The Hennepin County Alcohol and Drug Access and Intervention Unit (A.I.D.) established a special outreach project in March 1973 to provide assessment, intervention, referral, and followup care for the chemically dependent elderly in Hennepin County, Minnesota. The A.I.D. organization initially became involved with the chemically dependent elderly following requests by social workers, who had been receiving complaints from the residents of public housing projects concerning the disturbing behavior of intoxicated older residents. Intervening A.I.D. staff would often find the individual half-dressed, with bottles of pills on the cupboard or dresser, cans of opened food spoiling, and wastebaskets full of liquor bottles.

The A.I.D. program hired a chemical-dependency counselor whose main responsibility was to assist the A.I.D. director in developing an outreach program to train volunteers in assisting the intervention and followup processes of the special project.

The general program structure consists of six activities related to the objectives of access, intervention, referral, and followup for the chemically dependent elderly:

- The immediate call for help, either directly from the older person or through a referral, is handled by the A.I.D. Special Program Counselor.

- Intervention is handled by the counselor and a volunteer; the team approach is favored.

- Evaluation of the client is performed by the project counselor, with the assistance of A.I.D. staff members.

- Diagnosis of chemical dependency or other disorders requiring treatment is followed by a referral to an appropriate service agency—a hospital or nursing home detoxification center, drug treatment center, or other special program. Two outreach volunteers are available to assist the client to the appropriate treatment facility.

- Followup contact is maintained by the special program counselor, with the assistance of the volunteers. The followup program involves the chemically dependent person in growth groups modeled after those used in the treatment of alcoholics and drug addicts.

- Improved social functioning is measured by comparison of current and former behaviors.

Eleven satellite offices have been developed in the Minneapolis area. Transportation is provided for the handicapped or physically disabled, especially during the winter months. A.I.D. also operates a 24-hour answering service and conducts home interviews. Program services are provided on a continual basis, progress notes are kept on all client contacts, and group attendance records are maintained.

Between March 1, 1973, and November 1975, the A.I.D. program served 620 clients; 251

---

[1] Addresses and contacts are listed in appendix B.

men and 97 women are actively involved in the therapeutic groups, several of them volunteering their services. Other clients listed as inactive still receive followup contacts; half of this group shows improved social functioning, while others are active in AA-type groups and aftercare programs.

Since November 1975, the program has provided a series of informational seminars emphasizing the prevention of drug dependency. It also provides information on alcoholism and drug problems in high-rise residential settings, as well as information on health centers, homemaker programs, and other services for the aged.

Ramsey County Senior Chemical
Dependency Program (Minnesota)

Services provided by the Ramsey County Senior Chemical Dependency Program include prevention, intervention, counseling (both individual and group), transportation, client advocacy, aftercare, followup consultation, and education.

The program also acts as an advocate for clients who have been denied detoxification and medical treatment, possibly resulting in prolonged hospitalization and/or premature entrance into nursing homes or board-and-care units.

Ebenezer Society (Minnesota)

The Ebenezer Society serving older men and women, has recently initiated a chemical-dependency program called Intervention Plus. This program is designed to reduce drug misuse among the elderly of Hennepin County. The focus of the program is on outreach, evaluation, early intervention, nonresidential treatment, referral, followup, aftercare, coordination with other agencies, prevention, consultation, and education.

Northwestern Hospital (Minnesota)

Northwestern Hospital in Minneapolis operates a treatment program for chemically dependent patients referred to the hospital from detoxification centers, other hospitals, doctors, families, and the Hennepin County A.I.D. program.

Most arriving patients have been detoxified, but some require detoxification treatment. The program provides hospitalization and treatment for as long as 28 days, with possible extension of up to 2 weeks longer based on the evaluation of patient response at the end of the first 28 days. The program takes place in an age-integrated ward of the hospital,

which the program director believes facilitates social interaction and leads to more improvement among the older patients. Each patient is given a comprehensive physical and psychiatric examination on arrival and again at the time of discharge.

Program activities include three lectures daily on educational and therapy-oriented topics. Among the topics discussed are: adverse drug reactions, drug interactions, individual differences in physiology, and the problems of noncompliance, deliberate overuse, the potential misuse of over-the-counter drugs, and the Alcoholics Anonymous approach.

The program also offers individual consultation with trained chemical-dependency paraprofessionals to ease the clients' emotional problems and to determine their service needs. At the end of the 28-day period, a client is evaluated and judged ready to leave, and he or she is referred to Alcoholics Anonymous groups and/or to other service agencies for aftercare. A patient who requires still further treatment may remain for an additional 2 weeks. If s/he continues to require care and treatment after that time, s/he is referred to a local nursing home with a chemical-dependency program, or to the Hennepin County A.I.D., which will assist him/her in finding appropriate services and placement.

Queen Alcohol Treatment
Program (Minnesota)

The Queen Alcohol Treatment Center is representative of the small number of existing programs in nursing homes for the chemically dependent and physically or mentally impaired elderly. It was designed to treat the chronic alcoholic and chemically dependent older person. It maintains a 24-hour nursing staff and an 8-hour-a-day counseling staff for older persons who could not benefit from other programs because of significant physical and/or mental disorders related to past chemical abuse, and who have a medical disorder that is complicated by chronic alcoholism.

The initial effort of the program is toward physical improvement and an increased awareness of one's feelings. The focus is then broadened to include recognition and acceptance of living problems, and the importance of setting and achieving goals. Counseling and involvement in industrial and recreational therapies are also emphasized. Although the program emphasis appears to be on treatment of alcoholism, the staff are of the opinion that their treatment approach is also suitable for the elderly psychoactive drug abuser.

Upon admission to the program, clients are withdrawn under medical supervision from all mood-altering chemicals, with the exception of major tranquilizers prescribed for certain psychiatric disorders. In these cases, however, the patient is still evaluated for possible discontinuation, in order to assess the chemical dependence and treatment plan.

Prior to discharge, the client is required to join an AA chapter and complete the AA orientation program. If the patient needs vocational training, he is enrolled in an outside training program to acquire the desired skills. Housing arrangements are also made at this time. Followup contact, monthly or more often, assures the patient that he is welcome at the clinic at any time.

Camellia House (Minnesota)

One-third of the facilities at Camellia House nursing home are devoted to treating the chemically dependent patient. This is the second such home in Minnesota, and, like the Queen Alcohol Treatment Program, the goal is to establish and maintain patterns of living free from chemical dependency. The low-profile program at Camellia House is designed to overcome the feeling that treatment is associated with punishment.

The chemical-dependency program is geared to slower paced elderly patients and patients with temporary or permanent physical or mental disabilities. The program incorporates Alcoholics Anonymous program steps, group therapy, individual counseling, and educational lectures. Group therapy involves supportive confrontations directed toward encountering defense systems modifying behavior, and replacing the delusionary system with realistic awareness. Gestalt therapy is used as the basis for identifying and accepting the illness so that the patient can "come to grips with the conflict between values and behavior" with the discovery or rediscovery of himself as a thinking and feeling person. Weekly attendance in the AA group is required as part of group therapy.

Bridgeway Center (Minnesota)

The Bridgeway Center is a multidisciplinary chemical-dependency unit, operating in a facility under the ownership of King Care Centers, Inc., a private health care corporation. The program provides intervention services for the chemically dependent elderly and for other age groups. The program offers 30-day primary and extended care treatment programs that are oriented toward treatment of the physical, mental, and emotional illnesses of the chemically dependent person and that

provide one-to-one counseling and participation in group therapy.

At the end of the first 30 days, the client is evaluated and is either discharged or assigned to the continued care or the extended care program. The latter program lasts another 30 days. The program is designed to permit physical as well as mental recuperation. While the Northwestern program refers the patient to another program at the end of 6 weeks, the Bridgeway program attempts to carry out necessary treatment and rehabilitation within 2 months. If the client has not recuperated within that time, the patient is referred to a nursing home, such as the Camellia House.

State of Tennessee

In October 1976, representatives from four Tennessee mental health centers and three sections of the Department of Mental Health and Mental Retardation of the State of Tennessee met to plan a statewide program that addresses the problems of drug and alcohol abuse among the elderly. The mental health centers represented were Joe Johnson Mental Health Center in Chattanooga, Overlook Mental Health Center in Knoxville, Dede Wallace Mental Health Center in Memphis, and the University of Tennessee Mental Health Center. Together with representatives from the Geriatric Services Section, the Alcohol and Drug Abuse Section, and the Public Affairs Section of the State of Tennessee Department of Mental Health and Mental Retardation, they set the following objectives:

- To increase public awareness of alcohol and drug problems among the elderly, and to familiarize the public with resources and services available.

- To develop strategies and begin efforts to coordinate existing services.

- To develop specific plans and investigate the need for new programs and services.

Program planning is a cooperative venture, involving each of the participating agencies and mental health centers. In addition, the University of Tennessee Mental Health Center is conducting group sessions to deal with drug-related problems of the elderly; Overlook Mental Health Center is developing a screening process to detect alcohol and drug abuse problems; and Joe Johnson Mental Health Center is collecting data on the drug and alcohol problems of the over-60 population in their catchment area.

Augustana Hospital (Illinois)

Augustana Hospital in Chicago operates a program of health education, instructing elderly hospital patients in the effects and proper use of medications. It was soon noted, however, that the use of drugs within the hospital fostered dependency and made it difficult for the patients to benefit from the education program, which stressed independence. This realization resulted in a broadening of the program, which now addresses problems related to the independent functioning of senior citizens. Eleven health education topics have been developed: medication safety, the heart, high blood pressure, stress, laxatives and bowel preparations, analgesics and antibiotics, diabetes, consumer awareness, eye care, arthritis, and nutrition. Public attention has also been brought to the problems of the elderly through local television coverage and articles in a senior citizens' newspaper.

Medical counseling has been effective in building confidence in the health care system and encouraging greater use of these services.

A research program has been established to assess the health care needs of the elderly, to examine patterns of medication use, to evaluate the level and quality of services offered to the public by pharmacies, and to determine the factors contributing to noncompliance in medication use by the elderly.

Broome County Drug
Awareness Center (New York)

The program model designed at the Broome County Drug Awareness Center attempts to provide the elderly with health care information, particularly with regard to the safe and effective use of drugs, and also to aid them in developing a behavioral program for themselves and significant others.

THEE DOOR (Florida)

THEE DOOR is a service organization in Osceola County, Florida, addressing drug abuse problems in all age groups. Their facilities and programs include the Alpha Center for education and prevention of drug misuse, a center for individual and family counseling; a Youth Development Center with an alternative school and a residential program; a methadone center; and a Substance Abuse Program. THEE DOOR recently initiated an outpatient counseling center specifically oriented toward misuse of prescription medication by the elderly (overdosage, duplication of prescriptions, swapping of medications, and use of outdated drugs).

In addition to its direct counseling services, the counseling center provides educational services designed to be as accessible as possible to the elderly, through the use of an outreach program conducted at community centers in residential areas.

In March 1977, THEE DOOR began a training program for service providers to the elderly. Direct service workers (visiting nurses, county welfare workers, social and economic services workers, nursing home personnel, and others) participated in the training sessions. Training modules, with workbooks and cassette tapes have been developed for dissemination to other programs. In addition, the program has developed guidelines for the creation of a task force of elderly persons, to advise social service agencies and increase the effectiveness of referrals.

A Peer Counselor Approach (Florida)

"Management of Drug Abuse Among the Elderly: A Peer Counselor Approach" is a program organized by the Institute for the Study of Aging at the University of Miami, on behalf of 30 agencies in Dade County, Florida. It provides services to elderly persons identified as heavy users of drugs.

Drug use problems are attributed both to lack of information and to sociopsychological problems arising from isolation, physical disability, and economic difficulties. Intervention consists of the training of elderly persons as peer counselors, a method that has been effective among younger persons in both the prevention and the treatment of drug abuse.

Older Life Drug Experience Research
Project (OLDER) (Kentucky)

OLDER is a demonstration research program operating out of the Department of Psychiatry, University of Kentucky Medical Center, designed to study effectiveness of rational behavior therapy in the treatment of drug misuse problems among the elderly. The program operates under the hypothesis that learning an emotional self-help technique can enable the older person to cope with stresses of aging without the use of tranquilizers and nonprescription drugs. It is also hypothesized that these self-help techniques are best taught by laypersons rather than by mental health professionals, a belief that is supported by the success of such groups as Alcoholics Anonymous, etc.

This program also provides a systematic, factual, drug counseling effort designed to influence patterns of drug use. A 3-year research project will evaluate the effectiveness of this approach.

SUMMARY

The variety of programs now in existence to meet the problem of psychoactive drug abuse among the elderly suggest that the nature of and solution to the problem are not yet known. Evaluations of these existing programs are not yet available, and there are few guidelines against which the programs can be measured.

CONCLUSIONS

Programs addressing the problem of psychoactive drug misuse among the elderly fall into two broad categories: monitoring of drug use and intervention programs.

PROGRAMS THAT MONITOR THE DIAGNOSIS, PRESCRIPTION, AND ADMINISTRATION OF DRUGS

Considerable attention has been focused on the issue of more accurate diagnosis of psychiatric disorders in the elderly. This concern is centered on pairing a correctly diagnosed disorder with the most effective treatment, resulting in a decreased likelihood of incorrect or needless medication.

Increased physician awareness of the significance of accurate diagnostic procedures and appropriate therapeutic interventions for the aged has led them to recognize the role that individual physiological and psychological differences play in drug response. Consequently, physicians have developed formal and informal protocols to identify the correct drug for a given patient. They also have developed strategies adaptable for insuring correct drug administration and compliance. These include guidelines for selecting psychoactive drugs for the elderly and for determining the optimal quantities, duration, and structure of the drug regimen.

The increased volume of drug prescription and use, and the consequent increase in adverse reactions--due to drug/drug and drug/individual interactions--have provided an incentive for pharmacists and physicians to develop programs to monitor and evaluate drug consumption.

Interest on the part of Professional Standards Review Organizations has also promoted development of systematic methods of medication profile review and troubleshooting. With the growth of an extended pharmacy role in community health maintenance, and the increased availability of computer-operated monitoring systems, opportunity for encouraging appropriate or reduced use of psychoactive drugs in the elderly is enhanced.

PROGRAMS DESIGNED TO INTERVENE IN PSYCHOACTIVE DRUG MISUSE AMONG THE ELDERLY

The increase in public awareness of psychoactive drug use problems among the elderly has led to the creation of new intervention programs, designed strictly to serve the elderly drug user. These programs fall into five categories:

● Outreach and referral

● Hospital and nursing home treatment programs

● Educational programs in combination with another intervention such as health care, therapy, or a social activity

● Peer counseling

● "Rational" behavior training

There are at present, few active programs in the area of specific interventions and treatments for the elderly psychoactive drug user, other than the examples reviewed in this document, several of which originate in one State--Minnesota.

TRENDS

Several observations can be made concerning trends in the provision of services to prevent or intervene in psychoactive drug misuse among the elderly.

A Rational Approach to Prescription and Administration

There is an apparent trend to develop a more "rational" approach to the application and dispensation of psychoactive drugs that affect the elderly. This is manifested primarily in the development of enhanced information systems for use by physicians in prescribing medications; in the development of prospective monitoring and retrospective use studies; and in the increased role of health professionals in guiding and reviewing the prescription and use of drugs.

Improved prescription and monitoring systems will have a greater impact on the elderly drug users when three conditions are met: a) when the protocols for drug monitoring are used more universally and consistently;

b) when monitoring programs develop prescription criteria that take into consideration both the physiology and socioemotional status of the elderly consumer; and c) when drug/drug and drug/person interactions are considered in prescription. At the present time, very few pharmacies are capable of monitoring drug consumption in the community. This problem is complicated by the fact that drug consumers can move from pharmacy to pharmacy, and can obtain multiple prescriptions from different physicians. The need for centralized information in monitoring drugs must be seriously considered and evaluated in terms of the potential savings in lives and health care costs, as well as in terms of the issue of medication profile confidentiality. Should comprehensive drug monitoring systems be implemented, with guidelines for correct use and safeguards for privacy, the aged person will share the same benefits as other drug consumers.

Direct Intervention Programs

There is a growing interest in developing programs for direct intervention in psychoactive drug misuse by the elderly.

At the present time there are two major program thrusts: the first is toward identifying the drug misuser and placing him/her in contact with treatment resources and followup care; and the second is in the area of drug-use education. Many program developers are of the opinion that drug misuse in the elderly is attributable to lack of information as well as to emotional difficulties. The outreach programs recognize these factors, but the more immediate concern is with the existing cases of misuse that require immediate treatment. Patterns of future drug intervention for the aged may attempt to synthesize the identification component of the outreach programs with innovative therapeutic interventions and service referrals, followed by continuing education programs. Peer counseling and education will doubtless play an important role in all programs.

The most disconcerting aspect of the trend in development of drug interventions for elderly psychoactive drug misusers is the lack of central information clearinghouses where health care professionals can make contact and share their design concepts and service problems, as well as gather information on the aged. A second point of interest is the lack of contact between service providers in the field of direct intervention and pharmacists interested in promoting drug monitoring activities. Further interaction between those prescribing and dispensing drugs will facilitate more effective program interventions and alternatives for elderly psychoactive drug misusers. The U.S. Department of Health, Education, and Welfare Task Force on Prescription Drugs (1969) reported that at that time, over $3 billion a year was being spent to correct adverse response to therapeutically adminstered drugs. It is probable that the aged represent a significant portion of the population requiring corrective therapy for drug problems. Therefore, the personal and public savings to be derived from an integrated approach to monitoring and intervening in psychoactive drug use are apparent.

REFERENCES

Alexander, D.A. Senile dementia: A changing perspective. British Journal of Psychiatry, 121: 207-214, 1972.

Allen, M.D., and Greenblatt, D.J. Role of nurse and pharmacist monitors in the Boston Collaborative Drug Surveillance Program. Drug Intelligence and Clinical Pharmacy, 9:648-654, 1975.

American Pharmaceutical Association. Monitoring Drug Therapy of the Long-Term Care Patient. (A workbook for pharmacists.) Washington, D.C.: American Pharmaceutical Association, 1975.

Ayd, F.J. Oxazepam: An overview. Diseases of the Nervous System, 36:14, 1975.

Braunstein, M.L., and James, J.D. A computer-based system for screening outpatient drug utilization. Journal of the American Pharmaceutical Association, 16:82-85, 1976.

Brodie, D.C. Drug Utilization and Drug Utilization Review and Control. DHEW Publication No. (HSM)72-3002. Rockville, Md.: NCHSRO, HSMHA, Department of Health, Education, and Welfare, 1971.

Burville, P. Consecutive psychogeriatric admissions to psychiatric and geriatric hospitals. Geriatrics, 26:156-168, 1971.

De Groot, M.H.L. The clinical use of psychotherapeutic drugs in the elderly. Drugs, 8:132-138 1974.

Devenport, J.K., and Kane, R.L. The role of the clinical pharmacist on a nursing home care team. Drug Intelligence and Clinical Pharmacy, 10:268-271, 1976.

DiMascio, A., and Shader, R.L. Drug administration schedules. American Journal of Psychiatry 126:796-801, 1969.

Eisdorfer, C., and Stotsky, B.A. Intervention, treatment and rehabilitation of psychiatric disorders. In: Birren, J., and Schaie, W., eds. Handbook of Psychology of Aging. New York: Van Nostrand Reinhold, 1977.

Evans, R.L.; Kirk, R.F.; Walker, P.W.; Rosenbluth, S.A.; and McDonald, J. Medication maintenance of mentally ill patients by a pharmacist in a community setting. American Journal of Hospital Pharmacy, 33:635-638, 1976.

Fann, W.E.; Wheless, J.C.; and Richman, B.W. Treating the aged with psychotropic drugs. Gerontologist, 16:326, 1976.

Fish, K.H., Jr., and Cooper, J.W., Jr. A system for drug-drug interaction detection. Journal of the American Pharmaceutical Association, 15:28-31, 1975.

Foley, J. Differential diagnosis of the organic mental disorders in elderly patients. In: Gaitz, C., ed. Aging and the Brain. New York: Plenum Press, 1971.

Hall, M.R.P. Drug therapy in the elderly. British Medical Journal, 4:582-584, 1973.

Hull, H.J.; Brown, H.S., Jr.; Yarborough, F.F.; and Murry, W.J. Drug utilization review of Medicaid patients: Therapeutic implications and opportunities. North Carolina Medical Journal, 36:162-163, 1975.

Kabat, H.F.; Marttile, J.; and Stewart, J. Drug utilization review in skilled nursing facilities. Journal of the American Pharmaceutical Association, 15:34-37, 1975.

Kane, R.L.; Jorgensen, L.A.B.; and Pepper, G.A. Can nursing home care be cost effective. Journal of American Geriatric Society, 22:265-272, 1974.

Karig, A.W.; James, J.B.; Braunstein, M.L.; and Henderson, W.M. The pharmacist and computerized patient records: Training program and practise model. American Journal of Pharmacological Education, 38:161, 1974.

Knoben, J.E. Current status and relationship to assuring quality medical care. Drug Intelligence and Clinical Pharmacy, 10:222-228, 1976.

La Brie Associates. Drug Intake Management Evaluation System. Cambridge, Mass.: La Brie Associates, 1976.

Lamy, P.P., and Vestal, R.F. Drug prescribing for the elderly. Hospital Practice, 11:111-118, 1976.

Lawton, M.P. Coping behavior and the environment of older people. In: Schwartz, A., and Mensch, I., eds. Professional Obligations and Approaches to the Aged. Springfield, Ill.: Charles C Thomas, 1970.

Learoyd, M.B. Psychotropic drugs and the elderly patient. Medical Journal of Australia, 1:1131-1133, 1972.

Libow, L.S., and Mehl, B. Self-administration of medications by patients in hospitals or extended care facilities. Journal of the American Geriatrics Society, 18:81-85, 1970.

Martin, E.W. Hazards of Medication. Philadelphia: J.B. Lippincott Co., 1971.

Mechanic, D. Social psychologic factors affecting the presentation of bodily complaints. New England Journal of Medicine, 286:1132-1139, 1972.

Nelson, A., Jr.; Hutchinson, A.; Mahoney, D.; and Ringstrom, J. Evaluation of the utilization of medication profiles. Drug Intelligence and Clinical Pharmacy, 10:274-281, 1976.

Rawlings, J.L., and Frisk, P.A. Pharmaceutical services for skilled nursing facilities in compliance with federal regulations. American Journal of Hospital Pharmacy, 32:903-905, 1975.

Reilly, M.J. Drug utilization review by pharmacy and therapeutics committees. Drug information digest. American Journal of Hospital Pharmacy, 30:349-350, 1972.

Schuckit, M.A.; Miller, P.L.; and Hahlbohm, D. Unrecognized psychiatric illness in elderly medical-surgical patients. Journal of Gerontology, 30:655-660, 1975.

Solomon, D.K.; Baumgartner, R.P.; Glascock, L.M.; Glascock, S.A.; Briscoe, M.E.; and Billups, N.F. Use of medication profiles to detect potential therapeutic problems in ambulatory patients. American Journal of Hospital Pharmacy, 31:348-354, 1974.

Starr, K.J., and Petrie, J.C. Drug interactions in patients in a Medi-Cal population. California Pharmacist, 11:18-22, 1972.

Stewart, R.B., and Cluff, L.E. A review of medication errors and compliance in ambulant patients. Clinical Pharmacology and Therapeutics, 13:462-468, 1972.

Task Force on Prescription Drugs. Final Report. Washington, D.C.: Office of the Secretary, Department of Health, Education, and Welfare, 1969.

Tatro, D.S.; Briggs, R.L.; Chavez-Pardo, R.; Feinberg, L.S.; Hannigan, J.F.; Moore, T.N.; and Cohen, S.N. Detection and prevention of drug interactions utilizing an on-line computer system. Drugs Information Journal, Jan.-April 1975. pp. 10-15.

Trinca, C.; Bressler, R.; and Watson, P. The Drug Surveillance Program at the Arizona Medical Center. Arizona Medicine, 32:702-714, 1975.

Turbow, S.R. Geriatric group day care and its effect on independent living. Gerontologist, 15: 508-510, 1975.

Whelihan, W.M. "A Geriatric Consultation and Diagnostic Center: One Model for Assessment." Symposium presentation. American Psychological Association Meeting, Washington, D.C., September 1976.

Yarborough, F.F., and Laventuries, M.F. Peer review works via a committee of 7: 6 pharmacists plus one physician. Pharma Times, 40:58-63, 1974.

SELECTED BIBLIOGRAPHY

Bell, B.D. Medical care to the elderly: An evaluation. Gerontologist, 15:100-113, 1975.

Bender, D.A. The effect of increasing age on the distribution of peripheral blood flow in man. Journal of American Geriatric Society, 13:192-198, 1965.

Berger, M.M., and Berger, L.F. An innovative program for a private psychogeriatric day center. Journal of American Geriatric Society, 19:332-336, 1971.

Brickner, P.W.; Janeski, J.F.; Rich, G.; Dirque, T.; Starita, L.; LaRocco, R.; Flannery, T.; and Werlin, S. Home maintenance for the home-bound aged. Gerontologist, 16:25-29, 1976.

Brody, E.M.; Kleban, M.H.; and Liebowitz, B. Intermediate housing for the elderly: Satisfaction of those who moved in and those who did not. Gerontologist, 15:350-356, 1975.

California Pharmaceutical Association. Implementating Strategies for Intervention in Drug Misuse Situations, 1976.

California Pharmaceutical Association. Term Care Patient, 1975. (Syllabus.)

Cardoni, A.A.; Dugas, J.E.; and Pierpaoli, P.G. "Clinical Pharmacy Service for Psychiatric Inpatients at the Unversity of Connecticut Health Center." Presented at the Eighth Annual Midyear Clinical Meeting of the American Society of Hospital Pharmacists, New Orleans, La., December 1973.

Carp, F.M. A senior center in public housing for the elderly. Gerontologist, 16:243-249, 1976.

Chien, C.P.; Stotsky, B.A.; and Cole, J.O. Psychiatric treatment for nursing-home patients: Drug, alcohol and milieu. American Journal of Psychiatry, 130:543-548, 1973.

Chowinard, E. Family homes for adults. Social Rehabilitation Record, 2:10-15, 1975.

Cosin, L.Z. The place of the day hospital in geriatric unit. Practitioner, 172:552-554, 1954.

De Vries, H.A., and Adams, G.M. Electromyographic comparison of simple doses of exercise and meprobamate as to effects on muscular relaxation. American Journal of Physical Medicine, 51:130-141, 1972.

Epstein, L.J., and Simon, A. Alternatives to state hospitalization for the geriatric mentally ill. American Journal of Psychiatry, 124:955-961, 1968.

Firky, M.E., and Abduk-Wafa, M.H. Intestinal absorption in the old. Gerontologia Clinica, 7:171-178, 1965.

Gaitz, C.M., and Varner, R.V. A Multidisciplinary Mental Health Model. The Geriatric Program of the Texas Research Institute of Mental Sciences (TRIMS), December 1-5, 1975.

Garetz, F.J., and Peth, P.P. An outreach program of medical care for aged high-rise residents. Gerontologist, 14:404-409, 1974.

Gottesman, L.E. Milieu treatment of the aged in institutions. Gerontologist, 13:23-26, 1973.

Holloway, D.A. Drug problems in geriatric patients. Drug Intelligence and Clinical Pharmacy, 8:632-642, 1974.

Holmes, D. Nutrition and health screening services for the elderly. (Report of a demonstration project.) Journal of the American Dietetic Association, 60:301-305, 1972.

Kalson, L. The therapy of independent living for the elderly. Journal of American Geriatric Society, 20:394-397, 1972.

Kobrynski, B., and Cummings, E. Generation changes and geriatric care. Journal of American Geriatrics Society, 19:376-385, 1971.

Lasagna, L. Drug effects as modified by aging. Journal of Chronic Diseases, 3:567-574, 1956.

Lazarus, L.W. A program for the elderly at a private psychiatric hospital. Gerontologist, 16:125-131, 1976.

Liebowitz, B. "Implications of Community Housing for Planning and Policy." Unpublished, 1976.

MacLennan, W.J. Drug interactions. Gerontologia Clinica, 16:18-24, 1974.

McDonald, R.D.; Neulander, A.; Holod, O.; and Holcomb, N.S. Description of a non-residential psychogeriatric day care facility. Gerontologist, 11:322-327, 1971.

Novak, P. Aging, total body potassium, fat free mass and cell mass in males and females between the ages 18 and 85 years. Journal of Gerontology, 27:438-443, 1972.

Novick, L.J. Day care meets geriatric needs. Hospitals, 47:47-50, 1973.

Plutchick, R.; McCarthy, M.; Hall, B.; and Silverberg, S. Evaluation of a comprehensive psychiatric and health care program for elderly welfare tenants in a single-room occupancy hotel. Journal of American Geriatric Society, 21:452-459, 1973.

Rappaport, M.F. Community care homes. Hospitals, 44:56-59, 1970.

Rathbone-McCuan, and Levenson, J. Impact of socialization therapy in a geriatric day-care setting. Gerontologist, 15:338-342, 1975.

Riccitelli, M.L. Etiology and treatment of pyelonephritis: Modern concepts. Journal of the American Geriatrics Society, 19:252-263, 1971.

Rusk, H.A. Principles involved in teaching activities of daily living. In: Rusk, H.A., ed. Rehabilitation Medicine. St. Louis, Mo.: C.V. Mosby, 1958.

Salter, C. de, and Salter, C.A. Effects of an individualized activity program on elderly patients. Gerontologist, 15:404-406, 1975.

Schwartz, A.N. Planning micro-environments for the aged. In: Woodruff, D.S., and Birren, J.E., eds. Aging: Scientific Perspectives and Social Issues. New York: Van Nostrand Co., 1975.

Simon, A. Physical and socio-psychologic problems in aged mentally ill. California Mental Health Research Digest, 8:27-28, 1970.

Solomon, N. Keeping the elderly in the community and out of institutions. Geriatrics, 28:46, 1973.

Starin, I., and Kuo, N. The Queensbridge health maintenance service for the elderly, 1961-1965. Public Health Report, 81:75-82, 1966.

Sterne, R., and Woolf, L.M. Synthesizing hospital care with a senior center program. Gerontologist, 13:192-203, 1973.

Stiefel, J.B. Use and cost of AHS coordinated home care programs. Inquiry, 4:61-68, 1971.

Stotsky, B.A.A. Controlled study of factors in the successful adjustment of mental patients in nursing homes. American Journal of Psychiatry, 123:1243-1251, 1967.

Trager, B. Home care: Providing the right to stay home. Hospitals, Journal of the American Hospital Association, 49:94-98, 1975.

Van Dyke, F., and Brown, V. Organized home care: An alternative to institutions. Inquiry, 9:3-16, 1970.

Wilson, J.W. Starting a geriatric day care center within a State hospital. <u>Journal of American Geriatric Society</u>, 21:175-179, 1973.

Yeager, R. Hospital treats patients at home. <u>Modern Health Care</u>, 4:29-32, 1975.

Zung, W.W. A self-rating depression scale. <u>Archives of General Psychiatry</u>, 12:63-70, 1965.

Zusman, J. Some explanations of the changing appearances of psychotic patients: Antecedents of the social breakdown syndrome concepts. <u>International Journal of Psychiatry</u>, 3:216-237, 1967.

ANNOTATED BIBLIOGRAPHY

Aagaard, G.N. The Drug Spotlight Program. <u>Annals of Internal Medicine</u>, 78:603-605, 1973.

- The Drug Spotlight Program was established by the American Society for Clinical Pharmacology and Therapeutics in order to help hospitals develop policies and set standards appropriate to drug therapy that comply with the recommendations of the Joint Commission on Accreditation of Hospitals. This hospital-based continuing education program has both a national and a local hospital phase. The program's National Advisory Committee, comprised of its member organizations, is responsible for the national phase. This entails selecting the drugs that will be spotlighted, providing scientific papers that center on them, and publishing questions about their use that merit consideration at the local hospital level. For a 3-month period a drug or class of drugs will receive Spotlight attention. Relevant current information will be presented in scientific papers appearing in the following participating member group journals: <u>American Family Physician</u>, <u>American Journal of Hospital Pharmacy</u>, <u>American Journal of Nursing</u>, <u>Annals of Internal Medicine</u>, <u>Journal of American Medical Association</u>, and <u>Patient Care</u>. A videotape program will be offered by the Network for Continuing Medical Education consisting of a variety of viewpoints presented by numerous experts. The above publications as well as others of the participating organizations will, during the first month of each presentation, announce the upcoming drug subject for spotlighting, along with the questions to be considered. The local phase is planned to be carried out by each hospital's committee on pharmacology and therapeutics. A question relating to the spotlighted drug is chosen for study and its answer sought by gathering and analyzing data from hospital records. This important phase ends with its participants drawing conclusions and presenting them to the hospital staff.

Amin, M.H. Drug treatment of insomnia in old age. <u>Psychopharmacological Bulletin</u>, 12:52-54, 1976.

- It is estimated that 55 percent of persons over age 60 suffer from some degree of insomnia. The intensity of sleep processes is known to diminish with advancing age, and stage IV sleep in a 60-year-old is less than half that experienced at age 20. REM time begins to decline, while awake time in bed increases. Brain deterioration accompanying aging, regardless of its cause, is associated with greater disturbances in sleep. Treatment of insomnia with anxiolytic sedatives is made difficult and dangerous in part because of the likelihood of physical dependency on the barbiturates and also because of the longer half-life and period of percepto-motor as well as cognitive deficits associated with benzodiazepine use. These agents, during the first few weeks of administration, successfully increase stage II sleep and REM latency; but chronic use causes increased latency to sleep, increased number of awakenings, frequent stage shifts, continued suppression of REM sleep, and a dminished stage IV sleep. Withdrawal from these drugs produces unpleasant symptoms such as jitteriness, nervousness, difficulty in falling asleep, and fragmented sleep. An increased state I REM, i.e., REM rebound, and intensified REMs also occur during withdrawal, the rebound being dangerous because vegetative tone increases during REM sleep. Cardiac arrhythmias, anginal attacks as well as substantially increased acid secretion in duodenal ulcer patients occur with greater frequency during a REM period. Drugs such as the benzodiazepines, that particularly decrease slow wave sleep, only complicate the hyperthyroidism and uremia-associated insomnia that itself reults from decreased slow wave sleep. Meprobamate in doses not exceeding 800 mg, chloralhydrate at 500 mg and flurazepam at 15 mg, if administered for no longer than 2 to 6 weeks, are the best choices in instances where hypnotic use is absolutely unavoidable for elderly patients. Flurazepam, a benzodiazepine, does cause a reduction in slow wave sleep without REM rebound upon withdrawal. The hypnotic chloralhydrate decreases sleep latency and awake time while increasing total sleep time. Meprobamate possesses certain hypnotic properties. Small dosage levels of chlorpromazine (25 mg) or levomepromazine (10 mg) may have to be administered during the recommended gradual withdrawal period.

Bender, A.D. Pharmacodynamic principles of drug therapy in the aged. <u>Journal of the American Geriatrics Society</u>, 7:296-303, 1975.

● This paper presents a review of research concerning the functional, physiological, and pathological changes associated with increasing age and the pharmacologic aspects of aging. The discussion is oriented both to the effect of age on systems and events that influence the drug's concentration at its site of action and the age-related changes that affect systems and tissues directly or indirectly influenced by the drug's mechanism of action. Such factors as drug absorption, drug distribution, drug excretion and metabolism, and the effect of age on the activity of drugs are discussed. Among the findings reported are:

Absorption of some substances is reduced or delayed in the elderly.

Changes in drug activity with age are the result of impaired circulation and membrane permeability.

The rate at which drugs are metabolized and eliminated is decreased.

Changes in the number of receptors and concentration of substrate occur, thereby reducing the action of stimulants and enhancing the action of depressants.

This paper is directed toward the prescribing physician and emphasizes that fact that there may be an altered response in elderly and debilitated patients that requires adjustment in the patient's therapeutic regimen. (There are 72 references.)

Benson, R.A., and Brodie, D.C. Suicide by overdoses of medicines among the aged. Journal of the American Geriatrics Society, 23:304-308, 1975.

● The authors indicate that drugs rank third, after firearms and hanging, in suicide. Prescription drugs are used in one of three suicides in the United States. The elderly are prone to suicide because of failing health and diminished life satisfaction. The older white male, in particular, is called upon to adjust to income and status loss at a time when he is least able to adapt. The rate for suicides in this group exceeds that for all other combinations of age, sex, and race. Depression is often the only early clue or warning sign in a group whose attempts are almost always serious.

Prescriptions for hypnotics and psychotherapeutic drugs are readily available to the elderly. Barbiturate hypnotics accounted for over 20 million prescriptions filled in America during 1973; half of these were ordered for hypnotic purposes. The barbiturates an elderly insomniac consumes can actually produce or intensify any existing tendencies toward depression or suicide, particularly if combined with alcohol consumption.

Although there is evidence that the prescribing of barbiturates is slowly decreasing, the death rate per million prescriptions is on the rise. The prescribing physician is caught in the bind of deciding whether to make psychotropic drugs available to elderly patients, thus providing an easy means of suicide, or to withhold these drugs, leaving the patient alone in his struggle with depression and an often accompanying wish for death. Further complicating this dilemma is the difficulty surrounding the estimation of what constitutes a lethal dose of these drugs. It is suggested that elderly patients must be assessed on an individual basis by the prescribing physician so that treatment can be varied according to the patient's overall status.

Birkett, D.P., and Boltuch, B. Psychotropic drugs in old age. The Journal of the Medical Society of New Jersey, 70:647-648, 1973.

● Birkett and Boltuch conducted a study on the effects of psychotropic drugs on aged persons. Thirty psychogeriatric unit patients over age 65 participated in an open crossover study of the side effects of three antipsychotic drugs: thioridazine, chlorpromazine, and haloperidol. These subjects were not already stabilized on a psychotropic drug, their mental symptoms were more extensive than memory loss or confusion, they had no history of adverse reactions to phenothiazines, and they were free of any liver disease indications. Patients were not given phenothiazine-, butyrophenone-, or thioxanthine-type drugs during the week prior to the study. Ten patients each were then randomly assigned to three treatment groups where they followed study drug regimens for nine consecutive evenings. Each drug was administered separately for three consecutive evenings in the following amounts: haloperidol, 0.5 mg, 1 mg, 2 mg; thioridazine, 25 mg, 50 mg, 100 mg; and chlorpromazine, 25 mg, 50 mg, 100 mg. The above schedule was assigned to one of the groups while the other two followed schedules of either taking thioridazine first and then haloperidol and chlorpromazine, or of being administered chlorpromazine followed by thiroidazine and haloperidol. There were no significant differences between drugs in the severity of side effects they produced and none was particularly free of these problems. Both systolic and diastolic blood pressure fell most on thioridazine and least on chlorpromazine. Rigidity and unsteadiness on the feet were greatest on haloperidol, drowsiness was the most prominent on chlorpromazine, and tremor on thioridazine. No falls or accidents occured over the 9-day study period.

Boyd, J.R., et al. Drug defaulting. Part II: Analysis of noncompliance patterns. American Journal of Hospital Pharmacists, 31:485-491, 1974.

- Forty-two outpatients age 65 and over were included in a study of noncompliance with prescription instructions at an Oklahoma City teaching hospital. Pertinent information was gathered during patient home interviews within 7 to 10 days following a clinic visit where prescriptions were administered. A total of 380 prescriptions were written for the 134 participating patients, ranging in age from under 24 to 65 and over, of whom more than three-fourths were over 45 years old. Patients 65 and over received 107 prescriptions compared to the 63 patients age 45 to 64 who received 184. In all cases the association between comprehension and compliance was statistically significant (p=0.05). The 45 to 64 age group had the highest level of comprehension, significantly higher (p=0.05) than the lowest, age 65 and older, group. The 45 to 64 age group also had the smallest number of errors per prescription (p=0.001). The greater number of errors in the elderly population was attributed to a combination of more complex health problems and decreasing capacity for self-care.

Clinite, J.C., and Kabat, H.F. Prescribed drugs ... Errors during self-administration. Journal of the American Pharmaceutical Association, NS9:450-452, 1969.

- Thirty male outpatients ranging from 21 to 90 years old were interviewed about their prescription medication administering habits approximately 1 week after leaving a Veterans Administration hospital. Increasing age was not a factor in medication errors since patients over 70 had the lowest error rate. It was possible that they had more time than younger patients to carry out their therapeutic regimens correctly, and this may have accounted for their greater accuracy.

Covington, J.S. Alleviating agitation, apprehension, and related symptoms in geriatric patients: A double-blind comparison of a phenothiazine and a benzodiazepine. Southern Medical Journal, 68:719-724, 1975.

- In order to compare the efficacy of a phenothiazine (thioridazine or Mellaril) with a benzodiazepine tranquilizer (diazepam or Valium) in relieving geriatric apprehension and agitation, 40 senile, but nonpsychotic, nursing home patients were used as subjects in a 4-week, double-blind study. Patients were randomly assigned to treatment groups where 20 were administered diazepam and 20 received thioridazine in daily doses adjusted to each patient's need. These ranged from 10 to 80 mg of thioridazine, with a mean of 32.9 mg, and from 4 to 18 mg of diazepam, with a mean of 7.2 mg. Patients were evaluated before the study and at weekly intervals with a modified Hamilton Anxiety Rating Scale and a Modified Nurses' Observation Scale for Inpatient Evaluation (NOSIE). Global ratings were also made before and during the study of the degree of both illness and overall change.

A pretrial versus week-4 comparison based on the Hamilton Scale showed that thioridazine reduced the severity of all eight items more than diazepam, with significant reductions for the anxious mood and depressed mood items (p=0.10 or more). Thioridazine significantly reduced the severity (p=0.05 or better) of four of the eight items, but the diazepam group showed no significant reductions. A greater percentage of the thioridazine group (23 to 45 percent) than the diazepam group (15 to 30 percent) showed at least some improvement on each item. Time response trends differed, and significantly so (p=0.05 or better) for four items, with the thioridazine group generally showing a pattern of steady symptom improvement compared to a more erratic and less positive pattern in the diazepam group.

NOSIE results showed that after 4 weeks only thioridazine had significantly reduced the frequency of retardation (p=0.10) and this group had experienced more improvement on every factor, significantly more so (p=0.05 or better) on five of nine factors. Their time responses were significantly different (p=0.10 or better), favoring thioridazine for depressive manifestations and total positive factors. Separate global ratings by a physician and by nurses at the end of 4 weeks each showed a significant reduction (p=0.5 or better) in the degree of mental illness along with significant improvement (p=0.05 or better) in the degree of change in thioridazine patients, with a comparative significantly greater improvement (p=0.05) in these patients for both ratings. Worsening in these two ratings had occurred in the diazepam patients. No serious side effects of clinically significant changes in either vital signs or laboratory test results were found in either set of patients.

Davison, J.R.T., et al. Psychotropic drugs on general medical and surgical wards of a teaching hospital. _Archives of General Psychiatry_, 32:507-511, 1975.

- A 6-week study of psychotropic drug use on the wards of a 480-bed university teaching hospital was conducted to examine the prescribing patterns of gynecologists, surgeons, and internists. One hundred twenty-eight patients, or 9.4 percent of all 1,361 admissions, were administered psychotropic medicine. Preoperative and postoperative hypnotics were not included. They were administered the most frequently by the department of medicine, to 14.4 percent of their patients, followed by surgery (8.9 percent) and obstetrics-gynecology (4.7 percent). A ratio of 1:1.09 men to women received psychotropic drugs compared to the total admissions population ratio of 1:1.37. The ratios of black patients to white were 1:1.93 and 1:1.75, respectively. Generally, patient's age was not a determinant of choice of drug. The mean age of men patients was 45.9 and 47.7 for women. The 30- to 65-year-old admissions, comprising 45 percent of total admissions, were overrepresented in the psychotropic group (67 percent), whereas the over-65 patients were 14 percent of the total 15 percent of the psychotropic groups. Minor tranquilizers were the most widely used agents (72 percent); major tranquilizers comprised 16 percent of the prescriptions; barbiturates, used only for seizure disorders, represented another 6.7 percent and antidepressants, 5.3 percent.

Davison, W.T.D. Pitfalls to avoid in prescribing drugs in the elderly. _Geriatrics_, 1975. pp. 157-158.

- The author's editorial was directed toward geriatricians and emphasized both the importance of reviewing the patient's complete drug schedule and the need for constant questioning of every drug on the patient's prescription list, when prescribing medication. One special problem discussed is polypharmacy that results in a bigger drug burden, an increased risk of adverse drug reactions, and decreased patient compliance. Guidelines suggested to insure maximal response with minimal risk include: full knowledge of the diseases present, an understanding of drug actions, selectivity in drugs, the simplest drug schedule, and adequate supervision.

De Groot, M.H.L. The clinical use of psychotherapeutic drugs in the elderly. _Drugs_, 8:132-138, 1974.

- De Groot's article indicates that general principles of drug administration for the elderly patient apply as much to psychotherapeutic as to other drug classifications. The ability of the aging system to absorb, and particularly to detoxify and excrete, drugs is reduced; therefore, it is wise for the physician to be knowledgeable about the pharmacological action, metabolic and excretive characteristics of proposed drug therapy. The lowest effective dosage level should be established for each elderly patient, and complicated, multiple-drug regimens are best avoided.

Depression in the elderly patient is most effectively treated by the tricyclic antidepressants. A more pronounced sedative effect occurs with the use of amitriptyline, imipramine, trimipramine, and doxepin than results from using nortriptyline, protriptyline, and desipramine.

Initial low doses are recommended as hypotension can develop in elderly patients with unstable blood pressure. However, the action of adrenergic neuron blocking antihypertensive drugs can be antagonized by the presence of amitriptyline, imipramine, and derivatives. The tricyclic doxepin surmounts this problem if administered at the usual optimum dosage of 75 to 150 mg daily.

Atropine-like side effects can occur when these drugs are used along with other drugs possessing anticholinergic activity. Monoamine oxidase inhibitors are effective as antidepressants, but involve the dietary avoidance of foodstuffs rich in tyramine or dopamine and also the ingestion of preparations containing sympathomimetic amines. Only those elderly persons who are capable of remembering and carefully following instructions should be treated with these drugs. Elderly mania patients receiving lithium carbonate treatment require a lowered dosage due to their diminished ability to excrete the lithium ion. Use of barbiturates in these patients should be avoided as dependency is likely. The phenothiazines, although the most commonly used treatment in elderly schizophrenic patients, can produce extrapyramidal reactions that, particularly in older patients, are unresponsive to antiparkinsonian medication. Elderly endentulous female patients are particularly vulnerable to developing dyskinetic complications. Hypotension may occur in normotensive patients, and blood pressure control in hypertensives may be interfered with. The use of benzodiazepines or barbiturates in the treatment of anxiety in elderly patients can increase confusional states, thereby often increasing anxiety, creating dependency and even hostility.

Eisdorfer, C. Observations on the psychopharmacology of the aged. Journal of the American Geriatrics Society, 23:53-57, 1975.

- According to Eisdorfer, phenothiazines are currently the most widely used antipsychotic drugs. Side effects such as extrapyramidal motor signs, tardive dyskinesia, and akathisia are common. Difficulties are encountered in establishing a medical program for elderly psychotic patients. The acute stage of psychosis is best handled by commencing drug dosage at a low level, followed by a rapid increase up to an effective amount.

A chronic psychosis should be treated by using the lowest dosage level possible. A regime consisting of a single dose at bedtime along with no utilization over the weekend appears to maintain therapeutic effectiveness while diminishing unwanted side effects. The use of antiparkinson drugs to combat extrapyramidal side effects should be discouraged along with the administration of various psychotropic drugs from the same or even from different categories.

Psychotropic drug use in the elderly and in middle-aged, potentially chronic users should begin with a dosage level one-quarter to one-third less than the normal adult dosage and should gradually be raised according to individual tolerance. Side effects such as cardiovascular disorders, premonitory signs of glaucoma, or loss of libido should be watched for in elderly as well as in younger patients. Drug influence on cerebral circulation can make hypotension a particular danger for the elderly patient.

The aged are a population vulnerable not only to disease but to iatrogenic illness caused by both direct and indirect drug action. Although the elderly are more prone to drug induced side effects, clinical drug trials are usually conducted and dosage levels are developed based on results obtained from younger and healthier subjects. Older people have greater tissue storage of drugs due to a higher ratio of fat to muscle tissue, along with lower levels of metabolic function and a greater risk of metabolism related respiratory and renal systems diseases. The benefits of psychotropic drugs can best be realized in a program that includes a proper medical diagnosis formulated upon the patient's mental, emotional, and physical condition.

Fann, W.E. Interactions of psychotropic drugs in the elderly. Postgraduate Medicine, 53:182-186, 1973.

- Fann's article indicates that altered metabolism, blocked transport, altered excretion, altered mediator activity, and impaired gastrointestinal absorption may result from the multiple use of major psychotropic agents, particularly in the more vulnerable systems of older patients.

Liver microsomal metabolism of the anticonvulsant diphenylhydantoin, of tricyclic antidepressants, phenothiazines, and certain anticoagulants is retarded by the presence of methylphenidate, a mild central nervous system stimulant. When given to counter the sedative effect of a drug, it often increases sedation by blocking liver metabolism, thereby raising blood level of the sedative. Conversely, because the sedative phenobarbital accelerates liver microsomal metabolism in certain phenothiazines, warfarin, coumarin, and diphenylhydantoin, its use with a phenothiazine can lower that drug's serum level and reduce its clinical, including sedative, effect. The hypotensive effect of the antihypertensive drug guanethidine can be antagonized by the concurrent use of tricyclic antidepressants or certain phenothiazines. These drugs can prevent guanethidine from accumulating in the adrenergic neuron by blocking the activity of the adrenergic membrane transport system that would normally deliver it there. Since both depression and hypertension occur frequently in elderly persons, this interaction is a likely and dangerous one that physicians should be on the alert for, particularly in psychiatric outpatients.

Lithium therapy is useful in the treatment of cyclic affective disorders, but selective renal lithium reabsorption and toxicity can occur if the patient does not maintain a physiologically normal serum sodium level. Even though many elderly, cyclic affective disorder patients also have concurrent conditions demanding diuretic therapy, such treatment is contraindicated while lithium therapy is being administered.

Monoamine oxidase inhibiting compounds such as the antidepressant tranylcypromine and the anthypertensive drug pargyline, reduce intraneuronal breakdown of norepinephrine. These compounds potentiate the pharmacologic action of pressor amines, such as tyramine and amphetamine and its congeners, which in turn act to release the available norepinephrine.

Patients undergoing either of these treatments should be warned against eating certain tyramine-rich foods or ingesting sympathomimetic amines such as amphetamines, often available in over-the-counter cold remedies. The physician also must be careful not to prescribe such combinations as they can produce a hypertensive crisis. Desired absorption of the major tranquilizer chlorpromazine from the gastrointestinal tract can be threatened by gel antacids containing magnesium or aluminum. Further research is needed pertaining to cholestyramine, a hypercholesterolemia treatment agent, and its ability to interfere with absorption of psychotropic agents.

Fann, W.D. Pharmacotherapy in older depressed patients. Journal of Gerontology, 31:304-310, 1976.

- According to Fann, treatment for depressive conditions is generically the same for various age groups although dosage levels should be initially low and more gradually increased in elderly patients. Tricyclic antidepressants are a better treatment choice than the Monoamine Oxidase (MAO) inhibitors because they are safer; although in severe geriatric depression tricyclics may be more effective. Both have a 1 to several weeks lag time before therapeutic efficacy is noticeable.

Tricyclics are particularly effective in treating endogenous-type depressions. Nonsedating tricyclics such as protriptyline and imipramine are well suited to treatment of retarded or withdrawn depressives whereas the sedating amitriptyline or doxepin are more appropriate cases of agitated or hyperactive depression. Certain tricyclic side effects such as twitching, tremor, ataxia, hypotension, dry mouth, and atropine-like effects are especially troublesome in elderly patients. Reduced liver metabolism makes them more vulnerable to glaucoma, urinary retention, orthostatic hypotension during early treatment, constipation, and a central atropine-like delirium often mistaken for an increase in psychiatric symptoms. MAO inhibitors are dangerous because of their hepatoxicity and potentiating effect upon pressor amines, the latter resulting in hypertensive crises. All sympathomimetic agents are contraindicated during their use. A lowered initial starting dose should range from 10 to 25 mg a day and increase by 20 mg in 2 to 3 days if no side effects are evident.

The antianxiety agent diazepam has a slight advantage over the others in its antidepressant action but side effects such as habituation, sedation, aggravation of glaucoma, diplopia, blurred vision, and withdrawal phenomena can occur. Of the neuroleptics, thioridazine possesses helpful antidepressant properties. Certain piperazine derivatives, such as perphenazine and trifluoperazine, can be useful in agitated depression when administered with tricyclics. They must be used with care in the treatment of any underlying psychoses accompanying depression. Elderly patients are particularly vulnerable to the acute neuro-toxic and dyskinetic effects these drugs can cause. The parkinson-like syndrome is the most common. Late-onset hyperkinesis, or tardive dyskinesia is often irreversible, particularly in older persons with a history of treated psychosis.

Central nervous system stimulants are mainly helpful in cutting down tricyclic therapy lag time, but they can increase depression-related anorexia and induce short-lived mood elevation which is followed by severe emotional decline. Possible cardiovascular side effects make them a poor choice for elderly patients. Lithium is effective only in prophylaxis of endogenous depression and should not be used to treat reactive depressions. A lowered renal lithium clearance in elderly patients necessitates a careful monitoring for lithium toxicity.

Multiple system decompensation in elderly persons leads to a greater likelihood of their receiving multiple drug prescriptions. They are at greater risk for the occurrence of dangerous or treatment-impairing drug interactions. Many of the antidepressant agents, when used in combination with other drugs, can either block the transport of other drugs to their site of action, alter the excretion rate of the other drugs, alter their mediator activity, or interfere with their absorption from the gastrointestinal tract.

Fann, W.E.; Wheless, J.C.; and Richman, B.W. Treating the aged with psychotropic drugs. The Gerontologist, 16:322-328, 1976.

- The diagnosis and treatment of mental disturbances in the elderly are usually either incorrect or incomplete in nature. Insufficient attention is paid to the fact that chronic brain syndrome (cbs), or senility, is only one psychiatric disorder occurring in this population. Functional psychoses, affective disorders, and neuroses are as likely to be found in the elderly as they are in other age groups. When psychotropic drugs are applied to a cbs-diagnosed elderly patient and some improvement follows, it is not due to any real change in brain tissue function but rather to a beneficial effect upon other present psychiatric conditions.

When late paraphrenia develops in the elderly patient, it is important to distinguish whether it is caused by chronic brain syndrome or whether it accompanies a depressive state. Only chronic brain syndrome paraphrenia should be treated with antipsychotic medications. The phenothiazines are the most frequently used because of their ability to reduce symptomatic intensity in agitated, delusional, and hallucinating senile patients. As patients over age 65 have a great reduction in their ability to metabolize antipsychotic drugs, a lowered initial dosage level is not only adequate but far safer than levels administered to patients under age 65. Potential side effects due to physiological accumulation include dry mouth, urinary retention, constipation, nasal congestion, aggravation of glaucoma, drowsiness, lethargy, hypotension, and extrapyramidal symptoms. The elderly are especially vulnerable to the development of tardive dyskinesia, a syndrome including involuntary choreo-athetoid movements of the face, mouth, tongue, extremities, and trunk muscle groups. Even after medication withdrawal these symptoms may continue for an indefinite period, even becoming permanent in some instances. The use of phenothiazines in the particularly susceptible aged population can lead to a vicious circle of prescribing higher dosage levels to counteract what are actually drug-induced states of confusion and delirium.

Depression in elderly patients is most often treated by lowered starting doses of tricyclic antidepressants. Elderly persons who are restless and agitated receive the type which includes a sedative. Older patients with retarded depression are treated for the secondary problems of hypoactivity and hypomentation with a nonsedative tricyclic agent. Due to the 2- to 4-week lag time before results are apparent, these drugs are more useful in mild to moderate depression. They also possess potentially dangerous atropine-like and antiadrenergic actions. The inherent toxicity of monoamine oxidase inhibitors and their ability to potentiate pressor amines, along with the action of several unrelated drugs, e.g., anesthetics, barbiturates, adrenal coricosteroids, ganglion blocking agents, morphine, atropine, and 4-amino-quinoline compounds, causes them to be used less frequently. Also, the antidepressive and hypotensive effects of MAO inhibitors are potentiated by diuretics. However, the effectiveness of MAO inhibitors in the treatment of geriatric depression may still prove promising as elderly depression and the aging process itself are correlated with high MAO activity. Stimulant compounds are unpromising as antidepressants as their beneficial effects disappear quickly, drug tolerance or dependence is likely to occur, and they have potent pressor effects.

Numerous sedative, muscle relaxant, or anticonvulsant compounds have been clinically effective in treating anxiety in elderly patients. Chlordiazepoxide (Librium), a benzodiazepine, is frequently used due to its relative safeness. These agents can produce dependency and withdrawal symptoms which unfortunately mimic the onset of psychosis in elderly patients. Glaucoma can also be an unwanted side effect. Rauwolfia alkaloids possess some value as anxiolytics, particularly when blood pressure or pulse rate reduction is desirable, but gastrointestinal bleeding may occur along with other unwanted side effects. The use of any anxiolytic agent is very likely to cause a secondary clinical depression, especially in patients who have a history of affective illness episodes.

Fracchia, J., et al. Combination drug therapy. Journal of the American Geriatric Society, 13: 508-511, 1975.

- Data were gathered for a typical month on the most frequently used psychotropic drugs in 278 male and 624 female long-term, hospitalized psychogeriatric patients aged 60 years and over. T-tests were conducted to ascertain the significance of mean dosage differences for drugs used separately and in combinations. For females the use of 11 drugs was compared. The average multidrug dosage of 10 agents was higher than the single-drug dosage. It was significantly higher in four drugs: fluphenazine (Prolixin) and chlorprothixene (Taractan), t=2.95 and 2.78, p=.01; and thiothixene (Navane) and perphanazine (Trilafon), t=1.98 and 1.96, p.10. The average single-drug dosage of haloperidol (Haldol) was insignificantly higher than its average in combination. Only five drugs were compared for male patients, but the same general trend was in evidence. The average multidrug dosage of chlorpromazine (Thorazine) was significantly higher than the single-drug dosage (t=2.71, p=.01).

Greenblatt, D.J.; Shader, R.I.; and Koch-Weser, J. Psychotropic drug use in the Boston area. Archives of General Psychiatry, 32:518-521, 1975.

- The Boston Collaborative Drug Surveillance Program conducted interviews with 25,258 consecutively admitted patients aged 20- to 75-years-old during the first 10 months of 1972 to determine their use of prescribed psychotropic drugs prior to hospitalization. Patients with primary psychiatric diagnoses, those with psychogenic disorders, and those unable to identify drugs taken were excluded, leaving a population of 24,633 patients. Patients who were taking an identifiable antidepressant, antianxiety agent, antipsychotic, hypnotic, or stimulant were considered psychotropic drug users. Of the 24,633 patients analyzed, 5,079 or 20.6 percent reported taking a psychotropic drug at least once in the 3-month period prior to their interview. Women used these drugs more frequently than men (25 percent versus 15 percent), and use was highest in the 50 to 59 age group (women, 28 percent; men, 17 percent). The lowest female users were age 20 to 29 (19 percent), and 70- to 75-year-old and 60- to 69-year-old females were the second and third lowest, respectively (20 percent and 24 percent). The lowest male users were also age 20 to 29 (9 percent), and 70- to 75-year-old and 60- to 69-year-old males were the second and fifth lowest, respectively (12 percent and 16 percent).

Harenko, A. A comparison between chlormethiazole and nitrazepam as hypnotics in psychogeriatric patients. Current Medical Research and Opinion, 2:657-663, 1975.

- The hypnotic effects of chlormethiazole and nitrazepam were compared in a double-blind crossover study of 68 hospitalized demented elderly patients, averaging 77 years of age with a range of 62 to 91 years. Medications, consisting of two tablets nitrazepam 5 mg = 10 ml placebo mixture (syrup) and two tablets placebo = 10 ml chlormethiazole 5 percent mixture (syrup), were crossed over on alternate weeks. Six patients dropped out completely because of side effects or the manifestation of diseases, and 18 patients had to interrupt medication for 1 to 3 days. Twenty-one interruptions or discontinuations occurred during nitrazepam treatment, of which 15 were due to severe "hangover" effects. Two patients refused to take chlormethiazole because of its foul taste. Six of the forty-four uninterrupted cases experienced side effects, five of whom had muscular weakness, nausea, and worsening mental condition.

Over the 308-night test period, no significant differences pertaining to onset of sleep were noted in the 44 patients. Sleep more frequently lasted over 6 hours a night during chlormethiazole treatment, a significantly higher difference of 244 out of 308 nights compared to 163 out of 308 nights during nitrazepam treatment (x^2=46.35, p 0.001). Also, significantly more patients (36) were observed with "hangover" effects during nitrazepam treatment than during chlormethiazole treatment (2). A 10-mg dose of nitrazepam was judged to be at least two times higher than necessary for use in elderly patients. Excluding the 6 patients who dropped out, an overall judgment of suitability for 62 patients resulted in 37 cases assessed as faring better with chlormethiazole, 11 cases with nitrazepam, and 14 cases who could do equally well with either one.

Ingman, S.R., et al. A survey of the prescribing and administration of drugs in a long-term care institution for the elderly. Journal of the American Geriatrics Society, 13:309-316, 1975.

● On August 1, 1971, a survey was made of the prescribing and administering of drugs in a Connecticut nursing home as it pertained to residents. Primary focus was on the use of neuroactive drugs--anxiolytics, neuroleptics, antidepressants, psychostimulants, hypnotics, analgesics, skeletal muscle relaxants, antiparkinson drugs, autonomic agents, and cerebral stimulants in--severely brain-damaged persons, ambulatory and relatively self-sufficient residents, extended care unit patients, and recently hospitalized patients.

Doctors prescribed an average of 2.1 neuroactive drugs per patient but only an average 1.3 was administered. Analgesics and neuroleptics were prescribed the most frequently; phenothiazine derivatives (43 cases) and salicylates (37 cases) were the particular drugs most commonly prescribed.

Of the total 272 neuroactive drug prescriptions, 131 were actually administered, 145 were prescribed on a discretionary (p.r.n.) basis, and 96 (66 percent) of the p.r.n. group were not administered. Patients with relatively superior mentation and a greater measure of independence were prescribed significantly more neuroleptic substances (i.e., single chemical entities) and neuroleptic drugs than were patients with lower mentation and a greater amount of dependency (p < .05). There were 23 prescriptions for propoxyphene compound, a not-recommended drug by AMA Drug Evaluation standards. Fifty-four patients (41 percent) received prescriptions for fixed-dose combinations of drugs, which are frowned upon as an illogical drug therapy procedure. Variations in prescribing patterns among physicians were evident even when records of physicians with approximately the same number of patients were compared.

When the average number of all drugs prescribed on August 1, 1971 (4.9±6.3), was compared with the average number prescribed on October 1, 1970 (5.8±3.17), a significant average decline of 0.8 drug prescribed per patient had occurred (p < .001). The decline was subsequent to t' implementation of the JCAH recommended monthly rewriting of drug orders. A decr.ase of 0.14 p.r.n. drug occurred as well as a decrease of 0.27 fixed drug per patient. However, there was an increase in the number of drugs received per patient, rising from an average 2.55 (SD=2.3) to an average 2.9 (SD=1.4) drugs per patient. These results are based on the records of 112 patients who were in the nursing home on both dates.

Kral, V.A. An overview of psychopharmacology of old age. Psychopharmacology Bulletin, 12: 51-52, 1976.

● The functional psychoses, i.e., endogenous depressions, manic states, and the schizophrenic late paraphrenias, are the mental disorders of the aged most benefited by psychopharmacological treatment. Due to lessened metabolic efficiency and likely concurrent organic disease in these patients, the smallest yet effective dosage level of psychotropic drugs should be administered and the prescribing physician should be aware of all simultaneously prescribed drugs so as to avoid harmful drug interactions. Combinations of psychotropic drugs should be used only after each drug has been introduced separately to assess toler-ance.

Tricyclic antidepressants and the monoamine oxidase inhibitors are both used to treat endogenous depressions and must be administered at individually established levels. The therapeutic effects of tricyclics appear from 4 to 21 days after initial treatment, and admin-istration should continue until all target symptoms show definite improvement. A gradual tapering off is required, and a reduced maintenance dose for several months is often neces-sary.

Central nervous system side effects, such as ataxia, somnolence, and lassitude, occur with equal frequency in aged and younger patients. It is still questionable whether the drugs' anticholinergic action or an age-linked stress reaction is the causal agent in an acute con-fusional state occasionally occurring in elderly patients. The antidepressive effect of MAOIs is rapidly apparent, causing mood improvement but no allaying until later, and sometimes temporarily increasing the experience of anxiety. Treatment with MAOIs contraindicates the use of anesthetics and incurs the risk of hypotension in users. Combining antidepres-sants with a neuroleptic to treat agitated depressions can result in accident causing ortho-static hypotension and cerebral vascular accidents. Side effects are potentiated by the combined anticholinergic actions of tricyclic and the phenothiazines.

Lithium carbonate, although a successful treatment for manic states, is contraindicated in patients with compromised renal, hepatic, cardiovascular, and thyroid function. Complete recovery will occur in 3 weeks without serious side effects if the proper dosage is estab-lished and continued and serum lithium levels are monitored frequently. Without either careful monitoring or cautious patient selection, tremulousness, drowsiness, confusion, and extrapyramidal signs will occur. Aged schizophrenic patients, whose treatment is very similar to that for younger patients, share the risk of developing a neuroleptic-induced Parkinson syndrome. Often occurring shortly after therapy commencement, it is sometimes preceded or accompanied by a peculiar restless state. Although very responsive to tradi-tional antiparkinsonian medication, the combined anicholinergic action of both medications can produce an acute confusional state. Therefore the medication cannot be used in a pre-ventive manner and its use should be discontinued a few weeks after initial awareness of symptoms. Tardive dyskinesia is a neuroleptic-induced side effect presenting serious treat-ment difficulties and warranting a discontinuation of medication when feasible. Depressive or paranoid episodes accompanying a dementing process are treatable with antidepressants and/or tranquilizers, but their side effects may be more troublesome in such cases. A superimposed state of acute confusion warrants treatment with a neuroleptic along with the infusion of glucose.

Lamy, P.P. Geriatric drug therapy. Clinical Medicine, 81:52-57, 1974.

• The elderly patient frequently suffers from a multitude of morbid conditions or diseases at a time in life when reserve functional capacity, energy metabolism, and enzymatic processes are greatly reduced. The capacity to absorb, distribute, metabolize, and excrete drugs is very often impaired, resulting in an increase of adverse drug effects. Persons aged 70 to 79 experience adverse drug reactions at a rate seven times greater than persons aged 20 to 29 years, and the rate for those aged 60 to 70 years is twice that for persons aged 30 to 40 years. Age-related reduction in gastric juice acidity, a slowed stomach emptying rate, and a reduction in intestinal blood flow can lead to a delay or reduction in drug absorption.

Drug distribution can be affected by circulatory disturbances and the decreasing activities of several enzymes can hamper drug metabolism. Aging is accompanied by a decrease in kidney size, glomeruli, and tubule cells, and glomerular filtration rate, renal flow, and tubular secretion capacity fall below normal levels. Renal pathology and resulting dimin-ished renal function is the norm in elderly persons, and water imbalance along with general metabolism imbalances are frequently found. Reduced peristaltic activity, leading to con-stipation and diarrhea can also alter the elimination of drugs, especially those which exhibit enterohepatic circulation.

The establishment of drug dosage levels for the elderly patients is frequently accomplished by aiming at a uniform medium level which is often either too high or too low for at least half the population. There is no formula which can be followed for every patient, but the aim should be to arrive at the minimal effective dosage level. When prescribing antidepressants for elderly patients, lower than usual dosage levels are essential to avoid adverse reactions. Sedatives must be used with extreme caution in elderly persons. Barbiturates are generally contraindicated as they may cause severe and unexpected durg toxicity. A dependency liability is incurred with meprobamate and glutethimide use, and patients taking 20 or more tablets of the latter have a mortality rate of 45 percent. Paraldehyde, although unpalatable, is rapid, safe, and effective whereas chloral hydrate is a potential cardio-inhibitor and a gastric irritant.

Elderly patients with arteriosclerotic cerebral vessels or chronic obstructive pulmonary disease should not be administered sedatives which depress cardiac or respiratory function, and the insomnia which can occur due to an overly full bladder should not be treated with sedatives. When a decrease in anxiety, psychomotor activity, hallucinations, and delusions is needed, large initial, followed by smaller, doses of the phenothiazines are helpful. However, neurotic reactions, simple endogenous depression, and acute disturbances are not benefited by them. Possible dose-related side effects of the phenothiazines are jaundice, agranulocytosis, dermatitis, and photosensitivity, besides a general tendency to cause a high rate of extrapyramidal reactions and hypotension. Potentiation of epilepsy and mental depression, lowered body temperature, and exaggeration of cerebral anoxia can also occur, as well as irreversible parkinsonian symptoms. The phenothiazines and also chlordiazepoxide and diazepam can depress thyroid function, and small doses of the latter two are required to prevent ataxia development.

Lamy, P.P., and Kitler, M.E. Drugs and the geriatric patient. Journal of the American Geriatrics Society, 19:23-33, 1971.

- A survey of drug prescribing patterns centered upon 33 geriatric cardiac patients in a teaching hospital, 30 ambulatory patients over age 65, and 30 patients over 65 admitted to a geriatric care hospital. Although all drugs prescribed were found to be administered within the range of recommended dosage levels, there was no general reduction made because of the patients' elderly status. Barbiturates, particularly in combinations, were frequently administered to the ambulatory patient, whereas hospitalized patients received chloralhydrate on the rare occasions when barbiturates were prescribed.

Lamy, P.P., and Vestal, R.E. Drug prescribing for the elderly. Hospital Practice, 1976. pp. 111-118.

- Social Security Administration statistics show that during 1974 the aged population spent about $2.26 billion, or more than 20 percent of the national total, on drugs and drug sundries even though they comprise only 10 to 15 percent of the total population. Including renewals, they averaged over 13 prescriptions a year per capita, spending close to $100 for prescribed and over-the-counter drugs. The mere factor of multiple drug use, even when correctly prescribed at proper dosage levels, involves a strong possibility of toxic reactions, and studies have shown that drug-induced illness occurs with much greater frequency among elderly hospitalized patients.

Prescribing drugs for the elderly patient is both complicated and hazardous. Age-associated decrements in physiologic function as well as the effects of illness or trauma erase the reliability of the "average" dose for the "average" patient and require the physician to be able to weigh benefit and risk using a different set of parameters than s/he would apply to younger patients. Above all, s/he must approach the treatment of geriatric patients with a sense of caution accompanied by an awareness of knowledge that is available to help him/her formulate treatment regimens.

Because much research must still be done in order to fully understand the effects of aging on pharmacokinetics, quantitative answers to specific problems of dosage and drug selection are not yet available.

Learoyd, B.M. Psychotropic drugs and the elderly patient. The Medical Journal of Australia, 1:1131-1133, 1972.

- The Medical and Psychogeriatric Unit of the North Ryde Psychiatric Centre of North Ryde, New South Wales, reviewed case notes for all 236 patients over age 65 who had been admitted during the past 2 years to learn how many admissions had been the result of psychotropic drug intoxication. Thirty-seven, or 16 percent, met the criteria of having been administered psychotropic drugs prior to admission and then developing disturbed behavior with or without physical symptoms. Further, in the Centre this behavior must have subsided when these patients were removed from drugs followed by a discharge on a much smaller drug regimen. When admitted, seven of these patients were suffering from simple drug intoxication, and their confused mental state had often led to self-administered overdoses. Sixteen patients had, in addition to the above, incurred secondary effects from drug intoxication such as hypotensive syncope, related falls and three fractures, respiratory depression and associated chest infections, and urinary retention or gastrointestinal ileus. The remaining 14 patients had reactions which manifested as restlessness, agitation, paranoia, and aggression. Multiple psychotropic drug therapy was the rule, as only four patients were administered on drug alone. It is postulated that these admissions were made necessary because of elderly patients' reduced tolerance to the combinations of drugs, and because of ignorance about the effects that lead to further medication and increasing deterioration. Although the association was not as clearcut, it was estimated that another 4 percent of the 236 patients had been admitted mainly because of drug effects. Study findings lead to the postulation that many elderly admissions to general hospitals are for illnesses precipitated by excessive use of psychotropic drugs.

McKenney, J.M., and Harrison, W.L. Drug-related hospital admissions. American Journal of Hospital Pharmacy, 33:792-795, 1976.

- In a 2-month survey and analysis of the association between hospital admissions and drug-related problems there were a total of 216 admissions to a general medical ward, of which 59 (27.3 percent) were linked in some manner to drug usage. Seventeen percent of all patients were age 60 to 69, and 19 percent were age 70 or over. Their representation in the drug-linked admissions population, 15 percent and 11 percent, respectively, was not significantly different, nor was that of all other age groups. The age group 40 to 49 had the highest representation and comprised a quarter of the subpopulation. Adverse drug reactions (7.9 percent) and noncompliance (10.5 percent) seemed to be the major precipitating factors in hospital admissions for these 59 patients. Another 24 (11.1 percent) of the 59 patients had adverse drug reactions, but they did not cause their admission. Inadequate thereapy, improper or erroneous drug use and drug overdose had a somewhat weaker association with hospital admission.

Merlis, S. The use of oxazepam in elderly patients. Diseases of the Nervous System, 36:27-29, 1975.

- Oxazepam is a particularly effective and safe benzodiazine medication for use in elderly patients because of the following properties and characteristics: efficient absorption patterns, rapid metabolism to a psychopharmacologically inactive substance, favorable biotransformation characteristics, a wide margin of safety, and beneficial excretion patterns. Other characteristics surrounding its limited potential drug interactional effects with other therapeutic agents contribute to its efficacy without increased side effects. Earlier studies of oxazepam use in several hundred institutionalized geriatric subjects showed significantly superior overall results in reducing anxiety and tension occurring alone or anxiety concurrent with depression when compared with patients receiving another drug or placebo. In doses averaging 30 to 50 mgs daily, side effects were less prevalent than with other treatments, and vertigo, sedation, and nausea appeared less frequently. Some inhibition of hostility and aggressive behavior was evidenced, and paradoxical reactions, which sometimes occur with chlordiazepoxide use, rarely happened. Ambulatory noninstitutionalized elderly patients have also shown a high tolerance of oxazepam. It is useful in elderly patients who have sleep problems such as early awakening or restlessness at night. It possesses a short duration of action and at proper dosage levels there is no sedative or hangover effect in the morning.

Petersen, D.M., and Thomas, C.W. Acute drug reactions among the elderly. Journal of Gerontology, 30:552-556, 1975.

- Data were gathered for 60 persons age 50 and over who were admitted to a Dade County, Florida, hospital emergency room because of acute, nonfatal drug reactions during 1972. Ranging from 50 to 80 years old and averaging 59.6 years, they comprised only 5.4 percent of the total 1,128 overdose admissions whose average age was 27.6 years. Females outnumbered males (68.4 percent versus 31.6 percent) in the aged group and were more concentrated in the aged group than in the total population (68.4 percent versus 58.6 percent). Blacks comprised only 15 percent of the aged admissions compared to 33 percent of the total admissions. For both the aged group and all admissions, white females were the race/sex grouping most likely to be admitted, comprising 61.7 percent of aged admission and 38.4 percent of all admissions.

  Comparisons with 1970 Dade County census data showed that although the aged group was not overrepresented in total county emergency room admissions for acute drug reactions, over age 50 females (68.7 percent versus 55.3 percent) as well as white, over age 50 females (61.7 percent versus 51.4 percent). Similarly, blacks exceeded their Dade County distribution (15.0 percent versus 7.2 percent), black males (8.3 percent versus 3.3 percent) slightly more than black females (6.7 percent versus 3.9 percent). Aged admissions, though more likely to have reported multiple substance use prior to acute drug reaction (31.9 percent versus 23.5 percent of all admissions), were less likely to report alcohol use (8.3 percent versus 10.9 percent). The proportion of the aged group reporting their overdose as an attempt at suicide (35.0 percent) was only slightly greater than the 33.7 percent reported for all admissions.

  Legally available drugs, whether attainable by prescription or over the counter, were responsibile for all admissions among the aged group. The particulars of attainment were not available. Of every 10 of these drugs, 8 were psychotropic, either sedatives or tranquilizers, and one was a nonnarcotic analgesic. In descending order, Valium, Tuinal, phenobarbital, and Darvon were the most frequently abused. Among the aged group, whites and females were more likely to have overdosed on tranquilizers, sedatives, and nonnarcotic analgesics. Twenty percent of the admissions under age 50 had abused illicit substances.

Rada, R.T., and Kellner, R. Thiothixene in the treatment of geriatric patients with chronic organic brain syndrome. Journal of the American Geriatrics Society, 14:105-107, 1976.

- Forty-two hospitalized geriatric patients (21 male) with chronic organic brain syndrome (24 nonpsychotic) were randomly assigned to treatments in a double-blind, placebo-controlled 4-week study of the efficacy and safety of thiothixene (Navane) treatment. The mean age was 75.5 years, and duration of illness averaged 5.3 years. Demographic characteristics and the chronicity of illness did not significantly differ between the thiothixene and placebo group. Using a starting dosage of 2 mg three times daily during the first two weeks, which could then be increased to 5 mg three times daily, produced virtually no statistically significant improvement in the thiothixene group. The few side effects which occurred were mild in nature and developed in only seven thiothixene patients, compared to six placebo patients who experienced side effects.

Salzman, C., et al. Psychopharmacologic investigations in elderly volunteers: Effect of diazepam in males. Journal of the American Geriatrics Society, 13:451-457, 1975.

- Forty healthy elderly male volunteers over the age of 60 participated in a 2-week, double-blind study of diazepam (DZ) during which 20 were randomly assigned to a group receiving 12 mg of DZ daily and 20 received placebo (PBO). Various psychological scales and motor functioning tests were administered and mean change scores for both groups, statistically compared by t-test, were obtained by subtracting predrug ratings from 1-week and 2-week scores.

  Data were available for 38 patients. Overall analysis of significant results suggests that an increase in fatigue and decreases in memory and motor functions are produced by a daily 12 mg dose of DZ. After the 2-week period results from a revised MMPI depression scale showed a significantly higher number (9) of the 18 DZ recipients reporting decreased depression scores compared to only 2 of the 20 PBO recipients (p=.02).

Salzman, C., and Shader, R.I. Psychopharmacology in the aged--Research considerations in geriatric psychopharmacology. Journal of Geriatric Psychiatry, 7:165-184, 1974.

- The evaluation of drug effect in the elderly centers around the research problems of biologic variability, age, gender, dose, toxicity, polypharmacy, placebo effect, initial severity of symptoms, capacity to respond to drugs, and age-related problems of rating drug effect. Biologic and physiologic functioning among elderly persons who are the same chronological age can vary greatly according to the number and severity of chronic diseases and pathological processes present at any one time. This lack of biologic homogenity is a threat to the validity of research results unless given due consideration in research program design.

  Various psychotropic drug studies utilizing elderly subjects have found a differential response to treatment occurring in males and females, as well as in relatively younger and older aged subjects, suggesting that it is important to conduct a separate data analysis by gender and age so that these intrasample findings are revealed rather than cancelled out and overlooked in a total sample analysis. There is also evidence for a need to conduct separate treatment data analyses of patients who exhibit either high or low initial levels of symptoms.

  Findings from numerous studies suggest that patients exhibiting a high level of the target symptom or symptoms will show the greatest improvement following drug therapy, and an examination of only the overall "mean" drug effect can act to cancel out these variations. Elderly subjects are likely to be patients on various multiple drug regimens which are capable of affecting the action of psychotropic drugs. Also, elderly persons have a heightened sensitivity to the sedative side effects of psychotropic agents which may result in hampering their clinical efficacy. The elderly are also particularly vulnerable to potential extrapyramidal and hypotensive side effects caused by many antipsychotic and antidepressant drugs.

  It is wise for the researcher to establish dosage guidelines and learn of potential toxicity through a small preliminary pilot study. He should also be aware that high placebo response rates are common among attention-starved, elderly subjects, and one study's results suggest that it increases with the presence of psychopathology, institutionalization, and age. Any marginally greater improvement with active drug treatment over that with placebo is worthy of attention.

  The choice of rating scales to use for evaluation of drug effects in geriatric populations must be made with the variability of elderly subjects in mind. Although rating a relatively healthy and cooperative geriatric patient is similar to rating younger populations, there still exists a reduced attention span and a decreased tolerance for ambiguity. Very few scales have been designed especially for geriatric patients in the areas of behavioral, mood, and cognitive function rating.

Salzman, C., and Shader, R.I. Responses to psychotropic drugs in the normal elderly. In: Psychopharmacology and Aging. New York: Plenum Press, 1973. pp. 159-168.

- One hundred health volunteers over the age of 60 participated in a 1-week, double-blind study of mood-altering drugs administered in typical doses. Twenty-five subjects each were randomly assigned to treatment groups where they received either 2 mg t.i.d. of diazepam, 15 mg t.i.d. of phenobarbital, 5 mg t.i.d. of methylphenidate or a placebo three times each day. Psychological scales were administered before and after the study period, and the Bonferroni multiple comparison test was used to analyze mean change scores for the entire sample and for each sex. Each active drug was compared independently against placebo. Few statistically significant results were found. Diazepam showed a significant overall trend toward increasing both friendliness and fatigue and had a significant antidepressant effect on males. In females, diazepam and methylphenidate both significantly increased friendliness over placebo. Methylphenidate was found to be the best antidepressant and antianxiety agent for females, whereas diazepam was the more effective drug for males.

Salzman, C.; Shader, R.I.; and Van Der Kolk, B.A. Clinical psychopharmacology and the elderly patient. New York State Journal of Medicine, 76:71-77, 1976.

- Alterations in somatic functioning that occur due to the aging process can change the clinical and toxic effects of drugs or other agents. Changes in the gastrointestinal tract slow down and impair drug absorption and cause increased atropinergic sensitivity. The aging cardiovascular system can reduce or delay drug circulation and cause increased sensitivity to orthostatic stress. Albumin fraction is decreased in the aging hematopoietic system.

In the nervous system a decrease in neuronal tissue causes an increased sensitivity to clinical and toxic effects and also to side effects produced by the cholinergic blocking properties of certain drugs, such as neuroleptics and antidepressant agents. These drugs commonly cause blurred vision or a dry mouth, and the loosening of porcelain dental fillings is not unusual. Symptoms accompanying glaucoma or benign prostatic hypertrophy may be aggravated. Decreased gastrointestinal and bladder motility are less common, but possibly dangerous, side effects.

Potentially serious cardiovascular side effects can result from use of certain neuroleptics. Phenothiazines and the structurally related tricyclic antidepressants can cause occurrences of orthostatic hypotension, particularly in susceptible older persons with elevated blood pressure and resultant decreased elasticity of the arterial wall. Older people with impaired cardiovascular functioning are also more predisposed to arrythmia, a further side effect of both phenothiazines and tricyclic antidepressants.

Central nervous system disturbances are particularly prevalent in elderly neuroleptic users. Sedation, paradoxical excitement, delirium, dementia, assaultiveness, delusions, and hallucinations also occur with greater frequency in elderly patients taking psychoactive drugs. As no neuroleptic is free from side effects, and their clinical efficacy is about equal, choice of treatment should be based on knowledge of their differential production of sedative, hypotensive and extrapyramidal side effects, and the treatment needs and overall condition of each elderly patient. Tricyclic antidepressants are also approximately equal in effectiveness. Except for the risk in very old patients of producing severe hypotension or arrythmias, they are preferred in the treatment of elderly depression. They have potentially serious side effects, and they interact with many of the medical drugs that older persons commonly are administered.

The benzodiazepines are currently considered the drug treatment of choice for anxiety in both young and old patients. Elderly patients are more susceptible, however, to sedative side effects, making these drugs suitable for the treatment of mild insomnia as well. The hypnotic flurazepam as well as chlorpromazine or thioridazine in small doses is also extremely useful and safe. Generally, elderly patients should not be treated with babiturate and nonbarbiturate sleeping medications other than the benzodiazepines. Polypharmacy should be avoided as much as possible in order to prevent dangerous drug interactions.

Synder, B.D., and Harris, S. Treatable aspects of the dementia syndrome. Journal of the American Geriatrics Society, 14:179-184, 1976.

- Detailed case histories are presented of four geriatric patient referees to a general hospital from long-term care facilities due to the exhibiting of behavioral disturbances. The diagnosis of untreatable dementia was incorrect for two of these patients, one who had been administered five psychoactive drugs concurrently before hospital admission. The case histories illustrate the importance of proper diagnosis and exemplify improper, incomplete, and unsafe treatment as well as high-quality care which is thoughtfully planned and delivered with the individual patient in mind. The point is made that everything possible should be done to help both dementia, otherwise behaviorally impaired, demented and nondemented patients maintain their maximum level of overall health and independence.

Swanson, D.W.; Weddige, R.L.; and Morse, R.M. Abuse of prescription drugs. Mayo Clinic Proceedings, 48:359-367, 1973.

- A study was made of 225 patients ranging from 16 to 77 years old whose abuse of prescription medicines caused them to need inpatient psychiatric treatment between July 1, 1966, and July 1, 1972. Mean patient age was 45 years and 123, or 55 percent, of patients were females. Patients were categorized by the drug they abused into a sedative, analgesic, tranquilizer, stimulant, or miscellaneous grouping. The distribution by age decades and by sex was fairly even excepting that significantly more females (18) than males (6) had abused tranquilizers ($p < 0.05$), and the mean age of stimulant abusers was only 34.3 years, their ages ranging from 21 to only 53 years. The age at onset of drug abuse ranged from 14 to 73 years with a mean of 36.5. The duration of abuse ranged from 6 months to 35 years, and averaged 12.5 years. More patients abused sedatives and analgesics than the other categories.

APPENDIX A

RESEARCHERS INVOLVED IN PSYCHOACTIVE
DRUG USE BY THE ELDERLY

Aagaard, George N., M.D., Chairman, National Drug Spotlight Program National Advisory Committee (1973), and Professor of Medicine and Pharmacology and Head of the Division of Clinical Pharmacology, University of Washington, School of Medicine, Seattle, Washington.

Asnes, Daniel P., M.D., Psychiatrist-in-charge, Geriatric Unit, McLean Hospital, Belmont, Massachusetts.

Ayd, Frank J., Jr., M.D., Director of Professional Education and Research, Taylor Manor Hospital, Ellicott City, Maryland.

Balter, Mitchell, Ph.D., Chief, Special Studies Section, Psychopharmacology Research Branch, National Institute of Mental Health, Rockville, Maryland [(301) 443-3946].

Basen, Michelle M., Public Health Analyst, Services Research Branch, Division of Resource Development, National Institute on Drug Abuse, Rockville, Maryland.

Brands, Alvira, D.Sc., Program Analyst, Mental Health Care and Service Financing Branch, Division of Mental Health Service Programs, Room 11-95, National Institute of Mental Health, Rockville, Maryland [(301) 443-3657].

Brody, Stanley J., J.D., Professor, Departments of Physical Medicine and Rehabilitation and Psychiatry, School of Medicine, University of Pennsylvania, Philadelphia, Pennsylvania [(215) 243-5765].

Butler, Robert N., Ph.D., Director, National Institute on Aging, National Institute of Mental Health, Washington, D.C.

Carpenter, Linda, Coordinator, Rational Behavior Training Section, University of Kentucky Medical Center, Lexington, Kentucky [(606) 233-5000].

Cervera, A.A., M.D., Samuell Clinic, Dallas, Texas.

Cherkin, Arthur, M.D., Selpulveda Veterans Administration Hospital, Los Angeles, California.

Cheung, Alan, Pharmacist D., Associate Clinical Professor, School of Pharmacy, University of Southern California, Los Angeles, California [(213) 226-2561].

Clark, Walter, Assistant Chief, Mental Health Education Branch, Division of Scientific and Public Information, National Institute of Mental Health, Rockville, Maryland [(301) 443-4573].

Cohen, Dr. Gene, Chief, Center for Studies of Mental Health for Aging, National Institute of Mental Health, Rockville, Maryland [(301) 443-3823].

Cohen, Sidney, M.D., Department of Psychiatry, Neuropsychiatric Institute, UCLA School of Medicine, Los Angeles, California [(213) 825-0400].

Cole, Jonathan, M.D., Boston State Hospital, 591 Morton Street, Boston, Massachusetts.

Davis, John, Director of Research, Illinois State Psychiatric Institute, Chicago, Illinois, University of Chicago, School of Medicine.

Dunham, Katherine, Southern Illinois University, 411 E. Broadway, East St. Louis, Illinois [(618) 271-4400].

Eisdorfer, Carl, Ph.D., M.D., Chairman, Department of Psychiatry and Behavioral Sciences, School of Medicine, University of Washington, Seattle, Washington [(206) 543-3750].

English, Tom, Alcohol and Drug Coordinator, Joseph W. Johnson, Jr., Mental Health, Moccasin Bend Road, Chattanooga, Tennessee.

Fann, William E., M.D., Professor of Psychiatry, Associate Professor of Pharmacology, Baylor College of Medicine; Chief, Psychiatry Service, Veterans Administration Hospital, Houston, Texas.

Friedel, Robert, M.D., Vice Chairman, Department of Psychiatry and Behavioral Science, School of Medicine, University of Washington, Seattle, Washington [(206) 543-1570].

Gaetano, Ronald, Pharmacist, Broome County Drug Awareness Center, 22 Park Place, Johnson City, New York [(607) 798-7182].

Gerber, Carl, M.D., Chief of Staff, Veterans Administration Hospital, Tacoma, Washington [(206) 588-2185].

Gershon, Sam, M.D., Department of Psychiatry and Neurology, New York University Medical Center, New York, New York [(212) 679-3200, extension 3520].

Godes, Thomas H., Pharmacist Director, Consultants of Pharmacy, 420 South 7th Street, Minneapolis, Minnesota [(612) 333-4217 or 340-5454].

Greenblatt, David J., M.D., Assistant Professor, Harvard Medical School; Assistant in Medicine, Clinical Pharmacology, Massachusetts General Hospital, Boston, Massachusetts.

Guttman, David, DSW, National Catholic School of Social Services, Catholic University of America, Washington, D.C.

Haber, Paul, M.D., Assistant Chief Medical Director for Extended Care, Veterans Administration, 810 Vermont Avenue, N.W., Washington, D.C. [(202) 393-4120].

Hall, M.R.P., B.M., F.R.C.P. (Lond. Ed.), Professor of Geriatric Medicine, Faculty Medicine, Southampton General Hospital, Tremona Road, Southampton S09 4XY, England.

Hammel, Maxine, College of Pharmacy, University of Minnesota, Minneapolis, Minnesota [(612) 376-5316].

Hollister, Leo E., M.D., Veterans Administration Hospital, 3801 Serra Boulevard, Palo Alto, California [(415) 493-5000].

Holloway, Donald A., Pharm. D., The Methodist Retirement Home, Durham, North Carolina.

Jarvic, Lissy, M.D., Department of Psychiatry, UCLA Medical Center, Los Angeles, California [(213) 825-3885].

Jarvic, Murray, M.D., Department of Psychiatry, UCLA Medical Center, Los Angeles, California [(213) 825-2410].

Jefferson, Cherie, 120 Arch, St. Paul, Minnesota [(612) 227-6363].

Juni, Dr. Howard, Capitol Drug Center, 2023 E. County Road, White Bear Lake, Minnesota [(612) 777-8388].

Kabat, Dr. Hugh, University of Minnesota, School of Pharmacy, Department of Clinical Pharmacology, 115 Appleby Hall, Minneapolis, Minnesota [(612) 376-5312].

Kampf, Betty, M.D., Geriatric Coordinator, Overlook Mental Health Center, 5908 Lyons View Drive, Knoxville, Tennessee.

Kane, Robert L., M.D., Associate Professor of Community Medicine, University of Utah, College of Medicine, Salt Lake City, Utah.

Klett, C. James, Ph.D., Central Neuropsychiatric Research Laboratory, Veterans Administration Hospital, Perry Point, Maryland [(301) 642-2411, extension 353].

Lamy, Dr. Peter, Professor of Pharmacy, University of Maryland, School of Pharmacy, 636 W. Lombard Street, Baltimore, Maryland [(301) 528-7592].

Leech, Shirley, M.D., Geriatric Consultant, U.T. Mental Health Center, P.O. Box 4947, Knoxville, Tennessee.

Lehman, Heinz E., M.D., Clinical Director, Douglas Hospital, McGill University, Montreal, Quebec, Canada [(514) 716-6131, extension 128].

Levine, Dr. Ruth, Boston University, School of Medicine, Boston, Massachusetts.

Libow, L.S., M.D., Chief, Geriatric Division, Department of Medicine, Mount Sinai City Hospital Center, 79-01 Broadway, Elmhurst, New York.

Martilla, James, Pharmacist Director, Assistant Professor of Pharmacy, University of Minnesota, 318 Harvard Street, S.E., Minneapolis, Minnesota [(612) 376-5323].

McRae, Catherine E., Geriatric Services Section, State of Tennessee Department of Mental Health and Retardation, 501 Union Building, Nashville, Tennessee.

Mehl, B., R.P., Assistant Director, Mount Sinai Hospital, New York, New York.

Montero, E.F., M.D., Central State Hospital, Petersburg, Florida; National Building, 908 S. Florida Avenue, Lakeland, Florida.

Morrow, Gloria, Director of Research and Education, American Health Care Association, 1200 15th Street, N.W., Washington, D.C. [(202) 833-2050].

Parker, Jerry, Director of Senior Health Programs, Augustana Hospital, 411 W. Dickens, Chicago, Illinois [(312) 975-5056].

Pascarelli, Emil F., M.D., Director of Community Health Services, Department of Ambulatory Care, Roosevelt Hospital, New York, New York.

Penna, Dr. Dick, Director of Professional Affairs Division, American Pharmaceutical Association, 2215 Constitution Avenue, Washington, D.C. [(202) 628-4410].

Petersen, David M., Ph.D., Department of Sociology, Georgia State University, 33 Gilmer Street S.E., Atlanta, Georgia.

Phillipson, Richard V., M.D., Special Assistant for Scientific and Medical Affairs, Division of Resource Development, National Institute on Drug Abuse, 5600 Fishers Lane, Rockville, Maryland.

Prien, Robert, Ph.D., Psychopharmacology Research Branch, National Institute of Mental Health, Rockville, Maryland [(301) 443-3524].

Raskin, Allen, Ph.D., Research Psychologist, Psychopharmacology Research Branch, National Institute of Mental Health, Rockville, Maryland [(301) 443-3527].

Rawlings, John, and Associates Pharmaceutical Services, Nampa Drug Pharmacy, Box 115, Nampa, Idaho.

Reilly, Mary Jo, Editor, <u>American Hospital Formulary Service</u>, American Society of Hospital Pharmacists, 4630 Montgomery Avenue, Washington, D.C.

Reis, Barry, Ph.D., Albany College of Pharmacy [(518) 445-7211].

Ross, Hilda, University of Miami, Institute for Study on Aging, Miami, Florida [(305) 284-4011].

Rucher, T. Donald, Ph.D., Professor of Pharmacy Administration, Division of Administrative and Social Sciences, College of Pharmacy, Ohio State University, Columbus, Ohio.

Sathananthan, Dr. G.L., New York University, Department of Psychiatry, New York, New York [(212) 679-3919].

Schwartz, Doris, Associate Professor, Cornell-New York Hospital School of Nursing, New York, New York.

Shader, Richard, M.D., Director, Psychopharmacology Research Laboratory, Massachusetts Mental Health Center, Harvard Medical School, 25 Shattuck Street, Boston, Massachusetts [(617) 277-4378].

Sielski, Lestor, Ed.D., University of West Florida, Social Welfare Department [(904) 476-9500].

Smith, Roberta, M.D., Geriatric Coordinator, Dede Wallace Mental Health Center, 223 Madison Street, Madison, Tennessee.

Sprouse, Betsy, McBeath Institute on Aging and Adult Life, University of Wisconsin, 425 Henry Mall, Madison, Wisconsin [(608) 263-4020].

Stotsky, Bernard, M.D., St. Elizabeth's Hospital, Boston, Massachusetts.

Subby, Peg, Director, Hennepin County Alcohol and Drug Access and Intervention Unit, 1800 Chicago Avenue South, Minneapolis, Minnesota [(612) 348-8013].

Thomas, Doris Lang, M.S., Director of RPH Pharmacy, 515 Audubon Avenue, New York, New York [(212) 7819800].

Thompson, W. Leigh, Professor, Case Western Reserve, School of Medicine, Department of Pharmacology, Cleveland, Ohio.

Towery, Owen B., M.D., National Institute of Mental Health, Room 11-C 105, Parklawn Building, 5600 Fishers Lane, Rockville, Maryland.

Vestal, Robert, M.D., Research Fellow, School of Medicine, Vanderbilt University, Nashville, Tennessee.

Ward, Elliott, Ph.D., Director, Alcohol and Drug Section, Department of Mental Health and Mental Retardation, 501 Union Building, Nashville, Tennessee.

Wegner, Fred, Legislative Representative, NRTA-AARP, American Association of Retired Persons, Washington, D.C. [(202) 293-2390].

Wolfe, John C., Ph.D., Executive Director, National Council of Community Mental Health Centers, 2233 Wisconsin Avenue, N.W., Washington, D.C. [(202) 337-7530].

Wynne, Ronald D., Ph.D., Codirector, Wynne Associates, Washington, D.C. [(202) 966-7273].

Zung, William, M.D., School of Medicine, Duke University, School of Medicine, Durham, North Carolina [(919) 286-6359].

APPENDIX B

PROGRAMS SPECIFICALLY DESIGNED TO INTERVENE
IN PSYCHOACTIVE DRUG MISUSE/ABUSE BY THE ELDERLY

Alcohol and Drug Abuse and the Elderly Task Force. Catherine McRae, Geriatric Services, Tennessee Task Force, State of Tennessee, Department of Mental Health and Mental Retardation, 501 Union Boulevard, Nashville, Tennessee 37219.

Alcoholism, Inebriety, Drug Information and Referral Services (A.I.D.) of Hennepin County. Peg Subby, Director, 1810 Chicago Avenue, Minneapolis, Minnesota 55404.

Broome County Drug Awareness Center Programs. Ronald Gaetano, Director, 22 Park Lane, Johnson City, New York 13790.

Bridgeway. Douglas Laurenzo, Social Service Coordinator, 22 27th Avenue, S.E., Minneapolis, Minnesota 55414.

Camellia House Licensed Chemical Dependency Program. Patricia Hansen, Program Director, Camellia House Convalescent and Nursing Home, 1620 Oak Park Avenue, N., Minneapolis, Minnesota 55411.

DISC-Drugs and the Elderly Program. College of Pharmacy, University of Minnesota, Minneapolis, Minnesota 55455.

Intervention Plus Program: Ebenezer Society. Ken McArthur, Coordinator, Ebenezer Society, 2523 Portland Avenue, Minneapolis, Minnesota 55404.

Management of Drug Abuse Among the Elderly: A Peer Counselor Approach. Priscilla R. Perry, Director of the Institute for the Study of Aging, University of Miami, Coral Gables, Florida, P.O. Box 248106 (through the Florida Drug Abuse Prevention and Education Trust, 105½ East College Avenue, Tallahassee, Florida 32301).

Northwestern Hospital Chemical Dependency Treatment Program. Reverend Phil Hansen, Program Coordinator, Northwestern Hospital, 27th and Chicago Avenue, Minneapolis, Minnesota 55407.

Older Life Drug Experience Research (OLDER). Maxie C. Maultsby, M.D., Albert B. Chandler Medical Center, College of Medicine, Center for Rational Behavior Therapy Training, Office of Continuing Education, University of Kentucky, Lexington, Kentucky 40506.

Queen Treatment Program for the Chemically Dependent Elderly. Muriel L. Ganje, Administrator, Queen Treatment Center, 300 Queen Avenue, N., Minneapolis, Minnesota 55405.

Ramsey County Senior Chemical Dependency Program. Cherie Jefferson, Program Coordinator, 544 West Central Avenue, Suite 1105, St. Paul, Minnesota 55103.

Seniors' Health Program: Augustana Hospital. Betsy Epstein, Health Education Seniors' Health Program, Augustana Hospital and Health Care Center, 411 West Dickens Avenue, Chicago, Illinois 60614.

THEE DOOR, Substance Abuse Intervention. Carol Ann Cheek, Associate Executive Director, 1710 West Colonial Drive, Orlando, Florida 32894.